OTHER BOOKS BY LEWIS PUTNAM TURCO

The Museum of Ordinary People and Other Stories, 2008
Fearful Pleasures: The Complete Poems, 1959-2007
Fantaseers, A Book of Memories, 2005
The Collected Lyrics of Lewis Turco / Wesli Court, 2004
The Book of Dialogue, 2004
A Sheaf of Leaves, Literary Memoirs, 2004
The Green Maces of Autumn: Voices in an Old Maine House, 2002
The Book of Forms, A Handbook of Poetics, Third Edition, 2000
The Book of Literary Terms, 1999
A Book of Fears, 1998
Shaking the Family Tree, 1998
Bordello: A Portfolio of Poemprints, with George O'Connell, 1996
Emily Dickinson, Woman of Letters, 1993
The Public Poet, 1991
The Shifting Web: New and Selected Poems, 1989
The Fog: A Chamber Opera in One Act, with Walter Hekster, 1987
Visions and Revisions of American Poetry, 1986
The Compleat Melancholick, 1985
American Still Lifes, 1981
Poetry: An Introduction Through Writing, 1973
Pocoangelini: A Fantography & Other Poems, 1971
The Inhabitant, 1970
Awaken, Bells Falling: Poems 1959-1967, 1968
First Poems, 1960

Satan's Scourge

Satan's Scourge

A Narrative of the Age of Witchcraft
in England and New England 1580-1697

LEWIS PUTNAM TURCO

Professor Emeritus of English Writing Arts
State University of New York College at Oswego

STAR CLOUD PRESS
Scottsdale, Arizona
2009

Satan's Scourge

Copyright © 2009
by Lewis Putnam Turco

cover design by Trish Hadley

Cover art work: Examination of a Witch
T. H. Matteson
Oil on canvas
Peabody Essex Museum

All rights reserved. No part of this book may be used or reproduced in any manner whatsoever without written permission from the publisher, except in the case of brief quotations embodied in articles and reviews.

Published by

~ STAR CLOUD PRESS® ~

6137 East Mescal Street
Scottsdale, Arizona 85254-5418

www.StarCloudPress.com

Paperback: 978-1-932842-26-5 — $39.95

Cloth: 978-1-932842-27-2 — $ 54.95

Library of Congress Control Number: 2008943028

Printed in the United States of America

In loving memory of
"Mom May" Laura Putnam Turco
who might have liked this story of her family,
but then again, probably not.

FOREWORD AND ACKNOWLEDGMENTS

Satan's scourge, A Narrative of the Age of Witchcraft in England and New England 1580-1697 is a book of history, a chronicle of the period when the Age of Sympathetic Magic, which had been the system by which mankind operated from time immemorial, was beginning to shift over to the Age of Science, "The New Philosophy," by which the world would be increasingly governed from then forward. The main focus of the book is upon the Putnam family of Buckinghamshire, in England, from the birth of John Putnam, born in 1580, some of whose descendants would be deeply involved in the last gasp of sympathetic magic, the great witchcraft explosion of Salem Village, Massachusetts, in 1692, which is the climax of the book.

The volume not only looks at *all* the witchcraft cases in England and New England during the period covered, but it also tells the stories of the major scientists and Adepts of sympathetic magic (often the two were the same) in Europe and America. The effect is twofold: First, the method is strictly chronological, unfolding like a tapestry year by year. As one thread of the tapestry swells and tapers off, others appear and interweave with one another. Second, the history is told from the point of view of common people, the Puritans of England and New England primarily, but also the crystal gazers, alchemists, alleged witches and their accusers, and those ordinary citizens caught up in the webs woven by plotters, liars, "possessed" children and their parents, and, of course, the clerics.

Furthermore, this is the period when America was settled, when Oliver Cromwell and the Roundheads carried out their Puritan revolution, and all the politics and machinations of the relevant sovereigns and courtiers of the period are also a part of the tapestry here woven.

One is probably saying to oneself at this point, "It's too complicated and confusing." But when one begins to read the book one discovers that things start out clear, and they stay clear throughout. Everything in it is true. All the incidents took place in the real world, according to my historical sources (which are exhaustive — A bibliography is appended here), and this depiction of the Salem witchcraft trials is the most complete and accurate that has ever been written, many errors and misprisions having been corrected.

I wish to acknowledge those who have helped and inspired me in this project. The first person to encourage my writing on the subject was Dr. Eleanor Michel of Meriden, Connecticut, High School for whose 11th grade English class in 1950-51 I wrote an addendum — an extra concluding chapter, a postscript — to *The House of the Seven Gables*, in the style of Nathaniel Hawthorne.

At about the same time four of us at Meriden High founded the Fantaseers Science-Fiction Reading Club which grew to include (Rev.) Ben Barnes, Pierre Bennerup, Bill Burns, (Prof.) Lindsey Churchill, the late Phineas Gay, (Rev.) George Hangen, George Lallos, the late Jack Rule, (Rev.) Ray Staszewski, George Veillette, (Rev.) Arthur von Au, and Paul Wiese — the Black Thirteen who provided me with Faustian fellowship, evil escapades, vile volumes, and the opprobrious opportunity to do my second (very imaginative) writing on the subject of the Salem Village witchcrafts: A Senior Day skit, a photograph of which appears on page 139 of my book *Fantaseers, A Book of Memories*, published in 2005.

Next, I beg the indulgence of the Research Foundation of State University of New York for providing me with a Faculty Fellowship during the summer of 1974, under which I was to write a volume of poetry but, inasmuch as I had begun this book in the spring, I finished the first draft instead. I did nothing with it thereafter beyond query a few publishers who seemed not much interested in it because of its length, so I put it away until the spring of 2006 when I rewrote it as I typed it into my new MacBook Pro computer.

I wish to express my deep gratitude to several librarians for their help in my research: Eleanor S. Adams of the American Antiquarian Society, Worcester, Massachusetts, for her early and kind assistance; Dorothy Mozley, Genealogy and Local History Librarian of the Springfield City Library, Springfield, Massachusetts, for her help with the Springfield witchcraft cases of 1646 and 1651, and Cecilia Caneschi, Reference Librarian of the Meriden, Connecticut, Public Library for her great help with the Benham Wallingford witchcraft cases of 1691, 1692, and 1697.

The description of the Vale of Aylesbury at the beginning of this book is in fact very largely that of Eben Putnam, not myself, taken from his Putnam genealogies (see Bibliography, appended). Inasmuch as he explored the area, and I have not, I thought it as well to leave his descriptions largely as he wrote them. I thought it fitting, too, that this scholar of the Putnam family, who spent such enormous amounts of time and work researching his people, thus making the Putnams one of the most thoroughly documented families in America, ought to leave his imprint on these pages in some way other than statistically, for his two genealogies were published in limited editions (though I have made them available from University Microfilms International of Ann Arbor, Michigan).

Finally, over the years I have met or known many people who are descended from the folk depicted here including my dear friend, the late poet Constance Carrier of New Britain, Connecticut; Curtis Disbrow, the husband of my sister-in-law Anne Disbrow of Meriden; my cousin-in-law Gary Getchell of Cedar Grove, Maine; Lindsey Churchill and the late Jack Rule, both Fantaseers; the Maine artist Margaret Macy, a descendant of Rebecca Nurse; the Cleveland poet Mary Oliver; the late novelist John Cheever, who angrily informed me in my living room in Oswego, New York, that the character Ezekiel Cheever of Salem Village was fictional, having been invented by Arthur Miller for his play *The Crucible* — John did not stop fuming until I showed him his forebear's testimony in the Salem Witchraft trial records; my correspondent of almost forty years, the great fantasist Ray Bradbury, and there were two Drs. Mather, father and son (but doctors of medicine, not divinity — both Roman catholics!) in Oswego where I lived and taught for thirty-one years at the State University of New York College at Oswego, and where I wrote the first draft of this volume.

I wish to express my deepest gratitude to my wife, Jean, who helped me with the chore of working on the index of this book, the most grueling task she has suffered since the school year 1968-1969 when she carried most of the physical labor of typing and editing two manuscripts, *The Spiritual Autobiography of Luigi Turco*, my father, and *The Literature of New York: A Selective Bibliography of Colonial and Native New York State Authors*.

—Lewis Putnam Turco, Dresden Mills, Maine, December 2nd, 2008

Table of Contents

Foreword and Acknowledgments	
Prologue	i
Chapter One	1
Chapter Two	63
Chapter Three	108
Chapter Four	177
Chapter Five	243
Chapter Six	290
Chapter Seven	330
Chapter Eight	382
Chapter Nine	458
Chapter Ten	531
Chapter Eleven	606
Chapter Twelve	685
Epilogue	705
Appendix A:	
The Lineage of May Laura Putnam Turco	709
Bibliography	715
Index	725
About the Author	808

PROLOGUE

John Putnam was born, the second child and first son of Nicholas Putnam and Margaret Goodspeed Putnam in Wingrave, Buckinghamshire, England, in January of 1579 by the old reckoning, 1580 New Style, on the cusp of a new age.

The infant's Zodiacal sign was Capricorn, the goat of the mountains, an Earth Sign which was — according to the ancients, by whose system the universe still was perceived, even in John Putnam's day — the most important of the twelve signs of the Zodiac. Had the elder Putnams not been Puritans, they might have consulted the local astrologer — every community had one — and asked that a horoscope be cast for their newborn child; or, had they been less well-to-do than they were, they might have requested that the village's white witch, who cured by means of herb lore and charms, using some other method of divination look into the future and say what the baby's fate would be. Perhaps they did anyway. Without doubt, the attending midwife had her insights, and her opinions.

Capricorn was the prime quality of the Earth element; it was essentially negative, cold and dry; it was an obeying sign governed by Saturn, exalted by Mars; its detriment was the Moon and its fall, Jupiter. Given the fact that John Putnam had been born into a Puritan home, the symbolic interpretation of his sign was appropriate, for Capricorn signified the union of Jewish and Christian points of view: John Putnam would be an ambitious man, working for social position and worldly goods. He would regret the fall from Grace of his Brother, but this would not deter him from exacting his due in any case. He would be a practical man not given to change or experiment except in extenuating circumstances.

But he would not be too coldly calculating, for he would believe in the initiation of the Elect, in Justice and the Cosmic Order. Having been born in the third decan of his Sign, he would be an idealist, able to express his ideals concretely. His imagination would be strong and, joined with his propensity for great labor, he would do well for himself and his family. He would reach into the Infinite for knowledge.

Astrology was a branch of the universal system by which the world was governed in John Putnam's day, the system J. G. Frazer would study in the late nineteenth and early twentieth centuries and call, in *The Golden Bough*, the system of "sympathetic magic." By the time Frazer looked into magic, it would be dead for most of the western world, supplanted by a new system called "The New Philosophy" in its own day, Science in Frazer's. In 1580 The New Philosophy was just beginning to make inroads upon the mind of Man. John Putnam and his children and grandchildren would live in the span of time when the two ways of seeing would contend with one another, the old way fighting to remain viable and bursting forth resurgently, intermittently throughout the seventeenth century as the first of the great modern scientists, themselves of split minds, made discovery after discovery, each a plank in the coffin in which magic would at last be buried.

Although magic was part of every religion, it was not itself a religion. It was a worldview. Sympathetic magic was an essentially simple conception, depending on only two "laws," according to Frazer: The "Law of Similarity" and the "Law of Contact." Frazer says, "From the first of these principles, namely the Law of Similarity, the magician infers that he can produce any effect he desires merely by imitating it." Thus, if he wishes to produce rain, he may sprinkle water on the ground and expect the act to trigger the storm. The Law of Contact has as its basic premise the belief that an object or symbol, which is once in contact with some person or thing, maintains that connection, no matter what amounts of time or distance intervene. Hence, the magician "infers that whatever he does to a material object will affect equally the person with whom the object was once in contact, whether it formed part of his body or not." A witch, then, in order to hurt some person, needed only to obtain an article of that person's clothing, or some nail parings, or a bit of hair, and make a doll, a "poppit" as the New Englanders called it, containing the material. At that point, the object became the person, and the witch might stick pins — symbolic daggers — into the doll in order to bring about the person's death.

As with any system, belief in sympathetic magic was essential for it to work. If one believed the sorcerer or witch *could* do these things, often the things happened. The power of suggestion has always been more powerful than people have given it credit for. Mankind has tended to ascribe true powers to the magician, or to demons conjured by the magician when, in fact, it was Man's own mind that was the magic maker.

Frazer draws our attention to theory and practice: "Regarded as a system of natural law, that is, as a statement of the rules which determine the sequence of events throughout the world, it [magic] may be called Theoretical Magic; regarded as a set of precepts which human beings observe in order to compass their ends, it may be called Practical Magic." He names that branch of magic which is based on the Law of Similarity "Homeopathic Magic," and that based on the Laws of Contact "Contagious Magic." The whole system — theoretical and practical, homeopathic and contagious — Frazer labels "Sympathetic Magic."

Sympathetic magic had been universal throughout the world since prehistory, but it was not linked to "the Devil" until Christianity — and one of its early departures, Manichaeism — postulated his existence. To that point there had been no single Devil, God's Great Enemy, but merely demons. Each demon had its name and its particular domain, just as the various gods had their provinces until Judaism postulated the existence of the One God Who had dominion over all. But sympathetic magic had always been an essential ingredient of all religions, including Judaism and Christianity.

Under the Law of Contact there was the doctrine of the Secret Name: "In the beginning was the Word, and the Word was with God." Each god, demon, and person had two names — one was a practical, everyday name that one might say without fear. But the second, the Secret Name, was full of power, and it was the business of the sorcerer or priest to discover the Secret Name of any spirit he or she wished to invoke and control, for by naming the Name the spirit could be summoned and ordered to do what the manipulator wished; it was also his or her duty to guard the secret from all those who were not members of the Brotherhood / Sisterhood of the Initiate.

When the concept of the Devil had been developed, the old demons, and gods as well, became his legions. The Devil, therefore, was master, and his minions might not do the bidding of the sorcerer unless the Devil gave his consent. In order to obtain Satan's consent to conjure demons, the sorcerer was required to sign a pact with the Devil. In this bargain the conjuror bartered his or her "soul" in exchange for the right to conjure and control the spirits of Evil. At the moment he (or she) signed the devil's contract the conjuror became a "witch." In the same way, witchcraft was born out of sorcery, for the essential part of witchcraft in religious terms was the pact with the Powers of Darkness.

Witchcraft itself was seen in two lights by ordinary people, both of them arbitrary to the clergy: The "white witch" controlled spirits in order to do good — to heal, to foretell, to bring good weather; his or her practice was White Magic. The "black witch" practiced black magic and did evil for hire and for revenge, or simply out of malice.

However, witches and warlocks, whether white or black, could summon only evil spirits, for the good spirits, or angels, were under the control of God. Satan and his minions had theoretically once been angels themselves, but they had rebelled against God and had fallen from Grace. God (this word, even capitalized, is not a name at all, but merely a generic term standing in place of a name) would not permit His angels to be conjured for any purpose; therefore, the distinction between white magic and black was irrelevant from the point of view of the Church. Nor could one conjure God Himself, though He had His Secret Name as well. The everyday name of the God of the Hebrews was Adonai, but no one must ever speak the Sacred Name of Adonai, for to do so implied that a mere mortal aspired to control Him, which was rankest blasphemy — to speak the name of the Lord "in vain" — that is, in vain hope of invoking Him and His powers — was to curse rather than bless. It was, and is still considered by both Hebrews and Christians to be a sin.

Sympathetic magic was also part of the ritual of sacrifice: Offering to God or the gods a rightful share of the bountiful harvest for which He or they had been responsible and communing with God or the gods by eating ritually the Sacred Animal, whatever it might be in a particular culture: The Lamb, the Ox, the Bull, even the Crocodile, and thus absorbing the virtues contained in the animal's body, or even, if one were a cannibal, contained in a defeated enemy's body. In Judaism and Christianity the "animal" was often the Lamb and eventually, by extension, "the Lamb of God," or Christ himself, His blood transformed to wine, His flesh to bread — in imitation of the Last Supper with the Apostles — by means of the miracle and dogma of Transubstantiation.

Protestant dissenters such as the Putnams rejected this particular tenet of the Roman Catholic Church — that the bread and wine were the actual flesh and blood of Christ — on the grounds that it was itself blasphemous and cannibalistic. The Puritans preferred to leave the ritual on the abstract level of symbolism.

Chapter One

At the first opportunity Nicholas and Margaret Putnam took their first-born son to the village church in Wingrave to take communion themselves and to have him baptized in imitation of the immersion of Christ by John the Baptist —the blessed water symbolically washing him clean of Original Sin — on the 17th of January 1580. Afterward they took him home to begin a life of devotion and labor. The family numbered four. John's older sister Anne was two years of age. She was already a strong-willed child, adventuresome and difficult to control. Her disposition was sunny, however, and the Putnams found it difficult to be stern with her. It was the opinion of the uncles and aunts that John's coming would help his parents to be more even-handed with their daughter.

Home for the Putnams as far back as they could remember and beyond, into the dim past of generations, had been the Vale of Aylesbury. The range of the Chiltern Hills flanked the shires of Bedford and Hertford and was the eastern wall of the Vale in which lay the village of Puttenham. The hills cut off a strip of Hertfordshire about ten miles long and varying in width by from two to four miles. The hills jutted northwestwardly into Buckinghamshire where the ancient town of Tring, thirty-three miles north of London, had guarded the pass for centuries.

By following the road from Tring two miles toward Aylesbury, through pleasant countryside along the northern side of the Chilterns, one came to a road north that crossed the boundary between Hertfordshire and Buckinghamshire. The road descended rapidly till it bottomed out and permitted a glimpse of the old church of Drayton Beauchamp standing in a park to the left of the roadway.

Another two miles brought the traveler to a road going east and west through the parish of Puttenham. A footpath led from this point across the fields past the hoary tower of the church of Long Marston, to the road going toward Wingrave. Just before one reached Wingrave there was a sharp incline at the top of which stood Wingrave Church where John Putnam was baptized.

The road turned westward, continued to climb, and intersected the main road leading from Leighton Buzzard to Aylesbury. About a mile farther on, the traveler's progress seemed to be barred by high hedges and the lay of the land, but a way opened abruptly to the left, and another turn brought one into the village of Aston Abbots in which parish lay the lands John Putnam would one day own and work. The village, by this route, was so completely hidden that a traveler would be actually standing on the green before one knew one had arrived.

The manor house stood in its park to one side; the church was at the farther end of the green, to the left, a bit up the road that led out of town toward Cublington. The town of Aylesbury lay six miles south of Aston Abbotts; north ten miles as the crow flies was Tring. Nearby were Stewkeley and other small communities.

The whole area was full of Puritan sentiment. People were even beginning to think of following the course of the radical Separatist Robert Browne, who had founded a church in Norwich and was gathering a large congregation of followers. It was Browne's belief that nothing could be done from within the Church of England in the way of reform, on Calvinist principles. He had been traveling up and down the countryside, preaching in various spots in the shires of Norfolk and Suffolk, but particularly at Bury St. Edmunds, arguing that each community of worshippers ought to separate itself from the mother church in autonomous congregations which would enter into agreements, or "conventicles," to worship according to the doctrines of

John Calvin, as they had developed in England subsequent to his death in 1564.

It was little surprise, then, when Parliament reacted by banning conventicles or assemblies that gathered to worship in ways not prescribed by *The Book of Common Prayer* of the Anglican Church. The new law specified that, upon a first conviction, anyone attending such a gathering would be imprisoned; a second conviction meant banishment from England, and any person who returned to the country after banishment would be executed as a felon. England felt itself to be besieged in religious matters not only from the left, but from the right as well, for the Pope had begun sending Jesuit priests into the country to proselytize among Protestants, to give aid and comfort to English Catholics, and, in the popular mind, to conspire against Queen Elizabeth I.

Dr. John Dee, known as "Queen Elizabeth's Merlin" and regarded by most people merely as a sorcerer and alchemist, though he was in fact a famous mathematician as well, was living not far from London in Mortlake at the home of his mother, with his wife and children. He cast horoscopes for a living and was consultant to the Queen and the Court in matters mathematical and scientific. His interests ranged wide, however. He was a devoted antiquarian who, while on an excursion to Glastonbury Plain during the summer of 1580, discovered Merlin's secret as he was inspecting the ancient earthworks to be found there.

It occurred to Dr. Dee that the strange arrangement of the mounds was a representation of the Zodiac, in effect a planetarium molded in the earth, with the major stars raised above the plain by antediluvian hands. He painstakingly charted the entire district and wrote that "the stars which agree with their reproductions on the ground do lie only on the celestial path of the sun, moon, and planets; with the notable exceptions of Orion and Hercules…all the greater stars of Sagittarius fall in the hind quarters of the Horse, while Altair, Tarazed and Alschain from Aquilla do fall on its chest…thus is astrology and astronomy carefully and exactly married and measured in scientific reconstruction of the heavens, which shows that the ancients understood all which today the learned know to be facts."

This was Dee's aim: To fuse the ancient arts of the occult with the early science of his day, as it was the aim of some of the most learned men of the time, many of whom were his correspondents. Though Dee was no Puritan, his aim coincided with the aim of the educated Puritan leaders in this regard, for of all the religions of the late sixteenth and the seventeenth centuries, only Puritanism did not find in the newly emerging science a threat to dogma, a fact that might seem strange to those who did not understand that Puritanism's great enemy was, instead, medieval Aristotelianism with its emphasis on dialectic and logic based on false premises. This way of thinking had given rise to Scholasticism, and Scholasticism was the hard base of Catholicism. The mortal error, from the Puritans' point of view, was carried abroad primarily by the Jesuit priests, trained in Scholastic logic. The term "Jesuit" was equivalent, in the Puritan mind, with "Devil."

Thus, each discovery of the New Philosophy of science was greeted by the learned Puritan divines as further hard proof of the greatness and glory of God — proof not of the imagination and its labyrinthine rationalizations, but of hard fact. The Church of Rome was much more prone to find in any scientific discovery that undermined the basis of dogma and scholasticism a heresy, for if the theories of ages of church thinking were destroyed, would not the Church itself be destroyed as well?

The Puritans cared nothing at all for ages of Roman theorizing. They were interested in the Bible and its literal interpretation. Calvin had wished to sweep away the encrustations of dogma and ceremony built up through the centuries and return to the revealed Word of God. Where God was silent, there was no reason to reject the word of science. If Copernicus proved that the Earth revolved about the Sun, not vice-versa, and if astronomers showed that the Earth was merely a part of a greater universe, then how much greater the glory of God than had been supposed by Man in his cavernous ignorance?

But where science was silent, where mystery remained, there was no reason to reject tradition. Science had not driven out the occult, for there were many things science had not explained. It was therefore possible for a Puritan divine to believe both in astronomy and in Heaven. Though the stargazers may have shown that Paradise did not exist at some small distance above the clouds, they had not shown that it did not exist at a distance more remote and inscrutable. All science had done was to increase the vastness of the Fall of Satan and his hosts — and of Man. The imagination boggled in its attempt to encompass the cataclysmic nature of the doom of the dark angels, let alone Adam's decline from Grace — for if mankind had destroyed Bliss by eating of the Fruit of Knowledge, how small a bite science had begun to show it was. Evil became imponderable. It was Man's duty now to find God again by following the path he had chosen to the end, through the acquisition of knowledge about God's Creation. Many Puritan clerics were not only men of the cloth, but close observers of Nature as well, that Nature which, the Church had taught throughout the Middle Ages, was insignificant and unworthy of study, for Man's lot was merely to fix his thoughts on the life to come, not the life of the flesh.

Though in many ways the Puritans' view seemed, to outsiders, as dark as the views of medieval Catholicism, to the initiates they were not dark at all, merely stern. For Calvin taught the doctrine of Absolute Predestination, of the Salvation of the Elect. God had chosen a handful of men and women as His own; these were saved, and all others were doomed to destruction in the fires of Hell. No one could know absolutely if he or she were one of the Elect, and no one could be saved by doing good works or by merely living a Christian life. Nevertheless, in order to become a member of a Puritan congregation, one had to give testimony, to the satisfaction of the church members, that there were indications to show that the candidate was indeed one of the Chosen.

If his or her testimony seemed reasonable and likely, the postulant was welcomed.

Thus, if one's life were spotless; if one prospered in a trade or profession; if one were blessed with good children and a happy home; if one were of a charitable disposition, enjoyed being alive to partake of God's largesse in this world that He had made; if one gloried in the good things that happened and worried over the bad — if one asked oneself why God tried him or her in certain circumstances, and if one endeavored to correct any error into which one had fallen, then it was possible one was one of the Chosen. The true Puritan enjoyed what God had granted, but enjoyed it in the proper way. He or she made the best of the world, gave thanks that the opportunity had been offered, and praised God for His great bounty.

Dr. John Dee had many of these qualities in common with the Puritans — with people like Nicholas Putnam, but even more so with the Puritan intelligentsia. He differed from them mainly in what might be termed his impatience, though he was actually one of the most patient of men except in one regard: He aspired to the quality of Sainthood. He wished to speak directly with God. And he differed, also, in the method he used to effect his obsessive ambition: Though he was given to prayer, Dr. Dee also used sorcery.

The great sorrow of his life was that he lacked true Vision, for he was a mystic without the faculty of mysticism. Dr. Dee used his mind to come to a closer understanding of the nature of God, but he could not tap the wells of revelation. In desperation, he resorted to the ancient implements of the Magi — the Words of Power, the Secret Names, the alembic and the crucible, the symbols of the Zodiac and of Ouroboros, the Hermetic Dragon. He wished to speak with angels.

In 1580 John Dee's mother died, leaving her home in Mortlake to him. It already contained the doctor's very large library of books and manuscripts, which included many of the occult and alchemical books of Europe and England, "ancient and rare."

Dr. Dee and the Putnams shared not only certain attitudes, they shared the same shire. Mortlake, however, was a suburb of London, and Dr. Dee was no yeoman farmer. They might just as well have lived on different planets, for all their geographical proximity, except that both were influenced by the state of the nation, and things were changing rapidly in England, though in the more rural areas like Wingrave the changes might not be very apparent.

On September 26th Francis Drake returned to England from his epoch-making voyage around the world. He had left England in 1577, sailed across the Atlantic with five small ships, through the Straits of Magellan, and up the west coast of America, plundering Spanish ports as he went. When he had reached California, he had turned west, sailed across the Pacific and back to England. He had lost four of his ships on the voyage, but the one in which he returned was laden with fabulous treasures. The populace hailed Drake as a great hero, and Queen Elizabeth I came aboard his ship to bestow knighthood upon him.

As the year 1580 came to an end Margaret Putnam looked back upon it and thought what a difficult one it had been for her. She had had to cope with an infant and a small child simultaneously with her third pregnancy. The baby had been kicking vigorously for several weeks, and at Christmas time she had mentioned to her husband that it was a good thing the family was Puritan, not High Church, for she wouldn't otherwise have known how to deal with the holidays. As it was, she hadn't had to deal with them at all, for the Puritans believed Christmas to be nothing more than a Pagan holiday adopted, for its own purposes, by the Church of Rome.

Little John knew nothing about it, but Anne was just old enough to realize that some of her playmates had new toys while she had none. She had noticed and wondered at the glittering candles in the windows of some of the houses in Wingrave.

The year 1581 had not much more than begun when John and Anne were given a sister, Elizabeth, by the Lord God. It was almost like a holiday in the home, what with all the relatives coming and going, and one of the aunts in fact living-in during, and for a while after, the birth. On the 11th of February everyone made the baptismal trek to the church, and the ancient ceremony was repeated. Soon, things were back to normal in the household, if noisier and busier.

Also in February 1581 New Style, Dr. John Dee traveled to London to the Court on a matter of business and there met the visiting French demonologist Jean Bodin, author of the *Demonomania of Witches*, recently published and already famous. Dr. Dee availed himself of the opportunity to acquire a copy of the volume.

About the same time Robert Browne was imprisoned by the Bishop of Norwich for his activities on behalf of Separatism, but his confinement was short-lived, owing to the intervention of Browne's distant kinsman William Cecil, Lord Treasurer Burghley. Browne continued to get into trouble during the year, however, and before long he was imprisoned again.

In order to develop trade, Elizabeth I and Parliament had granted charters to monopolistic trading companies. These firms issued public stock and excluded from the monopoly other Englishmen not members of the corporation. The Turkey Company was organized in 1581 to trade with the eastern Mediterranean countries.

Nor was the religious issue subsiding. Laws were passed making it treason to attempt to convert a British subject to Catholicism; illegal to say or hear mass, and for Catholics to stay away from the services of the Church of England. Elizabeth I also laid down a special statute against foretelling the future and divination, with the same penalties as for Satanic witchcraft. To attempt to prophesy was treason, for it was in effect using sympathetic magic against a monarch: He who could tell — or even who thought he could tell — the future of the Queen might plot to bring her down at a propitious time. Since 1563 it had been illegal only for those in court circles to dabble in magic, but now, by extension, it was made to cover all those who might potentially wish to harm the State or its people. Not that anyone paid any attention to the law, however.

A necromancer, Edward Kelley, and a client of his, Paul Waring, ignored the new law and attempted to invoke demons in the park of Walton-in-the-Dale, Lancaster, in order to discover incidents in the future life, and the death-date, of a young nobleman, Waring's ward. They were unsuccessful in their conjuration — the magic circle drawn to ward off the powers invoked, the secret names pronounced to call forth the spirits. Kelley was puzzled. He might have better luck if he had a corpse. He asked a servant of Waring, a man who had accompanied them, whether it weren't true that the body of a poor man had been buried somewhere nearby recently. The servant, after some prompting, said it was so — the man had been put to rest that very day in the cemetery adjoining the park. Kelley made further preparations after the disinterment, said the proper things, and was at last successful: The cadaver spoke to them and foretold the future of Waring's ward.

Kelley, only twenty-six years of age, had been building a reputation for himself. He had studied, it was said, at Oxford when he was seventeen, and he had later studied law, becoming a notary in Lancaster. He had learned archaic English and Welsh and, using this knowledge had forged title deeds. When his crime was discovered, he had been indicted in Lancaster, sentenced to the pillory, and had his ears amputated by the authorities. Afterward, he had taken to wearing a black skull cap that covered his missing ears, which lent him a sinister appearance.

It wasn't long before Waring's servant began telling the story of Edward Kelley's latest adventure in the park in Walton-in-the-Dale, and when the authorities learned of it they looked diligently for the man in the black cap, but he was not to be found — no sooner had Waring paid him his fee than Kelly had disappeared to the southward.

In January of 1582 Robert Browne and his entire congregation migrated to Middleburgh in Zealand, Holland, where they organized a Calvinist church. Almost immediately, internal dissensions arose. Brown published in Middleburgh a book comprised of three tracts in which he propounded his radical system of Separatist Congregationalism. It wasn't long before copies of the book, and reports of the colony, began to circulate through the eastern shires of England and inland to London and the area of Wingrave.

In London Dr. John Dee had been busy attempting to persuade the Court to adopt the newly published policy that the Pope had proclaimed in a bull regarding the reformation of the old and inaccurate calendar. Nothing Catholic was likely to be listened to, given the situation in England, nor was it countenanced in this case; however, continental Europe began to change its way of reckoning dates, and so did Dr. Dee.

Elizabeth's Merlin had had more luck with finding a scryer and apprentice — a youth named Barnabas Saul, who could look into the crystal and see spirits. The relationship, unfortunately, was of short duration, for Barnabas soon got into trouble with the authorities and, in order to get himself out of his dilemma, he cried out on Dr. Dee, denouncing him as a sorcerer. The doctor, under the protection of the Queen, managed to extricate himself from the hostile law, and after only a few months he had to seek again for a partner in the occult.

Two days later Edward Kelley, by an extraordinary stroke of luck, introduced himself and said to the Doctor, "I understand that you seek one who scries, and I am such a one." Dr. Dee showed Kelley into his study and invited him to explain himself. Kelley told a strange story.

He had, he said, just come from Glastonbury, to which he had traveled from Lancaster far to the north. On his way there he had passed through Wales and one evening had stopped at an inn where he had had a few convivial glasses with the innkeeper, who, when he had discovered that Kelley was a scholar of antiquities, showed him an old manuscript which no one in the neighborhood had been able to read, it was couched in such archaic language. Kelley immediately recognized the script as ancient Welsh, and he was able to tell that it was, moreover, a discussion of the Philosopher's Stone and a treatise on the transmutation of base metals into gold.

The innkeeper, when Kelley had asked how he had come by the manuscript, told him that during one of the Protestant religious frenzies in the area the parchment had been discovered in the ransacked grave of an ancient bishop. The sepulcher had also contained two ivory caskets in one of which was a white, and in the other a red powder. The grave robbers had broken the casket containing the red powder, some of which had been lost. Unable to see what use any of this material was, they had sold it to the innkeeper for a flagon of wine.

Dr. Dee was fascinated. "What, then, became of these things?" he asked.

"I have them," Kelley replied. "I offered the man a guinea for the lot, and he accepted." As Kelley continued his story, he opened a bundle he had carried with him into the house and showed Dr. Dee the items it contained: A packet of red powder with a yellowish cast and a greasy feel, a small ivory box full of white powder, and an authentic-looking ancient manuscript.

"I have still not understood all that is written here," Kelly told the good doctor, for not only was the old language rather difficult, but since time immemorial true Adepts, as the doctor was sure to know, had couched their alchemical formulae in cryptic symbolism to keep their information from falling into ignorant and suspicious hands.

Dr. Dee was sure he had found his man at last. He asked Kelley when he would like to begin working. Kelley replied, "As soon as I have found lodging."

"Speak no more," Dr. Dee said, "you have found it. I wish to have you as close to hand as may be. You shall live in this house with my family."

Mrs. Jane Dee, a young and comely woman, was less than happy with the new arrangement, not to speak of the menacing stranger in the black cap he never removed, but her husband was delighted. He and his assistant began their work, but a small conflict of interests developed: Kelley was interested primarily in alchemy, Dee in speaking with spirits. He explained to Kelley that, though he was a deeply religious man, he did not have the psychic power. Kelley comforted him. "I can conjure angels," he said, "and I will scry for you."

In November Kelley and Dee prepared themselves. In Dr. Dee's study they prayed together. Then Kelley drew his circle, described his gestures as in the park in Walton-in-the-Dale, said the words, and conjured a cherub outside Dr. Dee's window.

"But I see nothing!" Dr. Dee cried.

"He is there," Kelley said, pointing toward the window. "He holds an egg of crystal."

"Describe the creature for me."

Kelley was pleased to comply, and from his description Dr. Dee recognized it as the angel Uriel. "He offers you the glass," Kelley said to the doctor. "Hold out your hand." Dr. Dee did so. Kelley reached to guide his arm to the spot, and lying on the windowsill Dr. Dee found an oval of pure crystal. "Do not be afraid of it," Kelley said, "pick it up. It is a gift of great price. Now we may scry." If he could truly have looked into the future, Dee would no doubt have been fascinated to know that his crystal would eventually be displayed at a new institution centuries later, the British Museum of London.

From that moment forward the conjurors scried nearly every day, and Dr. Dee began to keep a journal of their talks with the spirits. Kelley, however, found the inactivity of the scholarly home a bit wearing at times. He complained that the spirits often spoke to him in languages he did not understand; moreover, they sometimes denounced him right before Dr. Dee. To add insult to injury, Kelley's master insisted on taking down every word, so Kelley had to transmit the insults item by item, for Dr. Dee himself could discern nothing, although now and then he might see books moving in the study where one of the spirits stood, or hear a noise one of them made by knocking something over.

The spectres said on one occasion that Kelley was "a youngling, but old sinner," and that Dr. Dee's "sight" was more nearly perfect than that of Kelley, because purer. The situation was not one calculated to keep Kelley happy. He was subject to fits of unanticipated rage. Now and then he would disappear to look for treasure in the neighborhood — usually at night — but always he came back.

Dr. Dee and his wife Jane were pleased when they discovered that Edward Kelley had begun to take an interest in a young woman named Joan who lived nearby. It would be a steadying influence if he married her, for Jane in particular had been uncomfortable, on occasion, when she caught Edward staring at her.

Dr. Dee, like most of the New Philosophers of the day, was in touch not only with what was of interest in the Otherworld, but in this world as well. He was widely and deeply read, and he was constantly collecting intelligence and books. He was interested in two items of recent news from Italy and from Cologne. The first concerned an undergraduate student at the University of Pisa who, only last year having matriculated, had already isolated the principle of the isochronism of the pendulum. The young man's name was unusual: Galileo Galilei.

The news from Cologne was of a more immediately taking nature. One of Dee's continental colleagues, the Adept Hieronymous Scotus whose specialty was "magic dolls — effigies of the Medici, which he pierces with needles" in order to secure their deaths — had ingratiated himself with the Archbishop of Cologne, Gebhard Truchsess von Waldburg, by giving him a magic mirror in which the Archbishop saw the image of Canoness Agnes von Mansfield, "the fairest lady of Cologne." The Archbishop, falling madly in love, had courted her and, in order to be free to marry her, had left the Catholic Church and espoused Calvinism. The suit being successful, both the Archbishop and his wife had been excommunicated, and Scotus had been called to Prague by Emperor Rudolph II of Germany who, Dr. Dee long had known, was the greatest patron of alchemists and adepts in Europe.

Dr. Dee also came into possession of a chapbook published that year about a trial that had taken place in Chelmsford, Essex. Its author was known only by the initials: "W. W.," and it was entitled, *A True and Just Record*.

In Essex Ursula Kempe had been accused of witchcraft by Grace Thorlowe. Ursula was a wet nurse and a white witch who cured people by means of incantations and charms. One of her patients had been David Thorlowe, and she had told Grace, "I warrant thee, I, thy child shall do well enough." But when Grace had had a new baby, she hadn't asked Ursula to be its wet nurse. The infant girl had fallen out of its crib and broken its neck. Though Goodwife Thorlowe had her suspicions, she had nevertheless called Ursula Kempe in afterward to cure her arthritis, which had disappeared after the witch had treated it; however, Grace neglected to pay the witch her fee, and the arthritis had returned.

Goodwife Thorlowe complained of the situation to her master Brian Darcy, who was a judge of Common Sessions. He had ordered a preliminary examination of Ursula to be conducted by the Justice of the Peace who, having found probable cause, reported to Judge Darcy. Darcy in his turn had had her bound over to the County Sessions, and the trial had taken place.

Judge Darcy had succeeded in getting from Ursula's eight-year-old bastard son, Thomas Rabbet, some very strange stories about his mother. Ursula had denied the charges that she was a witch, but it had been only too obvious to everyone that she had been practicing the trade of "white" witch quite openly, and how far a step can it be from white magic to black? The judge told Ursula that "They who do confess the truth of their doings, they shall have much favor; but the other, they shall be burned and hanged."

Ursula, weeping, had confessed and told even more fantastic stories than her son had done, and she had implicated other women of her town of St. Osyth. Upon examination many of these women implicated others in a chain reaction. Of fourteen women accused, two had not been indicted for lack of evidence; two others had been released without indictments; four pleaded not guilty and were acquitted, and four had been convicted after pleading not guilty, but had been reprieved. Two, including Ursula Kempe, had been hanged.

Another new book Dr. Dee had debated buying, but had decided against as being an unnecessary expense, had been written by Richard Hakluyt. Its title was, *Diverse Voyages Touching the Discovery of America*.

Wingrave, where the Putnam family lived quietly, seemed an out-of-the-way place, but it was not so far off the beaten path as it might have appeared. It was, and still is, situated not a great distance north and west of London. Furthermore, the university town of Oxford was in the next shire, to the north and west also, and people journeying from one to the other passed close by Wingrave. Many people venturing out of the west from Hertfordshire and the coastal shire of Essex to Oxford had to pass directly through the town — and the ports of Essex were in constant touch with the southern coastal trading regions and the ports of Europe. News had a way of reaching Wingrave rather rapidly — news of the Puritan hotbeds in Norfolk, Essex, and Kent, where Calvin's doctrines had come in with the wool trade from Holland; news of the Court in London; news from the academics and clerics at Oxford.

The system of kinships being what it was, news of members of the family, no matter how distantly related, was always interesting, and might someday prove useful or important. The Putnams of Wingrave knew that they were related to the brothers Puttenham of Sherfield — Richard the elder and George the younger. Their own branch of the family, in fact, had not long ago spelled its name the same way, not that there was any standard of spelling at any rate. One spelled words as they sounded. *Putnam* would do well enough for yeoman farmers, and *Puttenham* for members of the gentry.

Richard Puttenham had been in and out of favor at Court for some years. He had married Mary , daughter of Sir William Warham of Malsanger and grandniece of the late old William Warham who had been Archbishop of Canterbury early in the century. Richard had been offered a knighthood but, since knighthood was more expensive to maintain than to pay a fine of forty pounds upon refusal of it, Richard had chosen to reject the offer and fall into disgrace at Court.

On February 15, 1560, Richard had leased his brother George his estate at Sherfield and shortly afterward had left England to go to the Continent, for he had fallen into further disgrace at Court and thought it best not to remain in the vicinity. He had left his wife behind in the care of George, who began to manage Sherfield in her, and his brother's, interest.

In 1567 Richard had secretly returned to England, and eventually he was successful in his search for a pardon for his offense to the Court. On the 22nd of October of that year he had sold his Sherfield estate to his son-in-law Francis Morris, under conditions subject to the lease he had made with George. According to the terms of the sale, Francis Morris was to pay "fifty pounds semi-annually at the tomb of Geoffrey Chaucer with the church of St. Peter, city of Westminster, also to deliver the carcass of a fallow deer, called a buck, being in season, yearly."

Neither of the Puttenham brothers was a Puritan, like their farmer cousins in Wingrave. On January 21, 1569, the Bishop of Winchester had protested against George's being placed in the Commission of the Peace because of his "evil life," for he was "a notorious enemy of God's truth."

George had been ordered to pay certain monies to Mary Puttenham, Richard's wife, because he had held back from the rents paid by the yeoman who farmed Sherfield a portion he considered his due for managing the estate. He felt he had been in the right, but in fact there was nothing in the lease he had signed that allowed him a fee. Francis Morris, in the belief that George had broken the terms of his contract with Richard and that he now owned the estate outright, had seized the property in 1570. George, when he discovered what Morris had done, attempted to enter the estate by force. Morris had resisted, subdued

George Puttenham and his men, and he had George thrown into prison for a short time; when he was released he had sued Morris, and lost.

George Puttenham, furious, had denounced the court and accused a man he had hired as go-between, Carl Hodges, of having sold out to Morris. Hodges, angry in turn, had denounced George as a member of a plot to kill William Cecil, Lord Burghley, Queen Elizabeth's Secretary. In addition, George had been accused of having armed his servants in order to harass Francis Morris, of harboring an accused murderer, and of attempting to hire Hodges to kill Cecil for 500 marks. George Puttenham had been subsequently tried and acquitted of all charges.

Feeling his first suit had been decided unfairly, George had again sued Morris, and, though the Privy Council felt there was a good deal of justice in Puttenham's view that he had been poorly used, George also lost the second suit. Morris immediately sold Sherfield to Thomas Colby, though the estate was still entailed in Mary Puttenham's name, and she was to have an income from it. Richard, through all his brother's troubles, had been unable to help, for he himself had been a prisoner before the King's Bench. in 1574 his wife Mary asked Thomas Colby "to pay her her pension fixed on the estate, as her estate is very poor."

And George was also having trouble with his own wife over her property. In 1578 he was before the Privy Council several times over the issue. Just as he had used force against Francis Morris over his brother's estate, Lady Elizabeth's son Thomas, Lord Paulet, had done the same against George. On one occasion when he had been summoned to attend the Privy Council George excused himself with the message that "My danger is not small in respect to my wife and my children, who have long desired my death." In a letter to his agent at Court, Sir John Throckmorton, he wrote, "I am now on the point of fifty years, and have been five or six times waylaid, twice by the Lord Thomas Paulet and his servants, and my goods taken away from me, and twice or thrice other times by Mrs. Paulet's servants, being assaulted with swords and daggers." Further, his wife and her favorites had slandered him at court, he wrote.

George was grateful to Sir John, who procured a safe conduct for him so that he could attend the Privy Council for a hearing. But a safe conduct was no guarantee of safety in London, and when he got to the city George had gone into hiding for three weeks instead of appearing before the Council. By means of a young French girl who was Puttenham's messenger, Throckmorton had found where he was hiding, had him arrested, and brought him before the Council.

In 1563 Throckmorton was able to effect a settlement between George and his wife, Lady Windsor, and George was allowed to occupy the estate of Herriard, part of her property. As soon as he could, George settled in and began to write a book about English poetry that he hoped would find favor at Court.

Rumors of the troubles of the infamous Puttenham brothers were always interesting to the Putnams of Wingrave, but of more moment was the news that the Spanish ambassador had been discovered to be involved in a plot to place Mary Queen of Scots on the English throne. Walsingham had uncovered this and other Catholic plots, and the Putnams were as one with the Queen on the issue of stern penalties for such Popish traitors. They heard that James Fitzmaurice's Irish Catholic rebellion, which had been flaring fitfully in southwestern Ireland for years, had finally been put down, brutally.

But in August Nicholas and Margaret were as apprehensive as their dissenting neighbors when news of the elevation of John Whitgift to the Archbishopric of Canterbury reached Wingrave. Though Whitgift himself was known to favor Calvinism, like all Church of England men he saw in Scottish Presbyterian Calvinism — with its competing hierarchical system — a threat to the established Anglican order. Nor did the Archbishop bear any love for separatists such as Robert Browne, whose experimental community in Holland had dissolved because of factional and ideological disputes.

Some of the Brownists had begun to drift back to England. The Putnams were appalled and dismayed when they heard that three Brownists had been hanged in Bury St. Edmunds, Suffolk, for circulating copies of the book Brown had published in Holland the previous year. It wasn't long before a copy or two of the book reached Wingrave and was surreptitiously passed about among the dissenters of the parish. Nicholas and Margaret were most shocked and outraged, however, when they learned in the church lecture that the Anglican minister, Samuel Harsnett, had preached against the Calvinist doctrine of Absolute Predestination, which he had called a "monstrous" tenet which required "that not one or two, but millions of men" not of God's "elect" should "fry in Hell" and that God had "made them for no other purpose."

During the summer Dr. John Dee had met Count Adalbert Lasky, a Polish nobleman and minion of Henry III of France, who was visiting the English Court. Lasky, Dee found, shared many of his own interests in matters arcane, and on the 31st of July Dee, feeling pressed, had agreed to have the Count for dinner — a dinner he could not really afford. Dee appealed to the Court for assistance, and he wrote a journal entry on the result:

"Her Majesty (An. 1583 *Julii ultimo*) being informed by the Right Honorable" Robert Dudley, "Earl of Leicester, that whereas the same day in the morning he had told me that his Honour and the Lord Lasky would dine with me within two days after, I confessed sincerely unto him that I was not able to prepare them a convenient dinner, unless I should presently sell some of my plate or some of my pewter...." But Queen Elizabeth I was compassionate, nor did she want her guest insulted, so she sent her Merlin twenty pounds.

The dinner was a great success. Lasky was profuse in his compliments and greatly admired the accomplishments of both Dr. Dee and Edward Kelley. The Count extended them an invitation to come with him to Prague to be presented to Emperor Rudolph II of Germany, patron of alchemists and sorcerers, seeker of the Philosopher's Stone. Dr. Dee, taken aback, professed himself to be uncertain, but Kelley was overjoyed — so much so that, while he cajoled his master, he ceased his rages and bickering.

Kelley hadn't to work long. Dr. Dee agreed to the adventure in August, and the household began to make preparations to depart. On Saturday, September 21st, Kelley, Dee, their wives — for Kelley had married Joan , the local girl he had met during the previous winter — and the Dee children left Mortlake "about three of the clock after noon." They thought everything was in order, but they had forgotten one important piece of business: No one had thought to ask permission of Queen Elizabeth I to leave the country, and the Queen was a jealous sovereign. That night the entourage met Count Lasky "on the water." By dark the party reached London "and in the dead of the night, by wherries, we went to Greenwich, to my friend Goodman Fern the potter in his house, where we refreshed ourselves," Dee wrote in his journal.

On Sunday the 22nd of September they went aboard their ships lying off Gravesend. Immediately they set sail and the next day ran into a gale that came close to foundering them, but they managed to put into Quinborough, and on the following Friday the vessel made Brielhaven on the continent. They began to coast, putting in at various ports. Finally, on Thursday, November 7th, the Dees and Kelleys, with Count Lasky, arrived at Lubeck.

In Wingrave the townsfolk heard nothing of Dr. Dee's sailing, or, if any of them did, there had been little reaction except perhaps a sigh of relief that the old warlock was safely out of the way for a while. But by the fall they had heard that Sir Humphrey Gilbert, Sir Walter Raleigh's half-brother, had been lost at sea attempting to plant an English colony in Newfoundland.

On the second of January, 1584, Dr. John Dee and his ménage arrived in Stetin, Pomerania. Almost unremittingly throughout the trip, and at every stopover, the sorcerer and his apprentice had been looking into the crystal egg, Edward Kelley had been talking to the spirits therein, and dictating their words to the good Doctor. Dee, in his journal, had been dating the entries according to the new calendar as well as the old, in cross-reference.

On an inauspicious day — Friday, the 13th of February, New Style — the caravan arrived in Cracow, Poland, and settled in to await Count Lasky who had gone to attend to an uprising in his province. Almost immediately Kelley, who had been becoming restive, began to receive slurs from his spirits. On the 19th of April he told Dr. Dee angrily that the spirits with whom they had been dealing "are all false and crafty, and if I had been in your place, I would burn my books." Dr. Dee managed to calm him down at last by telling him that he had had a message that Count Lasky was on his way to meet them.

On the 25th, a Wednesday, the Count arrived in the night, but only momentarily, for he was on his way to "recover Kesmark." Disappointed, the alchemists began another wait. In May they became involved in a rather large project: The spirits had been speaking to Kelley in a mystic language that Dr. Dee resolved to decode. Among many of the peculiar words there was one repeated seven times: "OHIO."

Toward the end of the month, the 24th of May, Kelley refused to look into the glass. Exasperated, Dr. Dee retired to his study where he was reading a little later when Kelley burst into the room waving a book by the Adept Agrippa. "I told you they were cozeners!" he shouted, "for I have found the names of the countries the spirits have given us are here!" Dr. Dee took the book and looked where Kelley pointed.

After a bit of perusal Dr. Dee came to an entirely different conclusion. He rebuked Kelley: "This is no proof of cozenage, but on the contrary, proof that the spirits are dealing fairly with us, as now we can assign the names of governing angels to the countries." But Kelley refused to believe his master, and after an argument he returned, muttering, to his own room.

As if this weren't enough, Dr. Dee received disastrous news from England: A howling mob, knowing full well the place was empty, had broken into his house at Mortlake screaming "Wizard!" and "Warlock!" They had ransacked the place and attacked his library, destroying the collection he had built for so many years. It was a great sorrow to him for, unlike many of his Brothers of the Stone, he had never been secretive about his work, and he had often lent his books to people who came to him for information about many things. Dee had been, in effect, a local librarian.

By the end of July the word had come that Dee and Kelley were to leave for Prague. On the first of August the sorcerer and his apprentice set off, leaving their families behind in Cracow, and on Thursday, the 9th, they arrived at their destination. By the middle of the month they were set up in a house lent them by D. Hageck. It was located in Bethlem, in Old Prague, and it had an excellent study for Dr. Dee which, it seemed to him, had been the studio of an Adept "skillful of the holy stone: A name was in diverse places of the study, noted in letters of gold and silver, 'Simon, Baccalaureate of Prague,' and among other things manifold written very fairly in the study (and very many Hieroglyphical Notes Philosophical, in birds, fishes, flowers, fruits, leaves, and six vessels, as for the Philosopher's works) these verses were over the door:

> "'Immortale Decus par gloriaque illi debentur
> Cikis ab ingenio est discolor his paries.'

"And of the Philosopher's work (on the south side of the study) in three lines, uppermost," there was written a long Latin passage. Dr. Dee was delighted. He summoned Edward Kelley to commence their work immediately.

Two days later, Dr. Dee wrote a letter to the Emperor Rudolph and sent it via the Spanish ambassador Don Guglielmo de San Clemente.

He settled back to wait for a reply, for he knew, from his traffic with the English Court, that these things took time.

On the 27th of August, ten days later, Dr. Dee received a great deal of mail — one letter from Count Lasky, one from his wife in Cracow, and one from his "brother"-in-law "Nicholas Fromonds in England: How Mr. Gilbert, Mr. Sledd, Mr. Andreas Firmorshem, my bookseller, used me very ill in diverse sorts.

"The dates of the letters from England," he wrote in his journal, "were of the 15th and 16th day of April 1584. My wife is in great sorrow for my brother Nicholas." But to balance out the bad news, Dr. Dee also received a message from the Spanish ambassador that within three or four days Dee might have an audience with the Emperor.

More than four days passed, and Dee had no further word from the Emperor. Then, on Sunday evening the 2nd of September, Edward Kelley went out to get drunk. His boon companion was Count Lasky's servant Alexander, and when they were well into their cups Kelley, becoming angry about something, threatened to cut off Alexander's head. Alexander took offense, went for his weapon, and was subdued by a blow from Kelley's staff.

A little later Dr. Dee, who had skipped supper and gone to his room, looked out and saw Alexander sitting on a stone outside the house. Dee called to him to approach, told him the rest of the members of the doctor's household were eating, and asked him what he wanted. Alexander informed Dee of what had happened, with a great deal of puffing and blowing, and Dr. Dee went out to see what he could do to straighten out the situation at Count Lasky's house. When he got there, he discovered Kelly lying in a drunken stupor. Seeing that the situation was hopeless for the moment, Dr. Dee said to Alexander, "Words spoken in drunkenness mean nothing. Do not be offended. Come and sleep at my house." Alexander was loudly unwilling to be persuaded, but after two hours of cajoling, and a warning from the night watch to keep the peace, he gave in and went with the doctor.

In the morning Kelley showed up at the house, found Alexander there, and was asked for an apology. Kelley swore he remembered nothing, but apologized for any insult he might have delivered. Dr. Dee told Kelley, "Why, you threatened poor Alexander that you would cut off his head, and Alexander had replied that before you could do it, he would cut you into pieces. I would be pleased if you would make peace between you."

But Kelley was astonished when he heard Alexander's reply, and no sooner had Dr. Dee finished speaking than he flew into a rage and dived for Alexander. Fortunately, there were several people in the room besides the frail doctor, including Americus Sontag, and they managed to keep him off Lasky's man. Kelley, however, tore loose from them and ran into the street dressed only in his doublet and hose, a rapier he had grabbed out of someone's sheath in his hand. Once outdoors he turned and screamed, "Alexander, come and fight! Come tear me in pieces, you swine!" Alexander went outdoors but refused and turned to leave — as soon as his back was turned Kelley picked up a stone and heaved it at him. When Alexander was gone, Kelley returned, still furious.

Dr. Dee spent most of the morning getting his scryer calm again. A letter from his wife in Cracow arrived about noon and, while he was resting, at 2 p.m. there came a message from the Emperor Rudolph summoning him…at 2 o'clock! Dee threw himself together, very distressed, and ran to the castle. In the guard chamber he was halted, told to wait, and word was sent in to the Chamberlain, Octavious Spinola, that Dr. Dee had arrived.

Presently Spinola appeared and, leading him, as the doctor described it in his journal, "by the skirt of the gown," brought him to the king in the privy chamber. Dr. Dee bowed three times, and the king received him kindly.

Emperor Rudolph was sitting holding Dr. Dee's letter and a copy of one of his books, *Monas Hieroglyphica*, which had been dedicated to Rudolph's father, Maximilian. The emperor commended him on the book but said, "It is too hard for me." Dr. Dee responded with a great, discursive monologue about his long journey toward the fount of knowledge, about his magnificent crystal, and he concluded with the information that in a recent session with his scryer, Edward Kelley, an angel of the Lord had given him a message for the emperor:

"The angel of the Lord hath appeared to me, and rebuketh you for your sins. If you will hear me, the Lord, the God that made Heaven and Earth (under whom you breathe, and have your spirit) putteth his foot against your breast, and will throw you headlong down from your seat.

"Moreover, the Lord hath made this covenant with me (by oath) that he will do and perform. If you will forsake your wickedness, and turn to him, your seat shall be the greatest that ever was, the Devil shall become your prisoner, which Devil I do conjecture to be the Great Turk. This, my commission, is from God; I feign nothing, neither am I an hypocrite, an ambitious man, or doting, or dreaming in this cause. If I speak otherwise than I have just cause, I forsake my salvation."

During his speech Dr. Dee had been greatly agitated, but the emperor's response was simply to say, "I do believe you. I think you love me unfeignedly." Dee's speech had not gone as smoothly as he afterwards put it down in his journal, for Rudolph at that point added, "You do not need so earnest protestations, and I would not willingly have you kneel so often as you do."

At last, after the good part of an hour, Dr. Dee understood that his audience was over. The king promised that Dr. Dee should have his rewards — or at least the mathematician thought the monarch had said something like that, but his Majesty had spoken in a voice so low that Dee hadn't quite made out his exact words.

The wizard, who had hoped to have another audience quite soon, by September 15th heard that Rudolph instead had designated Dr. Curtz as go-between to relay to the emperor what Dee's angels had to say. On that day Dee met Dr. Curtz and gave him a longer version of the story about his voyage toward the mystic land of knowledge and wisdom. He showed Curtz his crystal egg.

After six hours Dr. Curtz asked John Dee what summary of all these points he could give the emperor. Dr. Dee replied, "The king would do well to give ear to what my spirits say."

When the good doctor returned to his house he discovered that a "wicked tempter" who denied Christ had in the meantime visited Kelley and said that Kelley would use Dee "Like a serpent, and nothing good would ever come of the crystal gazing." But his master was not discouraged. Dee still had not caught on that Kelley wanted to practice alchemy, not scrying — or perhaps the good Doctor was purposely obtuse.

Twice, on the 17th and 18th of September, Dr. Dee sent Americus to see what he could find out about what Dr. Curtz had reported to Rudolph, but he could get no information. He began to suspect that Curtz was not his friend.

On Monday, the 24th, his suspicions were confirmed: Dr. Dee discovered that he had been slandered at the table of the Spanish ambassador, to the effect that he was "a conjuror and a bankrupt alchemist," one who had come to cheat the emperor out of something, Dee having sold his goods to bribe Lasky to intercede with Rudolph for him. As soon as he had word of this, Dr. Dee took the opportunity to complain of this treatment to the ambassador himself. Dee was reassured that the emperor thought kindly of him, "therefore you are not to regard these Dutchmen's ill tongues, who can hardly brook any stranger." He told Dee that he would like to see his stone, and Dr. Dee left, having made a dinner appointment for the next day.

When Dee got back to his home on Tuesday, September 25th, having returned to the ambassador's house, eaten with him, conversed, and shown him the crystal, he found Edward Kelley set to leave for England. He talked Kelley out of any precipitate moves, but his heart wasn't in it — for he was penniless, his patron Lasky nowhere in sight; he had heard that Queen Elizabeth I was unhappy that he had left England without her permission. Finally, he had information that the

Bishop of London intended to have him accused of being a conjuror, with "the secret assistance of you know whom," he wrote in his journal.

But his family had caught up with him at last, having traveled from Cracow, and that was some comfort. Toward the end of the month Dr. Curtz came to the house. Edward Kelley immediately disappeared into his room, and Dee took the visitor to the study where he complained of the doctor's great injury to him. But Dr. Curtz denied he had ever done anything against Dee. He said, further, that he had made a full report of their meeting to the emperor, but heard nothing in turn.

Dee had left some of his books with the emperor. Dr. Curtz had heard that he thought they were "either incredible or impossible," and wanted some time to consider them, together with other manuscripts. Dr. Dee, humiliated, replied, "They may not leave my hands, but I will make a copy for the emperor, at leisure." The two doctors finished by talking of mathematics. Dee showed Curtz a book he had published in Italy, let him borrow it, and Curtz left.

On Sunday, the 7th of October, they met again to discuss various matters. Dr. Dee told Curtz of his amazing mirror, with which one could communicate at long distances on a moonlit night. It was still in Cracow, but perhaps the emperor might like to see it. He asked Curtz if he might have from the emperor a safe conduct in his realm, gave him a note to deliver to Rudolph making the request, and they parted.

Soon things were looking much brighter, for Dr. Dee and Kelley left for Cracow in the fall and returned to Prague at the end of December — not in any mean way, either, but in a coach.

In Wingrave Nicholas Putnam found time to spare to think and talk with his neighbors about recent events, as for instance on the Monday after St. Peter's day during the summer after the Rush-Bearing ceremony at the church. On this day the parishioners gathered to scatter hay or rushes on the floor of the building in order to celebrate an old occurrence in the parish: One of the parishioners had gotten lost at night but managed to find her way home by following the church bells which were being rung. In gratitude, she had bequeathed to the parish the income from some of her nearby fields for the purpose of providing the church with floor covering.

By the fall, however, Margaret Putnam had little time to listen to gossip, for she could barely find a moment for herself. Their fourth child, Thomas, had been born in September and baptized on the 20th of that month. None of her children was yet old enough to be of any real help around the home. Anne, the eldest, was but six, very bright and active, but helter-skelter. No sooner had one asked her to do something than she forgot what she was about and was off into mischief. John was a solid, steady boy for his four years, and he loved to be entrusted with things to do, but there were few he was really capable of doing. As often as not Goodman Putnam took John with him into the fields where the boy tagged along quietly and was at least out from underfoot.

Elizabeth looked to be the more promising of the girls, but at three that promise was largely unfulfilled. She had a good imagination, however, and found things to interest her, which was a blessing. Goodwife Putnam wondered, sometimes, how many more children she would have, not that she minded a large family — she merely hoped the Lord would let the younger ones grow up a bit more first.

Her husband and his neighbors spoke in cautionary terms of the news. When the Protestant Prince William of Orange had been assassinated, some Englishmen had reacted by forming vigilante groups to avenge any attempts that might be made on Queen Elizabeth's life. These private armies were not, strictly speaking, illegal, but they were ominous, it seemed to the Puritans of Wingrave.

Robert Browne and some of his followers had gone to Scotland in January, stopping at Dundee and St. Andrews on their way to Edinburgh. He had attempted to put forth his views on Congregationalism — each local church to be an autonomous unit in the brotherhood of Puritanism, but Presbyterianism was well established in Scotland, and Browne had succeeded no better than he might. He had returned to England and settled in Stamford.

On the 4th of January, 1585, the Dee ménage rented a larger house in Prague for 70 thalers per year. Two days later Dee wrote a letter to "Dr. Jacob Kurtius," which was the proper way, he understood, to address the man he had been calling "Dr. Curtz." By the 12th they were moved into their new place and actively engaged in hatching spirits out of the crystal egg of the angel Uriel. But the scholar and the scryer had only a little over two months of worry-free study, for by the end of March they were penniless again. In desperation, they petitioned the spirits for sustenance: Perhaps it was to be found in alchemy — which is what Kelley had wanted all along, and what Rudolph was most interested in.

Dr. Dee had recorded in his journal on March 20th an alchemical recipe which he titled "Mysteria Stephanica" — where it came from was not recorded, nor who "Stephan" was. Perhaps it was the secret of Stephanus of Alexandria, the 7th century Arabian Alchemist, or perhaps the title was merely a dedication to the great King of Poland, Stephen Bathory. Like all the formulae of the adepts, certain words seemed to be in a cryptic language. Perhaps, if it could be deciphered in time, they would not have to go begging to Lasky or Rudolph once again:

"Take common audcal, purge and work it by rlodnr of four diverse digestions, continuing the last digestion for fourteen days, in one and a swift proportion, until it be dlasod fixed a most red and luminous body, the image of resurrection.

"Take also lulo of red roxtan, and work him through the four fiery degrees, until thou have his audcal, and there gather him.

"Then double every degree of your rlodnr, and by the law of coition and mixture work and continue them diligently together. Notwithstanding backward, through every degree, multiplying the lower and last rlodnr his due office finished by one degree more than the highest.

"So doth it become darr, the thing you seek for: A holy, most glorious, red, and dignified dlasod. But watch well, and gather him so, at the highest, for in one hour he descendeth, or ascendeth from the purpose.

"Take hold!"

As he pored over this text, Dr. Dee noticed that several words — rlodnr, dlasod — sounded like Welsh, and that the ultimate product was red, but perhaps he made no direct connection with Kelley's ancient manuscript *The Book of St. Dunstan*, and with the red powder that had purportedly been found in St. Dunstan's tomb in Wales.

Kelley himself put very little stock in the material they were getting from the crystal. He again asserted that the spirits were frauds, and he asked Dr. Dee to let him borrow one of his books to show to a Jesuit priest for his opinion. Dr. Dee, always cautious where priests were concerned, refused to lend him the volume, and Kelley flew into one of his typical rages. He shouted, "I will not leave this room until you give it me," and he went to shut the study door. Dr. Dee, who had been writing a letter to Queen Elizabeth when Kelley burst in, rose, took Kelley by the shoulders, and called for help. The household aroused, Kelley calmed down and began to work quietly again.

Somehow, the pair of wizards managed to raise some more money and again journeyed to Cracow. As they approached the city they saw whirlwinds, which proved to be an omen: When they arrived they discovered that the house they had leased was occupied by someone else. They insisted that they would stay there anyhow, and they did, but only until the next day, a Saturday, when the occupants evicted them. Dr. Dee complained to the Rector who immediately issued a citation for the occupants to answer Dee's complaint.

Fortunately, at this juncture Count Lasky arrived in Cracow. When Dr. Dee had acquainted him with the facts, the Count issued an order to the tenants to make room for Dee and Kelley. The tenants moved downstairs, the alchemists moved in upstairs. No sooner had they done so than Dee found that he had won his suit, and that Lasky had informed the King of Poland of the situation. The King apologized to Lasky for the inconvenience and told him he would like to meet the renowned pair.

The following Wednesday, Count Lasky and Dr. Dee were given an audience with King Stephen Bathory — which was all very good and well as far as prestige and Dr. Dee's social standing were concerned, but the first week in May Kelley was again in one of his great furies because Lasky had not paid him the money he owed, and partly, perhaps, because the "Mysteria Stephanica" had made little impression on the Polish king. His eyes flaming, his hands raised to the ceiling, Kelley shouted, "I curse God for this pass we have come to!" Dr. Dee, terrified and amazed, shrank back from his friend and moaned at the blasphemy.

By August, however, things were again relatively calm. They had returned to Prague and were scrying. Now and then some news from England would arrive — news of such things as voyages. In one of these Dr. Dee was particularly interested: Captain John Davis, the famous navigator, had sailed on a voyage to the Arctic in search of the Northwest Passage around America. Dr. Dee, who was a friend of the cartographer Mercator, had helped in the preparations for this voyage, which had been several years in the planning.

In the Vale of Aylesbury, too, there was a change of houses. Nicholas and Margaret Putnam packed up their possessions and children and moved to Stewkely, to a larger house. Goody Putnam was pregnant again, and there was simply no more room in the old place. Nicholas had acquired land in Aston Abbotts and sold the Wingrave property. Soon they had settled in, and the children were becoming accustomed to the new surroundings and the new faces.

The talk of the day was of the royal patent Sir Walter Raleigh had received to found a colony in the New World. The villagers shook their heads as they spoke of it. Raleigh had sent Sir Richard Grenville off to Roanoke Island with several planters. And there were tales of war as well: Queen Elizabeth had sent English troops to aid the Dutch in their war against the Catholic Philip of Spain who, harried and harassed by the English Queen, had decided — it was bruited about — to attack England when he had succeeded in defeating the heretical Hollanders.

Of even more moment to the Stewkeley dissenters was the fact that Robert Browne was again in prison. They had noticed that his views seemed to be changing of late, so it was not a great surprise, though a great disappointment, when on the 7th of October he made a submission with qualifications to the Church of England.

The rogue Richard Puttenham was again a prisoner as well. He had petitioned the Privy Council for relief.

The rumors continued all through the winter and into the fall of 1586. John Putnam, six years old, was too young to understand much of what his parents and their neighbors were talking about before the fire in the "hall" — the kitchen — or in the market when he accompanied them, but he was not too young to catch the note of concern in their voices when they talked of the armada of ships the King of Spain was amassing, of the plot against the Queen, led by Anthony Babington, and with Mary Queen of Scots and the King of Spain behind it all until Walsingham had uncovered it. Parliament had asked Elizabeth to execute Mary, and "Heads will roll!" was a phrase John heard over and over — the image troubled his sleep at night.

Nothing but bad news: Sir Francis Drake had had to rescue the survivors of the colony at Roanoke Island in America — an unlikely place at best, full of savages that worshipped the Devil. Nor was that the only place: There was Devil worship even in England, to hear tell of the trials of witches in Derbyshire. Though the judges had determined that fraud had taken place, still, "Where there is smoke, there is fire," and John Putnam imagined the Devil in Hell with witches all about.

For John Darrell, an itinerant preacher of Mansfield, Nottinghamshire, had been called in to pray with Catherine Wright who acted as though she were possessed, swooning and trembling in the neighboring shire. After a day of prayer and fasting, at Darrell's urging she had accused Margaret Roper of sending a demon named Middlecub to possess her.

Brought before the court and examined, Catherine had faltered and then admitted that her fits had been deliberately perpetrated, for she had discovered that "they made a severe father-in-law more kind." The magistrate had threatened Darrell with imprisonment should there be a recurrence of the event.

Indeed, the Devil was at work in England, for Robert Browne had made a further submission to the Church of England, and as his reward in November he was appointed Master of St. Olave's School in Southwark. But he was still a man in the middle, attacked by those who were High Church, and those who had originally followed and believed in him. But the Putnams had enough else to keep them preoccupied, for their fifth child and third son had arrived. They decided to name him Richard after Nicholas' younger brother who had died in 1576 and left him the Wingrave property.

Things had not been going well in Prague, which Dr. Dee and Edward Kelley, their wives and children, had left under a pall. Dr. Dee had given the Emperor Rudolph his two magic mirrors and an "astral magnet" with which, he assured the king, one was able to send "signals over long distances on moonlight nights."

On Tuesday, May 6th, the caravan arrived in Leipzig, and five days later Dee wrote to Sir Francis Walsingham, Queen Elizabeth's Secretary, in order to patch up any misunderstanding that might have arisen regarding his departure from the realm and his lengthy stay overseas.

Finally, on May 30th, Dr. Dee received a copy of his notice of exile from the dominions of the Emperor, for Pope Sixtus V had accused Dee of necromancy — raising the dead.

In England, on the 14th and 15th of October, Mary Queen of Scots was tried by Elizabeth at last, after long years of incarceration — tried for her purported role in various plots against the English queen, and for espousing the cause of the Spanish king. Elizabeth hesitated for some months still, and then, on the first of February, 1587, signed the death warrant. The people of Wingrave, Stewkeley, and the rest of England — those who were not Catholic — were gratified, for Mary had been a threat to the throne and to Protestantism.

No sooner had she put her hand to the warrant than Elizabeth wrote to Mary's jailer, taking him to task for not having taken Mary's death into his own hands earlier, thus relieving Elizabeth of the burden of conscience under which she labored. She suggested that he might still find a way to get the job done without the help of the Royal executioner, but the Puritan keeper of the Queen of Scots, Sir Amyas Paulet, declined the invitation to "shed blood without law or warrant." Admitting defeat, on the 7th of February the Queen sent two earls with the commission for execution, and the next morning sentence was carried out by the headsman.

John Putnam heard his parents talking about it, heard that one head had, indeed, rolled at last, and that it was a queen's head. Everyone was talking about the grisly scene — the missed stroke of the nervous executioner, the things that the head did after it had been severed from the body. John did not sleep well for several nights. The news put completely into the background the excitement he had felt when he heard that the great Sir Walter Raleigh was sending another colony to America to live.

The Dee party was in Trebona, Bohemia, by April, and on the fourth of that month Edward Kelley again refused to scry. This time it looked as though he meant it. Dr. Dee, in desperation, asked Kelley to train the doctor's son, Arthur Dee at first agreed, then refused to do even that, and Dr. Dee decided to attempt the training himself.

On the 15th Arthur Dee had his first look into the glass. After very long trying, he saw a few things, but not very much. On Friday the 17th Arthur again had little luck, which astonished Edward Kelley, for he had heard the Doctor and his son praying, had looked out, and seen "a great number of their usual spirits, including the girl Madimi, going in and out of the chapel, "in very filthy order; and Uriel appeared, and justified all to be of God, and good; and therefore I wonder if here you have no show — Perhaps," Kelley told the doctor, "there is somewhat, but Arthur seeth it not." Kelly was persuaded by this to scry into the glass, and the spirits spoke to him in Latin, very suggestively. Both Dee and Kelley were troubled in spirit.

The next day Arthur again sat to the glass, but saw nothing. Kelley, who had the previous day been instructed by the angels to bring a powder with him, arrived with the proper substance and took over. No sooner had he sat to scry than Madimi appeared, and the rest of the heavenly host with her. Suddenly, all but Madimi disappeared, and Kelley informed the doctor, "Madimi openeth all her apparel, and herself all naked, and showeth her shame also. Fie on thee, Devil!" Kelley cried into the stone, "Avoid hence with this filthiness!"

But Madimi replied, "In the name of God, why find you fault with me?"

Dee said, through his interpreter, "Because your yesterday's doings and words are provocations to sin, and unmeet for any godly creature to use."

"What is sin?" Madimi asked.

"To break the commandment of God."

"Set that down so," she said through her mouthpiece. "If the self-same God that gave you the law of Moses, and gave his New Covenant by Christ, who sealed it by his blood, and had his witnesses very many, and his Apostles instructed by his holy spirit, who admonished us of all uncleanness in words and works, yea and in thoughts, if by the same God, those former laws and doctrines be abrogated, and that sufficient proof and testimony may be had that it is the same God — then must the same God be obeyed, for only God is the Lord of lords, King of kings, and Governor of all things."

And what God now wanted was for the Kelleys and the Dees, all four, to live in a marriage commune, "that we two," the doctor and the scryer, "had our wives in each sort, as we might use them in common."

Kelley, shocked, repeated his vow never to scry again. Dr. Dee was confounded momentarily, but he thought they ought to ask the glass "whether the sense" of God's new commandment "were of carnal use (contrary to the law of the commandment), or of spiritual love, and charitable care and unity of minds, for advancing the service of God." They asked the question, and much to their dismay, the commandment was, indeed, to apply to everything, including carnal love.

The women, told of this development, reacted as might be expected: Amazed disbelief transfigured them. Dr. Dee wrote in his journal, "After all these, and many more things told me by the same Mr. E. K., we departed each to his bed, where I found my wife awake, attending to hear some new matter of me from Mr. Kelley's reports of the apparitions…I then told her, and said, 'Jane, I see that there is no other remedy, but as hath been said of our cross-matching, so it must needs be done.'

"Thereupon she fell a weeping and trembling for a quarter of an hour, and I pacified her as well as I could; and so, in the fear of God, and in believing of His admonishment, did persuade her that she show herself prettily resolved to be content, for God's sake and His secret purposes, to obey the admonishment."

On the 21st of April Dee and Kelley drew up a preliminary compact regarding the new marital order, but Kelley the next day wrote a disclaimer, saying he had always distrusted the spirits, but his master had persuaded him otherwise. In this statement he wrote that the women didn't wish to do anything against the spirits, but wanted more scrying on the subject before they submitted. Jane Dee had entered into a fast until she could be persuaded that this was, indeed, God's will. Kelley again swore he would scry no more.

Nevertheless, on April 24th there was another session at the crystal — sure enough, the spirits had meant precisely what they had been saying. Dee and Kelley had drawn up a long contract on the subject, with much supplication to the Lord God.

On the 3rd of May, a Sunday, all four people put their hands to the contract, but the women still had their doubts — they wanted to know specifically that God did not object. Speaking to angels was one thing, but direct word was quite another. And Kelley must scry yet again.

On the 20th of May the spirits tried to take away Dr. Dee's crystal, but it was supernaturally returned, for the sorcerer discovered it in his wife's room under her pillow, where she was resting.

Kelley, completely frustrated and unhappy, said that he was leaving the house forever, and this time he meant it. He returned to Prague; the Dees settled down to a relatively peaceful time in Trebona under the protection of Count Wilhelm von Rosenberg, Viceroy of Bohemia, but Dr. Dee missed his old friend, and Arthur, though a good and dutiful son, was completely unsatisfactory as a scryer.

Nevertheless, life was a good deal less hectic, and Dr. Dee could begin to pay attention to things he had let slip because of all the hours he had been spending in crystal gazing. For one thing, he could begin to collect books and rebuild the library he had lost in England, do some reading and corresponding with friends both scientific and occult, and ponder the political situation at home.

It didn't seem to him that the time had yet come for them to return, for in the fall of 1587 it was quite evident that King Philip of Spain was about to attack his country. The following year this rather safe prediction came true, but nothing he and Kelley had seen in the glass could have predicted the utter devastation that weather and the English fleet wrought upon the Spanish Armada. Dr. Dee was nearly as elated over the victory as were his countrymen back home.

Other word from the seven seas was not as good. Sir Walter Raleigh had named a part of America *Virginia*, after the Virgin Queen Elizabeth I, but the name could not obscure the fact that the colony at Roanoke

Island was in danger. The first English child to be born in America had been named Virginia Dare, appropriately enough, but the dare was in doubt. The child's grandfather, Deputy Governor John White, had gone back to England for supplies in 1586 and gotten caught up in the preparations for the Spanish invasion. He had sent back provision ships, but they had never reached the colony, having run afoul of Spanish men-of-war on the high seas.

Dr. Dee was of mixed feelings when he heard about the death of King Frederick II of Denmark, protector and patron of the great astronomer and astrologer Tycho Brahe. Dee knew that Frederick had some years in the past given Tycho the island of Hveen, together with an annual pension of 500 thalers, a canonry, and the income of an estate. Dee had always wished to visit the magnificent observatory Tycho had built and named Uraniborg, with its fabulous instruments for star study, but he also knew that Tycho was an arrogant man, and he wondered whether the new monarch, Christian IV, would prove so magnanimous as his predecessor.

The scientific news from Italy was of great interest. The young Galileo Galilei, already famous in his own land for having invented the hydrostatic balance, had published a treatise on the center of gravity in solids. The work had earned him the post of lecturer in mathematics — Dee allowed himself a twinge of envy — at the university in Pisa. The doctor looked forward to perusing the book at an early opportunity.

Considerably less worthy of note was the so-called "Martin Marprelate" war of satirical Puritan and Anglican pamphlets being published in England. Though Dee cared nothing for it, he knew that many people were purchasing the chapbooks, and that chapbook publication was meeting with an enthusiastic audience everywhere in England. Evidently his countrymen were becoming more literate, but not literate enough to understand the difference between the pursuit of knowledge and mere desultory reading on sensational topics. He wondered how his own books might be faring at home.

John Dee hadn't long to wait to find out. Having heard at last from the Queen that he had been forgiven, he left his host with many thanks for his hospitality, packed his goods and family, and in 1589 returned to England. It felt strange to be back. For one thing, though the Queen continued to war against Spain by sending an expedition against Philip's shipping and ports, there was an air of waiting expectancy, coupled with an exhilaration one could ascribe only to the great pride England was beginning to feel in herself as a naval power, a world power on a par with France, superior to the Dutch, Portugese and Spaniards. Perhaps superior even to the French, for the Protestant King Henry IV had asked Elizabeth to help him secure his throne, and she had sent troops.

In the New Philosophy, too, there were significant developments. Galileo had begun a series of experiments in Pisa that were bearing early fruit in the field of dynamics. Before the entire student body and faculty of the university he had dropped two bodies of unequal mass from the leaning tower and disproved the old theory that heavier bodies fall more swiftly than lighter ones. He was beginning to demolish all the old notions about the rates of projectiles and the weights of the elements. His work was starting, too, to earn him the bitter enmity of the Catholic Scholastic scholars whose tenets had been inherited from the Aristotelian philosophers of the middle ages.

Side by side with the new science, and often in the very persons of the scientists themselves, as in Dr. Dee, there existed the beliefs of the Middle Ages. Dr. Dee, during the course of the year, came into possession of one of the new chapbooks, *The Apprehension and Confession of Three Notorious Witches* by an anonymous author; it described the recent trial in Chelmsford, Essex. Ten people — nine women and a man — had been charged with murder by witchcraft. Many of the witnesses against these people had been children, and there were tales of imps and familiars, devil's marks and sorcery. Two boys had been commended by the court for giving evidence against their unwed mother, Alice Cunny, and their grandmother, Joan Cunny. Four of the witches had been sent to the gallows, three of them — all three interestingly named Joan — within two hours of being sentenced: Joan Upney, Joan Prentice, and Joan Cunny. Three others had been found not guilty of murder, but guilty of bewitchment in lesser degree. Reading the pamphlet, and remembering the mob that had sacked his house in his absence, Dr. Dee felt a bit uneasy and apprehensive. For a fleeting moment the doctor indulged himself in a fantasy: Would he, standing on the scaffold, be tempted to confess, like old Joan Cunny? Had he not, with Edward Kelley, raised spirits? He thrust the thought from him — of course not. His spirits had been angels, not demons.

The Stewkely folk, too, were talking among themselves of the witches, and of Robert Browne who had, in September, at last humbled himself completely before the Church of England. His mastership at St. Olave's had been terminated in June, and for a couple of months he had become rector of Little Castleton. But now he had accepted ordination in the Episcopal Church of England and had taken the proferred rectorship of Achurch-cum-Thorpe Waterfield in Northamptonshire.

John Putnam, nine now, listened to all this with the solemnity that had become his hallmark. Although he didn't know it, his kinsman George Puttenham had published a great book called *The Arte of English Poesy*. If he had known it he would have been hard-pressed to say what "poesy" was, unless it was the rhymes he sometimes said while playing with the other children of Stewkely. If John had been able to see the future in Dr. Dee's crystal egg, he would have been astonished to know that, though cousin George's line would soon die out, more than one of his own descendants would have to do with books and poesy in The New World of America.

By November there were further reports of witchcraft. Jane, the ten-year-old daughter of Robert Throckmorton of Warboys, Huntingdonshire, had the "falling sickness" — epilepsy — or "suffocation of the mother — hysteria. She would snort loudly for half an hour, then swoon for as long. She would arch her back and her belly would swell up — no one was strong enough to keep it from happening. Single parts of her body would tremble as though with the palsy.

A seventy-six-year-old neighbor, Mrs. Alice Samuel, came to visit, but Jane Throckmorton was hostile to her on sight. "Look where the old witch sitteth!" she cried. "Did you ever see one more like a witch than she is? Take off her black thrumbed cap, for I cannot abide to look on her!"

Her parents called in Dr. Philip Barrow and Master William Butler of the university at Cambridge, twenty miles away. Butler, though he had no doctorate, was reputed to be a great physician. Their examination of Jane perplexed them, and Barrow said, finally, "I have had some experience of the malice of witches. I verily believe," he told Goodman Throckmorton, "there is some sort of sorcery and witchcraft wrought toward your child."

By January of 1590 Jane Throckmorton's four sisters, aged nine to fifteen, had been infected by the fits, and seven servants likewise. All of them insisted that Mrs. Samuel was a witch. Henry Pickering of Christ's College — the maternal uncle of the children — interviewed Mrs. Samuel after he had seen them go into fits of torment and attempt to scratch the woman's hand to obtain relief, for it was believed that if the afflicted person could draw the witch's blood, she would stop hurting him. Others believed that the simple touch of the witch would suffice, her evil magnetism drawing back to herself the spell she had cast. Pickering accused Goody Samuel of torturing the children, but she denied it. "I am no witch," she told him.

"Then why do they act so?"

"It is out of wantonness. I know of naught else."

"Do you not see you should confess?" Pickering asked as the children screamed over and over, "She is a witch, and she hurts us by her shape!" for they saw the astral spirit of Goody Samuel floating out of her body toward them to pinch them and choke, though no one else in the room could see the phenomenon.

Receiving no satisfactory reply to his questions, Pickering blurted at last, "There is no way to prevent the judgments of God, but by your confession and repentance, which if you do not do in time, I hope one day to see you burned at the stake, and I myself will bring fire and wood, and the children shall blow the coals!"

In the early part of the year the children had fits in Goody Samuel's presence, but the pattern changed eventually, and they began to be tormented only in her absence, so the Throckmortons required her to live with the family. After she had moved in the children would periodically act as though they were possessed by demons. They would say, "Look you here, Mother Samuel, do you not see the thing that sits here by us?"

She said, "No, not I," shaking her head.

"Why, I marvel that you do not see it. Look how it leaps, skips, and plays up and down!"

During March King James VI of Scotland, the Protestant son of the late, Catholic Mary Queen of Scots, voyaged to Denmark to marry fifteen-year-old Princess Anne, daughter of Frederick II. The King of Scots was an avid follower of the craft of witches, and he may have suspected something when his ship at sea was driven by gales into a Norwegian port. But the storm was weathered, and the nuptials took place. On March 20th the King of Scotland went to visit Tycho Brahe in his observatory at Uraniborg and was vastly impressed.

In September Lady Cromwell, wife of Sir Henry Cromwell, visited the Throckmortons. There she confronted Mrs. Samuel, one of her tenants. "So there you are, you old witch!" she cried, striking off Alice's bonnet and cutting off some of the old woman's hair, which she ordered to be burned as a charm for warding off Goody Samuel's evil spell.

Mrs. Samuel said, "Madam, why do you use me thus? I never did you any harm — as yet." The episode passed, but shortly afterward Lady Cromwell began to feel ill, and her dreams turned bad.

By the time her monarch had returned Gillis Duncan, a young woman-servant of David Seaton, deputy-bailiff of the village of Tranent a few miles from Edinburgh, capital of Scotland, had begun to gather a reputation as one who could cure all sorts of illnesses. When her work was done in the evening she would slip off to give aid to some sufferer of the neighborhood, and Seaton, ever zealous in his office, became suspicious of her powers and of her activities after dimpse, so he decided to take action.

Seaton apprehended the girl and tied her down; then, putting a rope around her head, he commenced to "thraw" her — to jerk her head about in unexpected directions. He put her fingers in a special vice called "Pilniewinks" and tightened it. He conducted an examination of her body for the "mark of the Devil" where her familiar imp suckled her blood for its sustenance, and he found it on her throat. Gilly Duncan confessed to him at last that she had fallen victim to "the wicked allurements and enticements of the Devil."

To this point Seaton had acted unilaterally. Now, with hard evidence to back his accusations, he turned Gilly over to the proper authorities who soon had her naming her accomplices in what appeared to be a massive plot to kill King James VI by witchcraft. Many witches were immediately arrested and preliminary examinations begun. Most of the suspects were of good social standing in the area communities, and several were very well-connected. One was Dr. John Fian, schoolmaster of Saltpans; another was Agnes Sampson, a refined and thoughtful old woman; there were Barbara Napier, sister-in-law of the Laird of Carschogill, and Dame Euphane Macalzean, wife of the wealthy Patrick Moscrop and daughter of Lord Cliftonhall.

King James, when he discovered that he had unwittingly become a part of the witchhunt as an intended victim, took a deep interest in the case. He personally examined Agnes Sampson at Holyrood Castle. As the old woman had denied the charges, all her body hair was shaved off so that she could be closely inspected for the Devil's mark, which was discovered in her private parts. Stuck to the wall with a "witch's bridle" that had four iron prongs, two of which pressed into her tongue and two against her cheeks, she was requested to confess.

But she did not do so, whereupon she was thrawed and kept awake until she made her confession. King James found it to be incredible: Her "Black Paternoster" was a variant nursery rhyme; she told stories of sympathetic powders, of her imp named Elva who appeared in the shape of a black dog that lived in a well and came at her call, and, at last, of a witches' Sabbath, attended by near a hundred women and six men, on All Hallows Eve. The evil host had roistered, bibbed wine, and sailed the skies in sieves to North Berwick where they danced a reel to the music of Gilly Duncan played on the Jew's harp, the warlocks turning "nine times widdershins about, and the women six times."

Their meetinghouse alive with candles of black wax — the Devil, dressed like an ordinary man, demanding that his worshippers bend to buss his arse on the pulpit as the Cardinals must kiss the Pope's ring — the witches had each and all spoken of ways and means to raise a storm that would sink the ship carrying the King to Denmark to wed his Protestant bride, for this union would be the greatest threat in the world to the powers of darkness.

The skeptical King James checked Agnes' story by having Gilly Duncan play "Gillatripes" with sore fingers on her Jews' harp, but he was not convinced, though amazed, and pleasured by her performance. Still, it was clear to him that the witches were all "extreme liars" — till Agnes whispered into his ear the words James had said to his bride on the matrimonial night. The king "acknowledged her words to be most true, and therefore gave the more credit" to the witches' stories.

Agnes waxed even more lyrical in discussing her recipes for sympathetic magic: She had made a charmed powder with two joints of a corpse and a shroud; she had collected venom from a toad by suspending it by a string for three days over an oyster shell, intending to treat one of the king's garments, if she could get it, with the poison in order to make him feel "as if he had been lying upon sharp thorns and ends of needles"; she and her coven sisters had made and melted a waxen image of the king. Finally, by baptizing a cat, knitting four joints of a corpse to its paws, and casting it into the sea, they had raised the storm that had driven James into Norway.

The authorities determined that Dr. Fian was the ringleader of the coven and the center of the witches' plot against the crown. On December 26th he was indicted for attempted regicide by witchcraft in league with the Devil, "a mickle Black Man with a black beard sticking out like a goat's beard, and a high-ribbed nose, falling down sharp like the bill of a hawk, with a long, rumpled tail."

Dr. Fian was alleged to have cast horoscopes, seduced a widow by the black arts, borne magic candles by horseback — swooning into "ecstasies and trances, lying by the space of two or three hours dead, his spirit taken," and suffering himself to be "carried and transported to many mountains." He was accused of grave robbery for materials to make the witches' necrophiliac charms, of receiving the mark of the Devil, of plotting petty sorceries in revenge against a neighbor....

King James witnessed John Fian's examination: He was thrawed, his fingers crushed in pilniewinks; his feet and legs were crushed in the Spanish boots: Fian swooned after the third application, which was judged to be an attempt to escape interrogation, with the Devil's help. They searched him for his charm and found two pins thrust up into his palate — and he confessed before the king, renounced his sorcerer's craft.

On the following day, somehow, Dr. Fian escaped and went to his home in Saltpans. King James ordered that he be recaptured at once, and the refugee was easy to find. Brought again before the king, he recanted his confession and thereafter stood firm through every torture. The schoolmaster's fingernails were torn off with pincers. Into each exposed quick two large pins were driven; the boots were reapplied till "his legs were crushed and beaten as small as might be, and the bones and flesh so bruised that the blood and flesh spouted forth in great abundance, whereby they were made unserviceable for ever."

Dr. John Dee in Mortlake, hearing now and then rumors of the witchcraft cases coming out of Scotland and Essex, had great apprehensions. He added to his library a new book published during the year, Henry Holland's *Treatise Against Witchcraft*, which he read with some satisfaction, on the one hand, and some trepidation on the other.

On January 23, 1591 New Style, Dr. John Fian was executed in the traditional way of Scotland: He was first strangled, then his dead body was placed at the stake and burned. The various North Berwick witch cases were carried on, and other executions took place, including that of Agnes Sampson, but the jury that heard testimony against Barbara Napier found no case against her. King James recalled the court after her acquittal and demanded she be convicted. Those jurors who had voted to acquit were accused by the king of "willful error in assize: Acquitting a witch." The jury threw itself on the mercy of the monarch and did his bidding, but Mrs. Napier pled extenuating circumstances — she was pregnant. As in all such cases, her trial was continued until after the birth, for to kill an innocent babe in the womb, together with its mother, would have been a mortal sin and murder in itself.

Dame Euphane Macalzean was tried, and there was some difficulty in her case as well. Before the jury could bring in a verdict of guilty, after an all-night deliberation, the foreman had to be removed. Because she was a Catholic and the friend of the Earl of Bothwell, James' enemy — who had also been accused, but was lucky enough to escape trial A special punishment was reserved to Dame Macalzean: she was burned alive at the stake on a mound of faggots on July 25th. Burning at the stake was an exceedingly unusual punishment in England itself, though not so in continental Europe.

In Warboys, Essex, the Throckmorton children and Alice Samuel were the center of widespread interest. Many people came to visit and to wonder — ministers came to fast and pray with the children. But the situation, given the circumstances, remained stable.

Dr. John Dee bought another book, published that year, and read it with great interest. Another of the anonymous pamphlets, it was titled *News from Scotland* and recounted the North Berwick story. The aging crystal gazer, however, found it difficult to concentrate on matters of importance in the external world. He was sorry to learn, nevertheless, that the Scholastics had won at Pisa, that Galileo had been forced to resign his post, and that he had returned to Florence, his family home. But during the summer there was better news: Galileo had in July been offered the chair of mathematics at Padua university, and he had accepted.

In Stewkely, too, the folk had been keeping track of the witchcraft cases, but 11-year-old John Putnam wondered more at what had happened in America. John White, when he had returned to Roanoke Island, found no trace of Sir Walter Raleigh's colony or of any of the twelve settlers — no trace except the single word "CROATOAN" carved on a tree. The forests had apparently swallowed up the people, including the baby, Virginia Dare. Only the Satan-worshipping Indians and their witch doctors or "powwows" could know what the fate of the English planters had been, and John doubted they would ever tell.

John Putnam wondered what the word "CROATOAN" could mean. But if he could have seen a copy of a Dutch map titled "Norumbega et Virginia, 1595" from an atlas that would be published in a few years by Cornelius Wytfliet, he would have seen that it showed four islands that lay just east of Roanoke: Hatorask was northernmost, then Paqutwock; below that, *Croatoan*, and to the south, Wokakon. Nothing had happened to the colonists except that they had moved to an island that was not identified as Croatoan Island on the maps that John White was using. Nevertheless, they were gone, and no one would ever see them again.

The following February of 1592 in Scotland Richard Graham, who had been accused at the same time as Barbara Napier, was executed with a number of the other members of the coven. Mrs. Napier was luckier. She had somehow been more or less forgotten, and when the furor died down she was released from prison with her baby and allowed to go free.

In March a witch, Mother Atkins of Pinner, was found and tried in Middlesex. July saw a worsening of Lady Cromwell's long illness in Warboys, and she finally died, but things remained relatively quiet with the Throckmorton family until Christmas Eve. That day the parents told Mrs. Samuel they would like to have a nice Christmas, and they asked her if she wouldn't please stop giving the children fits for a while. Astonishingly, the fits stopped, proving to the family once and for all that she was certainly the cause of the trouble. The fact shocked Alice Samuel deeply enough so that she began to think the Throckmortons and the doctors had been correct in their isolation of her witchcraft. She said to Squire Throckmorton, "O sir, I *have* been the cause of all this trouble to your children! Dear sir, forgive me!"

In January of 1593 Dr. Dorrington, rector of Warboys, came to talk with Goody Samuel. He asked her to repeat, in public, the private confession that she had made of her witchcraft, and she agreed to do it. At the next meeting day she stood in the church while from the pulpit the minister read her acknowledgment of guilt, unwitting though it had been, and the congregation were pleased that another soul was on its way to being saved.

Unfortunately, the next day the Devil was resurgent. Goodwife Samuel, having thought it over, decided that she could not be so unknowingly a tool of evil, and she retracted her public confession. The church and the law were not to be treated with such disdain — she was arrested and taken before William Wickham, Bishop of Lincoln, Justice Francis Cromwell, and other notables. Frightened and intimidated, Goody Samuel re-confessed, even expanded upon her confession by naming her familiar demons: Three dun chickens named Pluck, Catch, and White.

Gratified, the authorities returned her to Huntingdonshire and threw her into jail together with her husband, John, and her daughter, Agnes Samuel, all three to await trial, for the Throckmorton children had implicated all of the family and charged that Goody Samuel had killed Lady Cromwell.

While the Samuel family were awaiting trial for witch murder, Archbishop Whitgift on April 1st hanged Henry Barrowe and John Greenwood, two Puritan Independent leaders and writers who had been kept in prison for years but who, nevertheless, managed to smuggle their writings out. Among the crowd at Tyburn were many Puritans who silently watched and marked the moment when the two martyrs gave up the ghost for the greater glory of God.

A few days later, on April 5th, the Samuels were tried. The Throckmorton children testified and showed the court how quickly they recovered from their fits when Mrs. Samuel or Agnes were required to say the formulaic, "Even as I am a witch and consented to the death of Lady Cromwell, so I charge thee, spirit, to depart and to let her be well." If the wording of this sentence were changed the slightest bit, for instance, "as I am *no* witch," and so forth, the fits would continue. And they would continue, as well, if anyone but one of the three Samuels recited the exorcism. Some neighbors also testified that Goody Samuel had bewitched their livestock, causing them great injury or death.

The jury deliberated five hours and found all three people guilty of the murder of Lady Cromwell. Goody Samuel confessed yet again, and went further: She said that the Devil had had "carnal knowledge of her body." Her daughter, Agnes, upon being urged by friends to plead pregnancy in order to escape execution, rejected the ploy: "Nay, that I will not do — it shall never be said that I was both a witch *and* a whore," for she was unmarried. All three were hanged. Sir Henry Cromwell, one of the richest commoners in England, immediately seized the property of the Samuels in order to endow an annual sermon "against the detestable practice, sin, and offense of witchcraft."

Dr. John Dee was shortly afterward able to add to his collection two books. One, a chapbook titled *The Most Strange and Admirable Discovery of the Three Witches of Warboys*, was written by the judge of the Samuel trial, Edward Fenner, and others. It was a complete record of what had happened. Unlike most of the chapbooks of the time, it was relatively long and balanced in its account — most such pamphlets were short and sensational. Dr. Dee was not the only one who found it fascinating — it became one of the more popular books, and it was often referred to by members of the legal profession.

The other volume was the *Dialogue Concerning Witches and Witchcrafts* by George Gifford, a highly regarded minister in Maldon, Essex. He believed that illnesses and deaths ascribed to sorcery were caused by natural illnesses; that spectral evidence — testimony by witnesses who claimed they had seen the disembodied spirits of suspected witches engaged in acts of *maleficium*, or simply wandering about or sitting on rafters — and hearsay evidence were not to be tolerated in courts of law. Yet, simultaneously, he believed in the reality of witches. He said the times were Devil-haunted. He wanted a very strict law against the art of darkness. His book was written in such a manner and style as to be accessible to common folk, and it, too, had a good sale.

John Dee, who had, after considerable importuning of the Queen, been appointed Chancellor of St. Paul's Cathedral, was interested in 1594 to note that some predictions that the celebrated astronomer Johannes Kepler had made in his annual astrological almanac published in Gratz, Germany, came true. Dr. Dee had heard that Kepler disliked astrology, but that he had nevertheless been required to produce an almanac each year as part of his duties. In his first almanac he had predicted a deep cold spell and an invasion by the Turks. The prophecies came to pass: Many of the inhabitants of Europe died of the intense winter and of the havoc wrought by the Turks from Vienna to Neustadt. Dr. Dee thought it ironic that he himself would have given anything to have such a power of seeing, but that Kepler wanted only to gaze at the stars in order to fix their positions and study their motions.

Dr. Dee, who at a distance had kept track of the hangings of the two Puritans and the three witches of Warboys; who had, further, read with misgivings of the call by George Gifford for even tighter laws against witchcraft than those that already existed, deemed it expedient to write Archbishop Whitgift a letter which said that, despite his alchemical researches, he, Dr. Dee, considered himself to be a good Christian.

In the fall the Putnams of Stewkely and Burstone had news of a relative: George Puttenham had died as the leaves began to fly.

In 1595 Dr. John Dee was transferred out of his sinecure at St. Paul's Cathedral to become Warden of the college at Manchester. No sooner had he been installed than he received word of the death of his scryer Edward Kelley. For a while Kelley had prospered with the Emperor Rudolph, had even been elevated to the rank of Marshall of Bohemia. He had claimed to be able to transmute metals, but when he failed to do so the Emperor threw him into the dungeons of the Castle of Zobeslau. Soon enough, however, Kelley was free again and attempting to manufacture the Philosopher's Stone, so-called, though it was actually a powder that was supposed to act as a catalyst in the process of turning lead into gold or silver.

The emperor, however, was wary, and he kept Kelley under close surveillance. In desperation, Kelley had attempted to escape and had murdered one of his guards in the attempt. Emperor Rudolph again had clapped him into durance, this time in a tower of the Castle of Zerner.

Dr. Dee had never forgotten his friend, nor stopped pleading with the Queen to intercede with Rudolph to allow Kelley to come home, as he was her subject. Finally, Elizabeth agreed and sent Captain Peter Gwinne to Prague. The emperor replied, though, that as Kelley was guilty of the murder of one of *his* subjects, he was not free to let him go. Rudolph had not executed Kelley because the alchemist maintained he was still capable of making the Philosopher's Stone. He would not do it, however, as long as he was kept a prisoner. Instead, he set to work in his cell to write a treatise on the Stone and actually did write *A Poem of Chemistry* and *A Poem of the Philosopher's Stone* that he dedicated to his "most gracious master, Rudolfus II."

It was not enough. In desperation on a stormy night in February 1595 Kelley attempted to make his escape a second time. He braided a rope of bed linens and let himself down by the window. Having grown fat over the years, however, and weak in his captivity, he fell from the tower, smashing his ribs and legs so badly that he died within a day or two at the age of forty-two.

When Captain Gwinne returned to England with his report, Dr. Dee wept. It was difficult for him to face a future devoid of the best scryer in the world. Nor was Dr. Dee's situation at Manchester easy to bear, for he was scoffed at and persecuted by the Fellows of the College. They had no use for crystal gazing, and they thought very little of Dee's old-fashioned mathematics — mere numerology, as they thought. The doctor's colleagues didn't even give him the credit the mob had done when it destroyed his library: His ability as a sorcerer was nil. He was merely a senile old man. Dr. Dee bore the insults patiently.

If his colleagues at Manchester College thought little of him, the local authorities regarded Dr. Dee as an expert in the fields of witchcraft and demonology. His library on the subject was again considerable, and in 1596 Edmund Hopwood, Deputy Lieutenant of Lancaster, of which shire Manchester was a part, came to the seer and asked to borrow some books. Dr. Dee, as always generous with his material goods, lent the Lieutenant three books, Johann Weyer's *De Praestigiis Daemonum*, which, though it did not deny witchcraft, distinguished between simple country herbalists and charmers who intended no eveil, and deliberate sorcerers; Girolamo Menghi's *Flagellum Daemonum: Exorcismos*, on exorcism; a book with the title *Fustis Daemonum*, and one of the most widely read books of its time, the *Malleus Maleficarum* or *Hammer of Witches* by Jacob Springer, a fifteenth-century Dean of the University at Cologne, and Prior Heinrich Kramer. It had gone through numerous editions, including several in English. The latest had been published in 1595, and Dr. Dee had made sure to get a copy.

One of the features of the *Hammer*, and doubtless the main reason Edmund Hopwood wanted to borrow it, was its detailing of the procedure to be used in trials for witchcraft. One could never tell when such information would come in handy. Witches were everywhere in England. A trial had begun on February 27th in Derbyshire:

Fourteeen-year-old Thomas Darling, out hunting with his uncle, had become separated from him in the woods and gotten lost. While wandering through the forest he had run into an old woman, Alice Goodrich, just as he broke wind. She had taken offense and said, "Gyp with a mischief and fart with a bell, / I will go to Heaven and thou shalt go to Hell."

Embarrassed, Thomas covered his discomfiture by taking the offensive. He replied, "Go to Hell thyself, thou old witch!"

Being fully equal to the repartee, Alice had told the boy, "Every boy doth call me witch, / But did I ever make thy arse itch?"

When Thomas got home at last he felt ill. The next day, the 28th, he began to have fits. He saw a green cat and green angels and, later, "a man come out of a chamber pot, flames of Hell, and the heavens open." The attending doctor thought Thomas had a case of worms, but this diagnosis was unacceptable. His people began casting about for another explanation, and Thomas eventually supplied it: His adventure in the woods with the person he described as "a little old woman with three warts on her face." A search for someone fitting the description was begun immediately.

On the 8th of April Alice Goodrich was apprehended and made to admit she had been in the woods that fateful day. Confronted by the boy, she was identified and accused of having bewitched him. His fits intensified and grew more numerous. Alice was searched for the witch's mark and given the test of reciting the Lord's Prayer, which no witch was supposed to be able to do. She failed. Other townspeople began to come in to look at her, and one accused her of having bewitched his cow. Sufficient evidence having been compiled against her, she was put to the torture. The authorities put a new pair of shoes on her feet and held them against the fire until she cried, "Release me! I will confess all." When she was released, however, she reneged. Further inducements to truth were applied.

At last Alice Goodrich confessed to having had some help from the Devil who appeared to her "in likeness of a little part-colored dog, red and white, and I callen him Minny." The dog of a neighbor, also called Minny, was immediately arrested, but released when Alice said she had gotten her dog from her mother, Elizabeth Wright. Given this lead, the authorities immediately took into custody Goody Wright and Goody Gooderich's husband, but only the two women could provoke Tom Darling to have fits, in which he had begun to have visions of Hell: "Yonder come Mother Red Cap," he cried. "Look how they beat her brains out! See what it is to be a witch! See how the toads gnaw the flesh from her bones!"

On the 27th of May John Darrell, the itinerant preacher who had been threatened with imprisonment by the judge who, in 1586, had detected fraud in the fits of Margaret Roper, arrived on the scene. He had not heeded the advice of the judge that he refrain from meddling with witches and had begun to build a reputation as England's solitary exorcist of the old school — not one who merely fasted and prayed with the afflicted persons, but one who actively made a business of finding witches and casting out demons. No sooner had he arrived than he got a conversation going among the several demon personalities who infested Tommy Darling. A little voice said, "Brother Glassap, we cannot prevail, his strength is so strong, and they fast and pray, and a preacher prayeth as fast as they."

A great hollow voice replied, "Brother Radulphus, I will go unto my master Beelzebub, and he shall double their tongues."

A third voice chimed in, "We cannot prevail! Let us go out of him, and enter into some of those here."

At last the voice of an angel said, "My son, arise up and walk; the evil spirit is gone from thee. Arise up and walk." The boy did so, though he was partially paralyzed for three months.

Alice Goodrich received a light sentence: Twelve months in jail. Not long afterward Thomas Darling was examined by Samuel Harsnett and the boy confessed to him that his fits had been fraudulent. But it was too late — Alice Goodrich had already died in prison.

Nothing much more happened during the year to interest Dr. Dee except that, by the winter, he had heard of Johannes Kepler's great discovery, made in Gratz. It was a mystical discovery, not a scientific one, regarding the relation of the "five major solids" and the number and distances of the known planets. The formula, when it was published, made Kepler famous, and he began to correspond with the astronomers Tycho Brahe and Galileo Galilei. Dr. Dee, when he had an opportunity to examine the formula, found it to contain just the proper blend of mathematics and mystic philosophy.

A book of great interest to Dr. Dee was published the next year. Titled *Demonology*, it had been written by King James VI of Scotland in answer to Reginald Scot's 1584 attack on credulousness, *Discovery of Witchcraft*, which had been the first book native to England to be devoted to the subject. It was, as well, considering the times, a rational work — even, in parts, satirical. King James' book was also a refutation of Johann Weyer's 1563 *De Praestigiis Daemonum*.

The *Demonology* defended in general the practices of the witchcraft inquisitions and insisted on the reality of the powers of diabolism in those who had signed the Devil's pact. Published in Edinburgh, copies soon began to circulate in England. These were of particular interest to those who were attached to the English Court, for James VI was heir apparent to the throne, and it never hurt a courtier to know the foibles and interests of the ruling monarch. Even Dr. Dee would have to consider the possibility that he might have to ask for James' patronage in the future.

By the time that the chapbook written on the Thomas Darling possession, *The Burton Boy*, was circulating, Harsnett had begun to expose Darrell by publishing the confession of fraud Darling had given him. Darrell replied that the confession had been forced from the boy — who had remained partially paralyzed for three months after his cure — during a seven-week imprisonment and threats of corporal punishment and murder. Darrell accused Harsnett of having gotten the boy to sign a blank page and of having filled it in afterwards.

But Darrell could not be troubled with petty hostilities — there was work still to be done. He had heard of another possession at Clayworth Hall, the home of Nicholas Starkey, at Leigh in Lancashire.

Edmund Hartlay, a conjuror, had been hired by Squire Starkey and asked to dispossess his son of the demons that possessed him. Hartlay had prepared himself and his paraphernalia, but something went wrong with the charm he had set to protect himself, and rather than ousting the demons, he himself was possessed and thrown into fits. The next day he felt better and decided on the tactic he would use to retaliate. He went into the woods, drew his magic circle on the ground, divided it into four, and in each quarter drew the image of a cross with his staff. When he was finished he brought Starkey to the circle and asked him to erase it, in order to exorcise the demons who had set upon him. "I may not tread it out myself," he told the squire, "for I will meet with them that went about my death."

Starkey, appalled, brought him before the authorities on charges of practicing witchcraft, and Hartlay was sentenced to be hanged. Brought to the gallows, Hartlay continued to protest his innocence of the charge, but it did no good. The executioner placed the rope about his neck, the trap was sprung…and the rope broke. Those present were astonished but not daunted. Before he was hanged the second time, Edmund Hartlay confessed.

John Darrell was nothing daunted, either. He stepped into the place Hartlay had vacated and found himself to be faced with an even greater challenge: Now seven members of the Starkey household had been possessed by the demons. Darrell's spectacular and successful exorcism attracted wide attention.

William Somers was an apprentice of a local musician of Nottingham. Disliking the work, he had run away, been brought back, and immediately commenced to have fits. The people of the neighborhood came to him with copies of *The Witches of Warboys* to compare his symptoms with those of the Throckmorton children. Willy Somers soon accused an old woman of having bewitched him "because I would not give her a hat band." On the 5th of November John Darrell arrived on the scene, having finished his engagement at Clayworth Hall. When he had introduced himself he was invited to try his hand at a new exorcism.

Before setting to work Darrell interviewed William Somers and told him how in all ways he was similar to the Boy of Burton, Thomas Darling. He described Darling's symptoms in detail and told Willy Somers that there was no doubt the apprentice was suffering for the people of Nottingham in the same way that Christ had suffered for all mankind. Darrell called for a day of solemn humiliation and prayer, desiring "all the people to refrain from the company of their wives that night, and the next day they would see strange sights."

On that day Darrell preached at St. Mary's Church on the subject of possession by demons. He listed fourteen symptoms, and his sermon was illustrated by William Somers who was also present. As Darrell ticked off the items one by one, Somers responded with swelling of the stomach, visions, lying in a swooning trance, and so forth. By the end of the service William had recovered — evidently the exorcism had been successful. However, Darrel warned that relapses might occur, and, before the congregation was dismissed, he passed the offering plate.

Darrell's prediction came true — there were relapses, and worse — the infection spread. Thirteen women were accused of bewitching. When witnesses pointed out that Somers somehow failed, on occasion, to have a fit when one of the accused persons approached him, there were others present who countered that the reason for this was the Devil who, in his wile, prevented the expected fit in order to confuse people and make them believe that Somers was feigning, and to "save the witches, and make God's work to be disbelieved."

Mary Cowper, Darrell's sister-in-law and follower, accused a local woman named Alice Freeman of being a witch. When Alice pleaded pregnancy Darrell responded by saying if it were so, it was the Devil who had induced the condition. Alice Freeman's brother, who was an alderman of Nottingham, incensed, arrested William Somers and had him thrown into the workhouse. The boy who had run away once to escape work informed the board of aldermen that he had counterfeited his fits. It was Darrell's turn to be incensed — he insisted the boy's possession had been real, and as the year came to an end the issue was still in doubt, at least in the minds of those who had not already made up their minds, but there were few of those.

While these things were going on Dr. John Dee heard from a European colleague that in Padua Galileo Galilei had invented a new mathematical instrument, the "proportional compass" or sector — a tool, rather simple in design, that could draw circles. It would be useful, Dr. Dee decided when he understood its principle, and would no doubt replace the nail-and-string method most people had used to date. He decided he would build one for himself.

The doctor raised his eyebrow in astonishment when his correspondent mentioned that Galileo had written Johannes Kepler that he was convinced of the truth of the Copernican theory of the solar system — that the planets revolve around the sun and not vice-versa — but he had refrained from saying so publicly, not because of a fear of persecution, but of ridicule.

In Stewkly by the end of the year there was sad news that was an omen of sadder news to come: Richard Puttenham had died. His younger brother George having died three years earlier, like himself without male issue, the family line of the Puttenhams of Sherfield, Southampton, came to an end.

Of much more grave concern was the fact that Nicholas Putnam had fallen ill and did not seem likely to recover. Margaret Putnam was in constant attendance, and the children did what they could to help. Anne, the eldest, was nineteen and managed the house. John, seventeen, was able to do nearly all the chores without help, though he had thirteen-year-old Thomas to help when a job required four hands. Richard was old enough, at eleven, to be able to do a good deal as well. Elizabeth, the third eldest, at fifteen, was assigned to keep track of his activities.

On the first of January, 1598 New Style, Nicholas made his will. He caused to be written, "I, Nicholas Putnam of Stewkely, being sick in body but of a perfect memory, thanks be to God, do deed and make this my last will and testament…." He left to his eldest son John his "house and lands, being in the field and town of Aston Abbotts when he cometh to age." Nicholas left to his wife Margaret all his goods "until such time as…John cometh to age and then he to have half." He wrote, further, "I will that if my wife and my son cannot agree to dwell together that then my son John shall pay unto my wife five pounds a year as long as she liveth if she keep her widowhood; if she marry, then my son to pay her 5 pounds a year so three years after her marriage and no longer."

He left to "Thomas, Richard, Anne, and Elizabeth…every one of them," ten pounds to be paid them by his wife and son John when the latter reached the age of twenty-one. Margaret and John were made executors; the witnesses were William Meade, Bennet Conley, John Meade and others.

But Nicholas lingered. John, Thomas and Richard during the spring plowed and planted the fields in Aston Abbotts. The crop was well up before Nicholas departed the Vales of Tears and Aylesbury. His three sons were among the pallbearers on the warm day when Nicholas, at the age of forty-eight, was put into the earth with the generations of his family who had gone before. He left a young widow of thirty-two years and five offspring, all of whom were old enough to be of comfort and aid to Margaret.

By harvest time John Putnam had taken up more or less permanent residence in the house on the Aston Abbots farm where he could more handily care for the property and livestock. In times of heavy labor Thomas came to stay with him, and Richard looked after the rest of the family at Stewkely, though he lent a hand at the farm when he was needed. The young men were far too busy to pay much attention to the news of the day. They heard that another rebellion had been raised in Ireland, but that was a long way off.

Dr. John Dee in Manchester was delighted to hear, via the mails, that the "magic mirror" telegraph system he had left with Emperor Rudolph II in Prague had been proved under stressful circumstances. Before Adjutant von Buchheim galloped up with the news that Gyor had been taken by Count Adolph von Schwarzenburg, the news had already been flashed across the moonlit miles, and the messenger had been astonished to find when he rode in that Rudolph was fully apprised of the situation.

Dr. Dee had been following as closely as possible the developments in the exorcism of William Somers in Nottingham. A public inquiry had been instituted to investigate the boy and the exorcist, John Darrell. Somers had confessed in the workhouse that his demonic possession had been counterfeited; he had recanted that confession subsequently because he had been told he "deserved to be hanged" if he had perpetrated fraud. Darrell had been most gratified by the recent turn of events.

The witches accused were tried, and at the trial William Somers again did an about-face. He recounted how some of his tricks had been performed: He had worked "the spittle in his mouth" until it foamed and "the froth ran down" his chin. His "prophecies" had been based on probabilities. Somers said, when he was examined in 1599 at Lambeth Palace by Whitgift, the Archbishop of Canterbury; Bancroft, the Bishop of London; his chaplain and Darrell's nemesis, Samuel Harsnett; two Lord Chief Justices and others, "I guessing by the time of Master

Darrell's departure, and by the distance of the way, and of the likelihood" that one of the women accused "would deny herself to be a witch, said to those that were present by me in one of my fits about eleven of the clock, that Millicent Horsley was in examining and that she denied herself to be a witch."

Of forty-four witnesses who appeared at the hearing, thirty-four had supported the exorcist. Furthermore, the trials were very popular, and the common folk had no doubts that witchcrafts had been perpetrated — most of them could tell their own tales, were anyone but to ask. Most parishioners of the local churches did not at all like the fact that the official policy of the Anglican Church with regard to exorcism was negative. Nevertheless, Darrell was denounced by the commission, defrocked, and sent to prison for a year, little to the surprise of Robert Cowper, Darrell's father-in-law, who remarked "I do verily think and believe in my conscience that William Somers did counterfeit all he did; that he was never possessed, dispossessed, nor repossessed, and that Mr. Darrell dealt very unjustly in all his course."

Samuel Harsnett wrote and published during the year his *Discovery of the Fraudulent Practices of John Darrell*, which Dr. Dee added to his steadily growing library. The book did next to nothing to sway the public's support for Darrell and his associate George More, who had been convicted with him; particularly it did nothing to move the Puritan public who remembered Harsnett's attack, in 1584, upon the doctrine of absolute predestination and the salvation of the elect alone.

Dr. Dee discovered, late in the year, that the Emperor Rudolph had extended an invitation to Tycho Brahe at Uraniborg to come to Prague. Tycho, who had become more and more impoverished since the death of his patron Frederick II of Denmark and the accession of Christian IV, decided at last to abandon his observatory and accept Rudolph's invitation. In June Tycho Brahe had arrived in Prague, and Rudolph had assigned him the Castle of Benatky for his work. He also gave the astronomer a pension of 3000 florins. The emperor sent to Uraniborg for all of Tycho's instruments as well, and when they arrived there were immediately set up. Tycho, who was no longer young, had asked Rudolph's permission to invite Johannes Kepler to come to Prague as well to be his assistant, and the monarch issued the invitation, which Kepler accepted. In August, Kepler set out from Gratz.

John Dee discovered himself to be melancholic as he thought of these developments — of what might have been if he and Edward Kelley had received this kind of treatment from the emperor. He gave himself up to the dark mood for a while.

Chapter Two

By the time that Kepler arrived in Prague in January, 1600, Tycho's instruments were in place and everything was well in order. It seemed to both the astronomers as they began their work that it was an auspicious way to begin the new century. If Tycho Brahe's health had been better he would have been looking forward eagerly to a long association with his colleague.

In England the seventeenth century hadn't begun, nor would it until March, for the nation continued to operate by the old calendar. In the State things were relatively quiet and stable. Queen Elizabeth chartered another new monopoly, the East India Company.

Richard Bancroft, Bishop of London, and his chaplain Samuel Harsnett, were greatly frustrated by the failure of Harsnett's book to destroy Darrell's reputation. They were further angered that, against orders, John Darrell and George More had in prison written rebuttals to Harsnett's book, smuggled them out, and had them printed.

Bancroft attacked by assigning John Deacon and John Walker to write two massive treatises against Darrell. But Thomas Harrison, a boy who lived in Norwich, Cheshire, began to have fits similar to those of William Somers, and there was no question which side the public chose to believe.

In 1601 the Deacon-Walker books, *A Summary Answer* and *Dialogical Discourse*, appeared and were immediately rebutted, as before, by Darrell. The general consensus was that Darrell was winner of the debate, for nowhere had Bishop Bancroft, Harsnett, or the two scholar-authors denied the reality of witchcraft as such. The dialogue on the part of the Anglicans was directed against exorcism, in which both the Puritans and the Catholics believed, but the Church of England did not. Unofficially, even many Anglican ministers had faith in their power to exorcise, so on this score the books failed even to convince the orthodox clergy. Further, the anti-Darrellites had gone so far as to deny the reality of all cases of possession, maintaining that even people who suffered from the falling sickness and suffocation of the mother were fraudulent. The debate had been, and was by many perceived, as political and religious rather than ethical and rational.

The case of Thomas Harrison of Norwich in Chester was being watched by a good many interested people. He was brought to the palace of Richard Vaughan, Bishop of Chester where for ten days he was carefully scrutinized. Eventually, no fraud being detected, the Bishop, ordered the boy's parish church to offer public prayers for Thomas at each church meeting. He also ordered seven ministers to rotate private visits with the boy to pray and fast with him. Eventually, the boy's fits ceased, and the watchers determined that a successful exorcism had been performed.

In Scotland, at Port Seton near Edinburgh, a Dutch ship piloted by Jacob Hanssen of Enkhuysen was cast away, and the people of the village organized themselves to rescue the crew. One of the villagers, a secret alchemist named Alexander Seton, had pulled Hanssen from the Firth of Forth, brought him to the Seton home, entertained him, even lent him money to get back to Holland. They became good friends. Hanssen invited Seton to visit him if ever the Scot should be in Holland, and Seton was pleased to accept.

In the fall of the year, October 24th, Tycho Brahe, Emperor Rudolph's astronomer, died in Prague. Rudolph ordered a state funeral for him and appointed Johannes Kepler to be his successor. Kepler set to work immediately to edit the work of the great scientist.

In Aston Abbotts the harvest was good, which was a great relief to John Putnam. He had put in a difficult year beginning in January when he had come of age and the terms of his father's will had to be fulfilled. To each of his four brothers and sisters he and his mother were required to pay ten pounds. It was impossible to do this in cash, of course. In order to fulfill his half of the money owed, he paid a portion in kind.

On the day of reckoning the family gathered in Stewkely and sat in the hall before the fire where accounts were calculated — so many cows, sheep, horses to Thomas and Richard; so many pieces of pewter, so many pieces of wooden ware and lengths of wool to Anne and Elizabeth, all before witnesses from the neighborhood and various relatives. Afterward the family prayed for the missing father and food was served.

In January also John had had to begin to accept his official place in the parish as the head of a household. The parish was the unit of local government — there was little distinction between church and civil affairs. The rector of the church was an important official. Two churchwardens elected by the congregation were his administrative assistants in charge of the building and properties of the church. It was they who set the "rates" or taxes required to keep everything in proper maintenance, including the parson, and it was they who, on the appointed day, collected the rates and checked the payment in the parish records.

The churchwardens were also delegated authority by the Queen in matters of local taxes and highway upkeep, village welfare, and other matters. The constables of the town kept the peace, but they were of much less importance than the church officials. A purely civil official was the surveyor of highways whose job it was to maintain the roads and to lay out new roads as they were needed.

In the larger unit, the shire or county, the Lord Lieutenant was in charge of raising and training the militia and of putting down any local rebellion that might arise. More important in everyday matters were the justices of the peace who were not only magistrates in all legal cases but, in effect, chiefs of police as well. They exercised jurisdiction over the buildings and grounds of the civil arm, set local wages and prices of goods, administered the welfare laws, and saw to it that proscribed activities of any kind, including religious activities, did not take place and, if they did, that those who took part in the activities were punished. The judges were by far the most powerful officials in the shire. The Crown appointed them, and the voters had nothing to say about their appointments. Though the wardens, constables, and coroners were locally elected, the magistrates supervised them and in effect ran the shire. It was the magistrate who appointed the surveyor of highways and the overseer of the poor. He, in turn, was responsible to the Privy Council in London. The magistrate's activities were recorded in the book kept by a deputy of the independent Keeper of the Rolls, an official, like the justices, of the Commission of the Peace, and these records were available to the Privy Council whenever they wished to be apprised of the magistrate's actions in a particular shire.

The magistrate, however, was not merely a tool of the Crown, for he was usually a member of the local gentry whose income was not dependent on the Crown. He therefore had as a rule the interests of the community foremost in his mind when he was called upon to settle a dispute, or collect a tax, or set the value of goods and services. John Putnam, like all the enfranchised freeholders of Buckinghamshire, soon came to know him and his personality well, even if he never had occasion to come into direct contact with him, which he was sure to do if he had any prolonged dispute with a neighbor over a boundary line or the price he charged for livestock.

John Putnam learned a good many things about his duties and obligations during the year. He had no time for petty gossip or even the news of war: 3000 Spanish troops landed in Ireland to help the

Catholics in their rebellion against the English Queen, but they arrived too late.

In March of 1602 Alexander Seton and his manservant William Hamilton arrived in Enkhuyssen, Holland, to visit Capt. Jacob Hanssen. The captain was delighted to see his friend, the man who had rescued him from his sinking ship in the Firth of Forth the previous year, and he welcomed Seton warmly.

When Seton had begun to feel at home and was assured that Hanssen was a friend indeed, the Scot revealed to the captain something he had kept close till then: He was an Adept of alchemy and had discovered the secret of transforming base metal into gold. Hanssen was astonished and not a little doubtful. Seton showed him his Philosopher's Stone: A red powder with a lemony-yellow cast to it and a greasy feel. Seton saw Hanssen's doubt and said, "As tomorrow is the 13th, I will give a demonstration. You may bring a witness, but be sure he is a man of discretion." Hanssen invited Dr. Van der Linden to his home the following afternoon.

At four p.m. Seton changed a lump of lead into what looked and felt like a piece of gold. He engraved the date and the time on it and gave it to Dr. Van der Linden, asking no recompense. Shortly afterward he took his leave of a convinced Capt. Hanssen in order to travel to Italy. From Italy Seton and Hamilton took ship for Germany. Aboard the ship he met a professor of medicine, Johann Wolfgang Dienheim of Freiburg, Breisgau. The professor was impressed with Seton, an "elderly, intelligent, and very modest man" of small stature but compact build. Seton, of a ruddy complexion, was pleasant in his conversation and demeanor. He wore a chestnut-colored, French-style beard and, when they first met, a flowered suit of silk. Seton's manservant, William Hamilton, had a flaming red beard and hair to match.

On the trip the conversation turned to alchemy, at which the professor scoffed, not realizing that Seton was an alchemist. The Scot listened patiently and said nothing to dissuade him until the party reached Basel where they took rooms at the Golden Stork. When they were all settled in, Seton availed himself of the first opportunity to address Prof. Dienheim.

"You will recall," he said, "how throughout our trip, and particularly on the boat, you have maligned alchemy and the alchemists. You will recall, too, that I promised to give you my answer, not in philosophic, logical conclusions, but in philosophic fact. The sun shall not set before I have carried out my promise. I am only waiting for someone who, like you, shall be witness to my demonstration, so that the opposition shall have the less reason to doubt the veracity of the matter."

It happened that Dienheim was slightly acquainted with a man who was living in the area, one who could be trusted, named Dr. Jacob Zwinger. Dr. Zwinger was sent for, and, as soon as he arrived, the party set out for a goldsmith's shop. Dr. Zwinger brought several sheets of lead.

At the shop Alexander Seton kept aloof from the proceedings, touching nothing, merely giving directions. Diener and Zwinger took one of the goldsmith's crucibles, some sulfur they had purchased on the way, and built a fire under the crucible. They put the lead and sulfur in alternate layers, applied the bellows, and melted the mass of lead and sulfur, stirring the while Seton quipped and made small talk for fifteen minutes until the pot was well melted, then he got out of his pocket a packet of powder and said, "Now throw this small envelope into the molten lead, but nicely in the center and not into the fire."

Diener and Zwinger did as they were told. They continued stirring for another fifteen minutes with a red-hot poker. At the end of the quarter-hour the goldsmith poured the contents of the crucible into another container: It looked and felt like pure gold. The goldsmith was asked to assay it, and his findings were that it was, indeed, the finest gold. Diener, Zwinger and the goldsmith stared at each other in dumbfounded amazement while Seton laughed.

"Now," he said, "take your silly philosophy and use sophistry to your heart's content! Here is the truth for you indeed, and it surpasses all, even your syllogisms." Seton had the goldsmith cut the gold into pieces; he gave one to each of the witnesses, and they returned to the inn. Shortly afterward Seton and his servant journeyed on to Strasbourg, and the alchemist began using a series of aliases so that the covetous German princes would not be able to trace him.

In Strasbourg he repeated his experiment in the shop of a goldsmith named Philipp Jakob Guestenhoever, with the same results. Guestenhoever had the audacity to ask Seton if he could buy some of the powder, at which the Scot laughed and handed him several packets. Guestenhoever was not a discrete man. He began to demonstrate his ability to transform metals, first, before friends who he thought could be trusted and, when these friends had spread the word about, the goldsmith was asked to perform before the city council, which he did. Unfortunately, he had been so liberal in his use of Seton's Philosopher's Stone that the powder ran out, but not before Emperor Rudolph II heard of his exploits in Prague. The Emperor sent for Guestenhoever, who declined to come, and Rudolph had him kidnapped.

Rudolph was not interested in the goldsmith's explanation that the powder, which he had gotten from a stranger, had run out, so that he could no longer make gold. Guestenhoever replaced Edward Kelley as an occupant of the prison tower. Rudolph's purpose in jailing the goldsmith was not to punish, but to give him the same opportunity, under duress, that Kelley had received — time and facilities to try to remember the secret formula for making gold. Like Kelley, Guestenhoever was closely guarded, but materials and equipment were made available to him, including books and paper. Two of the books, just published in Prague that year of 1602, were Kepler's first publication of his own *De Fundamentis Astrologiae* — which had little to do with science and everything to do with astrology, for Kepler was clever enough to know where his master Rudolph's inclinations lay — and the first volume of the works of Tycho Brahe which Kepler had edited, *Astronomiae Instaurate Progymnosmata*.

Alexander Seton had long since gone on his way. He visited Frankfurt, Cologne, Hamburg, and Munich, in each place conducting his demonstration and giving away his gold, never selling it until, in Munich, he fell in love with the daughter of a local burgher.

In Manchester, England, Dr. John Dee soon enough heard of the books of Kepler and Brahe, and the fantastic stories people were telling of the mysterious Scot who was wandering around Europe — no one knew why — transforming lead into gold and giving it away. Dr. Dee, though he was a credulous man, could scarcely credit such tales. Though his health was failing and, with it, the clarity of mind he had relied on all his life, Dee continued to struggle with the hostilities around him and with the body on which he could no longer rely.

Like the people of Aston Abbotts, Dr. Dee heard also of a new case of diabolical possession. Mary Glover, daughter of a London Fleet Street merchant, had been having strange seizures, and she had named one Elizabeth Jackson as her tormenter. The neighbors of the family urged them to bring charges against Elizabeth, but a doctor who had been called in on the case prevented it by telling the authorities he believed "the maid doth counterfeit." The magistrate who was examining the case ordered Sir John Croke, Recorder of London, to scrutinize the girl in his chamber at the Temple, and by the end of the year preparations were being made to do so.

Though this news of the Devil was curious, John Putnam was more taken with the exploits of Bartholomew Gosnold, commander of Sir Walter Raleigh's ship *Concord*, which had sailed in the spring for the New World. He had arrived, on May 15th, at a place he found to be teeming with fish and which he had named Cape Cod. In his coasting down the shores of North America he put in and traded with the Indians about Buzzard's Bay, and he returned to England with a large cargo of furs, sassafras, and other goods; then he began to proselytize among the members of the Court for a trading venture. His arguments interested a good many people, of whom one was Sir Ferdinando Gorges.

Puritans throughout England were talking also about the action taken by the Rev. Mr. John Robinson, the Separatist preacher who had had the temerity to lead his congregation at Gainesborough, Lincolnshire, out of association with the Church of England and into a conventicle of free worship.

In the new year 1603 Sir John Croke examined the possessed girl Mary Glover in the presence of the accused witch Elizabeth Jackson, various witnesses including neighbors of the girl, ministers, and people of rank. All of those present felt that there was no fraud involved. Croke asked the ministers to pray for the girl, and a successful exorcism was performed. Sir John, having carried out the duty he had been required to exercise sent one of the ministers present, the Rev. Mr. Lewis Hughes, to inform Bishop Bancroft of what had taken place. But the bishop had already been informed by the time Hughes arrived, and when the minister sent in word asking to see the bishop, Bancroft refused him an audience. Instead, the Bishop berated the minister, called him a "rascal" and a "varlet" and had him thrown into prison. But Bancroft did not interfere with Mother Jackson's arraignment and conviction for witchcraft. The Church of England did, however, ban from that time forward the rite of exorcism, citing the Harsnett book published four years earlier as its basis for so doing.

On the 24th of March, 1603, Queen Elizabeth died, and Alexander Seton's monarch, King James VI of Scotland, became King James I of England as well. With the accession, Dr. John Dee lost all hope of preferment, given James' reputation, and he lost, as well, his wardenship of Manchester College. He retired to his home in Mortlake — a widower by then — and began to eke out a living as he had done years before by casting horoscopes and, on occasion, selling one of his books. He could no longer hope to add to his library, so he had to pass up the new edition of George Gifford's *Dialogue Concerning Witches and Witchcrafts*.

In Germany Alexander Seton eloped to Stuttgart with the young woman with whom he had fallen in love and, running low on funds at last, broke his rule about not using his Philosopher's Stone to make money. Duke Frederick of Würtemburg, who was desperate for financing, had his own alchemical works in the Neckar Valley. Seton sought him out, demonstrated his ability to turn lead into gold, received a stipend to join the colony, and fled to Crossen.

The Electors of Saxony had also for years dabbled in alchemy, but the new Elector, Christian II, whose court was in Crossen, had little interest in the Philosopher's Art. He was twenty years old when Seton, his bride, and his manservant arrived. But when Hamilton, using his master's powder, turned lead to gold before his very eyes, he changed his mind and began to court Seton, suggesting in steadily rising degrees of imperative that it would be well if Seton divulged the secret of the red powder with the lemon tint.

Seton refused. The Elector had him carefully watched so that escape was impossible, but the manservant Hamilton mangaged to get away just before Christian II arrested Seton, threw him into a dungeon, and had him tortured: The Scot was put on the rack and administered the branding iron. Seton refused to speak and was again tortured two weeks after the first time. Still he said nothing. The Elector was afraid to attempt a third application, for Seton was so badly damaged it was feared he could not survive. Despite his condition Seton was closely guarded by forty men, nor permitted to see anyone, including his wife, who remained at the inn in the village. He remained in solitary confinement under the worst possible conditions.

While Seton was in prison a Polish nobleman, Michael Sendigovius, appeared and insinuated himself into the good graces of Christian II. At length he suggested to the elector that he might be able to pry Seton's secret out of him. Sendigovius was given permission to see the Scot. Once in the dungeon with him, he put a proposition: What would it be worth to Seton to be free again? Seton replied, "As much as will last you and your family for life."

Sendigovius left the dungeon, Seton, and Crossen, and returned to his home in Cracow where he sold his estate. With the money he had been able to raise he returned to Crossen. With the elector's permission, Sendigovius began to see Seton every day, reporting that he was becoming more and more friendly with the Scot and would have the secret if given enough time. The Pole was liberal with his money and became well known to the guards, who knew the Elector was his friend.

One day three months after Seton had been imprisoned, Sendigovius gave a riotous party for the guards and plied them with liquor until he had them all snoring on the floor. Then he unlocked the dungeon, helped the crippled Seton out to a waiting coach, and went to the inn. There Seton told his wife where he had hidden his Philosopher's Stone. She retrieved it, and the trio escaped to Cracow. Once there, Sendigovius informed Seton that the payment he expected was not merely a supply of the powder, but the secret itself. Seton refused, and paid him, as he had promised, an ounce of the Stone. But Seton was a dying man, and Sendigovius was a patient one. He knew that Mrs. Seton had more of the red powder; further, he had discovered that Seton also had a manuscript that contained the secret.

Seton's servant William Hamilton continued to travel after his escape from Crossen until he was again on British soil. He arrived in time to see King James asserting himself in many ways. No sooner had the new king ascended the throne than the rebellion in Ireland was crushed. A new English edition of the king's *Demonology* appeared.

James, who believed in the Divine Right of Kings to rule, had little use for Parliament, and he set about to increase the royal authority. A thousand Puritan clerics presented the king with the "Millenary Petition" which requested changes in *The Book of Common Prayer* of the Anglican Church, in the church ritual, and various other things of like nature. King James appointed a commission to consider the demands. He also set about the suppression of a book: He ordered that every copy of Reginald Scot's *Discovery of Witchcraft* that could be found, be burned. But James' reputation for being the nemesis of sorcerers seemed to many to be greatly exaggerated. He ignored Dr. Dee, only a few miles away in Mortlake, as he did the rest of the London dabblers in the mystic arts. In fact, one of the most notorious of them, Simon Forman, pulled a great coup out of his hat, right under James' nose, a fact that astonished John Dee.

Forman was a physician and astrologer of London, a former apothecary, schoolmaster, a student at Oxford and in Holland. He had been practicing in Philpot Lane for a number of years, but because he had done so without a license or diploma, he had been imprisoned on several occasions. Suddenly, on the 26th of June, Cambridge University issued him his license to practice medicine and, the next day, the university conferred on him the degree of M. D. Dr. Simon Forman returned from Cambridge to London and set up practice in both his specialties at Lambeth. Immediately, he built a large practice; many of his clients were persons of rank.

Dr. Dee could not fathom it. And he was disappointed in the second book of Tycho Brahe's published in Prague by Johannes in 1603 — it was, he was informed, nothing but a reprint of one of the astronomer's early books, first issued at Uraniborg in 1584, *De Mundi Aethereii*. The doctor got out his copy of the original issue and thumbed through it listlessly. An item of interest from Oxford scarcely registered when it came to his attention: Thomas Darling, the former possessed Boy of Burton, had been sentenced to a whipping and the loss of his ears for libeling the Vice Chancellor of the University.

In Aston Abbotts John Putnam and his neighbors had been discussing many things. They wondered what would be the outcome of the King's commission to study the Millenary Petition; they wondered what James would do about John Robinson's separation from the Church of England, and whether anyone would pay attention to the banning of exorcism now that the witchhunter was on the throne and his book was again circulating throughout the kingdom. John Putnam had his own private fascination, however, which had been with him since childhood: What of the New World? He understood that yet another mariner, Martin Pring, had sailed from England to explore the North American coast.

On Saturday, January 14, 1604 New Style, King James convened his lords, bishops, and other clergy at Hampton Court to consider the demands of the 1000 Puritan divines in their Millenary Petition. Nothing of any substance came of the talk of the first day, and the conference reconvened on the following Monday. Again the king would agree to very little, but when Dr. John Reynolds moved the approval of a new translation of the Bible, King James was quick to agree. On Wednesday the 18th the king and lords appointed a commission to proceed with the work. It was the only request the king granted.

In Cracow Alexander Seton died that same month, and Sendigovius looked forward to being granted his request, which was that the new widow marry him. She did so with alacrity, and the Pole came into possession thereupon of a large quantity of Seton's Philosopher's Stone and a manuscript that gave its formula. To his vast frustration, the ms. was couched in the traditional cryptic language, and he could make nothing of it. He did not discover the secret, but he did set up in Cracow as an alchemist, transmuting lead into gold with the red powder. He also wrote during the year and, in Prague — where he had been summoned by Rudolph — published a book, *Novum Lumen Chymicum*.

Also in January there was a wedding in Aston Abbotts. John Putnam's spinster sister Anne, twenty-six, married William Argett of the community. John and his mother were deeply gratified, for they had worried because Anne was so old. It had been difficult for them to raise her marriage portion, but it had been accomplished at last. The family stood in the church and heard the rector in a simple ceremony pronounce her a lawfully wedded wife. Afterward there was a small celebration in John's home, and at a decent hour the bridal couple, the relatives and friends, dispersed to their own dwellings in the village and surrounding communities.

When King James convened his first Parliament and discovered that it leaned toward Puritanism, it aroused the new monarch's hostility. As head of the Church of England James was not at all interested in people who wished to reform it, nor was he interested in the Scottish brand of Puritanism, Presbyterianism — if anything, the latter was worse, for it aspired to a monopoly of state religion. The House of Commons, no sooner than it had been convened, began to discuss moderate church reforms. Indignant, James informed the members that religion was no business of theirs at all; they were to attend strictly to secular affairs.

The Commons retreated, but slowly and not far. The House passed and sent to the king an "apology" in the form of a document that informed him Parliament had the right to discuss any thing or issue it saw fit to discuss. The Apology also considered "Divine Right" as James had defined it, and laid down ground rules for Parliament's own rights. James listened with less than half an ear. He had no sense at all of public opinion as expressed by the Commons or anyone else, but the populace considered that Catholicism was in no way to be propitiated, despite Divine Right; hence, when James negotiated a treaty of peace with Spain, few Englishmen regarded the practical wisdom of the pact with favor, but responded emotionally against it.

In late May and early June Parliament undertook legislation. Among the proposed laws was one that would make it illegal for any Englishman to "covenant with the Devil." While the law was being debated, on the 5th of June Dr. John Dee petitioned the king and asked that he be "tried and cleared of that horrible and damnable and, to me, most grievous and damaging slander — generally and for these many years last past, in this kingdom raised and continued, by report and print against me — namely, that I am or have been a conjuror or caller of Devils." Given the fact that the Church denied the possibility of any man's conjuring angels, it was as well that King James ignored the senile old man.

A new star, a nova, appeared in the sky in September, which gave Galileo the opportunity to attack the Scholastics' dogma of the "incorruptibility of the heavens," which he did in his correspondence primarily. In his public teaching at the university, however, he continued to cleave to the Church-sanctioned Ptolemaic theory of astronomy. In his mind and work the Earth spun about the Sun, but before his students a stunted sun rose and fell over an Earth as solid as the galactic turtle that in ancient myth had carried the globe on its back. One of Galileo's correspondents, Johannes Kepler, published his *Astronomiae Pars Optica* in Prague. The book was a very large step toward the theory of vision and the law of refraction of light.

Witches were once more abroad in the land of the English. Ann Gunter, a fourteen-year-old girl living in North Moreton, Berkshire, had an illness the doctors diagnosed as the falling sickness aggravated by suffocation of the mother. Her father, a gentleman, did not believe it — such things didn't happen in a good British home. He sent for the best witch experts money could pay for, and they arrived — along with many neighbors who carried in with them copies of the various witch chapbooks that had been published in recent years. They studied Ann's symptoms and read them to her out of their books: Her stomach swelled up; she snorted and voided uncontrollably; she foamed at the mouth, exuded pins from various orifices, went temporarily blind, went without eating up to twelve days, foretold events of the household.

Ann received a great deal of publicity, and she eventually identified the source of her torments — three women named Agnes Pepwell, Mary Pepwell, and Elizabeth Gregory. They and their imps haunted her unmercifully. They had also begun to haunt Richard Bancroft who, in November, was elevated to the Archbishopric of Canterbury, replacing the late Archbishop Whitgift who had died in March. Samuel Harsnett was automatically elevated as well — still the bishop's chaplain, he became minister to the Primate.

The case of Ann Gunter soon came to the attention of King James himself, always interested in incidents of the occult, whether fraudulent or demonstrably real. He was assiduous in unmasking the frauds on the grounds that, when fraud could not be proved, then witchcraft, contrarily, was. The accused witches were arraigned at Abingdon in 1605 and the jury found them "Not Guilty," but Ann continued to be tormented. She was committed by the court to the care of Henry Cotton, Bishop of Salisbury, a man who had ample experience of children, being himself the father of nineteen. While Ann was in his care the bishop collected every pin in the house, marked it, and was able to identify each one that Ann disgorged. He made his report and King James ordered the girl to be brought before him. After his examination on August 27th he gave her over to the care of Archbishop Bancroft and Minister Harsnett.

During the course of Bancroft's investigation, which lasted several months, Ann admitted that she had a natural disease which her father had coached her to exaggerate. She had developed such tricks as the vomiting of pins through experiment and practice.

The Archbishop lost his Minister during the fall, but it was a happy parting, for Harsnett was appointed to fill the vacancy of the mastership of Pembroke Hall, Cambridge, created by the death of the great divine, Launcelot Andrewes. The new master discovered that he had his work cut out for him inasmuch as the college was full of Puritan Fellows who were hostile to Harsnett's Anglican opinions on almost anything. But, too, a great work was underway there, for a portion of the Bible was in process of being translated at Cambridge. In the previous June translators had been appointed, about fifty of them. These had been divided into six groups, two groups to gather and work at each of three places — Westminster, Cambridge, and Oxford. By November of the preceding year the labor had begun, and Launcelot Andrewes had been one of the Cambridge translators before his death; a member of the second group was one John Bois.

Bois was the forty-four-year-old rector of Boxworth, near Cambridge. He had been a student and Fellow of St. John's College, Cambridge, and had been for ten years chief lecturer in Greek. He began to keep a journal of his work on the King James Bible.

A portion of another manuscript-in-the-making was published in England in 1605: The courtier Sir Francis Bacon issued *The Advancement of Learning* which began to assemble the theoretical framework for the study of science. Puritan clerics everywhere were speaking of the great works being undertaken and published, but the more ordinary variety of Puritan, such as John Putnam, cared only for the most obvious of King James' actions. The Catholics in England had organized themselves into an attempt on the king's life, the Gunpowder Plot, under the leadership of Guy Fawkes. They had planned to blow up the king, but the plot was exposed, and Parliament responded by passing stringent anti-Catholic laws. Much to the dismay of the folk in Aston Abbotts and elsewhere, it soon became apparent that James had no intention of enforcing those laws. Dismay was transformed to outrage, and then to suspicion. Puritans were as likely to be persecuted as any Romish traitor: Three-hundred nonconformist ministers were expelled from their churches. It passed almost unnoticed in the countryside that James had chartered two new corporations, the London and Plymouth Companies. A great fire began to smolder beneath the surface of English life.

In the following year King James granted all of the North American continent from 34° to 45° latitude to the London and Plymouth companies, the southern section to the former, and the northern to the latter. A prominent member of the Plymouth Company was Sir Ferdinando Gorges.

Within the realm James made a number of appointments, among them Sir Edward Coke to the post of Chief Justice of Common Pleas and Samuel Harsnett to the Vice Chancellorship of Cambridge University. Harsnett, who was involved both with the translation of the Bible and with the pending witchcraft case, saw the second resolved during the year: Ann Gunter and her father were charged with conspiracy by Coke, and the matter came to an end.

Early in November a rather ordinary incident took place. Toby Matthew of London lost 37 pounds, ten shillings by theft. He went to the establishment of the sorcerer Simon Reade who assured him he would be able to help discover the thief. On the 8th of November, by appointment, he held the first of several séances with Matthew, during the course of which he invoked the demons Heawelon, Fatemon, and Clevethon.

In Gainesborough the nonconformist church with which John Robinson was associated split into two groups. The congregation had been experiencing more and more hostility on the part of the authorities, and, among other things, there had been a good deal of debate among the people about what might best be done. Half of the church began to worship at Scrooby, a town near Gainesborough, and this group chose John Robinson as its pastor. They were thinking seriously of leaving the country.

The first week of January of the new year 1607 Toby Matthew, whose suspicions about Simon Reade's legitimacy had been growing for a month in reverse proportion to the thinning of his pocketbook, called a halt to the séances and the talks with the three demons he had come to know so well. He went to the authorities and charged Reade with fraud. Dr. John Dee followed the subsequent events as closely as his health would permit: On the 10th of January Simon Reade was tried for sorcery. At the trial he confessed that he was unable to conjure, that he had perpetrated a fraud on Matthew, and that consequently he could not possibly be convicted of trafficking with spirits. To Dr. Dee's astonishment, and much to Toby Matthew's chagrin, the court agreed and allowed Simon Reade to go free.

John Putnam was curious about a matter of greater moment. On the 19th of December the preceding year the London Company had sent three ships holding 160 colonists to Virginia under Christopher Newport, Bartholomew Gosnold, and James Ratcliffe. On the 26th of April the ships were blown into Chesapeake Bay. Their explorations had led them to a river, which they named the James after the king, and on May 13th a settlement, Jamestown, was established and a number of plantations laid out along the banks of the waterway.

Sir Ferdinando Gorges and the Plymouth Company sent their venture to the mouth of the Kennebec River in what would eventually be Maine. The colonists were headed by George Popham. They encountered a forbidding environment, and the winter set in very cold and stormy.

In England there were more rumors of witchcraft circulating. A namesake of the Virginia planter, a four-year-old child named John Smith of Husbands Bosworth, Leicestershire, began to have devilish traumas. His father, Sir Roger Smith, asked, "What ails you, boy?" and received the answer, "I am bewitched." He named several women as his tormenters. Sir Roger saw to it that the witches were brought to trial, but the jury saw to it that they were acquitted. The verdict did nothing to intimidate the precocious child.

On the 16th of December Thomas, Lord Windsor, grew quite ill in London. His friends and retainers, discussing the odd nature of the case, came to agreement by means of certain clues that Lord Windsor's enemies must have enlisted the services of the notorious sorcerer and alchemist Dr. John Lamb who had either bewitched or poisoned him.

By the end of the winter the Kennebec colony of Gov. Sir Ferdinando Gorges' Plymouth Company had failed. Its leader, George Popham, had died in the rigorous weather and from the virulent illness that struck the plantation — some called it Satan's scourge: smallpox. When the supply ship reached Maine in the spring of 1608 it took away what survivors there were. John Putnam was disappointed when they reached England and news of the debacle arrived at Aston Abbotts, but Sir Ferdinando Gorges in London merely became all the more determined to succeed. He immediately set about organizing other trading expeditions and planning for a permanent settlement.

On the 13th of May rumors were again abroad about the infamous Dr. John Lamb's meddling with demonology. He was a flamboyant man, a bachelor whose quarters were always alive with people coming and going, clients of the better social ranks. The people of London called him "The Duke's Devil," for he enjoyed the vacillating patronage of the Duke of Buckingham, serving him much as Dr. Dee had ministered to the wants, on various occasions, of the late Queen.

Dee and Lamb were aware of each other, as they could scarcely help being, and they were even acquainted. For years there had been a loose confederation, not only of the English astrologers/astronomers, alchemists / chemists, occultists and scientists in and around the areas of London, Oxford and Cambridge, but of overseas correspondents as well. This unofficial group was called by outsiders the "Invisible College," but traditionalists preferred to call it the "Hermetic Brotherhood," referring to the mythical Hermes Trismegistus, "thrice greatest Hermes," the Egyptian Thoth, author of the Sacred Books. In the Bible they were called the Magi, whence the word "magicians."

Greek tradition had it that Hermes Trismegistus had been the possessor of all knowledge and that he was the Scribe of the Gods. He was said to have written forty-two works in six categories, the first of which dealt with gods, laws, and the education of the priesthood in ten books. The second was a set of ten books dealing with ritual, prayer and incantation, and sacrifice. The third group, also of ten books, gathered together knowledge of geography, topography and cosmology. The fourth group, made up of four volumes, was devoted to astronomy and astrology; the fifth, of two books, collected hymns to the gods and discussed the ways of royalty. The last group of six books surveyed medicine.

Tradition had it as well that since Hermes' time there had been a direct chain of Hermeticism leading down through the ages and the various hands of the Magi — men of Wisdom — and Adepts. A complex symbology had been developed, both for purposes of ritual and to keep the secrets of the Brotherhood. Every astrologer or sorcerer who took himself seriously — and, with the advent of the seventeenth century, every scientist as well — kept close track of the doings of his counterparts everywhere. In fact, the London group held an annual banquet, so it was no news to Dr. John Lamb or to any of the other members that Dr. Dee would not last out the year.

News began to circulate also that the Frenchman Samuel de Champlain was attempting to plant a colony called Quebec in North America. In July he did so, in the same sort of climate that had driven off the Englishmen at Kennebec. John Putnam was interested and apprehensive, if not disappointed, in the news. He and his fellow parishioners began talking about the developments among John Robinson's followers at Scrooby: They had decided to leave England for Holland. But the authorities were watching and harassing them, so their move had to be surreptitious.

Robinson's congregation split into detachments and quietly went aboard various ships at sundry times during the year. Most of the congregation arrived in Amsterdam and assembled as a unit. The Puritans, particularly the Separatists of England, watched the situation closely. Many of them remembered what had happened to Robert Browne's original and early attempt to do the same thing. But John Robinson was esteemed as a wiser and steadier man, and there had been a great deal of development among the Puritans since that day. There was good hope that Robinson's venture would succeed, though whether the English Puritans could avoid assimilation into Dutch society over a generation or two was a question.

In Cambridge work on the translation of the Bible was proceeding apace. John Bois had finished his own portion of the work and was helping other groups unofficially. He was at last recognized among his colleagues and by the directors of the project as a more than ordinarily learned man who, moreover, cleaved to the King's course. It had not always been so. At the beginning of the project he was disdained by some of the Cambridge divines who saw him as nothing more than a country parson.

Bois had been assigned to do portions of the New Testament, and he kept in mind the penchant his king had for witches, as did many of the other translators. Inasmuch as witchcraft had not existed when the Old Testament had been written, and Satan in those books was a messenger of God, not a fallen angel, certain adjustments had to be made in the English words chosen to replace the Hebrew, Greek, and Latin words that referred to "poisoners," "sorcerers." "demons," "false gods," and so on, so that both halves of the Bible would be consistent, and so that current Protestant thinking on subjects such as Hell would be accurately reflected in the text.

This sort of process had been going on for millennia. It had always been evident to translators of the various versions and texts of the many manuscripts that went into making up the Old and New Testaments first, that it had been human beings who originally had written them, not the "Hand of God" Himself. History told translators that various churchmen, synods and conclaves over the centuries had perused these books and chosen those that were to be classified as canonical as distinguished from those that were "apocryphal." And common sense argued that, before the invention of printing, when scribes had to make copies of texts by hand, errors crept in and were often concretized in the language and compounded by the scriveners of a later date. Not that much was changed by the invention of printing in the fifteenth century, for printers committed as many "typographical" errors in texts as scribes had done manually. And then, of course, there were always the political and doctrinal considerations.

Of all King James' translators, only John Bois kept a permanent journal of his ruminations and decisions. When he was working on The Apocalypse of John, Chapter 20, Verse 13, he noted that the Greek word for Hades, the underworld, which had been translated in earlier versions as "the grave," Bois wrote, "I prefer *Hell*, on account of the following line." Thus, he had deliberately substituted the modern notion of Hell for the ancient word referring to the Greek underworld, which the spirits entered upon the death of the body, where they met the ferryman, Charon, who rowed them over the river Styx into the regions where the river Lethe, water of forgetfulness, flowed, and into which many of the spirits stepped, never to exist again.

The passage would be translated by others, "And the sea gave up the dead in it, Death and Hades [i.e., the grave] gave up the dead in them, and all were judged by what they had done." The following verse, 14, to which Bois referred, would read, "Then Death and Hades [the grave] were thrown into the lake of fire. This is the second death, the lake of fire."

The passage would be debated with many other passages throughout the following centuries, and some would point out that it seemed to them that it was not the spirits of the damned that burned in the lake of fire, but Death and the grave — in other words, that there would be no more Death, no more grave, for they would be utterly destroyed. The "second death" would be the death of Death itself.

But Bois translated the passage as it would appear in the King James version, "And the sea gave up the dead which were in it; and death and hell [not the grave] delivered up the dead which were in them; and they were judged every man according to their words. 14) And death and hell were cast into the lake of fire. This is the second death. 15) And whosoever was not found written in the book of life was cast into the lake of fire."

Even as the passage stood in Bois' translation, it could be pointed out that those who were "not found written in the Book of Life" — in other words, those who had wasted their lives, who might as well not have lived — would be consumed and forgotten in the same fire that destroyed death and Hell, not tormented forever in the fires of Hell. Those whose works on earth had been judged worthy would be granted immortality. All the rest would simply disappear into smoke.

The Bois version stood, and it would be referred to thousands of times by clerics who considered it to be the Word of God, though Puritan clerics would try to avoid the passage if they could, for even as it read it seemed to contradict the doctrine of Absolute Predestination, and to affirm, rather, a doctrine of Salvation by Works. But, then, Bois was an Anglican, not a Puritan. Many passages throughout the King James Bible were manipulated in just the same manner. They would feed the witchhunters for more than half a century in England and America.

Not only was the Bible being slanted in ways the translators felt King James, head of the Church of England, would approve, but most of the books on witchcraft published in England during his reign so far had been favorable to the belief in witchcraft. In 1608 another of these, William Perkins' *Discourse of the Damned Art of Witchcraft*, was published posthumously. Perkins had been a Puritan divine and a colleague of Bois at the University of Cambridge, but in Christ's College, not St. John's.

Though the book insisted on the reality and possibility of witchcraft, it made the point that evidence sufficient to indict was not necessarily sufficient to convict. Perkins insisted that the scriptural imperative, "Thou shalt not suffer a witch to live" must be enforced upon any conviction, however, even against "diviners, charmers, jugglers, all wizards commonly called wise men and wise women" — Magi or "magicians." His blanket coverage took care of all the possibilities that the translators of the King James Bible debated as they considered the Hebrew word they finally translated — as earlier translators of the various Christian Bibles had done — *witch*. There were scholars who insisted that the original word meant merely "poisoner," at worst "sorcerer" or "diviner."

Perkins' *Discourse* was published under the prestigious impress of the university at Cambridge, and it soon became a standard reference work on the subject; it circulated widely among Puritan leaders.

On the second of October an obscure event took place in Middleburg, Holland. An optician named Johannes Lippershey applied for a patent on an instrument designed to magnify the stars. The invention of the telescope did not remain in shadow for very long. Soon Lippershey and other Dutch opticians were manufacturing and selling them widely, and news of the machine spread even to Italy. Because of the proximity of England to Holland, and because of the many trading and religious connections between the two countries, not merely the news of the telescope arrived early, but the instruments themselves.

They arrived too late for Dr. John Dee. One evening in December, feeling ill and confused, he wandered about the rooms of his dilapidated house at Mortlake, touching his paraphernalia, opening one or two of his old books and staring at their pages in the lamplight. His tall, gaunt figure — dressed in an artist's gown with hanging sleeves — bent over the print, but he could not focus his eyes sufficiently to read. In the saffron light his normally fair complexion took on a sallow cast, and his long white beard gleamed like snow. He blew out the lamp, took a candle with him to his room, and went to bed. Soon he was asleep, and he never woke up.

Not many attended the simple funeral and interment near the Dee home by the river. There were a few neighbors, mostly curious about the eighty-one-year-old sorcerer whom they had avoided. John's son Arthur was there, a man following in the footsteps of his father, and some of Dee's other children. There were representatives, too, of the Brotherhood from London: Dr. John Lamb, Dr. Simon Forman, Simon Reade, William Hamilton. They were conspicuous among the townspeople.

In the following year, 1609, the London Company was reorganized. Its original charter had made the company a venture of the Crown, but now it became the first of the great monopolies to be made strictly a commercial corporation, which meant that the company could appoint its own governor and directors, provided, of course, that nothing were done that would infringe upon the rights of the Crown.

This information would have meant less than nothing to John Putnam even if he had heard it. What did take his attention, however, was the fact that John Robinson's community of Pilgrims, as they were beginning to be called, had moved from Amsterdam to Leyden. The change of site was in no way ominous, however, for his group was continuing to grow — Separatist Puritans in small groups, in couples and families, were leaving England to join Robinson, trickling out of nearly every shire month by month. There was next to nothing the authorities could do about damming the flow.

In June of 1609 the London Company sent nine ships with five hundred more colonists to Jamestown. The colony was beginning to get to its feet despite great losses among the settlers the first year, many of the deaths having been caused by smallpox — Satan's scourge. On the 11th of August the newcomers arrived and ousted John Smith from the position he had won. He slept in his boat because the newcomers had been planning to kill him in his bed, but even so one evening his powder bag somehow exploded, tore his thigh to pieces, and he was sent home to England. John Putnam listened avidly to the story when it was told him by his neighbor, Zaccheus Gould, who had just returned from London. John shook his head admiringly and said, "He may be a very Devil, but he is a brave man." He went back to work in his prospering fields, his head full of the adventures he had heard. John thought, also, as he tended his crops and livestock, of the English navigator Henry Hudson who had sailed to look for the Northwest Passage through North America to China.

Among the Brotherhood of Adepts there was other news. In June, when Galileo in Venice had been informed of the new astronomical invention that had come out of Holland, he became excited. That very night he went to bed and, instead of sleeping, thought about the description he had been given of the instrument. When he was sure he understood its principle in theory, he got up and began to work on one of his own. Shortly he had manufactured a 3X telescope and turned it to the skies. Immediately, revelations and discoveries began pouring down the tube into his eye and mind. He continued to build and refine better and better versions of the instrument. Its use spread like wildfire throughout Europe.

At the court of Rudolph II in Prague Johannes Kepler, too, began using the telescope. The same year he published his monumental *Astronomia Nova*, which described the laws of elliptical orbits and of equal areas. The volume was full of observations regarding the tides, planetary revolutions, and so forth.

In Cambridge work went forward speedily on the new Bible. Samuel Harsnett, Vice Chancellor of the University, was appointed to hold concurrently the bishopric of Chichester. In London at the Court, James continued to do unpopular things. His favorite, Sir Robert Carr, a Scot like the king and, in the opinion of many if not most Englishmen, a reprobate, was given the estate of Sherborne which James had semi-legally seized from the imprisoned Sir Walter Raleigh. Raleigh's wife was inadequately compensated for the property, and Carr took up residence there. He began an affair with a married woman, Frances Howard, Lady Essex, but managed to keep it secret for a while.

The talk of the Court, aside from politics, patronage, sea ventures, and expeditions to the New World, was of Dr. John Lamb who had been formally indicted at Worcester assizes for "wasting and consuming" Thomas, Lord Windsor, "by sorcery" and for "invoking and entertaining evil spirits," each a capital offense. Inasmuch as he did not, like Simon Reade, plead fraud, he was convicted on all counts. James, consistently inconsistent, saw to it that the sentence was commuted to imprisonment, and Lamb was thrown into the keep at Worcester Castle.

Within a year Dr. Lamb had been moved from Worcester Castle to King's Bench in London. As with all favored prisoners — such as Sir Walter Raleigh who had been kept in the Tower of London since 1603 and who had been free to have visitors, to write, and to experiment with alchemy — the terms of Dr. Lamb's confinement were easy. He set up once again as a practitioner of medicine and sorcery, and his clients, most of whom were highly placed, had access to him at will. Dr. Simon Forman, too, was doing excellent business at Lambeth. One of his clients was Frances Howard, the Countess of Essex who, during the year, often consulted him. She asked Forman to prepare her horoscope and to use other methods of divination in order to assure her success with the king's favorite, Sir Robert Carr. She also received medical advice and information about poisons.

Another of Forman's clients was a Mrs. Ernest Merchant, wife of a wealthy London gentleman, who told the sorcerer a strange story. Her husband had been traveling in Sussex some time before and had stayed overnight at an inn where someone had committed suicide. He was not told of the episode until after he had slept in the suicide's bed — the very bed where the man had cut his own throat and bled to death. Upon leaving the inn the husband had become aware of someone following him, but whenever he turned to confront the person he would slip into the shadows. Mr. Merchant became convinced that the ghost of the suicide was trailing him. Ever since, he had on occasion been seen to turn about and say to no one visible, "I defy thee!"

At last Mrs. Merchant had been able to stand it no longer. She asked Simon Forman for help, and he was happy to give it for a fee. He made a charm for the husband to wear and assured the matron the ghost would follow Mr. Merchant no more. Taking it home, Mrs. Merchant gave it to her husband, told him what she had done, and, handing the sigil to him, she bade him, "Wear it." He had put it on, turned around, and discovered that the Follower had disappeared. From that moment on he was never without Forman's amulet.

Forman and Lamb both heard soon enough of the book Galileo published in 1610, *Siderius Nuncius*, which discussed the discoveries he had made with the telescope. Nothing in the book astonished Europe more than Galileo's report of the discovery of the moons of Jupiter. In September Galileo left Padua after eighteen years of great success and acclaim at the university there. He had, in July, been named "Philosopher and Mathematician Extraordinary" to Cosimo II, Grand Duke of Tuscany. In his new post he almost immediately began to make a series of discoveries of such magnificence as to obliterate those in his past. If one had listened closely, one might have been able to hear the Earth begin to tremble.

Still another event of great significance took place on the opposite side of the Atlantic Ocean. In Jamestown, of all the colonists who had arrived the previous year, only sixty were left alive after a very hard winter and an epidemic of the smallpox. Totally discouraged, they decided to abandon the colony aboard ships that had recently arrived from the Bermudas. They boarded the ships and sailed out of the harbor. When John Putnam and his fellow parishioners heard of what had happened next, they saw that there had been a Divine Providence about it, and he said so to Zaccheus Gould who agreed with him: As the fleeing colonists reached the mouth of the river they met the fleet of the new governor, Thomas West, Lord De la Warre, arriving with more colonists and supplies. It was decided among the survivors that they would return and try again.

The Committee of Review at Cambridge, a member of which was John Bois, was midwifing yet another event: It was considering the final draft of the Bible. An occurrence of lesser significance to most, but of greatest to John Putnam was also taking shape. He was courting Priscilla Deacon of Corner Hall, Hemel Hempstead, Hertfordshire, which was a physically difficult proposition, Hemel Hempstead being at some remove from Aston Abbotts and Aylesbury. He had met her when she had visited her sister, Phoebe , who had married Zaccheus Gould of Aston Abbotts, John's neighbor and friend. Putnam's intended was of a good family, she was a good woman, and John was prosperous. He was also thirty years old.

In 1611 the King James version of the Bible was published and immediately recognized as a great accomplishment. James was delighted with it, and John Bois in Cambridge looked at his copy with quiet pride. The Vice Chancellor, Harsnett, had personally commended him for his work. Of this first edition the books of the Apocrypha, so-called, were an integral part, as they had been of all previous English editions since the 14th century, but no sooner had the Bible been published than there were heard among the voices of acclaim Puritan voices as well which complained that, because there were no Hebrew texts for the Apocrypha, only Greek texts, they should not have been included, for they were suspect as the Word of God. The Puritans had been using copies of the Geneva Bible with the Apocrypha dropped.

A few others were critical as well. These were likely to be scholars whose primary concern was accuracy rather than faultless style or orthodoxy. One section they were prone to point at had been translated by Bois: 1 Corinthians, Chapter 1, verse 20. In Hebrew it was argued that the word *Devils* in the verse, "and I would not have you partakers with the Devils," had originally been "idols," as in "false idols" or "false gods." Thus, they pointed out, the false idols of the early Christians were equated with the "demons" of the Greeks, including the whole panoply of Pagan gods, and Bois had thus made all the legions of the Great God Pan into Christian "Devils," thereby adopting into Christianity the Greek gods of nature and making them wholesale the underlings of Satan. Where originally the verse had been merely a re-emphasis of the commandment, "Thou shalt have no other gods before me," it was now a plank in the firmament of witchcraft persecution. But Bois was satisfied he had done the proper thing, and his critics found it politic not to press the issue. The King James Bible went forward to nearly universal praise.

James had little time to consider with pride its publication, for he had been having his troubles with Parliament which had been haggling over religion and money ever since it had been called into session in 1604. At last, frustrated and angry, the king dissolved Parliament and entered upon personal Royal rule of England. No sooner had the legislature been dissolved and its members returned to their communities to spread the word of the king's arrogant action than Sir Edward Coke, Chief Justice of the Common Pleas, stepped into the vacuum and began to use the courts in defense of the common law and the constitution and against the aggrandizement of the Royal Prerogative. King James was less than pleased.

James took another unpopular action during the year when, on the 25th of March, he elevated his favorite, Sir Robert Carr, to the title of Viscount Rochester. James' Court had begun to sniff out the liaison Carr had established with the Countess of Essex, Frances Howard. Sir Thomas Overbury, Carr's old friend and boon companion, had known about the affair almost from the first, and he had been violently, but privately, opposed. Now that Lady Essex, who was a notorious courtesan, had surfaced in Carr's bed, Overbury took the first chance he had to point out to him the quality of her reputation. Carr, like any lover, rejected his friend and informed the Countess of Overbury's words.

Sir Thomas, little daunted, wrote a poem titled "His Wife" which circulated through the Court in samisdat manuscript, the traditional method of Court publication. In the poem he depicted the virtues any woman ought to possess if a gentleman were thinking of marrying her. Copies of the poem soon found their way to the Countess who saw in it an attempt by Overbury to open Carr's eyes before it was too late. She became Overbury's deadly enemy. She went to consult about the situation with Dr. Simon Forman in the magus' studio.

In Aston Abbotts the talk was agitated and political; however, John Putnam was preoccupied with personal matters. He and his brothers and sisters, including Elizabeth with her intended, George Bottome; Anne with her husband, William Argett; his mother; the family and friends of the Deacons of Hemel Hempstead, his neighbors and relatives, gathered in the Aston Abbotts church where John and Priscilla pronounced the nuptial vows. After the ceremony Zaccheus Gould shook his brother-in-law's hand, and Phoebe Gould kissed her sister, welcoming her to the community. The bride smiled, blushed, and cast a glance at her new husbandman.

He was a big man, nearly six feet, strongly built and well-conditioned by his work in the fields. He had brown hair and eyes, a quiet demeanor. There was about him an air of sturdy capability. John, for his part, tried not to glance too often at his bride. He was pleased. She was a well-built, strong girl, not unshapely. She had a pleasant personality, she was young, and she would, John felt sure, make a good mother and a wise helpmeet. He congratulated himself for having waited long enough to make a good match.

The wedding party walked out from the church past the village green and along a cart track through the fields to the Putnam home where they entered, prayed together, and sat to drink cider and beer, to eat the cakes the women had baked, and to admire the goods Priscilla had brought with her as her portion: The fine pewter cups and dishes, the silver candlesticks, the spotless linens that covered the beds, the clothing. At a proper hour the guests took their leave, the women with curtsies and the men with winks and handshakes. John Putnam dropped his head, then raised it and looked them squarely in the eye. At the door Zaccheus said, "I would vouch for both sisters, John, to judge by the one I know." Zack stepped outdoors and closed the door, the last to leave, before John could collect his thoughts to reply. He stood a moment looking at the latch, then turned and went to Priscilla. He took her hand and looked down at her. "I am a happy man, Goodwife," he said. She laid her head on his chest and stood there holding him. It was the closest he had ever come to saying he loved her, but she was a Puritan, too, and it was close enough.

Things were happening elsewhere: In London one day Dr. Simon Forman stepped into a boat on the bank of the Thames to cross over and keep an appointment on the other side. In the middle of the river, while the boatman was rowing, the physician of Lambeth suddenly pitched forward and lay dead on the deck. In Rome in the Spring Galileo had exhibited in the gardens of the Quirinal Palace, to the admiration of an ardent Pontifical Court, the wonders of the new heavens, and in Augsberg Johannes Kepler published his treatise *Dioptrice*, which founded the science of optics.

In March of 1612 Elizabeth Southern of Lancashire, known as "Old Demdike" to her neighbors, was brought before a local justice, Roger Nowell, on suspicion of witchcraft. Old Demdike was eighty years old and blind. When she was accused and examined she admitted to having been a witch since 1560 when "a spirit or devil in the shape of a boy" received her soul. In 1565, she said, she had persuaded her gossip, Anne Whittle, known as "Old Chattox," to join her in her pact and practices. Ann was forthwith arraigned, and she, too, proved to be ancient and blind.

Not long after the two women had become the Devil's own, Old Demdike said, a coven of witches had been formed that included her daughter Elizabeth Device and Ann Whittle's daughter, Anne Redfearn, together with other friends and relatives. "Old Chattox" implicated her granddaughter, Alison Device. Soon there was arraigned before the court a host of witches. Goody Elizabeth Device had been born with a deformity: Her eyes were set at unequal heights in her face; one looked up and the other down. Alison was accused of laming an itinerant peddler who acted as though he had suffered a stroke, and she confessed. Old Chattox was indicted for the witch murder of Robert Nutter of Greenhead, in the forest of Pendle, Lancashire. Elizabeth Devise and Ann Redfearn were named as accessories to the murder. Old Demdike, Old Chattox, and Alison were sent to prison in Lancaster Castle, bound over to the next court session, but the rest were allowed to remain at liberty for lack of evidence.

Early in April Elizabeth Device was accused of calling an emergency meeting of the members of the coven who were still at large. They met in her mother's home in the forest of Pendle in order to plan a rescue of the imprisoned trio. Eighteen women and three men were in attendance at this first English "Sabbat" — they ate dinner: beef, bacon, roast mutton that had been stolen by James Device, which was in itself a capital crime. All in all, it seemed rather a subdued Sabbat, at least by Scottish standards. It didn't hold a candle to the Fian affair. Those at the gathering were said to have planned to kill the jailer of Lancaster

Castle, blow up the building with gunpowder — as Guy Fawkes had planned to do with King James — and free the accused. When the Sabbat broke up the witches agreed to meet in a year's time...but news of the gathering reached the ears of Justice Nowell.

On the 27th of April he arrested nine of the conspirators, sixteen of whom had been identified, but most of the rest fled before they could be apprehended. The trial began on August 17th. Primary witnesses were twenty-year-old James Device and his nine-year-old sister Janet. Their mother Elizabeth refused to confess to the charges until two of her other children joined the chorus. She broke down at that point, confessed, and then retracted her confession, but the judge allowed the original confession to stand as the main evidence against Mother Device. She was convicted and hanged, protesting her innocence. Though James and Janet Device had cooperated fully, naming the names of those who had attended the alleged Sabbat, their pliability earned them little leniency, but the jury acquitted Anne Redfearn of the Nutter murder, which infuriated Justice Nowell who had her retried on another charge: Bewitching Robert Nutter's father, Christopher Nutter, to death. The jury this time saw the wisdom of the charge and voted to convict.

Yet a further development in the Nutter case was the involvement of Christopher's wife Alice who was identified as having been at the Sabbat as well, for James Device said that his grandmother had told him Mrs. Nutter was a witch. The well-to-do, influential woman was convicted with the rest despite her insistence that she was completely innocent.

On the 20th of August the main trial was interrupted by the trial of the three Salmesbury witches who were accused of torturing a young woman by means of sympathetic magic. The judge interrogated the accuser who admitted she had accused falsely at the instigation of a Roman Catholic priest who, outraged at the conversion of the three to Protestantism, had attempted to be avenged. The testimony at this trial, however, had no effect upon the main case.

Ten of the accused in the original case were hanged, including Old Chattox, Anne Redfearn, Elizabeth Device, James Device, and Mrs. Nutter. Old Demdike died in jail before she could be executed. Two others were sentenced to one year in prison and four appearances in the pillory quarterly during that year. Seven of the total of twenty accused were acquitted.

While news of the Lancashire cases was circulating throughout the shires, also circulating was a chapbook with a long title about another case of 1612: *The Witches of Northamptonshsire: Agnes Browne, Joan Vaughan, Arthur Bill, Helen Jenkinson, Mary Barber, Witches, Who Were All Executed at Northampton the 22nd of July Last.*

There was a church gathering of the Putnam clan in Aston Abbotts on October 22nd: John's younger sister Elizabeth was married to a neighbor, Edward Bottome. She had been despaired of because, at the age of thirty-one, she appeared to be a confirmed spinster, but at last the prosperity of the Putnams and their influence in the community had induced the Bottomes to put forward their son for the match, and, to the great relief both of Mother Margaret Putnam and her eldest son, matters were at last settled.

No sooner had Elizabeth left Mother Putnam's home, however, than she began to find the living lonely. Her sons had all grown and gone their ways, and she was left at Stewkely in the old house to fend for herself at a distance of several miles from her son John's household. John soon stepped in. He arranged for the sale of the Stewkely property and moved his mother into the Aston Abbotts house where he could care for her and she, in turn, could help Priscilla with the impending arrival of the baby, an event that took place in December. The infant, a girl, was named in honor of John's sister Elizabeth and baptized in the church on the 20th of December. It was a happy Christmas season, even though it was in no way a holiday for the Puritan family.

During the year the ailing Emperor Rudolph II in Prague had been administered "a potion of ambergris and bezoar," which had been guaranteed by his alchemists and physicians to be the "universal panacea." Nevertheless, gangrene ultimately took his life, and a good many members of the Hermetic Brotherhood soon found themselves searching for other employment.

At the Court in London Robert Carr was appointed the king's secretary. He had made it known that he wished to marry Frances Howard, Lady Essex, and the king made no objection when she filed for an annulment of her marriage. Thomas Overbury continued to oppose the marriage, and to speak openly against it. The Countess feared him, for he threatened to expose some of her more unsavory actions, so the Lady began an intrigue that was aimed at disposing of Overbury's threat, and as the year came to an end the plot was in the weaving.

Two witchcraft chapbooks were published in 1613. The first, by John Potts, was titled *The Wonderful Discovery of Witches in the County of Lancashire*. It was very long for the genre, 186 pages, and quite detailed. The whole story of Old Demdike and Old Chattox was laid out for the public and for juries and judges as well. The second, anonymously authored as usual, was titled *A Book of the Witches Lately Condemned and Executed at Bedford*. It treated sensationally the case of three people who had gone to the gallows.

John Putnam kept track of the political news and the news from America where Dutch traders had erected some buildings on the Island of Manhattan, near the river Henry Hudson had explored and, briefly, hoped was the beginning of the Northwest Passage.

Sir Edward Coke, who had become a great thorn in the side of King James in his position as Chief Justice of the Common Pleas, was boosted upstairs to the Chief Justiceship of the King's Bench where, the King hoped, he would be more easily controllable and out of the way of sticky cases. Coke was also made a member of the Privy Council, in which position, too, he was answerable to the king.

Encouraged by his successes in Rome, Galileo Galilei published a book, *Letters on the Solar Spots*, in which he ventured to take sides with the Copernican theory as against the disproved — except where the Church was concerned — Ptolemaic theory. No sooner had he done so than the Jesuits and others detected discrepancies between what the Bible said regarding the heavens, and what Galileo was saying. Galileo had tried for years, and in his book he again tried, to avoid raising the religious issue, but once it had been raised by others he threw himself into the debate headlong. His enemies saw their chance.

At the Court in London the Countess of Essex sprang her trap on Sir Thomas Overbury. In the spring she manipulated him into a position where it seemed he had been disrespectful to the king. Finding himself unable to extricate himself, Overbury was thrown into the Tower of London where, for a while, his neighbor was Sir Walter Raleigh.

The Countess continued to develop her plan. On the 22nd of April she caused the governor of the tower, Sir William Wade, to be discharged and replaced by Sir Gervaise Elvis, whom she controlled. Sir Gervaise was aided by another new appointee, a jailer who was skilled in the administration of drugs. He began to feed Overbury small doses of sulfuric acid in the form of copper vitriol. The idea was to make it appear that Overbury had fallen ill and was dying a lingering death. But Overbury was constitutionally stronger than had been anticipated, and he lingered too long, in constant pain, all through the summer. At last the Countess lost patience. On the 15th of September Overbury was administered a large dose of poison and died. Ten days later, the countess' annulment was approved, and she began to plan for her wedding.

On the third of November Robert Carr was made Earl of Somerset, and in December the couple were married. As a wedding present, King James on December 23 appointed Carr Treasurer of Scotland.

Such things were not even dreamed of in Aston Abbotts. Life went on in the old way. From time to time neighbors dropped in to pass the time with Priscilla and Margaret Putnam. One of the rather frequent visitors was an older man, William Huxley, who was more than courteous to the widow Putnam. And in November Elizabeth Bottome had her first child who was named Richard.

The folk of Aston Abbotts found a good deal to gossip about during the following year. On April 5th King James summoned Parliament again, being in need of funding. Instead of debating supply, however, the Parliament — still very Puritan in its makeup — simply fell to debating the old issues of religion and parliamentary rights. On the fifth of June an irate sovereign threatened to dissolve again what he called the "addled" Parliament. His threat provoked no particular response on the part of the members. James waited two days, then carried out his threat. The Addled Parliament had accomplished nothing whatsoever, though they had engaged in some very bitter debates. Again the members dispersed to their communities, carrying with them the lees of bitterness for the home folk to drink. Again James added injury to insult: He once more honored Robert Carr, Earl of Somerset, who was appointed Lord Chamberlain of England.

John Putnam found more to be glad for in Sir Ferdinando Gorges' latest enterprise. The Governor of the Plymouth Company sent Captain John Smith on an expedition to explore New England, still called "Northern Virginia" in official documents. Capt. Smith coasted from Nova Scotia to Cape Cod charting the region and naming salient points: Plymouth, Cape Ann, the Charles River, Southampton, Barnstable, and many others. The colony at Jamestown, John Putnam noted, was seven years old, and the English had begun to colonize the Bermudas.

On the 8th of December John stood surety for his mother in her second marriage to Mr. William Huxley. Again there was a gathering of the family, and again the nuptial ceremony was performed. The house seemed peculiarly empty without Mother Putnam. Priscilla particularly missed her, for she found it difficult to do all that a yeoman's wife was supposed to do, being pregnant as she was. She found the strength to carry on, though, and John helped in the ways he could. Fortunately, they were surrounded by relatives who came to lend a hand and pass the time with Priscilla almost every day. At that, Mother Putnam hadn't been lost entirely for she, too, lived nearby.

Thomas Putnam was born early in March of 1615 and baptized in Aston Abbotts on the 7th of the month. John and Priscilla were excited and proud. It had been a difficult birth, as the boy was a large baby. The women of the village had seen her through, however, and all was well. The attending doctor characterized Thomas as "A strapping little lad," and John agreed silently as he looked at this first son lying cradled in its mother's arms.

Thomas was born under the sign of Pisces, second decan. The sign, interpreted symbolically, meant captivity and bondage. Thomas Putnam would be a quiet man, willing to live and let live. He would be given to prayer and self-denial. Words would not come easily to him, but he would be compassionate. He would accept the restrictions imposed upon him and look for others to assume as well. His gratification would come through helping those who needed help. He would throw himself into his work, but he would not be a particularly ambitious man. He would enjoy what he had, and he would willingly share it.

While he was squalling for his mother's breast the Tarrantine Indians of Maine were waging violent war on the other New England tribes. Thousands of their enemies were being slaughtered from the Penobscot River to the Charles. To protect themselves from Indian depredations the Dutch on the island of Manhattan built Fort Nassau.

In Italy Galileo had been called to Rome to answer charges before the Inquisition, and in Linz Johannes Kepler published a book that contributed to the development of higher mathematics, the *Nova Steriometria Doliorum*.

In London the murder of Sir Thomas Overbury came to light in September. Sir Edward Coke and Sir Francis Bacon — the greatest lawyer and the greatest scientific theorist in England — were assigned to find out the facts of the case. When they had done so, Robert Carr,

Earl of Somerset, and his lady were convicted and clapped into the Tower where they lived comfortably with one another.

In Rome on the 24th of February, 1616, the Holy Office published officially its finding regarding the Copernican theory of astronomy — not only was it absurd philosophically, it was also heretical theologically. Two days later Galileo was summoned by Pope Paul V from whom Galileo had expected much. He received a great deal — the Pope admonished him to refrain from teaching the proscribed theory. Galileo was induced to accede. On the fifth of March the Congregation of the Index published a decree that reinforced the findings of the Holy Office, with one change: The decree omitted the word "heretical." Copernicus' monumental scientific work *De Revolutionibus Orbium Coelestium* was placed on the index of banned books, and a treatise written by Fra Foscarini, a Carmelite monk, which discussed the Copernican theory from a religious point of view, was also proscribed.

In England on the 23rd of April one of the most popular playwrights of the age, William Shakespeare, died at his home in Stratford-upon-Avon.

Galileo in June returned to Florence where he attempted to scuttle the rumors being circulated by his enemies that he had had to grovel in the dust before the Inquisition. Then, like the Bard, he too entered into a still place.

During the summer John Smith of Leicester who, at the age of four in 1604, had been a child prodigy of demonic possession, was forced to resurface because he had again been bewitched by triple the number of witches that had originally bedeviled him. He accused nine women of afflicting him. Of these nine, six consorted with familiar spirits — a horse, a cat, a fish, a toad, a dog, and a polecat. Depending upon which woman it was who tormented him at a given time, John Smith would whinny, meow, blow bubbles, croak, bark, or fart. If the women were required to recite a particular incantation John's fits would be cured, but if the phrase varied in any way his torment would continue. John Smith was more successful in his second engagement with the powers of Hell: All nine of the women were convicted on July 18th.

Two weeks after their hanging, on the 15th of August, King James passed through the area on one of his progresses. He sent for the boy in order to examine him personally. John, awed by the Royal Presence, stumbled in his explanation of the phenomena he had experienced, and the king sent him to Lambeth to be examined by George Abbot, Archbishop of Canterbury, and his office. There, John's fraud was uncovered the second time. The king was informed that the boy could turn his fits on and off at will — for he was again having convulsions, had accused six other women of causing them, and the witches were awaiting trial at Leicester while the star witness was being detained in London. King James sent for the boy and urged him to perform, which he obligingly did.

In October the trial of the six took place with a representative of the archbishop present in the court. Eventually five of the Devil's Half-Dozen were released, but the sixth died in prison during the course of the proceedings. The magistrate, Sir Humphrey Winch, and his Sergeant, Sir Randolph Crew, who had presided over both trials, were discredited, but neither was punished for having sent six innocent people to the gallows.

A London judge was much more severely treated: Edward Coke, having denied in court the validity of a grant of a benefice by King James as a reward to the Bishop of Lichfield, was admonished with other judges who supported Coke's decision. All the judges submitted but Coke. King James dismissed him from all his offices on trumped-up charges.

In Aston Abbotts Priscilla Putnam was expecting for the third time. In all but this, 1616 had been a year of admonitions. There had been two publications in which some of the villagers were interested, one in which John Putnam was specifically interested: Captain John Smith published *A Description of New England*. Over the years there had been more and more speculation among Puritans concerning the New World.

Now that it had a name, some of them, the Separatists especially, were beginning to think in terms of colonization. Weren't the English colonies in Virginia and the Bermudas flourishing? Weren't the French in Quebec and the Dutch on Manhattan Island? Wasn't nearly all of Central and South America colonized by the Spanish and Portugese? Obviously, if it could be managed politically, a physical remove from England was feasible. But such talk was merely talk, though Sir Ferdinando Gorges was clearly ready to entertain a reasonable proposal — had been ready for years, in fact.

The other book that caused local talk — the Aston Abbotts parson owned a copy — was Alexander Roberts' *Treatise of Witchcraft* which reaffirmed everything that needed reaffirming.

John Robinson's Leyden Pilgrims in 1617 were thinking much harder about America than their English brethren. It was becoming clear that if they stayed in Holland much longer they would no longer be Englishmen — the children were already half Dutch. In their debates, Robinson's company discussed the merits of moving to Guiana or Virginia. The Dutch authorities attempted to influence the discussion — they wished the English to settle in Dutch territory on the Hudson River under the aegis of the Netherlands' West India Company. The majority of the Pilgrims preferred English territory, however, and at last the majority prevailed. Robinson's group applied to the London Company for a patent.

In New England the Tarrantine Indian War was over, but a plague of Satan's scourge, which had been brought to the New World by the Europeans, was ravaging the remains of the tribes. At no time within memory or tradition had the northeastern coast been so thinly populated by the native race. The Pawtucket tribe of the Cape Ann area numbered only a few hundred members out of the several thousand who had been living only a year or two earlier.

In Aston Abbotts on July 24th John Putnam and his wife took their second son, John Putnam, Jr., to the church to be initiated into the

Christian religion. The babe's father wondered whether this boy would set foot on the soil of the New England.

The witchcraft books were appearing at a steady rate. Thomas Cooper published his *Mystery of Witchcraft* which covered old ground — it was based on King James' *Demonology*, William Perkins' *Discourse of the Damned Art*, George Gifford's *Dialogue*, and it attacked the same book James had attacked, Reginald Scot's satirical *Discovery of Witchcraft*. Dr. Cooper had been an undergraduate at Christ Church, Oxford. While there he had as a roommate a student who had been obsessed with the study of the occult. Thomas had been seduced by his roommate's interest, and together they had pored over the ancient books and formulae, tried their hand at reciting the charms and the incantations of eld.

But the Lord had prevailed with Cooper, shown him the true light, and enabled him to say the equally ancient preventive charm, "Get thee behind me, Satan!" Not only had Cooper's soul been saved, but the Lord had led him to prevail with his roommate, who abjured the dark arts at last. Thenceforward, Thomas Cooper had studied from the other side of the ledger, becoming an avid follower of Perkins and a severe judge of those who transgressed.

At the end of the year the Leyden Pilgrims were informed that their patent had been granted. The year following was one of planning and preparation for Robinson's flock, their activities hastened by the threat of war, for the Tarrantine War of New England had its mirror image in Europe: The Thirty Years War had begun. In many spots on the Continent the Church was too preoccupied to pay a great deal of attention to the publication in Linz of the first volume of Johannes Kepler's *Epitome Astronomiae Copernicanae*, a textbook that set forth in plain terms the elements of the Copernican system. During the year three comets had appeared over Europe. While Kepler studied them, many another wondered what they portended.

Mother Putnam took ill suddenly as the year turned, and she died the first week. John Putnam mourned with his family when, on the 8th day of the month, most of the town turned out to lay the old woman away. She would have been sixty-three in August. The Goodspeed family came from Wingrave and surrounding communities. John in his forty-first year became the official head of his family, though he had been acting in his mother's behalf since Nicholas died. After the service, the eulogies and commiserations were over, the folk dispersed to continue their duties. Death was no stranger to the farmers of Aston Abbotts. The Putnams had been among the more fortunate of the families in this regard for many years.

In the spring of 1619 there was witchcraft at Lincoln. Involved were the Flowers of Belvoir Castle — two sisters named Margaret and Philippa. Some years earlier Margaret Flower had been dismissed from service at the castle by the Countess of Rutland. The girl's mother, Joan Flower, long notorious in the community as a practicing witch and a foul-mouthed hoyden, had planned revenge upon the family in the castle. Philippa confessed at her trial that she had brought out of the castle "the right hand glove of the Lord Henry Ross," eldest son of Francis Ross, Earl of Rutland, "which I did deliver to my mother, who presently rubbed it on the back of her spirit, Rutterkin, and then put it into hot boiling water" in order to induce fever in its owner. "Afterward she pricked it often and buried it in the yard, wishing the Lord Ross might never thrive." Eventually, the Earl's son had sickened and died, and the earl's second son and daughter had become ill as well. Rumors in the community had brought the case to the attention of the authorities.

The Flower sisters — Mother Flower being no longer alive — were tried at assizes by Sir Henry Hobart and Sir Edward Bromley, who convicted them and ordered them hanged. Soon after their execution another of the anonymous chapbooks appeared, *The Wonderful Discovery of the Witchcrafts of Margaret and Philip Flower*. Another book with a simple title also appeared. *Country Justice* by Michael Dalton was added to the shelf containing defenses of the prosecution of witches.

In continental Europe, too, two volumes came off the presses, both by Johannes Kepler. Published in Augsberg, the first was a scientific book, *De Cometis*, which recorded Kepler's observations of the comets of 1618. The second was a throwback to mysticism and astrology, *De Harmonica Mundi*, which Kepler dedicated to King James I of England. James, flattered by the dedication of the great astronomer, sent an invitation to Kepler to come to England, but the invitation was politely declined.

Nathaniel Putnam, third son and fourth child of John and Priscilla Putnam of Aston Abbotts was born under the sign of Libra and baptized on October 11th. The symbol of Libra was the scales in balance. Nathaniel would be a just man. He would also be willing to compromise to reach agreement if the compromise would not jeopardize his sense of what was proper in the situation. He would be willing to cooperate with people rather than compete with them, and he would therefore be successful in his enterprises.

But he would not be a mere toady, for, having been born in the second decan of his sign, he would be strong-willed and independent. His personality would be a dominating one, and he would not accept orders merely because they were given. He would, in fact, be a rebel against unreasonable restrictions and traditional values if those values seemed no longer to be viable. He would be a questioning man.

To add to his new burden of joy John Putnam had more news of America: The colony in Virginia, which had been totally male, was augmented during the year by the first female colonists in the form of "respectable maidens." A family man to the core of his being, John could only approve. Further, the House of Burgesses of Virginia was convened for the first time, the initial representative congress on the shores of the New World.

Chapter Three

The Robinson Pilgrims had been preparing to leave Leyden, and they were nearly ready. In Aston Abbotts one evening the Goulds came to visit the Putnams. All four seated themselves around the fire, the women busied themselves with needlework, and the men settled down to talk. Zaccheus said, "They soon will be upon their way, John. I would I was going with them."

John knew well of whom his friend was speaking. He nodded his head. "It is an adventure," he replied. "May the Lord protect them." He glanced at Pheobe and Priscilla, but they didn't lift their eyes. The fire in the ingle colored their cheeks and made the shadows dance among the folds of their gowns.

"Do not you wish you was a-going?" Zack asked. John's reply was noncommittal. "We prosper here, and the little ones are very young. America is a hard land to hear tell of it."

Zaccheus shook his head. "But the brethren are persecuted. There we might worship as we know to be a rightful manner." John had no answer. After a silence the conversation drifted to other things. They talked of the new Parliament that had been called, and of the fact that Sir Edward Coke had been elected a member from Liskeard. They expected that he would become a member of the party that defended the constitution against the king's prerogatives.

The plan among the Pilgrims was that half the group, or somewhat less, would leave for Northern Virginia that year and prepare the way for the rest. The preponderance of the first group would be younger people. Rev. John Robinson would remain behind for the time being with the mother community and would join the American Pilgrims when things were propitious.

On the 2nd of July, 1620, the first group of Pilgrims embarked for England. They took a sorrowful leave of their pastor and friends, but at the same time the atmosphere was filled with excitement — the salt air was electric as people and baggage were lowered into boats at the wharf and were rowed out to the ships riding the swell, at anchor in the harbor. John Robinson stood among the sounds of gulls screeching, pulleys screeling and oarlocks rattling, the swearing sailors, and watched his flock leave. Not until the sails had disappeared on the horizon did he turn to go back to Leyden. He considered his feelings to be odd for the situation, which was theoretically the beginning of the Salvation of the Elect. He was deeply melancholy. Something told him he had seen the last of these people, his friends and disciples.

The ships arrived in Southampton without difficulty, and the Pilgrims disembarked to wait for the ships that would carry them across the Atlantic. Most of the group was taken into the homes of friends, relatives, or simply other Puritans, where they waited impatiently for a month. Then, on the 3rd of August, they embarked upon their ships once more, the *Mayflower* and the *Speedwell*. The winds being favorable, the ships set out on their voyage, but not far from Southampton the *Speedwell* was discovered to be leaking, and both ships put about to return. The *Speedwell* needed refitting, so again the Pilgrims went ashore and waited.

While they were doing so, in Leicester a case of diabolical possession developed. A boy of Bilson named William Perry had accused Jane Clark, an old woman, of bewitching him and causing him to have convulsions in which he vomited rags, pins, thread, and straw. On the 10th of August Perry was brought before the magistrates at Stafford where he was closely examined. Very skeptical, the judges dismissed the charges against Goody Clark, and shortly afterward Perry confessed that his distress had been contrived.

At about the same time another boy of Leicester, William Lilly, eighteen years old of the town of Diseworth, left home after his father's death and burial. He traveled to London where he took a position with the former Mrs. Ernest Merchant, sometime client of Dr. Simon Forman, and at present the wife of an elderly man named Gilbert Wright. Lilly began to do his job well; his master and mistress were pleased with the apprentice, and they treated him like a son, for they had none of their own.

Among the members of the Invisible College there were developments as well, both on the continent and in England. Sir Francis Bacon, the English scientific theorist, published his landmark *Novum Organum* which called upon men to abandon their ancient "idols" in favor of the objective study of nature and its phenomena. There were various sorts of idols Man continued to worship; his prostration before these false gods prevented him from seeing the New Order that was before mankind, for men continued to worship cliché and truism unthinkingly, which Bacon called "the idols of the tribe." Those who worshipped the self and its limited individual consciousness worshipped "the idols of the cave." Others worshipped language and rhetoric, to the exclusion of intelligence and order, and these were the "idols of the market place." Those who fell down at the feet of tradition worshipped "idols of the theatre." The false gods must all be cast down before Man could embark upon the work of the future, the method of which would be science.

But even as people were reading these words, in Leonburg, Germany, Katherine Kepler, Kepler's mother, was being arrested on a charge of witchcraft. The astronomer hastened to travel to her defense.

When it had been refitted and repaired, the *Speedwell*, together with her sister ship, made another attempt to sail, but once more she developed a leak, and the vessels turned to Southampton. There, the decision was made to leave the *Speedwell* behind. One hundred and two passengers boarded the *Mayflower*, overcrowding her tremendously. Twenty of the Speedwell passengers had to be left ashore.

On the 6th of September the *Mayflower* put to sea yet again. This third time the voyage was about half completed before trouble developed. In the middle of the Atlantic the solitary voyager met heavy winds. Unable to carry canvas before the gales, the *Mayflower* drifted, pounded by high seas. At last the structure of the ship had taken too much and a main beam began to buckle.

There was consternation between decks. There seemed to be nothing that could be done until one passenger came forward and told the Captain he had brought with him from Holland a great screw-jack. The crew scurried to find it in the hold, hauled it out, set it in place, and forced the beam back into its proper position. The Pilgrims offered up prayers of thanksgiving to the Lord for his protection of the flock, and the Captain ordered an extra measure of grog dispensed to the crew. The storm weathered, the *Mayflower* continued on her track.

On the 3rd of November in England King James created the Council for the Affairs of New England with Sir Ferdinando Gorges and John Mason as its leaders. A grant of territory in New England was made over to the Council, the land to lie between 40° and 48° north latitude, as charted by Capt. John Smith. But the event had nothing to do with those aboard the Mayflower, inasmuch as they were bound for a position just below the 40th degree in the area of "Northern Virginia" that was in the purview of the London Company which had founded Jamestown.

There was yet another coming together of the Putnam family on the 5th of November in Aston Abbotts, but this time it was not for a baptism or a wedding, but for the funeral of Little John Putnam, Jr., who had died suddenly at the age of three after a brief and virulent illness which had been diagnosed as smallpox, but which was so frightening that members of the family called it "Satan's scourge." The Goulds and the Bottomes were present, and William Huxley. Thomas and Richard were there with their wives and families. When the rector pronounced the words "Ashes to ashes, dust to dust," dropping the first handful of soil on the coffin, Priscilla wept openly. John stood rigidly, his arm on his wife's waist, the tears glistening in the creases of his face. The parson said, "The Lord giveth, and he taketh away. Let us pray." In tableau the Puritans stood with their heads bared and bowed in a thin, cold, early winter wind, a drizzle of rain slowly seeping through their clothes.

On the ninth of November the *Mayflower* made landfall at Cape Cod, considerably above the point of their intended destination. The ship began to coast south and continued southerly for half a day, but the Captain soon found himself to be sailing among shoals. Alarmed, he held a quick conference with his mates and the Pilgrim leaders, and the ship put about to return to the Cape.

Two days later the *Mayflower* came to anchor in Cape Cod Bay. She lay there for two days while the Pilgrims debated among themselves on their next course of action. On Monday the 13th a number of them decided to go ashore and set up a camp. In order to do so, they had to wade part of the distance; they were completely chilled by the time they had gotten a fire built and set up shelters.

On the fifteenth Captain Miles Standish took sixteen men on a scouting expedition looking for a place to settle, and during the course of their wanderings they sighted Indians. The next day the party found Indian graves and, buried there, maize as well. They stopped, built a barricade and a fire, and camped overnight in a cold rain.

The next day, Friday, Standish and his men set out once again, but they soon realized they had become lost in the forests. They traveled to the east and eventually heard the breakers of the ocean booming through the underbrush and the immense boles of the trees. When they came to the shore they turned to follow the shoreline. At last they came back to the ship.

On Monday the 27th another party of scouts set out under the shipmaster, Captain Christopher Jones, in the *Mayflower*'s shallop. Aboard were twenty-four colonists and nine sailors. They had not gone far before foul weather forced them ashore to spend the night in wind and snow. The next day several of the men were ill. Nevertheless, they continued their trip toward the port they had set out to find, but when they arrived they discovered it to be unsuitable. The party landed, began to follow a creek inland; then, after they had traveled five miles, they stopped to camp for the night in a pine copse. Hunters among the party brought in three wild geese and six ducks, which the company devoured about the fire.

On Wednesday the 29th the Captain and fifteen others felt too ill to attempt to return to the ship. Eighteen of the scouts remained behind while the remainder set out for the *Mayflower*. The next day those who had remained behind felt well enough to continue their explorations. They marched inland five miles further, but found no Indians, whom they were desperate to contact, and returned to the shallop which they boarded to spend the night. On the first of December Capt. Jones returned to the ship. One of the party, Edward Thomson, died shortly afterward, and five others were soon gravely ill. Before the end of the month they, too, died.

On Wednesday, December 6th, a third party went scouting in extremely cold weather. They sighted Indians but could not make contact because the redmen, at sight of the English, disappeared into the forest. The next day the party split up, part following the shore, the rest coasting in the shallop offshore. During the day the two groups lost contact, but by nightfall they were reunited. They came together to camp on a creek, built a great fire and a barricade, and afterward wrapped themselves in blankets while their clothes, draped on the barricade, dried in the heat and the wind.

At five a. m. the next morning, the men were roused by the cry, "Indians!" Before the Englishmen could get to their muskets and other weapons the air was full of arrows, but the Indians, mistaking the clothes on the picket for the settlers themselves, hit no one. A barrage of shot drove the natives off. When the scouting party put on their clothes, they found them to be well ventilated with arrow holes. As quickly as possible they boarded the shallop and sailed off. By mid-afternoon a mixture of snow and rain was falling; the seas were rough. A rudder broke and the mast as well — the sail fell into the sea. Worse, the shallop was found to be drifting among shoals. At last, with oars, the scouts managed to get the shallop to the beach where some of them camped while the others remained in the boat. Over the weekend they remained where they were, and the Puritans among them made sure the Sabbath was kept.

The following Monday, the 11th of December, the party sounded the harbor they had entered, decided it was a good spot, and returned to the ship. When they arrived they discovered that in their absence Dorothy Bradford, wife of William Bradford, had somehow fallen overboard and drowned.

On the 15th the *Mayflower* weighed anchor for the port their scouts had discovered, but the ship was driven back by high winds. The crew persevered, and the next day, Saturday, the ship entered the harbor to drop anchor. On Sunday, despite the Puritans, scouting parties were put ashore. Others went to scout the next day as well. On Thursday, December 21st, twenty of the *Mayflower* people stepped ashore at Plymouth Rock. Before nightfall a wind and rainstorm blew up, forcing them to remain ashore. The storm continued the next day, so that it was not until Saturday that many of the colonists went ashore to begin hewing timber for their common house.

During the Lord's Day there was again the cry of "Indians," but none appeared. No one but the sailors troubled to observe that it was not only Sunday, but Christmas Eve as well. The settlers spent all of Christmas Day erecting their building, which was twenty feet square. There were more wind, more rain. As the men worked, the mud thickened and froze on their boots, moisture soaked clear through their clothing, chilling them so that frequently they had to resort to the fire that was kept roaring by a party assigned to cut and carry firewood. Their fingers and ears were frostbitten — even the yeomen among them had never experienced anything like this in England. Aboard ship the women and children waited to be told that their new communal home was ready for occupancy.

On Thursday the 28th Governor John Carver, William Bradford, and the other leaders of the group gathered to portion out house lots. By this time many among them were ill. At the end of the month Indian smoke had been sighted, but the community dwelling was finished. Most of the passengers were still aboard the *Mayflower* lying at anchor, but some were living ashore, and some had even begun building individual houses.

Two of the Pilgrims on Friday the 12th of January, 1621, set out to track a deer in the forest, got lost, and were forced to camp overnight. The next day, to the great relief of the others, they managed to find their way back to Plymouth.

The common house the Pilgrims had built was thatched. Sunday, the 14th of January, Gov. John Carver and William Bradford were asleep inside when a spark from the chimney landed on the roof. The building was immediately aflame. Within a short space of time it was entirely consumed, for there was a high wind and a low tide, so that those aboard the ship could not get ashore to help fight the fire. Those inside managed to get out in time, but the Pilgrims had to begin nearly from scratch again.

During the winter in England William Perry of Leicester had repeated his earlier act: He was again in convulsions. Thomas Morton, Bishop of Lichfield, was ordered to conduct an investigation, for the boy had his defenders despite the action of the court in the summer when his accusations had been thrown out, and despite the fact that Morton soon discovered Perry had been trained by a Catholic priest to feign diabolical possession.

The boy's partisans, however, were not convinced. If that were so, they asked, how was it possible for Perry to pass black urine? Even the physicians who had been called in thought that in this case "nature had left her usual operations." The bishop, frustrated, had resolved to go no further, but in the end he decided to try one more ploy.

The rest of the family having gone to church, one of the bishop's servants remained behind, stationed at a knothole that looked into Perry's room where the boy, exhausted from his ordeal, lay on the bed.

When the bishop returned from church, the spy informed him that, when everyone had gone, Perry "lifts up himself, and stares, and listens, at length gets out of bed, and in the straw or mat underneath it, takes out an inkpot and makes water in the chamber pot." The boy had added ink to the urine and, "for a reserve, if he should be forced to make water before company," soaked some cotton with ink and put it "into his prepuce, covering it with the foreskin."

In Plymouth the winter continued heavy. On the 16th of February a man out fowling sighted twelve Indians in the woods. The next day two Indians deliberately showed themselves and made signs for the whites to approach. Miles Standish and another man did so, but the Indians turned and fled.

By the end of the month a number of the company had died, and in March more followed. On the 16th of the month an Indian walked into the settlement and astonished everyone by calling out to them in English, "Welcome, Englishmen! Welcome, Englishmen!" — it was a phenomenon that would be repeated now and again, for English traders and ships had continually visited the coast for many years. The Indian's name was Samoset. He stayed overnight then left, but the following Sunday he returned with five friends. The Puritans would not trade, it being the Lord's day, and the Indians left after the Englishmen had asked them, through Samoset, to return later. They hadn't done so by Wednesday, and the colonists sent Samoset to find out why.

The third time Samoset returned he brought with him an Indian named Squanto who also spoke English, for Squanto had been taken to England by one of the English captains in 1614. Squanto and Samoset told the English that the chief of the local tribe, Massasoit, was nearby with his people. Within the hour Massasoit showed himself at the top of a hill.

For a while neither side, out of suspicion, would make a move, but eventually Squanto arranged a parley. Edward White was sent forward with gifts of knives, some cheap jewelry, and food. Eventually more members of both parties joined the negotiations, including Miles Standish and several musketeers, whereupon a treaty of peace and mutual assistance was agreed to.

By the end of March, fifty-one of the settlers had died. Yet, when the *Mayflower* on the fifth of April hoisted anchor to return to England, not a single Pilgrim returned with her. In April Governor Carver died, and a few weeks later his wife died as well. William Bradford was chosen Governor in Carver's place.

The *Mayflower* returned to England in time for its crew to hear about the last act of the Bilson Boy. witchcraft drama, if any of them were interested. On June 26th William Perry was required to make a public apology at the assizes in Stafford for having attempted to hoax the court and injure Mother Jane Clark

While the *Mayflower* had been gone King James had again run out of money and been forced to summon Parliament after a decade of personal rule. As it turned out, it was an amazingly loyal Parliament, but very hostile to monopolies; however, to attack monopolies was to attack James' favorites, to whom the corporations had been granted. The king arrogantly refused to listen and treated the House of Commons disdainfully over several issues. The good will with which Parliament had assembled evaporated, bickering set in, and debates over freedom of speech rose once more to the fore.

Sir Edward Coke was one of the leaders of Parliament, and it was he who led the House of Commons to pass "The Great Protestation," a manifesto in favor of the right of Parliament to debate the monarchy, the realm, religion, and nearly anything else it wanted to debate. When Parliament adjourned King James tore the page with The Great Protestation out of the record book but the things it said could not be torn out of the memories of those who had drafted, debated, and passed it. James cast Coke, John Pym, and Sir Edward Philips into prison for their insubordination.

During the year two important books had been published as well. Robert Burton of Christ Church, Oxford, brought out a book on which he had been working most of his life. Titled *The Anatomy of Melancholy*, it was a compendium of the knowledge of its time in science, philosophy, medicine, history, literature, and sympathetic magic. Arranged in three parts, the first had to do with the causes and symptoms of "melancholy," a term that included everything from depression to mania. The second part of the book dealt with cures for melancholy, and the third section sought to discuss love melancholy and religious melancholy.

Burton was a well-known scholar and cleric — a mathematician, astrologer, philologist. His book immediately became one of the most popular books of the day despite the fact that it was primarily a great listing of quotations by all other experts on melancholy throughout the ages pasted together with a quirky running commentary by Burton. A portion of his book defended the belief in witchcraft; other portions paradoxically mocked the idea of sympathetic magic. The tome is arguably the foundation of the social science of psychology.

On the 17th of November a vessel arrived in Plymouth with thirty-six new colonists aboard, some of them those who had been left behind with the failure of the *Speedwell*, but the ship had used all its supplies on the voyage over, and it could leave but little for the use of the new arrivals. The Plymotheans welcomed them, divided up their stocks among them, and found that the whole colony would have to go on half rations.

The Narragansett Indians, when they discovered that the ship had left no supplies and that the state of the settlers was nearly desperate, "sent the English a bundle of arrows, tied with a snake's skin." The settlers filled the skin with bullets and returned it to the Indians. the

Narragansetts would get nowhere near the token, which was moved after them as they retreated. Finally the skin got back to the English after it had been moved around several times, the Indians continually avoiding it, and all was quiet.

In Leonburg, Germany, Johannes Keppler struggled with the authorities over the issue of his mother's alleged witchcraft.

Early in the new year Kepler prevailed with the authorities who had imprisoned his mother. He came to fetch her home but found her to be weak and in poor health. Within a few months he stood beside her coffin as it was lowered into the earth on the 13th of April, 1622.

By spring it was clear that the Plymouth colony was going to survive, but by a narrow margin. It was too early for any crops to be harvested, and the colony faced famine. Just at the critical moment an English shallop was sighted off the coast. When it put into the harbor it was found to bear seven new planters for the colony, but no provisions. The planters had come over on an English fishing boat to which the shallop belonged.

Governor William Bradford sent Edward Winslow back to the trawler with the shallop to ask for supplies, but it could give them only biscuit enough for each colonist to eat half a pound a day until the harvest. When Winslow reported back to Bradford, he found the colony in worse shape than when he had left it. The people were living off shellfish mainly, the Indians were again making noises, and Massasoit seemed to have abandoned them.

In England King James had taken steps to revoke the charter of the London Company. Sir Ferdinando Gorges and his Council for New England issued its first grant of land to Thomas Weston who, during the summer, sent about fifty or sixty men who landed at Weymouth, disembarking from the *Charity* and the *Swan*, but the expedition had been poorly planned, organized and equipped. Before long the Weymouth camp was ill, hungry and desperate. Instead of getting themselves together in good order they stole from the Indians who began to plan to exterminate the white men. The Plymouth Colony, however, stepped in to help, and the massacre was avoided, but Thomas Weston himself was not quite so lucky. He had taken ship to join his plantation, but when the vessel reached the New England coast it was cast away near Naumkeag, the future site of Salem, where Indians discovered him on the beach and stripped him to his shirt.

With Weston's group at Weymouth was an English Squire named Thomas Morton — no relation to the Bishop of Lichfield of the same name. Like the others in his group, he was an adventurer, not a Puritan. During the summer Morton and a number of others went exploring in the area of what would one day be known as Boston Bay while they were waiting for the return of their ship the *Swan* which was exploring the coast, looking for a likely site for a permanent camp.

In August the *Swan* returned to Weymouth, having spotted a likely place at Wessagusset, near the mouth of the Monatiquot River. Morton's party having returned, all of the Weston people embarked for Wessagusset. Not long after they arrived the Indians began to complain to the Plymouth Colony of ill treatment at the hands of the Wessagusset settlers. Plymouth was forced to issue the Westonites a warning.

In England during the summer Edward Fairfax, a well-known English translator of the classics, accused six women at York assizes of having bewitched his two daughters. One of Fairfax's neighbors, John Jeffray, accused the women of having cast spells upon his daughter, Maud, as well. The grand jury, despite a cautionary statement on the part of the judge, found a true bill and the trial was scheduled.

It began on the 9th of August. In the courtroom the three girls went into a trance and had to be carried out. One of the judges, Sir George Ellis, together with some of his colleagues, followed the girls out to try to discover the fraud they suspected was taking place. On their return they declared that Maud Jeffray had confessed that she had perpetrated a hoax at the instigation of her parents. When Maud returned to the courtroom, however, she denied she had confessed. Nevertheless, John Jeffray was sent to jail. The Fairfax girls, though, had not confessed, so the trial proceeded until the judges threw the case out of court for lack of sufficient evidence beyond spectral evidence. The defendants were discharged.

Afterwards Fairfax told the authorities that he had discovered Maud Jeffray had influenced his eldest daughter to join her in her fits and trances, and that his eldest had in turn drawn the younger girl into the conspiracy of hysteria. He apologized to the court and the defendants and was exonerated of all blame for the incident. At home his daughters were given a number of forceful explanations about why it would be best if they refrained from being possessed by demons in the future.

During the year a chapbook was published which recounted the exposure that had taken place in the home of Bishop Thomas Morton. Its title was descriptive: *The Boy of Bilson, or A True Discovery of the Late Notorious Impostures of Certain Romish Priests in Their Pretended Exorcism or Expulsion of the Devil Out of a Young Boy, Named William Perry.* Dr. Lamb read his copy with curiosity.

In the eastern shires there was a serious depression and the government feared a rebellion. The economic situation; the good news from Plymouth; the knowledge that ships of all types were plying back and forth between Britain and New England on a regular basis with traders, adventurers, explorers and colonists; the continued persecution of the Puritans at home, caused many such as John Putnam to begin thinking in hard terms of a remove from England. The possibility no longer seemed merely something to dream of before the fire. Thomas Putnam was seven and Nathaniel, three. Elizabeth was ten. Perhaps, when the boys were older…but Priscilla was pregnant again.

In early March of 1623 the baby was born, a girl, whom the Putnams named Sarah and baptized in the church at Aston Abbotts on the 7th of the month. John and his neighbor Zaccheus Gould were keeping close track, now, of the developments in America. Their talk, when the Goulds came home with them after the baptism, was of the new expedition being organized by some merchants of Dorchester who intended to set up a permanent trading post in the land of Massasoit.

During the summer the company sent thirteen men overseas, but when they arrived at Cape Ann to begin their fishery and trading post, they discovered that a group of Plymouth people was already there doing the same thing. The Dorchester traders were, however, welcomed, room was made for them, and they got on well with one another for, like their predecessors, the new arrivals were Puritans. All were delighted to learn that Weston's colony at Wessagusset had failed.

The depression in England had reached into counties abutting the eastern shires, and it was merely one more incentive to the Putnams, Goulds, and others like them to continue to consider alternatives. Then King James made a move that frightened the Puritans exceedingly: He sent George Villiers, Duke of Buckingham, to Spain with his son Charles to woo the Catholic Infanta. Upon their arrival, worst of all, the priests set about attempting to convert Charles to Catholicism and would not let him see his intended bride until they had prevailed. Charles tried many ploys in his efforts to come close to the young woman, but a Protestant, to her, was the Devil incarnate, and she did nothing to encourage him while he was in the state of apostasy.

During the summer Dr. John Lamb — still imprisoned and doing good business in physic and sorcery — had more luck with a woman who visited him in his keep. A sexual encounter took place — very gratifying to one in confinement, especially one who was, unlike Robert Carr, a bachelor still.

Like others of the Invisible College, Dr. Lamb liked to have the news, and by the end of the year he had learned that Galileo in Italy had broken his long silence: In Rome, through the Academy of the Lincei — of which he was a member —the astronomer had published his *Saggiatore*. The volume was dedicated to the new Pope, Urban VIII. Since the few passages that defended the Copernican theory were soft-pedaled, the book received adulations both from clerics and scientists.

In 1624 James completed his revocation of the Virginia charter of the London Company and made the plantation a royal province. In return for a tobacco monopoly, however, he allowed the province to retain its representative House of Burgesses, so that in effect it was neither fish nor fowl — neither province nor company colony. Many Englishmen and other Europeans continued to travel to North America either to stay or to visit, among them eight Dutch who disembarked from the *New Netherland* at Manhattan and claimed the island in the name of Holland — a rather late claim inasmuch as the Dutch had been living there for some time. Their ship proceeded inland to a point upriver near what would become Albany.

In England Prince Charles and Buckingham returned from their fruitless voyage to Spain, both furious over the treatment they had received, but the nation was delighted that Charles had come back unmarried to a Catholic. He became an overnight hero and a champion of Protestantism. His father, the king began to fade out of the limelight — there were rumors he was not well.

Charles' companion in the Spanish adventure, Buckingham, was interested to find when he returned that his very own "Devil," Dr. John Lamb, had been cried out upon by the woman who had visited him in prison the previous year — she was charging rape. Brought to court, the jury convicted Lamb of the charge, but the judge of the case, the Chief Justice, demurred, perhaps at the hint of Buckingham. The judge considered that the evidence against the good doctor was rather slim and rather late. He succeeded in obtaining a pardon for the sorcerer.

Dr. Lamb was released, not only from the conviction, but from prison as well. No sooner had he gotten his freedom than he set up his practice and residence near Parliament House so as to be handy to his clients. He engaged a fifty-five-year-old married woman, Anne Bodenham, as his housekeeper. Dr. Lamb, who dressed as flamboyantly as his means would allow — and they allowed considerable — moved his effects out of his prison quarters and into the new digs. His pride was his library, but he had missed purchasing a book he had wanted when it first came out in 1612. Now, he was able to make up for the loss by buying the second edition of John Cotta's *A Trial of Witchcraft*. Mrs. Bodenham began to live-in, apart from her husband, and soon there was a good deal of gossip about her and her bachelor master. It wasn't long before people were calling the Duke's Devil's housekeeper "Dr. Lamb's Darling."

William Lilly, considerably Lamb's junior at the age of twenty-two, was saddened during the year by the death of the wife of his master Gilbert Wright, but his grief was mitigated by a bequest: A small scarlet bag containing various articles of occult paraphernalia including amulets and charms. One of these was made of gold, and it had belonged to her first husband, Ernest Merchant, who had been haunted by the ghost of a suicide until Dr. Simon Forman had manufactured the medal to ward off Merchant's silent stalker. Young Lilly sold the amulet for thirty-two shillings, but not until he had transcribed the runes engraved on it. When he investigated their meaning he discovered they were astrological. His interest was piqued and he began to look for more material on the subject.

In Aston Abbotts, the Putnams had been visited once more by the largesse of the Lord. Phoebe Putnam was baptized on the 28th of July and brought home to join her brothers and sisters in Christian charity.

March 1625 brought death to two important men. On the first of the month in Leyden, Holland, the Rev. Mr. John Robinson died. He had, perhaps, more to do with colonizing New England than any other single man. He had led his people out of corruption and into the new Zion, yet he himself had never seen the Promised Land.

In March, too, James I died, and on the 27th of the month Charles I ascended the throne of England. The people were delighted; everywhere the folk celebrated. In Aston Abbots the church bell summoned the Putnams and their neighbors to meeting to offer up prayers for the peace and tranquility of the realm and for the good health and wise leadership of the new sovereign. At last the people had a champion on the throne again.

But not for long. On the first of May Charles I married a Catholic after all — by proxy: His bride was Henrietta Maria of France, and on the 13th of June he welcomed her to England at Canterbury.

Five days later Charles called for Parliament to convene. No sooner had it assembled than he began to treat the House of Commons more arrogantly than his father had. He asked for money but refused to say what it would be used for. The Puritans in the House were present in much greater numbers than ever before, reflecting the spread of the movement throughout England, but present in the country also was an Anglican group called "The New School," and it, too, was growing.

One of the tenets of The New School was that the Roman Catholic Church, like the Church of England, was a "true Church," though it was "corrupt and unsound in its doctrines." The New School leaned toward elaboration of ritual, and it supported the king and his claims to rule by Divine Right. The members of the New School perceived their position to be a moderate one, but from the Puritan point of view it was a Roman Catholic view and therefore extreme.

With no regard at all for the wishes of the Puritans or other Anglicans, Charles began to appoint New Scholars to positions of authority despite the known fact that he personally leaned toward Calvinism. It was a question of polity vs. conviction: Charles was appointing those who supported his position as monarch.

The Commons responded by arresting Richard Montague, a cleric who had written pamphlets in support of the views of the New School. Charles escalated by making Montague his personal chaplain. The Parliament thereupon voted only small sums for supply, refusing to give Charles what he had asked for and, in fact, needed. The king dissolved Parliament on August 12th.

To add to the confusion and dismay, plague broke out in London. Gilbert Wright, William Lilly's master, fled the city leaving his apprentice in charge. William enjoyed the vacation. He played at bowls in Lincoln's Inn Fields with Wat the cobbler, bought a bass viol and took music lessons and, in his spare time, studied astrology with Master Evans.

In Massachusetts during the spring John Lyford and some of his followers who had left Plymouth Colony to settle at Nantasket, decided the location didn't suit them and moved to Cape Ann to join the growing settlement there. Lyford, Thomas Gardner, and the other Puritans at Cape Ann felt they would like to have the Pilgrim entrepreneur Roger Conant join them. He was invited, and in the fall he joined the settlement. Conant had large plans for establishing fisheries; his interference soon caused disputes between the Pilgrims and the Dorchester men, and these arguments grew so virulent that Miles Standish had to be sent for.

When Standish arrived with his soldiers the Pilgrims decided they would separate from the Dorchesterians to form their own settlement, but the settlement failed and the Dorchester people, too, decided to give up and to go home to England. They left behind a few herdsmen to tend the livestock. Roger Conant suggested to all who were left that they try again at another location. Conant sent out scouts who came back with news of "a fruitful neck of land" called Naumkeag to the west, near where Weston had been cast away and stripped to his shirt by the Indians. It was agreed: They would abandon Cape Ann.

The situation in England was so bad by the end of the year that interest in New England was spreading everywhere among the Puritans…and among other Englishmen as well. During the summer Thomas Morton returned with new adventurers to begin a settlement on Boston Bay at Mount Wollaston, not far from Weston's old settlement of Wessagusset where a few stragglers still lurked in the woods.

In the new year Charles I, in great need of money, summoned his second Parliament which convened on the 6th of February, 1626, but even while it was gathering there was trouble over the terms of his marriage contract and an abortive raid that the Duke of Buckingham, George Villiers, had carried out against Spain with obsolete ships the previous fall. The Parliament, when it met, blamed the Duke for giving bad advice to the king and wished to impeach him.

Charles asked the Parliament to provide him with money to run the government, but Commons fell to debating the other issues. When Charles asked the house to stop their bickering and get to money, Parliament, including the House of Lords, refused to do so until several of its leaders, who had been arrested by the king, were released.

Sir Francis Bacon, who had been out of power for years in a forced retirement, despite his having petitioned James often, spent his time writing and experimenting. In March he caught cold while stuffing a fowl with snow near Highgate in order to observe the effect of cold on the preservation of flesh. He died on April 9th at the home of Thomas Howard, Earl of Arundel, not far from the place where he had been working — Arundel was one of those whom the Lords and Commons forced King Charles to release from the Tower.

On the fourth of May in North America the Dutchman Pieter Minuit set foot on Manhattan Island, and on the 6th he purchased the land from the owners, the native Americans, a step which the Puritans of Massachusetts had fatefully neglected to take.

At about the same time Roger Conant and his Dorchester fishermen completed their move from Cape Ann to Naumkeag and commenced to erect a settlement. It was good land, a neck that jutted out into the sea, with a good harbor and islands offshore where the fishing was excellent. Soon the village was doing well. Word had reached Plymouth in April, a year late, of the death of John Robinson, and no sooner had Conant's colony been founded than it received the sad news, relayed from Plymouth.

In June King Charles dissolved the Parliament and began casting about for other means of laying hold of funds. He notified the Justices of the Peace in each shire to ask the inhabitants for a money gift to the crown, but most of the people, upset by the king's high-handed ways and dissatisfied with conditions, refused to make the offering. Charles then attempted to make the "gift" mandatory. A few shires agreed grudgingly, but when the arrogant sovereign required that the justices sign a statement that this form of taxation was legal, they refused to do so and opposition coalesced among the remaining shires which then refused to comply with the original request. The treasury was bare.

At least the plague had run its course in London and in the city things returned to normal. Gilbert Wright, William Lilly's master, returned home and brought with him a young bride whom the young apprentice was anxious to please.

Among the Puritans of Lincolnshire in 1627 there was serious talk about "the planting of the Gospel in New England." It was not long before Puritans in London, Buckinghamshire, and many other counties to the west were involved in the discussion. The Dorchester merchants who had financed the Cape Ann venture got in touch with the interested Puritans upon the arrival in England of John Woodbury who had been sent by the Naumkeag planters to inform the merchants of their situation. Plans were immediately undertaken to send reinforcements to Massachusetts.

John Putnam again found himself unable to take advantage of events, for his wife was once more about to give birth. As he worked in his fields and barns, doing the spring planting and preparing for the heavy summer, he listened carefully to the rumors and items of news that Zaccheus Gould, Zaccheus' younger brother Jeremy Gould, and his other neighbors brought to him. But he kept his peace and was not involved much in the talk himself.

In America on the 11th of May Thomas Morton changed the name of Mount Wollaston to "Ma-Re Mount," a pun on the Latin *mare*, meaning sea, and the English *merry*. In order to celebrate the name change Morton and his merry men set up a Maypole — an eighty-foot pine. The Indians in the area were invited to the celebration and helped the Englishmen drag the pole to the top of the hill near the village, drums reverberating and firearms exploding.

When the Maypole of Merry Mount was ready to be raised it was decked with ribbons and garlands, the antlers of a spreading buck nailed to its top. Then, with a will, those present erected their totem and Thomas Morton, who had written a poem for the occasion — a poem no one could understand — nailed a copy of his offering to the pole. The crowd danced around it singing a song of revelry Morton also had written for the occasion.

When they heard of the pagan celebration the Plymotheans forty miles away were outraged. They were more than outraged, however, when they discovered that Morton had begun to deal in firearms and to trade them with the Indians.

Toward the end of the month Priscilla Putnam bore her husband another son who was baptized in Aston Abbotts on the 27th of May and named — like his dead brother — John Putnam Jr., for the Putnams were not superstitious people. Had they been, they might have been interested to know that their new child had been born in the first decan of Gemini, the sign of the twins. John Putnam the younger would be a good-humored man, of changeable moods and interests, a gregarious person, outgoing and interested in taking center stage — the opposite of his father in other words. He would be extremely competent, intelligent, and able to understand how things worked. Once he had mastered anything, he would make it his own.

John's older brothers Thomas and Nathaniel were twelve and eight years old respectively. They were witnesses to the baby's initiation into the mysteries of life and religion, and Thomas was old enough to be able to sense a certain ambivalence toward the new child on the part of his father — there was pride, but beneath the surface the tug of something like frustration as well. Old John was forty-seven, well into middle age.

In London William Lilly's master, Gilbert Wright, died suddenly leaving behind a young wife and twenty pounds in an annuity for the young astrologer. Lilly saw no reason to change addresses, so he stayed on and married the second Mrs. Wright. But he now needed an occupation of his own, so he dived into his hobby and began to study astrology seriously — he read everything he could find on the subject and collected as many books as he could afford, which was not an inconsiderable number, for Mrs. Lilly had come into a fair fortune. Two new volumes in which Lilly was interested — published during the year — were Richard Bernard's *Guide to Grandjurymen*, which discussed witchcraft, and Johannes Kepler's *Rudolphine Tables*, published in Ulm, which Lilly wanted desperately to get hold of when he heard of it, for it was a landmark set of astronomical calculations to which were appended tables of logarithms and of refractions, together with a catalogue of over a thousand stars. William Lilly was willing to learn to read German if he could not soon buy a translation.

On the fourth of March 1628 the group of Puritans who had been negotiating with the Dorchester merchants were successful in obtaining a grant from Sir Ferdinando Gorges and his New England Council, but it was not an outright grant, for they were not incorporated with governmental powers. They were to be merely tenants of the Council. Of the Dorchesterians, only the son-in-law of the Earl of Lincoln, John Humphrey, was associated with both the Cape Ann venture and the proposed augmentation of the Naumkeag colony.

While these negotiations were going on Charles I summoned his third Parliament, and it assembled on March 17th. Elected to the Commons as a member from Buckinghamshire was Sir Edward Coke. Another M. P. was a man named Oliver Cromwell, grandson of the Lady Cromwell who had been bewitched to death in 1590. Both men immediately took prominent roles.

The Parliament in England had its mirror image in Massachusetts. A meeting of representatives from the settlements was called to discuss the growing danger at Merry Mount. The representatives from Naumkeag were Roger Conant, Peter Palfrey, and John Balch. The

Council decided to ask Plymouth Plantation to take action against Thomas Morton before there were too many guns distributed among Morton's Indian friends and too many desperadoes attracted to the rollicking settlement.

When Plymouth officially received the council's request it sent a "friendly" warning to Morton who replied that he would trade with the Indians as he saw fit, and that it was none of Plymouth's business. Plymouth replied sternly that he was breaking an English law by selling guns to the natives and endangering the safety of the plantations. Thomas Morton, in effect, told the colonists to enter into a hot place.

At the end of May Miles Standish set out for Merry Mount with a squad of eight men. Having been apprised that Morton would be found at Wessagusset, Standish arrived there and surprised Morton, placing him under arrest, but at night Morton managed to escape and make his way back to Merry Mount — he was an English squire who loved the outdoors and had come to America very largely because it offered marvelous hunting and tramping about in virgin forest. He had no difficulty over terrain that he knew. When he arrived back home he prepared to resist. Among his preparations a prominent article was a quantity of alcohol.

The next morning Standish and his squad merely marched up to Morton's house and knocked on the door, demanding that he give himself up. Most of Morton's crew was off elsewhere when the Plymotheans arrived. Morton had only two cronies to aid in the defense, and one of those surrendered. The other was too drunk to help. Morton, nevertheless, scoffed at Standish's demand until the Captain threatened to break down the door. Morton opened the door and came outside carrying his musket, his drunken aide-de-camp staggering behind him — Standish grabbed the toper who stumbled and ran his nose against the soldier's sword: It would leave an interesting scar. When the squad took Morton's gun away from him they found that it was stuffed halfway up the barrel with powder and would very likely have blown up like a bomb if he had fired it. Obviously, Morton himself had been doing a little imbibing while he waited for the militia to show up. Captain Standish and his sturdy band took Morton along to Plymouth, making sure that he didn't escape again. Early in June Morton was sent back to England with John Oldham.

In England, while the invasion of Merry Mount was taking place, John Endicott of the Massachusetts Bay Company was preparing to sail for America, and in Parliament there had been major developments. Sir Edward Coke had been instrumental in drawing up a Petition of Right, which had been passed. It asked the king to observe four principles: That there be no "taxation without Parliamentary representation"; that there be no imprisonment for anyone without just cause shown; that there be no forced billeting of soldiers among the people, and that there be no martial law imposed on the nation in time of peace. Charles, after backing and filling for a time, finally agreed to the Petition of Right on June 7th, and the Parliament immediately voted him taxes. Then it returned to debating grievances, among which was the growing power of the New School clerics and courtiers, particularly William Laud, Bishop of London, who in April had also been made Chancellor of Oxford University. The growing power of these New Scholars angered not only the Puritan members, but other Anglican members as well.

The promotion of another old enemy this year also irritated the Puritans: Samuel Harsnett had been made Bishop of York and his new book, *Considerations for the Better Settling of Church Government*, was ordered circulated among the English bishops. For his own part, Harsnett was deeply embittered over the growth of Puritanism.

In the midst of all the noise and furor John Endicott and his wife sailed with a hundred colonists for Naumkeag aboard the *Abigail*. Their ship passed that carrying Thomas Morton going in the opposite direction.

On the 26th of June Charles prorogued the Parliament, which dispersed. Sir Edward Coke retired to his home at Stoke Poges to write books on the law.

George Villiers, Duke of Buckingham, on the 23rd of August was assassinated after breakfast by John Felton who — having heard that Parliament had proscribed the Duke as an enemy of the people, and harboring a grudge about monies unpaid him — stabbed the courtier through the heart as he left the table.

The Duke's Devil, Dr. John Lamb, returning from an evening at the Fortune Theatre, was recognized on the street by a hostile mob. Voices in the crowd were raised — "Look! 'Tis the warlock! Get him! Get the Duke's Devil!" Startled, Dr. Lamb backed off, his scarlet cloak swirling about his knees; when he saw the crowd break for him he turned and ran. But he was no longer a young man and by the time he had reached St. Paul's Cross he was exhausted. He sank to his knees panting, and the crowd caught him. They began pelting him with cobbles and stones.

The watch could do nothing — they ran to get help. The king was informed; he mounted and rode out, but by the time he arrived Dr. Lamb was lying dead in a pool of blood, his body crushed and broken. The king ordered that the leaders of the mob be taken and punished, but the crowd had dispersed and the authorities were unable to respond. Charles, ever open to an opportunity to raise funds, fined the city of London 600 pounds for its failure to catch the criminals.

Dr. Lamb's Darling, Anne Bodenham, was out of a job, a home, and a master, but Dr. Lamb had indulged her to the extent that he had taught her some of his conjuring tricks and given her a book of charms. A resourceful woman, she immediately capitalized on her notoriety and Dr. Lamb's fame and set up a shop herself as a witch. Goody Bodenham was well acquainted with herb lore — she had been the doctor's gardener as well as housekeeper — and soon she had a respectable business going. Respectable, that is, in terms of numbers of clients. She wore about her neck a green bag with a toad in it.

On the 6th of September the John Endicotts arrived at Naumkeag. Roger Conant greeted John Endicott, and shortly the new colonists disembarked while the Naumkeag Indians watched, puzzled, from the opposite shore. It was impossible for them to comprehend why these white men had come. John Endicott had been elected resident governor of Naumkeag in England by the company he represented, and when he had settled in he assumed the reins of government, to the umbrage of the Dorchesterians whom the newcomers were already calling the "Old Planters." The Old Planters wanted Roger Conant as their leader; they closed ranks against John Endicott, but being in a minority they could not control the situation. Nevertheless, politics was born in Massachusetts as the Old Planters and the New Planters entered into contention.

In January of the next year, 1629, King Charles I recalled the Parliament and asked for funds, but the House of Commons began debating religious issues despite an order from the king that they keep silent on such matters. Commons paid no attention, merely pointing out that the Petition of Right, to which the king had agreed, gave them the right to debate as they chose, and one of the things they wanted was an edition of the King James Bible with the Apocrypha dropped.

By March, the debate still waxing strong, Charles was exasperated and he ordered the Parliament to be dissolved. A purely *pro forma* vote had to be taken by Parliament on the command, and Commons astonished everyone, especially the king, by violating tradition and voting *nay* to its dissolution. When the Speaker of the House had put the question and been voted down, he attempted to leave the assembly, but the Commons forced him back into his seat, locked the doors against the king's messengers, and brought forth three resolutions, namely, that anyone who introduced innovations in religion — meaning specifically the New School people — was a capital enemy; the same for anyone who advised the king to levy "tonnage and poundage" taxes — which had been one of Charles' ploys in order to raise money without Parliament; and, third, the same for anyone who willingly paid such taxes. When these resolutions had been passed Parliament allowed itself to be dissolved. King Charles immediately set to work to ignore the resolutions.

Charles and Parliament were all the folk talked about in Aston Abbotts — except for the disastrous defeat in France of the Protestant Huguenots. The subject of secession from the country was rife among the Puritans, especially when Charles arrested nine parliamentary leaders, refusing to let them go free until they had sworn they would stay out of trouble thenceforth — meaning out of Charles' hair. Of the nine three, including Sir John Eliot, the major leader in the House, refused to submit.

In order to raise money without Parliament the king began to revive strange old laws, including compulsory distraint of knighthood — the law that Richard Puttenham had run afoul of in the last century: Each man whose income from land was 40 pounds or more annually was compelled to accept knighthood or pay a fine. Inasmuch as the cost of being a knight far exceeded the fine, like Puttenham most refused the honor. John Putnam wondered when and whether the law that had haunted his kinsman would be turned against him in his turn, for his income from lands exceeded the minimum. He soon found out.

Not long after the law was reinvoked, John was notified that he was to appear before the magistrate in Aston Abbotts. There, he discovered a number of his neighbors waiting before the court. Zaccheus Gould was there, and they exchanged nods, but neither spoke, nor did any of the other men except to say "How do" to friends. When the assemblage was complete, the justice spoke to them. "You know why you are gathered here. There is little to say. I am sorry this must be done, but it must. Is there any man here who would become a knight?" No one replied. "Then we must to it. Every man is hereby fined forty pounds. Step forward."

Some of the villagers could not pay in cash, but the judge refused to accept goods or chattels. The king needed hard currency. "If you cannot pay in gold," the magistrate said, "you must pay in silver. If you cannot pay in silver today, you will pay today week. If you cannot pay then, your estates will be seized and sold." Both Zaccheus Gould and John Putnam had come prepared, and when it was their turn, they paid in coin of the realm. When they left together, both were silent for a while as they walked. Then Zack said, "This ruinous tax has nigh broken me, John."

John, who was in better condition, said, "I am sorry for it. It has wasted my estate as well."

"I believe I shall go for America," Zack said.

Again there was a silence. Then John said, "I would I could go as well. It may be I shall yet do it." Neither man slept well that night for thinking about the future.

The next thing King Charles did was to order his court of Star Chamber to punish severely those Puritans who criticized the Anglican Church.

During the month of March several east England men, including Sir Richard Saltonstall, Matthew Cradock, Isaac Johnson, George Nowell, Richard Bellingham, Samuel Vassall, Theophilus Eaton and William Pynchon, began to make solid plans for evacuation, not without feelings of guilt, for they found themselves impaled on the horns of a dilemma: All good Puritans were needed in England to stand together against the usurpation of power by the haughty monarch. At the same time the New Zion beckoned — the land where Puritans could worship as they chose; where they, in fact, would be in command of worship and could exclude wrongful forms from infecting the purity of the people.

When Charles granted them a charter that confirmed the territorial grant already given their company for a colony at Naumkeag, and when he added, besides, complete corporate and governmental rights, like those previously granted the Plymouth and London companies; when, further, the king forgot to include a clause requiring that the governors and charter of the company remain in England, their minds were made up for them once and for all. A party of them took ship for Naumkeag on April 25th.

On the 30th of April John Endicott, in Naumkeag, was elected Governor of the Plantation in the Massachusetts Bay. In England on the

13th of May Matthew Cradock was elected governor of the Massachusetts Bay Company "for the year following."

On June 29th the *Talbot* anchored in the harbor of Naumkeag and disembarked its passengers and freight: three hundred men, eighty women, twenty-six children, one-hundred-forty head of cattle, and provisions. They found a village of a dozen or so houses, including a "fair house" for the governor. Not long after the arrival of these latest newcomers, the name of the settlement was changed from Naumkeag to Salem to memorialize the settlement of the differences between the Old Planters and the new.

The next thing the town of Salem needed to do was to organize its church. The nineteenth day of July was designated a solemn day of humiliation and prayer, and on the 20th the corporate members of the colony — all non-members of the company were excluded — organized the First Congregational church, not only of Salem, but of the New World. The Rev. Mr. Samuel Skelton, who had arrived in another ship, the *George*, was chosen first pastor, and Francis Higginson, first teacher, for all Puritan churches of any size had two ministers, one to deliver the Sunday sermon, and the other to deliver the weekly Lecture Day talk.

In effect, the Pastor was the theoretician of the flock, and the Teacher was the catechizer. The election of Skelton and Higginson was the first time the secret ballot had been used in America. The members of the congregation voted, writing the name of the man who was their choice for pastor on a slip of paper, the same for teacher, and the ballots were tallied.

When the choices had been made Mr. Higginson and several church elders gathered to Mr. Skelton and laid hands upon him, offering up prayers for his blessing and success in the leadership of the flock. When the ceremony was finished, it was repeated for Mr. Higginson. It was Charles Gott's opinion that "Here was a right foundation laid." He hoped that God's people would say, "these two blessed servants of the Lord came in at the door, and not at the window."

In England on July 28th Matthew Cradock, Governor of the company, met with the board of directors, or General Court, which included the Governor and his Assistants — the other board members. He discussed a proposal for "the encouragement of persons of wealth and quality to remove themselves and families thither...that the government of the Plantation should be transferred to those that shall inhabit there." But the discussion was kept secret while the General Court made certain that all stock in the company made its way into the hands of those who were prepared to leave for America.

John Winthrop of London, a barrister, and other members of the corporation met in Cambridge and agreed among themselves to take ship for Salem the March following "on condition that the government and patent be removed to the colony." On August 29th the agreement was voted and passed.

On the 30th of October, with Matthew Cradock present, Winthrop was elected by the corporation resident Governor of the colony of Massachusetts Bay. Though Wintrhop himself wasn't ready to sail, a good many others were making their way across the Atlantic. Salem was beginning to boom. A brickyard was operating; ships were coming and going; the fisheries were functioning and fish were being salted. Governor John Endicott found he had to pay attention to a good deal of detail — and his wife was ill. There being no doctor in town, Dr. Samuel Fuller of Plymouth was sent for, but he could do little.

John Endicott was a bluff, blustery man, a combination of zealot and maverick, as likely to act in a passionate manner as to be practical. When he discovered that Thomas Morton had returned to New England and was living in Plymouth under the protection of Isaac Allerton, who had brought Morton with him from England, John Endicott was outraged, his colony of Puritans was scandalized, and the Governor laid plans to get his hands on Morton when the chance offered.

When Allerton returned to England and Morton returned to Merry Mount, rejoining the remnants of his band of rogues still living in the area, John Endicott requested that Morton abide by the trade regulations the Massachusetts settlements had agreed upon. Morton answered in his customary fashion.

In December John Endicott sent another arresting party to Merry Mount, but Morton was nowhere to be found. The squad ransacked Morton's house, left him nothing but some reject corn, tore down the offending Maypole, and returned to Salem. Morton, a fine hunter and the first man in America to train hawks in falconry, survived the winter on game and with the aid of his Indian friends. In Salem there was famine and illness. The winter was a heavy one, amazing the English with its intensity. Twenty-five percent of the colony died during the winter, many of Satan's scourge, smallpox.

In March of 1630 four ships assembled at Cowes, England: the *Talbot, Ambrose, Jewel,* and *Eagle*, renamed the *Arbella* in honor of its distinguished passenger, Lady Arbella, wife of Isaac Johnson, also aboard: They were some of the "people of quality" who were traveling to live in America. On the 30th of the month the fleet sailed. The passage was a stormy one, but on the 6th of June the ships made landfall at Nova Scotia, or Acadia as it was called, and by the eighth they were cruising southwest.

On the 12th of June the *Arbella* and her sister vessels anchored in Salem harbor with the charter of the plantation and the remainder of the company's government aboard. Strawberries were in season in New England — the passengers disembarked and fell to in the fields, on hands and knees, regaling themselves upon the wild fruit, rejoicing in the bounty of the land after their long trip on salt meat and hardtack. But they found, when they turned back to the town, that all was not strawberries and cream: During the winter eighty people had died, the Rev. Mr. Francis Higginson was ill, and there was grain left for only two more weeks.

During those two weeks, however, seven more ships arrived, and during the rest of the summer many other ships dropped anchor in the harbor, a number sent by the Massachusetts Bay Company. Aboard were a thousand new colonists together with supplies and livestock. Of the two hundred head of cattle aboard Winthrop's fleet, seventy had died on the voyage. A similar proportion hadn't made it to the New World on the other ships, but a good many had, and the town herds increased rapidly. As they did so, just as it was in England, they began to pollute the local water sources. No one in England drank water if they could help it, nor did the Salemites. Beer, cider, and sack were the order of the day.

On the 17th of June a party of the newcomers cruised up the Mystic River looking for a likely spot to plant a new town, and on the first of July Henry Winthrop, son of the governor — for John Endicott had relinquished *de facto* rule to John Winthrop when he had arrived, though technically John Endicott had not been removed from office — arrived in Salem. The next day, in attempting to canoe across the North River to an Indian camp on the opposite shore, Henry Winthrop capsized and drowned. By the end of August the Lady Arbella had died as well, and her husband, Lord Arbella, was ill.

On the 23rd of August the first Court of Assistants of the Massachusetts Bay Company met at Charlestown. The Court of Assistants would not, however, be the complete government of Massachusetts. A second group of elected representatives, the Deputies, would meet with the Assistants as a single group to pass the laws. The Deputies would represent the various settlements, and the Assistants would be the local judges as well as legislators and Magistrates of the colony, very similar to the justices of the peace in England. In fact, very little was changed in local government. The village magistrates would be responsible to the central government. The innovation was that, when the magistrates assembled as the Court of Assistants, they, together with the Governor and the Deputies, *were* the central government, for England and the Crown were a long way off. Though it was technically still beholden to the Crown, the Government of Massachusetts Bay

Colony was, for all intents and purposes, autonomous. The colonists proposed to keep it that way for as long as possible.

The Parish was likewise little changed from the parish organization in England. There were the local preacher, his teacher, the two deacons, and the various functionaries of the church including the parish clerk, the beadle, and the sexton. In the course of things, the ministers as a group had a large say in the government — though they held no official positions, since church and state were as one, the ministers had in fact a great deal to say on every topic, in every situation.

With regard to franchise, the town and parish were also as one. Only church members had a say in parish affairs, and only freemen could be voters in town meeting. Landholders could be admitted as freemen to the town, but *freeman* was not synonymous with *church member*, though in fact the one usually followed the other. In any case, no one was allowed to live in town without the express permission of the Board of Selectmen, which was elected by the voters of the town. The Selectmen were empowered to take care of routine matters in the absence of a town meeting, but no matter of any consequence could be undertaken without a town meeting on the subject.

The town meeting was comprised, then, of precisely the same people as those that made up the parish meeting. It was the parish meeting that agreed to pay the minister his salary, but it was the town meeting that levied the rate to pay that salary. A town meeting was as likely to conduct church business as town business. The town meeting elected the Deputies to the General Court, a commissioner to serve with the Selectmen to set rates, highway commissioners, constables, grand and petit jurors; it appointed the town herdsman, night watch and bell-ringer; settled local land disputes; granted land; deputed special agents to treat with other towns in case of boundary disputes; levied rates not only for the minister but for public works and welfare; arranged to have the meetinghouse built and kept in repair — anything and everything too small to send to the Court of Assistants or the General Court, or too large to be handled by the Board of Selectmen.

On the 17th of September, John Endicott having caught up with him, Thomas Morton was arraigned before the Court of Assistants. Morton faced not only John Endicott but magistrates William Pynchon, Thomas Dudley, Simon Bradstreet and a number of other staunch Puritans. The disposition of his case was a foregone conclusion — Morton was, again, sentenced to be transported to England after a term of sitting in the stocks. All his goods were seized and his house condemned to be burned to the ground, though he was allowed to live in it until his transportation could be arranged.

On the 30th of September Lady Arbella's spouse, Isaac Johnson, followed her into death. A number of others died during the summer and fall as well, including the Teacher of the Salem Church, Francis Higginson. A replacement for him was needed.

In November Governor Winthrop settled in Charlestown rather than in Salem, which place had too many bitter memories of his son's death. In December Thomas Morton was deported, his house in flames behind him as he left it. He could not have known it, nor would he have cared, but in Ratisbon, Germany, only a few weeks before, one of the greatest astronomers of the age, Johannes Kepler, had died: he would be followed into the starry heavens by a good many Salemites before the winter was over. The weather settled in bitterly in New England. In Salem that winter wolves killed six calves; the inhabitants were able to kill only one wolf.

On the fifth of February 1631 the radical young Puritan preacher Roger Williams arrived in Nantasket with his wife Mary aboard the *Lyon*, Capt. William Pierce commanding. The long cold snap had not broken for months, and the couple was appalled by the weather. Williams' reputation had preceded him. In England he had been an outspoken Separatist, a view that did not sit well with Winthrop and the other Massachusetts Bay clergy whose political interests did not lie in that direction. Whereas the Plymouth colonists were Separatists, the Massachusetts people continued to insist — despite their separation physically from England — on the one hand, that they were merely Puritans working from within the framework of the Church of England in order to change the errors of worship into which the mother church had fallen but, on the other hand, they were adamantly opposed to the establishment of the Church of England in Massachusetts.

The issue had already been joined in Salem in 1629. No sooner had the church there been organized than friction had broken out between Skelton and Higginson on one side, and John and Samuel Browne on the other. The Brownes had attempted to organize a rival church in Salem that utilized the liturgy and *Book of Common Prayer* of the Anglican church. The Brownes had been summarily packed off back to England.

Roger Williams' views were anathema as well. It would have been one thing if he had held them and kept them to himself, but he insisted on speaking his mind, and the Massachusetts Bay Colony would not countenance such public declarations, for if the king heard about them he might become aware of the *de facto* separation of the New England Puritans from the Church of England and decide to do something about it. It was the purpose of the Bay people to do one thing and say another, a condition that Williams saw to be hypocrisy. He would have none of it. He was quite unpopular in the colony.

The government of the Bay Colony had been moved during the winter from Salem to Charlestown, and then to Boston when Gov. Winthrop decided the site of Boston was a more likely spot for a capital. Winthrop's followers — some of them — grumblingly trekked after their perambulating leader; others remained in one spot or the other. Eventually, though, Boston was officially chosen for the capital and a church begun there under the Rev. Mr. John Cotton.

Hardly had Roger Williams stepped ashore than he refused a call to assist Cotton at the Boston church because that congregation would not come out for Separatism nor admit the error of their ways when they had worshipped in England in the Anglican church. Roger Williams made himself some fast friends and hard enemies immediately.

By the middle of February the brittle weather broke, but the dying was not over among the colonists. On the 15th of March in Salem Mrs. Skelton died. Roger Williams accepted a call from the Salem church to assist Rev. Samuel Skelton, and he settled there — against the will of the rigid governor — on the 12th of April. He immediately became a popular preacher, one of his staunchest supporters being former governor John Endicott.

For most of the winter the Massachusetts Bay Colony had technically been without a governor. The elections were held annually in the spring, and the governor's term was for one year only. Before Winthrop had sailed, John Endicott had been elected in the spring, and the following fall Winthrop had been elected in England as governor. When Winthrop arrived, John Endicott had stepped aside — his view was that the English election took precedence. However, the following spring Winthrop's term, which had begun in the fall, was not over, so elections were not held; then, in October, Winthrop's term did end, but elections could not be held till the spring of 1631. As a result, from October to May Winthrop acted as governor without legal authority. No one mentioned anything about the situation as it was an embarrassing and potentially volatile situation, but on Wednesday, May 18th, 1631, elections were held, Winthrop was re-elected, and the mess was cleared up.

No sooner had Winthrop a mandate than he and the Court made things uncomfortable for Roger Williams who decided to leave the Bay for Plymouth which was avowedly Separatist. During the summer he removed himself and his family and was warmly greeted by the younger people of Plymouth, though some of the older folk regarded his views as too radical even for a Separatist community.

Behind him in Salem he left good friends and rancor. The Salem settlement had begun in contention over Roger Conant and the split with some of the Dorchester people at Cape Ann. The resentment had continued with the arrival of John Endicott and the split between Old Planters and new, with the rejection of Salem by Winthrop as the site for the capital, and with the church fight with the Brownes. The Roger Williams persecution caused the Salemites to add one more grievance to the list, which was a long one considering the age of the town.

On the fourth of July Governor Winthrop began the maritime history of the colony by launching on the Mystic River his 60-ton bark *Blessing of the Bay*, the first ship of any size built in New England. There were a good many other ships about, however. On the 27th of May a Virginia pinnace laden with corn and tobacco put into Salem harbor and sold its grain for 10 shillings per bushel. On the 26th of July John Elston's Salem bark capsized. It had been carrying oil and did not sink. Within forty-eight hours Henry Way in his boat rescued Elston and the two fishermen who were aboard with him.

Three days later in England, though the news would not reach the New World till later, Captain John Smith, who had given New England its name, died and was buried in London. A month later, on August 31, Winthrop's *Blessing of the Bay* set out on its maiden voyage "to Eastward."

Winthrop and the General Court had been busy during the spring and late summer passing laws "not inimical to the laws of England," as the charter required. One of these was that Saturday would be militia training day, for protection was needed from the Indians, some of whom were hostile. Another was that "no man shall be admitted to this body politic but such as are members of some of the churches." On the 6th of September Gov. Winthrop received the Bay Company's first grant of land "near his house at Mystic." It was a tract of some six hundred acres.

The same day, in Salem, the pinnace of the town set sail for Cape Cod to trade for corn. Contrary winds, however, forced it to change course for Plymouth. When it arrived, Gov. William Bradford took umbrage at the captain and crew and forbade them to trade. If they attempted to do so he threatened them with violence, "even to the spending of their lives," according to Winthrop. The pinnace returned, its captain complained to Winthrop, and the Governor wrote to Bradford about the incident which was settled between them.

In the fall, on the 25th of October, Governor Winthrop, Captain John Underhill, and several others chose to hike through the beautiful weather from Boston to Lynn, a new settlement that abutted upon Salem to the south — for all practical purposes, at the time it was a part of Salem. From Lynn on the 26th the group went to Salem where they were "beautifully entertained" by John Endicott, and on the 28th they returned to Boston, noticing in the fields as they went evidence of a "plentiful crop" soon to be harvested — a Providence of God.

In England things were ominously quiet. The exodus to New England continued into the fall. William Lilly was building his clientele and was interested to note that a new book had been published in Paris by a man with a famous family name: Arthur Dee had written an alchemical anthology titled *Fasciculus Chemicus*. Lilly wanted a copy.

In Aston Abbotts John Putnam carried on as usual. His youngest child, John, Jr., was four years old, and his eldest, Elizabeth, was nearly nineteen. Zaccheus Gould still had not left, for he had been unable to raise sufficient money for the voyage, but he and John, and now Jeremy, Zack's younger brother, talked about the trip often.

The year 1632 was a relatively quiet one on both sides of the Atlantic — at least in England and New England. In Plymouth Roger Williams was working among the Indians and gaining their devotion. He had set himself to learning their tongue and to compiling notes toward a book that he titled tentatively, *Key into the Language of America*.

There was a good deal of movement between Plymouth Colony and the settlements of Massachusetts Bay. Daniel Ray came to Salem from Plymouth. Thomas Dudley, Deputy Governor of the Bay, received the second grant of land — 200 acres "on the west side of Charles River," over against Newton, and John Endicott received 300 acres in Salem at about the same time in early June. He called his estate Orchard Farm. Rev. Samuel Skelton, too, was granted 200 acres.

It was not until the end of the year that news from England and the Continent began to filter into the Colonies: In January Galileo had published his great book, *Dialogo Dei Due Massimi Sistemi del Mondo*, to which Europe had responded with lavish praise — except for the Catholic Church, for in the book Galileo had flouted the edict of silence on the subject of Copernicism which had been laid upon him. By the end of August the book had been banned, and on the first of October the Inquisition had summoned him to Rome. Galileo had pleaded his age, but no excuses were allowed, and he was forced to go.

In England in November there occurred, like an explosion, an event that shattered the peace of the realm. Sir John Eliot, who had refused to buy his freedom from Charles I, died in prison under highly suspicious circumstances. He immediately became the martyr the Puritans had been waiting for. Charles was so insensitive and vindictive that he added oil to the fire by refusing to give up Sir John's body to the family for burial in their family sepulcher. Puritans throughout England responded like banshees. In Aston Abbotts the people, when the news came, rushed from house to house, speaking of it. The authorities grew uneasy and ordered the constables and the watch to report immediately any disturbances that might occur.

John Putnam went to the home of his neighbor, Zaccheus Gould, to discuss the situation. A man slow to anger, he knocked on the door rather more loudly than he had intended. Phoebe let him in. Zaccheus was standing by the fire smoking a pipe. "Zack," he began, but his friend held up a hand.

"Say no more, John. I know what you will say. I agree. We must begin to make plans."

John, startled, stopped in his tracks, then snorted and nodded. "Let us begin," he said.

It was another cold and deep winter in New England. In early January of 1633 Rev. Samuel Skelton's maidservant, on an errand to Lynn — or Saugus, as the Indians called it — became lost in the woods and was missing for a week. Mr. Skelton and a good many Salemites hunted for her, but the snow came down so hard among the boles of the tremendous trees that soon all tracks ere obliterated, and after looking for two days the search —and hope — was abandoned.

But after seven days the young woman turned up! She had been without food but had munched snow for water. She had slept in the snow. Some mornings, when she had waked, she had been so nearly frozen to death that it had taken her an hour or more just to be able to get to her feet. Her survival was accounted a miracle by some; after a little while she seemed to be none the worse for her experience. She was the talk of the settlement.

William Lilly in England was keeping track of the Galileo affair. The astronomer had arrived in Rome on the 13th of February and lodged with the Tuscan papal ambassador. On April 12th he was placed under arrest in the Palace of the Inquisition where he was examined closely for eighteen days. On the 30th of April he was allowed to return to the home of the ambassador until June the 21st when he was recalled by the Inquisition and again examined, this time under the threat of torture.

The next day Galileo Galilei recanted in the church of Santa Maria sopra Minerva. Afterward he was sentenced to incarceration at the pleasure of the tribunal and sentenced to recite once each week for three years the seven Penitential Psalms. Early in July he was allowed to leave Rome for Sienna, but not for Florence.

Lilly considered the whole performance to be educative, to say the least. While he was gathering the news piecemeal as it came in, he was also conducting his own business and caring for his wife, who had become ill. He had also met a fellow astrologer, Nicholas Fiske, who had come to London and begun to develop a reputation as a reliable caster of horoscopes. The two astrologers met frequently after their introduction, to swap astrological tidbits and gossip. Both men were fascinated with the latest witchcraft episode.

In Hoarstones, Lancashire, in the Pendle Forest district, ten-year-old Edmund Robinson claimed he had been beating two greyhounds because they would not course a hare when, suddenly, the dogs were transformed into a woman and a boy. The pair of were-dogs offered Edmund a bribe if he would keep to himself what had happened, but Edmund had refused. The witch had then changed her companion into a horse, mounted herself and Edmund on its back, and whisked him off to a Sabbat: Sixty people gathered in a barnyard.

The witch had bade Edmund dismount, and when they had done so they entered the barn — there were six witches pulling on six ropes that rose up to the ceiling and disappeared into shadow. As they pulled and chanted their terrible charms, meat, butter and eggs appeared, flying from the ropes and neatly falling into basins underneath. In the hubbub going on, Edmund managed to run out of the barn and steal home.

The witches were identified and accused in a written deposition that Edmund's father endorsed. Neither of them knew the names of all the witches; hence, the court authorized Edmund to go forth into the countryside, accompanied by constables, and point out those witches he recognized as having been at the Sabbat.

One of those he discovered on his peregrinations was Mary Spencer, a girl who, when she went out to fetch water, would run down the hill in front of her rolling pail, to which she would turn and call, "Do follow me, and don't be running off to the side like that!" Another was Janet Device who, as a girl in 1612, had herself been a chief child accuser and witness in the trials that had hanged her mother and others.

On his witchhunting tour Edmund Robinson dropped in on the church service of the Rev. John Webster in Kildwick accompanied by "two very unlikely persons," as the minister described them. The boy was set on a stall to look the congregation over — a situation that led to some disturbance. After the prayer service Mr. Webster made some inquiries about the boy, then went to see him but was refused a private session. The minister agreed to talk with Edmund with witnesses present. The Rev. Mr. Webster asked, "Goode boy, tell me truly and in earnest, did you see and hear such strange things of the meeting of witches as is reported by many? Or did not some person teach you to say such things of yourself?"

Edmund's two bodyguards prevented him from answering. They took him away and said to the minister, "He has been examined by two able justices, and they did never ask him such a question."

Mr. Webster replied, "The persons accused had therefore the more wrong."

Edmund Robinson accused thirty people, of whom seventeen were convicted primarily because "Devil's marks" or "witch teats" — unusual growths or spots where familiar demons purportedly sucked blood — were found on them. But the local justices had begun to share the Rev. Mr. Webster's skepticism, and they sent the cases forward to the King's Council for further consideration. The Right Rev. John Bridgeman, Bishop of Chester, examined both the accuser and the convicted witches. He decided that there was malice involved, but not that of witches or devils.

Mary Spencer and three others were sent to London where the king's physician could find no evidence of any unnatural marks on the convicts, and this was not only the opinion of Dr. Harvey, but of King Charles I himself, who examined them in person.

Edmund was questioned under sterner circumstances, and he broke down. He admitted that he had been put up to the whole thing by his father for purposes of "money, revenge, and hope of gain." Edmund, in fact, had been gathering plums at the very time the Sabbat was alleged to have been held. All the convictions were reversed and the women accused of being witches freed.

While the trial had been going on William Lilly's wife had died. Having had no children by Mr. Wright, and Mr. Wright having had no offspring by his first wife, Lilly inherited the considerable estate and was transformed into a wealthy astrologer.

In August William Laud was elevated to the position of Archbishop of Canterbury, and with the act the New School's control of the Church of England was complete, although the group still was a minority. Laud let it be known he expected rigid conformity to the practices of the new order, and he began a program of local visits to determine how services were being conducted in the parishes.

In Aston Abbotts during the fall John Putnam's family attended a church service that seemed to them to be strained, though it was the normal service — a rather plain affair, along Puritan lines, but not truly non-conformist. *The Book of Common Prayer* was used in the Aston Abbots church. John and Priscilla Putnam wondered who the man was who sat at the head of the church during the service dressed in clerical robes — a visiting preacher, no doubt. But when the service ended and the rector had failed to identify the man, the Putnams inquired of their neighbors as they were leaving.

"That be the Archbishop's man, John," one of them said. "Our parson will be punished."

The Puritans in Aston Abbotts and elsewhere were upset enough with Laud and his repression when two more events took place to rub salt into their wounds. The name of Robert Browne, the original separatist, rose out of the obscurity in which it had been buried at Achurch-cum-Thorpe Waterfield in Northamptonshire since 1589. The octogenarian had a dispute with a local constable over a rate, and he struck the official. Robinson was haled before the magistrate where he behaved so stubbornly that he was thrown into Northampton jail. In October he died in prison and was buried in St. Giles churchyard. The older parishioners of Aston Abbotts were heard to remark, with not a little smugness and bitterness, that it was a pity he had not been half so stubborn before he scraped his belly to the bishops.

Worse, however, was happening to William Prynne, the well-known Puritan writer and barb-thrower. He had published a book during the year titled *Histrio-Mastix* which attacked the stage and made the point that those rulers who were devoted to the theatre often were prone to violent death. Charles I read himself between the lines, and he read Henrietta Marie in the violent words that were directed at actresses, for Charles' consort was rehearsing to take part in a ballet such as those that were often performed among the nobility at masques and balls in the great houses of England. The king took Prynne and threw him into prison to wait for trial. At the time, few people rushed to Prynne's defense, for he was not the most popular man in England.

In New England immigrants continued to arrive in large numbers — many of them men and women of rank and substance — and to settle new towns. Ipswich was founded in 1633 and several stockholders in the Bay Company settled there including John Winthrop, Jr., Richard Saltonstall, Richard Bellingham, and Samuel Symonds; the town thus held four of the magistrates who sat on the Court of Assistants.

In August Roger Williams returned to Salem to become assistant to the Rev. Samuel Skelton. Both of the Salem preachers saw fit to object during the fall to an innovation of the ministers of the Bay: They had begun to gather each fortnight in round-robin visits to discuss a specified question. The Salem ministers demurred on the grounds that it sounded as though it might develop into a Presbyterian-style synod. They were assured it would not, and Winthrop made a notation of the matter in his journal.

A good many projects were underway throughout the Bay. One of these was the building of a fort at Castle Island in Boston Harbor. The General Court had levied rates against each township to help pay for the structure, but again Salem, together with Lynn, found itself on the opposite side of an issue. The two towns refused to contribute their share.

Governor Winthrop, who was at feud with his Deputy Governor Thomas Dudley of Salem, wrote a letter asking for a conference. John Haynes and Rev. Thomas Hooker kept the appointment, but bore a bitter letter from Dudley. Winthrop, greatly insulted by the letter, returned it to the messengers and told them the matter would keep until the next General Court. Eventually, however, the contretemps was glossed over and the towns paid their portions.

In November a plague of Satan's scourge infected the local Indian tribes. The English managed to save some of the children of the natives, but many died of the pox, as did the adults including Chickatabot, Sagamore of Naponsett, and James, Sagamore of Saugus. He left a small son who was to be brought up by the whites.

In December the quarterly General Court met in Boston to consider the case of Roger Williams who had written a tract in which he stated that the English had no right to inhabit the land unless they first purchased it from the natives. The Court decided to order Williams to come before the next session to be censured. Winthrop wrote to John Endicott, Williams' friend and defender, asking him to work on the Teacher of Salem and persuade him to retract.

Williams responded by writing that the tract had been intended only for the eyes of Gov. William Bradford of Plymouth Plantation, not for the Bay Colony. He offered to burn the tract, Winthrop wrote in his journal very smugly. If what the Governor had written were true, Williams had his reflection at exactly the same time in Italy, where Galileo Galilei was allowed by the Inquisition to return to Florence at last.

Archbishop Laud had been given another important office by King Charles I: The Lords Commissioners for Plantations in General had been created to replace Gorges' old Council for New England, and Laud was placed in command. Gorges retained a seat on the commission, and one of the first things Laud did, at Gorges' instigation, was to inform Matthew Cradock that the Lords Commissioners, having heard complaints out of New England that the Puritans were running things with a high hand, wished to examine the colony's charter — would he please send for it. Obediently, Cradock sent a letter to the government of Massachusetts Bay.

The same month, February 1634, Star Chamber sentenced the curmudgeon William Prynne to be imprisoned for life, to be outlawed from the legal profession and expelled from Lincoln's Inn, and to have his B. A. from Oxford rescinded. He was sentenced also to be placed in the pillory and to have his ears shorn off. On the 7th day of May the sentence was executed.

The Lords Commissioners issued an order that ships traveling to New England were to be prevented from sailing, but the ship captains, maintaining that the fishing industry would be destroyed if they were not allowed to sail, managed to have the order withdrawn; thus, commerce continued — as well as the exodus from England, at which the order had been aimed in the first place.

In June fourteen "great ships" arrived in Massachusetts Bay, one of them in Salem Harbor. John Humphrey and his wife Susan, sister of the Lady Arbella, immigrated and brought with them a quantity of guns and ammunition. Thomas Dudley, who had been elected governor, also received letters from English and Scots people signifying their intent to immigrate, and the flood out of England began to reach high tide. But the people of "better quality" whom the colonists had hoped to attract were beginning to reverse the flow by returning to England, because of hardship for one thing, but also because things seemed to be coming to a head in the Puritan movement, and many felt it was their duty to go home to lend a hand in whatever was going to take place as well as to protect their estates.

Matthew Cradock's letter arrived in July and Dudley met with his Council of Assistants to discuss it. They decided to answer Cradock, but to stall for time, so they replied that nothing could be done until the next General Court, which was to be held in September. Rumors of invasion by England began to circulate immediately among the colonists, and Richard Davenport of Salem was made Ensign of the Colony.

In September a copy of the commission given Laud to regulate the colonies arrived and it looked exceedingly ominous to the Puritans of

Massachusetts. Winthrop wrote in his journal that the receipt of the commission "occasioned the magistrates and deputies to hasten our fortifications, and to discover our minds each to other." What they discovered was that they were ready to fight.

But in England Charles was busy doing a good many other irritating things and a reaction was beginning to set in heavily. Still hard-pressed for funding, and still ruling by personal fiat rather than by act of Parliament, the king continued to disinter and refurbish old laws that violated the Petition of Right, in order to raise money. His latest ploy was to call for "Ship Money" — a wartime law illegal in peacetime that called for port towns each to provide the Crown with a ship of a size that could be found only in London, or its equivalent in cash. The ports managed to raise the tax, but not without encountering a great deal of resistance.

In the New England wilderness, the Indians were encountering something that was more lethal. The Plymouth Colony had an outpost, a trading-house, at Windsor on the Connecticut River, and William Bradford, in his journal, wrote that the tribes there "fell sick of the small pox and died most miserably; for a sorer disease cannot befall them, they fear it more than the plague. For usually they that have this disease have them in abundance, and for want of bedding and linen and other helps they fall into a lamentable condition as they lie on their hard mats, the pox breaking and mattering and running into one another, their skin cleaving by reason thereof to the mats they lie on. When they turn them, a whole side will flay off at once as it were, and they will be all of a gore blood, most fearful to behold. And then being very sore, what with cold and other distempers, they die like rotten sheep. The condition of this people was so lamentable and they fell down so generally of this disease as they were in the end not able to help one another, no not to make a fire nor to fetch a little water to drink, nor any to bury the dead. But would strive as long as they could, and when they could procure no other means to make fire, they would burn the wooden trays and dishes they ate their meat in, and their very bows and arrows. And some would crawl out on all fours to get a little water, and sometimes die by the way and not be able to get in again.

"But of those of the English house, though at first they were afraid of the infection, yet seeing their woeful and sad condition and hearing their pitiful cries and lamentations, they had compassion of them, and daily fetched them wood and water and made them fires, got them victuals whilst they lived; and buried them when they died. For very few of them escaped, notwithstanding they did what they could for them to the hazard of themselves. The chief sachem himself now died and almost all his friends and kindred. But by the marvelous goodness and providence of God, not one of the English was so much as sick or in the least measure tainted with this disease, though they daily did these offices for them for many weeks together. And this mercy which they showed them was kindly taken and thankfully acknowledged of all the Indians that knew or heard of the same. And their masters here did much commend and reward them for the same." Truly, small pox *did* look and act like a disease out of Hell.

In the fall there was further bad news out of England: Word reached Massachusetts that the old defender of the constitution, Sir Edward Coke, had died at his home in Stoke Poges. Among the many colonists who arrived in the fall was a woman named Anne Hutchinson, a brilliant and vivacious young woman who settled in Boston. In the late summer Samuel Skelton, rector of Salem, died, and the congregation chose Roger Williams to replace him.

On the 20th of October a great accident took place in Salem, which grieved the community. When six men of the town went out fowling in a large canoe toward Kettle Island the canoe overturned and five of them were drowned, but there were many good things happening in Salem as well. Houses were being built, the town government was making important decisions at every meeting, new industries were springing up and land was being cleared. The waterfront was a bustling hive of boats and, often, ships. Fishermen put out every day and brought home their catches to be sold or salted. Roads were being laid out, the market place growing: There was already a merchant class in the town, doing very well, though the farmers were experiencing something of a depression: The crop had been so good that maize was selling for 4 shillings per bushel or cheaper.

Francis Weston, Roger Conant and John Holgrave were chosen Deputies to the Court from Salem. In November the Court of Assistants heard a complaint that at Salem the English flag had been defaced, and Ensign Richard Davenport was ordered to appear at the next court session to explain. The Bay government did not need provocations of this kind reaching the ears of the English government — and there were beginning to be a good many people in Massachusetts who were only too glad to be able to send adverse reports back to Britain.

The Court had also to consider the case of Roger Williams who had begun to say more strange things: That the Magistrates should not administer the oath to men who were unregenerate, for oath-taking, like prayer, is a form of worship. Both the clergy and the magistrates were infuriated by the proposition.

The year had hardly turned when the town of Salem, on January 25th, 1635, granted Roger Conant, Peter Palfrey, William Trask, John Woodbury, and John Balch each 200 acres of land in the township. As these were the original settlers from Cape Ann, their properties became known eftsoons as the Old Planters' Farms. These grants were nearly the last that had to be approved by the Bay government, for on the 3rd of March the General Court gave to the towns the exclusive right to grant lands within their boundaries.

The General Court had also determined that it was John Endicott who had cut the cross out of the British flag, not Davenport himself, though he had been involved, and it summoned the former governor to explain himself. He informed the court that the cross was an idolatrous image and that in a fit of passion he had sliced it out of the Jack. This suggestion was not a great deal different in kind from Williams' stand on oath-taking but, inconsistently, Winthrop and others were suitably impressed with the argument — they had assumed that John Endicott's action had been some sort of act of defiance against the crown because of the way things were trending in England; they hadn't thought of a good religious reason for it. As soon as John Endicott gave them one, however, the magistrates couldn't decide whether to lay aside the flags or not. They tabled the matter and followed up by creating the Military Commission. No sooner had it come into being than the Commission ordered that the British flags be laid aside.

There were, however, some acts of defiance that the Bay government refused to stand for, one of these being the Salem church's choosing Roger Williams as its pastor, which was judged to be "a great contempt of authority." Williams was ordered before the Court of Assistants. On the same day that Williams was officially covenanted by the Salem Church the court rejected a petition by the town of Salem that the land claimed by the town on Marblehead Neck be officially sanctioned. The Court informed Salem that it would reconsider its decision when "proper submission" was made "on the question of Mr. Williams."

It was a feud, then. Salem gave its approval to the new minister to write letters of protest to all the churches of the colony that had in their congregations magistrates of the General Court. It was not long before retaliation set in: The Court ordered the freemen of Salem to disclaim the letters or suffer the unseating of the town's deputies. Salem backed off and left Roger Williams standing in the open alone. The ministers of the colony were invited to attend a special session of the Court to hear the case, and most of them accepted.

On the sixth of May the Court admonished John Endicott for his impetuous, if understandable, irritation with the flag of Britain and prepared itself to meet with the Rev. Mr. Williams in July. The encounter took place on the 8th. Williams and the Rev. Thomas Hooker engaged in a debate, but Williams failed to see the error of his ways and was given until October to think things over and recant.

People from England were still arriving in large numbers despite the Crown's attempts to stem the flow. The Rev. Hugh Peter and Sir Henry

Vane, young men both, came to Salem which covered a large area and was beginning to have other centers of settlement besides downtown. Salem and the other towns were also expanding their rosters of professions and trades. In July Richard Graves, a pewterer, arrived in Salem aboard the *Abigail*. Edmond Farrington, a fellmonger — dealer in hides — set up shop in nearby Lynn. A number of others, who had become settled citizens like Townsend Bishop, were admitted as freemen. Not only were the English using the town, but the Indians of the area were doing the same — they came in to trade their hides for utensils, food, and jewelry.

In August for a few days, however, business came to a standstill as an enormous hurricane hit town. The winds and high seas wrought havoc on the waterfront, destroying shipping and wharving, knocking down trees. The rains swamped those boats that weren't damaged and flooded low-lying areas of the township, beating down the crops that were growing toward harvest. It was a great disaster, but as soon as the tempest passed the people got out and began to help each other clean up. By the end of the month most of the damage had been repaired and the town had begun to hum again.

By the time that the Court had specified in October, Roger Williams still had not apologized and he was ordered banished within six weeks. But the minister was in poor health, and the limit was extended to the spring of the next year. Williams had had time to think about what he would do, and he was prepared to do it: Found a new colony. The Rev. Mr. Hugh Peter was chosen to replace him as minister of the Salem Church.

On the 26th of November Hugh Peter had had enough of the seamen's monopoly on fishing in the colony. He called for a company to be formed among the colonists to break the cartel's hold on the industry. The year ended quietly and coldly in Salem with a grant of 300 acres to Robert Cole.

Things had been anything but quiet in England, however, during the entire year, for Charles had decided to call for ship tax again, only this time he extended it to cover the inland towns as well as those of the coast. There was no possible excuse for this flagrant violation of the clause in the Petition of Right guaranteeing the people that they would be exempt from taxation without parliamentary representation. There was outrage everywhere.

In Aston Abbotts Jeremy Gould came to see John Putnam and his family. When Jeremy knocked on the door he was invited to come in and sit. When he had done so and been offered a glass of ale, he took a quaff and got to the point.

"I am off for New England, John, at last. Wish me well."

John stared at him. "I do, and more."

Jeremy looked about him at the family gathered there: Thomas Putnam, twenty years old and built like a bear, as compassionate a young man as ever lived and the best man with livestock in the village; Elizabeth Putnam, homely as a vegetable garden — for whom *he* felt compassion — blushing as he looked at her; Nathaniel the young spark of sixteen, eyes flashing, ready to get up and pack a sack if Jeremy but gave the word.

John the younger, eight years old, sat at the hearth with the girls, Sarah twelve and Phoebe eleven, toying with yarn or sticks, half listening. And old John. And Priscilla. These were good people. They would be missed.

"Do you think you will go? The children are growing into their flesh."

Old John merely grunted and cast his eyes toward Priscilla. "We may yet be driven out. The king will see to it." He lapsed into silence.

"Where will you go?" Thomas asked.

"To Massachusetts Bay. To the town of Salem."

"When?" Nathaniel was leaning forward.

"My ship puts to sea in a fortnight." There was silence again as the flames crackled in the ingle.

"Will you have another glass?" Priscilla began to rise but Jeremy motioned for her to remain seated.

"I thank you, but I must go now. At dawn we leave for the ship." He rose himself and extended his hand. Old John heaved to his feet and took Jeremy's grasp.

"The Lord go with thee," he said. "It may be Zack and I shall follow." Jeremy dropped his gaze and went to the door; the boys and John followed him.

"My prayers shall be with you in the other land," Jeremy said. He opened the door, closed it, and did not look back.

Word reached Governor John Haynes and the Court of Assistants that, despite an injunction against his holding forth publicly on his opinions, Roger Williams had been having a group of people drop in for religious discussions at his home during the winter. Surreptitiously, the Court decided it would be best if they broke their promise that Williams might stay in Salem until the spring of 1636. They made arrangements for him to be arrested and transported to England.

The Court's decision was made partly because Williams had been gaining a good number of converts to his cause in the Bay, and in Salem particularly, but the greater reason was that there were rumors Williams intended to take his followers and begin a new plantation on Narragansett Bay in Plymouth jurisdiction "from whence," as Winthrop wrote in his journal, "the infection would easily spread into these churches, (the people being, many of them, much taken with the apprehension of his Godliness)."

Capt. John Underhill was sent in a pinnace to take Williams prisoner and bring him to the ship that would take him back to England, but Williams had his friends, and when Underhill arrived at the minister's home he found that Williams had left three days earlier. The Court had no idea where Williams had gone. He had, in fact, taken four followers and traveled through the New England winter to Manton's Neck in Plymouth colony.

The Williams affair was not the only religious controversy with which the government had to deal. In 1635 a commission of ministers from the settlements had gone to Lynn to investigate a squabble there; in 1636 that problem had flared up again. Rev. Stephen Batchellor had come to Lynn; his original followers fell out with the rest of the congregation, and they requested permission to separate themselves from the church. Permission was granted on the assumption the minister intended to leave town; however, he had not done so. He had begun another church instead. The inhabitants of the town, greatly disturbed, complained; Batchellor refused to capitulate and the Court sent a marshal after him. When the marshal arrived, Batchellor submitted and agreed to leave town within three months.

Because of the controversies at Salem and Lynn, and with the added pragmatic reason that maize was scarce, the church Elders called for a general fast throughout the Bay on the 25th of February, but not all was stress and contention — Salem continued to grant land to its outstanding citizens: Richard Davenport was allowed eighty acres, and Thomas Gardner, a hundred. William Hathorne was received as a member of Salem Church.

On the third of March the General Court ordered that the boundaries of Salem, Ipswich and Newbury should extend six miles into the countryside, which was taken to mean six miles from the meeting houses of the towns. It was an ambiguous situation at best, however, and a good many people were confused as to where the boundaries lay. There were more overriding issues, though — in Salem there was still discontent at the church, and in Boston Church a great storm was brewing.

Anne Hutchinson had been holding each week at her home what amounted to a religious salon where people gathered to discuss the sermon of the previous Sunday. Mrs. Hutchinson was a brilliant woman, as deeply knowledgeable of the Bible as any minister in the colony, and she could hold her own in debate with anyone. It was her contention that most of the Massachusetts ministers were preaching a doctrine of Salvation by Works rather than of Salvation by Grace. She had attracted a number of interesting and interested people into her circle, including Sir Henry Vane, the young and highly attractive — to the people of the colony — aristocrat who had arrived the previous year. Mrs. Hutchinson also had a large following in some of the neighboring towns, including Salem. The government was watching the situation closely. A number of the Bay ministers took tremendous exception to this female's taking them to task over their Puritan unorthodoxy, as she saw it.

Around the same time the Court managed to pass a law that made many citizens angry: It was ruled that a certain few magistrates were to hold term for life. Consequently, Sir Henry Vane was elected Governor for the year to follow — a great rebuke to Winthrop; Vane, Winthrop, and Thomas Dudley were elected to the life terms.

Petit quarterly courts were established in some of the towns, including Salem, to handle local issues. In Salem, too, Rev. Hugh Peter had organized trading and fishing to the point where these had to be regulated. On Winter Island there was development — Fish Street was laid out, warehouses were built there, and permission granted to establish taverns.

News got back to town during the summer that Roger Williams had founded a settlement called Providence. A few of the inhabitants set about leaving town and traveling to Rhode Island. It was a dangerous time to be on the road: One of Roger Conant's Old Planters, John Oldham, originally a Plymouth colonist, was killed by Pequot Indians and another, John Tilly, overseer of Salem fishing, was captured, tortured, and killed.

Governor Vane sent three armed boats to find the Indians whom scouts had reported to be camped on Block Island. John Endicott of Salem was put in command of the expedition. When he arrived he found an Indian village deserted and put it to the torch. A later expedition under the command of Capt. John Underhill, Old Planter John Mason, and Capt. William Trask of Salem, leader of the Essex

County company of militia, managed to engage the Pequots and succeeded in nearly annihilating the tribe.

On the 27th of June the Selectmen of Salem ordered that on July 4th all canoes in Salem were to be brought to the waterfront for a safety inspection. The day of the inspection brought the population together for a great social gathering. While the inspectors examined each boat and marked those that passed muster with a special seal, the young men of the community raced through the sunny day and the chill Atlantic waters while the folk stood on the beach and docks watching and applauding. The women were dressed in their finest clothes — bright colors were everywhere — and the younger ladies encouraged their swains circumspectly but unmistakably as they vied with one another.

Other boats of all descriptions joined the show, parading past the waterfront under full sail. When a canoe capsized, its occupants were immediately pulled from the swell by the closest boat and the canoe righted. The young men, dripping wet, would re-embark and set out for another tilt. The salt air whetted the appetites both of onlookers and participants; picnic lunches were spread along the beaches; neighbors dropped by to chat and share food. It was a grand day. Dr. George Emery, the new physician in town, found himself called upon to examine wrenched knees and cut fingers, but nothing serious. He enjoyed the outing as much as anyone else, for he soon understood that he was asked to look at a child not so much because anything was wrong, but because his new neighbors wanted the opportunity to look him over.

People talked for the rest of the summer about that Fourth of July celebration, and most remarked they hoped it would become an annual feature. By the fall, however, most were talking about the high price of food and commodities and about the prospects for the harvest. Merchants were scalping the newcomers who were arriving steadily and paying the charges, being ignorant of the local market and, for the moment, most of them were flush from having sold their estates in England. The inflation was spilling over into the settled community.

New grants of land continued to be assigned throughout the year. Townsend Bishop was allowed 300 acres in Salem, his property bounding the properties of the late Rev. Samuel Skelton and John Endicott. Bishop had been named a local justice, a deputy to the General Court, and admitted to the Salem congregation. Thomas Scruggs had also been given 300 acres; his neighbor, William Alford, received 200 — both men were in agreement on the subject of Anne Hutchinson, whom they supported. Scruggs had attempted, through a land swap, to help Salem capture the proposed college of the Colony, but the deal had fallen through, and it was decided that the school would be established in Newton.

By November the situation in Lynn had been settled to the satisfaction of the Court — a new church had been formed and the Rev. Thomas Whiting was chosen minister. The government could turn its attention wholly upon the issue of Anne Hutchinson and what people were beginning to call the "Antinomian controversy."

Judge William Pynchon was a strange sort of man, even for his own times, which were filled with odd folk. His was a charismatic and overpowering personality. He tended to dominate attention whenever he was present with other people. In addition he held some unorthodox religious beliefs, though he kept these to himself. In 1636 he gathered about him a group of settlers who were ready to follow him into the wilderness to found a new community at a considerable remove from Boston. Not being himself a minister, Pynchon brought with him the Rev. George Moxon, a strong-willed man himself and a sawyer-brickmaker named Hugh Parsons. Parsons was a dour man with peculiar habits and a vengeful streak that manifested itself not in actions but in mutterings to the effect that he would "be even" with anyone who crossed him.

The first settlement of Pynchon's group was on the west bank of the Connecticut River in western Massachusetts Bay, at the confluence of the Agawam River where a tribe of Indians was close by. It soon became apparent to the Englishmen that the Indian god of Evil, whom they called Hobbamock and whom the Puritans called the Devil, was aroused against the settlement. The Indians of New England worshipped Hobbamock, not because he was a good spirit, but because he was evil and needed to be appeased so that he would do them no harm. His name had entered the colonists' vocabulary in a shortened form, for parents often told their children to "stop raising Hobb." But Hobb was raised in Springfield, for that was to be the name of Pynchon's town.

No sooner had the folk built shelters than they began to be plagued with a series of inexplicable incidents, the chief of which had to do with their cattle getting loose and straying into the Indians' cornfields, doing a great deal of damage. The natives were angry. Their drums, with accompanying menacing dances, could be heard summoning other tribes to a rendezvous. The medicine men or "powwows" could be seen and heard singing before blazing fires. The Springfielders decided to move across the river.

There they found barren, stony ground. At great cost in health and labor, they attempted to settle in. Many spoke of returning to the Boston area and muttered that the Devil had chosen their band for particular punishment. Nothing but Judge Pynchon's force of will prevented a mass exit from the new town.

By the end of the year newcomers had brought to Massachusetts word from England that King Charles had again attempted to impose ship money taxes on the towns and that many had refused to pay it.

In Aston Abbotts John Putnam received a letter from Jeremy Gould that said he had settled in a place called Rhode Island. It was a name that was unfamiliar to old John.

Women were getting to be a great problem in the Massachusetts Bay. In January 1637 the Selectmen of Salem were brought squarely up against a dilemma: Deborah Holmes had asked that she be granted land in Salem. The problem was that she wasn't married, therefore was not asking in the name of a husband who was temporarily absent for some reason. The all-male town meeting came down firmly astride the problem. The town recorder noted in his records that Miss Holmes was refused, "being a maid, but had four bushels of corn granted her," one each by John Endicott, Elias Stileman, John Woodbury, and Philip Veren, Sr., for it "would be a bad precedent, to keep house alone."

And by the spring the tide had begun to turn against Anne Hutchinson in Boston. In May the opposition showed its strength by voting young Sir Henry Vane out of office and turning once more to John Winthrop. No one could say precisely what the "Antinomian" controversy was all about, for Goodwife Hutchinson was, if anything, more orthodox in her views of Puritanism than most of the ministers. She insisted on Salvation by the Grace of God alone, not by any display of good works. In her debates with the clergy the argument revolved about fine points of doctrine with many Biblical references of a nicety that confused all but the most learned. Nevertheless, the government sensed a threat to its authority, and once it was well organized her opposition coalesced into an imponderable force.

Daily life in the villages, however, went on while the Antinomian maelstrom whirled in Boston. The summer brought a new flood of immigrants, and news of Charles' latest madness: John Hampden had sued the Crown over the issue of ship money and had failed. Throughout the shires Puritans packed their bags. The Scots began to do likewise: In the fall of 1636 Charles had published the Church of England's new *Book of Canons* which required practices that were contrary to Puritan worship. When, in May 1637, the book arrived in Scotland and the king showed that he intended to enforce it, the entire Presbyterian Church rose up against him.

Among the recent arrivals in New England was the thirty-year-old Rev. John Harvard, M. A. of Emmanuel College, Cambridge. A great many educated commoners were arriving in New England, though members of the gentry, discouraged by the hardship of the country and anxious about their English estates, were continuing to return to England.

Salem got its second physician when the Rev. John Fiske stepped ashore. He found a robust little frontier town and, despite the problems the settlers faced, a good deal of growth, optimism, and activity. Thomas Gardner, one of the deputies from Salem, had a thriving farm in the western section of Salem including a portion in what was becoming known as Salem Farms. Richard Graves, likewise, had been granted land and was working it. At Salem Neck Richard Hollingsworth had begun a shipyard and was building boats, and Goodman Stephens was also given permission to begin a shipyard on the Neck. A customs shed, the Port House, had been erected on the South River. Mr. Fiske discovered, when he stepped into the village streets, that New England could produce rather hot weather.

He took his place immediately among the discernible middle class members of the community; it was not long before he discovered who was who, and where the power lay. John Endicott had been elected to the office of Magistrate for Life under the new law. Rev. Edward Norris had been appointed master of the new Salem Latin Grammar School that stood on School House Lane. Mr. Fiske was pleased to accept a position under Mr. Norris as first teacher of the school. Nearly every inhabitant, like Mr. Fiske, doubled in occupation. All the farmers had a second trade — brick-laying, carpentry, shoemaking, dying, milling; the housewives, too, often worked in industrial crafts, such as cloth-weaving.

Mr. Fiske had an opportunity to meet Gov. Winthrop when, in June, he and others of Boston again toured the area, visiting Salem, Lynn and Ipswich, between the 23rd and the 28th. The new school teacher, like everyone else in the village proper, was always on hand at the waterfront to greet a new ship out of England and get the news, which continued bad…or good, depending on one's point of view.

William Prynne in England had continued to write his lambasting articles and tracts, even in prison, and in June he was once more brought before the courts, on charges of sedition, together with two others. On the 30th of June the stumps of his ears were shaved off and his cheeks branded with the letters *S. L.* for "seditious libeler." Prynne preferred to regard them as meaning "stigmata laudis" — wounds of praise. At his punishment the crowds, once indifferent to him, demonstrated violently in his behalf before he was carted back to his dungeon. On the 23rd of July in Scotland another riot took place when, at St. Giles' Cathedral, the king attempted to enforce the use of his *Book of Canons*. Several more people were punished by the English authorities.

Salem was doing its share of punishing as well. On the 21st of August John Getchell was fined ten shillings "for building upon the Town ground without leave." The recorder noted the leniency of his punishment, however, when he wrote, "And in case he shall cut off his long hair of his head into a civil frame in the mean time, shall have [his fine] abated five shillings, his fine to be paid in to the Town meeting within two months from this time[, Getchell] to have leave to go on in his building in the mean time."

The town was treated to some public spectacles as well. Isaac Robinson, servant of Goodman Woods, was whipped for having run away and for urging others to do likewise. Robinson's whipping was by way of warning to the other indentured servants in the colony, of whom there were many, and of whom few were Puritans. Often they were Irish — even Irish Catholics — or Scots.

The most upsetting occurrence of the year, however, concerned Dorothy Talby, a "distracted" woman. She was brought before the salem court for having attempted to murder her husband. The court was lenient — it admonished her, sentenced her to be chained to a post and to remain there except for church services until she repented. No sooner had she been released than she again attacked her husband. Brought back to court, she was sentenced to a whipping. It evidently did little good. People felt that she was suffering from melancholia.

By the end of the year there was strong news out of Scotland: The people had signed a National Covenant, refusing to worship according to the king's new book. Charles had been forced to retreat ignominiously on the issue.

A good many others in New England besides Dorothy Talby suffered from something like melancholia during the winter, which settled down hard on the fourth of November and did not let up for months. Somehow Capt. Peirce, in his ship *Desire* out of Salem, made it through the weather on his return voyage from the West Indies. Having been gone for seven months, he anchored in Salem Harbor on the 26th of February 1638 and began to unload his cargo. Part of it walked out of the holds under its own power: He had brought back a load of black slaves for sale in the Bay. Certainly, the Negroes had never before seen anything like what confronted them.

The snow lay packed on the ground, driven by the gales off the ocean, eighteen to thirty-six inches deep. Most of the slaves were very nearly frozen to death — those that had survived — and were wrapped in whatever the sailors could find to cover them. The winter continued deep until the 23rd of March, the day after Anne Hutchinson was excommunicated. Within a few days she had been banished as well.

The day before she was to leave, however, on the 27th of March, a horrible rumor reached out of Boston and began to spread like an inferno through Salem — one of Anne Hutchinson's disciples, Mary Dyer, had labored and been delivered of a stillborn monster. It was a Providence of God. The rumors started with Jane Hawkins, another Hutchinson follower — the attending midwife. A church Elder had gotten wind of it and questioned Mrs. Hutchinson as she was preparing to leave the colony. Mrs. Hutchinson admitted the monstrous birth but said she had kept still on the advice of the Rev. Mr. John Cotton, who felt no good could come of the event being made public.

The Elder had informed Gov. Winthrop who had summoned the midwife and examined her. At first all she would admit was that the child had been born deformed, but when she was told that Anne Hutchinson had already told all, the midwife had said that the baby had been a female, two months premature, stillborn. "It came hiplings till I turned it," she said. "It was of ordinary bigness, had a face, but no head, and the ears stood upon the shoulders and were like an ape's; it had no forehead, but over the eyes four horns, hard and sharp, two of them being above one inch long, the other two shorter, the eyes standing out, and the mouth also.

"The nose hooked upward; all over, the breast and back full of sharp pricks and scales, like a thornback; the navel and all the belly, with the sex, were where the back should be, and the back and hips before, where the belly should have been. Behind, between the shoulders, it had two mouths, and in each of them a piece of red flesh sticking out. It had arms and legs as other children, but instead of toes it had on each foot three claws, like a young fowl, with sharp talons."

Winthrop was astonished. When he asked Mr. Cotton why he had told Mrs. Hutchinson to conceal the birth the minister replied that it was because he saw a Providence of God in the fact that, with the women coming and going out of the birthing room, at the time of the delivery only Mrs. Hawkins had been present. He also felt that, if it had been his own case, he would have wanted it kept quiet. Finally, he knew of other monstrous births that had been concealed, and he thought that God might intend such things to be meant for the instruction and chastisement of the parents only.

Winthrop thought otherwise, but he allowed Mrs. Hutchinson to depart the jurisdiction for Rhode Island on March 28th. On the 2nd of April the corpse of the baby was disinterred. Because the winter had been so cold and the spring so late, the body was in a relatively good condition of preservation — enough for the witnesses to confirm the midwife's description of it as factual, not fantastic. The governor pursued his investigation and discovered the reason why the many women present before the birth had been absent at the time of the delivery. He wrote in his journal, "When it died in the mother's body, (which was about two hours before the birth), the bed whereon the mother lay did shake, and withal there was such a noisome savor, as most of the women were taken with extreme vomiting and purging, so as they were forced to depart; and others of them their children were taken with convulsions, (which they never had before nor after), and so were sent for home, so as by these occasions it came to be concealed." The midwife was indicted for witchcraft for her part in the horrible affair, but rather than suffering death, she was banished from the Bay Colony, to Winthrop's mind a punishment that was more than just, "for," he wrote in his journal, "it was known that she used to give young women oil of mandrakes" — the mandrake being a cleft root that, because it looked like a man, had entered the pharmacopia as much for its magical as for its medicinal properties — "and other stuff to cause conception; and she grew into great suspicion to be a witch, for it was credibly reported that, when she gave any medicines, (for she practiced physic), she would ask the party if she did believe, she could help her, and so forth."

Francis Weston of Salem, for being a supporter of Hutchinson, was ordered to leave the colony also. He did, but his wife refused and was placed in the stocks "two hours at Boston and two at Salem" on Lecture Day. On the second of May John Winthrop was elected Governor again, and the name of Newton, site of the proposed College, was changed to Cambridge.

A month later, on the first of June, the earth began to shake. The tremors rolled over New England from west to east. In the houses the shelves of pewter and crockery trembled and the dishes and plates rolled off to shatter on the floor or to be bent and dented. The livestock panicked and stampeded into the roads and fields and felt their legs bobbling beneath them; some fell down and hugged the earth fearfully. The children cried; their parents, bewildered, tried to comfort them. It was surely another judgment of God, but no one could settle on what it was they were being judged for. Eventually the heavy temblors subsided, but on and off throughout the summer and fall minor aftershocks continued to be felt. The great earthquake of 1638 became a watershed of conversation; Anne Hutchinson and the monstrous birth receded to second and third places in the rumor mill.

The earthquake did nothing to prevent the new settlers, still arriving in great numbers, from spreading out over the countryside and taking up residence. Few cared even to think of returning to England. During the summer twenty large ships arrived, bringing over three thousand newcomers. The merchant George Corwin arrived and stayed in Salem. He opened a shop and began to trade.

Richard Davenport was allowed a second grant of 220 acres in the town, and, in anticipation of their arrival, Emanuel Downing and his wife Lucy, sister of the governor, were granted 500 acres on the 16th of July. When they disembarked in August they were pleased to accept the grant and become members of the community at once. On the 6th of September Bray Wilkins was authorized by the town to set up a house and keep a ferry at Neponset River where he was to have "a penny a person" in fare.

Elsewhere in the colony Rev. Nathaniel Ward of Ipswich was given the assignment of drawing up a body of laws for the government. Stephen Day of Cambridge set up the first press in New England and printed "The Freeman's Oath," the first document of Massachusetts Bay Colony to be set in type. In Cambridge, too, the college opened and held its first classes under the tutelage of Nathaniel Eaton. On the 14th of September the recent immigrant John Harvard died and bequeathed the college four hundred books and 780 pounds, which was half of his estate.

In the early fall rumors began to circulate again — Anne Hutchinson in Roger Williams' colony had herself given birth to a monster. The voices of the villagers were hushed and excited as they swapped stories. They were also talking about the problem over in Lynn.

Like their neighbors in Salem the people of Lynn cooperated in keeping cattle, taking turns at herding. Goodman Gillow had his turn, and while he was driving the herd a neighbor stopped him to chat. As they talked, the cattle strayed into a cornfield, and when the herdsman turned to try to round them up, the neighbor left without helping. He had, however, laughingly told someone else about Gillow's predicament, and eventually help arrived — not, however, before the cattle had eaten so much that two of them became ill and one of them died. It happened that both these cows belonged to the neighbor who had stopped to talk, and he haled Gillow before the court for malfeasance. The court, however, got the particulars straight, and, to the delight of both Salem and Lynn, penalized the man who had brought suit. Poetic justice — the hand of God in it.

For six weeks in September and October the weather was cold and rainy; there was even snow. The Salemites were certain the situation was owing to the earthquake. On the fourth of November the church admitted Emanuel and Lucy Downing, the governor's brother-in-law and sister, as members and appointed Emanuel a judge in the Salem court. He found himself involved immediately in the recurrence of the Dorothy Talby affair: The woman had murdered her own child, a girl who had been named Difficulty.

Mrs. Talby had herself been a member of the Salem church before she had taken to assaulting her husband. She had quit eating meat because, she said, it had been revealed to her that she should do so. After her whipping she had acted, for a time, like a devoted wife and mother, but she had become, in Winthrop's words, "possessed of Satan" once again, and the devil had "persuaded her (by his delusions, which she listened to as revelations from God) to break the neck of her own child, that she might free it from future misery."

When she was arraigned Mrs. Talby stood mute, refusing to plead innocent or guilty until Winthrop reminded her of English law: Those who stand mute at the bar will be pressed with weights until they agree to plead, or until they are dead. Then she confessed. When she was sentenced, she kept her face covered and refused to rise.

On the sixth of December the woman was brought to the scaffold, which was not a platform but a ladder. There were no true scaffolds at Massachusetts hangings. Often it was a tree that was used, the noose dangling from a limb, and a ladder propped against the tree. The hangman waited on the ladder for the condemned person to climb it, turned him or her around to face the spectators of all ages, affixed the rope, and gave the condemned a chance to say some last words. Then the person to be executed would be "turned off" the ladder — given a turning shove so that the ladder wouldn't be dislodged. The condemned person would fall several feet, come up hard at the jerk of the rope and, if the knot had been placed properly beneath one ear and he or she were lucky, the neck would be broken instantly. If all went well, the death would be almost painless.

Dorothy Talby stood with the noose about her neck, reached up and took off her hood, and tried to wad it between the noose and her throat. She said to the hangman, "I desire to be beheaded instead. It is not so painful or shameful a thing." That was out of the question, so she was "turned off" the ladder, but her neck was not broken, as it was supposed to be, and she swung back and forth several times, then reached out to catch at a rung.

Her neighbors, standing witness, were horrified. They had brought their children, for it was considered an education to see an execution or two. Her pastor, the Rev. Hugh Peter, stood before the crowd and instructed them to take heed of these revelations and of the consequences of "despising the ordinance of excommunication" as Mrs. Talby had done when, in church, she had heard it pronounced against her, had turned her back upon the minister, and would have left the church if the beadle and others hadn't stopped her.

"See!" Peter cried as she swung in the winter wind, "These are the wages of sin!" Goody Talby at last stopped struggling — she had strangled to death. Her face was black, her eyes popping out, her tongue blue and thrust out between her teeth.

There seemed to be no end of trouble-making women in Salem. In June Mary Oliver had begun to kick up a ruckus, and no sooner had Dorothy Talby been disposed of than Mrs. Oliver stood forth in a manner that required stern action. Before she had immigrated Goody

Oliver had gotten herself into trouble in England for refusing to bow her head in prayer. She was a bright, argumentative, and lively person and, despite her quirk, religious. She was, however, poor as well and knew few people in Salem. She had been denied the right to become a member of Salem church. One Sunday she stood up in church meeting and demanded that she be allowed to give public testimony of her right to enter into the church covenant. She refused to be still when the congregation and Rev. Peter attempted to silence her. John Endicott, who was present, threatened to call the constable to take her away and she finally subsided.

Shortly after, though, she had been brought before the court and examined. She had given such pert, and impertinent answers to the questions put to her that she was thrown into jail for a few days, until her husband Thomas made her bond for good behavior and she was released. The Governor, however, discovered that she hadn't really mended her ways and that she continued to say, among other things, that everyone in town who believed in Christ ought to be allowed to receive the sacrament, and that "if Paul were at Salem, he would call all the inhabitants there saints," not just a few. In December Mary Oliver was censured again.

In the same month the pewterer Richard Graves gave Salem more to gossip about. He went to Peter Busgutt's house for a visit and wound up giving him a licking. When the neighbors reported the fight to the constable he came and hauled both men before the magistrate who sentenced Graves to a session in the town stocks. Peter dared to pass some satirical remarks of his own, directed against the court — he was whipped through the streets by the constable. On the fifteenth of the month a great blizzard put an end to most of the hilarity. A number of ships were cast away in the storm.

Across the seas that year Galileo published in Leyden his great book on mechanics and his early experiments, *Dialoghi delle Nuove Science*. John Milton, the English Puritan poet, went to visit him at Arcetri and discovered that the great astronomer was totally blind. In Aston Abbotts the Putnam family was finally making ready to leave for Salem in Massachusetts Bay.

Chapter Four

The second thing to be issued from Stephen Day's press in Cambridge, Massachusetts, was an almanac for the year 1639, "Calculated by Mr. Peirce, Mariner." Captain William Peirce was none other than the man who had brought Roger Williams and a cargo of black slaves to the New World. Being a navigator, Capt. Peirce naturally was interested in astronomy, and in astrology as well — at least to the degree of making weather predictions rather than horoscopes. Still, his almanac carried the mandatory "Man of the Signs," without which no such pamphlet could be expected to sell. The Man stood there with his bowels open to view. Surrounding him were the symbols for the twelve houses of the Zodiac with lines going toward those parts of the body over which each sign ruled. The almanac had a quick sale, and every copy was so well thumbed by the spring that there was a good deal of doubt they would last out the year.

On the 14th of January the earthquake renewed itself. The snow shook out of the trees and startled people and livestock underneath. Again dishes fell to the floors and broke in the country houses, the people rushed out to meet the judgment of God, and again the shocks subsided. But in Brookline James Everell and others saw during the month a sight, rumors of which swiftly traveled throughout the colony. They witnessed "a great light in the night" that began as a square, then turned into the figure of a swine that ran off toward Charlestown and continued to run to and fro for two or three hours.

On the fourth of February the town fathers of Salem decided they needed a larger meeting house on the site of the old one, and they signed a contract with John Pickering to build it. It was countersigned by John Endicott, Roger Conant, William Hathorne, John Woodbury, and Lawrence Leach. The new house was to be twenty-five feet long, with a gallery, and equally wide. It would have a catted chimney (a wooden chimney with a mud inner facing) twelve feet long, four feet to project above the roof, and the chimney would be backed with brick or stone. There were to be six windows, two on each side and two at the front end. Two stairways were to ascend to the gallery on either side of the front door. The building would be covered with one-and-one-half-inch plank and one-inch boards, not overlapping but butted edge-to-edge.

At about the same time in Aston Abbotts excitement was running high among the young people of the Putnam family, and misgiving equally high among the elders. There was nothing for it, however, but to go, as the property had been disposed of and most of the gear purchased for the expedition. Thomas, Nathaniel, and Old John checked each item in the stacks, barrels, and boxes over and over as the winter dragged into spring. They had attempted to cover every possible contingency. There were a bellows, a scoop, a large pail and casting shovel, sacks, lanterns, several hoes and axes of various varieties, three saws including a whipsaw, a file and wrest, hammers, augurs, an axle tree and cartwheels — for wheelwrights, they had heard, were scarce in New England; furthermore, they understood that, as soon as they landed on the dock, it would be well to build a cart and carry their gear along with them. There were, then, oxen as well as other livestock going with the family. There was a wheelbarrow, an oaken ladder, a plough, three shovels and two spades, chisels, gimlets, hatchets, knives, froes and handbills.

Thomas stuck a pinhole into the paper beside the name of each item as Nathaniel called them off — the paper was so well pricked that it threatened, in its margins, to disintegrate: There were all kinds of nails, spikes and pins, locks, curry combs, a branding iron, a hand vise, two pickaxes, pitchforks, a chain and lock for a boat, two extra ploughshares, and a 10-pound coulter.

Priscilla's gear included an iron pot and a great copper kettle, some smaller kettles, a spider, a huge cast-iron frying pan that had legs so that it could stand alone in the fireplace or "ingle," large and small frying pans, a brass mortar with a wooden pestle, a spit, a gridiron, skillets, platters, dishes, and spoons of woodenware.

The men's clothing consisted of shoes — four pairs each, the same for stockings, Norwich gaiters, cambric shirts; suits, doublets and hose of leather lined with oilskin and fastened with hooks and eyes; various other suits, bands, handkerchiefs, waistcoats, leather girdles, Monmouth caps, knit caps and black hats lined with leather, gloves, greatcoats, breeches of cloth and leather, to say nothing of the women's wear, and not all of it plainstyle, either. The young men looked up at their father. "I think we have done what can be done," Thomas told him.

Old John nodded. "It is a considerable investment," he said. Priscilla paused in her work and looked about the house. Nathaniel said, "We will build you another, Mother." "A greater one," Little John added. She smiled at them both, sighed, then went about her business.

On the sixteenth of March in Massachusetts Bay there was a violent wind in the evening, and it continued to rise until midnight. The great gale tore up houses and fences, knocked over barns and outbuildings, uprooted trees, devastated the Salem waterfront once more. Following the storm, flooding rains.

In May the omen was succeeded by another order from the Commission in England that Massachusetts Bay send its patent back immediately. However, because the letter had not been entrusted to a particular messenger to deliver to Gov. Winthrop, but merely by

Matthew Cradock's messenger in a load of other correspondence, the Court requested the messenger, when he reported to England, simply to omit mentioning anything about his having delivered the message at all. The Court laid the matter aside once again.

In June there were again many ships and many passengers. Lady Deborah Moody stepped ashore; so did John Putnam, Sr., with his wife, three sons, and three daughters. Zaccheus and Phoebe Gould stood right behind them with their family. What they found was a town that was nearly surrounded by water, since it was situated between two inlets of the sea — the North and South rivers. To the main part of town was attached a spit called The Neck, where the boatyards were, and a public pasture.

Salem was a low-lying town, but it rose to a hill that commanded a broad prospect of the territory. A few people had already begun to call it Gallows Hill, for it was there that the hangman did his work. The streets in town were meandering and irregular, especially Essex Street, which was the only one that ran all the way through the town. The harbor was excellent — ships found it a fine anchorage. Thomas thought his parents looked bewildered, so he said, "I will look after the shipping. Do you go and find where we must go, father." Old John nodded as Thomas turned back to the boats.

Priscilla said, "There is some shade, children. We will wait there." She, Phoebe, and the girls gathered the portable luggage, Nathaniel picked up the heavier parcels, and they moved off. Young John Putnam Jr., said, "May I come too?" His father nodded, said, "Will you come, Zack, or stay?" Zaccheus said, "I will come. Boys, help the women." The men turned and went off, young John tagging behind.

When they returned — and they had been gone a long time — they found the afternoon wearing on and two carts assembled and waiting: Nathaniel and Thomas had expedited matters with the sailors. The gear was nearly loaded, the rest of it was quickly stowed; the oxen were backed into their places, and the other livestock were tethered and hobbled. John Putnam looked at his family and the Goulds. He said, "We go to Lynn. We will sleep in the fields tonight."

"Where is Lynn?" Nathaniel asked.

"Not far," John said.

"While you were gone, there was a madwoman here," Thomas informed the men.

"A madwoman?" Zaccheus asked.

""Aye," Nathaniel pointed toward Essex Street. "She came to the wharves and called out to those who were coming off the ships. She told us we should never find redemption in Salem, for true believers were not welcome, but only such as were well-to-do."

Priscilla and Phoebe shook their heads. "We was frighted for the children," Phoebe said.

"A woman of quality named Lady Moody was greatly disturbed," Priscilla told John.

"The constable came and took the mad woman." Thomas leaned against the wheel of one of the wagons. "He told us her name was Oliver and she had made trouble before this."

"Well," John said, "it is over. We must begin to move if we would get to Lynn soon." In a few minutes the two families began to move off up the road away from the water, but slowly, for the cattle followed at their own pace.

Lynn lay five miles from Salem to the southwest. When the Putnams and the Goulds arrived there the next day they found it to be a pleasant place lying on a plain surrounded by rising land except towards the east where it opened on Lynn Bay, the peninsula of Nahant, and a point of land that jutted out into the Atlantic. The Saugus River watered the town and the main street was broad.

But the women were astonished when they saw where they were going to dwell for the first while: Zaccheus and John led the two families to a hill outside of town. When Priscilla asked, "Why do we stop here?" John replied, "This is where we will live."

"And where is that?" Priscilla cast her eyes about the spot, and her sister Phoebe did likewise.

"Inside the hill," Zaccheus said. "Pitch in, boys." Tom and Nathaniel laughed at the looks of astonishment on the women's faces as they went to unload picks and shovels. It took a couple of weeks, but at the end of that time a good-sized cave had been hollowed in the side of the hill, lined with boards, and a chimney punched through from the hearth. The entrance to the cave was a rectangular door swung on leather hinges and hung in a wooden frame, like the door of a house: The front of the cave — one entire side — was a wooden wall with a window in it as well as the door.

Zaccheus and John made arrangements with the town to put their livestock with the town herd on Nahant, and they began to look around for employment, for they could not plant crops so late, even if they had a land grant. They applied for permission to live in the town and set about exploring the area. John Putnam saw some likely property at Salem Farms, and Zaccheus thought some Ipswich property looked promising. Salem was larger than Lynn, and there was often occasion for the men to go there. Thomas generally stayed in Lynn and began to make acquaintances. He was highly esteemed for his willingness to help the neighbors when an extra hand was needed.

Zack and John, Sr., found that Salem was a much more highly diversified community than Aston Abbotts had been. A glass factory was in operation, manufacturing primarily bottles, and beads for trade with the Indians. The glass was a dark brownish-black. The new meetinghouse was being constructed — John and Nathaniel Putnam lent a hand with that for a day or two.

The harbor continued busy. The first imports of sugar and indigo came ashore that summer from ships owned in Salem. All season new passengers came ashore. The waterfront had several taverns, and the behavior of the seamen was in marked contrast to that of the townspeople, though a good many ship's officers and sailors had wives, families, and homes in the town. These generally behaved circumspectly, but the transient crews were roisterous.

John and Priscilla began to attend services at the Salem meetinghouse. There, they were introduced one lecture day to New England justice: George Dill had been sentenced for drunkenness and loud behavior to "stand at the meeting house door...with a cleft stick upon his tongue, and a paper upon his hat" on which was written, "For Gross Lying."

Jane James, wife of Erasmus James of Marblehead across the bay, was accused of setting her sons to steal from the home of Anthony Thatcher. The parents were bound to their good behavior, and the court ordered that Erasmus whip all his male children soundly.

Land continued to be granted regularly, which gave John, Sr., good hope of receiving some in the near future. Richard Davenport received 150 acres more for his service during the Pequot War. John began to meet a good many of the men and women of Salem and was considered by the church people to be a sound man. One of his acquaintances was a newcomer like himself, Edward Bishop, who was no relative of Townsend Bishop, a pillar of the community.

In September the Salem fishing fleet had great success during the mackerel runs. Whole schools were caught in nets, and many townspeople went out with lines to catch strings of the fish. Nathaniel brought home a bucketful several times, and the two families regaled themselves.

There were two cases of interest in September: Mary Oliver was sentenced to prison in Boston "indefinitely, for her speeches at the arrival of some newcomers." And Marmaduke Perry of Salem was arraigned for the murder of his apprentice. The jury, however, could not agree on whether he ought to received death or imprisonment, and it adjourned until December.

Harvard college did not open for the fall term as it was being reorganized, but in Salem new businesses continued to be developed. On the first of October the first tannery in town was opened.

During the fall the ships began to bring in news of King Charles' new adviser. Thomas Wentworth, Lord Strafford, who had been a leader in Parliament when it produced the Petition of Right, had become much more ambitious since those days and therefore more pro-crown. He had been appointed President of the Council of the North and Lord Deputy of Ireland where he had been employed in ruthlessly subjugating the Irish. In September Charles called him back to London to be his chief advisor about how best to humble the rebellious Scots as well as his own Puritans. Strafford advised the king to treat the English in the same way Strafford had treated the Irish. The suggestion earned him the title "Black Tom Tyrant." Later the New Englanders learned that Black Tom had also advised the calling up of Parliament.

On the 5th of November the Court of Massachusetts accepted the report of a commission whose members, William Hathorne and Richard Davenport, had recommended the laying out of an 800-acre farm in Salem for Richard Bellingham, formerly Deputy Governor and currently a magistrate. It was to be located on Salem Head, northwest of town, "there being in it a hill, an Indian Plantation, and a pond." Nathaniel Putnam fretted, in a hurry to move to a parcel of the Putnams' own land, but his father urged him to be calm, for all would work itself out in its own time.

On the same day the General Court passed an order that unwittingly conflicted with its previous "six-mile extent" boundary order of 1636, and the inhabitants of Salem Farms, five miles from town, began to push out beyond the "extent." The magistrate-for-life law was rescinded during the year because of its unpopularity, and as the winter set in the jury reassembled in the Marmaduke Perry murder case. New evidence had been introduced that tended to clear Perry, but two jurors disagreed with the majority.

Perry's apprentice had been treated very hard by his master and fed on a poor diet. An autopsy had shown that, when he died, he had a concussion, which he had told some people he had received from a measuring stick wielded by his master, but he had evidently told others he had hurt himself in a fall from a tree. There was no other evidence. The two hung jurors remained silent and Perry was freed.

The winter settled in. The Putnams and the Goulds were cramped, but surprisingly warm, in their cave in Lynn.

Nathaniel Putnam impatiently watched as others were given land in Salem. But John and Thomas Putnam and Zaccheus Gould were stoical. They were building bridges to the communities.

By summer news began to arrive in New England of the calling of Parliament on the 13th of April. The King had asked for money before the body began to debate grievances, but Commons desired the reverse order, and after three weeks of argument and harangue the exasperated King Charles I dissolved the body, which became known as the Short Parliament among the populace.

Joseph Grafton of Salem set something of a record for a voyage to Maine. On May 2nd he set sail from Salem harbor to Pemaquid in his 40-ton ketch. He and his crew — three men and a boy — arrived the next morning, took aboard twenty cattle, hay, and water, and got back to Salem on the afternoon of the sixth. The port town was trading up and down the coast as well as overseas. It had opened routes to the Bermudas, Virginia, the West Indies and Antigua. A good many more things than the mere necessities were available in the local shops. Whereas many ships continued to put in from England as well, now very few carried much more than supplies and goods — the flood of immigrants was reduced to a trickle as matters in England began to build to a climax, which everyone on both sides of the water sensed.

On the 13th of May Thomas Dudley was elected Governor of the colony. Those who had already arrived continued to be assimilated. The Lady Deborah Moody, among others, was admitted a member of the Salem assembly. The church folk in Salem as elsewhere had their first true native book in 1640: Stephen Day in Cambridge issued the *Bay Psalm Book* which took its place alongside the Bible in many homes.

Gov. Dudley had to contend with a lack of specie in the Bay; therefore, the General Court made Indian wampum legal tender. The barter system — at controlled standard rates — was also given official sanction. Joseph Bois was in July granted ten acres at Cape Ann, but no land grants were forthcoming for the Putnams. Nathaniel continued to fret.

William Osgood of Andover, not far from Salem Farms, was building a barn for John Spencer during the month of August when John Godfrey, Spencer's herdsman, came to where the men were at work on the frame of the building and began what seemed at first to be a bantering conversation. Godfrey said, "I have gotten a new master against the time when I have done with keeping cows."

Osgood asked, "Who is it?"

"I know not," Godfrey replied.

"Then were does he dwell?"

"I do not know."

"Well, then, what is his name? You must know his name."

"No, I know not what his name is," Godfrey told him.

Frustrated, Osgood asked, "How, then, will you go to him when your time is out?"

"The man will come," Godfrey said mysteriously, "and fetch me then."

"Have you made an absolute bargain?"

Godfrey nodded. "A covenant has been made; I have set my hand to it."

"Have you not a counter-Covenant?" Osgood was beginning to get the drift of the conversation.

Godfrey shook his head. "No," he said.

Osgood was appalled. "What a mad fellow you are to make a covenant in this manner!"

The herdsman looked thoughtful. "He is an honest man," he mused at last.

"How know you that?"

"He looks like one."

"I am persuaded," Osgood said, backing off, "you have made a covenant with the Devil!"

The answer filled Godfrey with delight. "I profess!" he chortled, skipping about like a goat, "I profess!"

On the 27th of August the college in Cambridge received as president Mr. Henry Dunster, a newcomer who had been educated in England at Cambridge University. He prepared to open the school, which had been renamed in honor of its first benefactor, the late Rev. John Harvard, after it had lain fallow for a year. The following month Salem, always on the lookout for new industries, deputed three people — John Balch, John Gedney, and Ralph Fogg — to look into the matter of "fustian spinsters" before the next town meeting.

In England King Charles impressed an army and marched against the Scots, but he had been unable to raise enough money to train and equip his troops properly. Further, not all of his men were monarchists, by any means. When the two armies met at the border the English troops refused to fight. The Scots advanced and occupied the northern English shires. The king was forced to negotiate in order to stop the invasion, but the Scots refused to sign any agreement that was not ratified by Parliament.

On November 3rd, then, King Charles was forced to call for Parliament to assemble. The first thing that the Parliament did was to call for the release of political prisoners, of whom William Prynne was one. On the 28th of November he entered London in triumph, crowds cheering in the streets. The next thing Parliament wanted was Strafford's head. There were great demonstrations and mobs and threats against the life of the queen. Charles capitulated and handed Commons his advisor. The king was practically helpless before Parliament — he had, by his arrogant actions and illegal taxes over the years, united the entire nation against him. Parliament demanded constitutional reforms and the king agreed once more.

Then the Parliament ran into its own snag: Everyone wanted the religious question settled, and nearly everyone was against the New School, but no one could agree on what should replace it. By the end of the year the debates were growing very hot, but the weather in New England was very cold and it was difficult for the colonists to keep abreast of developments overseas, for very few ships or boats of any kind were arriving from England; however, now and then one straggled in. Twenty-five-thousand English colonials waited eagerly for the latest information to spread outward from the port towns into the countryside. From Aquiday in Rhode Island, though, there was news of a different kind: Anne Hutchinson and two men named Collins and Hales were accused of being witches, but the colony's government did not seem to be interested in prosecuting the affair.

The first thing in the new year John Putnam received his grant of land: On the 20th of January 1641 he was given fifty acres of upland and five acres of meadow in the section known as Salem Farms, which some were beginning to call as well Salem Village, to distinguish it from the Town of Salem, of which it was a part. Salem was not laid out in a fashion that was typical of New England villages, most of which copied the old manorial layout of towns in England, with a central village and, around it, the farming land to which the farmers could walk from their homes in the town. Because Salem was built on a peninsula, the farms had to be at a greater remove and, for convenience, most of the farmers preferred to build their houses in the countryside outside the town. As a result, Salem Village was becoming quite a settlement in itself.

The Putnams prepared to move, all except Thomas who had decided to remain in Lynn for the time being. The Goulds were to go to Ipswich as soon as the weather would permit. There were a good many things to do before the spring thaw and everyone was busy through February.

When the sap was beginning to run in the maples the Rev. Mr. Nathaniel Ward of Ipswich, who had been commissioned to draw up a body of laws for Massachusetts, completed his task and submitted the code to the government, which began to consider it. In February, too, the government requested the Rev. Hugh Peter of Salem to serve in a delegation to be sent to England to treat with Parliament in behalf of the colony and to further the colony's interests.

There was great opposition to the plan in Salem. John Endicott was against it on the ground that ministers should not be taken away from their congregations to serve civil ends. The main fear of the church, however, was that Peter would remain in England permanently, for John Humphrey was to go back with Peter, and it was known Humphrey planned to stay, arguing that good men were needed to help in the coming revolution. He and John Endicott confronted one another in the meetinghouse over the issue, and the argument was hot. Soon there was such dissension spread abroad by the fight that the magistrates let the issue lapse for the time being.

As soon as the snow was off the ground John Putnam, Sr., and his sons packed their tools and gear into one of the carts and left the women behind while they went into the woods near Davenport Hill in Salem Village to raise their house. Inasmuch as the cart could not be gotten to their homestead site through the wilderness, they first went to a spot on Frost Fish Brook and built a large dugout canoe Indian-fashion. They cut down a pine of an appropriate size and built a fire, then charred the ends of the tree and shaped it by chiseling the charcoal off. They did the same with the interior, burning it in layers and scraping out the burned wood until it was hollow. When they had finished, they launched the canoe and loaded it, then made their way up the stream to Mile Brook. When they got to a spot opposite their site they trekked the materials they needed through the trees and, as they went, blazed first a trail and then, in succeeding trips, cut a path through the undergrowth.

When they were ready with their materials they first set themselves to building a camp with an English wigwam. They cut saplings, stuck the thick inds into the earth in a circle, bent the tops over and tied them together. Then they covered it with hides, built a frame door and a fireplace inside, and were ready to get down to the business of building their house. Old and young John and Nathaniel lived in the wigwam while Thomas commuted in the canoe back and forth to Lynn while the house was being framed.

A clearing was carved out of the forest, a cellar dug, and a foundation laid of stones. The timbers of the house were formed out of logs of appropriate size, squared and roughly shaped by hand with axes and hatchets. When the framing timbers were done, they were morticed and tenoned on the ground, lying in such positions that they merely needed to be raised and fitted together when upright, and fastened.

Next, a great fireplace was built of stone — it was nearly the same length as the house, which was relatively small and only about eight feet high. But when the frame was raised, the fireplace would need only to have a chimney attached to be ready for use.

The Putnams erected a saw frame of rough timbers, strong enough to hold a large log just high enough so that the men would not have to bend to saw. When the frame was ready they jockeyed a tree trunk onto the frame using pulleys and winches. One man stood on each side of the log holding one end of a huge, double-handled saw. The sawteeth were set horizontally to the end of the log, and they walked down the length of it sawing while a third man wedged open the split end so that the saw could work freely. It was a huge labor just to square the log, but eventually there were enough boards for the house to be covered.

When all was ready, the neighbors arrived for the house-raising. It was a great picnic in the woods. The weather was warm at last, and the insects were fierce, but no one let that stop him. The women brought and made food of all sorts while the children played their games and the men worked raising the frame, then covering it, and at last roofing the house. The Putnams' roof was not thatched, like many another dwelling, but covered with wooden shakes. The whole job, once it was begun, was completed by nightfall.

The Goulds stayed overnight with their friends, and the next morning they said their goodbyes. John shook hands with Zack and said, "When your house is raised, I will be there with my sons." The Goulds would be in Ipswich, not a great distance from Salem Village.

Zack replied, "Well, John, here we are at last, and one has a house already in the new land. The Lord has been good."

John nodded his agreement. Priscilla kissed Phoebe. "We will stay close, sister," she said. "Take our blessing and our love."

Phoebe smiled, squeezed her sister's hand, and gathered her family together. The Putnams stood in the yard waving as their lifelong Aston Abbotts relatives walked through the woods of Salem Village to the brook, but they did not stand there long, for there were fields to be cleared, crops to be planted, barns to raise, and a life to begin.

The fields were cleared slowly. At first, the trees over a stretch of ground were cut, but the stumps left where they were. The rows — if one could call them that — of the field simply went around the stumps, which were left to rot after they had been burned as close to the ground as possible. John and his boys had a great deal to do just to get seed into the earth that first year, but they had also to build fences, raise outbuildings, transport livestock, clear the barnyard and do a host of other things such as chop firewood and put in a truck garden. Everyone in the family spent many a night simply lying awake aching in every muscle.

Sundays, the days of rest, and Thursdays, lecture days, the family also had to try to get in to Salem for services, which they managed most of the time, for they had applied for church membership and wanted to make a good impression. Further, those were the days when they heard the town gossip, the women visiting with other women in their halls, the men having a mug of beer or cider in the nearby tavern — there was always one of those handy for these all-day affairs with breaks in between sessions. Everyone was amazed to hear in April that a black woman servant of Israel Stoughton of Dorchester had been baptized and admitted to the church there.

Richard Bellingham was chosen governor of the colony in June, at about the same time that Hugh Peter, against the wishes of his congregation, accepted the commission to go to England with William Hibbins of Boston. He resigned his ministry amid many complaints, and the Rev. Edward Norris, Salem's schoolmaster, was chosen to replace him — the fourth pastor of the Salem church meeting.

The Rev. Mr. Peter could leave, however, with a clear conscience. He had done much to help the town grow. When he left he could see the signs of progress. Salem was producing salt for the fisheries, in which he had been so interested, by evaporating salt water from the ocean. John Pride had begun a pottery in town. Richard Hollingsworth, the Salem shipwright, had built and launched a tremendous ship of 300 tons. All of Peter's flock was active in the town, and many of the young men were at work for other families — Joseph Houlton was, for instance, a servant of Richard Ingersoll. A few were not so fortunate: The Lady Deborah Moody's farm was failing — it was a wet summer, not good for crops — and, discouraged, she was considering a remove.

Not all the inhabitants were keeping their hands and minds on their own and God's business, however. Word reached the authorities through William Allen that "Richard Graves kissed Goody Gent twice." Haled before the court, the troublesome pewterer confessed and was sentenced to a fine or whipping, whichever he could best afford. But there was worse.

Daniel Fairfield, who was half Dutch and forty years old, lived in Salem with his lusty young wife not far from John Humphrey's farm. Humphrey was a poor father who left his three young daughters to their own devices much of the time. All the girls were under ten years of age, and Humphrey trusted his servants to care for them, which they seldom did. For two years Fairfield had been visiting the girls and entertaining them sexually. He had even allowed a couple of male servants to join in the games on occasion.

Blissfully ignorant of what was going on under his nose, Humphrey left his family behind while he went to England. No sooner was he out of sight than the youngest of the three young Humphrey girls, nine years old, confessed to her older sister what had been going on, and she took the matter to the governor.

As soon as word got out about the affair, the people of Salem and Boston began to talk about lynching. John Putnam, thinking about his own daughters, smoldered deeply and angrily as he talked with his neighbors about it. But the authorities proceeded methodically with an investigation and, afterwards, canvassed the ministers of all the colonies down to New Haven and Connecticut. After having gathered as much evidence and clerical opinion as possible, the court concluded that there was no Biblical justification for a death sentence, even if it could be shown that rape had been committed — and there was doubt it had.

But Fairfield wished that he might have been hanged. He was sentenced to be "severely whipped at Boston and at Salem, and confined to Boston neck, upon pain of death," if he tried to escape. He was to "have one nostril slit and seared at Boston, and the other at Salem, and to wear an halter" — a noose — "about his neck visibly all his life, or to be whipped every time he were seen abroad without it, and to die, if he attempted the like upon any person, and 40 pounds to Mr. Humphrey." The other two defendants were fined and sentenced to whippings at Boston and Salem. One of them was to wear a noose, like Fairfield, and to be confined to Lynn.

Salem and the surrounding towns gathered themselves together, in a great mass of people from the area, at Gallows Hill for the public punishment. Everyone agreed the convicts bore the whippings well — each received forty stripes, which was a great number — and afterward gave a public confession, saying that their sin had been much greater than the punishment. They could hardly speak. The blood ran off their hips in rivulets into the soil, and they had to be supported by the executioner: A great "Oh!" went up from the crowd as he slashed Fairfield's nose with his knife and the blood spouted over the prisoner's chin. When the crowd dispersed, it was with a sense that something had been released and they were once again washed clean. It was a good deal like a church service but somehow more satisfying.

The ships from England were bringing in reports about the debates in Parliament during the summer. The radicals in Commons wanted to abolish Episcopacy, but many others merely wished to remove Laud's New School innovations and keep the Anglican church as it had always been. Finally Parliament adjourned. While the members were at home or at the Court, local disturbances took place throughout the realm. There were demonstrations of Puritan fanaticism here and there. Splinter sects began to arise, and many individual churches began to invent strange forms of worship. One of the most zealous Puritans was John Weir, an officer in the Scottish Presbyterian army, but he noted only with disapproval what he saw going on among the madmen of England. Many moderates began to grow conservative. In late summer Ireland revolted again. On the second of September the General Court of the Massachusetts Bay Colony called for a day of Thanksgiving to celebrate events in England.

There were other occurrences in England and elsewhere, however, and two of these were of interest to William Lilly, the astrologer of London. The first was the publication of a new book, a tract titled *The Prophecy of Mother Shipton in the Reign of Henry VIII*, which was full of prophecies of things that had happened, and things to come. Lilly considered that Mother Shipton's existence was problematical, but he had to admit to his friend Nicholas Fiske that her book was intriguing. "And popular," Fiske added. "Many copies have been sold." The remark gave Lilly pause. He had often thought about the possibility of publishing popular books. The second thing in which he was interested, and that he and Fiske discussed, had to do with the child prodigy Robert Boyle, fourteen years old and a younger son of Richard Boyle, Earl of Cork. Lilly had heard that the boy was in Florence studying "the paradoxes of the great star gazer" Galileo.

Events of this nature were of no interest to the Putnams and their neighbors. They reserved their curiosity for the sale of Townsend Bishop's property in Salem to Richard Ingersoll, and for the crop situation, which was poor — it had been a chilly, wet summer. On the 12th of November, with most of the harvest in, the countryside was struck by a great wind and rainstorm, and a huge tide battered the waterfront, damaging shipping and wharving and flooding the streets downtown.

The Body of Liberties of Massachusetts Bay was promulgated at last. The colony now had a set of laws that the towns and counties could refer to in their courts, but not everyone was satisfied. William Hathorne of Salem wanted to have set penalties for such crimes as lying, swearing, and so forth, on the grounds that magistrates should not have too much leeway in deciding what penalties to impose, for what was fair for one man ought to be fair for another. Many opposed this view, pointing out that not every case was precisely the same and magistrates ought to have the right to make the punishment fit the circumstances of each particular case.

Another Hathorne suggestion angered a good many people: He wished to force the retirement of two of the older magistrates because they had become poor men and were no longer propertied. He was publicly chastised by the Rev. John Cotton of the Boston Church for his lack of Christian charity.

The winter of 1641-2 was a deep one. There was heavy freezing and a great deal of snow. It was difficult in Salem to get news from England. The people heard that on the 22nd of November last — Saint Cecilia's Day — Parliament had passed a "Grand Remonstrance" which set forth their grievances against the king and demanded a government acceptable to the Parliament and a settlement of the religious question. The monarch promised to abide by the new rules and to do nothing without Parliament's consent.

He lied. On the 5th of January he personally tried to arrest five parliamentary leaders including John Pym and John Hampden. However, spies at court had warned Parliament of the impending raid, and the members were ready: The five took refuge, and when Charles arrived, he was confounded by their absence. The next day he tried to have the refugees arrested in London but was again unsuccessful. His invasion of Parliament was the first time in history such a thing had been done, the people were more than outraged. There was a general strike of merchants and workers in London; the tradesmen stood in the doorways of their shops with swords drawn and halberds at the ready. On January 10th Charles fled Whitehall to prepare to wage civil war.

The Parliament was divided now into two major factions — the Royalists or Cavaliers, on the one hand, who backed the king, and the Puritans or Roundheads. Oliver Cromwell had gathered a troop of horse for the Puritans — the best-trained band in England, and his men called themselves the Ironsides.

The people of New England watched developments as closely as they could, but meanwhile life went on as it had to. In Salem old John Putnam had made arrangements with John Endicott to have his youngest son, John Putnam Jr., apprenticed on the John Endicott farm. In February, when the sap began to run, he went into the woods with the men and learned how to tap maples and boil the sap for syrup.

A hollow, narrow box was chiseled into the trunk of each tree, its base slanting downward, so that the sap would collect in the bottom of the box. Near the bottom of the box a tap was inserted, and beneath the tree troughs made of hollowed-out logs were laid to collect the sap. When eventually the troughs were nearly full, everyone on the farms went into the forest, made temporary wigwams, and built large fires over which were slung great copper kettles such as the one the Putnams had brought from England. Everyone camped out while the sap was boiled down into various consistencies of syrup or cakes of solid sugar.

The Putnams, though, did not have to camp out, for they were in the midst of the forest already. It felt good when John, Sr., and Nathaniel Putnam came in out of the weather and spread themselves on the settle before the fire in the huge fireplace. It was usually Nathaniel who built up the fire in the morning from its banking the evening before. When he had to start it fresh he and his father hauled in a log six feet long and put it into the fireplace as a backlog, using handspikes. A smaller backstick was placed above it, the andirons set with an iron bar and a forestick at the front, then the firewood was arranged so that there were ample spaces between for the fire to breathe, and kindling was placed on top of the pile — never below it. Finally the fire was lighted with tinder made of charred rags kept, with the flint and steel, in the tinder niche in the fireplace itself.

One could walk into the fireplace and sit down, for at either end there were benches built in the chimney corners. Also built into the back of the chimney was the brick oven, the door of which could be opened when it was hot enough to bake, and the food to be prepared inserted.

The settle was a high-backed bench that faced the fire — high-backed to keep the winter drafts off one's back, and it was reserved in the evenings for the older folks. Priscilla and the girls cooked over the open fire. There were cranes, hooks, and pulleys built into the fireplace at various heights, and there was always water boiling. Meat was roasted on a spit that rested in brackets built as part of the back of the andirons; the drippings were caught in a crock. Potatoes were wrapped in wet leaves and roasted in the ashes.

A winter meal consisted often of broth or porridge — a bean soup flavored with summer savory; Indian pudding with sauce; boiled pork and beef, turnips, and a few potatoes. Cider was the chief drink. It had been made in the fall from the wild apples of the woods, which the English settlers were amazed to discover were very tasty. John and Nathaniel had turned a grove of them into an orchard; they planned at some time in the future to try grafting English stock on the New England trees, but meantime the result of their first efforts was good enough.

The fare was varied with game that had been trapped in the woods, or shot on fowling expeditions. Young John was good at trapping rabbits. He would find a rabbit run in the snow and cut notches in two small trees on either side. He would put a cross-stick into the notches, bend a sapling over, and tie it to the cross-stick. He would drop a stiff horsehair noose with a slipknot down from the cross-stick in the center of the path. When the rabbit came running along, its head would go into the noose, its ears would knock the cross-stick out of the notches, the sapling would snap upright, and the rabbit would be found hanging high out of the reach of vermin when young John came to collect his prey.

John was wise in the lore of rabbit and hare. He knew the differences between them — that the hare was larger and lived in the open, not in a burrow, hence he would find no "hare runs" — but he could follow the noise of hares thumping in the woods and shoot them. He kept in his pocket a rabbit's foot — the left hind one, though it was one of his own, not one taken from a hare killed in the full moon by a cross-eyed man: That was the most efficacious kind, he had been told. Still, a rabbit's foot was a rabbit's foot.

The farm meals were varied as much as possible, which was not much — a bowl of cider with toasted cornbread in it, cheese manufactured on the premises. There was almost never wheat flour available to Goody Putnam. She baked Indian bannock by mixing cornmeal with water, spreading it an inch thick on an inclined board in front of the fire and, when it was done, serving it as milk toast. If most of the meals were dull, they were nourishing, considering the circumstances.

Things were anything but dull overseas during the spring. Parliament passed a bill that gave itself the power to appoint the commanders of the Army. King Charles refused to sign the bill, and Parliament illegally declared the Militia Bill to be the law of the land without the king's signature. By the end of April revolution began to seem inevitable and imminent.

While momentous events continued to move swiftly forward in the mother country, Massachusetts waited and listened. Immigration came nearly to a dead halt. From the few ships fresh from England — fishers mostly — the New England folk got what news was to be had. The people of Salem were interested to learn that their former minister,

Hugh Peter, had been appointed Chaplain of Oliver Cromwell's Parliamentary army.

The first senior class of Harvard College was graduated — nine Bachelors took their degrees, and one of these was George Downing of Salem, son of Emanuel Downing. Boston was struck by a great thunderstorm. Another ship was launched at Salem. Ensign Richard Davenport was granted a third allotment of 80 acres. In Lynn Thomas Putnam was admitted to the body politic by being made a freeman. He was becoming quite active in civic affairs.

There continued to be new businesses started, and old ones prospered. William Jones of Salem had set up as a tailor and was doing well. The colony, however, continued to suffer from an insufficiency of currency, even though Indian wampum was legal tender for debts under 40 shillings. John Putnam, when he came into town to trade during the summer had occasion to do business with William Jones, whom he paid with white and black wampum. The white was made of the stems of periwinkles with the shell taken off and strung. At first six periwinkle beads was equivalent to a penny, but inflation had taken the value up to eight strung beads per penny. The blue-black wampum was fashioned out of the shells of quahogs, three beads to the penny at first, and later four. A fathom of these beads was equivalent to five shillings. The graduating seniors and the other students at Harvard had paid their tuition largely in wampum, and the College found itself with surpluses of it.

The summer scandal of Salem was the case of Robert Cocker who was sued for breach of promise. Priscilla Putnam and the other women between services on Sunday discussed the affair. Cocker had betrothed himself to one of the Salem maidens, then turned around and married another. It was Priscilla's understanding that he had decided not to marry the first girl because she had a widow's peak: He feared he would die soon after their marriage and she would then remarry. Priscilla suspected the story was nonsense and that Cocker was merely fickle. He was sentenced to a public whipping, which everyone attended, and fined five pounds, which he had to pay to Thomas King who had married Cocker's first fiancée. Much less interesting was the fact that John Winthrop had once again been chosen governor.

In England on the ninth of June Parliament submitted nineteen propositions to the king as a basis for the reconstruction of the government; according to the bill, Privy Councilors, the principal Crown officers, judges, and peers might be appointed only with Parliamentary approval. On the 22nd of August Charles had had enough of such rebellion and effrontery: The Revolution began at Nottingham where the king raised his battle standard and joined the issue with force. The tide of war went his way as he had superior ground forces, though Cromwell's Ironsides troop was well-disciplined and trained, and though Parliament controlled the Navy.

In London William Lilly was experiencing a private revolution. Shortly after Galileo had died on the 8th of January and the news of his death reached Lilly in the spring, the astrologer had begun to read Valentine Nabod's *Commentary on Alchabitius*. Lilly soon found him to be "the profoundest author" he had ever come upon. He had begun to revise his notions about astrology and to devise a system of his own — a system of divination by the stars based upon the ideas of Nabod.

Of less interest to Lilly, but of considerably more to the scientific community, was the publication of the young Thomas Browne's *Religio Medici* which established him as one of the foremost members of the Invisible College. Browne was not a Puritan, nor was he less split in his mind than the other proponents of the New Philosophy. He had no personal doubts about the existence of guardian angels and witches.

When the Massachusetts colonists heard how the war was going in England, many of them wondered whether the powers of darkness were not stronger than they had thought. It was frustrating to the Putnams and their neighbors to be so helpless to aid their brethren in the great struggle. Nothing momentous was taking place in the Bay itself early in

1643, and the colonists waited impatiently for the spring thaw which would bring ships with news of the fighting. On the fifth of February the tedium was broken in Salem when Margaret Page incurred the wrath of the magistrates and it was ordered that she be sent "to Boston jail as a lazy, idle, and loitering person, where she may be set to work for a living," but the titillation was meager.

On the 28th of the same month, however, Richard Graves was back before the courts accused of "Oppression in his trade of pewtering." This time he was acquitted, but the court admonished him on another occasion for stealing fence rails from the lot of Christopher Young of Wenham — a weaver by trade, and an amateur alchemist by hobby. The court administered Graves at the same session a fine for taking wood from Thomas Edwards and calling him "a base fellow — one might run a pike half in his belly and never touch his heart."

It was to be a big year for Thomas Putnam. In the spring he was chosen one of the seven Selectmen of Lynn, and on the third of April he was admitted to membership in the First Church of Salem. Furthermore, the banns had been posted for his marriage, in the fall, to Ann Holyoke, daughter of Edward and Prudence Holyoke who were members of one of the most prominent families in the colony.

Mistress Holyoke had completed the collection of articles in her hope chest — the garments and linens she would need to begin her married life, none to be worn or used until the wedding day for fear she would die an old maid. As each item had been sewn and stitched, folded and finished, it had been laid away to wait for the great day, though it did not lie still in the chest, for each article had been taken out and shown to cousins and sisters and aunts very often, and the occasions increased as the wedding day approached. There was no woman in the village who did not know precisely how many quilts, cloths, pieces of wearing apparel and so forth with which the Thomas Putnams would begin their life together.

By the tenth of May more momentous things were happening in Massachusetts, however — the governments of Massachusetts Bay,

Plymouth Colony, New Haven and Hartford were drafting Articles of Confederation; on the 19th of the month the articles were adopted, and the New England Confederation was formed to protect each other against the Indians, the Dutch, and all other enemies, and to provide for the capture and extradition of criminals and fugitives.

It was a great step forward for law and order, but there were those for whom the term seemed meaningless — the Putnams' old acquaintance Mary Oliver had once again defied the magistrates, reproached them publicly, and been sentenced to a public whipping. Thomas Putnam made sure he was on hand to see it. He had to admit to his father and brothers that "It was a marvel," for the Oliver woman had stood to her lashing without being tied, seemed rather to glory in her punishment. John, who had been unable to be at the scene, shook his head and owned, "Mary Oliver is an unbending rod, but one day she will be broken." When he attended Lecture Day it seemed to him his prediction had already come true, for she was forced to stand with a cleft stick on her tongue for a half hour after the lecture, and she looked decidedly hangdog.

The Salemites received interesting news from Plymouth before they got anything substantial from England: they were astonished to hear that Thomas Morton of Merry Mount had yet once more appeared in New England. He, too, they heard, seemed an unhealthy and probably broken person, old and poverty-stricken — so much so that the authorities took pity on him and allowed him to remain until the following spring.

The folk of Salem were made of sterner stuff: They had their own returned exile — the Antinomian Francis Weston. No sooner had he been seen back in town than the constable apprehended him, took him before the magistrate, and clapped him in irons at hard labor. The authorities could see no improvement in his beliefs. After a while he was again scourged out of the settlement.

Old John's friend Zaccheus Gould had settled in Ipswich, in that section some called Topsfield. Now, John and his sons began to see a conflict of interests emerging: The General Court having allowed the Salem Village people the right in 1639 to push over the "six-mile extent" boundaries, the same right was in 1643 given to the Ipswich townspeople. They began to develop Topsfield on the same territory, for now Salem Village and Topsfield overlapped. The situation was the subject of angry conversation in many Village halls, especially in those whose masters owned — or thought they owned — some of the disputed land. The problem did not dismay Ensign Richard Davenport, however, for he moved out of Salem Town and into Salem Village.

There was plenty else to argue about locally. One of the most prominent members of Salem Church, Lady Deborah Moody, had joined the procession of contentious Massachusetts women. She had dared to say that nowhere in the scriptures was infant baptism mentioned; rather, that baptism by total immersion as an adult was the ritual of the Lord, and she would not back off from that position.

The church people were taken aback that they had an Anabaptist in their very bosom. The Rev. Edward Norris first admonished her, then suspended her from the fellowship, and at last, in a solemn ceremony, after the service on a Sunday morning, excommunicated her. Almost no one in the congregation would be able to forget the ritual; it was a simple act, but impressive and frightening. Priscilla and her daughters discussed it over and over in the farmhouse in the woods. They could not understand such behavior, nor such dire heresy. Everyone in the communities of Salem and Lynn kept track of Lady Deborah's transactions — the selling of her property, her preparations to depart, and at last the start of her journey out of the jurisdiction toward Long Island. Clearly, there was to be no such thing as "Religious Freedom" in Massachusetts Bay except for those who were card-carrying Puritans of a particular stripe.

The news was bad out of England. In the spring, when the fighting had been renewed, the king had continued to do well, taking up where he had left off at the beginning of the winter. Some of the sailors brought word of a local hero: Roger Williams had gone to England for the purpose of obtaining a charter from the Long Parliament for his colony of Rhode Island. He had met the great Puritan poet John Milton and Oliver Cromwell and succeeded in his quest. It was his purpose to attempt to run his colony on the principle of the separation of powers between Church and State. Many of the Massachusetts clergy and elders looked upon that idea as a greater heresy than that of Lady Deborah — for was not the New Jerusalem to be founded upon the Covenant with God? How could a colony be run by the masses who were, most of them, not even members of local churches? How could the people be governed by leaders not of the Covenant? They shook their heads, these leaders, and knew they had been right to banish the renegade minister; yet, withal, he was giving the Devil foothold on New England's shores, just as they had feared. Nor could they forgive *their* Parliament for helping him to do it. They could not even imagine the reasons for Parliament's action.

The ships docking in Salem now and then brought a book for sale, or stowed in some seaman's ditty chest, and it was by means of one of these, a pamphlet titled *A Most Certain, Strange, and True Discovery of a Witch, Being Overtaken by Some of the Parliamentary Forces*, that the Salemites learned of a fantastic wartime episode, a battle waged with the Devil, as it were, between times in the Revolution: A portion of Cromwell's army, under Robert Devereux, Earl of Essex, had been in Newbury. Some of the soldiers had seen a woman apparently walking on the water. According to the pamphlet, "They could perceive there was a plank or deal overshadowed with a little shallow water that she stood upon…turning and winding it which way she pleased." The men had decided she must be a witch, used her for target practice, and dispatched her.

In the early fall there was news from New Haven, another Providence of God: Indians had murdered the notorious Antinomian heretic and suspected witch Anne Hutchinson in an August raid. No sooner had God made known his will in this case, however, than the Massachusetts government found it necessary to convoke a synod at

Cambridge which the Rev. Mr. Edward Norris attended. Its purpose was to discuss tactics to be invoked in the Newbury, Massachusetts, case: Presbyterianism was being introduced into the colony — there could be no greater threat to the idea of Congregational Puritanism than a hierarchical State Puritanism with its Protestant mimicry of the priestly classes of Rome. At the synod one of the lesser ministers was heard to remark on the peculiar coincidence of place names in the recent English witch episode and the Presbyterian threat, "Newbury." He was glared to silence, but later in the fall his witticism was recalled with dread when news reached New England of the Long Parliament's latest action: In order to win Scotland's alliance in the war with King Charles it had subscribed to the Solemn League and Covenant which promised, in effect, that England would be governed by the Presbyterian system after the great victory. Governor Winthrop and the General Court, the clergy, the elders, and most church members reacted with shocked outrage and bafflement to the bulletin.

On the 17th of October the Putnams put aside all these and other considerations to gather at the meetinghouse in Lynn for the marriage of Thomas Putnam and Ann Holyoke. The ceremony was conducted in the bride's church by the controversial and contentious Rev. Thomas Cobbett who had, only a bit earlier, sworn out two complaints, one against William Winter of Lynn for having said Mr. Cobbett spoke against the ordinance of infant baptism, and the other against Henry Walton for having stated publicly, "I would as leave to hear a dog bark as to hear Master Cobbett preach."

Priscilla and the girls wept quietly at the ceremony; old John looked proud, Nathaniel was solemn, and John, Jr., blushed. Thomas, when he carried the bride over the threshold, was careful to step across the sill with his right foot first. He realized it was foolish to think that evil would follow if he did it left foot first, but there was no sense in tempting fate.

There was a poor harvest in the land that year, and food was scarce for most, but Thomas Putnam and his family prospered nevertheless.

William Lilly had perfected his astrological system, and he brought out for the year 1644 the first of his projected annual series of almanacs, *Merlinus Anglicus Junior*, full of prophecies and predictions about everything from weather to war. It attracted the attention of the public and sold very well; it even aroused the interest of some influential members of the Long Parliament, including Elias Ashmole who had acquired a number of the books in the library of the late Dr. John Dee, including one of the old seer's diaries.

Lilly's "system" was not entirely dependent upon readings of the stars, however. He was an avaricious follower of current events; he was developing a network of domestic and foreign correspondents that kept him informed of what was happening abroad and in various parts of the Realm, and he was an astute analyst of trends and likelihoods. As the year went on people began to speak of the accuracy of his forecasts.

The New Englanders kept their eyes on significant events of an omenical nature as well. Capt. John Chaddock's 30-ton pinnace lay in Boston harbor, manned and fitted, ready to weigh anchor for Trinidad. The captain went ashore and while he was gone his crew of eight fell to drinking and carousing. One of the men struck a light with his pistol and two nearby barrels of gunpowder blew up. Five in the cabin were killed, but three who were forward managed to save themselves in a boat. Governor Winthrop saw in the event God's vengeance upon irreligious men.

On the 18th day of January, sixteen days after the Chaddock pinnace was blasted, there were strange lights and voices in the sky near the scene of the explosion. A ghostly voice was heard to say, "Boy, boy, come away!" Rumors had been circulating that the man who had struck the light had been known to profess himself a necromancer — one who called up the dead. A Virginian, he was suspected of having murdered his master there and fled. The Boston magistrates had not been notified of the act, however, until after the man had blown himself up. The authorities noted that four of the five bodies had been found, but the murderer's had not been.

On the 21st day of March the Massachusetts General Court was reorganized over an insignificant case that had been in litigation for a long while. A suit over a sow owned by Goodwife Sherman had resulted in the Assistants voting one way, and the Deputies voting another. As a result, the two bodies were divided into two houses, and the Colony was thenceforth to be governed by a bicameral legislature. The House of Deputies chose William Hathorne of Salem as its first Speaker. In the Spring John Endicott of Salem was elected Governor.

John Endicott was keeping his eye on Thomas Morton in Plymouth. Just as he suspected, Morton did not ship for England but prepared to go to Maine. John Endicott lay in wait for him if he should enter Massachusetts jurisdiction — which Morton did by touching at Gloucester, but John Endicott missed him.

In England King Charles' forces began to move, and the tide of war shifted against him in favor of the Puritans. The Scots had come into the battle on the promise of fulfillment of the Solemn League and Covenant. Oliver Cromwell had emerged as a brilliant commander, and he had begun to whip into shape the entire Eastern Army. He and his Ironsides linked up with the Scottish army at Marston Moor, and the combined forces scored a brilliant victory over the Royalists. Charles was forced to go on the defensive. The entire Puritan army was reorganized on the example of the Ironsides, and it began to be called the New Model.

In London on the king's birthday, May 29th, three mock suns were seen in the heavens. William Lilly in June, following up on the success of his astrological almanac, published two books, *Supernatural Sight* and *The White King's Prophecy* which sold 1800 copies in three days. The prodigy Robert Boyle, who had been touring the continent for several years, returned to England at the age of seventeen and discovered that in his absence his father, the Earl of Cork, had died and left him the manor of Stalbridge in Dorsetshire. Robert settled into it and began to devote his life to the study of The New Philosophy.

The war in England nearly came to New England on the 23rd of May, but it was narrowly averted. Captain Stagg in a London ship carrying a privateer warrant from Parliament came alongside a Royalist merchantman off Charlestown and took her as a prize. A crowd of colonists collected on Windmill Hill to watch what they thought would be a battle, and some Bostonians with goods aboard the merchantman began to riot. However, the authorities managed to calm people down and overt trouble was avoided. Within a few days the magistrates and the elders of the church met at Salem to debate what was to be done. Stagg warned that to prevent him from keeping his prize was to defy Parliament. On the other hand, not to allow him to keep it would mean that the colony was siding with the king. The issue was decided at length in favor of Capt. Stagg, inasmuch as the colony was already in trouble with the king, and it could not afford to defy Parliament as well, especially inasmuch as Parliament was doing so well in the field. It was thought good, however, to keep Castle Island in Boston Harbor ready for any future emergencies of the kind, and Ensign Richard Davenport of Salem was made commander of the fortification.

Old John Putnam, was appointed to patrol Salem with Emanuel Downing and others. Otherwise, things there proceeded normally — births and deaths occurred, among the latter being that of Nathaniel Ingersoll, Sr.

In August Thomas Morton dared to set foot in Boston itself, and John Endicott had him. He was taken before the Court to be tried — now that the colony had definitely taken sides — as a king's man. He was thrown into prison and heavily fined. Considering Morton's patent poverty, the magistrates had no hope of recovering the fine.

On the 26th of August there was another omen. At 9:00 p.m., John Winthrop wrote in his journal, "there fell a great flame of fire down towards Pullen Point; it lighted the air far about it: It was no lightning, for the sky was very clear."

At the end of September in Salem it was "ordered that a note be published on the next lecture day that such as have children to be kept at school, would bring in their names and what they will give for one whole year; and also that, if any poor body hath children or a child to be put to school and not able to pay for their schooling, that the Town will pay it by a rate" or levy.

At about the same time that school was opening and the crops ripening toward harvest, Goodman Cornish of Agamenticus was discovered slain. When his wife and her purported lover, a man named Footman, were brought into the presence of the corpse, the body was observed to bleed freshly again, a sure sign of their guilt to accompany testimony regarding Goody Cornish's lascivious carriage and lewdness. She was convicted and executed.

Matthew Hopkins, an unsuccessful barrister of Manningtree in Essex, England, and a Puritan, had during the winter been reading several books on the subject of witchcraft. By the spring of 1645 he had finished King James' *Demonology*, Potts' account of the Lancashire witches, and Bernard's *Guide to Grandjurymen*. Thus prepared, he set out to become the Witch-Finder General of England in the midst of the Revolution.

His first discovery was Elizabeth Clarke who had but one leg. Hopkins roused the neighbors to denounce her, set up a grilling system, and soon had five other women suspects besides Mother Clarke. His success attracted the attention of John Stearne who joined him in his activities. Before long they had a list of thiry-two suspects, all of whom, after preliminary examinations, were bound over to Chelmsford Sessions.

The principal method Hopkins and Stearne used was discovery on the bodies of the suspects the witch teat or Devil's mark — some sort of seemingly unnatural excrescence on the body, said to be cold and unfeeling, where the witch's familiar demons were supposed to suckle blood. Goody Clarke had such a growth, and on the 25th of March she was hanged after she had been induced to admit she had had "carnal copulation with the Devil six or seven years," according to Hopkins, "three or four times a week...in the shape of a proper gentleman." Such cases of sexual intercourse with incubi were said to be common on the part of women, and with succubi, rather common on the part of men who had made a pact with Satan. The demons came in the night, masked in dreams, and traces of their activities could often be found upon the bed. At the trial of Mother Clarke, Hopkins and Stearne swore that they had seen various imps in animal shape about the woman — shapes that vanished as people approached. Such testimony was corroborated by neighbors and by a new member of the detective agency, Mary Phillips.

A majority of the Chelmsford witches confessed after they had been tested: At first one of Hopkins' favorite methods of testing, besides searching for the witch teat, was "swimming" — the women were thrown into a pond or stream after their hands had been tied by the thumbs behind them so that they could not swim. If they sank, and possibly drowned, the women were innocent; if they floated, they were guilty, for the water, out of sympathy with holy water used in baptism, had rejected them.

By the time that hostilities had recommenced after the winter truce, the New Model army was in excellent shape and fine morale. Oliver Cromwell had been made Lieutenant General in Command of the Parliamentary cavalry, and the Commander-in-chief was Thomas Fairfax. The New Model met the Royalist army at Naseby, and the king was soundly defeated. Charles managed to escape from the battlefield to Scotland where he was offered the opportunity to put his signature to the Solemn League and Covenant, which he refused to do. Meanwhile, Oliver Cromwell met the last organized body of Royalists under Sir Jacob Astley at Stow-on-the-Wold and utterly destroyed it.

In London William Lilly was tending to business while the battles raged, as were most people. He brought out a reprint of Mother Shipton's *Prophecy*, and another book of his own, *Starry Messenger*, which was an interpretation of the significance of the mock suns that had been seen over London the previous year. Unfortunately, it was not an interpretation that pleased Parliament; Lilly was summoned before the Parliamentary Committee on a charge of publishing treasonable material, but he argued well, and the charge was dropped.

The General Court of Massachusetts Bay decided to rotate its sessions among the towns of Boston, Cambridge, and Salem successively, and in the latter place on the 6th of April there was a fire at the home of Emanuel Downing. His family was at church when his catted chimney caught fire and burned the dwelling to the ground. George Downing, his son and a Harvard graduate, left for England to become Chaplain in Sir Thomas Fairfax's troops, for the regiment of Colonel Okye.

William Hathorne was once more chosen Speaker of the House of Deputies, and he sat for the trial of one of his Salem neighbors, Townsend Bishop, who had conceived doubts about the rite of infant baptism. Mr. Bishop was induced to leave town permanently. Another Bishop — Edward Bishop, Sr., no relative of Townsend — was admitted to the Salem church.

On the 18th of June the General Court appointed Thomas Putnam, Thomas Leighton, and Edward Burcham justices of small causes for the town of Lynn for one year. Richard Graves traveled to Boston to take part in a dispute over some bronze molds used in his trade of pewtering. It was a relatively dull summer in Massachusetts, and the main topic of conversation was the foreign news — both the Puritan victories and the witchcraft trials.

On the 26th of July the trials resumed at Chelmsford in Essex, but Hopkins had been busy elsewhere as well, and a new trial began at Bury

St. Edmunds, Suffolk, Justice Matthew Hale presiding. The Parliamentary Commission of Oyer and Terminer objected in August to Hopkins' method of testing for witches by swimming suspects, but it allowed other methods: Starvation, solitary confinement, forced walking to exhaustion, continuous cross-legged stool sitting, and watching the suspects to keep them awake till they confessed.

In addition, Judge Hale ruled that spectral evidence was admissible as proof of witchcraft. People who had been "possessed" by the Devil and who were tormented by the specters of the witches, made accusations against the witches. Since no one but they — certainly not the Court — could see the specters, if such evidence were dismissed there would be nothing on which to base convictions except testimony regarding maleficia conducted by the witches against cattle, persons, and so forth.

The question was, could the Devil, with God's permission, send specters in the shapes of the witches *and of innocent people* to torment afflicted persons, or could the Devil send only the specters of true witches — those who had made a pact with Satan — to do harm? Judge Hale resolved the dilemma by ruling in favor of the latter situation. The jury was instructed to convict on the basis of spectral evidence, even spectral evidence that took place in court before the jury's very eyes, where the possessed people writhed and screamed (in pain) on the floor and pointed to the person sitting in the prisoner's box as the source of their afflictions.

On the 29th of July many of the Chelmsford witches were accused of murder by means of sympathetic magic. Eight were accused, in addition, of having incubi; nine of merely entertaining familiars. Two of these latter were found guilty but reprieved. All of the women's familiars were either pets or other small animals such as squirrels, mice, or moles. One woman who, when rescued from Hopkins by her friends and neighbors, said, after her recovery, that she had confessed only under torture. When she was informed that she had sworn to having a familiar called Nan, she replied, "I know of nothing of that name, but I have a pullet that sometimes I call Nan."

Bishop Francis Hutchinson gave it as his opinion that "when the witch finders had kept the poor people without meat or sleep till they knew not well what they said, then, to ease themselves of their tortures, they told them tales of their dogs and cats and kittens." The judges — Robert Rich, Earl of Warwick, and Sir Harbottle Grimston — sentenced nineteen of the Chelmsford witches to death by hanging; eight were bound over to the next session; one was found not guilty and released, and four died in prison before the trial began.

By the time the Chelmsford trial ended Hopkins and his band of witch-prickers had roused a veritable storm of witchcraft in Essex, Norfolk and Suffolk, sometimes visiting towns on request but more often freelancing, collecting fees for each witch discovered. The Witch-Finder General was growing wealthy. At Suffolk Sessions in Bury St. Edmunds two hundred people were under suspicion of being witches. One of these was John Lowes, a seventy-year-old minister who was forced to confession by means of watching and forced running for several consecutive days. At last he admitted he had signed a pact with the Devil; suckled four demons named Flo, Bess, Tom and Mary; cast spells on livestock, and sent specters to sink a ship off Harwich with the loss of fourteen lives. Though he retracted his confession, he was denied benefit of clergy at his execution. On the scaffold he therefore recited his own burial service.

On the eighth of September Hopkins was in Aldeburgh, Suffolk, where he left his assistant witch-pricker, Mary Phillips, to gather evidence: When a witch teat was found she stuck it with a pin to see if the suspect felt pain. If the person did not, it was considered proof of witchery. During the same month the *Moderate Intelligencer*, a newsmagazine of Parliament, raised a mild demurrer to Hopkins' activities. "Diverse are condemned," it said, "and some are executed, and more like to be. Life is precious, and there is need of great inquisition before it is taken away."

But Matthew Hopkins was too quick for such trifling criticism. In Faversham, Kent, three witches were under indictment — Joan Coriden, Jane Hold, and Joan Williford. On the 24th of September Joan Williford confessed that seven years earlier a demon had appeared to her in the shape of a small dog. She had made a pact with him; her pet name for the familiar was Bunny. Later she contradicted herself and said the pact had in fact been made twenty years earlier. She implicated others including Jane Holt, Elizabeth Harris, and Joan Argoll who, in company with her, had indulged in the practice of various maleficia by means of their familiars. She, Joan Coriden and Jane Holt were hanged on September 29th.

During this time in Massachusetts Thomas Morton had been brought from jail before the magistrates, freed, and rebanished, but he was not transported to England; rather, he left for Agamenticus in Maine, south of Casco on the coast, Mount Agamenticus being a set of three moderate elevations four miles from the sea and a well-known landmark to mariners.

On the 25th of August Ann Putnam was born, the first child of Thomas and Ann Holyoke Putnam. The family gathered to await the birth. Old John and his sons sat in the dooryard or wandered around the farm waiting for word from the women who attended the young wife. At last Phoebe notified them that the birth had gone well. "It is a fine girl," she said, but the men thought they detected a note of disappointment in her voice. Thomas was amazed at the sense of relief he felt — he did not at all regret that it was a girl. He had been thinking primarily of his wife. His first question was, "Is my wife well?"

"Very well, but tired," Phoebe told him. "You may come and see her." Nathaniel took Tom's hand and pumped it, as did young John. The father put his arm about his eldest son and said, "The Lord has been merciful and kind. I have a grandchild and you have a daughter. Let us see the child and then give thanks." They followed Phoebe into the house and into the birthing room. When the men walked in the women gathered about the bed parted to allow Thomas passage.

He stood next to the bed and noted with astonishment the immense and mysterious radiance that shone from the face of his wife. The small head of a flat-faced infant lay swaddled beside her, cradled in her right arm. "Well done, woman," he said.

Ann noticed that his voice cracked. "I am sorry it is not a son," she said, but Thomas could detect no trace of true sorrow about her.

"The next child will be a son. This one is a delight to behold." He stooped to peer into the baby's dark eyes. Ann laughed tiredly at the look of bewilderment on his face. She reached over with her left hand and took his. Neither said anything.

"She needs to rest now," Priscilla said. Thomas squeezed Ann's fingers. "I shall be nearby," he said. The baby was asleep. As he left the room he turned to see that his wife was falling asleep as well, and the circle of women had reformed.

Springfield on the 27th of October witnessed the marriage by the Rev. George Moxon of the town's sawyer and brickmaker, Hugh Parsons, with a young woman named Mary Lewis. It was a significant event in the village by the river, lost in the woods of the west. Hugh had a reputation as an odd person, but a good many townsfolk thought Mary even stranger. It was certainly an interesting match. One or two of the villagers were known to suspect that Hugh Parsons had some kind of occult traffic, for he sharpened his saws in the night when decent men were asleep and out of the noxious vapors of darkness. Mary, too, had come in for her share of speculation. But the Parsonses settled into a routine, and soon the harvest was upon the people.

The war had not been forgotten, nor the danger of Indian attacks. On November 3rd the town of Salem ordered that the ordnance and cannon they had been assembling be mounted. Two days later the General Court gave villagers living in portions of Ipswich and Salem at a distance from the centers of the towns permission to begin a church of their own. Ipswich was unhappy about it, but the Court was adamant, and Topsfield Parish was organized.

Margaret Page was back in town, and the Selectmen felt it to be their duty to see that she was kept busy. On the 15th of December they agreed "that if Brother Browning do accept of 50 shillings for Margaret Page to keep her at work this year, then she shall not be sent to the prison, and the town is willing to give it; otherwise it is agreed she shall be sent to prison."

John Winthrop wrote in his journal that, on the same day, "There appeared about noon, upon the north side of the sun, a great part of a circle like a rainbow, with the horns reversed, and upon each side of the sun, east and west, a bright light." He noted, further, "This was the earliest and sharpest winter we had since we arrived in the country, and it was as vehement cold to the southward as here."

On the 20th of December Matthew Hopkins, who was still on the road in England, dropped back in on his assistant Mary Phillips, still testing for witches at Aldeburgh, Kent, to see how the hunt was progressing. It had been a most impressive year, as the productions of the presses testified. By the end of the year three pamphlets had been published. One, which dealt with the Faversham witches, was titled, *The Examination, Confession, Trial, and Execution of Joan Williford, Joan Coriden, and Jane Holt*; another, *A True and Exact Relation*, treated of the Chelmsford trials, but it was the third, *A True Relation of the Arraignment of Eighteen Witches at St. Edmundsbury*, that detailed Sir Matthew Hale's handling of the trials using spectral evidence that attracted most attention both in England and Massachusetts Bay. It was not long before several copies were circulating in New England among the clergy and others.

Matthew Hopkins hadn't stayed overlong on his second trip to Aldeburgh, for he was a busy man, but he found time in his schedule to make a third stop there on the 7th of January, 1646. He took reports from Mary Phillips on local progress, made suggestions, and pointed out how matters might be expedited in particular instances. He had done very well elsewhere, for in Suffolk alone he had been responsible for at least one-hundred-twenty-four accusations of witchcraft and sixty-eight hangings. He had also been extending his operations into the counties of Bedford, Cambridge, Huntingdon and Northampton.

There were omens once again in New England. About the middle of January Winthrop wrote that there "were seen three suns, about the sun-setting." It seemed that nothing could happen in England without its belated reflections in the Bay Colony.

In Casco, Maine, a young woman named Mary Martin had been left with her sister in the house of her father when he had been called to England on business. Mary's family was well connected, her grandfather having been the mayor of Plymouth, England. When her father left, there was living in the house with the Martin sisters a Mr. Mitton who wasted little time in seducing Mary. Not long afterward Mary made arrangements to come to Boston to be the servant of Mrs. Nehemiah Bourne who, when the young woman arrived, found she liked her very much. Mary was in Boston in time to witness the phenomenon Winthrop wrote about in his diary for the middle of February when there were seen to be "two suns at sun-rising; the one continued close to the horizon while the other (which was the true sun) arose about half an hour."

Nor was this all. "At Ipswich there was a calf brought forth with one head, and three mouths, three noses, and six eyes. What these prodigies portended," Winthrop wrote, "the Lord only knows, which in his due time he will manifest." Meanwhile, there was an epidemic to worry about, which he described as "a malignant fever" from which people generally "died within a few days, but if they passed the crisis on the 8th day, they recovered."

Not all cases of Satan's scourge were alike, and some of them were difficult to diagnose as one illness, not another. A normal case required an incubation period of from ten to fourteen days during which time the sufferer might or might not complain of discomfort. Suddenly, there would be a rigor and a high fever, sometimes hot enough to cause permanent damage to the brain. The pulse would be fast, there would be intense headache, vomiting, severe back pains. On occasion there would be convulsions accompanied by delirium during which the patient would rave, sometimes talking nonsense, at other times roaring of demons and nightmares. These symptoms continued for two full days with varying intensity. Sometimes one would notice on the sufferer, in the regions of the lower abdomen and inner thighs, a diffuse scarlet and slight spots like those of scarlet fever.

The third day the redness spread to the forehead and roots of the hair, then to the face, breaking upward at last into what looked like pimples over the entire body — there was fever and itching. The eruption continued for two more days. Then the pimples changed and became blisters filled with clear fluid, each about the bigness of a pea; gradually the fluid darkened until the eighth or ninth day when they became larger and pus-filled. The flesh generally swelled and flamed, transforming the victim into an unrecognizable travesty of his or her former self. Nor were the pustules confined to the skin of the body, for the mouth, nostrils and throat were filled with them as well, sometimes to the point where the sufferer was choked to death at that time. The blisters began to break, and the odor was terrible, a musky, fetid stench. The patient drooled excessively and his voice was changed into a harsh rasp. Fever returned on the eight or ninth day as well, sometimes severely.

Again there would often be convulsions, delirium, coma, or restive trembling of the limbs and head. If this crisis were passed, as Winthrop noted, the patient would stand a good chance of living if complications did not set in. The broken blisters would begin to stop oozing and to dry up on the ninth or tenth day, leaving behind the characteristic pock marks covered by scabs which eventually would drop off, leaving their scars exposed.

It was a fearful disease, and a rabid one, native to Asia, and now it began to wreak its havoc in the New World as well as the old. It would often run through an entire family, killing some and leaving others behind scarred for life both physically and emotionally, sometimes mentally as well. Children who witnessed it would understand it not much worse than the adults, but the images of the convulsed and raving members would remain in their memories for a long while, if the youngsters were old enough to remember anything at all. It seemed to them — and to the adults as well — that demons had been loosed among them.

The war in England had about run its course. In the spring Parliament's forces mopped up the last few Royalist strongholds. No sooner had the enemy without been defeated, however, than the Puritans had to face the conflicts among their own factions. Protestants of various hues had come together against the King, but now that he had been removed from immediate concern the sects began to fall away from one another. Most of the Puritans were still loyal to the Church of England, but Parliament had agreed to do away with Episcopacy and substitute Presbyterianism. Some Puritans were independents who wanted every parish to be autonomous within a loose Congregational structure. Other small groups, such as the Baptists, disagreed with strict Calvinist doctrine. No one seemed to be able to agree with anyone else on what should be done with the state church.

One minister in Huntingdonshire, however, had had enough of Matthew Hopkins, the "Witch-Finder General." In April the Rev. John Gaule stood in the pulpit and denounced him, and in retaliation Hopkins threatened to descend upon the town to force Gaule to retract. The minister was unintimidated, and he published a booklet titled *Select Cases of Conscience* which exposed Hopkins and his methods.

Suddenly, the mania ceased, and Hopkins' bookings collapsed. Judges in court began to question Hopkins about his tortures and the fees he collected. During the summer the Witch-Finder General found it expedient to retire, a wealthy man, to his home in Manningtree to begin to write a reply to Gaule's book. John Stearne, on the other hand, feared animosity in Manningtree and retired to Bury St. Edmunds.

In New England another minister published a book of quite a different kind from that of John Gaule. The Rev. John Eliot had been doing missionary work among the Indians, and in order to do his job well he had learned their language. Further, he had transcribed their vocabulary to the English alphabet, and he published the *Algonquin Grammar* which attracted a good deal of interest both at home and in England.

During the spring William Hathorne of Salem had again been chosen Speaker of the House of Deputies. The General Court established a fine of five shillings for every church absence, and Mary Oliver once again became a public spectacle when she was sentenced to be tied to the whipping post with a slit stick on her tongue for saying, "All ministers in the country be bloodthirsty men."

Thomas and Mary Bowen testified in court against Jane James of Marblehead. The previous year John Bartoll had said in court, "I can prove Jane James is a common liar, thief, and a false and forsworn woman." Goodwife James had been before the court earlier, in 1639, for her children's thievery in the home of Anthony Thatcher. Now, Thomas Bowen and his wife gave their oath that she had spoken evilly to William Barber in Bowen's house, and Barber had shouted at her, "Get out of doors, you filthy old bawd, or else I will cuttle your hide, you filthy old baggage!" He had picked up a firebrand from the ingle and made as if to throw it at her, but had restrained himself.

On the nineteenth of May Dr. Robert Child and six others presented the Assistants and the General Court with a petition complaining "of the suppression of liberty and the exercise of arbitrary authority" by the theocratic government of the colony. Havoc reigned in the pulpits throughout the Bay. It was not long before the petitioners were carried before the Court and ruinously fined. Then the magistrates made the discovery that Child had drawn up another petition to Parliament and was preparing to sail for England. He and one other petitioner were arrested, their baggage searched, and the petition confiscated.

But Thomas Fowle, a third member of the group, managed to elude the authorities and sail with copies of both petitions. On the voyage a storm arose to threaten the ship. Some of the passengers aboard recalled that the Rev. John Cotton, in his Thursday lecture, had said that if any ship had aboard it any complaint against God's people, it would be the cause of great storms. When this became generally known aboard ship the passengers crowded about Fowle, clamoring for him to throw the papers overboard. But Fowle had a great deal of presence of mind. Since he had several copies of the petition to the General Court, he threw one over the side. The passengers were greatly relieved when at last the winds subsided. Upon the ship's reaching England some of the passengers spread the report that a miracle had taken place at sea. Fowle went about taking the steps necessary to present his petitions to Parliament.

When Elias Ashmole at last met William Lilly, whose almanacs he greatly admired, they spoke of several things having to do with the scientific and the occult. One of these was the recent death in Europe of Sendigovius, the successor of Alexander Seton. Ashmole was able to interest Lilly with conversation of the antiquities Elias had been studying, of some manuscripts Ashmole had managed to get hold of that had belonged to Dr. John Dee and his son Arthur Dee, of the Hopkins-Gaule affair — they avoided the topic of the Revolution. It was a pleasant encounter.

New England in July had two unpleasant encounters. In the heat of the summer there had come a caterpillar scourge to blight the crops — Biblical precedents were scoured and cited from the pulpit. The second conflict was even more curious: The General Court called for a synod of the churches, but the Child-Fowle treason had somehow begun to spread insidiously, for the Boston and Salem churches took offense on the ground that the civil government was not to interfere with church matters, though it was quite all right for the churches to have their say in matters governmental. Further, the idea had originally come from some of the church elders, and it looked as though the elders intended to have the Court pass ecclesiastical laws derived from the proceedings of the synod. Altogether, it looked very Presbyterian and, sure enough, the Presbyterians objected on the grounds that not to hold a synod might anger Parliament. The synod was set for September first, but the struggle continued. Boston, Salem, and Hingam churches refused to send delegates, and the synod was adjourned until the 8th of June of the following year, since nothing could be accomplished at the current session.

Fall set in and the harvest was gathered. The maples flamed red, the beeches yellow, the oaks russet. The stooks stood in the field, and the wind began to chill. Then, On November fourth, it rose to a great gale and blew the roof off the house where the Lady Deborah Moody had lived — blew it off with people inside who never woke until the morning when they were astonished to see the sky instead of the ceiling over their heads. Everyone in Salem talked about the amazing phenomenon.

Rumors began to percolate up from the valley of the Connecticut River that in Windsor, the town between Springfield and Hartford that had originally been a Plymouth Colony trading post, Alice Young and others had been accused of witchcraft. The news reached Springfield much sooner than it did Salem, and it served to confirm the opinions of many of Judge William Pynchon's followers. Pynchon still ran his town with an iron hand, notwithstanding the fact that a board of Selectmen had been duly elected. It was the old man who set town policy, not the citizenry who were well cowed. Now and then one or two would furtively exchange grumbles or take a complaint to the Rev. George Moxon, but he would do nothing to interfere with the civil arm. So long as Pynchon kept to the secular side of the road, Moxon could not see his way clear to step across the line dividing it from the spiritual. Besides, his eldest daughter, Martha, ever since she had heard of the Windsor witches, had been acting in a peculiar manner, and he was too busy worrying about the Devil to bother much about a dictator.

During the fall in Boston Mrs. Nehemiah Bourne was approached by an acquaintance, a local midwife, who informed her that her maid, Mary Martin, was obviously pregnant and, since she was unmarried, there was obviously something she didn't know about going on in her house. Mrs. Bourne was outraged at the suggestion, no matter how delicately put, and politely but firmly sent the midwife out of her home. Nevertheless, on December 10th Mary delivered herself of her infant in a back room of the Bourne home. It was born alive and healthy. Mary attempted to kill it, but was at first unsuccessful. A second attempt succeeded, and she hid the body in a chest. The midwife immediately spotted the change in Mary's body, but Mrs. Bourne noticed nothing, for she was too busy preparing to leave for England to join her husband who had returned to serve in the Puritan army.

No sooner had Mrs. Bourne left than Mary moved into another house, and the midwife publicly accused Mistress Martin of having murdered her child. When Mary was examined, she confessed to having burned the body of a stillborn child, but the authorities conducted a search and discovered the baby's corpse. The midwife reported the baby had bled afresh when its mother approached. Mary Martin was accused of witchcraft and murder.

Terrified, the young woman broke down and confessed to the murder; she even admitted she had had carnal relations with another man besides the child's father, Mr. Mitton — a person named Sears — but she denied any knowledge of witchcraft. She was thrown into prison and bound over for trial.

The Salem people added the Mary Martin affair to their stock of lore regarding witches — it had been a banner year in this respect, not only locally but abroad as well. True, there was not much of substance to the rumors at home, but from abroad the witchcraft pamphlets had begun to come in aboard the ships and to circulate among the villagers of the Bay. The most recent was entitled, *The Witches of Huntingdon*. It was much better received than the Rev. Mr. Gaule's debunking of Matthew Hopkins.

By the end of February 1647 the Salem artillery had still not been mounted on its carriages. Fortunately, no enemy was in sight, and the town Selectmen continued to try to get their defenses in order. Too, they were having trouble with Margaret Page, still in town, and still a burden. Someone among the Selectmen came up with a brilliant idea — or perhaps it was Mary Oliver's own to make a little money. At any rate, it was decided that the two women deserved each other, and "Capt. Hathorne and Mr. Corwin, being appointed to make an agreement with Goodwife Oliver for the entertaining of Margaret Page, have made this agreement: viz., the said G. Oliver is to give Margaret Page house room and to keep her to work for sixpence per week; and hath sold" Margaret "bed and bolster for six shillings sixpence and two blankets of cotton cloth to cover her at three shillings per yard; and this to be paid in Indian corn at two shillings eightpence per bushel. And in case Margaret Page be removed from thence, the bedding to be removed as being the Town's. Capt. Hathorne and Mr. Jonathan Corwin have engaged themselfes for the payment of it, and the town is to pay them back again."

By March the news that the petitions of the previous year had made a stir in England had gotten back to Massachusetts. Two Salemites who had signed one of the complaining documents, Samuel Maverick and William Clark, were arraigned before the General Court and bound over for trial.

March 18th was set for the day of Mary Martin's execution. On that day, before the hanging, Rev. William Thomson of Braintree exhorted her to confess to the charge of witchcraft as well as to fornication and murder, but Mary was adamant in denying it. However, she freely agreed that she deserved death for her other crimes, and she met it bravely.

All did not go well with Mary Martin. After she had been turned off the gallows ladder she swung but was not choked, nor was her neck snapped. She stared forward as she dangled and turned in the air and croaked, "What do you mean to do?" Her words stirred several in the horrified crowd to action. They stepped forward and lifted her up by the ankles to take the tension off the rope; the hangman bent down to readjust the knot; her holders let go, and at last she strangled in the spring air.

The day after, a barn in Salem was struck by a sheet of lightning that ignited the thatch and destroyed it and all its contents of maize and hay. On April 4th old John Putnam was admitted to the fellowship of the Salem church.

In Springfield during the spring Martha Moxon, eldest daughter of the Rev. George Moxon, went into convulsions, began to rave that she was tormented by demons. It was as folk had feared — there were more witches in New England than had come to light at Windsor, Connecticut. But what an awesome thing it was to see Satan possessing the body of the minister's child! For his part Moxon had no doubt as to the reality of Martha's torment. He prayed and fasted with her, but it seemed to do little good. Soon the entire village was drawn into the situation with neighbors crowding into the parsonage to witness the terrible struggles of the girl — and then her sister as well! — with the Serpent.

The Scottish army had gone home in January leaving King Charles behind. He was taken into protective custody by the Parliamentary Commissioners, and forthwith he entered into negotiations with Parliament which had ordered the New Model army disbanded without back pay, for the treasury was empty. The army refused, however, to disperse. The soldiers organized themselves, elected leaders, and charged them to prepare plans of action.

Parliament, transformed suddenly from a government with an army to a government with no army, no money, and no king, attempted to come to terms with Charles with regard to establishing Presbyterianism for a certain number of years and other matters, but on June 3rd the army arrested the monarch. Then the army turned to occupy London and to overwhelm Parliament. The King was placed under guard in Hampton Court. Charles began to intrigue, playing the army and Parliament off against each other, making deals secretly with one, then the other.

On the 26th of May Alice Young of Windsor, Connecticut, gained the distinction of becoming the first witch to be hanged in British North America. She had been tried, condemned, and executed in Hartford. Connecticut had managed to set a precedent, though only because Mary Martin had been obdurate in her denials-to-the-death at Boston. A good many Springfield people were present at Alice Young's hanging, having come by water down the Connecticut River. Among these were the Rev. George Moxon and Judge William Pynchon.

When they returned to Springfield the minister was insistent that his daughters Martha Moxon and Rebecca Moxon tell him who it was that tormented them. At last they spoke — it was the brickmaker, Hugh Parsons, who appeared to them in their visions. The parson swore out a complaint against Parsons who was placed under arrest and questioned in a preliminary examination by Judge Pynchon.

The Springfield settlement was still an unstable one, and Judge Pynchon knew it. He doubted whether a witchhunt would improve matters much. Aside from unsubstantiated claims on the part of some townspeople to the effect that Hugh Parsons did such strange things as grind his saws in the night and mutter threats under his breath against people who he thought were doing him ill, there was only the spectral evidence of Martha and Rebecca Moxon to stand against him. Judge Pynchon did not allow spectral evidence, despite the impressive spectacle of the preacher's girls writhing on the floor of the courthouse. He dismissed the charge.

The Rev. Mr. Moxon was amazed and infuriated. The judge had, in effect, called his daughters liars. Since the minister supported his children's testimony and had sworn in affidavits that, in his judgment, the torments were real, Pynchon had not only called into question his integrity, but he had undermined the church's authority among the parishioners. Nevertheless, Judge Pynchon refused to be swayed from his course, and he forcefully put down all objections. For the first time since the founding of Springfield Judge Pynchon had an open enemy, and a powerful one; others were only slightly less vocal — they were as sure that witchcraft was being performed as Moxon, but there was nothing they could do, for the judge had been well within his rights to act as he had — he was able to cite as recent a case as that of Hopkins in England and Rev. John Gaule's opinions of what constituted proper evidence in a court of law and in the sight of the Puritan church.

The case never reached the General Court, which made a concession to democracy during the year by passing a law that gave men who were not freemen, but were of good character, the right to act as jurymen, to vote in town meetings, and to act as town officers. Still, many were not satisfied, for only church members continued to have universal franchise. The legislature also passed anti-Catholic regulations. Many of the colony's Irish indentured servants were Catholic.

A Salem town meeting finally decided it had to do something drastic about Margaret Page, and it was decided that she should be shipped back to England. The town also decided to attach "the goods of Mr. Hugh Peter," their former minister, at that moment Chaplain to the New Model, "...for a debt due to the town concerning part of a barque that Robert Codman hath."

Christopher Young, the man from whom Richard Graves was supposed to have stolen fence rails, died in Wenham, and his alchemical hobby came to light, for he had several pewter alchemy spoons, plus a pipkin and some other shabby laboratory equipment. It was a poor estate. Matthew Whipple of Ipswich, who also died, was found to have owned 21 brass alchemical spoons.

On the 14th of November compulsory education was voted for the Massachusetts Bay Colony. Elementary education was required of towns of one hundred or more; secondary schools were to be required as well. The preamble of the law read, "It being one chief prospect of the old deluder Satan to keep men from the knowledge of the Scriptures, as in former times by keeping [the scriptures] in an unknown tongue…that the true sense and meaning of the original might be clouded by false glosses of saint-seeming deceivers, that learning may not be buried in the grave[s] of our fathers…."

In England Matthew Hopkins died of tuberculosis in Manningtree, but not before he had completed his book which was published by the end of the year. Titled, *The Discovery of Witches* it rebutted John Gaule's tract, but it appeared too late to do either Hopkins or the Rev. George Moxon of Springfield much good.

King Charles on the day after Christmas sealed his fate with another of his secret agreements. He signed a document with the Scottish Commissioners agreeing to establish Presbyterianism as the state church of England for a period of three years and to suppress all other sects in return for their restoring him to the throne.

In 1648 four of the eight Chelmsford witches who had been remanded to the next sessions for trial in July of 1645 were still in prison, the English were still pondering the fate of their king, and Charles continued to play both ends against the middle.

In Massachusetts Bay on March 2nd Mary Oliver was before the courts again, this time for a whole series of offenses: She had abused Capt. William Hathorne, Speaker of the House of Deputies; she had abused Goodman Gutch by telling him, "I hope to tear your flesh in pieces, and all such as you are!" Mary had gone to his house in a joyful good mood, under some sort of religious ecstasy. There she had found some townspeople who, like her, were not members of the church, and she had cried, "Lift up your heads! Your salvation draweth near!"

When Gutch reminded her that she had already been punished for this sort of thing she replied, "I came out of that with a scarf and a ring." One word had led to another, and Gutch had done his duty. Driven to a fine rage, Mary condemned the whole country by spitting out, "You in New England are thieves and robbers!" Before the local magistrates Mary was told to give bond for her good behavior but, refusing to do it, she was sent to Boston jail to await trial at the next Salem sessions of the Court.

At that session Margaret Jones of Charlestown was tried for witchcraft. Evidence was given in that after an argument with some of her neighbors their livestock took sick and died. When a portion of the enchanted animals' anatomy had been burned, Margaret had been drawn to the fire by sympathetic magnetism as the person who had cast the spell, and suspicion was vindicated.

The woman had long been suspected of witchcraft. She had such a malignant touch that if she laid her hands upon anyone in anger, whether man, woman, child or beast, soon that being would be taken with attacks of nausea and vomiting, or would fall violently ill in some other way. Further, she had long practiced folk medicine openly. Though her remedies were of the most ordinary sort — herb simples and such — they had effects far stronger than were warranted. She told her patients that if they wouldn't use her medicines they would never be healed, and several who had dared to defy her testified that what she said was true.

Beyond her practice of physic, Margaret Jones told fortunes and made forecasts. She knew and heard things she could not, in the opinions of her accusers, possibly have known and heard. Before her trial she had been given a body search and a witch teat had been found in her "secret parts." While she was in prison, according to John Winthrop, "in the clear daylight, there was seen in her arms, she sitting on the floor, and her clothes up, etc., a little child, which ran from her into another room, and the officer following it, it was vanished. The like child was seen in two other places to which she had relation; and one maid that saw it fell sick upon it and was cured by...Margaret, who used means to be employed to that end." Which meant that a young woman had fallen to fits while being tormented by Margaret's specter, and was cured by the witch's touch.

"Her behavior at her trial was very intemperate — lying notoriously and railing upon the jury and witnesses...." The judges were outraged by her behavior and impressed with Matthew Hopkins' successes as detailed in his book. Margaret Jones was certainly a witch; she was convicted, and the court set June 15th as the date for her execution. Her husband, Thomas Jones, also indicted, was not to be tried.

In Springfield in March Hugh Parsons visited the home of Rice and Blanche Bodortha to discuss a complaint Rice had about some bricks Parsons had sold him. Mrs. Bodortha thought nothing of inserting an insulting remark about the bricks into the conversation and Hugh turned upon her to say, "Gammer, you needed not have said anything. I spoke not to you, but I shall remember you when you little think on it." Rice was incensed at Parsons for speaking so threateningly to his wife.

Not long after Parsons' visit — a few days — Blanche one night was preparing for bed. She took off her waistcoat of red shag cotton and went to hang it up on a pin when, holding it, she saw a flickering, like candlelight, cross the inside of the waistcoat three times. Evidently she was unfamiliar with the phenomenon of static electricity. She laid the waistcoat down, picked the garment up again to see if firelight might not have caused the effect, but decided not, inasmuch as there was a double Indian blanket hung across the bed between her and the fire. It was much too early in the year for fireflies. On several other nights she tried the same experiment, but could not reproduce the phenomenon.

On a Friday in April Mrs. Bodortha, who was expecting a child, lay down in bed and nodded off, but within an hour she woke and felt, as she described it, "a soreness about her heart." The pain increased and spread to her left shoulder and her neck. She sat up to ease the pain, which felt like knives, and found she couldn't lie back down but had to be propped up with a bag of cotton wool. A neighbor, Widow Thomas Marshfield, was called in to attend her during the days over the weekend while the pain continued. About noon on Monday it began to abate at last, and by Tuesday it was, she said, "pretty well gone." At that point she had a sudden flash of revelation: Hugh Parsons had threatened to "remember" her when she least expected it. She confided this thought to her gossip, Widow Marshfield, who nodded grimly — it was no wonder.

The story soon got around town, and eventually it reached Mary, Hugh Parsons' wife. Indignant, she said to several, "It must have been the Widow Marshfield that bewitched her, not my husband, for it was Goody Marshfield who was there when she had her pains."

Thomas Putnam, Thomas Leighton, and Edward Burcham had their terms renewed as justices of small claims in Lynn for the following year. Thomas' brother Nathaniel had been married to Elizabeth, daughter of Richard and Alice Hutchinson of Salem Village, and both were admitted to the fellowship of the Salem church. Young John Putnam reached legal age at twenty-one on the 27th of May, and his apprenticeship to Governor John Endicott was ended. Things were progressing very well for the family who had become important members of the twin communities of Salem and Lynn.

In Springfield Mary Parsons gave birth to her second child and first son, Samuel, on the 8th of June. On the 15th young John Putnam journeyed up to Boston to witness the hanging of Margaret Jones. A number of other Salemites went as well, and so did 12-year-old John Hale of Charlestown who was attended by his parents. Many children were present, for hangings were considered to be exemplary to the young. Before she was taken to the gallows her Charlestown minister and neighbors attempted to persuade Margaret to confess the charges against her. They were unsuccessful; John Hale was bewildered and awed by her behavior.

The witch acted just as badly at her execution. When she was given the opportunity to address the crowd as she stood on the ladder, she denied her guilt vehemently and railed at the crowd until she was turned off. According to Gov. John Winthrop, "The same day and hour she was executed there was a very great tempest at Connecticut which blew down many trees, etc." But Margaret Jones' friend Alice Stratton was unimpressed by such phenomena, because she continued to defend her by saying that Margaret "died wrongfully" and that "her blood would be required at the magistrates' hands." Alice Stratton would be the next witch to be considered by the magistrates.

There had been other signs and portents recently. On the day the oft-postponed synod finally met the Rev. John Allen of Dedham was preaching when a snake got up into the pew behind the preacher where the Elders were sitting. Some of them shifted to avoid it, but one of the Elders, Goodman Thomson of Braintree, stepped on its head and stuck it with a fish spear, killing it. Winthrop saw this as a Divine Providence, the snake being the Devil who, having failed twice before to keep the synod from going on, tried a third time. Eventually the synod concluded its business and drew up the "Cambridge Platform" which added a synod to Congregationalism but not a permanent one as in Presbyterianism. It would be an emergency colloquium, to be convened only when necessary. The document agreed with the English Westminster Confession in matters of faith, but objected to the Parliamentary agreement with the Scots with regard to church organization.

On the 24th of June Margaret, daughter of Mr. & Mrs. Henry Smith of Springfield, died. Four days later the *Welcome* of Boston, a 300-ton ship at anchor in Boston Harbor off Charlestown, where Margaret Jones had lived, began rolling in calm weather. The crew shifted the ballast, added more, but the violent rolling continued.

The county court of Boston heard of it, and they heard, too, that Margaret Jones' widower, Thomas, was aboard, attempting to leave the colony. They issued a warrant to take him off the ship — one of the judges said the ship would quit heaving as soon as he was off it and in prison. A constable was sent to the ship and, according to Winthrop, "as the officer went and was passing over the ferry, one said to him, 'You can tame men sometimes; can't you tame a ship?' The officer answered, 'I have that here that — it may be — will tame her and make her be quiet,' and with that showed his warrant. And at the same instant, she began to stop and presently stayed, and after he was put in prison, moved no more."

Winthrop continued, "There appeared over the harbor of New Haven, in the evening, the form of a keel of a ship with three masts, in which were suddenly added all the tackling and sails, and presently after, upon the top of the poop, a man standing with one hand akimbo under his left side, and in his right hand a sword stretched out toward the sea. Then from the side of the ship which was away from the town there arose a great smoke which covered all the ship, and in that smoke she vanished away, but some saw her keel sink into the water. This was seen by many men and women, and it continued about a quarter of an hour."

Two days later — six days after the death of her sister — Sarah Smith of Springfield died. Mary Parsons began to think that perhaps her neighbors were right about her husband and suspected he might, indeed, have witch-murdered the girls, for hadn't she heard him say he would get even with Mr. Smith for sundry petty reasons? At the first opportunity Mary Parsons inspected her husband's body in his sleep, searching for the Devil's mark, but she could find none, unless they were in his "secret parts." She began to participate in the village gossip, spreading hints of her suspicions. When Hugh Parsons heard of it at last he said, "My wife is the worst enemy that I have. If anybody bespeak evil of me, she will speak as ill and as much as anybody else."

The Scots invaded England in support of King Charles I, and his perfidy became known. Cromwell, however, had little difficulty in defeating them and the remaining Royalists who had risen again. The

Independents were disgusted with Parliament for negotiating with the king, and they resolved to pull him all the way down.

William Lilly, unlike the Independents, was completely satisfied with Parliament, for the Council of State in London bestowed on him a pension of 100 pounds per annum and a grant of fifty pounds for his astrological services.

Thomas and Ann Holyoke Putnam of Lynn baptized their second child, another daughter, on the 23rd of July. She was christened Sarah by her parents. Priscilla Putnam doted on her and fretted that the two families lived so far apart. Old John, John, Jr., and Nathaniel were apprehensive about the harvest. Grain was in short supply because so much of it was being shipped out of Boston and Salem to the West Indies. In August, when the first harvest had been taken, great flocks of carrier pigeons arrived in the forests.

The Putnams, like all other men who could carry fowling pieces, took to the woods, and there was a slaughter of the birds, feathers falling out of the sky like snow, and birds like a great hail. The forests and meadows echoed to the reports — if there were no bread during the winter, there would be meat.

After such bounty there came a plague of locusts, or what many at first thought was a plague. The cicada — the seven-year-locust — arrived, and the sound of its call ratcheted through the countryside. Now the farmers regretted that the birds had been killed, for they would have combated the insects. But nothing happened. The locusts did not touch the crops, and the people gave thanks for their preservation.

In September there was a great discovery in Salem: A copper lode was found on the property of Governor John Endicott; a mine was dug and men put to work immediately. On the fourth of October John Endicott took some of his new wealth and bought Henry Chickering's property in Salem for 160 pounds, a considerable sum.

With the fall there arose a new case of witchcraft: Mary Johnson and John and Joan Carrington of Wethersfield, Connecticut, were indicted at Hartford for conducting the Devil's business. It was no time at all till the news arrived in Springfield. Hugh Parsons dropped in on a neighbor where the family and other visitors were talking about it. There was a break in the conversation when Parsons walked in, but discussion resumed eventually. He did not participate, merely listened.

When he went home he told his wife Mary about the visit and the gossip. When he had finished speaking she said, "I hope that God will find out all such wicked persons and purge New England ere it be long."

Parsons cast her a cutting glance but did not respond. Then he bent over, picked up a block of wood from the hearth, and feinted as though to throw it at her. Instead, he threw it onto the hearth. Mary, who had flinched, stood stock-still and glared at him. Finally he told her, "If any trouble do come to me, it will be by your means. You will be the means to hang me."

In Salem on the 11th of November Thomas Putnam was chosen grand juryman. He made it a point to avail himself of Bernard's *Guide to Grandjurymen* and, considering the events recently, to bone up on the proofs of witchcraft contained in it. For a while it looked as though the information might come in handy, for Mary Oliver had left her husband, Thomas, who took ship for England, and she continued contentious. The problem was brought before the magistrates and she was ordered to go back to him, wherever he was, before the next court was held.

In December she counter-attacked. She sued John Robinson for false imprisonment — taking her violently and putting her in the stocks without warrant. The court awarded her ten shillings in damages, which infuriated a good many people. While Mary Oliver's case was in litigation, Mary Johnson of Wethersfield, Connecticut, was convicted of witchcraft on her own confession. The others accused with her were exonerated and freed.

In England on Christmas day the Puritans' purged Parliament attempted once more to come to terms with King Charles, but the effort was a failure. A day or two after Christmas John Aubrey was hunting with friends in Wiltshire. He was not searching for anything but game; nevertheless, as he rode through the village of Avebury he noticed something even the inhabitants had never seen: An enormous prehistoric temple, the greatest in Europe. It was not hidden, certainly, for Avebury was built among its ruins. It was simply that no one had noticed it before, but once Aubrey saw it for what it was, everyone could see.

A new almanac, the first in New England since Capt. Peirce's, was published for the year 1649, and in England Lilly's *Merlinus Anglicus Junior* continued in series. Neither of them dared to predict what everyone seemed to think was inevitable. Indeed, what was left of the army-purged Parliament on the first of January passed a resolution that King Charles I was guilty of treason for having waged war against Parliament and the realm. On the fourth Parliament declared its right to legislate without a sovereign, and on January 6th it formed a special court to try the king. Once matters began to move in this direction they moved swiftly and inexorably. On the 20th the trial began without the benefit of judges, all of whom refused to participate. Charles laughed aloud when he heard himself publicly called a traitor, and he asked by what authority he was being tried, since he *was* the authority. The king was told he was being tried by the people of England who had elected him king. Charles replied that he had not been elected; he was king by inheritance, and England had been so governed for a thousand years. The discussion was curtailed by an abrupt adjournment.

On the 23rd the trial was resumed, but Charles refused still to plead one way or the other; he merely raised his former objections and added others. It was becoming evident that the nation was not united in favor of the trial, for when Charles passed through the ranks of soldiers they shouted, "Justice! Justice!" but the citizens standing behind them cried, "Long live the King!" Among the members of the court itself there was dissension. It was resolved by the 26th, however, and unanimously decided, that he was to be executed.

The next day Charles was brought before the tribunal to hear his sentence read. He asked to be tried before the houses of Parliament and Lords, but he was denied. He attempted to answer the charges against him, but he was silenced and the sentence read. As the soldiers removed him from the chamber Charles said, "I am not suffered to speak. Expect what justice other people will have!"

The king turned stoic during his last days, and his bearing impressed everyone; some of his attendants said he was borne up in his hour of trial by supernatural power. At ten in the morning on the 30th of January he crossed from St. James to Whitehall, telling his guard to "Walk apace!" At two in the afternoon he stepped out of the middle window of Banqueting House onto the scaffold built there. Rank upon rank of Cromwell's soldiers separated him from the enormous crowd, which he was given the opportunity to address. He believed in freedom and liberty as much as anyone, he told them, "but," he said, "I must tell you that their liberty and freedom consists in having government.... It is not their having a share in the government; that is nothing appertaining unto them. A subject and a sovereign are clean different things."

His deportment was resigned and calmly majestic. Few of the spectators were unmoved when he knelt to receive the beheading blow — a great groan rose into the air from the people. The soldiers immediately turned and, with other troops who were waiting, marched upon the multitudes to disperse them by force. At that moment Charles I became a martyr. The Irish, both Catholic and Protestant, lost no time in declaring Charles II in exile to be king, and they attacked the small Puritan army in Ireland. The Scots, too, began to rumble. Among the Puritan forces guarding Edinburgh was Major Thomas Weir, a fierce Presbyterian and adjudged to be as upright a man as any that ever walked the cobbles. Oliver Cromwell turned upon Ireland and, in a bloodbath at Rogheda, proceeded without mercy to put down the rebellion. Parliament turned its attention to governance, and even to giving consideration to its colonies in America. It provided money for the purposes of Christianizing the Indians and founding an Indian Agricultural School.

Witchcraft continued as a major issue in Massachusetts Bay. John Bradstreet was indicted at Ipswich for "having familiarity with the Devil," but he was let off with a sentence of a fine or a whipping, having been convicted only of lying. During the month of May John Matthews in Springfield spoke with Mary Parsons about witches. She said to him, "My husband is a witch."

"How do you know?" Matthews asked.

"The Devil came to him in the night," she replied, "at the bed, and sucked him one night and made him cry out one time — I cannot tell what it should be else but the Devil. He is often tormented in his bowels and cries out as if he were pricked with pins and daggers, and I know not what else it should be, unless it were the Devil that should torment him so."

Sometime toward the end of the month her husband went to the home of Sarah and Alexander Edwards in Long Meadow to buy some milk. Sarah told him, "I will give you a halfpenny worth, but I cannot let you have any more at this time." Hugh, who was working in the area, appeared to be displeased, but he took the milk and left.

Goodwife Edwards had a cow that normally gave three quarts a meal, but the next meal after Parsons' visit it gave only about a quart, and that was of a saffron color. The next meal the milk was diminished in quantity again, and it was of a still different color. At succeeding meals there were less and less milk and stranger and stranger hues — a veritable rainbow dairy! — but the cow appeared to be healthy. After a week the milk returned to its normal white, the quantity increased, and Sarah couldn't think what might have been responsible unless it were Hugh Parsons.

By June the Widow Marshfield had heard of Mary Parsons' allegations regarding her witchcraft, and she took action: She sued Hugh Parsons for his wife's libel. She won the suit and Judge William

Pynchon awarded her damages in the amount of twenty-four bushels of Indian maize.

The General Court of Massachusetts was still uninvolved in the Springfield controversies. It passed a law regulating animal experiments on the part of physicians and detached the town of Marblehead from Salem, among other things.

In Salem itself Richard Hollingsworth was admonished for sleeping at public meeting and for absenting himself therefrom upon occasion. He pled illness and bodily infirmity. Mary Oliver was brought back before the magistrates in July and ordered to return to her husband in England. She was to take the next ship on penalty of a twenty-pound fine.

Hugh Parsons and Anthony Dorchester, together with two other men of Springfield, in September bought equal shares of a butchered cow, including its manure. Dorchester and his consumptive wife Sarah lived with the Parsonses in Springfield. Hugh wanted the root of the tongue of the cow, but it fell through lots to Dorchester's share instead. He took it home, salted the meat, and put it into the meat barrel. On a Sunday afterward, the Dorchesters and the Parsonses were together in the house, but Sarah Dorchester was too ill with tuberculosis to get out of bed without help; the other three adults were preparing to attend Rev. Mr. George Moxon's morning service.

Hugh and Mary left the house with their infant son Samuel first. Before he left, Dorchester took the tongue out of the salt barrel and put it into a boiling pot on the fire, then he followed the Parsonses, leaving his wife behind. After service Dorchester was the first to return. When he entered the house he discovered the tongue was missing from the pot. A few minutes later Mary Parsons came home with the baby, and Dorchester told her the meat was missing. She said, "I wonder how it can be gone?" She went to check the salt barrel in case Dorchester were mistaken, but he was not.

Dorchester said, "I am sure I put it into the boiling kettle."

Mary, musing, replied, "Yes, come to think on it, I saw you pick it and wash it." She paused, then continued, "I fear my husband took it." She told Dorchester that Hugh, who had been carrying the baby when they left, gave it to her when they got near the house of Thomas Merrick. Hugh had been unusually pleasant, she said, but at Merrick's he left her, handing her the baby, and she went on alone — she hadn't seen him again till meeting was almost over. He had come in and sat down on the men's side of the meetinghouse, and afterwards she hadn't seen him either.

When Hugh got home Dorchester suspiciously told him about the missing meat, but Parsons wasn't particularly interested. All he said was, "I think you did not put it in," and dismissed the affair.

Not long afterward in the fall the Parsonses lost their second child, Samuel, to disease. At eight or nine in the morning Jonathan Burt went to the Long Meadow where Hugh Parsons had spent the night alone while his baby was dying. Burt found Parsons under a great oak not far from the Coultons' house. He approached Parsons and told him his child was dead.

Immediately Parsons hurried — "after a light manner," it seemed to Burt — to the Coultons' house and went in. He said to them, "I hear my child is dead, but I will cut a pipe of tobacco first before I go home." His seeming offhandedness amazed and offended the Coultons. When he got home he found a house full of neighbors and a keening, hysterical wife who, when Hugh walked in, cried at him, "Where were you? Do you not know that our baby is dead?" Hugh stood still in the middle of the room, quiet and staring at her, swaying. "You show no sorrow," Mary said. "You have killed him."

On the thirteenth of November, in Salem, Mary Oliver was back in court again, this time accused of having stolen some goats instead of having left for England. She was found guilty and fined. Either she was innocent or she had great gall, for afterward she railed against the governor, calling him "unjust, corrupt, and a wretch." Furthermore, she maintained, "He made me pay for stealing two goats when there was no proof in the world of it."

Her insubordination got her before the judges again; they sentenced her to be whipped next lecture day — not exceeding twenty stripes. Capt. William Hathorne and Emanuel Downing were to see to the execution of the sentence. To add to her woes, Mary was charged by George Ropes with not having returned a spade she had borrowed: She was fined five shillings. But Mary had a way about her, and the whipping was not carried out.

The town made some further grants on the 26th of November. Nathaniel Putnam was allowed fifty acres of land "lying beyond Elias Stileman's farm, bounding upon Mr. Thorndyke and so upon Capt. Hathorne's farm." At the same time Giles Corey received twenty acres.

During the winter in Springfield Hugh Parsons went to pay his fine to the Widow Marshfield. He asked her to abate him twenty shillings, but she refused. "I will not abate anything," she said, "because I have heard that your wife has said the witnesses had taken a false oath" during the lawsuit.

Parsons replied, "Well, if you will not, it had been as good you had — it will be but as wildfire in your house, and as a moth in a garment, and it will do you no good, I'll warrant it. Make account — it is but lent you."

A neighbor of Parsons was Griffin Jones. One Sunday after morning service he went home to have dinner, but his wife stayed to visit and have dinner with a neighbor, before the afternoon service. When he got home Jones laid out his dinner "on a little table made on the cradle head." He looked for a knife, but couldn't find one, though he knew he owned more than two. Finally he went to his shoe repair basket and there found a rusty knife to use.

After he had eaten he put away the leftovers and set the rusty knife on a corner of the table "to cut a pip of tobacco." Before he cut it, though, he stepped outside — not far from the door — to tend to a pig. When he returned, there lay three knives together on the table, which made him blush. He went to cut his tobacco and Hugh Parsons walked in saying, "Where *is* the man?" When he spotted Jones he asked, "Are you ready to go to meeting?"

Jones looked up and replied, "By and by, as soon as I have taken a pipe of tobacco." Hugh sat down and joined him for a smoke.

Another Springfielder, William Branch, went to bed one evening, but before he went to sleep there was a bright light in his room, like fire. A thing like a little boy clambered upon the bed — it had "a face as red as fire." It put its hand under Branch's chin; Branch felt something like scalding water on his back and heard a voice say, "It is done! It is done!" When he could move again Branch woke his wife and told her about his experience. He began to feel ill. He recalled that Hugh Parsons had often come to his house to ask favors, and that he had found it impossible to say no to him.

In England Elias Ashmole was excited about Aubrey's discovery of last year in the town of Avebury. It was a great revelation and a boon to the new science of archeology. Ashmole recalled Dr. John Dee's remarks about the planetarium the ancients had constructed on Glastonbury Plain, and he realized that the old wizard was, in fact, the founder of the science. Ashmole continued to work with his manuscripts, including those by the elder and younger Dee, and to add to his very large collections of books, coins, and other antiquities. During the year he purchased a copy of a new pamphlet titled *The Devil's Delusions*, which detailed the trial and execution of John Palmer and Elizabeth Knot at St. Albans. Elias Ashmole was an indefatigable collector and researcher.

There was a great deal of Satan's scourge of smallpox in New England during the year 1649, most of it confined to Boston, but there it was of epidemic proportions.

Chapter Five

On the 21st of February 1650 the Salem Board of Selectmen assigned William Dodge, Jacob Barney, and Nathaniel Putnam to lay out a highway from the former Townsend Bishop farm to Crane River. Nathaniel was a busy man. At every opportunity — when the weather would permit — he went to his land to clear trees and underbrush, to lay out as much lumber as he could for his house-raising, and to prepare to move into his own home in the spring.

A week after his assignment as highway surveyor, on the 28th, Mary Oliver — who had not yet had her whipping — was the subject of a request on the part of Edmund Batter: He asked that her sentence be respited. The magistrates agreed on condition that she leave Salem on Capt. Joseph Hardy's ship when it sailed, otherwise Capt. William Hathorne and George Downing were to call her forth for her punishment. If ever she returned, her whipping would be waiting for her. On the first of March Mary's fine was remitted so that she could afford to transport herself and her children out of the colony within three weeks.

In Springfield Sara Marshfield, the daughter of Widow Marshfield, was taken with diabolical fits. It was obvious that evil spirits had possessed her. The family recalled what Hugh Parsons had said in the winter when he came to pay his fine. The possessions began to spread.

In April the two-year-old son of Rice and Blanche Bodortha saw an invisible black dog. When Rice asked him whose dog it was he said, "It is Lombard's dog."

Rice told him, "Lombard has no dog."

"No," the child said, "It is Parsons' dog." He continued to see the dog thereafter, sometimes saying, "It is under the stool," or "It is under the cradle," or other places. No adults seemed to remember that when they were children they, too, had had invisible friends or pets.

William Hathorne of Salem was once more chosen as Speaker of the House of Deputies in the spring. Thomas and Ann Holyoke Putnam had another daughter, Mary, and she was baptized in the Salem church on the 19th of May.

In June the inevitable happened: Mary Oliver, who had not yet left, was accused of witchcraft. She was given a preliminary examination — a long one — and at last the truth came out: She confessed to the crime. It was as almost everyone in Salem had long suspected. The Putnams and their neighbors spoke of the situation in ominous tones, heads shaking grimly.

The General Court was in a quandary about what to do with her. Mary was under sentence of exile already. Ought they to hang her? After a great deal of discussion it was decided that the thing to do was to carry out her prior sentence, send her back to England where her husband Thomas had gone, and let the English courts do what they would.

At the first opportunity Mary Oliver was put aboard a ship in chains, together with her children, and the captain was handed a document addressed to the authorities in England explaining the situation. It was a worn and broken woman who settled into her corner between decks to sail toward a questionable fate. There was relief in Salem.

By the time Mary Oliver got to England the Revolution was entering its last stages. Oliver Cromwell was mopping up in Ireland. When he finished he turned to attend to the Scots, for Charles II had arrived in Scotland in person. At Dunbar Cromwell met and defeated an army twice the size of his own. In Edinburgh Major John Weir heard the news and expected the worst.

In London William Lilly, too, experienced reverses: The Council of State terminated its pension to him, but in fact Lilly hardly noticed what to most other men would have been a financial calamity. He had grown so wealthy as an astrologer that he bought a country estate at Hersham in Surrey. Lilly was beginning to get on in years, but others were waiting offstage to step into the astrological starlight. At that very time John Gadbury was the pupil of Nicholas Fiske.

Thomas Lothrop of Salem had come to England for a visit, and when he returned he brought back his sister Ellen with him. They brought back with them two new books, one of them published by Elias Ashmole — a tract on the philosopher's stone by Dr. Arthur Dee; the other was Nathaniel Homes' *Demonology and Theology*, a book critical of the methods in use in cases concerning witchcraft.

Judge William Pynchon in Springfield published a book as well, a religious treatise, though he was no minister. It said some things about religious liberty that the Rev. Mr. George Moxon found to be obnoxious, if not outright heretical. All the antagonism between the men that had been steeping during the past few years broke into the open air when Mr. Moxon denounced Pynchon's book from the pulpit. That public display of hostility encouraged the latent animosities in the congregation to manifest themselves, and opposition to the judge formed rapidly in the community.

During the summer John Lombard laid a trowel and a stick just outside his door. Shortly, two Indians stopped by and came in for a few minutes on business. When he went to look for his trowel, the stick was still there, but the trowel was missing. He and his wife looked for it everywhere but couldn't find it. They assumed the Indians had made off with it. Two days later Hugh Parsons stopped by. As he was standing in the door Lombard saw, over Parsons' shoulder, that the same two Indians were passing by. He called to them. Parsons said, "What do you want of them?"

Lombard answered, "They have stolen my trowel."

Parsons, pointing to the ground beside the door, said, "Look, here it is," and there it was, right where Lombard had left it. Lombard was confounded.

Around the same time Parsons struck a bargain with the Rev. Mr. Moxon to make bricks for the parsonage chimney. As it turned out, Parsons got the worst of the bargain, and he attempted to renege. John Matthews, who was working with Parsons, in discussing the situation said, "Mr. Moxon will hold you to your bargain."

Hugh replied, "If he do, I will be even with him." The same week, Martha Moxon had a new attack of diabolical possession. Not long afterward her sister Rebecca was infected as well. Not only had Moxon had words with Hugh over the bricks, but he had also had to have a talk with Mary Parsons "about another matter." The circumstances were more than suspicious but, despite everything, Judge Pynchon managed to keep the lid on things for a while longer.

William Branch one day that summer went to the Long Meadow. As he passed Parsons' house he was taken with "a strange stiffness" in his thighs, "as if two stakes had been bound" to them. He walked on with great difficulty. His feet burned, and the condition lasted for some time.

Toward the end of the summer Henry Smith, Pynchon's son-in-law, was at the mill to get some meal ground. Parsons was there as well, and he asked Smith to help him out by carrying a sack of meal home for him on his horse, since he was passing not far off. Smith coldly refused and Parsons was offended. Smith rode off with his own sack of meal. He went five or six rods, and then the horse stumbled and fell down. The meal fell off. Smith repacked his sack, remounted, and started again. Two or three rods farther on the horse fell down again. Once more Smith re-stowed his meal and remounted — the same thing happened yet again. Finally, after one more try, they managed to go on without mishap.

On October 26th Mary Parsons gave birth to another son, Joshua, who appeared to be a normally healthy baby. But the new child did nothing to diminish her despair over the loss of her two other children. She believed that Hugh had bewitched them to death, just as he had done to the Smith children.

While things were taking such turns in Springfield, there was abortive diabolism in Marblehead. In September Henry Pease deposed that he had heard Peter Pitford say that Goodwife Jane James was a witch and that he saw her in a boat at sea in the likeness of a cat. Further, Pitford had maintained, according to Pease, that so long as he lived near Mrs. James his garden fruits had not prospered. Pease had heard Pitford call her "Jesabel." When these things came to the attention of Erasmus James, Jane's husband, he sued Pease for slander and won his case.

George and Hannah Langdon of Springfield on the 11th of February 1651 made two puddings in a bag. Because she was holding the baby Mr. Langdon slipped the pudding out of the bag and "it fell into two pieces, lengthwise, and in appearance it was cut straight along as if it had been cut with a knife. It was cut straight along almost the whole length — it lacked but very little."

When he took the second pudding out it, too, was sliced the same way. A neighbor came by and they showed the puddings to him. He agreed it looked as though preternatural forces were at work, but he knew how to break the spell and make the witch show herself: He took a piece of one of the puddings and threw it into the fire. Shortly afterwards George Langdon went out with the neighbor and Goody Bessy Sewall dropped in to sit with Hannah. An hour after the episode with the puddings the two women heard someone at the door. Goody Sewall, who was closest, answered it. Hannah called, "Who is it?"

Mrs. Sewall answered, "It is Hugh Parsons.

Hannah went to the door and Parsons asked, "Is Goodman Langdon to home?"

Hannah replied, "No. What is your errand?" But Parsons spoke of other things. Asked a second tome to state his business, again he changed the subject. The third time she asked, Mrs. Langdon was insistent, and Hugh said, "I came to get some hay of him, but as he is not here, I will ask him another time." He tipped his hat and left.

The next day, the 12th, Hugh spoke to George Langdon, but he mentioned no hay, On the 13th Parsons again met Langdon, but hay was not among the subjects of conversation.

Not long afterward Thomas Miller, Hugh Parsons, Thomas Cooper and others were in the forest felling timber. They stopped for noon dinner and were rather jolly. Parsons took his seat on a log that was stacked somewhat higher than those the rest were sitting on. One of the men said in a low voice, "I wonder why he sits there?"

Miller replied, "To see what we have," and fell to discussing the pudding episode which was the talk of the village. Thomas Cooper began to fidget, feeling uncomfortable that Miller spoke so plainly in front of Parsons, but Hugh at first didn't seem to mind. He joked back at the men. Eventually, though, he grew silent and pensive. When they went back to work a half hour later, Miller cut his leg with an axe.

A day or two later Parsons went to ask Judge Pynchon for enough whiteleather to make a cap for a flail. Pynchon, who spoke to him in the doorway of his home, was quite willing and told Hugh, "Go see my servant Simon Beaumont for it."

Beaumont was in the barnyard hitching up a cart when Parsons found him and made his request. Beaumont replied, "I cannot now stay to give it you, but another time I shall."

Parsons, after some argument, turned sullenly and went home. He told his wife of the episode and said, "It had been as good he had, for he shall get nothing by it."

Mary replied, "Husband, why do you threaten the fellow so? It is likely he was busy."

Later the same day Beaumont was returning to the Pynchon farm with a load of timber when the horses shied at nothing he could see; they broke into a wild run. He was thrown off the wagon and the cartwheels just missed running over him — it ran over the flap of his jacket.

The Parsonses had great trouble of their own at home, for their second son was ill. George Coulton went to their house on an errand. When he went in he found Mary Parsons sitting by the fire with her baby on her lap. Coulton was amazed at the child's condition: "The child's secrets did rot, or were consumed," he told people.

While he was still there Mary told him right in front of her husband, "Though my child be so ill, and I have much to do with it, yet my husband keeps ado at me to help him about his corn." He wanted her, once in a while, to go to the door and throw a handful of corn to the chickens. Mary turned to Hugh and scolded him, insulting him before their guest, but Parsons replied nothing, which made Coulton think there must be something in what Mary said, for he ought to have reproved her for her behavior.

In Salem there was some trouble too — Giles Corey, who lived on Essex Street, had been the victim of a contretemps, and he had taken it to court. He had been in company with Edward Norris, the minister's son and schoolmaster of Salem, Corey testified, on February 26th. "Mr. Edward Norris and I were going towards the brick-kiln," he told the court, when "John Kitchen, going with us, fell a-nipping and pinching of us. And when we came back again, John Kitchen struck up Mr. Edward Norris' heels and mine and fell upon me and catched me by the throat, and held me so long till he had almost stopped my breath. And I said unto John Kitchen, 'This is not good jesting.' And John Kitchen replied, 'This is nothing — I do owe you more than this of old; this is not half of that which you shall have afterwards.' After this he went into his house, and he took stinking water and threw [it] upon us, and took me and thrust me out of doors, and I went my ways. And John Kitchen followed me halfway up the lane or thereabouts.

"Perceiving him to follow me, I went to go over the rails. He took me again and threw me down off the rails and fell a-beating of me until I was all bloody. And, Thomas Bishop being present, I desired him to bear witness of what he saw. Upon my words, he let me rise. As soon as I was up, he fell a-beating of me again."

The Rev. Mr. Moxon's daughters Martha and Rebecca continued in the throes of violent fits in Springfield. They cried, "Hugh Parsons has bewitched his own baby! We will tell! He is there," they cried, pointing at nothing anyone else could see, "Oh! He pinches! He bites! He wants us to sign the Devil's book!"

On Friday, the 21st of February, Parsons went to work with Jonathan Taylor in Constable Thomas Merrick's barn. He said to Taylor, "I desire to ask you a question — who are my accusers?"

Taylor said, "I cannot tell."

"Why do you say so?" Hugh asked. "You can tell — I know you can tell. Was it ever known that a man should be accused and not know his accusers? Tell me who they are, for whatever you tell me shall be as in my own breast."

Taylor shook his head. "I wonder you are so earnest with me to tell you," he said. "You will know soon enough. I will not tell you anything, but I believe your wife will be the biggest accuser."

Just at that moment Hugh saw his wife, through the open barn doors, passing by with Merrick to be examined by Judge Pynchon. He said, "It is likely I shall be examined now. I have often been afraid," Hugh continued, "that my wife is a witch. I have so far suspected her that I tried to examine her body for the Devil's mark, but she resisted saying it was an immodest thing."

That night as they were about to go home Taylor asked Mrs. Merrick for some beer. She said, "Go down into the cellar and draw it." Taylor went, but found he could not draw the tap, no matter how hard he tried. He took a board and knocked the tap to loosen it and tried again — he tried until his hand was raw, but couldn't budge it. He went back up the ladder to the kitchen and told Mrs. Merrick, "I cannot get the tap out."

She laughed and replied, "I am persuaded I will fetch it out with my little finger."

Taylor shook his head. "It is impossible."

"Light a candle and let us go see," she said to Taylor and Parsons. Taylor lit the candle; he, Mrs. Merrick and Hugh went down cellar; Parsons reached out and pulled the tap.

"What!" Taylor asked Goody Merrick, "Are you a witch?"

When they got upstairs again Goody Merrick said to Taylor, "Let me see your hand." She examined it. "I confess it is tender," she said; then, turning to Hugh, "The blood stands in his hand, but I would not have you think it was by witchery, for I think the least child in this house might have got it out."

When Taylor arrived at home full of Goody Merrick's beer, he blew out the lights, went to bed beside his sleeping, pregnant wife — and sat up startled to see the room lighted as though with daylight. He looked at the floor and saw three snakes. He was amazed to see snakes abroad so early in the year. Two of them were large and the other small with blackish and yellow streaks — a garter snake. It came up to the bedside, climbed onto the covers. Taylor knocked it off again. He began to be afraid his wife would wake, see the snakes, and be frightened, so he lay back down and thought, "Let God do what he will." God evidently would do *delirium tremens* whenever it suited Him.

The small snake got back up on the bed and struck him on the forehead — its bite pricked like a needle — and Taylor heard a voice that sounded like Parsons' say, "Death!"

Taylor replied to the invisible voice, "Death? That is a lie. It was never known that such a snake killed a man."

Suddenly, it was dark in the room again and Taylor was "taken with such a strange shaking as if every limb had been pulled in pieces."

Goody Taylor woke and said, "Husband, what ails you that you shake so? Are you cold?"

"No," he replied, "I am hot enough, but I am very ill."

"Shall I rise," she asked, "and warm you some clothes?"

"No," Taylor answered, but he continued to tremble the rest of the night.

The next morning, Saturday, Mrs. Taylor got up and called in some neighbors to witness Jonathan's fever. It lasted the weekend with fits of violent trembling, one of which began at the spot where the snake bit him, and another at his knees.

The Same Saturday, February 22, Hugh Parsons was arrested. As he and Constable Merrick were passing by the Stebbins' house Goody Stebbins cried as he went by the gate, "Ah! Witch! Ah! Witch!" Thereupon she fell into a fit, the first she had ever had.

Judge William Pynchon examined Parsons who asked him, "Do you think there was not some witchcraft in the distemper of Mr. Moxon's children?"

"I question not," Hugh said, "but that there is witchcraft in it; but I wish the saddle may be set upon the right horse."

"Who is the right horse? Do you know of anybody else?"

"No, I am clear for myself, neither do I suspect any other."

"Do you have any grounds to suspect your wife?"

"No," parsons replied, "I do not know that ever I had any such thought of her."

On March 3rd Parsons was in jail in chains, lying by the fire and watched by Thomas Merrick. Hugh groaned and said, twice, "I have a great pain in my belly."

Merrick told him, "If you will go forth to ease yourself, I'll take off the chains and let you go."

"No," Parsons said, "I have no need that way."

Tuesday the 4th of March had been declared by Rev. Mr. Moxon to be a day of public humiliation and fasting. A special service had been called in the village meetinghouse. Jonathan Taylor told his wife, "Though I be ill, I will go thither; I am persuaded I shall be better." And so he was, though not completely well.

That same day Joshua, the Parsonses' son, died of his wasting disease.

On March 15th Thomas Cooper was assigned to watch Mary Parsons under arrest. She told him, "I am now hampered for relating so much as I have done against my husband at Mr. Pynchon's, but if that dumb dog could have but spoken, it would have been better with me than it is. If I might but speak with him before Mr. Pynchon, face to face, I would make that dumb dog to speak!"

Cooper asked her, "Why do you speak so of your husband? Methinks if he were a witch there would be some apparent sign or mark of it appear on his body, for they say witches have teats upon some part of their body, but as far as I hear, there is not any such apparent thing upon his body."

Mary replied, "It is not always so. But why do I say so? For I have no skill in witchery. But why may it not be with him as it was with me that night when I was at Goodman Ashley's? The Devil may come into his body only like a wind and go forth again — for so the Devil told me that night. I think I should have been a witch afore now but that I was afraid to see the Devil lest he should fright me.

"But the Devil told me I should not fear that — 'I will not come in any apparition,' said he, 'but only come into thy body like a wind, and trouble thee but a little while, and presently go forth again.'

"And so I consented, and that night I was with my husband and Goodwife Merrick and Bessy Sewall in John Stebbins' lot — and we were a-plotting for some good cheer — and they made me to go barefoot and make the fires because I had declared so much at Mr. Pynchon's"

Cooper practically fell over himself getting to the door to tell Judge Pynchon what Mary Parsons had just told him. The next day Rebecca and Martha Moxon accused Mary Parsons of tormenting them and giving them fits. It seemed that nearly all the children in town and some of the women were having fits including Mary Bliss Parsons, wife of the well-to-do merchant Joseph Parsons — though she and the accused witch shared a name they were not related. On March 17th Sarah Miller had one of a number of fits she had been tormented with. She cried out, "Get thee gone, Hugh Parsons, get thee gone! If thou wilt not go, I will go to Mr. Pynchon, and he shall have thee away!"

Life was proceeding at a much slower pace in Salem Village. On the 24th of March Nathaniel Putnam was granted "five acres of meadow near Ipswich River." All was in readiness for his house-raising which would be held at the first spate of good weather. Things were quiet in town now that Mary Oliver was gone. Great as the distance was, news of the Springfield disorders had arrived, and the villagers gossiped about them.

On March 27th at Springfield Sarah Miller, wife of Thomas, was visiting at Prudence Morgan's home. While she was there Sarah was taken with some of her fits. Between times on one occasion she looked out of a window and cried, "Look you! There is a man at Goodman Cooper's barn!"

Prudence looked and replied, "No, there is no man there that I can see."

"You might see him if you would," Sarah responded, "but now he is gone." She fell into another fit. When she came back to herself she said again, "Look you! There he is!"

"Who is it?" Prudence asked, peering at nothing.

"It is one in a red waistcoat and a lined cap. It is like Hugh Parsons. He points his finger at me! He would have me come to him!"

"There is nobody there that I can see," Prudence said.

"Yes, there he is, there he is!" Sarah cried.

Mrs. John Stebbins was having fits at home as well. She looked up the chimney. John asked her, "What do you look at?" He noticed that her eye was fixed on something and asked her again.

Finally she replied, with a gesture of strange wonderment, "O, dear! There hangs Hugh Parsons upon the pole." Her husband looked and saw a small pole standing upright in the chimney corner. Just then his wife gave a start backwards and said, "Oh! He will fall down upon me!" She fell into a fit.

On April 4th Jonathan Taylor was watching Mary Parsons overnight. She said, "I have two things to say to you. One is, I forgive you the wrong you have done me; the other is about the three snakes that you saw — they were three witches."

"Who were they?" Taylor asked.

"One was my husband."

"Who were the others?"

"I have pointed at them already," Mary answered, "but you will not believe me." Taylor knew well she meant Goody Merrick and Bessy Sewall, one the wife of the constable and the other a member of an important family. "I am counted but as a dreamer," Mary continued, "but when this dreamer is hanged, then remember what I said to you — the town will not be clear yet. If you had believed that voice that spake to you, you would have died, but seeing you spake to it, and resisted it, it had not power to kill you, for you do not know how my husband hath threatened you."

On the 6th of April Mary Parsons was sent to Boston to be tried for witchcraft, for she was accused of having tormented Martha and Rebecca Moxon and others. The following May 13th Mary was indicted and she entered a plea of innocent. She had been taken gravely ill. Judge William Pynchon was present in the courtroom, silent for the most part, for he was himself in great trouble with the General Court over the publication of his book. It was apparent that he was unhappy about the necessity of his being there, but he had little choice: Pynchon could sit in court under duress as a silent witness, or he could sit there as a defendant on charges of heresy.

Mary Parsons was acquitted on the charge of witchcraft, despite the fact that she was reported to have told the court that when she lost her first baby she grieved greatly and said, "Oh, that I might see my child again!" Whereupon "The Devil in my child's guise came to my bedside and talked with me and asked to get into bed with me, which I allowed for several nights together. And so I entered into a pact with Satan." the court charged her with the murder of her son Joshua, and she confessed she had done it at the command of the Devil. She was convicted and sentenced to be hanged. But the next witch to be executed was not Mary

Parsons, for she was so ill in prison she was reprieved until May 29th; rather, it was Goodwife Basset of Stratford, Connecticut, who went to meet her Maker on May fifteenth. Roger Ludlow had cried out upon her. Under duress she had confessed and implicated others — the town was split with dissension and mutual recrimination, just as was the case in Springfield.

Judge Pynchon took the news of Mary Parsons' confession to Springfield — he had been dismissed as a magistrate, and on the 27th of May Hugh Parsons was cleared of killing his child. On the charge of witchcraft the Springfield jury found him not "legally" guilty; however, his neighbors, Particularly Rev. George Moxon, were not convinced he was not a witch. They decided to send him to Boston for the General Court to handle.

Early in June Hugh arrived in Boston. The grand jury there decided he had had "familiar and wicked converse with the Devil and did diverse devilish practices and witchcraft to the hurt of diverse persons," and they did "leave him to the Court for his further trial for his life. It was not long thereafter that there were rumors that Mary Parsons had died in her cell.

The General Court had been busy with other matters besides the Springfield witchcrafts and Pynchon's heresy. It had approved the *Book of Discipline* and the *Platform of Church Government* which laid out as punishable crimes "idolatry, blasphemy, schism, heresy, venting of corrupt and pernicious opinions, profanation of the Lord's Day," and so forth. Judge William Pynchon saw his name written between the lines of some of these charges, and he decided that the best place for him would be England. He began to get his estate in order.

There was great bitterness in town directed against him on the one hand, and against Rev. George Moxon on the other, for it seemed that everyone was heaping accusations upon everyone else for things that had been said in court, for libelous rumors against one-another, and so forth. Among others, the Widow Marshfield, Goody Merrick and her family, Goody Sewall and hers, and Mary Bliss Parsons had all been tainted.

The possessed children were under suspicion of duplicity, particularly Rebecca and Martha Moxon and Sara Marshfield. The whole atmosphere of the village had been poisoned.

In Salem William Nichols bought two hundred acres of land from Henry Bartholomew, part of it in Salem Village, but most of it beyond the "six-mile extent," and consequently in Topsfield. George Corwin had set up a shop in Salem. His stock included fabrics, hardware, toys, all sorts of locks — in other words, it was a general store. Business was good. John Putnam came in a cart filled with twelve bushels of rye through the woods from Salem Village. He brought his grain into Corwin's store and bartered it for goods — sugar for Priscilla and, for his grandchildren, a doll and a bird whistle.

In the midst of such mundane activities, however, were darker events. Old John and George Corwin, after they had transacted their business, stopped to chat, and they talked of John Getchell's recent accusation against Goodwife Jane James of Marblehead. Getchell had said, "Jane James is an old witch, and I have seen her going in a boat upon the water to Boston," though the woman had been in her yard at home at the time. Erasmus James had brought another suit, this time against Getchell, and won a judgment against him.

Oliver Cromwell in England gained another great victory over the Scots at Worcester, for the Scottish army had invaded England. They capitulated. Because they were Protestant Puritans, the terms they received were generous — not like the brutal repressions that had been heaped upon the Catholic Irish.

The insurrections finally being over, Parliament turned its attention to other matters, including her overseas colonies. It passed the Navigation Act which prohibited goods from being carried between England, her colonies, and Asia, Africa, or America in any but English or English Colonial ships which were to be manned by similar crews.

The astrologer William Poole died and left his books to one Dr. Arder on condition that, "If Dr. Arder gives my wife anything that is mine, I wish the Devil may fetch him body and soul." The doctor cautiously gave Poole's books to William Lilly who in turn handed them over to the Widow Poole. William Poole had been a link between Lilly and Dr. John Dee, for Poole had been a friend of Charles Sledd, and Lilly was sorry at his passing.

William Lilly published during the year a book titled *Monarchy or No Monarchy* that contained, among other things, illustrations of burials after an epidemic and a great fire. A new edition of another book appeared in 1651 as well: Robert Burton's *The Anatomy of Melancholy*, having gone through six editions and revisions since 1621, was published in its final, classic form.

In Lanark, Scotland, a woman entered a barn and stopped dead in her tracks, astonished beyond measure. What she saw was the godly Major Thomas Weir standing on a barrel and having sexual intercourse with a mare. The woman spun about and went immediately to the authorities with her story. It was so preposterous that measures were taken immediately to have her whipped through town by the hangman for lying. Worse had happened to Alice Lake of Dorchester in Massachusetts — she had fallen into the Devil's trap, for he, "appearing to her in the likeness, and acting the part, of a child of hers then lately dead, on whom her heart was much set," had laid his snare in the same way he had for Mary Parsons. Alice Lake, however, did not die in jail, but upon the gallows tree.

Early in 1652 Elizabeth Kendal of Cambridge was accused of the witchcraft murder of a child by the child's nurse who testified that "Mrs. Kendal did make much of the child" and soon afterward it had turned blue and died.

One of Mrs. Kendal's neighbors had been troubled with cats in the night, so he had kept a light burning in his bedroom and a sword handy. One night a cat came close enough for him to strike at it — he hit and wounded it with his blade. The next day he heard Widow Kendal had a sore back. He testified at her trial that he believed in striking the cat he had struck the witch. Widow Kendal's doctor, however, testified that the woman had come to him with her sore back that, on examination, he found to be due to a boil. He let it ripen, lanced it, and she was cured. Nevertheless the evidence was considered to be sufficient against her and things came to a boil: She was convicted and hanged.

The parents of the dead child were Goodman and Goodwife Jennings of Watertown — they were not called to testify at Mrs. Kendal's trial. Richard Brown, who knew the widow and had hoped better of her, made a point of inquiring of the Jenningses — too late, unfortunately — whether they judged Mrs. Kendal had murdered their child. They answered, "No."

The baby's nurse, the night before its death, had "carried out the child and kept it abroad in the cold a long time. The red gum was come out upon it, and the cold had stuck in the gum, and this we judge the cause of the child's death. And Widow Kendal did come that day and make much of the child," but her efforts had been in vain.

Brown discovered that, while he was conducting his investigation, the nurse had been put in prison for adultery, and she had given birth to her bastard in her cell. Richard Brown went down to see her; he told her, "It is just with God to leave you to this wickedness for your murdering Goody Kendal by your false swearing." Shortly thereafter the nurse died in prison of childbed fever and nothing more was done — nothing was left to be done.

There was another birth in Salem Village on March 12th: Thomas Putnam, Jr., first son of Thomas and Ann Holyoke Putnam was born, his parents having moved from Lynn. He was a second decan Pisces. He was in every way a chip off the old block. He was born to bondage and would be an inhibited person. He would have few open feelings, and his response to matters would be silence, but what happened inwardly would not be mirrored by externals, for he would be a contradictory creature, having great depths of imagination. Young Thomas would do his duty by others always, without flinching, and he would be loyal to his family. His introversion and unwillingness to act in his own behalf would leave him open to manipulation by the strong-willed. If he married a demanding woman, she would lead him, and he would do as he was bade.

Back in the Putnams' old county, Buckinghamshire, England, Joan Peterson was well-known as a white witch — her specialties were curing headache and taking hexes off enchanted cattle. But she incurred the hostility of some of her neighbors, and she was indicted in London on charges of trafficking with evil spirits. The Puritan government took an interest in the case. At her trial, quite unexpectedly, the authorities seated on the bench Sir John Danvers who was a member of Oliver Cromwell's council. Friendly witnesses were discouraged from appearing in Joan's defense; Danvers intimidated his fellow judges, and Mrs. Peterson was found guilty. On Monday, April 12th, she was hanged at Tyburn. After another outbreak of witchcraft many years later, no doubt as a pure coincidence, the name of Salem Village would be changed to Danvers, Massachusetts.

Anne Bodenham, "Dr. Lamb's darling," was, like Goody Peterson, a practicing white witch — though the question was how white that was. She lived in Fisherton Anger, Wiltshire, where she was well patronized as a fortune-teller and herb doctor. In her capacity as an herbalogist Anne had become expert in the knowledge of poisons — on occasion she was consulted on the subject by neighbors, as need arose.

A particular client in this regard was Mrs. Goddard who had become convinced that her two daughters were attempting to poison her. She bought from Anne Bodenham three packets containing dried vervain, dried dill, and nail parings to be used in a charm or amulet.

Nicholas Culpepper published a new book titled *The English Physician*, a compendium of herbs listed together with the astrological signs governing, and planetary influences upon, each herb; descriptions of the herbs' physical and medicinal characteristics, and so forth. It was immediately an immensely popular book, destined never to go out of print as far into the distant future as any seer could look. Anne Bodenham owned a copy of the first edition.

According to Culpepper's book the dill that Anne sold Mrs. Goddard was "a gallant expeller of wind" and an excellent laxative; the vervain was an effective antidote to poison. Obviously, Mrs. Goddard's measures against her daughters' suspected murderous intentions were, at that point, purely defensive, and no prescription for poison had passed between the witch and the afflicted woman.

Oliver Cromwell had come up with a plan for Ireland: He proceeded to "settle" the land by forcing rebels to move to other parts from their home territories; by expropriating the rebels' property and moving in English settlers upon it, and by enforcing the penal laws against Catholics. It was a diabolical plan, it seemed to many, particularly to the Irish who were affected.

John Gadbury, who had been living in London where he was a member of William Lilly's group of astrologers, which some called the Invisible College, decided that, considering the climate of the times, it were better for him to leave town. He returned to his native place, Wheatley, near Oxford.

Hugh Parsons was tried at last before the Court of Assistants in Boston on May 12th. The jury decided that there was so much evidence against him that he had to be convicted, but they had certain doubts about the validity of some of the written evidence, so they left the matter up to the General Court.

On the seventeenth of May in Salem Village John Putnam, Sr., was granted some compensatory land by the Salem Selectmen because it had turned out that his original grant of land had not come to fifty full acres. The General Court appointed May 31st, the day when Hugh Parsons' case was to come before it for review, as a Day of Humiliation in consideration, among other things, "of the extent to which Satan prevails among us in respect of witchcraft." But much to everyone's astonishment, the Court reversed his conviction by the Assistants, and he was discharged upon payment of court fees. When he did get out of prison Parsons did not return to Springfield, but eventually settled in Watertown and became as plain a citizen as possible.

Judge William Pynchon also disappeared — into England, leaving the town of Springfield in the hands of his son John. He had no desire to stay to be prosecuted for heresy by Moxon or the Boston clergy; furthermore, his authority had been totally destroyed during the Parsons affair. George fared little better himself. He, too, found the situation impossible, and a while after Pynchon left Moxon gathered up his family — his wife and five children — and embarked for England.

Massachusetts began, against the laws of England, to coin "pine tree money," because of the lack of hard English currency in the colony. Business was growing constantly, and legal — or even illegal — tender was utterly necessary. A shoe mill had been started in Salem; the waterfront was humming, not only with merchant and fishing ships but with such occupations as rigging and sail-making. But landmarks were passing as well. Mrs. Daniel Fairfield petitioned that her husband be allowed to take off the noose he had been wearing in public since his conviction in 1641 for dallying with John Humphrey's young daughters. Mrs. Fairfield's request was granted, but to the folk of Boston and Roxbury, to which towns he was confined, the missing noose changed nothing — Daniel Fairfield was still a pariah.

In Salem Joseph Houlton married Sarah Haynes, daughter of Richard Ingersoll, for whom Joseph had worked as a servant, as John Putnam, Jr., had worked for Gov. John Endicott. Sarah had been married before, being the widow of William Haynes. And on the third of September there was yet another marriage in the Putnam family: John, Jr., took to wife Rebecca Prince, stepdaughter of John Gedney.

In September, too, John Bradstreet of Rowley was indicted again on his own word for having familiarity with the Devil. At his trial on the 28th witnesses against him said that Bradstreet was wont to read in a book of magic and that he maintained he had heard a voice asking him what work Bradstreet had for it to do. Bradstreet had allegedly answered the spirit fearfully, "Go make a bridge of sand over the sea; go make a ladder of sand up to heaven and come down no more." The court ordered that Bradstreet be whipped for a chronic liar, or pay a fine of 20 shillings. It was his second conviction.

On November 18th Ezekiel Cheever, a widower, married Ellen Lothrop, the sister that Capt. Thomas Lothrop had brought back with him from England in 1650. However Salem, gaining on the one hand, lost what it had gained on the other: Emanuel Downing joined the procession of colonists who were returning to England now that the Revolution was successful and the Puritans in power.

By the time he got back to the old country, Downing might have read a chapbook, *A Prodigious and Tragical History* by E. G., Gent., which detailed the recent witchcraft cases in Kent: In Maidstone several people had been accused of witchcraft and murder by sorcery. Elizabeth Hynes of Thorpe had been indicted for having two familiar spirits — a white kitten named Bess and a black one called Katt. The jurors reported "no true bill" in this case, but six other people were indicted for witch murder and hanged.

Another chapbook was published as well, *The Witch of Wapping*, which told the story of Joan Peterson. Late in the year Elias Ashmole published his chemistry compendium, *Theatrum Chemicum Britannicum*, on which he had been working for years. It was a collection of all the unpublished works of the English alchemists and chemists. Once it was out of the way Ashmole turned more or less away from the occult and semi-occult and began to devote most of his time to the study of antiquities and archeology.

The Rump Parliament was no longer representative of any group in England. The army forced Cromwell to dissolve it by force, and to replace it Cromwell called the Barebone Parliament in 1653 which consisted of a hundred and forty members chosen by the army's officers from a nomination list draw up by Independent congregations nationwide. It was a Parliament of reformers and fanatics, and it drew up the Instrument of Government that was the first modern-style constitution. The English Commonwealth was ended, the Protectorate begun with Oliver Cromwell as the first Lord Protector. He immediately launched a war with Spain at sea upon the Spanish Main. It soon became apparent that, despite the existence of a democratic constitution, England was in fact ruled by a military dictatorship that had few friends outside the New Model.

In Fisherton Anger a man named Mason came to see Anne Bodenham — by then an old woman of about eighty — regarding a lawsuit he was contemplating against his father-in-law, Mr. Goddard, the husband of the woman who feared poisoning at the hands of her daughters. Anne made preparation to divine the future: She made an appointment with Mason and when he arrived she took her staff, drew with it a circle upon the earthen floor of her cottage, then she laid a green glass on her book of charms, put an earthen pot full of burning coals inside the circle, and threw a handful of powder into the pot calling, simultaneously, "Beelzebub, Tormentor, Satan, Lucifer — appear! I conjure you!"

Suddenly the back door flew open and the demons materialized in the form of five boys of different sizes who ran around the circle on the floor. The old woman threw some scraps of bread on the floor; the boys picked them up, leaped into the circle over the pot of coals, then ran out of the house the way they had come. Anne Bodenham said to Mr. Mason, "It is clear then — demand of him 1500 pounds at once, and each year 150 pounds, or else you will sue." Their business complete, Mason paid her three shillings for the consultation.

Meanwhile, Goddard's wife had gone from defense to offense. She sent her servant, Ann Styles, to buy some arsenic from Anne Bodenham. When the Goddard girls discovered what their mother was up to, they began to make inquiries.

Ann Styles panicked, stole some of the Goddards' silverware, and ran away. The authorities were alerted, and soon she was apprehended. Upon examination the girl accused Anne Bodenham of witchcraft.

Mistress Styles claimed that Mrs. Bodenham had at one time turned herself into a cat in order to tempt her to serve Satan. The witch then pricked her finger and made her make her mark in a red book containing the roster of people who had sold their souls to the Devil. One of the witch's imps, who were like "great boys with long, shagged black hair," according to Ann Styles, guided her fingers as she signed. When she had done, the company said "Amen," and the imp gave her a coin of silver.

In the ensuing trial Ann Styles went into fits, shouting that a beardless "Black Man" was contending for her soul. When Mrs. Bodenham came near her the girl swooned and recovered when the witch left her vicinity. Anne Bodenham was given a physical examination, and two witch teats were discovered, one on her shoulder and another in her pudenda. The final pieces of evidence were the prick mark on the finger of Ann Styles and the silver coin.

Dr. Lamb's darling was condemned and taken to the scaffold in Salisbury. She pled for beer so that she would be drunk when she was hanged, but she was refused. When she was asked if she wanted a psalm she replied, "Let no psalm be sung, for you are hypocrites. I never have served the Devil, but you serve him. May you be his lackeys in Hell forever!"

Not long after her execution Edmund Bowen published a chapbook with the title *Doctor Lamb's Darling*. The second edition of Culpepper's *English Physician* was also published, for the first edition had disappeared rapidly. The new issue, too, had an enormous popularity. The presses continued to run off a number of other occult books as well; one of these — Henry More's *Antidote against Atheism* — was in favor of the strictest kinds of repression of witchcraft, but another, Robert Filmer's *Advertisement to the Jurymen of England*, was much more moderate and gave an answer to William Perkins' 1608 book.

Much more moderate too were events in Salem Village during the spring of 1653. On the 18th of February Nathaniel and Elizabeth

Hutchinson Putnam had their first child, a son whom they named Samuel. He was baptized in the Salem Church on the 17th of April. Now that the future seemed assured, and he was so old, John Putnam Sr., decided it was time he settled his land upon his sons. He gave the homestead to young John, Jr., who lived with him still, and divided the rest between Thomas and Nathaniel. Henceforward Old John would be titular head of the family only. On the 28th of May John, Jr., and Rebecca Prince Putnam became the parents of a daughter who was christened Rebecca Putnam the Younger, after her mother. She was born eight months after her parents had been married.

John Endicott, Jr., the former Governor's eldest son, married Elizabeth Hawkins of Boston and received the Chickering-Townsend Bishop farm in Salem Village as a wedding gift, but it was not given outright, merely for "present possession."

His neighbors were still reviling the Rev. Mr. Thomas Cobbett of Lynn and he was still hauling them into court for slander and calumny. He had a renewal of his 1643 war with Thomas Wheeler who was convicted of and fined for "profane and foolish dancing, singing, and wanton speeches, probably being drunk" — one of the speeches being an outburst against Mr. Cobbett. Wheeler was ordered to stand at meeting in Lynn while the minister read his confession from the pulpit:

"Whereas I, Thomas Wheeler of Lynn, have been convicted at the last court at Salem for speaking sinful and reproachful speeches against Master Cobbett, calumniating the doctrine by him delivered…., I do acknowledge my great sin and offense in so speaking, humbly entreating those whom it doth concern to pass it by…, promising for the time to come — God helping me — to be more watchful over my words and speeches…."

Edward Bishop, Jr., with his wife Hannah, got into trouble in Salem and was fined for "depredating upon the premises of his neighbors." In Lynn Christopher Collins sued Enoch Golden for the slander of calling Goodwife Collins a witch, but the suit went against him. Something like the same thing happened in New Haven on the fourth of August:

Elizabeth Godman was always willing to see the hand of the Devil in any unusual thing. She had implied that various people in town were witches, but when Mrs. Atwater said, "Elizabeth Godman is a witch, and Hobbamock is her husband," Elizabeth sued for slander. The court, however, decided it was more likely she *was* a witch than that her neighbors were lying, though there was not overwhelming evidence of her having sold her soul to the Devil. The court let her off with a warning to refrain from meddling in her neighbors' affairs.

Charles Browne was sitting one Sabbath day listening to a boring sermon in the gallery of the meetinghouse in Rowley, Massachusetts. Browne sat in the first row and was letting his eyes rove. Suddenly the man beside him — John Godfrey — threw his head back and was seized of a tremendous yawn. Browne was startled by what he saw: Beneath Godfrey's tongue was a strange excrescence of some kind.

Christopher Collins tried to sue Enoch Coldan again in the fall at the court in Salem, but once more the suit was squelched, and he and his wife had to eat gall. More of the same sorts of actions had been taken in Gloucester where several local women, including Agnes Evans, Grace Dutch, Elizabeth Perkins, and Sarah Vinson had brought suit against their neighbors for saying that they were members in good standing of a witches' coven.

The cauldron of Windsor, Connecticut, continued to boil in 1654 — Lydia Golbert had been accused of witchcraft, and her trial would end in an execution. In Salem on the 20th of February John Putnam Jr., was granted "twenty or thirty acres of land" adjoining Capt. Hathorne's farm "in consideration of 12 shillings due for bridge work, and in regard he had none granted formerly." If things were slow in Salem, Connecticut continued to heat up, for Roger Ludlow, who seemed to have some pretensions to the title of Witchfinder General of Connecticut, accused Elizabeth Knapp of Fairfield of witchcraft. She was forced to undergo a body search, and witch teats were found. Eventually she confessed and was convicted.

At her hanging Ludlow said that Goody Knapp had descended the gallows ladder just before she was dispatched and confided to him the name of another witch of the town: Mary Staples. Furthermore, he maintained that when Goody Knapp had been cut down Goody Staples and other women had gone to the graveside where the corpse lay and had examined the body. He said Mrs. Staples had said to her neighbors, "Will you say these are witch's teats? I have such myself, and so have you."

Goodwife Lockwood was said to have replied, "If I had such I would be hanged, and deserve it, too."

Goodwife Odell was supposed to have remarked further that, "No honest woman has such teats." Then all the other women had chimed in and Mrs. Staples had fallen silent.

A number of people corroborated Ludlow's story in court, but others contradicted it. Hester Ward testified that Mrs. Knapp told her Mrs. Staples had been given "two little things, brighter than the day" by an Indian who told her they were Indian gods and that, if she kept them, she would be "so big rich, all one god."

But Roger Ludlow was convicted of slander and ordered "to pay to Thomas Staples, by way of fine, for reparation of his wife's name ten pounds, and for his trouble and charge in following the suit, five pounds more." At the next court session he was fined an additional ten pounds for lying. The community, like Stratford and Springfield before, was rent by dissension and mutual recrimination. Roger Ludlow found it expedient to decamp for Virginia at the earliest opportunity.

Meanwhile, the drought of scandal had broken in Salem: Cornelius Hulett was tried, convicted, and sentenced to be whipped for fornication with Mrs. Elizabeth Due who had confessed her guilt to Rev. Edward Norris, Jr., Master of Salem Latin School, and to others.

In England Oliver Cromwell appointed the witch judge Sir Matthew Hale to be Justice of Common Pleas. Robert Boyle, the prodigy grown to young manhood and membership in the Invisible College of scientists in the new disciplines then emerging, decided to leave his manor, Stalbridge, in Dorset and, like John Gadbury, move to Oxford where he would be nearer his colleagues, some of whom met at Oxford on occasion; all of whom met for more or less regular sessions at Gresham College in London.

The fourth of July in Salem saw the birth of Edward, second son of Thomas and Ann Holyoke Putnam. Edward was a second decan Cancerian and as such would be gripped in struggle with his sexual feelings. He would be the next thing to a poet, full of energy, resourceful and emotional. He would be in tune with the supernatural, subject to revelations, changeful, quick to form opinions, and just as quick to cast them aside when they were no longer useful or viable.

While the Putnams were admiring this latest arrival of the clan, Thomas Wheeler and Rev. Cobbett of Lynn were at it again in the courts. Wheeler had not been true to the conditions of his confession and had taken the liberty of comparing Cobbett to Korah of the Book of Numbers, leader of a revolt against Moses. Once more Wheeler was required to confess his error in meeting, admitting that he had committed evil, "to my own shame and hope for time to come shall be more careful."

On the fourth of September the Putnams once more welcomed a new arrival, this time a girl named Sarah, second child of John, Jr., and Rebecca; she was named after her cousin, born to Thomas and Elizabeth, who had lived for only a short time.

Elizabeth Due next astonished Salem by claiming that the father of her child was Zerbubabel, a son of the old Governor. Zerubabel was a physician who kept a journal in which he listed recipes for all sorts of diseases. One of these was "A powder for the dizziness of the head, falling sickness, and heart qualms that have been oft used." Some of the ingredients included white amber, diarrhodian, seeds of peony, mistletoe, and the filings of a dead man's skull. One was to "Make all into a very fine powder and take of it as much as will lie on a shilling two or three nights together before the new; and before the full moon take it in Saxony or betony water."

Zerubabel had a number of such sympathetic magic medicaments, which he prescribed for patients, as "for a person that is distracted, if it be a woman:

"Take milk of a nurse that gives suck to a male child, and also take a tomcat and cut off one of his ears or a piece of it and let it bleed into the milk, and then let the sick woman drink it — do this three times.

"For sharp and difficult travail in woman with child," Dr. Zerubabel Endicott recommended, "Take a lock of virgin's hair on any part of the head — of half the age of the woman in travail; cut it very small to fine powder, then take twelve ants eggs dried in an oven after the bread is drawn, or otherwise make them dry, and make them to powder with the hair. Give this with a quarter of a pint of red cow's milk, or for want of it, give it in strong ale wort."

Dr. Zerubabel Endicott was outraged by Elizabeth Due's charges, and he brought her to court. She was convicted of slander against this pillar of the community, publicly whipped, and required to stand before the congregation on lecture day with a sign pinned to her hat that read in capital letters, 'A SLANDERER OF MR. ZERUBABEL ENDICOTT."

On the second of October John Putnam Jr., traded the land he had received earlier in the year for "thirty acres of upland" near the farms of Capt. Hathorne, John Bucke, and William Nichols.

In Hampton, New Hampshire, Eunice Cole, wife of William Cole, was a scandal to the town, supposed by many to be able to perform preternatural acts. The town mothers used her name to quiet their screaming children and to get their recalcitrant sons off to school. She was a virago with a nasty disposition — perhaps her poverty and that of her husband had something to do with her nature — and it was rumored that she had made a pact with the Devil.

On the 26th of February 1655 old John Putnam, with partners, bought some rocky land on speculation from the pewterer Richard Graves. They met in John Gedney's tavern in Salem to seal the bargain, and when they were through they drank a glass of beer together. Clearly, Graves thought he had gotten the better of the bargain, and he began to wax loud. John Gedney came over to him and said, "Goodman Graves, you have been overly boisterous in my house before now, and suffered for it. Will not you be calmer?"

Old John clapped Graves, who was glowering at Mr. Gedney, on the shoulder. "Come, let us drink another glass and be done."

"Nay," Graves replied, "I will play you at shovel board, the loser to pay for our beer."

John shook his head, "I will not wager, nor play at games." But one of the other men present took Graves up on his offer and John sat down to watch. When he had finished his glass of beer he exchanged a few friendly words with his youngest son's father-in-law — or, rather, stepfather-in-law — Mr. Gedney, then he took his leave.

During the spring the Selectmen of Hampton, New Hampshire, were having a meeting at the house of Robert Drake. Suddenly the door flew open and Eunice Cole walked in, confronted the men, and demanded that they give her some town aid in the form of firewood and other items. The Selectmen told her, "You have an estate of your own, and need no help of the town."

Eunice snorted. "You can help Goodman Roby, being a lusty man, and I may have none. It should not do."

A few days later Mr. Roby lost a cow and a sheep in what some considered a strange way. One of her neighbors said to Eunice, "You should look for the hand of God in it, for that the town people withdrew their hearts from helping of you."

Eunice answered, "No, 'twas the Devil did it."

Nathaniel Putnam, Jr., second son of Nathaniel and Elizabeth Hutchinson Putnam, was born in Salem Village on the 24th of April and the family rejoiced. Next door, the town of Salem was still having trouble getting its guns and artillery in order. On May 17th the Selectmen ordered that the fortification of Winter Island "be finished with all speed." Ten days later Nathaniel Putnam, Jr., was baptized at Salem meetinghouse. New businesses were continuing to open in town — James Underwood began a bakery. On June 13th Nathaniel Putnam, Sr., was chosen trial juryman of Salem, and on the 17th of August Thomas Putnam, Sr., was made grand juryman. John, Jr., was chosen trial juryman in November.

In New Haven Gammer Godman was again called before the court, having been accused by Mr. Hooke of staling his beer. She was again admonished, as in 1653, for her suspicious carriage, but was freed for lack of evidence.

Ann Hibbins of Boston was the widow of William Hibbins who had been a magistrate of the Court of Assistants and a prominent merchant. Ann was also the sister of Richard Bellingham, Deputy Governor. Her husband, who had died the year previous, had had reverses in his last years and become quite poor.

Mrs. Hibbins, naturally cantankerous, had become increasingly "turbulent and quarrelsome" in her eld and had been censured for her behavior by her church. At last her neighbors accused her of witchcraft. Among other things, two women of her neighborhood had been talking together in the street when Widow Hibbins saw them glancing up at her window. As soon as the opportunity presented itself, Mrs. Hibbins told them, "I know that you were speaking about me." The women told the court that the only way she could have known what the subject of their conversation had been was by witchcraft, not by observation.

Joshua Scottow, a Selectman, gave testimony at Mrs. Hibbins' trial that tended to support her. He was ordered by the Court to write an apology for his witness in favor of the widow who was convicted by the Assistants. However, her case was appealed to the General Court and Widow Hibbins was put into jail to await her new trial.

The Putnams continued to receive the recognition of their fellow townsmen right up to the end of the year, for on the tenth of December

Thomas Putnam, Sr. became the town constable, replacing William Bowen — a member of the town grand jury thus became the town policeman as well.

In New Haven Colony there continued to be ramifications arising out of the Godman witchcraft case, for Nicholas Bailey and his wife were tried, but this time the jury voted to acquit. Closer to Salem, in Ipswich, Goodwife Batchelor was accused of the same crime, but nothing came of it.

In England during the year an important book was published. Its title was *A Candle in the Dark*, and its author was Thomas Ady. It was a book skeptical of many aspects of witchcraft and witchcraft trials, and Ady acknowledged his debt to Reginald Scot's book of 1584, *The Discovery of Witchcraft*. Ady's book was a reply to King James' *Demonology* and Michael Dalton's *Country Justice*, published in 1619.

Thomas Putnam, Sr., was becoming a highly respected member of the Greater Salem community — on March 13th, 1656, he was appointed, with John Porter, Thomas Gardner, and Jacob Barney to lay out roads through John Endicott's farm and the property of others down to the "Great River."

Susannah Trimmings of Dover, New Hampshire, had a strange experience on Sunday, the 30th of March. She was returning home at night with her baby in her arms when she heard a rustling in the woods. She assumed the noise was caused by swine. Shortly, however, an old woman whom she recognized appeared — it was Joan Walford, wife of Thomas Walford: She was wearing a white linen hood over a black hat, the hood tied under her chin. A red waistcoat and petticoat, and a green apron completed her costume. Mrs. Walford approached and asked Susannah, "Where is your consort?"

"I have none," Mrs. Trimmings replied.

"Thy consort is at home by this time," the old woman told her. "Lend me a pound of cotton."

Mrs. Trimmings said, "I have but two pounds in the house, and I would not spare any to my mother."

"You had better have done it," Mrs. Walford answered, shaking her head, "for your sorrow is very great already, and it shall be greater, for you are going on a great journey, but shall never come there." Goody Walford turned to leave, and Susannah felt a "clap of fire" on her back. The witch vanished toward the water in the shape of a cat.

When Susannah managed to get home she was in shock. She moved past her husband silently when he asked, "What is the matter?" She put the baby on the bed and Oliver caught her in his arms and asked again. "What is the trouble?" He had to support her. A third time he said, desperately, "Tell me! Speak! What ails you?" But Susannah was gasping as though something were caught in her throat.

Oliver unlaced her clothes and sat her down. Finally Susannah said, "Lord have mercy upon me, this wicked woman will kill me."

"What woman?"

"Goodwife Walford."

"It is only your weakness makes you say so," Oliver replied.

"No," Susannah said, and she told him what had just happened on the path. "My back is as a flame of fire, and my legs have no feeling."

Oliver pinched her legs, but Susannah felt nothing and didn't flinch. The next day the Trimmingses swore out a complaint against the old woman. On the 18th of April Mrs. Walford was given a preliminary interrogation before the magistrates. Several of her neighbors testified against her, and she was bound over to the next court in Portsmouth in June.

On the 14th of May the case of Ann Hibbins of Boston, which had been pending for a year, was suddenly brought before the General Court. John Endicott, the Governor; Mrs. Hibbins' brother, Richard Bellingham, Deputy Governor, and the rest reviewed the record of her previous trial and asked her how she pleaded. She replied, "Not guilty." But the Court upheld the verdict of the Assistants and Governor John Endicott condemned her to death. The father of the witch-doctor of

Salem ordered the Marshal General to see to it that she "hang till she was dead" on "the 5th day next come fortnight, presently after the lecture at Boston, being the 19th of June next."

On the 6th of June Nathaniel Putnam replaced his brother as constable of Salem. Daniel Fairfield, former resident fornicator, had discovered over the years that the removal of the noose he had been wearing had done nothing to change his status in Boston and Roxbury, so he had petitioned the authorities to allow him to leave for England. His request was granted provided that he never return. The General Court also proclaimed that June 11th was to be "a public day of humiliation" in consideration that the people were "to seek the face of God in behalf of our native country in reference to the abounding of errors, especially those of the Ranters and Quakers that the Protector" — Oliver Cromwell — "may be preserved from the machinations of evil-minded persons...."

Giles Corey was the Salem herdsman, but he found the job not to his liking, so he, too, petitioned — that he be relieved of his responsibility. The Selectmen replied that if he could find a suitable replacement he might quit. And William Brown signed a contract with the Selectmen to repair the Salem meetinghouse.

In Portsmouth in June Mrs. Walford's case was again put off until September, but Ann Hibbins was hanged in Boston on June 19th. It was the opinion of the Rev. Mr. John Norton that her only crime — referring to the telepathic episode when Widow Hibbins spied her neighbors gossiping about her in the street — was in "having more wit than her neighbors." He said this publicly which made those who heard him cringe, for he was an important man, and he was criticizing the government. On the same day that Widow Hibbins was hanged a seventeen-year-old young man named Increase Mather graduated with his class from Harvard College.

There were other social events in the area that summer: Thomas Andrews, the "scholar musician" played at a merriment held at the home of John Andrews in Ipswich, and in Rowley John Godfrey had occasion to be at the house of Mr. & Mrs. Charles Browne. Goodman Browne had cause to believe John Godfrey might be a witch, for he had seen a strange excrescence under Godfrey's tongue three years earlier when Godfrey had yawned at meeting. Browne steered the subject around to witches, and Godfrey was pleased to follow; indeed, he conducted a learned monologue on the topic.

"If witches are not kindly entertained," Godfrey said, "the Devil will appear unto them and ask them if they were grieved or vexed with anybody, and ask them what he should do for them. And, if they would not give them beer and victuals, they might let all the beer run out of the cellar."

"Would you have a glass of beer? some cheese?" Browne asked his guest.

"Aye, that would touch the right place," Godfrey replied, staring at his host. After a long draught he went on, "If witches look steadfastly upon any creature, it will die; and, if it were hard to some witches to take away life, either of man or beast, yet, when they once begin it, then it is easy to them."

Browne looked uneasily away toward his wife who was sitting, with a stiff, blanched look about her, upon the settle.

Mary Bliss Parsons had moved with her husband, Joseph, from Springfield to the new western Massachusetts settlement of Northampton. Notwithstanding the fact that she was the wife of a wealthy man and a matron with numerous children, her reputation as a strange woman had followed her — during the witchcraft episode involving Mary Lewis Parsons and her husband Hugh, Mary Bliss had been the victim of fits and attacks, like the much younger Moxon girls. No one put it into so many words, but there was something unseemly, or, to put it another way, even more unseemly about an adult woman acting like teenage girls, allowing herself to be pitched about by invisible "shapes." One neighbor in particular, Sarah Bridgeman, remembered Mary Bliss from the old days, for she, too, had relocated in Northampton from Springfield with her family. The difference was this:

That, though the two women had very similar backgrounds, Mary Bliss Parsons had all the luck, or so it seemed, at least, to Goody Bridgeman, who wagged her tongue to the effect that Mary was a witch. Mary, through her husband Joseph, prepared to take the matter to court in an action for slander.

Beverly, like Salem Village an outlying district of Salem, was given permission to build its own meetinghouse and to hold services there, but Salem Church insisted that this was being allowed only for the convenience of the settlers; the new church would remain legally merely a branch church of the main body in Salem.

On the 11th of July Deputy Governor Richard Bellingham staved off an invasion of the Massachusetts Bay Colony, having been forewarned. He sent officers to board the small sailing ship *Swallow*, Capt. Simon Kempthorne commanding, to arrest two women named Mary Fisher and Ann Austin before they could come ashore to spread the new blasphemy that people called Quakerism. They were thrown into Boston jail without trial and held for five weeks until arrangements could be made to transport them back "whence they came," to England. Meanwhile it was ordered that their "corrupt books" be "forthwith burnt and destroyed by the common executioner." In jail the women were given a body search to determine if there were witch teats present, but none were found.

On the fifth of September Thomas and Ann Holyoke Putnam were blessed with another baby, a daughter whom they aptly named Deliverance. On the same day in Hampton, New Hampshire, Thomas Coleman accused Eunice Cole of witchcraft. Though nearly everyone in town believed she was a witch, she was "suffered to live" nevertheless, and at about the same time Goody Walford of Dover was finally tried in Portsmouth Court. It was decided that there was insufficient evidence to convict her, and she was released on her good behavior.

At the fall sessions of the General Court the Massachusetts Bay Colony published, on October 21st, some very harsh laws against the heresy of Quakerism. The year ended in Salem with an order on December 29th from the Board of Selectmen: "It is ordered that Lawrence Southwick shall have two shillings per week for keeping of John Talby till the town take further course."

The fourth of March 1657 saw another Putnam enter the world: Priscilla, third child of John, and Rebecca Prince Putnam, was born, and she was followed twenty-two days later by "Little John", another third child, this time of Nathaniel and Elizabeth Hutchinson Putnam. To distinguish him from his uncle and his grandfather, relatives immediately began calling him "Little" John.

Little John Putnam was a first decan Aries, and those in Salem Village who kept track of such things noted that his astrological sign boded him little good. He would be a choleric man, quick to anger, quick to act without thought: His symbol was the rams-horns, and, like a ram, he would burst headlong into contention. Little John Putnam would be egocentric and adventurous; he would brook no opposition to his desires. He would be a brave man, zealous in his duties, hyperactive, and it was written in the stars that he would meet with great misfortune and notoriety. Bridget Wasselby, who was reputed to have insight into such matters, spoke ominously of the birth.

The town ordnance still had not been mounted, but Thomas Oliver was back in town and operating as the bell-ringer of Salem — it was said he considered that Mrs. Wasselby was a handsome young woman, yet nothing was looked for in that direction inasmuch as Bridget was married. Thomas Oliver had returned from England without his wife Mary, and he would not speak of her when he was asked, so people did not know whether to consider him a bachelor or a husbandman. Some of the villagers — Priscilla Putnam in particular — professed to see certain similarities between Mary Oliver and Bridget Wasselby.

William Hathorne was elected Speaker of the House of Deputies for the sixth time. A boy named Thomas West was apprehended in Salem and charged with burglary and stealing on the Sabbath Day — he lost an ear for his iniquity, and Francis Usselton was convicted at Salem Sessions for cursing at Henry Haggett's sow — "A pox of God upon her," he had cried, "and the Devil take her!"

A woman many people called "Mother Goose" lived in town; her real name was Elizabeth Vergoose, but no one called her that. She was a widow, an old woman and a town charge. All the lore of the children of Salem surrounded her, aided and abetted by the mothers. When their children were ill with colds they took goose grease and turpentine, mixed it together into a balm, rubbed it on the children's chests, and wrapped them with flannel cloth. When the youngsters protested they were told, "Mrs. Goose says it must be so," and they were quieted, for mystery surrounded the old woman. Nor was this the only remedy attributed to Goody Goose. It was believed that the upper vertebra of a goose could cure cramps as long as it had never touched the earth since the goose had been killed. For burns, people took elder bark and goose dung, mixed them, and fried them in May butter; more, keeping some on hand from one May to the next protected against fire.

Some of the children predicted the weather by means of the breastbone of a goose — preferably one bought or stolen from Mother Goose. If it were thick in November, there would be a heavy winter. Pink bones forecast mild weather, red ones cold and stormy. A tuft of thick down at the point on the quill where feather began likewise told of a heavy winter. If geese flew south early in the late summer, the Indians foretold a cold and snowy winter; if they returned in the spring in great, high flocks, spring would be wet and long.

One or two of the younger children believed that Mrs. Goose was a witch — at least a white one, but others knew that if she were approached in the proper way she would tell strange stories about animals and fairies, stories the Puritan parents did not much approve of. The old woman was a storehouse of songs and catches as well, and the children of Salem sang a rhyme she had taught them:

"Cups and saucers,
Saucers and cups,
Saucers for kittens,
And cups for pups."

It was a tongue-twister, a game they played to see how many times the lines could be repeated correctly.

Deliverance Putnam was baptized in Salem church on the tenth of May, and the next day Thomas Putnam, Sr. and John Parker were assigned to assess the damage to a town road and cause it to be repaired. The town meeting also "voted that Mr. George Corwin and Jacob Barney are to appear at Ipswich Court to inform the Court of the condition of John Talby, and to advise about his being put in the house of correction at Ipswich."

In June John Hale of Charlestown, who had as a boy witnessed the hanging of a witch, was graduated from Harvard College at the age of twenty-one. He was of an age, and he owned credentials enough, to express himself on matters of doctrine and be listened to with a modicum of respect. There was much to discuss, for the Quakers had begun to invade Massachusetts in increasing numbers, drawn by a lust for martyrdom and the likelihood of it in light of Massachusetts' stringent new laws against their religion.

An elderly couple of Salem, Lawrence and Cassandra Southwick, had dared to entertain two of the berserkers, Christopher Holder and John Copeland. The Southwicks were members of Salem church. When their transgression became known they were arrested and thrown into prison. Laurence was let go soon, but his wife was held seven weeks and fined 40 shillings for owning a tract written by Holder and Copeland. Salem town meeting passed a law, on June 20th, making it a misdemeanor for anyone to entertain a stranger in town without permission from the Selectmen. Now Salem became a particular target for the Quakers, and Magistrate William Hathorne dealt with Anne Coleman, Mary Clark, and three others by having them whipped through the streets of Salem, Dedham, and Boston. Everyone who could walk turned out for the spectacle. The Devil was again threatening Massachusetts Bay.

The town Selectmen on September 14th ordered that Nathaniel Putnam, William Flint, and John Porter meet with representatives of the town of Reading in order to reach agreement on a new highway that was to link the two towns. There was some sort of disagreement between Porter and Nathaniel's father, for eight days later it was "Ordered that the difference betwixt John Porter and John Putnam about a highway over Mr. Sharp's hill shall be viewed by Capt. Trask sometime betwixt this and the last day of the month."

The General Court on the fourteenth of October decided to increase the penalties against Quakerism — the Quakers were beginning to be everywhere — and the convicts could expect thenceforward to be gagged, diseneared, whipped, and/or to have their tongues bored through with a hot iron, depending on the offense and the number of prior convictions.

The government was beset by its own people as well, many of whom continued to complain that they were disenfranchised still. A synod of churches was convened, and it came up with a compromise bill, the Halfway Covenant, which it recommended to the legislature. The Covenant would allow people who had been baptized in infancy, who reaffirmed the baptism as adults, and who had led good lives, to become church members and bring their own children to the church for baptism. The compromise pleased very few on either side. Many church members objected strenuously to this loosening of qualifications for church membership, for it would allow converts as well as lifetime members to vote.

In Easthampton, Long Island, her neighbors accused Elizabeth Garlick of witchcraft. Upon due consideration, the town court decided it was incompetent to judge in such matters. The magistrates being inexperienced in the legal niceties involved and unskilled in occult doctrines. They referred the matter to the General Court of Connecticut.

A popular nonconformist minister of London took ill while he was preaching in the pulpit one Sunday, and not long after he died of a lung infection. His name was Richard Gilpin, and he left behind him a book, *Daemonologia Sacra*, which went exhaustively into the attributes and wiles of Satan and defended the belief in witchcraft in the most fiendish terms. And in Oxford Robert Boyle read about a new German invention, the air pump. He immediately built one himself and began to experiment with it, making improvements in the design as he went along.

On the 17th of February, 1658, Thomas Putnam, Sr., was one of several men asked to canvass Salem for a subscription of money to provide for "the Elders' maintenance." He was asked to handle Salem Village with the help of George Porter. The town settled with Nathaniel Putnam, for the year he was constable, in the amount of one pound 16 shillings.

The relative peace and calm of the Village was rudely shattered when the General Court created the town of Topsfield in the territory that had been in dispute between Salem and Ipswich since 1643. Not only did the Putnams and others own land there, but the entire farms of a number of people who had considered themselves to be residents of Salem Village now belonged to a strange town with which they had no connection at all. Disputes and public furor broke out into the open; letters and petitions were addressed to the Court, to no avail whatsoever.

On the 22nd of the following month Thomas Putnam, Sr., and Jacob Barney were appointed surveyors "for the bridges about the Governor's farm," and they went out to inspect the area about John Endicott's before they turned in their report to the Selectmen. John Putnam Jr., deeded twenty acres to Robert Prince, and then there was a recurrence of Quakerism in the town of Salem. Christopher Holder and John Copeland went to Salem church of a Sabbath, and there were fewer coughs and sneezes in the congregation than usual throughout the service, but nothing untoward happened until the Rev. Mr. Edward Norris had finished. At that moment Holder rose to speak. No sooner had he gotten to his feet than hands took him by the hair behind him, jerked his head back and his body down into the pew, and thrust a glove and a handkerchief into his mouth, gagging him.

Holder and Copeland were immediately sent off to Boston jail where they were thrown into a room with John Rouse. On the 7th of July all three were tried before the Court of Assistants where they debated every point the magistrates made. Three days later they were brought back into Court again and the argument continued — some dared to say the Assistants got the worst of the words. But the Quakers got the worst of the sentence: On July 16th all three of them had their right ears lopped off and were whipped thirty stripes each with a knotted cord. John Burton of Salem — not himself a Quaker — decided that, in conscience, he had to share their exile in Rhode Island as a protest.

In Connecticut the pending trial of Elizabeth Garlick of Long Island was brought up before the General Court. Goody Garlick had been a servant in the home of Capt. Lyon Gardiner. Another of Gardiner's servants had lost a child and had accused Mrs. Garlick of having bewitched it to death. Upon investigation, however, the Court discovered the old woman's accuser had displaced her suckling babe at her breast in favor of an Indian child whom she had accepted pay to nurse, and she had in fact starved her own baby. Mrs. Garlick was found to be not guilty, but her accuser was thrown into prison.

Thomas Putnam, Sr., in Salem on the 18th of August was chosen for grand juryman; five days later Francis Nurse and Richard Sibley were fined for cutting trees in the town Commons. The Southwicks, together with their son Josiah, withdrew from the Salem church to worship in privacy, but it was not to be allowed: They were fined five shillings per week during their absence, sent to prison in Boston, whipped with knotted cords, and their goods — to a value of four pounds thirteen shillings — were expropriated for missing public worship. They were not the only ones: A total of a dozen people of Salem were fined an aggregate of 40 pounds 19 shillings for absenting themselves from services.

On the 3rd of September the Protector Oliver Cromwell, who had rejected the offer of the Crown of England some years earlier, died and his inept son, Richard, succeeded him, but the news did not reach Salem and Massachusetts Bay until much later in the fall. By the 20th of November people knew, and they wondered what would now become of the Protectorate. Nathaniel Putnam was chosen trial juror on November 21st, and Francis Nurse, who had not much liked his last fine, was again fined "for his abusive carriage in the town meeting."

In December — in the town of Andover, which was not far from Salem Village — John Godfrey was haled into court for preternatural reasons. Godfrey had gone to the home of Henry Blaisdell, who owed him money, and demanded payment of the debt. Blaisdell was embarrassed, for he had guests that night, Isabel Holdred and her husband. Godfrey informed Blaisdell that a warrant was out against him for the money, and Constable Lord was on his way. "Will you not pay me?" he asked.

Blaisdell blustered before his guests and his wife. "Yes," he said, "tonight or tomorrow — if we had it; for I believe we shall not have it soon, and so we are in your debt still."

"That is a bitter word," Godfrey said, "I must begin and must send Goodman Lord."

"When thou wilt," Blaisdell returned, "I fear thee not, nor all the Devils in Hell!"

Two days later Isabel Holdred began to have fits and to see apparitions — on the first night a humble-bee, and on the second a bear that grinned at her and shook its claw in her face saying, "Thou sayest thou art not afraid. Thou thinkest Harry Blaisdell's house will save thee!"

Isabel replied, "I hope the Lord Jesus Christ will save me."

The bear was ferocious in its reply: "Thou sayest thou art not afraid of all the devils in Hell, but I will have thy heart's blood within a few hours!"

The next thing Isabel saw was a great snake that frightened her so that she "skipped to Nathan Gould, who was in the opposite chimney-corner, and caught hold of the hair of his head; and her speech was taken away for the space of half an hour."

Fourth, there appeared a great horse. Inasmuch as Thomas Haynes was present, Isabel told him of it, for he could see nothing. Haynes picked up a stick, asked, "Where be it?" She pointed and he swung; she saw him strike it a glancing blow and the "great horse" galloped under the table. She pointed, cried, "There it goes! and, as Haynes prepared to deliver a second blow the horse cantered off to another piece of furniture and made it shake. There were other incidents of similar kind, and Jonathan Singletary told a strange tale about some of them. Godfrey was thrown into jail where he had plenty of time to consider the folly of asking that a debt be repaid him.

Salem appointed a committee of the 29th of January, 1659, which was assigned to treat with the town of Topsfield and settle the border dispute between the towns. The composition of the committee was not calculated to deal with the Topsfielders in a spirit of Christian charity: Two of the four committeemen were Thomas and Nathaniel Putnam; the other two were Jeffrey Massey and Joseph Hutchinson. Nevertheless, the negotiations got under way, and so did the trial of John Godfrey of Andover. Matters proceeded slowly in both instances.

On March 17th reinforcements arrived for the Putnams: Jonathan Putnam, fourth child and first son of John, Jr., and Rebecca Prince Putnam was born. He, too, was a first decan Aries, like Little John, with whom he shared a name. He, too, would be overzealous, overactive, over-adventurous, and doomed to be tainted with dishonor. However, having been born on the cusp of Pisces, the fish, the traits he shared with Little John would be muted by inhibitions and by the Infinite, for

Jonathan would be troubled by whispers from beyond himself. He would act quickly, but if he paused to think before he acted, he would become indecisive and uncertain. As long as he kept his eyes fixed on the physical world he would be like Little John, but if his gaze turned inward, he would be another man — and a stranger one.

In April the negotiations with Topsfield had completed a first round and the selectmen "Ordered that Thomas Putnam shall have 20 shillings allowed him for entertaining of the men that run the line between Topsfield and us, and Joseph Gardner, 30 shillings."

The Quakers continued to come seeking abuse and martyrdom. William Brend got more than his share when he held a Friends meeting in Salem. He was taken to Boston, clapped into irons, "one on each thigh and another about his neck," all three latched with a "horse lock" that left "no more room betwixt the irons than the lock allowed," and thrown into a cell in this doubled-over contortion for sixteen hours.

Nevertheless, the punishment failed to break his spirit or make him recant, so the jailer gave him a vicious beating with a corded whip. Most people lost count of the blows, but at least one counted 117 stripes. One witness said, "…his flesh was beaten black and as into jelly, and under his arms the bruised flesh and blood hung down, clotted as it were into bags; and it was so beaten into one mass that the signs of one particular blow could not be seen."

Brend lay unconscious and seemingly dead on the floor. Someone informed the Governor who sent a doctor. When the physician went in the crowd pushed in behind him and stood looking on in horror until the Rev. John Wilson told them it was all right — all that had been done was to beat Brend black and blue as he had beaten the laws of God. The doctor shook his head, turned, and walked away — it seemed clear to him there was nothing he could do…but somehow Brend survived.

In May six Salem Quakers, one of whom was Samuel Shattuck whose house was on Essex Street, were banished from the Colony. The General Court sat to consider and approve the death penalty for recalcitrant Quakers. One of the new law's most ardent proponents was John Endicott of Salem.

The Essex County trial of John Godfrey continued to drag along under the reluctant aegis of Simon Bradstreet — though, in fact, the word "trial" was inappropriate, for though Bradstreet took depositions, it was more an investigation than even a preliminary examination. A number of witnesses appeared against Godfrey, including several out of his past such as Charles Browne and William Osgood. Job Tyler and his family — Mary, his wife; Moses, his son, aged seventeen; and Mary Tyler the younger, his fifteen-year-old daughter — testified that they had seen a "thing like a bird" — a bat — "as big as a pigeon," come into their house with Godfrey. Godfrey had tried to catch it, but it had vanished through a chink in the wall. Job had asked, "Wherefore did it come?"

"It came to suck your wife," Godfrey had replied. The case came up to the County Court at Salem on the 28th of June, but Bradstreet squelched it.

On the 7th of July the Selectmen ordered that "the footbridge over the marsh at Nathaniel Putnam's farm be speedily mended: William Flint and Samuel Cutler" were appointed to do the work.

In England John Gadbury published a book in August titled *The Nativity of the Late King Charles Astrologically and Faithfully Performed*, which some were mean enough to point out was as accurate a horoscope as hindsight would allow, which was at least as accurate as those Gadbury composed ahead of time. Another Oxonian, Robert Boyle, had been spending his time in perfecting his "pneumatical engine" the air pump, and he had begun a series of studies of the properties of air. And in London Mericus Casaubon's edition of Dr. John Dee's *A True and Faithful Relation* appeared posthumously; it chronicled the crystal-gazing he and Edward Kelley had done back in Elizabeth's day and transcribed the conversations they had had with Madimi, Uriel, and the other angels and angelical beings whose acquaintance they had cultivated.

The Salem folk on August 15th had appointed Nathaniel Putnam grand juryman again. The Rev. Edward Norris, pastor of the church, died and was replaced by the Rev. John Higginson, Son of the Rev. Francis Higginson. Giles Corey had sold his town house and moved out to Salem Village, and on the 30th of August the child of Thomas Putnam and Ann Holyoke Putnam, Elizabeth, entered the Puritan world of New England to join her four sisters and two brothers.

Elizabeth Putnam was a first decan Virgo. She would be a thinking woman, able to discriminate and to analyze situations. She would achieve what she set out to accomplish — the tasks she chose would not be small.

The Putnams were well used to the visits of Mother Goose's stork by now; that legendary bird, in fact, was the most salient feature of the Putnam coat of arms which was described in heraldic terms as "Sable, a stork argent, beaked and legged gules, within an orle of eight crosslets fitches or, on a chief embattled of the second, a roman fasces in fess proper. Crest: A wolf's head gules, couped at the neck, per fess embattled, gules and or." Still another visit of the family bird impended, and in October it settled on the roof of Nathaniel and Elizabeth Hutchinson Putnam to lay its burden, a son, in the waiting cradle. A few days later, on November 7th, its uncle Thomas was appointed to the trial jury of the town. At the end of the month business received a boost in Salem when George Corwin and two others were given permission to build a gristmill on the South River "above Mr. Rucke's house." It would not rise until at least spring, however, for winter was settling down hard over the waterfront and among the silent fields and forests.

Before the fires of autumn, upon their own settles, the Putnams and their Salem Village neighbors could pass the time — and frighten themselves — by discussing the witchcraft case of Cambridge that year. Winifred Holman and her daughter, Mary, were accused by the people who lived nearest them, the Gibsons and the Stearnses, of bewitching and bedeviling them, in small ways and in large.

Mary was often in the Gibsons' hall, to borrow a skillet or to make a fuss over the baby in its cradle "every morning, and sometimes twice in the day." Nor was Winifred far behind. "How do your daughter?" she would ask. "I will prescribe some herbs for her, if you wish." But the Gibsons did not wish, though they did wish to keep tabs on the Holmans who were known to act quite oddly at times. Goody Stearns thought so too, for there were times when she "looked out of her window and saw Mary Holman running about." She obviously was casting a spell, for "presently" Goody Stearns "was taken sick, almost struck dead as she thought."

Nothing the Holmans did escaped their neighbors' notice, whether they were gardening or harvesting, shucking corn, "carrying sand" or "digging a hole in the common," making a U-turn at the oak tree, or "sitting at a hole of water" for who knew what reason and, even more ominously, "going out towards night into swamps and byways." Often she dressed peculiarly. Once, on the Sabbath when it was raining, she dared go out "without any hat on her head." John Gibson testified that he was often "afflicted with Goody Holman's hens," for he could not keep them from getting into his barns and damaging his corn.

But his affliction was as nothing compared with that of Goody Rebecca Stearns who really did become ill, exhibiting many of the symptoms of Satan's scourge. Mostly she blamed it upon the Holmans, but she also was "carried with rage against her parents and her brothers and sisters," so much so that the family "were fain to tie her hands." Thus she lay, talking on against Goody Winifred and Mary Holman to everyone who crowded around to see and hear these amazing things, crying out "that they were witches and must be hanged, and so she told them to their faces, and could not be stilled." She would cry out "with a loud voice to the Lord for help." And Rebecca would demand from time to time that Goody Holman be sent for. "And so she cried on until her body gave up its ghost into the arms of the Lord." The Holmans were indicted, but the Salem Villagers heard that the magistrates did not convict them.

Chapter Six

Bray Wilkins and John Gingle, both residents of Lynn, on the 9th of March 1660 bought the Richard Bellingham farm for twenty-four pounds in bar iron and one pound in cash as down payment of the purchase price, which was 250 pounds. The rest they mortgaged.

In Salem John Porter and Thomas Putnam, Sr., were made highway surveyors for the town, and Edward Bishop, Sr., became constable. William Hathorne was elected Speaker of the House of Deputies for Massachusetts Bay once more, and George Corwin, the merchant, who had done very well indeed, purchased a lot on Essex Street in Salem from Widow Ann Woodbury; he proceeded to erect a mansion near the corner of Norman Street.

The Rev. John Higginson, having proved acceptable to the congregation, was ordained minister of Salem Church, but the ceremony was spoiled by a Quaker of the town, John Smith, who rose from his pew and cried out, "What you are going about to set up, our God is pulling down!" Edward Bishop, who was present, immediately apprehended him and put him into jail.

On April 3rd Joseph Miller was convicted for entertaining "a stranger, a Scot" for several weeks. He was fined 20 shillings and ordered "to clear the town of him." Likewise, "John Southwick brought into this town Joseph Nicholson's companion, a woman great with child, about the 18th day of March last past, for which disorder" he was "to pay 20 shillings per week from that time and so long as she is in town," and Thomas Spooner was "fined 10 shillings for entertaining of a strange woman, that is to say, Goody Finch," and he was "to be made — together with others that have entertained her — to give security to discharge the town of her."

While Salem was evicting its guests, Richard Cromwell, the Protector of England, abdicated; Charles II landed at Dover on the 25th of May, claimed the crown, and the monarchy was restored. He immediately set about a purge of rebels — particularly those who had had a hand in the regicide of his father. One of those selected for execution was Cromwell's chaplain and Salem's former pastor, Hugh Peter.

While the King was acquiring a kingdom, John Partridge, the apprentice of a Covent Garden shoemaker, was acquiring an education by poring over every almanac, book or pamphlet on astrology that he could lay his hands on. His great idol was William Lilly whose success was as a beacon before his eyes.

Robert Boyle in Oxford published his *New Experiments Phsyico-Mechanical Touching the Spring of Air and Its Effect.* Numerous people attacked it including a Jesuit priest. In answering the priest's blast Boyle enunciated what soon became known as "Boyle's Law" — that the volume of gas varies inversely as the pressure. And on September 3rd Joan Neville was hanged for having committed murder by witchcraft.

Two of the English regicides escaped during the summer: Edward Whalley and William Goffe managed to get to Boston where Governor John Endicott welcomed them warmly and put them up at Harvard College — their quarters were immediately a popular spot for visitors, but not everyone was happy about their arrival. Capt. Breedon was bold enough to criticize the colony publicly for harboring fugitives. He soon found himself facing John Endicott who cholerically denounced him as "malignant." The marshal, who stood at Breedon's elbow, leered into his face and said, "Speak against Whalley and Goffe if ye dare, if ye dare, if ye dare!" The Captain was purple-faced but silent.

In Scituate, Plymouth Colony, Dinah Sylvester accused Mrs. William Holmes of appearing to her in the shape of a bear, "about a stone's throw from the path." In court Dinah was asked, "What manner of tail did the bear have?"

She replied, "I could not tell because the bear's head was towards me." It was evident to the court that the woman's answers left something to be desired, and she was required to pay court costs and be whipped, or apologize publicly to Mrs. Holmes. Dinah chose the apology.

Long Island found itself once more confronted by the Devil's work. Mary and Hannah Wright of Oyster Bay were accused of witchcraft. Once again the authorities felt themselves incompetent to judge, as in the case of Goody Garlick in 1657, but this time, rather than referring the case to the Connecticut courts, they sent the woman to Boston for trial.

Among the holdings of the Putnams in Topsfield were two farmhouses, meadows, orchards, and fields. Other land in the area was considered both by Topsfield and Salem to be Town Commons. One day in February of 1661 Isaac Burton heard a tree fall as he was passing near the home of John Nichols and he went into the woods to see what was going on, for there were angry voices as well.

When he got to the spot he found John Putnam, Jr., very red-faced, glaring angrily at Jacob Towne and John Howe of Topsfield who had impudently felled a tree Putnam knew to be on Salem land, but which Topsfield disputed. The Topsfielders had cut the tree before Putnam's very eyes and against his specific warning. John was outmanned at the moment, so he merely spun about and stalked off, to the derisive remarks of Towne and Howe.

Not long after that incident the sound of many axes rang in the woods, and the Topsfield men went to see what was going on. When they arrived at the scene they found trees falling in all directions and the woods swarming with Putnams and other Salem Villagers swinging axes. This time the odds did not favor the Topsfielders who were only four in number: Isaac Easty, Sr., John Easty, John Towne, and Joseph Towne, Jr. They ordered John Putnam to cease and desist forthwith, but he wasn't interested.

"The timber now and here cut down has been felled by me and my orders," he said, "and I will keep cutting and carrying away from this land until next March."

"What! By violence?" he was asked.

"Ay, by violence," John Putnam. replied. "You may sue me — you know where I dwell." He spun on his heel and said to his people, who had paused to listen, "Fall on!" and the axes rang again. The Topsfielders retreated in mute fury and disarray.

In April, on the 22nd, the Selectman of Salem ordered that John Putnam. and James Simons were to attend the board's next meeting to answer "for cutting timber contrary to orders." On the 3rd of May Simons was fined for felling trees on the Commons, but nothing was done about Putnam.

Four days later the town appointed all-night watches; Thomas Oliver was the Salem street-cleaner. On the 22nd Bray Wilkins and John Gingle petitioned the General Court asking that the Richard Bellingham farm which they had purchased — 700 acres plus 150 acres of meadow, the whole known as "Will's Hill" — "may be laid to, and appointed to belong to, Salem, being nigh its lands, and the petitioners of its society." Eventually the request was granted.

During the spring in England the Cavalier Parliament was elected. It reestablished the Anglican Church and ended toleration of other Protestant sects. It was as Massachusetts had feared; nevertheless, on the 8th of June the colony recognized the king in a public ceremony. John Gadbury published his *Britain's Royal Star, or An Astrological Demonstration of England's Future Felicity*, which purported to be based on the positions of the stars on the date Charles II had been proclaimed king.

Robert Boyle published a book as well, this one titled *The Skeptical Chemist*. It attacked the precepts and premises of Paracelsus' system. A third book written by the Quaker George Bishop and titled *New England Judged* told the story of the Quaker persecutions in the American Puritan colonies. It was a prophecy of dire events to follow, for the country had to be punished for its sins. Bishop's was not the only complaint registered. Others were lodged with King Charles II by Sir Ferdinando Gorges and people who had been ill-treated or banished by Massachusetts.

Charles listened and sent an order to Governor John Endicott that imprisoned Quakers were to be released immediately. John Endicott trembled angrily as he read the letter that had been delivered to him by his fellow townsman Samuel Shattuck. For a few moments Shattuck gleefully thought John Endicott would suffer an apoplectic stroke, but the crisis passed.

The two young women of Easthampton, Mary and Hannah Wright, who had been sent to Boston by the Long Island authorities to be tried on charges of witchcraft the year before, had stood trial. They were not, however, convicted of the original charge, but rather for being Quakers. They had been put into prison, but the King's order released them along with the many others of their sect who were kept in durance vile.

The General Court, long used to circumventing orders from England, passed the Vagabond Act which suspended the death penalties for Quakers but hedged it round with ambiguous language.

In Salem itself John Putnam Jr., was chosen trial juryman on June 10th; Nathaniel Putnam was grand juryman as of August 17th. On the fourth of September James Putnam, fifth child and second son of John, Jr., and Rebecca Prince Putnam, was born at the family homestead, Oak Knoll. The 18th of November Nathaniel Putnam was appointed to the trial jury of Salem. It was in December that he and his brothers decided they had had enough of the pack of wolves that had been roaming the outskirts of the Village.

The men of the family gathered on some of the Topsfield land and dug a large trench or elongated pit. When it was wide and deep they cut down a number of small trees, topped them, stripped them of bark so that they would be slippery, and lined the pit with them vertically so that the wolves would not be able to scrabble out. On top of the wolf pit they built, out of the branches they had accumulated, a framework that would support a certain amount of weight, and the framework was covered with brush, grass, and woodland debris until it looked very much like the terrain. Pieces of meat were placed in the center of the false ground.

During the night many of the villagers could hear the pack baying in the moon. Suddenly, there was a sound like all the devils of Hell screaming in the woods — growls, whines, high-pitched yelps and barks — the noise continued for hours, and finally, just before dawn, it died down. The children who had not fallen off to sleep trembling finally could close their eyes.

In the morning the Village men gathered at the pit and looked down into the gleaming yellow eyes and bared fangs beneath them. The wolves jumped to their feet and again furiously assaulted the slippery sides, but at last fell back exhausted. The men raised their muskets and began firing at the evil faces that looked at them with pure malice. Again, it was like the bowels of Hades in the pit, until at last there was nothing left but blood and riddled carcasses. The Putnams and the others filled the pit back in with soil and debris so that other predators wouldn't be attracted to the site. It was snowing. An hour after the men left the woods not even their tracks could be found.

Giles Corey at the end of the first month of the new year 1662 was compensated by the Board of Selectmen for a strip of his land that had been taken to make a new road in Salem Village. He received two acres. A month later, on the last day of February, a tired stork deposited

Prudence with Thomas and Ann Holyoke Putnam — their eighth child. Their oldest, Ann Putnam the younger, was seventeen years old, and Thomas, Jr., the eldest boy, was ten.

Salem continued to grow and expand. On the 3rd of March John Buttolph was given permission to begin a tannery, and plans were laid to erect a shipyard with warehouses, shops, and wharves at Burying Point. Thomas Oliver resigned as bell-ringer of Salem.

In England in March two elderly widows of Lowestoft, Suffolk — Rose Cullender and Amy Duny — were accused of being witches. They were arrested and taken to Bury St. Edmunds sessions where they were arraigned before Sir Matthew Hale. Dorothy Durent had accused the women. She said that she had hired Amy Duny to babysit. Against instructions the old woman had tried to nurse the baby — an exercise in futility at any rate — and Mrs. Durent had chastised her for it. Amy had replied, "You had as good to have done otherwise than to have found fault with me."

Shortly afterward the infant had had convulsions. Mrs. Durent took it to "Dr." Jacob, a white witch, for a consultation. He recommended that Mother Durent wrap the baby in a blanket that had been prepared by hanging it in the chimney nook. Dr. Jacob told her to burn anything that fell out of the blanket as it hung.

Goody Durent followed the instructions, and she found a toad in the fireplace. She took it, threw it onto the fire, and it exploded. The next time Dorothy Durent saw Amy Duny she noticed that the old woman's face, legs, and thighs were scorched.

At the trial a nine-year-old girl, Deborah Pacy, said she had been sitting in the sun for her lameness when Amy Duny came to the house to purchase some herrings of her fisherman father. Because Amy was reputed to be a witch, she was denied the fish three times, and finally she had left muttering under her breath. At that moment Deborah had been pitched into a fit and experienced severe cramps. The girl accused

Amy of having hexed her. In court, she had fits when Amy confronted her.

The wife of Amy's landlord said that Amy had told her, "If you look not to the chimney in your house, it will fall."

"But," the woman had replied, "it is a new one." She thought no more about it and they parted, but soon the chimney did fall.

Deborah Pacy's eleven-year-old sister Elizabeth caught the fits and was at various times, with her sibling, blind, sore, lame, speechless, racked by coughs, and they even vomited pins and a twopenny nail. Another girl accuser, Jane Bocking, seemed to eat no food for several weeks. All of them could read the Bible until they came to one of the names of God or Christ, at which they would be struck dumb and go into convulsions, but any of the Devil's names had a salutary effect; the girls would say, "This bites, but makes me feel right well."

Mary Chandler, mother of another of the juvenile accusers, Susan Chandler, was given the task of searching Amy Duny for witch teats — she found one, an inch long, on the old woman's lower abdomen. When Judge Hale questioned Amy about it she said it was a rupture that had been caused by carrying water, but three more were found in her privy parts. The longest of these had a "little hole" in the end of it, and it appeared "as if it had been lately sucked, and upon the straining of it there issued out some white milky matter."

Sir Matthew and the other judges were quite willing to admit spectral evidence against the witches. Elizabeth and Deborah Pacy both maintained that they had seen the disembodied spirits of the two witches hurting them. In their fits they would cry out, "There stands Amy Duny!" or "There stands Rose Cullender!" while they pointed at nothing anyone else but another afflicted person could see. They would run to the empty spots and attempt to strike the specters while the witches' apparitions mocked at them.

Rose Cullender had also been refused fish at the Durents' cottage, and Ann Durent said she, too, had seen Mrs. Cullender's apparition threatening her.

John Soam of Lowestoft, a farmer, said that the last harvest time he had three carts to bring in his crops, but as they were passing Rose Cullender's house to go into the fields for loading, one of the carts had scraped the witch's window. The woman had come out in a rage and threatened Soam. When the carts were loaded two of them got home all right and came back for new loads, but the culprit cart kept turning over, and as it was going through the gate it stuck so fast the men had to take down a post to get it through. When at last they got it home they couldn't get it close to the place where they wished to unload it, but had to unload at a distance instead. They had such difficulty unloading it that their noses bled, and they had to leave the cart till the next day when they finished the job without difficulty.

Robert Sherringham believed that the huge lice with which he had been plagued two years earlier could be laid at Rose's door.

Several of the judges suspected that the children might have been faking their fits, so they tried an experiment. Lord Cornwallis, Sir Edmund Bacon, Sergeant Keeling and some others took one of the girls to the back of the hall while she was having a fit. The witches' touch caused them to scream, so they put an apron over the child's eyes, brought Amy Duny forward, and then had a different person touch the girl — she screamed just as though it had been the witch who touched her.

Nevertheless, Sir Matthew Hale was the principal judge and a believer, so on the tenth of March he charged the jury, and in thirty minutes Rose Cullender and Amy Duny were convicted on thirteen counts of sorcery and witchcraft. On the fourteenth of March they were hanged.

The trial attracted a great deal of attention. Shortly afterward a pamphlet, *A Trial of Witches at the Assizes Held at Bury St. Edmunds*, was published. It was quite long for its genre — sixty pages — and it was well-documented; it contained a number of the trial records. It was immediately a bestseller in England, and copies began to find their way aboard ships bound for New England.

During the same month a vagabond drummer named William Drury was making his way through the shires doing sleight-of-hand and gymnastic tricks, beating his drum to attract attention. He was a veteran soldier without a regiment to drum for, but soon he had a host of people following his activities. He was arrested in Tedworth, Wiltshire, on charges of working a confidence game with counterfeited documents as he passed through on his way to Portsmouth. The local magistrate, John Momperson, set the drummer free, but confiscated his drum.

Immediately, strange things began to happen in the Momperson home: There were drummings, levitations; a horse was found with one of its legs stuck into its mouth. Momperson took action: The drum was obviously enchanted, so he destroyed it. Things got worse at once.

The signs and omens appearing in Salem that spring were of a much less significant order: On April 7th John Milk was appointed to be town herdsman, and thereafter numbers of tiresome jests were coined regarding the town's "Milk cows." Three days after, Governor John Endicott made out his will prudently ahead of time. The document carried through his wedding gift to his son and deeded him, "his heirs and assigns forever," the Townsend Bishop farm. The apothecary in town, William Woodcock, knew nothing of such things as milk bars, but he made application for the right, and was granted permission, to distill and sell "strong water" at retail prices. In June John Putnam, Jr., and others were given leave to "build a seat by the south gallery in our meeting house," for space in church was assigned according to social ranking, and he had been accepted as a member in good standing. His niece Prudence was baptized in the church on the 29th. Fortunately she was too young to appreciate the spectacle that summer of Deborah Wilson, the Quaker lady, walking through town naked in order to make her point, whatever it was.

The General Court plugged a loophole during the year by passing a law that required anything printed in the colony to be licensed, for literature, too, was strong water. A book appeared in Massachusetts that passed all tests, both legal and popular: Michael Wigglesworth's *The Day of Doom* appeared and was a runaway best seller in Puritan homes. It made explicit the horrors that awaited the unchosen in the hereafter, though its craftsmanship as literature left something to be desired. This, however, was of no moment to most of its readers, few of whom had any notion of literature at all.

Rebecca Greensmith of Hartford was thrown into durance vile on charges of witchcraft. Shortly afterward Ann Cole, daughter of John Cole, was possessed of the Devil. At first Goody Greensmith had denied all charges, but when she was confronted by the diabolical convulsions and accusations of Ann Cole face to face, she broke down and confessed her guilt. Thereupon she went into detail about her situation *vis-à-vis* Satan: Although she hadn't made a formal covenant, she had promised to be ready at his call; she was to have, in return, "high frolic" at Christmas when the final contract was to be signed between them. Mrs. Greensmith implicated her husband Nathaniel and told the authorities that she and others had had sexual intercourse with a succubus "with much seeming delight to herself."

The demons that possessed Ann Cole — who lived next door to a Dutch family — were wont at times to speak in Dutch, at other times in English, and even in a third language that no one understood. The demons were three in number, and at times they spoke with each other in the presence of witnesses. Several ministers in attendance took down what the voices that issued out of Ann said. A goodly number of the words were recognizable as the names of townspeople.

The Greensmiths — and others who were accused but did not immediately leave town and flee to New York jurisdiction — were searched for witch teats and three were tested by the ordeal of swimming, hands and feet bound together behind them. One man and a woman floated; a second man sank. The Greensmiths were convicted.

On the 11th of August Elizabeth — fifth child and first daughter of Nathaniel and Elizabeth Hutchinson Putnam — was born in Salem Village. In England on August 24th, St. Barholomew's Day, the Cavalier Parliament passed an act requiring religious uniformity throughout the kingdom. Two thousand dissenting ministers were relieved of their livings. A good many of these began to prepare to leave for the New England colonies; one, Mr. Charles Nicolet, set his course for Salem.

Rev. John Norton and Simon Bradstreet had gone to England to attempt to persuade the new king to reaffirm the charter of the Massachusetts Bay colony. After six months they returned to Boston with a letter that directed the government to give complete religious freedom to all the Anglicans in the colony. The General Court responded by passing a law that had the effect of leaving matters exactly as they had been.

On September 27th Thomas Putnam, Sr., was chosen trial juryman, and a few days later the militia of Salem, Lynn, and surrounding settlements was organized, the troops putting forward to the General Court the names of the officers they had chosen to lead them. The Captain of the company was to be George Corwin; Thomas Putnam, Sr., was chosen to be Lieutenant — a title he would bear forever after, and Walter Price was made Cornet.

John Godfrey, having come off unscathed from his day in court as an accused witch of Andover, commenced slander actions against William and Samuel Simons, and against Jonathan Singletary, "for calling him 'witch' and saying of him, 'Is this witch on this side of Boston gallows yet?'" In both cases Godfrey was victor and damages were assessed; the Simonses were to pay two shillings and court costs — the damages were small because the jury did "conceive that, by the testimonies" rendered, Godfrey was "rendered suspicious." Singletary had either to make public acknowledgment of his error at Haverhill within a month or pay ten shillings damages, plus court costs.

On December 23rd old John Putnam, Richard Hutchinson and others completed engineering a complicated swap of lands. One week later, on the 30th, John "ate his supper, went to prayer with his family, and died before he went to sleep." Never had there been greater mourning in Salem Village — sons and daughters, nieces and nephews, grandchildren and in-laws gathered from all parts of the greater Salem area — the Goulds came from Topsfield and Ipswich; neighbors arrived from far and near to mark the passing of one of the patriarchs of Salem. John Putnam had lived to see his family grow to be one of the largest and most powerful in the area of New England that he had chosen in his elder years to inhabit.

Not so lucky was William Cole of Hampton, New Hampshire, who died and left his widow Eunice to the mercies of the town children who called her "the Old Witch" and lost no opportunity to torment her. Not long after his death Eunice was sent to the House of Correction by the court.

When John Putnam's will was read early in 1663 it was discovered that he had left a double portion — as was not uncommon — to his eldest son Thomas. As the eldest living Putnam Thomas also inherited from his father the family honorific "Landlord," which would stand among his relatives in place of the rank title Lieutenant. As Bridget Wasselby was wont to say, misquoting the Bible — whether intentionally or accidentally was the question — "What God taken away on the one hand he giveth with the other": Hannah, sixth child of John, Jr., and Rebecca Prince Putnam, was born on the 2nd of February.

Ten days later the pastor of the Boston North Church, Increase Mather, became the father of a son whom he named Cotton after the child's maternal grandfather John Cotton. Cotton Mather was a third decan Aquarian, and his symbol was the Water Bearer: He would be a servant of humanity, a great humanitarian, his will governed by reason — but the reasoning might be accurate or specious, depending on the premises upon which his logic was built.

Nevertheless, once he had thought out his course, according to his lights, he would bring all his genius to bear upon his fellows so that they might see the light as well. He would perceive humanity as an extension of his own self — all part of a greater Self that included flesh and soul, but the spirit would predominate. He was to be Superman, but, being born in the third decan of his Sign, he would be a repressed person. His best expression would be achieved in his associations with womankind. His wife would be a lucky woman, and he would love her as himself.

Increase Mather was inordinately proud of his son. He rendered up thanks unto the Lord for the greatness of His bounty and promised that this boy should be a treasure of the Elect. Increase was a busy and a deeply read man. He had recently managed to get hold of a copy of *A Trial of Witches* that told of Sir Matthew Hale's Bury St. Edmunds cases. Hale was greatly admired in the Bay, and Increase had entered into a correspondence with the famous jurist. He trusted his new child would wish one day to follow in its father's footsteps along the path of righteousness, would wish to learn all that there was to learn of the spirit and its temptations, and of the ways in which evil was dealt with in this world.

There had been altogether too many fires in the colony and in the town of Salem of recent months. There had long been a law against thatched roofs and catted chimneys, but it was usually unenforced. Even if neither of these hazards was present, however, the building up of soot in the chimneys was a great danger, and on the 10th of February the Salem Selectmen had begun to require that chimneys be swept at least once each month from the first of October to the 31st of March, and once each two months from April 1st to September 20th. In order to enforce the edict the Selectmen offered incentives for the neighbors to spy upon each other: Informers against those who failed to comply would receive the 12 pence fine that would be imposed. John Milk, the herdsman, was appointed town sweep for those who didn't want to, or couldn't, clean their own chimneys.

Rumors began immediately to circulate among some of the matrons of a certain class that one ought to beware of a few of their society, for Elizabeth Vergoose, Bridget Wasselby, and one or two others had taken up with drop-in visits. They would seat themselves before the hearth and wait their moment when their hostess' back was turned, it was alleged. In a twinkling, the visitors would be over in the chimney, head cocked at an odd angle, looking up the flue, and then back into their chairs before the housewife turned around again. There were many wary episodes in the halls of Salem and Salem Village after the law was passed.

At the Essex County Court held at Salem on March 4th a young man of Salem named John Porter, Jr., was brought before magistrate William Hathorne, accused of the most vile behavior toward his parents that Hathorne had ever heard of. Porter, when asked what he had to say to it, told Hathorne, "You are a base, corrupt fellow, and I care not a turd for you!" Hathorne apoplectically committed him to the Ipswich House of Correction.

On the 24th of March Nathaniel Putnam was chosen to "seal weights and measures for the year ensuing," a position of great trust. Henry Kenny, Francis Nurse, and several others petitioned the Selectmen that John Putnam Jr., claimed "more meadow than was laid out to him." Francis Kerry, Henry Kenny, Francis Nurse, and Henry Batholomew were ordered to survey the property in question.

In England William Drury, the former regimental drummer, was arrested for rustling swine and convicted, but he was not sentenced to death for this capital crime in Gloucester, the scene of his depredations; rather, he was lucky enough to be sentenced to transportation overseas, to one of the colonies. On the convict ship he jumped overboard and swam to shore at Uffcot, not far from Tedworth. There he bought a drum and went into his old act. Within a day Justice John Momperson heard of his presence and had him picked up. The magistrate threw him into Salisbury jail and accused him of witchcraft.

In April he was tried and acquitted for lack of evidence, despite the fact that the local parson and other notables testified against him, and that the poltergeist phenomena at Mr. Momperson's home persisted — once, when some wood moved in the judge's presence, he fired a pistol at it, and blood was found beneath the wood and on the stairs. Drury was, however, reconvicted on the original charge of pig rustling and again sentenced to transportation to Virginia. No sooner had sentence been passed against the Drummer of Tedworth than the strange occurrences stopped.

In London the astrologer John Booker, a friend of William Lilly, predicted the solar eclipse that took place during the year and prophesied that the event presaged the deaths of two kings — of Sweden and Bohemia. The Invisible College became visible in 1663. Robert Boyle and others organized it as the Royal Society of London for Improving Natural Knowledge. It was immediately the focal point for scientific investigations in England and in her colonies, and its publications became vastly important. John Winthrop, Jr., who had been studying in England and was a Fellow of the Royal Society, when he returned to Massachusetts Bay took with him the first celestial telescope to appear in North America.

In Hartford, Connecticut, Rebecca Greensmith and her husband Nathaniel were hanged for their crime. A number of others who had been accused of maleficia, including Judith Varlet, a relative of Gov. Pieter Stuyvesant of New Netherlands, managed to elude the authorities until after the Greensmiths were dead and Ann Cole's fits had stopped.

Another book came off the press in Cambridge: Apostle John Eliot published a translation of the Bible written in the language of the Algonquin Indians. Quakerism still was rife, and Rev. John Higginson wrote the General Court that Salem was "a nest of Quakers." Philip Veren, Jr., became a public spectacle in the town when he made a scene and was sentenced "to be set by the heels in the stocks one hour for disowning the country's power, in open court, about forcing any to come to the public worship." Veren had been in trouble before for not attending services and for defending the Quakers.

On August 22nd John Putnam Jr. was appointed to the Grand Jury, and the surveyors of his meadow reported that, after all, it was no larger than he had claimed it to be and it was rightfully his. On the eighth of

October the town gave its permission for a second mill to be built on the South River, and the second week in November Nathaniel Putnam was "chosen Clerk of the Market for the year ensuing."

Caleb Moody was a neighbor of William and Elizabeth Morse of Newbury. He had a difference of opinion with Morse, and the next day he found one of his best hogs lying "dead in the yard, and no natural cause" thereof that Moody could discover.

In the fall John Porter, Jr., was released from the Ipswich House of Correction. He came back home to his father's house in Salem, began to frequent the taverns of the town, drinking and playing shovel board, and abusing his parents once again. Again John Porter, Sr., found it necessary at last to go to the authorities. This time, on the 20th of November, he was sent to Boston prison, bound over for trial the following March.

And in Setauket, Long Island, in Suffolk County — which had been settled by New Englanders — there was a strange death: On Christmas Day George Wood was suddenly taken ill; a few days later he died leaving his widow to carry on alone. She had her suspicions about Ralph Hall.

George Gardner and Nathaniel Putnam were reappointed Salem town surveyors in February of 1664, but they could do little until the winter had let up some. Rumors of a new war in the offing began to circulate in the colonies, this time a war with the Dutch that might very well touch New England's shores.

The conflict began in July. King Charles II had sent four commissioners, Col, Richard Nichols, Sir Robert Carr, George Cartwright, and Samuel Maverick — formerly of Salem — "to hear and determine complaints and appeals in all causes, as well military as criminal and civil." they were greeted with barely covered hostility when they set foot in Boston. The presence of Samuel Maverick was particularly galling to the government, for he had been one of the signers of the Child petition in 1646, and his name was already synonymous in Salem, and in Massachusetts Bay as a whole, with one who bucked authority. In fact, "maverick" soon came to mean *renegade*, if not outright *traitor*.

On the fourth of March in Boston the trial of John Porter, Jr., — a maverick of horrendous proportions — began to expose the enormity of this other Salemite's actions. He was a bachelor of about thirty years who lived with his parents. When he had come of age his father had given him 400 pounds as his portion, which the young man was to use to make his fortune in the world. Instead, he had gone down to the waterfront and shipped aboard a sailing vessel twice to the Barbados Islands and England, where he had squandered the money in riotous living. In England he had run himself into debt and was thrown into prison. He was rescued from his cell by friends of his father on the promise that John Porter, Sr., would make good all his son's debts, which he did.

The younger Porter returned to Salem and was received home with affection and forgiveness. But the young man was not appreciative and "did carry himself very perversely, stubbornly, and rebelliously towards his natural parents," according to the records of the General Court. Worse, "He called his father thief, liar, and simple ape, shitabed."

Frequently he threatened to burn his father's house, "to cut down his house and barn, to kill his cattle and horses, and did with an axe cut down his fence several times, and did set fire of a pile of wood near the dwelling house, greatly endangering it...."

But Junior did not leave it at that, for he turned upon his mother as well, calling her "rambugger, Gammer Shithouse, Gammer Pisshouse, Gammer Two Shoes, and told her her tongue went like a pear monger, and said she was the rankest sow in the town, and these abusive names he used frequently." When one of his brothers dared to object to his actions, Junior attempted to stab him in a drunken rage; he "reviled, and abused, and beat his father's servants," nearly killing one of them.

Porter got away with this behavior for several years, his temper and drunkenness approaching crescendo through 1662 and 1663. But finally his father had taken all the abuse he could stand. At first the elder Porter went quietly to the authorities for help, but matters had escalated into furor.

At the trial "The complaints against him...were produced, the witnesses brought face to face, and his charge proved; also, his own natural father openly complained of the stubbornness and rebellion of this his son, and craved justice and relief against him, being over pressed thereunto by his unheard-of and unparalleled outrages...."

The younger Porter, given the opportunity to defend himself, "impudently denied some things, others he excused by vain pretences, and some he owned, but gave no sign of true repentance; whereupon the...Court proceeded to give sentence against him, the sum whereof was, to stand upon the gallows, with a rope about his neck, for one hour, and afterwards to be severely whipped, and so committed to the House of Correction, to be kept closely to work, with the diet of that house, and not thence to be released without special order from the Court of Assistants or the General Court, and to pay to the country as a fine two hundred pounds."

The Court noted that, "If the mother of Porter had not been overmoved by her tender and motherly affections to forbear, but had joined with his father in complaining and craving justice, the Court must necessarily have proceeded with him as a capital offender, according to our law, being grounded upon and expressed in the Word of God...'" i.e., "thou shalt honor thy father and thy mother."

But before all of the sentence could be executed John Porter, Jr., "found means to make escape out of the prison in Boston, and presented himself before three of His Majesty's Commissioners, then at Warwick" in Rhode Island, "with complaints of injustice, unto whom they granted a warrant, under their hands, for a hearing of his case at Boston, before themselves, the 8th of May, 1665, and in the interim granted him protection against all authority, officers, and people...." By their action the King's Commissioners did nothing to improve the Government's disposition toward them. The General Court began to conspire among themselves for the downfall of the Commission, whose members had given them the opening they needed.

The Commissioners did not stay overlong on their first visit to New England, however, for in August they boarded their ships to sail down to Manhattan Island to relieve the Dutch and Governor Stuyvesant of New Netherlands, which was shortly renamed New York.

On Long Island Widow Ann Wood, whose husband George had died so oddly the previous year, married a man named Goodman Rogers. Not long afterward her child died, and she was sure it was not a natural death — she accused Ralph Hall of having murdered her first husband by sorcery, and both Ralph and his wife Mary of murdering her child.

Meanwhile, in Salem, despite King Charles' orders and the imminence of the King's commissioners, the repression of Quakers and others went on. Richard Waterman, a "dissenter from the prevalent creed" was condemned to a term of imprisonment and subsequent banishment. When he was released he, like young John Porter, left for Rhode Island.

The new church in Beverly invited the Rev. John Hale to come to preach to them with a view to eventual ordination if the congregation decided it were kindly disposed toward him after a period of probation. He was pleased to accept.

Priscilla Putnam, who had been waning since the death of her husband, took to bed in the heat of the summer and, after a week or two of fading, died quietly in her sleep. Again the clan gathered to mourn. The funeral service at the Salem church drew nearly the whole town, and the Rev. John Higginson was eloquent in praise of the scrupulous and godly life the old woman had led. She was truly and deeply mourned by her three sons who stood at the grave with their sisters, wives and children to watch Mr. Higginson say the old words and cast a handful of soil onto the coffin.

In England there was beginning to be clearly a split in the Invisible College that had at one time included all of the "old school" alchemists, sorcerers, astrologers and various occultists as well as the "new philosophers" — but the split was not yet very wide. The Philomaths, or old-school people, had long held a yearly banquet, a sort of occult convention, which was attended as well by Elias Ashmole who had become relatively respectable in terms of the new sciences. Lady Ann Conway, further, held spiritualist sessions at Ragley Castle to which she invited various guests including Dr. Henry More, author of the witchcraft book *Antidote Against Atheism*, and the scientist Robert Boyle. But since the founding of the Royal Society the Philomaths had begun to become open laughing stock, and William Lilly with his crew of stargazers fell further and further into disrepute — a fact that nevertheless did nothing to hurt the sales of their books and almanacs. One of the younger members of Lady Conway's group was Joseph Glanvill who promised fair to become a power to reckon with in the field of witchcraft. He was interested to hear during the year that a sorceress of Somerset named Elizabeth Style had openly stated that she was the Devil's own, that he had promised her money, and that "I should live gallantly, and have the pleasure of the world for twelve years if I would with blood sign his paper," pledging her soul to him.

There were great disruptions in England, for the plague had come among the people again and was decimating the city of London and other metropolises. Crowds of people who could afford it fled into the country to wait until the disease followed its course and sank again into the sewers beneath the streets. Those who could not flee — and many of those who did — tried to find ways to ward off the evil clouds that spread the sickness. The New World provided them with what many felt was a sure-fire antidote: Tobacco chewing spread its brown stain into the finest salons.

The year ended in Salem with typical events: Nathaniel Putnam was trial juror in November, and on Christmas Eve Benjamin Putnam was delivered to Nathaniel and his wife. Benjamin was born in the first decan of his sign which was, like that of his late grandfather, Capricorn. He would have many of the same qualities — pragmatism, the union of Christian and Jewish points of view: He would be a patriarch, but he would also be well organized and well balanced. He would presage finer things to come, and his best talent would be an ability to bring contending parties together in a spirit of conciliation. Though Puritans were not supposed to expect Christmas presents, Nathaniel and Elizabeth accepted this one with a good grace.

Samuel Danforth published his *New England Almanac* for the year 1665, and in it he attempted to blend the old with the new: He maintained that, though comets had been proved to be natural occurrences, still they were "portentous signals of great and notable changes." He did not try to settle the question this raised about predestination as versus free will, inasmuch as comets were regularly appearing phenomena.

Early in the year the King's Commissioners returned from New York, prepared to do business and straighten out the Massachusetts government. They soon found their task to be easier to contemplate than to accomplish — they met with frustration after frustration; runaround and doubletalk was what they encountered whenever they attempted to get information or action.

In Salem on the sixth of March the Selectmen ordered "that Lt. Thomas Putnam shall have 30 shillings allowed him out of this year's rates for his charges in attending the Court" — meaning the General Court — "in behalf of our town, in defending our case betwixt us and Topsfield." He had served so well that the town was pleased to elect him Selectman for the ensuing year.

At about the same time in Hartford, Connecticut, Elizabeth Seger was indicted on a charge of witchcraft and brought to trial. The jury found her guilty as charged, but the judges disagreed — they overrode the jury's verdict and set the woman free.

On the fifteenth of March Governor John Endicott died. When his will — which had been written in 1659 — was submitted to probate it was discovered to be unwitnessed, and the court over the summer studied its provisions, which were to enforce the deed he had made to his eldest son of the Townsend Bishop estate.

The Parliament of England was having its troubles with dissenters, and it took action by passing the Conventicle Act making it illegal for groups of more than five persons to come together in worship services other than those of the Church of England.

The Philomath William Lilly, who had been suffering from ill health of late, decided to leave the noxious fumes of London behind and settle on his country estate. A fellow Philomath, the quack doctor William Saffold, bought Lilly's town house in Blackfriars, and Lilly moved out. Once he was nicely settled into his new rural quarters Lilly turned to the study of medicine himself.

In May the Church at Beverly came to the conclusion that it liked Rev. Mr. John Hale well enough to ask him to stay on permanently as its minister, and he accepted the offer.

On the fifth of May in Boston the Porter case, that of New England's most prodigal son, came up for review before the King's Commissioners, and they held that the General Court had been unjust. On the 30th the Government spread the whole sordid story of John Porter, Jr., upon the public records. The Government mounted a full-scale attack upon the Commission, sparing nothing in the way of detail about Junior's actions towards his parents and others. The Commissioners were accused of being criminals as bad as Porter himself, unable to know right from wrong, or to uphold the King's laws — they were nothing more nor less than accomplices in one of the worst crimes the colony had ever had to deal with.

Not only was the Court over-lenient in Porter's case — at his mother's behest — and far from being cruel in terms of the punishment that had been handed down, it was positively seraphic in the quality of mercy. The Commissioners, on the other hand, were truly evil in that they had let Porter go scart free for a year.

The Commissioners were clearly in the wrong. Whatever they did in the way of explaining their actions was turned against them. The Court made a public statement that charged the Commission with "obstructing the sentence of justice passed against that notorious offender" John Porter, Jr.; with condoning "his rebellion against his natural parents"; with holding in contempt a court of the country and unilaterally absolving the people "from their oaths whereby they had sworn obedience to His Majesty's authority according to the Constitution of his Royal Charter," and — moving away from the Porter case into larger issues — with in fact invading New England and, with military force, attempting to do away with Englishmen's liberties.

The Commissioners could not have chosen a better case than Porter's with which to exercise their arrogance and give the Puritans a grip by which they might be overthrown. Their power and influence were utterly destroyed, and they prepared to leave. Porter was thrown back into prison to finish serving his sentence.

John Putnam Jr., on the 17th of June was chosen to sit on a trial jury. Then, in July, an amazing Providence of God took place, but what it could signify baffled everyone in Salem and Boston: Ensign Richard Davenport, Commander of the Fort at Castle Island in Boston Harbor, was killed at his post by a stroke of lightning. Perhaps there was some connection with the case of the infamous Salemite John Porter, Jr., but if so, few could fathom what it was.

On the first of August John Endicott's will was not approved by the General Court, and the whole issue was cast into utter confusion.

Eunice Cole, in Hampton, New Hampshire, was still a prisoner of the town, and a great burden both to it and to her warder, William Salter, for Hampton had to pay for her maintenance inasmuch as the old woman was impoverished.

The John Godfrey witchcraft case of 1659 was reopened in Boston with the family of Job Tyler again the principal accusers. At least one other witness, however, failed to arrive from Andover to testify, and, though Simon Bradstreet's records of the case were reviewed, Godfrey was once again found not legally guilty, though the court noted that there were grounds for suspicion because he was a notorious common swearer and had been in court many times before on a host of charges ranging from theft and drunkenness to suborning witnesses and witchcraft.

James Brown, an eighteen-year-old boy, took a trip from his hometown of Salisbury to Newbury, where he proposed to have a high old time away from the watchful eyes of his family and neighbors. The next day he came home and had occasion to go to the house of Elizabeth Morse. She told him she knew what he had been up to on his night out, and she related a few of his "misdemeanors" of the previous night.

Brown asked her, "How could you tell of 'em?"

"Everybody says it is true," Mrs. Morse told him.

"Everybody," James replied, "says you are a witch."

Goody Morse had the last word: "Our Savior Christ was belied, and so are you and I." It seemed a reasonable compromise, and they changed the subject.

On the 26th of August Nathaniel Putnam was made a grand juryman for Salem. A few days later, on the first of September, his sister-in-law Ann Holyoke Putnam died after a brief illness, and the family came together once more to mourn. Lt. Thomas went into a period of seclusion. John, Jr., and Rebecca Prince Putnam brought another child into the world, named him Eleazer Putnam, and the baby's father became a Freeman of Salem near the same time.

On the 2nd of October Ralph and Mary Hall of Setauket, Long Island, were tried in New York for the witch-murder of George Wood and the baby of his widow, Mrs. Ann Rogers. Ralph was found innocent, and the evidence against his wife was found to be insufficient for conviction, but sufficient to establish suspicion of guilt. The Halls posted bond for Mary's good behavior and they were set at liberty.

Later in the month John Endicott, Jr., petitioned the General Court to settle his father's estate. The Court responded by making "Mrs. Elizabeth Endicott and her two sons, John and Zerubabel," executors. Zerubabel was one of the practicing witches in Salem, though not many people knew about his sympathetic magic medicines, for he kept quiet about them. Nevertheless, there was good proof among his manuscripts that he believed in and practiced occult chirurgery. If any one thought of doing anything about it, they thought twice because he was a member of a powerful family.

He was no more free of gossip than Elizabeth Vergoose and Bridget Wasselby, however, for he had something of a checkered past — people remembered Elizabeth Due's accusation that he was her child's father, and where there was smoke.... The current troubles he was undergoing with his father's will made him a prime topic of conversation before the town hearths in 1665.

In December the King's Commissioners reported to England that they had failed in their mission and that the colonial government of Massachusetts regarded itself as autonomous.

New England was growing strong at its distance from the mother country. There were three hundred vessels trading with Barbados, Virginia, Madeira, Acadia, and so forth, not to mention thirteen-hundred smaller craft off fishing at Cape Sable alone. England was in the throes of the Great Plague that had destroyed 100,000 Londoners: The golden leaf from Virginia had not been the Panacea after all.

Nathaniel and Lt. Thomas Putnam were two of three surveyors appointed early in 1666 to view the bounds between Salem and Topsfield: There would obviously be no settlement of the issue that year. Then, in the middle of March, Nathaniel having done his duty once again, he was made one of the Selectmen of Salem.

In April Charles II acted on the report of his Commissioners, and it was obvious the colony had won once again, for the letter he wrote was quite conciliatory. The sovereign had too many problems at home to wish to attempt to bring Massachusetts Bay to heel just then.

In May Salem lost one of its Old Planters: William Trask was buried on the 16th of the month. On the 23rd Widow Elizabeth Endicott and her son Zerubabel petitioned the General Court to honor the old governor's unwitnessed will. The Court decided to do so with certain exceptions. The Townsend Bishop farm was to go to John Endicott, Jr., "his heirs and assigns for ever," thus making it impossible for Zerubabel to inherit the property if his brother died without issue. The widow was made sole administratrix of the rest of the estate.

The town of Salem gained an inhabitant when John Proctor moved from Ipswich into town to work the Downing farm. Bridget Wasselby's husband had died — there were rumors that she had bewitched the man to death, but no one dared say so publicly — and Thomas Oliver proved to be a bachelor after all, for he married the grieving Widow Wasselby. It seemed to some of the local matrons to be a scandalously appropriate match. Bridget Proctor did not have polite access to a great number of Salem homes.

Thomas Putnam had come out of his period of mourning to sit on a trial jury on the 18th of June, just after he posted the banns for his marriage to Mary Veren, widow of Nathaniel Veren who had formerly been of Salem. It was decided on the 14th of August that John Putnam, Jr., was to be the commissioner who would join the Selectmen in setting a rate for the town.

In September in England there was the Great Fire of London which, following on the heels of the plague, destroyed over 13,000 private houses and public buildings, and 89 churches. Grave suspicion fell upon the almanac makers of England, some of whom had predicted something like the Great Plague and the Fire, and they were rounded up. William Lilly was one of these, for in one of his books he had published pictures of devastation such as had just taken place. Some members of Parliament thought that it was just possible Lilly or others had set the fire in order to be sure their predictions would come true.

On Friday, October 25th, the committee of the House of Commons that had been appointed to inquire into the fire examined Lilly. The astrologer was ushered into the presence of Sir Robert Brooke who said to him, "Mr. Lilly, this committee thought fit to summon you to appear before them this day to know if you can say anything as to the cause of the late fire or whether there might be any design therein. You are called rather hither, because in a book of yours long since printed, you hinted some such thing by one of your hieroglyphics."

Lilly had a speech ready. He replied, "After the beheading of the late King, considering that in the three subsequent years the Parliament acted nothing which concerned the settlement of the Nation's peace, I was desirous, according to the best knowledge God has given me, to make inquiry by the art I studied, what might from that time happen unto the Parliament and the Nation in general. At last, having satisfied myself and perfected my judgment therein, I thought it most convenient to signify my intentions and conceptions thereof in forms, shapes, types, hieroglyphics, etc., without any commentary, that so my judgment might be concealed from the vulgar and made manifest to the wise. Having found, sir, that the great city of London should be sadly afflicted with a great plague, and not long after with an exorbitant fire, I framed these two hieroglyphics which in effect have proved true."

One of the committee members asked, "Did you foresee the year?"

"I did not, nor was desirous of that," Lilly said. "I made no scrutiny. Now, sirs," he went on, "whether there was any design of burning the city or any employed to that purpose, I must deal ingenuously with you, that since the fire I have taken such pains in the search thereof, but cannot or could not give myself the least satisfaction therein. I conclude that it was the finger of God only, but what instruments He used thereunto, I am ignorant."

Lilly's testimony must have been convincing to the committee members, if they understood what he had said, for he was released to return to his retirement, but two other almanac makers were not so lucky, and they were hanged.

In Newbury, Massachusetts, Mrs. William Chandler tacked a horseshoe over her door to keep witches away. Goody Chandler took note that, as long as it was in place, her neighbor Elizabeth Morse refused to enter the house. It was as Mrs. Chandler had suspected — Goody Morse was the cause of the sore wound she had. Mrs. Chandler had a fit over it, and while in the throes of her possession she accused Goody Morse of having wounded her. The accusation did not, however, leave the family.

Lt. Thomas Putnam on November 14th took as his second wife Widow Mary Veren who was wealthy and had property in Jamaica and Barbados. He himself was a man of no inconsiderable means, having done very well since he had arrived in New England, and having inherited a double portion at the death of his father. The honeymoon lasted a very little while, for on Christmas Day — a working day for the Selectmen — Thomas was appointed to be a member of a committee that was to discuss with Andover the laying-out of a road between the two towns.

About the middle of the first month of the new year — January 18th, 1667 — the Putnam family came together with the Trasks to celebrate another marriage: Lt. Thomas Putnam's daughter Ann was to marry William Trask of Salem, son of Capt. William Trask and Sarah Trask. The Rev. John Higginson officiated at the ceremony: Thomas gave away the bride as his own bride stood by dry-eyed, and another landmark was passed: The twenty-two-year-old maiden was the first of the third generation of New England Putnams to be wed.

On the 12th of February Major William Hathorne, Harry Bartholomew, and Nathaniel Putnam were chosen by the Selectmen to settle an intra-family dispute that had broken out between William King and his relatives. Nathaniel was busy the following month, also; the third week of March he was requested to be surveyor of fences for Salem Village, or "The Farms" as some still called the settlement. He would arbitrate any boundary disputes that might have broken out between neighbors. Any fence that separated two properties had to be kept in good repair; one of the farmers would be responsible for half the length of the fence, and the other would be responsible for the second half.

In the spring, when the ground had thawed and cattle were to be put out of the barn to graze, the neighbors would get together, each on his own side of the fence, and walk the line, each to be satisfied that the other had properly complied with his duty. Should the fence be a stone one, and not rails — or, on occasion, a hedge — as the men walked down the fence and they came to stones that had fallen from frostheave or accident, they would stoop to pick them up and replace them.

Nathaniel continued as Selectman in May, and Lt. Thomas' house was selected as the site for a meeting, with Andover residents, at which were to be settled the route and details of the country highway that was proposed to bind the towns together.

The Salem Church lost a member when Edward Bishop, Sr., transferred to the Beverly church, which was more convenient for him. On the 17th of June Jane James of Marblehead brought Richard Rowland before the bar of justice and charged him with defamation "for saying that plaintiff came in at a hole in the window in Rowland's house, took him by the throat, and almost choked him as he lay in his bed." He had also called her an "old hag."

Jane James had witnesses on her side in this case — witnesses who were ready to testify; she was also fortunate in having a judge who was unwilling to admit spectral evidence. "Capt. James Smith, aged about forty-three years, deposed that he, Samuel Aborne, Sr., and Richard Rowland were in bed together when suddenly the latter screeched, started up, and said he was almost choked with the old hag, Goody James, who, he said, had come in through a hole in the window and had him fast by the throat, etc. Deponent saw nothing, although the room was very bright with the light of the moon." Aborne backed Smith's testimony, and John Furbush swore he "had often heard Richard Rowland and his wife call Jane James "Jezabel" and "Devil." Goodwife James collected damages.

While these things were going on Nathaniel Putnam and Edmund Batter had been "empowered to perfect the agreement with Goodman Fuller about the highway between Salem and Andover," and they had been endeavoring to get the job done quickly.

In London the Dutch utterly humiliated Charles and the English nation by sailing a fleet into the Thames River, burning shipping, and threatening the capital. It was a temporary distraction, however, and business went on. The astrologer John Booker died, and Elias Ashmole bought his entire library. Richard Head published a biography titled *The Life and Death of Mother Shipton* — the good Mother, who probably had not ever been born, refused to die and, indeed, was alive and kicking on stage as well as between covers, for Thomas Thompson wrote a play that year called "Mother Shipton, Her Life."

John Putnam Jr. had become a great trial and worry to his family and to the Rev. John Higginson over the past several years — he had been acting strangely with regard to the baptism of his children. In fact, none of them had yet been baptized. Higginson feared that Putnam might possibly secretly be troubled with the old Anabaptist heresy that infants ought not to be baptized.

A good deal of pressure had been brought to bear upon John to take his children to the church for the rite. Then, when his new son was born on July 14th, the situation was brought to a climax. The family and the Rev. Mr. Higginson, who was informed of the birth and who came personally to the old homestead Oak Knoll, plied John with enormous pressure. In suppressed anger John bowed and broke. He rounded up his six children — Rebecca, Hannah, Sarah, Priscilla the younger,

Jonathan, and James Putnam; he snatched his new son, John, out of its mother's arms, and he rode, with a contingent of the family, Mr. Higginson leading, into Salem from Salem Village.

The neighbors along the route marveled at the procession, whole families coming out to the road to lean on their gates and watch, some of them falling into line behind. When they all arrived at the Salem meetinghouse everyone went inside and Mr. Higginson conducted a mass baptism. "There," John was heard to mutter under his breath, "Now I may be left in peace." His sisters and brothers were greatly relieved.

On September 21st John, who had been made a corporal in the town militia, was also appointed a constable of Salem with three other men of the town.

John Endicott, Jr., precipitated another crisis in his family by falling ill in January of 1668, making out his will on the 27th of the month and expiring shortly afterward, for he died without issue, thus throwing the Townsend Bishop estate — as per the General Court's decision with regard to his father's unattested will — into the control of his wife, Elizabeth Hawkins Endicott, and out of the control of Zerubabel and his mother, for the will of John Endicott, Jr., specified that his whole estate was to go to his widow.

Exasperation was mixed with sorrow at the home of Zerubabel when his brother's will was probated on February 29th — for 1668 was a leap year. It soon became apparent that Widow Elizabeth Endicott was prepared to leap. It was the accepted social custom in New England that widows and widowers be reattached to spouses as soon as it was reasonably possible, for in this way the land would be populated, according to God's holy ordinance and directive, and estates were protected. Still, Widow Endicott's haste seemed unseemly to a degree. If it were not that she had chosen as her next husband the Rev. James Allen of the Boston First Church, people might have gossiped more than they did, which was considerable at any rate. Mr. Allen was no poor man, for he had significant assets, among which was the press in Cambridge, of which he was proprietor.

Salem became smaller in 1668, for the settlement of Beverly was detached from it to become an autonomous community. It was suggested that Salem parish become even smaller, a proposition that did not sit well with the minister: The Putnam brothers and others of Salem Village petitioned that the Village be granted the right to have its own permanent minister. On the tenth of March the Putnams managed to put some teeth into their request by getting the Salem Villagers to back them *en masse* for seats on the Board of Selectmen. Corporal John and Nathaniel were elected. Five days later Lt. Thomas was appointed surveyor once again.

While contention was building in Salem Village over a new church, an old enemy was rearing his head in the new town of Beverly where John Samson lived at the home of William and Dorcas Hoar. Samson was the owner of a book of palmistry and fortunetelling. Mrs. Hoar was fascinated with it, and she asked permission to borrow it from Samson, which he allowed her to do. The first thing Goody Hoar did with the book was to tell her own fortune: She forecast that she would "live poorly" so long as her husband lived, but that he would die before she did, and after that she would live a better life. The next thing she did was to begin telling the fortunes of some of her neighbors, including those of Ensign Corning and his wife — she predicted that Corning's wife would die before he did.

On the first of June the jury for a new trial was selected, and Lt. Thomas Putnam was chosen as one of its members. The case of a local doctor was a spectacular one — it appeared that physicians in Salem were particularly susceptible to the Devil's wiles, for an old resident — Dr. George Emery, who had been in town since 1636 — was convicted of an unnatural crime and was sentenced to sit upon the gallows with a rope around his neck. Rumors had it that Dr. Emery, like Samson and many others, owned strange books, one of which was believed to be Mericus Casaubon's 1659 edition of Dr. John Dee's *A True and Faithful*

Relation, in the pages of which the conversations of spirits were recorded as Dee's necromancing partner Edward Kelley had dictated them to the old seer. In England Dr. Casaubon was still active. He was Prebend of Canterbury, and during the year 1668 he published another book, *Credulity and Incredulity*, an affirmation of the reality of witchcraft and demonology.

It had been decided in Salem that a new prison was necessary, so the community built one in the center of town, not far from the site of the first meetinghouse. None too soon, either, for peculiar things were beginning to happen in the area: An Ipswich man had a stroke of lightning snatch away part of his Bible during a thunderstorm.

In order to pay for the prison and to ascertain tax rates, Salem ordered on June 24th that a census be taken and an assessment made of the property of the townspeople. Property was greatly at issue, too, when, on August 31st, Widow Elizabeth Endicott married the Rev. Mr. James Allen, himself a widower whose first wife, Hannah Dummer Allen, had died in March and left him 500 acres of land.

Salem continued to have money and minister troubles, for some of the Villagers had not been paying their rates for the support of the pastor. Corporal John Putnam, Jr., and three others were appointed on September 12th to a committee charged with the responsibility of checking on those folks who had not volunteered contributions for Mr. Higginson's maintenance. Three days Mary, seventh child of Nathaniel and Elizabeth Hutchinson Putnam peeped into this Vale of Tears and decided to stay.

Fifty-six-year-old William Brown of Salisbury was living quietly with his wife Elizabeth until one fall day, going from their home to Salisbury mill, Mrs. Brown met Susannah Martin of Amesbury on the road. Mrs. Martin — to Goodwife Brown's vast astonishment and terror — seemed to vanish before her very eyes. From that moment Susannah's specter began to haunt Goody Brown in her very own home.

John Pressey of Amesbury had an even more impressive encounter with the enchanting Susannah Martin. Of a Saturday evening at dimpse he was about three miles from his home, to which he was returning. Just after he passed the field owned by George and Susannah Martin, at Goodall's Hill, he lost his way, though he was quite familiar with the territory. He wandered about in a circle till he came back to the spot where he went wrong, which he was able to recognize by certain "stooping trees."

Pressey set out again, steering by the bright moon, but he lost himself a second, and then a third, time. At last he set a correct course, but within a half mile he saw a light, about the size of a bushel, burning to his left at no great distance. He paid no attention and kept going. The light reappeared twice more, and finally, at its fourth appearance, he approached it and beat at it with his walking-stick — the light bobbed about like "a turkey cock when he spreads his tail," but it did not give way.

Finally Pressey gave up and turned to leave, but just as he did so his feet were knocked out from under him and he fell on his back into a pit or depression in the earth, but he managed to save himself from rolling to the bottom by snatching at some brush growing in the side of the hole. However, the coat he had been carrying over his arm was lost. Pressey got up and walked back to the light — still flickering — in wonderment, for he knew no pit was to be found in the area. There, near to the light, he found his coat lying. Pressey staggered to it and retrieved it, his head spinning.

He managed to grope along his way home for five or six rods, and then he saw Susannah Martin standing to his left, looking at him, just as the lights had stood. She said nothing, just followed him with her eyes, staring at his erratic behavior.

When Pressey made it to his own land he somehow managed to overshoot his house, but he got back to it all right, reeling all the way. At the door he was seized with fear of what might be waiting for him inside; he stood in the open doorway, unable to speak until his wife addressed him. The whole family was fearful as well, he was in such a condition.

The next day Pressey made sure the story of his night out got back to town, and the rumor spread that Susannah Martin's whole body was so sore from some drubbing she had taken that she had to be swabbed.

Susannah Martin continued to haunt Goodwife Elizabeth Brown of Salisbury into the new year of 1669, but in February the haunting changed in radical ways: Instead of appearing in her spectral shape, she began to materialize in the form of birds that pecked Goody Brown's legs or slapped her with their wings. She felt pain where the birds had nipped her, and the pain spread upward into her stomach — they felt like nails or pins. Then they rose farther, into her throat "in a bunch, like a pullet's egg." In the midst of one of her seizures Goody Brown cried, "Witch! You shan't choke me!" At last complaint was made to her pastor who appointed a day of humiliation, which the church observed in Goody Brown's behalf — and the trouble ceased for a while.

By the ninth of March, when Salem town elections were held, so much opposition to the Salem Village petition of the year before had arisen that no Putnam was chosen to sit on the Board of Selectmen. Benjamin Felton was appointed to be the keeper of the Salem prison.

Susannah Martin began to torment Goody Brown again in April. This time the Browns swore out a formal complaint against her to the court, a summons was issued, and she was called to account, but the hearing went nowhere; Susannah was released. Not long afterward Goody Brown was milking her cow at the farm when Susannah came up behind her, weeping, and said to the woman, "I will make you the miserablest creature for defaming my name at the court!"

Newlywed twenty-two-year-old John Kimball of the adjoining town of Newbury had meanwhile struck a bargain to buy some land in Amesbury from Susannah's husband George Martin; he was to pay for it in cash or kind in the following March.

Corporal John Putnam, Jr., was chosen to serve as petty juryman in Salem on June 12th. The trial was unimportant, but the Susannah Martin hearing continued to generate issues in Newbury and Amesbury, for Robert Downer, twenty-eight, who had attended the court's session, took the occasion to tell the accused witch, among other things, that he believed the testimony that had been given in against her, despite the court's dismissal of the case. Goody Martin replied, "A She-devil will fetch you away." Downer was not impressed, but the next night, as he was lying in bed, a cat came in through the window and lay on his chest. It seemed a common enough occurrence at first, but when he remembered Susannah's threat he cried out, throwing off the bedclothes, "Avoid! Thou she-devil, in the name of the Father, the Son, and the Holy Ghost!" The cat jumped off him and scatted out the window.

In June Harvard College graduated the class of 1669, one member of which was a young man named James Bailey who intended to find a position as minister of a church as soon as possible. During the same month William Brown of Salisbury had to make a prolonged trip to Hampton. He did not much like leaving his wife alone in the condition into which she had fallen, but it had to be done. When, in July, he returned to his farm, his wife refused to accept him back — she said, "Have you not met Mr. Bent of Abbey, in England, by whom you are divorced?" Brown was confounded by his obviously demented wife, and he called in for consultation Dr. Fuller and Dr. Crosby. They, too, were baffled so that at last they were driven to the ultimate defense of their ignorance: Their diagnosis was that her distemper was supernatural, not physical. Some evil person had bewitched her.

Nathaniel Putnam and two other men were appointed highway repair overseers in Salem on July 21st. There was a good bit of work to be done on the roads during the summer that remained.

In Dover, New Hampshire, Joan Walford of Portsmouth brought suit against Robert Couch for slander. He had been talking around town and saying malicious things such as that "Goody Walford is a witch."

the court found for the plaintiff, and Couch was fined heavily — five pounds — and made to pay court costs.

John Mitchell went to work one day at William Morse's farm in Newbury — he was to hew shingles. He worked without incident through the day, but when he was about to leave in the evening Mrs. Elizabeth Morse urged him to stay the night so that he could help her son first thing in the morning. Mitchell was unwilling to stay, but Goody Morse was importunate, and he was driven to invent excuses. Finally he told her that he had a mare that had been tied up in his barn all day, and he needed to get back to water it. Reluctantly, Goody Morse told him, "Well, be sure to come again tomorrow!" Mitchell went home.

He did not appear at the Morse farm the next day, nor any day afterward — for he had not at all liked the way he had been handled nor Goody Morse's tone — though she sent for him on several occasions. The last time she sent a message it was to tell Mitchell she was very angry with him. Shortly thereafter Mitchell found one of his calves in terrible condition — it had lost all the hair and skin on its back. Under normal circumstances he might have attributed this affliction to the work of a bobcat, but no matter what he did, the wound would not heal; instead, the calf grew worse and worse till "at last his eyes came out of his head." This was not the worst of the problems that began to beset Mitchell — one of his cows gored another, "and the dung ran out of her side." Soon he had scarcely an animal that wasn't ill one way or another.

Lt. Thomas Putnam was chosen commissioner of rates in Salem on August 27th, and in Wethersfield, Connecticut, Katherine Harrison was accused of witchcraft. She was imprisoned, convicted, and sentenced to death, but the court overruled the jury and merely banished her — for her own safety, the town was so aroused against her. She traveled to Westchester, New York, at the earliest moment.

Lt. Thomas and his second wife, Mary Veren Putnam, had thair first child, Joseph, on September 14th. He was born under the Sign of Virgo — the virgin — in the third decan of that sign. It was the sign of the Messiah.

Joseph Putnam was born to eschew everything else in order to accomplish his duty to others. He would wear, eventually, the Crown of Thorns, and he would suffer for doing what he knew to be right. He would in no way be superstitious, but devoted to the scientific view, and whatever he did would be done without thought of personal reward. He would be the light of Salem when everyone else was wandering about in darkness; eventually their eyes would be opened, and they would see Joseph Putnam beckoning to them to come out of the shadows into the sunlight. Slowly, one by one, the Salem Villagers and the people of Salem would respond — where once they had been ready to crucify him, they would walk toward the man and be saved from themselves.

On the first of November the witchcraft lightning that had been striking throughout New England during the year finally dropped a bolt upon Salem when Dr. Philip Reed accused his medical competition, Goodwife Burt, of dealing in witchcraft. Dr. Reed was not the only one who believed that Goody Burt had been working her evil in Salem, Lynn, and Marblehead, for Madeline Pearson testified as well: She said that her father had taken her sister-in-law, Sarah Townsend Pearson, to the white witch to be cured of a sore foot and odd fits she had been having. Goody Burt had put her to bed and said to her, "Sarah, if you will believe in my god, I will cure you body and soul. But if you tell of it, you shall be as a distracted body as long as you live. Your husband does not believe in my god, and he will not be cured."

Goody Burt's god was evidently Hobbamock, for she prescribed Indian remedies, and on Sarah's foot she used a compound made of blue flag iris. Goody Burt prepared it by boiling the root, then pulverizing it with mortar and pestle and applying it in a wet dressing. Madeline testified that Sarah had believed in Goody Burt's god and was cured of both her wound and her fits. When she had been home some time in good health, the witch had dropped by, offered her a pipe, and said, "Sarah, will you smoke it?" Sarah should perhaps have known better, for she had, against orders, been talking about her cure, but she took the witch's pipe, smoked it, and had immediately fallen into fits again.

Sarah vowed that Goody Burt had brought the Devil to her to torment her; Dr. Reed agreed. Nevertheless, the court dismissed the case.

In England John Wagstaffe continued the debate pro and con aspects of witchcraft by publishing a book that was essentially negative, *The Question of Witchcraft Debated.*

Henry Coley — mathematician, astrologer, and an adopted son of William Lilly, who had, like his former master, been "adopting" promising young men for many years in order to give them the breaks he had himself been lucky enough to receive — also published a book, *Clavis Astrologiae Elimata or, A Key to the Whole Art of Astrology* which Captain Bubb, a charlatan astrologer of Lambeth Marsh, envied. Both were Philomaths, but Captain Bubb was a confidence man as well. A butcher came to him to discover who who had stolen forty pounds from him as he was on his way to a fair. Bubb was happy to help after a deposit of ten pounds had been left with him.

Bubb told the butcher to be at a particular place at a particular moment, and the thief would show up there. The butcher did as he was bade and, sure enough, at precisely the moment forecast, a man on horseback came riding by at a great gallop. The butcher stepped out, knocked the rider off the horse with a club, and took him prisoner. Unfortunately, the butcher was supposed to have been unsuccessful in this capture, because the rider turned out to be Captain Bubb's manservant. Bubb was sentenced to stand in the pillory for conspiracy to defraud.

The Philomaths, like the rest of Europe, were aghast at the news out of Sweden where there had been a horrendous outbreak of witchcraft at Mora: Eighty-five people were burned at the stake because they had enticed three hundred children to fly to the mountain called the Blocula to worship the Devil. The infection began to spread throughout Scandinavia.

Chapter Seven

The Putnams were back in the good graces of a majority of the Salem constituency by March 7th of 1670, for Corporal John Putnam Jr., was chosen as a Selectman; they were back, too, with another petition that requested a minister for Salem Village.

The preternatural phenomena in Newbury involving Susannah Martin continued into March as well when John Kimball, having completed his move from Newbury to Amesbury, was to pay George Martin for the property he had purchased. On the day appointed George and Susannah Martin came to collect; Kimball offered them the choice of three cows and other cattle, but he reserved two other cows with which he did not feel free to part, for they were the first cows the Kimballs had ever had. George Martin was satisfied with the terms of the payment, but Susannah was irritated. She said to Kimball, "It had been as good that you had given us the other cow, for she will never do you any more good."

Not long afterward Kimball — who had not yet built his own house and was living in the home of Edmund Elliot in Amesbury — went to buy a dog for his host. He had heard that Susannah Martin's bitch had whelped, so he went there first. Goody Martin, however, was still disgruntled with him, and she refused to let him have his choice of the pups, reserving some of them, just as Kimball had done to her. But it was one of the reserved pups that Kimball wanted, so he walked away in a huff and went to Goodman Blaisdell, who also had puppies for sale.

While Kimball was dickering with Blaisdell it happened that George Martin came by and asked him whether he wouldn't rather have one of his wife's puppies. Kimball replied, coldly, "No."

Later the same day Edmund Elliot dropped in on the Martins at home; while he was there he overheard George ask his wife, "Is John Kimball not to have one of your puppies?"

"He is," Susannah replied.

"Well, he have got one at Goodman Blaisdell's. I saw him choose it and mark it."

"If I live," Susannah said in a pet, "I'll give him puppies enough!" Elliot returned home and told the story to his houseguest.

A few days later John Kimball was coming back home to the Elliots' farm from the site of his future house in the woods. It was almost sunset of a clear day, but suddenly a small black cloud arose in the northwest, and the wind began to blow. As Kimball was walking the road between the house of John Woods and the Amesbury meetinghouse a few drops of rain began to fall. There were stumps of trees by the wayside, and for no seeming reason he began to stumble over the stumps one after another. As he was carrying an axe, which was dangerous, he resolved not to trip over the next stump — but it happened anyway.

A little below the meetinghouse a black puppy suddenly scooted between his legs; it ran around and round and repeated the maneuver till Kimball was so put out he tried to hit it with his axe — he missed, but the puppy disappeared. A bit farther on down the road another black puppy — seemingly larger than the first — again jumped up on him, and again Kimball found he could not hit it. He began to be afraid. He ran to the fence and called on God and Jesus Christ — the dog disappeared. Kimball decided not to mention the incident when he got home for fear of fretting his wife. He slept late the day after but finally awoke with a headache.

In the morning Edmund Elliot, going toward the barn of his neighbors the Martins to look at oxen, stepped into their kitchen to light his pipe. Susannah asked him, "Where is Kimball?"

"Abed with his wife, for aught I know," Elliot said.

"They say," Susannah remarked, "he was affrighted last night."

"With what?" Elliot asked.

"With puppies."

"I have heard nothing of it," Elliot said. "Where did you hear of it?"

"About the town," was her reply.

After a time Elliot left and told the story elsewhere. Kimball, who had been working in the woods alone all day building the frame for his house, heard the story when he returned, for by then it was truly all over town.

The Royal Society of London in March published in its *Philosophical Transactions* some extracts from a letter that John Winthrop, Jr. — an American Fellow of the Society — had sent in regarding a number of natural objects and observations. Winthrop had sent along, as well, several samples. He had struck up a correspondence with English and European scientists including Johann Rudolph Glauber the chemist, and the astronomers Johann Hevelius and Johannes Kepler, Jr.

William Lilly had changed his entire life style since he had moved to his estate in Hersham. He completed his study of medicine, and during 1670 he received a license to practice from Gilbert Sheldon, Archbishop of Canterbury. Lilly's life was that of the country gentleman except on Saturdays when he traveled to Kingston to give medical advice to anyone who wished to consult him. In Hersham it was his custom to treat any and all of his neighbors free of charge.

Major Thomas Weir, the 76-year-old Presbyterian stalwart and Puritan par excellence suddenly was struck in Scotland with fearful attacks of remorse and conscience. He voluntarily came forward and began to confess to the most depraved and diabolical life that anyone had ever heard of. His activities had commenced at the age of ten when he attempted to rape his sister, eventually seduced her, and lived with her in incest from the age of 16 to 50 when, at last, he began to loathe her because she was so old. He had otherwise to turn, however, for he had also committed sexual acts with Margaret Bourdon — his stepchild, the daughter of his dead wife — and with various others, including Bessie Weems, his live-in maidservant for twenty years. When human partners were unavailable, he used animals, including a mare he had once ridden into the west country near New Mills. In 1651 a woman had caught him in a barn with his mare *in flagrante delicto*, but no one had believed her and she had been whipped for lying.

No one but a witch could have committed such atrocities. He and his sister were indicted on April 9th for various of these crimes, "but most especially, consulting witches, necromancers, and devils." The confessions of Thomas and Jane Weir were enough to convict them, but others testified as well, including Weir's sister-in-law Margaret who deposed that when she was a young woman she "found the Major…and Jane, lying together in the barn at Wicket-Shaw, and…they were both naked in the bed together." Margaret had been above them in the barn, unseen, and she saw "that the bed did shake" and she heard "some scandalous language between them."

Jane Weir told stories in court of having a Devil's imp that aided her in spinning "extraordinary quantities of yarn" for her "in a shorter time than three or four women could have done the same." Long ago she had signed a pact with the Devil, selling her soul to him, and her brother owned a magic staff of thornwood carved in heads that everyone remembered him leaning upon to pray, but they had thought he was praying to God!

Major Weir was strangled and burned on April 11th, and his sister Jane followed the next day, but while she stood on the ladder she said to the gathered multitude, "I see a great crowd of people come hither today to behold a poor old miserable creature's death, but I trow there be few among you who are weeping and mourning for the broken Covenant."

In Amesbury, Massachusetts, John Pressey and his wife Marah received a visit from Susannah Martin who took them to task for having given in false evidence against her at her hearing the year before. She said to them, "You shall never prosper for doing it, and if you are never so likely to have more, yet you shall never obtain it!"

On the fifth of April, just before the Weir executions, Thomas Oliver in Salem was "chosen to go from house to house about the town once a month to inquire what strangers do come or have privily thrust themselves into the town, and to give notice to the Selectmen...." Oliver was a good choice, for in appointing him they in effect appointed a team, for his wife, Bridget, took a good deal of pleasure in keeping her eyes open and feeding in tips to her husband.

In June Harvard College graduated its class of 1670. Among the new holders of the baccalaureate degree was a young man who had distinguished himself, while at the school, as an athlete and gymnast. George Burroughs was a small man in stature, but solidly built. More than that, he liked to astonish people with his feats of strength, and he had a teasing streak in him as well. When folk marveled at his abilities in anything he was wont to be mysterious about how he did what he did. Yet, all in all, he was an affable young man who was likely to do well as the parson of a village — one of the lesser ones, probably.

Daniel Epps was hired as schoolmaster of Salem on July 18th. It was a hot summer, but he immediately set to work to prepare himself for the upcoming school year. In July, too, Katherine Harrison of Wethersfield, Connecticut, banished to Westchester, found that her reputation as a witch had followed her, and her neighbors were complaining to the authorities that she ought to be sent back whence she had come. The fact that Mrs. Harrison was single — a widow — and wealthy did nothing to endear her to the Westchester matrons. Worse still, she was the houseguest of a man of the town. In August she was summoned to New York, and her host, "Capt. Richard Danton, at whose house she resideth," was requested to accompany her on her visit to court. There, the magistrate referred the matter to the next General Court, which was to meet in October.

Dorcas Hoar went to Rev. John Hale in Lynn to confess and repent of her past sins. Goody Hoar told the minister that she had some time back borrowed a book of palmistry from which she had learned to divine the future. Hale, shaking his head sadly, said, "It is an evil book and art." Dorcas agreed and promised to do better in the future.

The Putnam family celebrated two events on the fourth of September: Joseph Putnam was baptized in Salem Church by the Rev. Mr. Higginson at about the same time that his aunt, Rebecca Prince Putnam, was giving birth to a girl cousin named Susannah.

The General Court of New York met in October and considered the matter of Mrs. Katherine Harrison and Capt. Richard Danton. The records of her having been cleared by the Connecticut General Court had arrived; they were reviewed by the New York magistrates, and Mrs. Harrison was once more cleared. She was told to go back to Westchester if she wished.

In Salem in November Thomas Oliver had been diligent in his role as town spy, for he had managed to find a stranger living in the midst of Salem. Francis Skerry was fined for having allowed the interloper to live with him for three weeks without town permission. Two days later Nathaniel Putnam was made a petty juryman, and the year ended on December 30th with the Selectmen making arrangements for the care and feeding of one of the town's odd birds, Elizabeth Vergoose.

On the 12th of April 1671 the Indian chief named Metacom, son of the great chief Massasoit and known as "King Philip," signed a peace treaty with the Massachusetts government at Taunton. It was a great relief to the settlers, for there had been rumblings of trouble from time to time over the past few years.

In the late spring two of the Putnam cousins — Edward, who was fourteen, and Little John, Nathaniel's son, eleven — decided that they would go hunting for wild beehives. They knew what to do. First, they prepared a smudge pot by putting moist, oily rags into a crock, then they went out into the meadow to follow a bee home. It sounded easier than it was. They managed to follow several bees a short way into the woods, but invariably when they dodged a branch or tried to fold aside a patch of underbrush, the bee would get away.

The day was a hot one, and the meadow they had chosen lay next to Mile Brook, not far from Oak Knoll. The boys had about decided to give it up when, more by luck than anything else, they stopped to pant in the steamy woods just after they had lost another bee — and heard not far away a droning noise. They followed their ears and saw, hanging from the branch of a small maple, a good-sized hive with the workers going in and out in great activity.

The boys got excited and Edward said, "Have you the smoke pot ready?" Little John looked at him with consternation: He had left it in the meadow. "Go and get it," Edward told him disdainfully, "it is no matter, for we must wait till they be sleeping at any rate."

Little John made his way to the bank of the brook, made a mark on a tree, and took landmarks so he could find his way back, then followed Mile Brook to the meadow. He got back with the pot all right, but by then he was so hot and sweaty and the black flies were biting so badly he said, "It is a long time to wait till the sun sets. Let's go to swim in the brook."

Edward thought that was a fine idea, and that was what they did. They swam and frolicked in the water till at last they were bored, put their clothes back on, and returned to the hive. The sun was just at the horizon when they got there, and the cousins began to think the bees were settling down — almost none were going in. Finally, they thought it was all right — that was their first mistake; their second was to try to light the smudge pot directly under the hive rather than at a distance and carry it there.

Little John was the first to be stung as he held his hand cupped around the wood shavings while Edward struck steel against flint. He let out a howl and slapped at the back of his neck. Edward looked up with surprise at the noise and immediately joined in with his own cry of anguish. As they made for Mile Brook, crashing through the woods, the boys were surrounded by a cloud of angry insects. It seemed forever till they were able to dive into the water — dive down deep and swim for all they were worth with the current. Edward came up for air once, too soon, and went back under. When finally they both surfaced the bees were gone. They waded in the shallows, Little John weeping and Edward moaning, till they struck the trail to Uncle John's.

When they came in the door Aunt Rebecca Putnam and Mother Elizabeth Vergoose, who was visiting, could hardly recognize who they were they were so covered with stings. There was no time to waste with fancier remedies, and too great an area to be covered anyway, so Rebecca ordered her two eldest daughters, Rebecca and Sarah, to "Go to the spring and get half a bucket of water. Make some mud of it — go quickly!" The young women turned and ran out the door. Rebecca stripped the boys naked. Mother Goose said to Priscilla, who was Edward's age, "do not stare. Come and help me." the old woman took Priscilla by the elbow and, picking up a large pot from the ingle, they went out the door.

Sarah and Rebecca came rushing back in with a bucket full of mud and all three of them plastered the exhausted, groaning boys with it. Outdoors Mother Goose and Priscilla were stripping the leaves off the trumpet honeysuckle vines in the clearing. When they had a pot full of them — the younger children helped, so the job was done quickly — Mother Goose gathered some mint, added it to the honeysuckle leaves, and got two washing sticks. She handed one to Priscilla, and they began to pound the pot full of leaves into a green paste. She added a little beer, said, "Spit is better, but this will do," and took it inside.

The boys were washed off, the paste applied, and they were put to bed. When Uncle John got home he was sent to get Nathaniel and Thomas. By the time they arrived the boys were feverish, but the men had brought Dr. Zerubabel Endicott, with them, and he knew what to do to bring it down: He bled them. In the morning Little John and Edward were ill, but it became apparent they would survive. John hugged his wife, and everyone thanked Mother Goose for her help. Dr.

Endicott asked her, "What remedy was it you used?" She told him. He nodded his head. "It is an Indian cure," he said; "I have heard of it."

Salem had been having its troubles with the minister, Mr. Higginson, for some time about the terms of his maintenance. On the seventeenth of July Nathaniel Putnam, Edmund Batter, and Henry Bartholomew were appointed to make him an offer of 100 pounds per annum, to be paid quarterly, plus 40 cords of wood. Higginson dickered with them and made a counter-proposal. At the end of August John Corwin refused to pay a bill he had been assessed by the town and Corporal John Putnam, Jr. served on a jury.

On the thirtieth of October Mistress Elizabeth Knapp, a young woman of Groton — whose namesake had in 1654 been hanged for witchcraft in Fairfield, Connecticut — suddenly began to manifest signs of diabolical possession. She wept and laughed uncontrollably, roared, had violent fits, and screamed "Money! Money!" The minister of the town, the Rev. Mr. Samuel Willard, was called in the same day and that evening, just before bedtime, he was sitting with Elizabeth before the fire when suddenly she cried, "Oh! My legs!" and grabbed at them; then, "Oh! My breast" and grasped it; finally, "Oh! I am strangled!" and clutched at her throat.

Two days later, the day after Halloween, Mistress Knapp in her fits began to accuse a local woman of having bewitched her. The test of the witch's touch was administered: Though Elizabeth's eyes were closed when the woman laid hands upon her, Elizabeth was able to identify her. Rev. Mr. Willard, who was sure Elizabeth hadn't peeked, asked accused and accuser to pray together, however, and afterward Elizabeth admitted that she had been deluded by the Devil — this nice old woman never had hurt her. It was the Devil himself who afflicted her. The Devil, Elizabeth said to the minister, had been after her for years to sign a pact with him, and she had been often tempted to set her hand to the page.

During the next two weeks Elizabeth Knapp's condition continued and got worse. On the fifteenth her tongue was drawn up towards the roof of her mouth so powerfully that grown men who tried could not loosen it with their fingers. Six men could scarcely hold her down in the midst of one of her fits, and if they let loose she would jump up, her face contorted, and skip about the house.

On the 20th of November Nathaniel Putnam was a trial juryman, but he and his neighbors were more interested in the Groton case, about which rumors had begun circulating, than in local misdemeanors: On the 29th a witch in the shape of a dog appeared to Elizabeth Knapp and tried to strangle her — a difficult maneuver with paws. Evidently the invisible dog was uncommonly resourceful, however, because before witnesses she gagged and gasped.

Early in December Elizabeth again accused someone in town of tormenting her, but this time it was noticed that her fit was a particularly violent one, so more credence was given her statement than the last time she had pointed her finger. Rev. Samuel Willard investigated personally. He found "two evident and clear mistakes" in Elizabeth's accusation, and these served to exonerate the accused person.

It was Willard's opinion that the girl had not been bewitched by anyone, but that she had been possessed by a demon. He delivered a sermon to his congregation, the main point of it being that he and they ought to take the example of Mistress Knapp to heart. "Let us all," he said, "examine by this Providence what sins they have been that have given Satan so much footing in this poor place."

The Devil kept his footing. On December 17th Elizabeth's tongue was extruded to an enormous extent, and a demon began speaking through her, though her lips did not seem to move. The ungodly thing railed at Samuel Willard, uttering the deepest blasphemies, claiming it was greater than God. "I," said the demon buried in Elizabeth, "am greater than your God," and her eyes blazed up into the preacher's face.

Ministers throughout the colony were interested in the case. One of the most interested was Increase Mather of Boston; another was the Rev. Deodat Lawson of Martha's Vineyard.

Sir Matthew Hale, the great Witch Judge of England, would have been interested too, had he known about it. He had prospered during the year, as he had done under both King and Parliament. This time Charles II appointed him to be Chief Justice. Sir Ferdinando Gorges — an elderly man by then — began to renew his grievances against Massachusetts and her government. It was his contention that the colony had illegally intruded itself into his lands in Maine, and it was true: The Massachusetts Bay government did indeed act as though it were the legal government of the northern territories of New England. Charles was interested, but his war with Holland was of more moment.

Henry Coley, one of Lilly's adopted sons, published an almanac for 1672 that competed with Lilly's annual ephemeron, but the two men were still on good terms. On the 26th of January a fire destroyed a portion of Elias Ashmole's library and collection of 9000 coins and other antiquities in his quarters at the Middle Temple, but his most valuable manuscripts and coins remained safe at his home in South Lambeth.

On the 14th of March Corporal John Putnam, Jr. was elected a Salem Selectman again. About a week later, on the 22nd, Salem Church gave its permission to Salem Village to set itself off as a separate parish, to a degree. The new parish was not, however, to be autonomous, but — as in the earlier case of Beverly — merely a branch parish of the mother church in Salem which was to retain final control over everything. One of Salem church's greatest concerns was the rate burden of its parishioners, for if Salem Village were allowed to detach itself completely, its ratepayers would go with it and the rates of the Salem citizens would need to be increased to make up for the loss. John Higginson had been having difficulty enough with his parishioners over his maintenance without wishing to add this as well.

The net effect of the proposed new arrangement — which still had to be ratified by the General Court — was that the parishioners of

Salem and Salem Village both were to pay rates for the upkeep of Rev. Mr. Higginson; the Salem Villagers, in addition, were to pay rates for their own minister's maintenance as well as for the building of a meetinghouse and its maintenance. It was a patently unfair situation for the Salem Villagers, but some of the most zealous of them jumped at the chance anyway, without thinking of the consequences. One of these was Thomas Putnam. His brother, Nathaniel, was more prudent, but he represented a minority view.

John Allen of Salisbury, a 25-year-old man, was working hauling timber for George Carr who was building a boat in Amesbury. Having finished, and getting ready to go home, he was accosted by Susannah Martin who asked him if he would cart staves for her and her husband, George. Allen excused himself on the grounds that his oxen were weak and needed building up before they did any more heavy labor. Susannah was not satisfied and she muttered, "You had been as good you had, for your oxen will never do you much more service."

Allen replied, "Dost threaten me, thou old witch?" He made a grab at her to throw her into the nearby brook, but Susannah skipped away and over the bridge.

On his way home one of Allen's oxen grew so weary that it had to be unyoked and led. When Allen and his team reached home he put the oxen out to graze with other cattle in the marsh grass on Salisbury beach. A few days later, when he and his help went to round the cattle up they found that the tracks of the beasts led to the mouth of the Merrimac River and stopped, seemingly at the river's brink.

Allen assumed that the cattle were drowned, but a further search showed that they had gone ashore at Plum Island. The party followed the tracks clear across the island and part way back again, where they found the cattle lying down. They tried to herd them, but the beasts refused to budge or even to get to their feet. Without warning, then, the herd heaved upright and stampeded clear into the ocean. All the animals swam out to sea except two old oxen that left the herd. One of the swimming cattle returned and barged off into the interior, through

Newbury, and into the forest beyond where, a few days later, it was found. Of all the herd, only those three were saved.

On April 22nd Rebecca, eldest child of Corporal John and Rebecca Prince Putnam, was married to John Fuller, but in Salisbury another love match came to nothing. James Carr dropped in on John Wheelwright and his daughter, the Widow Maverick. She was quite nice to him and invited him to come more often — "You are such a stranger," she told him. A few days later James Carr complied, only to discover that William Bradbury was also there. Carr didn't know it, but Bradbury was the widow's suitor; when Carr came in, nevertheless, she proceeded to be rude to Bradbury, and eventually he left in high dudgeon. Carr stayed, had a nice visit, and left somewhat later.

A few days afterward he began to manifest strange symptoms of an illness. He went to see Dr. Crosby who treated him with no result — even a simple made of tobacco steeped in water helped not a whit. Frustrated, Dr. Crosby told James Carr, "I believe you are behagged."

Carr replied, "I had thought so a good while."

"By whom?" the doctor inquired.

"I do not care to speak of it," said the patient, "for she is counted an honest woman." Crosby, however, pressed the issue, and finally Carr said, "Goody Bradbury," William's mother.

Dr. Crosby nodded wisely. "I do believe Mary Bradbury is a great deal worse than Goody Martin."

Several nights later Carr was in bed when he felt something — perhaps a cat — on the stead with him. He tried to strike at it and believed he hit it. Immediately, Dr. Crosby's medicines began to take effect and Carr started to mend.

In July Corporal John lost another daughter on the bridal path — his second eldest, Sarah Putnam, became the wife of John Hutchinson of Salem Village.

Corruption was uncovered in Salem public affairs when in a trial it was testified that the jailkeeper, Benjamin Felton, "had often been known to take prisoners out of the prison to help him about his own occasions, and sometimes men have run away in the meantime." On the 17th of August Lt. Thomas Putnam was made a grand juryman; the town of Salem decided to build a new schoolhouse and watch house, and to tear down the old meetinghouse. In expectation that the General Court would put its stamp of approval on the new Salem Village parish, Salem donated the Villagers their old pulpit.

In England Charles II issued a declaration of indulgence which suspended strictures against Catholics and Puritan dissenters. Abstractly, the declaration might have seemed fair, but the people didn't care for it — they believed the king was about to try to reestablish Catholicism in England.

Dr. Mericus Casaubon's 1668 book was reissued under the title, *A Treatise Proving Spirits, Witches, and Supernatural Operations by Pregnant Instances and Evidences.* There had been few instances of witchcraft in England since the Restoration, but there were those who, if they did not care for the reestablishment of Catholicism, would not at all have objected to the rejuvenation of an old folk belief.

On October 8th the General Court ratified the establishment of the Salem Village parish, along with all of the strictures attached to the proposal. On the 11th of November Lt. Thomas Putnam was made chairman of the Parish Committee, and the Rev. James Bailey of Newbury was chosen by the committee and a majority of the parishioners to come to preach on probation, but not everyone was happy with the choice, in particular Nathaniel Putnam — at loggerheads with his brother over the issue — and Bray Wilkins. The families of these two men in themselves constituted a sizeable dissident minority. Objectors to Rev. Mr. Bailey did not at all care for the way the Parish Committee overrode their demurrers, and a hard grievance settled in to stay, some of it directed toward the Rev. John Higginson, who concurred in the choice of Bailey, but much more of it aimed inward.

The chief bone of contention between the dissidents and the majority was in calling a minister to the Village before a meetinghouse was built and before satisfactory arrangements had been made to provide for his support and to end rate-paying by Villagers of Mr. Higginson's maintenance in Salem. Nathaniel Putnam felt his brother Thomas and his supporters had been far too hasty.

Mrs. Mary Carr Bailey's 11-year-old sister, Ann Carr — whose Salisbury brothers were particularly prone to be the objects of the maleficia of witches — had herself been born in Salisbury on June 15, 1661; she was thus a third decan Gemini, and in all ways but one she was completely typical of her Zodiacal Sign. The Geminian was changeable, egocentric — always wanting to be the center of attention, like Ann Carr. But in addition the third decan Geminian was supposed to be a rational person, intelligent and objective.

In no way was the girl objective — she was spoiled. She would have her way no matter what. Though Ann was intelligent, rationality could not be said to have much of a place in her life: She was moody and mysterious, giving instances of flights of fancy that delighted anyone who was with her at the time, though there was no indication that Ann Carr felt there was anything out of the usual about her imaginary creations. The girl was, like most of the Carrs, subject to violent passions. Altogether, Ann combined a number of attributes remarkable for a Puritan maid.

Late in the year Katherine Harrison of Westchester, New York, was again accused of practicing witchcraft. She was charged and bound over to the next court sessions.

In Newbury, Massachusetts, Jonathan Woodman was going home on a dark night. A cat came up to him and rubbed against his legs. He tried to shoo it away, but it wouldn't leave, so he finally fetched it a kick that sent it into a fence. The cat gave a shriek, disappeared, and bothered him no more. At about the same moment William Morse sent for a doctor to look at a wound in the head of his wife, Elizabeth. When Woodman heard of it he became suspicious until he learned that Goody

Morse had originally been hurt several days before when she was hit by bricks that fell out of her chimney. Nevertheless, Woodman thought it peculiar she should have grown worse that same night he kicked the cat.

A grievance was given in at Salem on February 18th when "Joseph Herrick and Edward Bishop made complaint to the Selectmen that they were opposed by William Fisk, James Friend, and several others of Wenham, from felling trees in the Great Swamp nigh Wenham and from bringing away some which they had felled." The men were Salem Villagers, and the border dispute between Salem Village and Topsfield continued as well, so that there was constant friction among the abutting territories.

At the same town meeting Nathaniel Ingersoll was "allowed to sell beer and cider by the quart for the time while the farmers are a-building of their meeting house, and on Lord's Days thereafter." Ingersoll's tavern was next door to the meetinghouse and was handy to thirsty men working on the new building. After morning services of a Sunday the parish men could drop in to have a pint of refreshment and wait for the afternoon service to begin. Though it was seldom said aloud, it was well known that some of the men felt the taverns that were nearly always located near the meetinghouses in New England villages were a true Godsend, for the Lord only knew how a body could get through two long-winded speeches in a single day without a little inner support in the form of been or cider, not to mention the fact that public water was still normally polluted. The women generally went home and took with them a wife or two from the outlying districts to gossip while the men drank and exchanged rumors.

Corporal John Putnam, Jr. was made Selectman of Salem at the end of March. Not long after, on April 5th, Elizabeth Allen, wife of Boston's Rev. James Allen and the former widow of John Endicott, Jr., took her leave of the world and left her whole estate, including the Townsend Bishop farm, to her husband.

Now and then Salem allowed a new resident within its precincts, and one of these was Samuel Getchell who, on April 15th, was admitted as an inhabitant.

The case of Eunice Cole of Hampton, New Hampshire, was brought up for hearing at last when some of her neighbors formally denounced her as a witch. She was taken before the bar at a Salisbury county court and sent to Boston jail to await action by a grand jury. Eventually she was indicted for "familiarity with the Devil" by the Massachusetts Court of Assistants and tried. The Court decided that, though there were "just grounds for suspicion of her having had familiarity with the Devil," it proceeded no further against her than to require that she "depart from and abide out of this jurisdiction" — which meant that she was still New Hampshire's problem.

The colony's first dancing school was opened in Boston and just as quickly closed down. There would be no dancing in Massachusetts if the government could help it. In Salem on May 26th Nathaniel Putnam was relieved of his position as layer-out of land — that is, surveyor. Anna Edmunds was accused of witchcraft and tried, found not guilty, and her accusers ordered to pay court costs.

What the King's Commissioners had earlier done, a Dutch fleet undid on July 30th when New York was retaken and renamed New Amsterdam. The defenses of Salem — never what one might call threatening — had fallen into disrepair. The coming of war to the shores of North America — though it was not a terrifically violent one so far — shook Salem into action when the General Court ordered that the town repair its fort at Winter Island, mend the platform, and fit up its artillery. August, too, was the month when Ruth Putnam, the tenth child of Corporal John Putnam and Rebecca Prince Putnam, opened her eyes upon Salem Village and the world.

The case of Katherine Harrison, who had for a third time been accused of witchcraft in 1672, was brought before the new Dutch military governor of New Amsterdam, Capt. Anthony Colve, rather than a court of law. His practically immediate dismissal of the complaint in August was taken huffily by the complainants as indicative of a certain amount of contempt on his part.

The 11th day of September the wealthy minister of Boston James Allen took a wife for the third time: Sarah Hawlins. Allen settled into parish life as in Salem gnashed his teeth in anguish over the passing of what he considered to be his property to utter strangers.

Nathaniel Putnam sat on a trial jury in litigious Salem in the middle of November, and in England the Parliament had passed the "Test Act" which required that anyone holding civil or military office in British territory was required to be a communicant of the Anglican Church. When Massachusetts heard of it there was rage in the bosoms of the Puritan government leaders, the elders, ministers and church members — nearly anyone who was anyone, in fact, none of whom were Anglican communicants.

Apostle John Eliot had, however, made Puritan converts among 4000 New England Indians by 1674, a fact that did not sit well with the rest of the Indians who were more hostile to whites as the numbers of settlers increased and encroached further and further upon Indian hunting territories and living space.

A sad case of poverty was brought before the Selectmen of Salem in March, a kind of poverty through business reverse that was quite common in the port town. When a seaman sank everything he owned into a ship and that ship was lost at sea, or the cargo rendered unsalvageable, or some such situation, often the Salem town fathers did as they did now when they noted, "The Selectmen considering how that, by the Providence of God, Capt. Moore is brought very low, they judge it meet to grant him liberty for the keeping of a public house of entertainment for the selling of beer, wine, and cider, this to be done for the first year upon trial...." There were many taverns in Salem and its vicinity.

Sarah Atkinson of Newbury received a springtime visit from Susannah Martin in the most inclement, wet weather available, and

Susannah's appearance astonished Goody Atkinson. She asked, "Did you come from Amesbury afoot?":

"I did," Susannah answered.

"How could you come in this time afoot?" Sarah inquired, clearing away children from the fire so that Susannah could dry out her petticoats, but Susannah spread them and said, "I am as dry as you." She turned her coats to show Sarah who noticed that not even the woman's shoes were wet.

Startled, Sarah said, "I should have been wet up to my knees if I should have come so far on foot!"

Susannah laughed. "I scorn to have a drabbled tail," she told her hostess.

The objections to rate-paying among Salem Villagers broke into litigation on March 27th when Nathaniel Putnam and his brother John, Jr, refused to give the Salem constable their portions of the rate assessed to pay for the building of the new Salem meetinghouse, and the brothers were brought before the bar at Ipswich Sessions of the Court.

Capt. Brown, the ruined ship's master turned tavern keeper soon had company in tribulation, for on the 9th of April the Selectmen again wrote that, "Considering how that William Hollingsworth, by several losses at sea, is brought low, the Selectmen have granted liberty to his wife to draw beer and cider, and Ipswich Court allowed of it while the Court was at Salem."

A case of sympathetic magic surfaced in Suffolk County when Edward Peggy was convicted for "using indirect means by powders, or other ways unlawful, to engage the affections or desires of women kind to him, and for begetting Ruth Hemingway of Roxbury with child."

Jonathan Corwin bought the Richard Davenport property in Salem Village; and Hannah Grey, for acting lasciviously, was sentenced to wear a sign on her cap at public meeting in Salem and Beverly: "I STAND HERE FOR MY LASCIVIOUS AND WANTON CARRIAGES" the sign read, spelled out in capital letters. She had been convicted for enticing the Harvard "scholar boys," using "bawdy language," and being seen acting wantonly with Andrew Davis.

Corporal John Putnam Jr. was rising fast in the world. In partnership with Simon Bradstreet and Daniel Dennison he began an iron works at Rowley. John and his brothers, though they could not compete in wealth with such residents of Salem proper as the merchants George Corwin and Philip English, nevertheless were becoming the wealthiest and most powerful members of the Salem Village community.

The strange incidents at Newbury continued during 1674: Joshua Richardson was driving his sheep to Hampton, and he decided to corral his sheep in William Morse's barn because the boat he was to use to float them downriver was nearby the Morse property. He went into the barn to be sure it was empty before he used it, then drove his herd inside. Elizabeth Morse spotted him from the house and came hustling outside. She spat angrily at Richardson, "You had better ask leave!" She went on to give him a tongue-lashing for his presumption.

Richardson disgustedly drove his sheep out and got them to Hampton all right, but when they had been there only a little while they began to grow ill and to foam at the mouth about two hours later. One of the sheep died. The Hampton folk asked him where he had penned his sheep, and Richardson replied, "In Morse's cow house." Everyone took it for granted the sheep had been bewitched.

In June Sir Joseph Williamson was appointed by King Charles to the post of Secretary of State, and he became interested in the Massachusetts problem. He wanted to know the answers to certain questions about the colonists: How many laws did they break? In what ways had they usurped the King's authority? He held hearings and many witnesses were eager to testify before the Council of Plantations to give evidence against the haughty colonists of Massachusetts Bay.

A witch named Ann Foster was tried and hanged in Northampton for having set fire to the barns of a grazier who had provoked her, destroyed by magic his hay and grain, and bewitched a flock of sheep.

A pamphlet telling her story was soon in the streets; it was titled, *A Full and True Relation*....

The namesake of Ann Foster's town had its own troubles with witches at the same time: In Northampton, Massachusetts, Mary, the wife of Samuel Bartlett, died of an illness the doctors could not diagnose. As in many such situations, they opined that the cause was witchcraft. In this case the witch was determined to be — another coincidence — a woman of respectable citizenship named Mrs. Mary Bliss Parsons, wife of Joseph Parsons, a leading member of the western Massachusetts community. While the Devil was moving forward in the Northamptons, Salem turned to psychology: The town appointed Lt. Thomas Putnam rate commissioner on the 15th of August. But if the Selectmen of the town hoped to lay to rest the rate-paying hostilities between Town and Farms with such a move, they were wide of the mark.

The Northampton case was taken up by the court in Springfield on the 28th of September, and Samuel Bartlett submitted depositions against Mrs. Mary Parsons who appeared in person without waiting to be summoned. She addressed the court to declare, "I do assert my innocency. I am clear of any such crime as witchcraft. The righteous God knows I am not guilty, and I leave my cause in His hands." The court was unimpressed. It appointed a committee of women to conduct a body search of Mary. Witch teats were found, they made their report to the court, and she was bound over to the Court of Assistants in Boston.

In the fall George Jacobs, Jr., of Salem Village dared to take on Nathaniel Putnam. He had become irritated about a trespass and had driven Nathaniel's horses into the river, threatening to drown them. One of the horses did drown and others were lost. He was taken to court and fined 20 shillings court costs, but no damages were assessed, much to Nathaniel's humiliation.

John March, a native of Newbury, twenty-two years old, was working in Boston with John Wells who sent him home to Newbury on an errand. While he was there he stayed with Goody Wells who told him before he went to bed, "I do not question but that you shall see something in your chamber at night."

March's bedmate that night was Daniel Greenleaf. While they were lying and talking they heard a noise and saw "several cats and rats at play together in the chamber, running after one another; the rats after the cats." March and Greenleaf were "much amazed," but they overcame their emotions sufficiently to throw shoes and other things at the animals and hit some of them, at which, oddly enough, they disappeared.

Next morning, before they left the room, the two men heard Goody Wells and Goody Elizabeth Morse outside the door, arguing. They heard Mrs. Wells call Goody Morse a witch. When John March went downstairs Mrs. Wells asked him, "Did you see cats and rats at play last night?"

Astonished again, March queried back, "Why do you ask me?"

"Goody Morse said you saw cats and rats in the night. When I said, 'How do you know?' she said, 'I heard so.'" March could not fathom it at all, for neither he nor Greenleaf had been out of the room to tell anyone anything. It did not occur to him to ask himself how Goody Wells had known in the first place, before he had gone to bed, that he would "see something" in his chamber that night. Mrs. Wells continued, "I have often been to Goody Morse's house to fetch water and have seen some small creatures like mice or rats run into the house after her and run under her coats."

It was not long before the story was all over town, as usual. When William Morse heard it, he prosecuted Mrs. Wells for slander.

In November the Dutch returned New York to the British under the Treaty of Westminster. And in Essex County Court held in Salem on the 24th, "Christopher Brown, having reported that he had been trafficking or discoursing with one whom he apprehended to be the

Devil, which came like a gentleman" in order to get Brown to bind himself to him as a servant, "upon his examination, his discourse seeming inconsistent with truth etc., the court gave him good counsel and caution and, for the present, dismissed him."

On the second day of March, 1675, the case of Mary Bliss Parsons of Northampton was brought before the Boston Court of Assistants on an indictment by the grand jury, and she was put into prison to await trial.

Five days later the General Court decided that the Salem Militia was to be divided into two companies, an upper one, to include Salem Village, and a lower. Joseph Getchell was appointed drummer to the upper company, and John Gedney's tavern was "appointed for a house of entertainment for the upper company." The following 10th of April Lt. Thomas Putnam was appointed to a committee that was to settle the Lynn boundary with inhabitants of that community, and he was also chosen commissioner to raise a rate.

Mary Bliss Parsons came to trial on the 13th of May on charges "that she had, not having the fear of God before her eyes, entered into familiarity with the Devil, and committed sundry acts of witchcraft on the persons of one or more." Despite the ominous sound of the indictment the jury acquitted her. Subsequently charges of witchcraft were leveled at her son John, but the evidence was so skimpy that the county court back home dismissed the case.

John Samson, who had lived with the Hoars in Beverly five years earlier, had gone to Casco, Maine, on some occasion; there he sold the book of palmistry that Dorcas Hoar had borrowed from him in 1668 and that she had returned two years later, stricken with conscience. Casco was an outpost of New England civilization — a backward, insignificant settlement surrounded on three sides by dense forest filled with hostile Indians, and on the fourth by the chill ocean. The Rev. George Burroughs had chosen this place in which to do his work. He was held in awe by many of the inhabitants, not only because he was a man of God, but because he could do things with his muscle that few ordinary men could do.

One May morning Little John Putnam faced his father, Nathaniel, and his mother in the door of their home. Over his shoulder there was flung a cloth sack and at his feet there was a medium-sized wooden chest. "Goodbye," he said to them, "I am for the Carolinas." Nathaniel smiled in a concerned way and Elizabeth had creases in her brow.

"Well, once I was a voyager," Nathaniel said, "and I found fortune in a strange land. It may be you will do as well."

"I shall," Little John said, "but this is not so far as you went, and I shall come back." Elizabeth took him by the shoulders, looked into his eyes, then hugged him.

"We are farm folk," she told him, "and know little of the sea, though it lies at our very door. But God goes with you. Take good care."

Little John kissed her, shook his father's hand, and stooped to pick up his chest. A cart was waiting for him at the gate, for Nathaniel's man was going into town. Little John had asked his parents to stay away from the waterfront and say their goodbyes here, in the dooryard, to prevent embarrassment among the sailors with whom, at the age of eighteen, he was shipping on a voyage to the southward.

He turned and got into the cart, waved, and was soon swallowed by a turn in the road.

He could not have known it, but he left just in time to avoid trouble, for in June King Philip Metacom broke the Taunton treaty and led his braves on the warpath. In Salem and the rest of Massachusetts the preparations for war that had been started in order to meet the Dutch threat were intensified to meet the much more present enemy.

Caleb Moody had lived for years near the farm of William and Elizabeth Morse in Newbury — they had not been the friendliest of neighbors. Moody had a four-year-old heifer with calf in 1675, and he went into the woods where they were grazing to bring the animals back to the farm and good pasture, near the Morse farm.

When the animals had been fattened up Moody went to the pasture to bring in the calf and butcher it for veal. The heifer took no notice of Moody's fetching it away, a fact which struck him as curious, for "she was very fond of her calf."

Having finished butchering the animal, Caleb went back to see if anything ailed its mother. He found her lying among thorn bushes, tried to raise her head and, as he did so, spotted Elizabeth Morse not far off in her field. After a good deal of striving he managed to get the heifer to her feet and drive her a short distance to good grass, but she refused to eat. He left her there and, later, came back to check on her — she was back in the thorns, and Mrs. Morse was back as well. A third attempt produced the same result. Caleb Moody became suspicious that something untoward was going on.

While country witchcraft was in the air, the Flower of Essex was summoned to the field to fight the Indians — a hundred men, picked from the towns of Essex County, who rendezvoused at Hadley in order to save the towns of the Connecticut River Valley. Capt. Thomas Lothrop of Beverly commanded one company of men, and Capt. Richard Beers of Watertown, another. On August 26th the two outfits pursued a band of Indians into a swamp ten miles from Hatfield in western Massachusetts, beneath Sugar Loaf Hill. At the cost of ten men, the settlers killed twenty-six braves and scattered the rest who went on to deprate lone farmhouses and small settlements.

On September 18th Lothrop's company set out to convoy a wagon train from Deerfield consisting of eighteen wagons full of grain and furniture belonging to refugees. Despite scouting parties, the Indians managed to ambush Lothrop's party as it was crossing a stream. Hiding in the woods, the vastly superior Indian force simply picked off all but eight of Lothrop's men — Lothrop himself was one of the first to fall. Nine young men from Salem Village were lost in the ambush at Bloody Brook, as the stream was called ever after.

Harvard College, when it enrolled the new class of freshmen, welcomed through its portals with the others a twelve-year-old boy named Cotton, the son of Boston's Increase Mather. The child was said to be a prodigy, and he lost little time in proving it to his tutors.

In October Apostle John Eliot's Christian Indians — three-hundred-fifty of them, including men, women and children, were taken to Deer Island in Boston Harbor and interned for the duration of King Philip's War, despite the fact that the Massachusetts Indians were loyal to their messiah and to the English colonists. They were the first of a long list of "foreigners" who would be interned in their own American homeland over the centuries.

Another prisoner, James Booth, who was an inhabitant of Salem Prison, broke out — a relatively easy thing to do in Colonial jails, as they were mostly poor wooden structures, often laxly attended — and Constable Clifford raised a hue and cry after him as he was required to do. He sent out a description of the man: "He is of middle stature, brownish hair and complexion, a blemish in one of his eyes, of a drawning speech, a tailor by trade."

The slaughter at Bloody Brook aroused the country which recognized that unless something great were done immediately, the colonies in New England were faced with destruction at the hands of Hobbamock's forces of darkness. The Indians were victorious everywhere among the outlying settlements, and on occasion they would launch vicious attacks into the heartlands. A scouting report by Lt. Phineas Upham of Malden, made on October first, said that "Now, seeing that in all our marches we find no Indians, we verily think that they are drawn together into great bodies remote from these parts." Other reports confirmed the guess, and at last the main body of King Philip's warriors was discovered to be in Narragansett country, in Rhode Island.

The New England Confederation made plans to attack the Indians in the winter before they could gather themselves for a spring offensive. Massachusetts contributed 527 men to an allied force, one member of which was twenty-three-year-old Thomas Putnam, Jr.; Connecticut, 315, and Plymouth Colony, 158 men in companies, respectively, of one cavalry and six infantry; five infantry and two infantry. Governor Josiah Winslow of Plymouth was made commander-in-Chief of the combined troops. Much to its disgrace, Rhode Island, in whose jurisdiction the main fight was to take place, raised no troops for the Confederation.

The winter was an early one, cold and snowy. On December 10th the seven Massachusetts companies, under Major Samuel Appleton of Ipswich, set out for the Narragansett country, rendezvousing with the Plymouth forces on December 12th at Wickford Hill in North Kingston, Rhode Island. The next day Gov. Winslow marched for battle. Five days later the Connecticut troops caught up with the main body, and scouts were sent out to locate the exact spot of the Indian encampment.

Despite deep snow, it was found to be on a low rise surrounded by a swamp in South Kingston. Young Thomas Putnam when he saw the fortification he and his comrades would have to storm felt great anxiety — a combination of trepidation and exhilaration, for the camp was defended by a double palisade and a hedge — it was an obstacle course; worse, there was only one evident entrance to the camp, and that could only be reached one at a time over a slippery log spanning a ditch. But the Indians must have had other entrances — they sent out snipers to flank the Colonial army which was forced to camp in the open at the last minute before the battle because the garrison in which they had expected to pass the night fifteen miles to the rear had been destroyed two days previously by King Philip, and the seventeen guards massacred.

On Sunday, December 19th, the army of the New England Confederation was without supplies, for their provisions had been taken when the garrison fell. At five-thirty a.m. the troops commenced their assault through deep drifts and continuing snow only to find that the extreme cold weather had frozen the swamp and made it more easily passable than they had anticipated. Still, the going was hard enough; Thomas was worn and hungry, like his fellows, and it was early afternoon before they came upon the Indian camp. Without waiting for anything, Governor Winslow ordered an immediate attack.

Massachusetts spearheaded the drive, the Plymotheans were in the center, and Connecticut brought up the rear. They found that the Indians had built a blockhouse at the entryway and filled it with riflemen; there were sharpshooters along the palisades as well. The companies of Samuel Mosely and Nathaniel Davenport led the charge. Davenport fell just inside the entrance, shot three times, but Mosely made it through. The first man to get into the fort proper was John Raymond of Salem Village; Tom Putnam wasn't far behind. Isaac Johnson, the Roxbury company's captain, was shot while he ran along the log, as were many others, but under a colonial fusillade Tom and many others breached the Indians' defenses and engaged in hand-to-hand combat inside the fort.

For three hours the incredible fight continued in the deep chill, blood staining the snow, the ground inside the fort stirred to ochre mud by moccasins and boots, by the exhausted frenzy of single combat. Tom had no time to think of what his next action would be — he and the others simply fended and thrust. There was little time for anyone to load a gun, so the firing was sparse; the fight was all tomahawks and knives, hands and feet, bursting lungs and sweat. The cries of dying men and moans of the wounded, the sounds of blows rose and sank until the Indians turned and ran with the setting sun. Hundreds of them lay killed inside the fort, and those who fled into the wintry swamp left to starve without provisions in the New England forests.

Eighty colonists had been killed outright, and a hundred-fifty were wounded. Phineas Upham, who had given in the original scouting report, was one of the Colonials mortally wounded. Dr. Daniel Weld of Salem, chief surgeon of the army, could not save him. Salem Villagers who lay dead on the spongy floor of the fort were Charles Knight, Thomas Flint, and Joseph Houlton, Jr. Many others from towns surrounding Salem fell as well, including men from Marblehead, Wenham, Cape Ann, Topsfield, Lynn, Andover, and Beverly. Joseph Peirce and Samuel Pikeworth of Salem itself were among the dead.

One of the survivors of the fight was Thomas Putnam, Jr., of Salem Village, and others of his fellow townsmen who lived to tell the tale before their hearths that winter were John Dodge and William Dodge, Jr., William, Thomas, and John Raymond, Joseph Herrick, Thomas Abbey, Robert Leach, and Peter Prescott. They were welcomed home as heroes and saviors of the society, for with the debacle at Kingston King Philip Metacom's power was broken and his war lost.

By the time the soldiers came home a sailor had returned as well — Little John Putnam had come back from his voyage to the Carolinas. He had decided that the life of a sailor was not his style, but at least the adventure had done one thing for him — he had lost the appellation "Little" John, which he loathed, and he was known thenceforward to one and all as "Carolina" John Putnam. It was his intention to settle down in the Village and ply the trade of weaver.

In England during 1675 Mary Baguley was hanged for witchcraft, and a young man named John Case, fifteen years old, came from Lyme Regis to London to seek his fortune. He took lodgings in Lambeth and began to study medicine and astrology.

Early in 1676 young Jacob Goodell left his home, where he lived with his father, Robert, and the rest of his family, to go to work at Giles Corey's farm in Salem Village. He was reluctant to leave that day, for he felt unwell, but his parents insisted he go as they needed his wages and they suspected he was merely being lazy.

When work was over Goody Martha Corey offered to give him a ride home, which Goodell gratefully accepted. On their way they stopped for a few minutes at the home of John Proctor. Eventually Jacob Goodell was deposited at his home looking very ill. Shortly afterward, he died. Immediately rumors began to circulate through the Village that Giles Corey had beaten him to death.

A grand jury was empanelled to investigate and view the body. When it was done it gave in the report that Goodell had died "with clodders about the heart," and it appeared that Goodell had been kicked and beaten to death. Giles Corey was arrested on suspicion of having committed murder.

At about the same time in Casco, Maine, a band of Indians fell upon the community and destroyed it. Thirty-two people were killed or captured; others managed to escape into the forest. The Rev. Mr. George Burroughs was able to get to an island in Casco Bay from which he was eventually rescued by a party from the mainland. He was asked to write a report of the raid for the authorities in Boston, which he was glad to do.

John Putnam, Jr., was made a Selectman of Salem on March 20th, but the town had a more difficult time in arranging to draft a police force, for on the 24th John Cromwell was chosen to be a constable, refused the position, and was fined five pounds. The job of constable was often a thankless task, and there were rumors in the air that it was going to be more thankless than ever if the wishes of Rev. John Higginson were to be enforced — he had been complaining mightily at the absences of many members of his congregation on Lord's and Lecture Days; it would be the duty of the constables to be sure their neighbors came to church. On March 29th the Selectmen chose Samuel Archer to fill one of the open positions; he, too, refused and was fined on April 14th. That same day John Ingersoll was offered the job and declined it. The town was getting rich from the stiff fines, but it needed a constable. Finally, Henry Skerry, Jr., accepted the post and was paid five pounds.

Six days later the Selectmen ordered the constables to guard the three doors of the meetinghouse each Sunday and to make sure that nobody left until service was over unless there were a very good reason for a person's doing so. Regardless, anyone who left was to be reported to the town's officers, and this was to apply both to afternoon and forenoon services. Furthermore, Reuben Guppy was given the responsibility to see that all the town boys sat on the three pairs of stairs of the meetinghouse during services. He was also to keep order among the boys and to keep dogs out of the building. For these duties his rate was remitted for the year.

On April 28th two of the Selectmen warned "the new baker to depart the town," and they warned Thomas Cromwell also not to allow him to remain in his home any longer. On the same day Corporal John Putnam, Jr. was chosen trial juryman.

At his trial a number of witnesses testified against Giles Corey, but others introduced conflicting evidence. The Proctors said that when Martha Corey and Jacob Goodell stopped at their house they saw no evidence of ill-will between the two at that point, and no one was suggesting that it was Martha Corey who beat him between the Proctors' place and Goodell's home. Further, there was some indication that Goodell might have received his beating *after* he got home, not before. Finally, some witnesses believed that Goodell hadn't died of a beating at all, but of ordinary disease. Corey was not a popular man in Salem Village, yet, despite public feeling against him, he was released for lack of evidence but fined, nevertheless, for the suspicion.

In Newbury William Morse had occasion to be at the home of Mrs. Jane Sewall, and the conversation concerned his wife and her reputation as a white witch. He said to Goody Sewall, "My wife is accounted a witch, but I wonder that she should be both a healing and destroying witch." He told a story:

Mrs. Thomas Wells had been in labor a long time and could not be delivered of her baby. Her people had put off asking for the attendance of Mrs. Morse whose specialty was midwifery, but eventually they sent for her. She was miffed at not having been asked sooner, yet she attended. When she arrived she prepared a strong drink compounded of squawroot tea and alcohol, gave it to the expectant mother, and shortly afterward the baby was born safely. Under the circumstances, Morse asked Goody Sewall, did it seem likely that a woman who could do so much good would also wish to do evil?

Bray Wilkins and John Gingle managed to pay off the mortgage they had taken on the Richard Bellingham farm some years earlier, and as soon as that transaction was completed Wilkins bought out Gingle's share, thus obtaining clear title to the property. It was not a good year for farming, however, as New England suffered in the grasp of a deep drought. The land lay baking beneath the sun, crops withered, and dry cracks appeared in the fields that looked and felt like stone.

Edward Randolph arrived in Boston on June 10th, having been appointed special messenger and investigator to Massachusetts by the English Lords of Trade and Plantations. He soon proved to be a tenacious and energetic man. The first thing Randolph did was to deliver his credentials and a letter from the King to the colonial government, then he began poking into the affairs of the colony at every moment, despite obstacles and road blocks thrown in his way by the Governor and the General Court. Shortly he began sending adverse reports back to the Lords.

Salem finally took action to refurbish its dilapidated prison on June 19th. The Selectmen agreed that John Marston would undertake to move the prison to the field of Benjamin Felton, still the jailer, and to put a new floor in it.

The Wampanoag Indians, King Philip's tribe, were in poor shape by the summer of 1676, despite the fact that they had been aided in their war by the French and the Dutch. The colonists had harried them from point to point so that they could grow no crops, and they were without food. Furthermore, the colonists had made treaties with the Natick and Niantic tribes.

King Philip went into hiding. On August the first his wife and nine-year-old son were captured. Ten days later an Indian traitor led Captain Benjamin Church, the Indian fighter, to Philip's hiding place, and on the 12th the chief was captured under Mount Hope in Rhode Island. Philip tried to escape and was killed by another Indian. His head was severed, sent to Plymouth, and put on public display, skewered on a pole. The Indian who had killed him was given Philip's right hand, which he preserved in rum and began exhibiting from village to village.

In September Major William Hathorne led a large force of 1200 men against what remained of the Indian resistance and surprised 400 of them. He executed several of the leaders, sent 200 of those he considered "perfidious" to Boston to be sold into slavery. The war was over, the the last casualty did not take place until the first week in October. On a Friday a Salem boy was out fowling and he saw a man with black hair standing by a pond — he jumped to the conclusion that it was an Indian, shot at him, and ran away. The next day the man's body was found where the boy said he had fired his shot; however, it was found not to be that of an Indian but of an Englishman. The boy was put into prison.

The town of Salem made an agreement on November 10th "with Arthur Hughes to be bellman for the town; that he "shall begin to take his walk about ten of the clock at night, from the bridge to Henry Moses' house, passing through all the streets and lanes within the circumference of the town, to give notice of the time of night, with weather and so forth, according to custom, and to take special care to prevent fire and any disorder in the night by giving timely notice thereof, his perambulation to continue till daybreak."

Ann Putnam Trask, Thomas Putnam's daughter and the wife of William Trask, died on November 14th. Both families gathered to mourn her passing at the early age of thirty-one. On Christmas Day Selectman John Putnam, Jr. was appointed to prosecute Nicholas Manning at the next court sessions for a debt he owed to the town.

Edmund Halley in England published a paper in which John Winthrop, Jr., of Connecticut would have been interested had he lasted out the year. The treatise dealt with the orbits of the principal planets of the Solar System. He was nineteen years old, and the paper appeared in the *Philosophical Transactions* of the Royal Society.

Salem got a new superintendent of schools on the 24th of January, 1677, when the town chose John Putnam Jr. to take responsibility for enforcing education.

In the spring one of the very few cases of witchcraft and possession to trouble the Plymouth Colony emerged when Mary Ingham of Scituate was prosecuted for having "maliciously procured much hurt, mischief, and pain unto the body of Mehitabel Woodworth" which caused the afflicted person "to fall into violent fits" and which "almost bereaved her of her senses." The jury considered the evidence and, despite spectacular scenes of possession in the very courtroom, found the defendant not guilty.

Daniel Epps was renewed as Salem Schoolmaster on the 7th of April, and the government of the colony ordered that Salem make sure that all was in readiness in its fort at Winter Island, for now that the Indians had been taken care of, there were the Dutch to worry about once again: They had been raiding the coast of Virginia and had taken a number of ships as prizes. Some of these were Salem ships whose crews were pressed into service in the Dutch men-of-war, leaving a good number of families in Salem without heads and without money. Furthermore, Satan's scourge was taking its toll more than normally heavily in the colonies. The plight of families thus reduced in circumstance was such that news of them reached as far as England and Ireland, and the Irish people donated 44 pounds, 5 shillings for the relief of New England families who were without means of support.

On June 2nd Nathaniel Putnam was chosen trial juryman. George Jacobs was tried for assault and battery, having become provoked with someone and struck him. Jacobs was convicted and fined. Susannah Buswell, wife of Isaac, was convicted in another case and sentenced to sit in Salem meetinghouse at lecture, "about the middle of the aisle," with a paper pinned to her head which read, FOR BURGLARY AND LYING.

The Salem Constables on June 11th were issued warrants to warn "the several persons chosen in their several wards, to have inspection of those families appointed them according to law, and to attend the next County Court the last Thursday of this instant month to receive their orders...." The purpose of the warrants was to implement a system of town spying to be sure that everyone was doing what he was supposed to be doing — including observing the Sabbath. Two of the spies for Salem Village were Lt. Thomas Putnam and Nathaniel Putnam.

The government of Massachusetts Bay in July sent William Stoughton and Peter Bulkely to England to reply to the charges that had been made against the colony by Sir Ferdinando Gorges, Edward Randolph and others.

John Webster published a book in England in 1677 titled *Displaying of Supposed Witchcraft* which was directed against Mericus Casaubon's book. Nevertheless, he believed that angels existed in a corporeal sense and were not spirits except "in a relative and respective sense," as was the case also with devils. Thus, "they may move and agitate other bodies," but their strength to do so was limited. Webster also believed in ghosts.

John Webster, who had been involved in the Edmund Robinson case in 1633, defended certain aspects of sympathetic magic — he was certain that dead bodies bled when their murderers approached, and he was certain of the existence of witchcraft, though he did not believe witches could do half the things with which they were credited — that included the signing of a material pact with Satan or having sexual intercourse with him. He did not believe they could suckle imps, be transformed into were-animals, or fly through the air on a broom or off.

There were certainly, on the other hand, malignant people whose hearts were with the Devil, but the evil they did was not performed by magic means; rather, by means of poisons and so forth. So-called "witches" were, in Webster's opinion, technicians of abstruse knowledge, such as herb lore, not adepts of the occult. He could not deny the existence of sympathetic magic, however, for many natural objects had powers and magnetisms few people other than students of such things could understand. Webster himself was a student of medicine, and he upheld Paracelsus' dictum that only through experimentation could mankind discover cures and medicines — not by mindless adherence to the worthless dogmas of traditions.

Elias Ashmole at his home in South Lambeth began to keep a meteorological notebook of weather observations. For the most part he had become a scientist, but on occasion he dipped into his enormous collection of books on astrology, including the volumes he had obtained in the purchase of the estate of John Booker in 1667.

John Putnam Jr., since he had had his children baptized, had become a more and more cooperative man, at the same time that his brothers did less and less for Salem Town, preferring to see the Village as a more or less separate entity and to tie their lot up with it. On the 25th of August John was chosen commissioner of the country rate — meaning the Salem Village rate — and Thomas was chosen grand juryman…but he refused to serve. Duty well performed was rewarded, and on October 10th John was elected Deputy to the General Court, to serve until the next election. His brothers did not begrudge him.

All three men often met during the fall at the husking bees of the neighborhoods. In the sun-burnished afternoons families and neighbors gathered after the harvest of hay and grain to help each other with the maize harvest. The men and boys harvested the cobs and carted them up to the farmyards were women and children waited to strip the corn-silk and leaves from the ears and fill the corncribs to bursting. The stalks in the fields were bound in bunches with a cord at the center; these "stooks" stood in the fields like the sentinels of autumn.

As the new year 1678 began in Salem, twenty-two-year-old William Stacey caught Satan's scourge. He was visited with the standard ambiguous symptoms of smallpox and by Bridget Oliver as well, who made a point of giving him what comfort she could — Stacey felt it was more than the occasion, or their acquaintance, warranted. When he recovered, Goody Oliver hired him to do some work for her, paying him threepence for his efforts. He left the Oliver farm and had not gone very far on his way when he discovered that his money was missing from his pocket. He retraced his steps but could find no sign of it.

In April Corporal John, Jr. and Lt. Thomas Putnam were chosen to perambulate the boundary between Salem Village and Topsfield with residents of that town.

Something of much more moment to New England than the feud between two towns was happening in England at the same time: The Attorney General and the Solicitor General were asked by the Lords of Trade and Plantations to give their legal opinions on the question, Was the Charter of Massachusetts Bay not abrogated in 1635 by the *quo warranto* proceedings which had been brought against it in that year?

At the end of April Rev. James Allen sold the John Endicott-Townsend Bishop property on easy terms — a land contract — to Francis Nurse. His wife, Rebecca, was delighted, and was frustrated by the agreement which kept Allen as ultimate controller of the property until the contract had been completely executed. The Nurses soon had cause to be thankful that this was the case, for it became apparent that the grants made to Governor John Endicott, whose property was controlled by Zerubabel; to Townsend Bishop; and to Elias Stileman, whose property was owned in 1678 by Nathaniel Putnam, in fact overlapped.

No sooner had the overlapping been seen to exist than suits for trespass and various other charges began to clog up the court calendar. They were brought by , Nathaniel Putnam, and by Rev. James Allen in behalf of Francis Nurse. Nor were these the only litigations in which citizens of the town, and the town itself, were engaged. On May first Corporal John Putnam Jr. and Samuel Gardner, Sr., were appointed to represent Salem at the Court in Boston in a dispute with the town of Beverly.

The banns were posted in May for the marriage of a local hero, a veteran of the Great Swamp Fight, Thomas Putnam, Jr., to seventeen-year-old Ann Carr, sister of the Salem Village minister's wife, Mary Carr Bailey. The Putnams — at least some of them — looked forward to this linking of the Lord's local family with the local lords' family. It could not be said that the proposed alliance did much to sweeten the disposition of Nathaniel Putnam to the minister, though Nathaniel did feel sorry for the pastor's wife, for she had had several miscarriages and stillbirths since she had come to Salem Village, and the matrons spoke in whispers about the situation between services, over tea or cider in the halls near the meetinghouse, while their husbands spoke of crops and weather at Ingersoll's Ordinary.

On the 31st of May John Putnam Jr. was a trial juryman once again. Bridget Oliver got into trouble with the law when, on a Sabbath Day, she called her husband various "opprobrious names" such as "old rogue" and "old devil." She was sentenced to stand in the marketplace at Salem with a gag in her mouth, much to the delight of many citizens, both male and female.

Bridget's husband Thomas was drafted into service as proclaimer of a local rebellion on June 20th when he walked the streets to announce a meeting called by a petition that had been signed by Nathaniel and John, Jr. and a number of others. The petitioners believed they were calling the meeting legally, "according to a law made in 1660 entitled, 'Township Privileges,'" which stated that the majority of those who were proprietors in the Town Commons may call such a meeting. The issue of rate-paying for the upkeep both of Bailey and Higginson on the part of Salem Villagers was very hot — so hot that the Selectmen did not want to deal with it in an open town meeting.

But the issue was joined with Oliver's announcement, and the next day the Selectmen met and judged that "proceedings of this nature is very irregular illegal and tends to the disturbance of the peace and quiet of this town." They posted a notice on the door of the meetinghouse forbidding the proposed rebel conclave. A week later, on the 28th of

June, the Selectmen appointed Captain George Corwin to present the case of the petitioners to the Salem Court, which was to be held the next day and ask the court its opinion regarding the law of tithing. The opinion was rendered, and it did not favor the point of view of the Salem Villagers. The farmers were not satisfied.

A queer thing happened to Samuel Gray near the same time — he woke up in the night and saw a woman standing between the baby's cradle and the bed; she seemed to be looking at Gray. As he rose up in bed she vanished. Gray got out of bed, went to check the door — it was bolted. He unlocked it, opened it, went to the front door of the house, looked out…and there the woman was, in the dooryard. He said to her, "In the name of God, what do you come for?" Again she vanished.

Still half asleep, he returned to bed and lay down. He was dropping off when he felt something cold on his lips. He started awake and saw the same woman again at the bedside, holding something she had between her hands against his mouth. At Gray's motion she moved as well, the baby shrieked in its cradle, and for the third time the witch vanished. The baby continued to cry, and for hours Gray tried to soothe it. Eventually, somewhere around dawn, he was successful, but within a few days the infant began to sicken.

The Harvard College Class of 1678 was graduated in June, and among the new baccalaureates was a young man, aged fifteen, named Cotton Mather. Having entered the College when he was twelve years old, the boy had distinguished himself among his older classmates and completed all requirements for his degree within three years.

Litigations multiplied in Salem: John Gloyd, who had worked for Giles Corey, sued his employer over wages, and the issue was submitted to a panel of arbitration for settlement out of court. Gloyd chose John Proctor as one of the arbitrators; Corey chose Edmund Bridges, and Nathaniel Putnam was agreed upon mutually as the third arbitrator. The decision of the panel was to be binding, and it was rendered against Giles Corey, but he accepted it with a good grace.

At least, at the time it seemed so, but a few days later John Proctor's barn was burned to the ground and local tongues had it that Corey had set the fire. Proctor, beside himself, agreed it must be so, and swore out a warrant for Corey's arrest. As in Corey's previous trial, conflicting evidence, most of it circumstantial, was introduced.

John Phelps and Thomas Fuller, who lived over toward Ipswich, had raised the alarm two hours before dawn as they walked to market with their goods and had stopped to help fight the blaze. It was the opinion of Thomas Flint and Thomas Gould that "an evil hand" had set the fire, given the hour it was discovered, but Caleb and Jane Moore, and James Poland, testified that they heard Proctor tell someone that his boy had accidentally started the fire with a lanthorn.

The theory of Corey's motive for setting the fire — revenge for the disadvantageous decision over Gloyd's wages — was undermined by the deposition of Nathaniel Putnam and Edmund Bridges which stated that the agreement "was greatly to the satisfaction of the parties concerned; and Giles Corey did manifest, to our observation, as much satisfaction to John Proctor as he did to the rest of the arbitrators." Captain Moore, in whose tavern on the Salem waterfront the arbitrators had met with the claimants to render their verdict, backed the testimony of Putnam and Bridges, for he swore, "I did see and take notice of the abundance of love manifested from Corey to Proctor, and from Proctor to Corey, for they drank wine together, and Proctor paid for part, and Corey part."

Finally, Corey came up with an ironclad alibi for his whereabouts at the time of the fire. Abraham Walcott testified that, "Tuesday night last was a week, I lodged at Giles Corey's house, which night John Proctor's house was damaged by fire; and Giles Corey went to bed before nine o'clock, and rose about sunrise again, and could not have gone out of the house but I should have heard him. It must have been impossible that he should have gone to Proctor's house that night, for he cannot in a long time go afoot, and, as for his horse-kind, they were all in the woods." His wife swore he was in bed from nine p.m. to sunrise. Several other witnesses — John Parker, Abraham Walcott, even John Gloyd, testified to the impossibility of Corey's being anywhere near the scene at the time that the fire was started. The jury could do nothing but acquit him, which it did.

The Attorney General and the Solicitor General of England had been considering the question put to them by the Lords of Trade and Plantations, and in July they rendered the opinion that Massachusetts Bay was responsible for "many transgressions and forfeitures" — sufficient, certainly, to declare the Charter null and void.

In Beverly the Rev. Mr. John Hale discovered that one of his servants and some of Dorcas Hoar's children had been stealing things from the minister's household. Hale asked his preadolescent daughter, Rebecca, if she knew anything about it. "Yes," she answered, "but I durst not reveal it because Goody Hoar is a witch and has a book by which she can tell what I tell. If I did tell you of the stealing, Goody Hoar would raise the Devil to bewitch me."

Hale asked, "Did you see the book?"

"Yes," the girl said, "I was showed it. There are many streaks and pictures in it by which Goody Hoar can reveal and work witchcrafts."

"How big is the book?"

"Like that grammar that lies on the table." She pointed. "Now I have told you of the stealing, Goody Hoar will bewitch me."

Hale, who still hoped better of the woman, told his daughter, "Do not think so hardly of her."

Rebecca replied, "I know Goody Hoar is a witch," and she began to recount stories of strange occurrences in the house when her parents were away. Rebecca accounted these to be omens and warnings to her to be silent.

In thinking about the situation Hale recalled Dorcas' confession to him in 1670 that she had borrowed a book on palmistry. He went to talk with Goodman Hoar and ask whether he knew if his wife had a book of fortune telling. He told the minister, "Yea, she has such a kind of book with streaks and pictures in it, and it is about the bigness of such a book" — he pointed out a small book lying nearby.

In no time at all word of the situation was spread all around town, though it was not the minister who spread it. One of his parishioners told the story to Major Daniel Dennison who took the first opportunity to question William Hoar about his wife's book. He told the Major, "The book was John Samson's, and my wife returned it to him long ago." Slowly, with the minister's reluctance to prosecute, the matter was dropped, but the gossip continued.

On the second day of September the two Putnam brothers, Nathaniel and John, appealed to the Court of Assistants in Boston to protest their having to pay Salem rates in addition to their own rates in Salem Village. The Selectmen, having heard of a smallpox epidemic in the Capital, were unwilling to go to the court in person to present the Town's side of the case, so they did the next best thing — they appointed Major William Hathorne to do it for them.

After the grain harvest William Stacey met Bridget Oliver on the street as she was going to his father's mill. She stopped him to ask whether he thought his father would grind her grist for her.

"Why do you ask?" Stacey inquired. "I don't question but my father will grind it," Stacey told her and whipped up his horse, for he was driving a cart with a small load on it. When he had traveled about six rods, one of the wheels sank into a pothole in the road. Stacey got off, found someone to help him push the cart out, and went on his way. When he returned along the same road, he could find no pothole anywhere near the spot where he had been stuck.

On the 7th of October thirty-six men of "the reserve of Salem Old Troop" successfully petitioned the General Court to revive and reorganize the militia as a troop of cavalry with William Brown, Jr., as Captain, and John Putnam, Jr., as Lieutenant. Despite everything Lt. John Putnam continued to gather-in honors and responsibilities, for at the end of October he was chosen as a member of a committee to represent Salem in a boundary dispute with Wenham and Beverly at the General Court. His brother, Nathaniel Putnam, was made a grand juryman.

By November word of the danger the charter was in had arrived in Massachusetts, and the Court proclaimed November 21st as a day of humiliation during which the inhabitants were directed to fast and pray for the salvation of their document of government. Four days later Sgt. Thomas Putnam, Jr., took to wife the Rev. Mr. Bailey's sister-in-law Ann Carr in a marriage rite at Salem Church where Rev. John Higginson officiated, and Mr. Bailey gave away the bride. It seemed to many who were present that the ceremony brought together in a focus nearly all of the frictions that were besetting the Village and Town, and most of the persons involved as well.

During the winter William Stacey had a strange dream that Bridget Oliver was sitting at the foot of his bed. Though it was night, it seemed as bright as day, and he saw that she was wearing a black cap and hat and a red coat. Suddenly, she clasped the coat to her, hopped around the room, and then went out. It was so curious a dream that he simply had to tell people about it. When the story got to Bridget she sought Stacey out and asked him if the rumors were true.

"Yes," he replied, "deny it if you dare!"

Bridget didn't deny it; she got angry instead. She told the young man, "You do me more mischief than any other body."

"Why?" he asked.

"Because," the woman shook her head, "folks will believe you before anybody else."

The child of Samuel Gray, meanwhile, had died after several months of languishing. Gray had no idea who the woman was who had appeared in his bedroom to put the hex on his child until, a week after its death, he saw her walking the streets of Salem. He inquired of a passerby who the woman was. The man cast a look at her and replied, "Oh, that is Goody Oliver."

On the second day of December Carolina John Putnam, weaver of Salem Village, twenty-one years old — former bee-hunter, former seaman — took to his hearth to be his helpmeet and mate Hannah Cutler of Salem, two years his senior, daughter of Samuel and Eliza Cutler.

In England Robert Boyle had turned momentarily from the study of air pumps and such scientific gadgetry to write and publish a book titled *The Historic Report of a Break-Down of Gold by Means of an Anti-Elixir*. An important element in the alchemical processes described in the volume was a red powder, like that which had belonged to Alexander Seton and, before him, Edward Kelley. Boyle's fellow experimenter in the occult, Joseph Glanvill, was appointed Chaplain to King Charles during the year and, despite all their bluster, the Lords of Trade and Plantations did nothing against the Charter of Massachusetts Bay.

All in all, William Stoughton and Rev. Peter Bulkeley felt they had done a creditable job of staving off action yet again, but when they left London and returned to Boston on December 23rd they found themselves to be under fire for having yielded too much to the Lords. They brought with them, and handed over to the government, a letter of rebuke from Charles and the evil news that Edward Randolph had been appointed Royal Collector of Customs for New England. The Governor and the Court were roused to wrath against their ambassadors.

Early in the spring of 1679 John Stebbins of Northampton was working in a sawmill when he began to have trouble with the logs and boards with which he was working. They began to act up in strange ways — falling down by themselves, writhing out of his hands. He complained of the situation to his wife and neighbors. On March 7th he was found dead. His body was covered with hundreds of spots, "as though made with small shot." The grand jury, one of whose members was Dr. Thomas Hastings of Hatfield, scraped some of the spots and beneath them found "holes under them into the body." Stebbins' wife was the sister of Samuel Bartlett who had unsuccessfully prosecuted Mrs. Mary Bliss Parsons in 1674. He was, of course, convinced that his brother-in-law's death was caused by witchcraft, not smallpox, and he brought an action against one of his neighbors in the county court.

The parish controversy in Salem Village had grown considerably since Rev. James Bailey had come to town, and a hard bitterness had set in over the issues involved between Nathaniel and John Putnam Jr., on the one hand, and Lt. Thomas on the other. The situation Nathaniel had foreseen when he objected to the calling of a minister to the Village so precipitately had come to pass: The Village still had no meetinghouse of its own, and the Villagers were still paying rates to Mr. Higginson in Salem, as well as to Mr. Bailey.

Nor was Lt. Thomas in any mood or position to back off at this stage, for his son, Sgt. Tom, Jr., had married into the Village minister's family, and his brothers had brought suit against the laws of tithing and the agreement Thomas and the Parish Committee of the Village had made with Salem when the Village had been set off as a separate parish. Lt. Thomas was committed, and overcommitted, for he was also Clerk of the Salem Village Parish.

The legal appeals on the parts of Nathaniel and John having been unsuccessful, the focus of the warfare settled on Mr. Bailey, the Village minister, and the factions were adamant in their points of view. On March 10th both sides appealed to Salem Church for advice. Three papers were presented — one, with sixteen signatures, by Bailey's opponents; one, with thirty-nine names, by his supporters in the Village, and one, also favorable, by ten people living in Topsfield who resided near the Village and attended services there rather than in their own town. The resulting debate was intense, and "There was such agitation on both sides, and diverse things were spoken of by the brethren; but the business being long, and many of the brethren gone, we could not make a church act of advice in the case" for lack of a quorum; "therefore, it was left to another time," the record read.

Salem and the Village turned to other matters for a while. On March 13th Lt. Thomas was appointed to a committee that was charged to search land titles and parcels still ungranted in the town for property that might have been lost among other property but still, in fact, belonged to the town. All three Putnam brothers were chosen on the 27th to perambulate the town line with Beverlyans. Then, on April 4th the conflict erupted again when Thomas and John, Jr., Daniel Andrews and Nathaniel Ingersoll brought a suit against Henry Kenny "for slandering our minister, Mr. Bailey, by reporting that he doth not perform family duties" — prayer duties — "in his family."

At the trial a young woman parishioner testified that, "Being at Mr. Bailey's house three weeks together, I never heard Mr. Bailey read a chapter, nor expound on any part of the Scripture, which was a great relief to me."

Others, however, testified that, "Having, for a year, some more, some less, since Mr. Bailey's coming to Salem Farms, lived at his house, we testify to our knowledge that he hath continually performed family duties, morning and evening, unless sickness or some other unavoidable providence hath prevented." Two of these witnesses went on to be much more specific in their defense of the minister.

Henry Kenney lost the battle. Inasmuch as John Putnam. had joined Thomas in the suit against Kenny, it was obvious that, of the three brothers, he was the only one who was objective in the matter. He felt put upon by the situation that the Village was in, but he was not malignantly disposed toward Rev. Mr. Bailey who was, in fact, merely caught in the middle.

At another meeting on April 22nd Salem Church advised Nathaniel, Bray Wilkins, and the rest of the anti-Bailey faction "to submit to the generality for the present" — until they built their own church, but the request went unheeded by the dissidents and the fight wore on. The Beverly perambulation took place on April 28th, but only Thomas and

John showed up to walk with other Salemites and the Beverly people — Nathaniel absented himself.

In May Simon Bradstreet of Ipswich — husband of the first American poet, Anne Bradstreet — became Governor of Massachusetts Bay Colony, and Lt. John Putnam, Jr., was elected Deputy from Salem to the General Court, succeeding Bartholomew Gedney. He was also assigned by the town to represent Salem in boundary disputes before the Court in Boston. Lt. John and Simon were partners together in the Rowley iron works, and they looked forward to close cooperation in their governmental duties. One of the first things that Bradstreet saw cross his desk was the Springfield County Court's referral of the John Stebbins case in Northampton to the General Court. Bradstreet, as he had done earlier in situations of the kind, quietly quashed the whole business.

But the Allen-John Endicott-Putnam dispute over the boundaries of the various properties belonging to Francis Nurse, and Nathaniel were unquashable and had been litigated to shreds in the courts. In May a Special Commission was formed to recommend a settlement; the General Court accepted its report and was the major loser; Nathaniel and the Allen-Nurse combine were favorably treated. This was adding insult to injury, for the Allen-Nurse property — the former Townsend Bishop estate — had early-on been John Endicott property as well. Now Zerubabel saw his own property diminished at the behest of usurpers. It drove him to furious distraction, but he calmed down sufficiently to petition for a new hearing.

On May 19th Lt. John. and Daniel Andrews were selected to represent Salem at the General Court in a Wenham boundary dispute, and a month later a new Putnam stepped into the civic scene: Sgt. Thomas Putnam, Jr., was made a trial juryman. At about the same time, of a Sunday, John Endicott, Jr., involved himself with the occult:

Relations between George Carr and Mary Bradbury, both of Salisbury, had long been poor, and one Lord's Day afternoon the elder Carr, his son Richard Carr — both kinfolk of Ann Carr, Sgt. Thomas' wife — and Zerubabel Endicott, Jr., were riding past the Capt. Thomas Bradbury place when they saw Mary Bradbury go through her gate and turn a corner. Immediately, a blue boar shot out of the gate and darted at the legs of George Carr's horse, which stumbled. Carr called out, "Boys! What did you see?"

They answered, "A blue boar!"

"I am glad you see it as well as I," Carr hinted darkly. They rode on, conversing, and eventually agreed that the boar must have been Goody Bradbury in animal shape.

Salem lost one of its founders during the year when Roger Conant, the Old Planter, died at the age of eighty-seven. Thomas Oliver died as well, and it was no time at all before the town gossips were saying Bridget had wished him to death, just as she had done to her first husband, Goodman Wasselby.

Moving Salem Prison to Benjamin Felton's field and putting a new floor into it had done little to improve conditions in it. Joseph Getchell hated it, so he broke out and escaped. A hue and cry was raised after him; he was recaptured, fined, and recommitted for a week. Getchell complained bitterly about the "noisome place" which was "not fit for a Christian man to breathe in." It was "impossible," he said, "that any human creature should endure to live in so pestiferous a stink."

Salem imposed a curfew for Indians beginning in the middle of August: None were to be allowed in town between sundown and sunup. Not long afterward, on the 22nd, Carolina John and Hannah Cutler Putnam had their first child, a girl named Hannah Putnam, who arrived about a month earlier than had been anticipated, which started several tongues wagging. In the middle of October Philip Cromwell and John Hathorne were appointed by the Selectmen "to advise and assist Goody Oliver in the sale of her land to pay her debts due to the town…." Things were beginning to look desperate for Bridget.

The next day, October 15th, the General Court rendered its decision in the matter of the Rev. Mr. James Bailey. He was, the Court said, "orthodox, and competently able, and of a blameless and self-denying conversation...." It was ordered that he "be continued and settled the minister" of Salem Village, for he had never been ordained and was still serving his probationary term, and that "he be allowed sixty pounds per annum for his maintenance, one-third part thereof in money, the other two-thirds in provisions of all sorts, such as a family needs, at equal prices, and fuel for his family's occasions, this sum to be paid by the inhabitants" of the Village. The decision astonished Nathaniel Putnam, Bray Wilkins, and the other dissidents, for no one had ever suggested such a vast sum of money for the preacher's upkeep, not even his partisans.

The Court further ordered that a committee of three or five men be formed which would set the rate and collect it. If this arrangement didn't work, then the Court appointed Edmund Batter, Capt. Jonathan Corwin, and Capt. Walter Price of the mother parish to set the rate and enforce it with the full power of the Salem constabulary and the county marshal to attach property and use arrest powers to collect, if any were so foolish as to continue to refuse.

There were further stringent regulations established in the matter in order to be utterly certain Mr. Bailey got his salary. But an escape clause was appended: "This order," the Court directed, "shall continue for one year only from the last of September past. In the mean while, all parties," it was hoped, would "endeavor an agreement in him or some other meet person for a minister among them," and the whole Village was to pay the court costs of the litigation.

The dissidents paid no attention whatever to the court order.

In the middle of everything Ann Putnam, daughter of Sgt. Thomas Putnam, Jr,, and Ann Carr Putnam decided to be born on October 18th. No more significant birth ever took place in Salem Village — or in Salem, for that matter.

Ann Putnam, Jr. — Annie Putnam, as she was soon called to distinguish her from her mother — was a third decan Libra. Annie Putnam's Sign was ordinarily that of one who was born to conciliate, not to cause dissension, but this was truer of the first decan Libran, less so of the second decan. The child of the third decan, however — though superior in qualities of the mind associated with literature and the arts — was born to make slaves of others through the imagination. The outcome of this enslavement would be death, and the Libran would one day come to ask forgiveness, to confess and expiate grave sins committed against her fellow man.

Though no one read the stars at the time of Annie Putnam Putnam's birth, the midwife and attending women were well aware that Annie Putnam's birth was portentous, for the child was born with a caul which meant that she would have double sight and powers of prophecy; she would never die by drowning. But the caul was not lucky red — it was of a blackish cast. Annie Putnam would be the victim of ill fortune, and her life would not be a long one.

On November 3rd the infant's grandfather, Lt. Thomas, was made a grand juryman and, a bit later in the month, twice-widowed Bridget Oliver married Edward Bishop, Jr., a sawyer of Salem Village and a widower. The matrons were confounded — the witch had captured another man and she had yet again found a way out of her difficulties.

William Morse, the shoemaker of Newbury, and his wife Elizabeth had taken into their home to live with them their grandson, a boy named John Styles. Not long afterward a poltergeist began to haunt the house: An awl fell down the chimney, stones rattled against the walls, pots and kettles danced on the cranes in the fireplace, rods clattered in pans, jumped out and fell to the floor, a pig got into the locked house, chests opened and shut seemingly by themselves.

When Caleb Powell, a ship's mate who lived in town, heard about the case between voyages, he decided to take a hand in it. He went to the Morse house and, before knocking, glanced in the window. There, inside, he saw the old couple with some neighbors kneeling, eyes closed, in prayer. Caleb decided it wouldn't be proper to intrude at that moment, so he waited and watched. His eyes were attracted to a movement in the room and Powell noticed John Styles slyly pick up a shoe, chuck it at his grandfather's head, and quickly reassume a prayerful posture before the shoe even landed.

The *thunk*, Morse's cry, and the shoe ricocheting off his head to the floor disrupted the prayer, but it was resumed, and when it was finished Caleb Powell knocked. As soon as he was in the house Powell said to the old couple, "Poor old man! Poor old woman! This boy" — he pointed at young Styles — "is the occasion of your grief, for he hath done these things, and hath caused his good old grandmother to be counted a witch."

"Then," Morse asked, "how can all these things be done by him?"

"Although he may not have done all, yet most of them," Powell said, "for this boy is a young rogue, a vile rogue — I have watched him and see him do things as to come up and down."

"I am persuaded it is witchcraft," Morse replied.

Powell switched tactics to placate the old man. "I am a navigator," he said, "and a mariner and have understanding in astrology and astronomy. I know the working of spirits, some in one country, some in another." He looked at Styles and continued, "You young rogue, to begin so soon!" Then, turning back to Morse, "If you be willing to let me have this boy, I will undertake you shall be free from any trouble of this kind while he is with me."

At first the Morses were unwilling to let the boy go, but Powell urged them, and when he assured them as to where he would lodge the boy, how he would be employed, and with whom he would be associating, they agreed. No sooner had Powell taken John Styles away from the Morse home than the poltergeist phenomena stopped. Instead of making the logical assumption, the Morses jumped to an even more obvious conclusion: It was Caleb Powell who was the witch. Hadn't he said he knew all about the occult? On the 3rd of December the Morses swore out a warrant for his arrest.

Caleb Powell on December 8th appeared for examination before Justice John Woodbridge of Newbury. He was charged with trafficking with the Devil, his testimony was taken, and he was bound over for trial the following March. Instead of being jailed, however, Powell was released on 20 pounds bail.

In England John Gadbury the astrologer was not so lucky. He had been cast into prison on suspicion of being mixed up in Catholic plots.

Chapter Eight

By the time the year 1680 got under weigh John Styles had been taken away from Caleb Powell, given back to his grandparents, and the weird events had resumed at the Morse home. Now the neighbors jumped to the same conclusion the Morses had jumped to except that their suspicions fell upon the old white witch Elizabeth Morse as a much more likely candidate for the gallows than Powell, for she had a reputation — and a practice of midwifery and herb medicine dispensing — that stretched back through the years. Judge Woodbridge kept surveillance of the situation and conducted further hearings and investigations, took depositions from the local folk against Goody Morse on January 7th. On the 6th of March he issued a warrant for her arrest.

The last week in March Caleb Powell's case came up for action. After trial by the County Court at Ipswich, a verdict was handed down: "In the case of Caleb Powell, though the Court do not see sufficient to charge further, yet find so much suspicion as that he pay the charges. The ordering of the charges left to Dr. John Woodbridge." That left no one but Elizabeth Morse, for somehow everyone was overlooking the possible culpability of John Styles. On April 2nd the old woman was taken into custody.

There was an epidemic of Satan's scourge in the Barbados that threatened Salem through the ships that docked at her wharves. On April 23rd the Selectmen prohibited Barbados ships from tying up at dockside or anchoring in the harbor and forbade the crews or passengers on such ships to come ashore.

By May the minister of Salem Village had fallen victim to the epidemic of hostility directed toward him by a minority of his parishioners. Tired of all the contention, he decided not merely to retire from the fray but from the ministry as well. He was poverty stricken, for his whole salary had never been paid and he saw greater opportunities in the study and field of medicine, which he determined to enter into and practice at Roxbury. Having prevailed over superior odds, Nathaniel Putnam magnanimously joined his brothers Thomas and John, as well as Thomas Fuller, Sr., and Joseph Hutchinson, Sr., in deeding Bailey some land in the Village to make up for things.

On May 6th John Putnam Jr., . was re-elected Deputy to the House of Deputies from Salem, and five days later he was once more appointed a member of the team representing Salem in the Wenham border dispute before the General Court. His brothers were made Salem Village highway surveyors.

Elizabeth Morse's trial commenced on May 20th. Several of her neighbors complained that she had caused them to have fits. John Chase swore he had had the bloody flux since the day he first gave testimony against the witch. Further, he said that his wife's breast had rotted off, and the other had had to be cut off. It was a short trial — she was convicted the same day.

Governor Simon Bradstreet, on May 27th "after lecture" very uncharacteristically condemned the woman to death. It became evident on the first of June, however, that his condemnation was merely a political expedient, taken in view of public opinion in the case and not meant to stand, for he and the Court of Assistants voted Goody Morse a reprieve. There was a public outcry against this action, especially when the next session of the Court of Assistants extended the reprieve. The House of Deputies protested the action of the Magistrates.

Eunice Cole of Hampton, New Hampshire, was brought before the bar once more on the same old charge. Again, the Court decided that there was "no full proof" of her witchcraft, and once more she was remanded to the custody of her town, with "a lock kept on her leg" at the pleasure of the Court. The Selectmen of Hampton were "to take care to provide for her as formerly." The old woman was allowed to return to her own shack — with a manacle about her leg — rather than to the local jail.

Samuel Shattuck, the Quaker, had returned to live in Salem after his adventures. Still a young man — under thirty — he had become a dyer. One day, in the line of business, he received a visit from Bridget Bishop, alias Oliver, alias Wasselby. She told him she wanted to buy an old barrel of him. Shattuck was willing to sell it, cheap, but somehow Bridget worked the conversation in such a way that they never got down to serious dickering and she left without purchasing it. On several subsequent days Bridget renewed her visit, on slight occasion, and the Shattucks were at a loss to explain the situation.

At last Bridget brought Shattuck some pieces of wool to dye — they were so small that the dyer was puzzled, since they were obviously not meant to be made into clothes for a grown person or even a child. Perhaps dolls.... Shattuck did the job and Bridget paid him twopence. Shattuck took the money and gave it to Henry Williams, who lived with the Shattucks, for some work he had done. Williams put the coins into a purse, locked the purse in a box, as he recalled, and the purse disappeared. He could find it nowhere.

Bridget Bishop was brought to trial on a charge of witchcraft and discharged into the community immediately, as the accusation did not take, much to the chagrin of the more righteous members of the town. Clemency was evidently in the air, for Joseph Getchell, who despised Salem Prison, was sentenced to be put back into it for a week, having been convicted on a charge of "reviling and reproachful speeches against the magistrates and ministry." The prospect was more than he could bear. Very contritely he petitioned the court that, since he had "neither house nor home," and his spouse was "a very weak woman," then "should he be now imprisoned for the week, his wife and poor babe must perish." The court took pity on him and his sentence was commuted. However, William Nelson, who had been convicted of the rape of a child of less than ten years, was administered a grievous public whipping before he was allowed to rejoin society.

The people of Hampton, New Hampshire, thought it peculiar that they hadn't seen Eunice Cole abroad for the past several days. At last it was reluctantly decided that the authorities had to go and check on her since she was, after all, a charge of the town. With a great deal of trepidation the locked door of her shack was broken down and the worst discovered: The witch had died — she had been dead for quite a while.

After a muffled and irritable conference among the Selectmen and other officials, a grave was dug in her dooryard, Eunice's corpse was dragged from the shack and tumbled into the open hole without a burial service. Instead, before they shoveled the dirt in upon her, the townspeople drove a wooden stake through her heart.

Having lost one witch, the town needed a replacement, so Rachel Fuller was indicted on July 13th for the murder of a child belonging to one John Godfry. The grand jury drew up the bill of indictment after the members had viewed the one-year-old child and found "grounds of suspicion that the said child was murdered by witchcraft: First, in part by what we saw by the dead corpse; second, something we perceived by the party suspected, which was then present and was examined by authority; and third, by what was said by the witnesses." On the following day Rachel's husband, John Fuller, was also indicted.

Elizabeth Denham and Mary Godfry deposed that, in a conversation with Goody Fuller some time previously, she had told them how it was that witches were able to "go abroad at night" by putting "their husbands and children asleep," evidently an unusual thing to do in the evening in Hampton. She had also told them, "I reckon there are witches and wizards in this town to the number of eight women and two men including Eunice Cole; Mrs. Benjamin Evans and her daughters; Goodwife Coulter and her daughter, Mrs. Prescott; Goodwife Towle, and another person, now dead."

Nathaniel Smith testified that Rachel had once told him, "The other night there was a great rout at Henry Roby's when first Dr. Reed was at this town. They pulled Dr. Reed out of the bed and, with an enchanted bridle, did intend to lead a jaunt. He got one by the coat but could not hold her." When she was asked who it was that Dr. Philip Reed had caught, Goody Fuller had turned away and laughed — or so it seemed to Mr. Smith.

Dr. Reed had originally been called into town to treat John Godfry's virulently ill baby, and he had treated it with a medicine derived from the root of the pitcher plant, but his treatment, and the prayers of the parents, had failed, so the family turned to sympathetic magic as a last resort. Mary and Sarah Godfry, the wife and daughter, respectively, of John, testified that Dr. Reed had in bafflement at last diagnosed witchcraft, so they had mixed the child's urine with other ingredients, and "by and by" — through occult magnetism — Rachel Fuller came in and looked very strangely; bending, daubed her face with molasses, as she judged it, so as she almost daubed up one of her eyes"; but of course she had dipped into the magic anti-elixir, not molasses, "and she sat down by Goody Godfry, who had the sick child in her lap, and took the child by the hand, and Goodwife Godfry…put her hand off from the child, and wrapped the child's hand in her apron.

"Then…Rachel turned her about, and smote the back of her hands together sundry times, and spat in the fire. Then, having herbs in her hands, rubbed and strewed them about the hearth by the fire. Then she sat down again, and said, 'Woman, the child will be well.' She then went behind the house. Mehitabel Godfry then told her mother that Goody Fuller was acting strangely. Then Mary Godfry and Sarah, looking out, saw Rachel Fuller standing with her face towards the house, beating herself with her arms, as men do to warm their hands. This she did three times. Then, gathering something from the ground, went home."

Further, Mary Godfry said that the next day her children told her that Rachel had told them that "if they did lay sweet bays under the threshold, it would keep a witch from coming in. One of the girls said, 'Mother, I will try it,' and she laid bays under the threshold of the back door, all the way and half way of the breadth of the foredoor; and soon after, Rachel Fuller came to the house, and she always had formerly come in at the back door, which is next her house, but now she went about to the foredoor, and though the door stood open, but she crowded in on that side where the bays lay not, and rubbed her back against the post, so as that she rubbed off her hat, and then she sat her down and made ugly faces, and nestled about, and would have looked on the child" — the sick baby — "but I not suffering her, she went out rubbing against the post of the door as she came in, and beat off her hat again, and I never saw her in the house since."

Hazen Levitt testified that, "Riding up to his lot in July last, sun about an hour high, I saw John Fuller's wife upon her hands and knees, scrambling to and fro, first one way and then another, and seemed to me to be mighty lazy. But after she spied me she left off that manner of acting and seemed to take up her apron with one of her hands, and with the other, to gather up something."

Rachel had a baby with her, Levitt said, and "She gave me a frowning look at first," and when he continued on his way she laughed at him. Levitt stopped a short distance away, took to cover, and watched the woman. He saw "a thing like a little dog" come from the gate into her yard, and it went to her while she was still trying to put things into her apron.

The Hampton coven was in a fair way to being broken up, for Isabella Towle was committed to custody along with Rachel Fuller.

The main thing in the air at Salem Village was not witches, but an adventure. A number of people, one of whom was Jonathan Putnam, son of Lt. John, had petitioned the General Court that they be allowed to begin a township at Casco Bay, on the Swagustago River. Settlers in the area, Sir Ferdinando Gorges' men, when they got wind of the project, protested and the Court turned the petitioners down but granted them permission to begin one on the north side of Casco Bay instead. Bartholomew Gedney was named to a committee to supervise the settlement. Jonathan did not intend himself to settle in Maine, but he did hope to make some money from the project.

On the 26th of September Jonathan's cousin, Carolina John Putnam, and his wife Hannah Putnam, were blessed with their second child, another daughter whom they named Elizabeth.

Dr. Philip Reed, not having stayed in Hampton long enough to enjoy the rout of indictments that followed upon his adventure with the enchanted bridle and his diagnosis of witchcraft, came home to Salem where he sought to make up for his lapse from duty by accusing Ipswich's Margaret Gifford of occult practices. His first accusation of the kind — that against Goody Burt — having come to frustration in 1669, Dr. Reed determined that this time nothing would go wrong. However, it did, for the Gifford woman never appeared in court to answer the charges brought against her, and nothing whatever happened.

The Rev. Deodat Lawson took the Freeman's Oath in the town of his habitation, Boston, and one of his former colleagues of the cloth, James Bailey, moved from Salem Village to Roxbury, though he kept the property the Putnams and others had given him. He held few grudges and determined to visit his Salem holdings from time to time, even to reside there for short periods in order to extend his practice of medicine, for doctors were in short supply and they often traveled, like Dr. Reed, to other communities to treat patients. Bailey left behind a dilapidated parsonage that would need extensive repair before the next minister could move in.

That minister, it had been decided, would be the Rev. Mr. George Burroughs of Casco, Maine, whose acquaintance Jonathan Putnam had made on his trips to the area. Mr. Burroughs was called to Salem Village in November by the Parish Committee, and when he arrived in town he and his wife moved in with Lt.. John Putnam, Jr.'s family until the parsonage could be repaired. On the 25th of November Lt. Thomas Putnam and Jonathan Walcott were chosen deacons of the Salem

Village Church on a pro-tem basis, their tenure to extend only through the following year. On December 3rd Nathaniel Putnam and Lt. John Putnam, Jr.., were still involved with the wearisome Wenham boundary dispute.

Joseph Glanvill, King Charles' chaplain, had died in November in Bath, England, leaving behind him an important manuscript. Early in the year John Gadbury, after two months in jail, had been released for lack of evidence that he was involved in plotting against the king. John Partridge, who had admired and envied William Lilly for years, now that his master was on the wane had stepped in with his own almanac, *Merlinus Liberatus*; the title was meant to capitalize on Lilly's *Merlinus Anglicus Junior*.

In Paris Edmund Halley and his elder colleague, Giovanni Domenico Cassini, observed the great comet of 1680. Halley predicted its return, and it was given his name. In England a volume was published that sided with witches; its title was, deceptively, *Discovery of the Imposture of Witches*, and its author was John Brinley.

The new year began auspiciously for Sgt. Thomas Putnam, Jr., and his wife Ann Carr Putnam. Since their marriage in 1678 Ann, like her sister Mary, had experienced a miscarriage or two, but on February 9th, 1681, she was delivered of a healthy son who was christened Thomas Putnam III. The next day the Salem Village Parish voted the Rev. Mr. George Burroughs, their new minister, his salary for the year. All was not harmony in the Village, however, for Mr. Burroughs, though he like Bailey before him was the majority choice, was nevertheless not the unanimous choice. He soon found that he had automatic enemies in Thomas Putnam, Bailey's prime backer, and in Ann Carr Putnam, Mary Bailey's sister. With both his father and his wife opposed to Burroughs, Sgt. Thomas Putnam, Jr., of course was entered in the opposing lists as well.

Furthermore, there was friction developing between Burroughs and Lt. John Putnam, Jr., in whose house Burroughs continued to live while the parish wrangled over the refurbishment of the parsonage. Neither John nor his wife, Rebecca, cared for the way Burroughs treated his wife who was something of a gossip. Burroughs had a strong sense of privacy, and he objected to his spouse's telling Rebecca all the family grievances. He chastised her for her loose tongue on several occasions — and, naturally, Mrs. Burroughs relayed these lectures to Rebecca who passed them on to John. Their sympathies lay with the oppressed wife, not the secretive minister.

The political situation in England between Parliament and the King had been deteriorating slowly for years, and in March it reached a crisis. The House of Commons in the recent elections had been confirmed as Whig, and the king's Tory party was out of power. The Commons arrived to assemble in Oxford, and it was summoned to the Bodleian Tower where the House of Lords gathered and King Charles II sat.

The Commons suspected nothing, but when its members arrived they discovered that Charles was dressed in his robes of state, which he had donned secretly — it was a signal that Parliament was to be dissolved before it had even gotten underway. Before anyone could do anything the monarch dissolved the body, and the "Second Stuart Despotism" was inaugurated.

William Lilly in Hersham was struck blind and, shortly afterward, he suffered another stroke that paralyzed him. At his first affliction his adopted son, Henry Coley, had rushed to his side to be the astrologer-physician's amanuensis, and he stayed by the old man's side throughout his ordeal.

Lt. John Putnam, Jr. on March 21st was elected a selectman of Salem, and Bridget Bishop sold a piece of her land to Daniel Epps the schoolmaster in order to pay her debts to the town. In April the Salem

Village parsonage was ready for habitation and the Burroughs family moved into it.

Nothing, however, had yet been settled in the Powell-Morse case in Newbury. William Morse on May 18th petitioned the Court to settle his wife's situation one way or the other — Elizabeth was still in jail waiting to find out whether her reprieve was to be permanent or the execution carried out. A few days later, on the 24th, she was released from prison, but still under penalty — the House of Deputies had voted to try her again, but the Assistants and Governor Bradstreet refused to concur. At least the witch had her liberty and her life.

William Lilly died in Hersham, England, on the 9th of June and was interred in the chancel of Walton Church. He left his almanac, *Merlinus Anglicus Junior*, which had appeared for thirty-six consecutive years, to Henry Coley. Lilly's friend, Elias Ashmole, erected a slab of black marble to mark the astrologer's grave.

The Wenham boundary dispute continued to vex Salem, and on June 9th Lt. John Putnam. and Israel Porter were assigned to prosecute the case of Joseph Porter who lived in the disputed territory — Salem claimed he ought to pay its rates, Wenham objected. John had also been given the responsibility of laying out a highway at Royal Side. When June 14th dawned, the day's eye saw Lt. Thomas Putnam's son Edward married to Mary Hale. Two weeks later, Major William Hathorne died at the age of seventy-four, and his passing was observed by most of the town.

Capt. Samuel Smith of Boston was preparing to voyage to Barbados, and Mary Bradbury of Salisbury went to Boston to sell him two firkins of butter that were put aboard. The vessel sailed, and after they had been at sea for three weeks the crew discovered that one of the firkins had not been completely churned — it had spoiled and was full of maggots. The seamen were considerably irritated, and they mumbled among themselves that they had often heard Goody Bradbury was a witch. It must be true, they inferred — exercising their infallible mariners' logic — or she would not have dared to sell their captain such goods.

Four days later the ship hit a hard gale — the mainmast was lost, together with the rigging and fifteen horses that the ship was transporting. Two weeks later the vessel came so close to colliding with another ship that two of its mizzen shrouds and one of the leaches of the new mainsail were carried away.

The ill-fated voyager put into Barbados at last, landed its cargo and, the morning after, sprang a leak in the hold, ruining several tons of salt. In order to repair the leak the crew had to unload once more. Finally, Capt. Smith weighed anchor for home. The return was uneventful, but as the ship neared Boston one of the seamen, Samuel John Endicott, could have sworn he saw a witch come aboard.

Jonathan Dunen was a member of Case's Crew, a splinter sect of Quakers who had detached themselves from the main body to follow Thomas Case, their prophet, to live at Southold, Long Island. Dunen was suddenly taken with The Spirit, and he saw that it was his destiny to go into Plymouth Colony to work miracles. In Marshfield he seduced a woman away from her husband, and another woman named Mary Ross soon joined the couple.

Mary was taken with a spirit even more violent than that which had possessed Dunen. She burned her clothes, declared that she was Christ come anew, and rechristened the members of Dunen's growing band with the names of the Apostles. She prophesied that she would die and be resurrected after three days — glories would be seen when she returned. She raised her hand in farewell and fell into a trance.

When at last Mary Ross returned to herself, she ordered Dunen to sacrifice a dog to her. After he had done so, she and the women of the band danced naked together until a bilious constable surprised them and took the whole lot of them into custody. He carried them, with Dunen uttering blasphemies all the way, before the magistrates. In court Dunen himself went into a dead trance for an hour which he put to good use figuring out what to do. When he came to, he declared that Mary Ross had ordered him to do what he had done; she had cast a spell on him, and thereby forced him to carry out her directions.

The Boston clergy had for some time been concerned about the rising tide of rationalism that threatened their religion. Clearly, something had to be done about the situation. Increase Mather came up with a proposal: Why not ask the ministers of New England to gather together all the supernatural evidence they could find and put it into a collection of personal experiences, ghost stories, tales of diabolical possessions, Providences of God, and so forth? The people to whom Mather made the suggestion thought it was a fine idea.

During the summer Jonathan Putnam married Elizabeth Whipple and looked forward to the not-too-distant day when he would be the head of a family of his own. Luke Perkins in Ipswich spoke his mind about the Rev. Thomas Cobbett who, he said, "was more fit to be in a hogsty than a pulpit; he was a vile man in his former days." Perkins was unwise in his selection of confidants, and he was publicly whipped as soon as ever the minister heard the story from the gossipmongers and complained to the authorities.

In September Mrs. George Burroughs died in Salem Village and the minister was in deep trouble. He was totally broke, for no one had collected the rates he had been voted earlier in the year, and he had not been paid his salary. He and his existed on the charity of Capt. John Putnam, Jr. ,as best he could; now, he had to bury his helpmeet. He was forced to go further into debt.

It was the end. He foresaw no possibility of his being able to stay on in Salem Village and appease the warring parishioners. When he had come he had been wise enough to realize this might be the case, so he had had an escape clause written into his contract with the Village: "All is to be understood so long as I have Gospel encouragement." He had had no encouragement whatsoever. As soon as he could get his affairs in order he left Salem Village, without even calling a parish meeting to try to settle the wages owed him, and went back to Maine — but not before he had taken another wife, the sister of Thomas Rucke. Burroughs' abrupt departure did nothing at all to sweeten the atmosphere of the parish, and the minister left in his wake a number of implacable enemies, including his new brother-in-law.

In October King Charles sent the Massachusetts Government an angry letter telling them to send agents to London within three months if they intended to defend their Charter. William Stoughton was named again, and Joseph Dudley, but Stoughton, recalling the way he had been treated on the last occasion, rejected the appointment.

Nathaniel Putnam was empowered to build a horse bridge over Crane River on November 4th and made a grand juryman two days later. That same day Samuel Gardner and Nathaniel's brother John were appointed to prosecute several former Salem constables who had collected rates from citizens but had never turned them in to the town treasury. On the 27th of the following month Jonathan Walcott and Lt. Thomas were renewed as deacons pro-tem of the Salem Village Church.

Two pro-witchcraft books had appeared In England during the year, Joseph Glanvill's posthumous *Saducismus Triumphatus* and Henry Hallywell's *Melampronoeia*. The latter book purported to be a "scientific" explanation of why and how familiar imps suckled witches' blood. Glanvill's book had been written in collaboration with his friend, Dr. Henry More. Its subtitle was, *A Full and Plain Evidence Concerning Witches*; it seemed to many to put the perfect case for witchcraft and cast it in a scientific and philosophical light. It became popular immediately on both sides of the Atlantic, and it was not long before the Rev. John Hale of Beverly owned a copy. The peculiar thing about the book was that neither of its co-authors was a Puritan.

In November Anthony Ashley Cooper, Earl of Shaftesbury, the parliamentary leader, was driven into exile by King Charles.

In February 1682, a month late, Massachusetts succeeded in appointing the emissaries King Charles had mandated. John Richards and Joseph Dudley were instructed to proceed to England forthwith, but they were not given the power to make binding agreements with the English government. In effect, they were merely high-grade couriers.

Carolina John and Hannah Putnam were blessed with a third daughter, Abigail, on February 26th. On March 14th his uncle John, together with various other Putnams and Salem Villagers, petitioned that the Village be officially detached from Salem. The petition carried a fair amount of weight, if the first published Salem Village tax list were any indication, for the wealthiest men in the Village were, in order, Lt. Thomas Putnam, Nathaniel Putnam, Thomas Fuller, and Lt. John Putnam.

If the Putnams of Salem Village were doing well in a financial way, Salisbury's William Osgood was turning away business, for one day George Martin dropped in to ask if he might buy some of Martin's beef. He was refused and he left in a huff. The next day — as might have been expected — Osgood and his boarder, Bernard Veach, found that one of Osgood's cows was in such a fright that they had a hard time catching her and getting her tethered in his barn. The following morning the cow was let out with the other cattle to browse, and when the herd returned in the evening she was ill — there were sores under her eyes as big as walnuts. Later in the night the cow died.

In April Prudence Putnam, Lt. Thomas' daughter, married William Wyman of Woburn and moved to that town. As one cycle thus began, another ended — or ought to have when Thomas Tuck of Beverly died. Not long after the funeral, however, Dorcas Hoar saw what she believed to be Tuck's ghost coming to talk with her about some land he had mentioned to her before his death. Dorcas ought to have had enough familiarity with the World Beyond to keep her nerve, but that was not the case. She ran before the phantom could tell her what was on its mind. Old Thomas Tuck presumably returned to his place of rest, for he was not seen thereafter. However, Mother Nature abhors a vacuum, so on April 29th Mary Hale Putnam, wife of young Edward Putnam, brought the couple's first child into the world, and they called him Edward, Jr.

In May the commission that had been appointed to reconsider the Court's decision in the Allen-Putnam-John Endicott land squabble, at long last came in with its report: It was even more unfavorable to Dr. Zerubabel Endicott than the original had been. Zerubabel was beside himself with impotent fury.

Hannah Putnam, on May 13th, was married in Salisbury to Henry Brown. Her father, Lt. John, and mother, Rebecca, journeyed to the town for the ceremony along with her uncles, aunts, and a contingent of cousins.

Poltergeists were rampant in New Hampshire in 1682. Mary Hortado, wife of Antonio Hortado of Salmon Falls, was initiated into the psychic world when first she heard a voice at her door saying, "What do you there?" When she looked to see who it was, no one was in sight. An hour later she was again standing at the door when she was hit in the eye and knocked to the floor by an unseen hand.

Two or three days later a stone fell down the chimney, but when she went to pick it up it was gone. All the members of her family were in the house at the time. Shortly, a frying pan hung in the chimney rang so loudly it could be heard across the river more than a hundred rods away. Mary and her husband got into a canoe a little later to cross the river. Part way across they saw ahead of them in the water the shaved head of a man and, a yard behind the head, the tail of a white cat. When they returned across the river the bald head and the tail followed them until they reached shore and the phenomena disappeared.

While she was standing in her yard Mary was bitten black and blue on both arms, the teethmarks visible. As she tried to make it back into the house she was bitten and scratched on her breast. Antonio and Mary decided to abandon their house. They packed themselves and their family off across the river to stay with a neighbor, but not long after they arrived there a woman "clothed with a green safeguard, a short blue cloak and white cap" appeared to Mary — the apparition brandished a firebrand as though to hit Goody Hortado, but she refrained. The same phantom appeared the next day, but in a different costume: A gray gown, a white apron, and a white headdress. She laughed, but there was no noise of laughter. Quite abruptly after this, however, for some reason Mary ceased being plagued.

Unfortunately, though, on June 11th the poltergeists tried to break up a convention of important Quakers who had gathered at the home of George Walton who lived at Grand Island, Newcastle, New Hampshire. There were many important people present including Richard Chamberlain, Secretary of the Province; Samuel Jennings, Governor of West Jersey; Walter Clark, Deputy Governor of Rhode Island, and Thomas Maule of Salem.

The mystic manifestations began with a shower of stones in the night, thrown against the roof and walls of the Walton home. When they went out to investigate, the people who were gathered there discovered the gate was torn off its hinges. More stones fell among them, but no one was hurt. The stones moved indoors with the guests shattering glass, bending the lead casements of the windows. A large hammer just missed one of the men, knocking a candlestick near him to the floor.

Nine of the stones were picked up — some of them proved to be hot — and marked. They were laid on a table, and soon the marked stones were flying about again. Despite the excitement of the occasion, eventually people tired and went to bed, but they were to have no rest, for a great rock smashed through one of the bedroom doors and a brickbat followed. Mr. Walton came and collected the stone, took it to his own room, and locked it in. It refused to stay put but went whooshing off into the next room instead.

The spit in the fireplace flew up the chimney, came hurtling down again point first, and stuck in the backlog; then it flew out the window. Such phenomena continued for several days, and the guests began to notice that the stones were thickest where Walton walked. Once they saw a black cat and shot at it but missed; another time some of the folk saw a hand throw a stone through the hall window but they could find no one there.

At night there were "dismal howlings," the sounds of trotting and snorting horses. When Walton went up to the Great Bay for timber in his boat, the stone shower followed him, and when he attempted to return home his anchor jumped overboard. Eventually, when he made it back through adversity, he discovered his haycocks hanging from the branches of trees, and a stirrup iron he had left in his boat "came jingling after him through the woods."

In order to get rid of the poltergeists, Walton's guests turned to sympathetic magic. They set a pot of urine on the fire, dropped some crooked pins into the brew so that they would attract magnetically and turn the spell of whatever witch it was that vexed them back upon herself. They waited for the pot to boil, for when it did the witch would be hurt and forced to cancel her enchantment. But just as the pot was heating up a stone hit it, broke the spout, and knocked it over. A goodly supply of the pot's liquid contents had been held in reserve, so the occultists tried again. This time a stone broke the pot's handle and knocked it over. Grimly the guests girded their loins for a third attempt, but the phantom had by that time zeroed in on the pot and the next stone smashed it.

The first child of Jonathan and Elizabeth Whipple Putnam was born on August 8th in Salem Village, but there was great trouble with the birth and the mother died after the delivery, to the enormous grief of Jonathan and his family. The next few days were days of lamentation, for not only had Elizabeth's funeral to be held, but there was grave doubt that the baby would survive. It was terribly hurt and weak, but somehow it kept alive, though it did not seem to grow better. The Putnams did not need the services of Samuel Wardwell of Andover to foresee what was likely to happen soon.

Wardwell was Andover's fortuneteller, and his specialty was the reading of palms. It was the opinion of Dorothy Eames that Wardwell was a witch "or else," she told her friends, "he could never tell what he does," for his predictions were sometimes uncannily accurate. Wardwell never took money for his services, and he particularly liked telling the fortunes of young people, seeming to do it for sport more than anything else. He would peer at a person's hand, then look at the ground before he told what was going to happen in one's life — he told Ephraim Foster that his wife would have five daughters before she had a son, and he told Dorothy Eames' fortune as well. The gossips had it that palmistry was not his only talent, for he could make cattle and animals come to him whenever he pleased.

Job Tookey of Marblehead was a servant, but not, in his opinion, cut out simply to be a menial, for he was a highly articulate and, at times, presumptuous man. At last his master had enough of his rebelliousness, took him to the Essex County Court, and had him thrown into Salem Prison for an extended visit. The place offended him no less than it had Joseph Getchell. He began to bombard his master with letters of complaint and appeal. "No one alive," he said with some exaggeration, "knows or is able to express what I have suffered since I came into this place, and still daily do…." Though he had "an extraordinary pain" in his side, he had never been allowed to see a doctor since his incarceration.

There were no toilet facilities in his cell, and he was not allowed to use the outhouse, so after he had been ten weeks locked into his quarters he was "almost poisoned with the stink" and had not even "so much as a minute's time to take the air since I came into this dolesome place." Having survived fourteen weeks in Salem prison, he at last petitioned the court to take pity on "this sad, miserable, and deplorable condition" in which he found himself.

On November 30th Jonathan's infant son, having languished through the late summer and early fall, finally succumbed to the damage his birth had wrought upon him. It was a hard thing to bear, but in some ways a relief. Had it survived the child would never have been healthy and whole.

During the year in England Sir Francis North had sentenced three witches to be hanged, and a pamphlet had been published describing the trials and executions; its title was *The Trial, Condemnation, and Execution of Three Witches; viz., Temperance Lloyd, Mary Lloyd, and Susanna Edwards*. A late entry in the witch pamphlet parade was *The Bury St. Edmunds Witches* that told the story, twenty years late, of Rose Cullender and Amy Duny. England was running out of witches.

Rev. Cotton Mather was the editor of an almanac for 1683, the *Boston Ephemeris*, and this was an indication of the anomaly of his nature. He epitomized the paradox of Puritanism as a whole, which made it a relatively unstable religion. On the one hand, Cotton Mather was a mystic, utterly committed to revelations and providences — his guide in these was the Bible. But the Bible was more than an evidence of the World of Spirits, it was a book of rules as well, so Cotton was a dogmatist to boot. In themselves, these two elements of his religion brought him into conflict with himself, as it did many Puritans, for fortune-telling and divining were strictly prohibited by the Scriptures; yet it was through such things that the Bible's revelations often took place: Readings of the stars, burning bushes, heavenly phenomena. So Cotton Mather published an almanac and practiced a forbidden form of divining — Bibliomancy.

Yet he could not practice Bibliomancy deliberately; therefore, when he just "happened" to let his Bible fall open and his eyes light accidentally on a particular passage — a frequent occurrence — it seemed like one of God's Providences when the passage happened to be relevant to his situation at the moment. He was forever aware of coincidences, which never seemed to be merely coincidence.

If Mather were a mystic and a dogmatist, he was also devoted to the New Philosophy of Science, and he was a correspondent of the Royal Society in London. He believed that knowledge was important in and of itself, for knowledge of God's world could not be evil. It was, in fact, mandatory that God's people acquire knowledge, for learning was itself a form of revelation. Hence, Mather could believe that comets were, at one and the same time, natural phenomena that recurred at regular intervals, and portents of things to come. If his mind at times tripped over the inherent inconsistency of this position — that there were regularly recurring portents of things to come — and what that inconsistency did to the doctrine of Free Will, he always found a way out for himself, even if whatever loophole it was he found didn't really clear matters up completely. Mystery was an essential element of his belief. If science explained one thing that had been mysterious, it also uncovered something else heretofore unknown that was even more mysterious. And so on and on.

Hence, Cotton Mather — like his father, Increase — was mystic, dogmatist, *and* scientist. Further, he was a humanitarian, believing that God's greatest creation, Man, was put on Earth to be led out of darkness by the Chosen men, of whom Cotton was certainly one. Add, then, to the list of his attributes the fact that he was a supreme egotist, and his personality was nearly complete, except for one final feature: Cotton Mather truly believed he was an humble man…misunderstood, often disliked for his pomposity and self-righteousness, but withal, humble.

In February Edward Randolph, King Charles' trouble-shooter for New England, left Boston for London to be present at the proceedings against the Massachusetts Charter. By the time he arrived there Charles had discovered the blunted authority Massachusetts had given its emissaries Dudley and Richards. He informed them that they were to obtain full authority to negotiate immediately, or the Charter would fall instantly.

When news of this situation got back to Boston there was consternation and turmoil in the government. Finally, it bluntly refused to grant Dudley and Richards the power that the king had ordered. Charles backed down to a degree, and he sent Randoph back to Boston once more with a compromise proposal. On the day he arrived a fire destroyed a large part of Boston. Rumor had it that, if he were not directly to blame, at least it was an obvious Providence of God and portent of things to come.

Western Massachusetts, too, was having its share of occult phenomena. William and Mary Webster were inhabitants of Hadley; the couple was very poor and, to boot, Mary was a scold — needless to say their neighbors thought she was a witch: Horses balked outside her house, cattle refused to be driven past. But the Hadleyans had discovered a process that was effective when applied to these occurrences, for when they happened the drivers would enter Mary's home and beat her, or threaten to, and then she would take off her spell so that they could drive on by. Once when Mary had overturned a load of hay the farmer came in to beat her but discovered, when he looked back, that his cart had preternaturally been put back upright.

On another occasion, when Goody Webster had looked at a child in its cradle, the baby had levitated three times. A hen had come squawking down the chimney of one of the townsfolk and scalded itself in a pot of boiling water — Mary had suffered a scald at the same time. In April the townsfolk had had enough. She was accused, sent to jail, given a body search that revealed witch teats, and bound over for trial before the Court of Assistants in Boston.

At Ipswich Session of the Essex County Court in April the Salem Villagers petitioned for relief from their lack of ministry and asked the magistrates that "they be pleased to write to Mr. Burroughs, requiring him to attend an orderly hearing and clearing up the case" and to settle accounts with them in respect to his salary and debts. It was to be a balancing of the books prior to the Village's calling another minister. The Court agreed, and it summoned Mr. Burroughs from Casco; however, the "orderly hearing" was anything but that.

On April 24th Burroughs appeared for the accounting, a letter from the Court was read directing the participants to settle accounts, and Burroughs asked his former parishioners, "Do you take up with the advice of the court, given in the letter, or do you reject it?"

"Yes," the Villagers answered him, "we take up with it," and no man demurred. They worked out a proposed settlement, and "the second, third, and fourth days of the following week were agreed upon by Mr.

Burroughs and the people to be the days for every man to come in and to reckon with the said Burroughs; and so they adjourned the meeting to the last of the aforesaid three days, in the afternoon, then to make up the whole account in public."

So May 2nd was the day of reckoning. As the Villagers were gathered to complete the accounting and payments, Henry Skerry, the county marshal, came in the door, walked up to Lt. John Putnam, and whispered something to him. Putnam said aloud, "You know what you have to do! Do your office."

Reluctantly, the marshal went over to Burroughs and said to him, "Sir, I have a writing to read to you." It was an attachment of the salary the Village owed Burroughs, sworn out by John Putnam. for debts Burroughs purportedly owed him for the time the minister had lived with the Putnam family, and for money that had been borrowed to pay for the funeral of Mr. Burroughs' first wife.

When Marshal Skerry had read the document, Burroughs turned to Lt. Putnam and asked, "What money is it that you attach me for?"

Putnam replied, "For five pounds and odd money at Shippen's at Boston, and for thirteen shillings at my father-in-law Gedney's, and for twenty-four shillings at Mrs. Darby's."

Burroughs turned again to the marshal and told him, "I have no goods to show, but I am now reckoning with the inhabitants, for we do not know yet who is in debt," he paused for a breath and said, "but here is my body." He spread his arms wide.

Nathaniel Ingersoll stood up and faced John Putnam. "Lieutenant," he said, "I wonder that you attach Mr. Burroughs for the money at Darby's and your father Gedney's, when, to my knowledge, you and Mr. Burroughs have reckoned and balanced accounts two or three times since — as you say — it was due, and you never made any mention of it when you reckoned with Mr. Burroughs."

It was true. Furthermore, Ingersoll and his wife, Hannah, had been present when Burroughs borrowed the money for Shippen as well. Ingersoll had heard Burroughs ask for a draft to be presented to Mr.

Shippen, and Putnam had inquired, "How much will you take up at Shippen's?"

Burroughs had answered, "It might be five pounds," but when he had done some more figuring he had said, "It may be it might come to more, therefore I will have to give him a draft to the value of five or six pounds."

Putnam had replied, "It is all one to me," and he had written the draft, read it to Burroughs, and said, "This will go for a part of the 33 pounds, 6 shillings, eight-pence the Parish owes you."

There was nothing John Putnam. could reply to Ingersoll — they were both well aware that the parish owed Burroughs much more than Burroughs owed Putnam. The two men stood looking at one another for a moment, and Putnam finally said, "It is true, and I own it." But John Putnam was not about to let a small matter of equity interfere with what he had made up his mind to do.

The incident had broken up the meeting with nothing settled, and people were getting up to leave, most of them in great embarrassment, when Mr. Burroughs said, "Well, what will you do with me?"

The marshal approached John Putnam. uncertainly and asked, "What shall I do?"

Putnam replied, "You know your business." He tossed his head in the direction of the minister, then went over to his brother Thomas, tugged at his coat, and they went outdoors to confer while the marshal arrested Burroughs. The Putnam brothers came back in a moment later, and John Putnam. said, "Marshal, take your prisoner and have him up to the Ordinary" — Ingersoll's Inn — "and secure him till the morning."

The marshal took Burroughs out, shouldering through the knots of citizens who stood about and looked angrily or reproachfully upon the proceedings. Some of the Villagers decided to do something about it. They followed Burroughs and Marshal Skerry to Ingersoll's where they drew up a bond:

"We whose names are underwritten do bind ourselves jointly and severally to Henry Skerry, Marshal of Salem, our heirs, executors, and administrators, in the sum of fourteen pounds money, that George Burroughs shall appear at the next court at Salem, to answer to Lieutenant John Putnam, according to the summons of this attachment, and to abide the order of the court therein, and not to depart without license; as witness our hands this 2nd of May, 1693." The bond was signed by Burroughs, Ingersoll, John Buxton, Thomas Haynes, Samuel and William Sibley, and William Ireland, Jr. The Casco minister was set at local liberty for the time being.

If Dorcas Hoar had been present at the meeting of Salem Villagers, perhaps she could have predicted what would eventually happen, but she was busy in Beverly. She was present in the home of John Giles when a thirty-nine-year-old matron, Marie Wood, dropped in with her son Joshua for a visit. No sooner had the general conversation commenced when, peering into the boy's face, Dorcas said, "The child is not long-lived."

Marie, startled, asked, "How do you know?"

Dorcas simply shook her head and said, "It will not live long. Mark the end of it."

On May 22nd in Boston Mary Webster of Hadley was indicted before Governor Bradstreet and the Court of Assistants on the charge of practicing witchcraft. Two days later the Salem Village parish voted to levy a rate to raise fifteen pounds owed to George Burroughs for his last quarter's preaching in the Village.

The specters that had haunted Mary Hortado in Salmon Falls, New Hampshire, the year previous returned to the Hortado home, but this time it was her husband Antonio that they were after. Goodman Hortado heard a man walking in the room above him, and the boards buckled under the walker's feet, but when Antonio and others went to look, no one was there. It was enough to send the Hortados back across the river again, to the home of their neighbor, for an extended visit, but Antonio commuted to his farm in order to put in the spring crop despite the merry pranks of Robin Goodfellow or Hobbamock, or whoever it was that pulled down his fencing so the cattle got into the corn. Mary made many attempts to ward off the spirits by strewing fresh bay leaves about the house. It was an effective method until the leaves dried out and the devils raised winds to blow them away.

On May 29th Sgt. Thomas and Ann Carr Putnam ushered their third child, a daughter named Elizabeth, into the world. Nothing much untoward was happening in Salem Village at the time, but in Hartford the poltergeists — leaping over Massachusetts — attacked Nicholas Disbrow and caught him in a shower of "stones, pieces of earth, cobs of Indian corn," and so forth. He could not escape, for the baleful storm followed him indoors through doors, windows, and the chimney; it followed him into the barn, the fields — wherever he went, until an escalation set in and a fire burned a good deal of his property.

Nicholas did not resort to magic in order to lay the evil spirits to rest — he simply returned an article he had illegally seized from a neighbor, and the evil events came to an end. Other neighbors whispered among themselves when he died later the same year that witchcraft was certainly involved in the case.

It was a measure of John's vindictiveness when, in June, in Essex County Court, he brought a suit against George Burroughs for a "debt for two gallons of Canary wine, and cloth, &c., bought of Mr. Gedney on John Putnam's account, for the funeral of Mrs. Burroughs."

At about the same time in Beverly Mrs. Marie Wood's child Joshua died, as Dorcas Hoar had predicted it would. In Salem Village widower Jonathan Putnam took, as his second wife, Lydia Potter of Ipswich; shortly afterward he was chosen grand juryman in Salem Village. Samuel Beadle, "who lost his health in the Narragansett expedition," was "allowed to take the place of Mr. Stephens as an innkeeper" in Salem.

On September 4th Mary Webster of Hadley was tried before Gov. Simon Bradstreet and the magistrates; she was acquitted. At the end of the month Edward and Mary Hale Putnam had their second child, a boy they named Holyoke, and in Beverly Marie Wood ran across

Dorcas Hoar again, accosted her, and asked, "How could you have known that my child would die?"

Dorcas told her, "I have acquaintance with a doctor that taught me to know, and I have a doctor's book by me." It was clear that if, indeed, she had ever returned John Samson's book of fortunetelling to him — the book he was supposed to have sold in Casco — she had acquired a replacement for it.

It had twice been settled in the courts that Zerubabel Endicott could have no title to the Townsend Bishop land, owned by Francis Nurse and Nathaniel Putnam, but after the second decision he had manically appealed the decision of the Court a third time and the date of the new hearing was set for November 24th. Before that day Zerubabel sent men out to cut timber on that portion of the disputed territory that Nathaniel Putnam owned, though the General Court had specifically instructed him not to engage in unilateral actions of the kind.

Zerubabel's men worked unmolested for a few days. They cut down a number of trees, dressed them, and hewed them to make beams and timbers for a house that Zerubabel planned to build there as proof of *de facto* ownership. But one morning when the men arrived for work the whole place had been cleared out, including the house frame. They followed sign, and a mile away they found the wood piled neatly beside Nathaniel Putnam's house.

Nothing deterred, Zerubabel again sent men to cut timber on the land, but this time he chose to contest the issue with Francis Nurse instead of Nathaniel. Zerubabel's teams went to take out a quantity of winter firewood, but when they had finished "Thomas Preston and John Tarbell," Nurse kin, "came in a violent manner and hauled the wood" out of Endicott's sleds; "and Francis Nurse, being present, demanded whose men" they were. "Mr Endicott, being present, answered they were his men." For two days Endicott's people cut wood, loaded it, and watched it being pitched back off by Nurse's men. It was a wild scene in the woods of New England.

On November 24th, the day set for the rehearing before the General Court, Zerubabel was ill in bed and unable to attend. It made no difference: The previous court settlement remained in effect. Zerubabel sued Nathaniel and Francis, again to no effect. Nothing, however, made Dr. Zerubabel Endicott change his mind that the whole issue was unfinished business. In December the Salem Villagers voted to take care of some other unfinished business: They would raise a rate among them to pay the parish debts.

The University of Oxford in 1683 completed a repository for the antiquities of Elias Ashmole and, by agreement, he donated much of his collection to begin the first public institution of its kind, the Ashmolean Museum. His countryman, Edmund Halley, published his theory of the variation of the magnet.

On December 27th in Pennsylvania, the Quaker colony, two old Swedish women were brought before William Penn on charges of witchcraft. The Quakers were chary of the belief in witchcraft as a general rule, at least in Pennsylvania, for too many of them had been accused themselves of being witches. It was said that "the Quaker revelation doth arise in them only when the witchcraft fit is upon them," and people believed that they used a magic Quaker powder to gain converts.

The old women were acquitted, and the story began to circulate that Penn's examination of them had been unorthodox. He was said to have asked one of them, "art thou a witch? Hast thou ridden through the air on a broomstick?"

"Yea," the woman was said to have replied.

"Well," Penn replied, "thou hast a perfect right to ride on a broomstick, for there is no law against it."

Zerubabel Endicott never again left his bed for any amount of time, for he was dead as 1684 got under weigh. The Rev. George Burroughs was still very much on the scene, however, and living in Salem Village, for though he was free on bond, he could not leave town until John Putnam Jr.'s suit was settled. The minister was, therefore, existing again largely on charity, for he was without a salary and he had to continue to send money back to Casco for the support of his family as well.

On February 22nd the Salem Village parish again voted to raise "fifteen pounds for Mr. Burroughs" so that he could continue to exist while he awaited trial. In the meantime the parish committee had received permission to call another minister to preach in the Village, and it had settled upon Deodat Lawson who was, however, reluctant to respond to the call, for the notoriety of the settlement as a place of pastoral contention was widespread. Lawson was importuned to accept, however, and at last, reluctantly, he did so. At the same meeting that voted Burroughs funds, a committee of parish members was formed to arrange to have Lawson's worldly goods transported into town from Boston.

Although Lawson didn't know it at the time, the Village church members had found something else to wrangle about: They were arguing over the entries in their parish records. Some people had complained that there were errors and discrepancies in the parish book stretching all the way back to Rev. Mr. Bailey's tenure — missing votes, inaccurate notes, and so forth. There were so many meetings called to argue about the subject that some of the farmers were having difficulty getting ready for spring planting. Some members insisted that the inaccurate entries be wiped off the record while others argued that they ought to be correctly inserted.

Then there was trouble over the lands owned by the parish. Every church had to have land on which the minister could live, and which he could work or lease out for part of his living. Joseph Houlton had donated the church lands, but he had never gotten the title straightened out — he had no copy of the deed, and the original had gotten lost. Nor had the question of tithing with regard to the Salem church been resolved. Deodat Lawson was about to step into a whirlpool the dimensions of which he could not fully understand.

In April Mr. Burroughs, who wanted nothing more than to get out of town, proposed a solution to his own particular problem: He authorized Lt. Thomas Putnam to receive from the parish the money due him by "the inhabitants of Salem Farms." Thus, Thomas could pay his brother John whatever the Court decided Burroughs owed him, if anything, and send the rest up to Casco. Burroughs was not fool enough, however, to think that he would receive much of anything by mail. If by chance he did, fine; if not, at least he would be free of the toils of Salem Village, or so he surmised.

In Boston the General Court decided that it would retain a London barrister to defend the Massachusetts Charter against the king and the Lords of Trade, though lawyers were banned from practicing in the colony itself and every person had to be his or her own lawyer. The process was set in motion.

Zerubabel Endicott's will had been proved on March 27th and it contained a curious clause: "Whereas my late father, by his last will, bequeathed to me his farm called Bishop's or Chickering's farm, I do give the said farm to my five sons, to be equally divided among them." Zerubabel had gone to his grave regarding the lost Townsend Bishop estate as his own, despite years of adverse rulings by every court available.

The General Court's action in regard to its charter proved to be too little and too late. On April 16th a *scire facias* action was introduced into the English courts against the charter, and the proceedings ground swiftly to an inevitable conclusion. On June 10th the charter fell. When news arrived in Boston despair reigned, for Massachusetts was transformed from a self-governing corporation into merely a Royal Colony. The law of England obtained in New England, not the law of the Puritan Bible.

During the summer John Londer, a young man, was living in the household of John and Susannah Gedney, John Putnam Jr.'s step-sibling-in-law. Gedney's orchard adjoined that of Edward and Bridget Bishop, and Goody Bishop was much on Londer's mind. One night he dreamed that Bridget was sitting on his stomach and trying to choke him.

Bridget and the Gedney family had not been getting along well, and at the first opportunity Susannah Gedney informed Bridget of Londer's nocturnal visitation. Bridget denied that any such thing had really happened, but Londer was called into the dispute and affirmed to the witch's face that what he had dreamed was a fact.

Bridget was furious in the face of such pigheaded stupidity, and in the heat of her anger she made threats. Soon Londer received other spectral visits including a black pig and a monkey-like creature with rooster claws and the face of a man. It spoke to him and made him an offer: "If you are ruled by me you shall want for nothing in the world."

Londer, however, was made of sterner stuff; he clapped his hands at the specter and cried, "You Devil, I will kill you!" He attempted to grab it, but its form was insubstantial.

It jumped out the window, immediately reappeared from the porch and said, "You had better take my council." Londer hit at the demon with a stick but succeeded only in breaking the stick on the sill. Suddenly, he found himself to be paralyzed, and the specter vanished.

When Londer had recovered himself he went outdoors to see if the demon were still in the neighborhood, and he saw Bridget Bishop walking through her orchard toward her house. Again he was struck with paralysis. Coming out of the spell at last he turned and went back indoors — and there was the monkey-creature! Londer cried out, "The whole army of God to be between me and you!" The shape sprang back at this oath, flung dust in Londer's face with its rooster claws, and sailed out the door over the apple trees, knocking many apples to the ground. For three days Londer was struck dumb and could not tell his hosts what had happened.

More than two years after her birth Abigail Putnam, daughter of Carolina John and Hannah, was baptized in Salem on July 6th, and around the same time Richard Coman, twenty-four, was inaugurated into the world of preternatural visitations. He had locked the door in the evening and gone to bed. He was lying beside his wife, and a lamp was on in the room. Suddenly, Bridget Bishop and two other women who were strangers came into the room — Coman recognized Bridget by the clothes she was wearing. The lamp was blown out and in the darkness Bridget came and lay upon Coman in the bed — at least Coman assumed it was Bridget. The event disturbed his wife not at all, and Coman could neither speak nor stir to waken her. The next night the same thing happened, only this time Bridget tried to choke him and pull him out of bed.

He told his kinsman William Coman of these tenebrous perambulations, and William offered to stay with Richard on the third night, a Saturday. William told Richard, "Lay your sword athwart your body" in the bed. They went to bed and were talking when in came the three women again. William was struck speechless — either that, or had had fallen asleep. The women tried to take Richard's sword away from him, but he held on. He cried to his wife and to Sarah Phillips, who was sleeping with Mrs. Coman that night, and he called to William. They heard his cries dimly, but somehow they couldn't get out of bed to come to his aid. Finally, Sarah roused herself sufficiently to call out, "In the name of God, Goodman Coman, what is the matter with you?" whereupon the three witches vanished away and did not return.

One summer Thursday James Howe, Jr., of Ipswich went to the home of Deacon Isaac Cummings to borrow a horse, but the Deacon was not at home and he spoke to Cummings' son, Isaac Cummings, Jr. Howe asked, "Does your father have ever a horse?"

"No," the young man replied.

"Has he ever a mare, then?"

"Yes," Isaac Junior replied.

"Do you think your father would lend me his mare?" Howe persisted.

"I do not think he would," Isaac replied, for it was the only steed the elder Cummings had available.

On Friday Goodman Cummings and his wife rode the mare in question a mile to a neighbor's house and back again, and when they got home the mare was set out to graze. The next morning the mare was standing outside the door of the house, showing signs of having been ridden hard. She had a sore mouth. The elder Cummings put the mare into the barn and fed it fodder, but it would consume nothing. It obviously was ill, and expert advice was necessary, so Deacon Cummings called upon his brother-in-law, Thomas Andrews of Boxford.

Andrews treated the mare for its illness, which he at first diagnosed as "the belly ache," but his medications were of no avail. Andrews shook his head and said to Cummings, "I will try one thing more. I'll take a pipe of tobacco and light it and put it into the fundament of the mare."

Cummings replied, "I think it is not lawful," and he was right, for it was a sympathetic magic cure: The fire in the bowl of the pipe would attract the evil spirits that infested the mare and draw them out of her belly —or perhaps it would attract the methane gas in her digestive system.

Andrews was of an opposite opinion. "It is lawful for man or beast," he said.

Cummings went to get a clean clay pipe from the house; he filled and lit it, then handed it to Andrews who took it, inserted the stem into the mare's rectum, and — the tobacco blazed and turned blue!

Startled, Cummings said, "You shall try no more! It is not lawful!"

"I will try once again," Andrews contradicted him, and he did so.

Later, when Cummings told the story, he said, "There arose a blaze from the pipe of tobacco which seemed to me to cover the buttocks of the mare. The blaze went upward towards the roof of the barn, and in the roof of the barn there arose a great crackling, as if the barn would have fallen or been burnt," or so it seemed to the onlookers, both inside and outside the barn. Cummings told Thomas Andrews, "I had rather lose my mare than my barn!" The great farrier's operation was over at last, and the gathering broke up, everyone discussing the amazing exhibition.

At church services the next day Cummings asked Andrews to come and look at his mare once more, for she was worse. Andrews came and tried another of his spectacular remedies, to no effect. That night a neighbor, John Hawkins, came to view the mare, and he suggested still another occult remedy for taking the spell off her — "If I were as you," he told Cummings, "I would cut off a piece of the mare and burn it," for to burn a part, according to the rules of sympathetic magic, was to burn the whole.

It was a drastic step, so Cummings replied, "No, not today, but if she lives till tomorrow morning I might cut off a piece of her and burn it." As he spoke these words he and Hawkins stepped out of the barn, and at the same moment the mare fell down dead, no doubt preferring to die immediately than be burnt alive a piece at a time.

Increase Mather in Boston had finished his portion of the great compendium of supernatural phenomena he and other New England divines had begun to gather in 1681, and he had so much material he decided to publish it as a separate volume. It appeared with a long title, *Essay for the Recording of Illustrious Providences: Wherein an Account Is Given of Many Remarkable and Very Memorable Events Which Have Happened in This Last Age, Especially in New England*, but folk called it merely *Illustrious Providences,* and it was an immediate best seller. It was obvious to everyone who read it that the Age of Miracles was not yet over.

One day in Salem John Westgate was in Samuel Beadle's tavern with John Parker and others, enjoying a pint of brew, when Parker's wife Mary came in, very angry, and began to scold him for frequenting such a place with such people. She irritated everyone, and finally Westgate broke in — since Parker was saying nothing — and told her, "It is an unbecoming thing for you to come after your husband to the tavern and rail after that rate."

Mary Parker turned upon him. She leaned into his face, arms akimbo, and spat out, "Rogue! Mind your own business! You had better have said nothing!"

Later, when the party had broken up and he was walking near John Robinson's house, Westgate heard a great noise and saw a black hog with open mouth running at him. Panicked — and having had perhaps a drop too much at Beadle's — he stumbled and fell on his knife in its sheath. The blade cut the stitching in the leather and ran into his hip, up to the haft.

Unable to walk, Westgate crawled, bleeding copiously, up to Essex Street, past the Salem Common, along the stone fence, down an alley and to his own house. When he got there his dog went wild, for the black hog had followed Westgate home, but it was unimpressed by the barking and yelping. When Westgate managed to get inside he pulled the knife, still partly in its sheaf, out of his leg. The sheaf fell apart, and Westgate managed to attend to his wound.

Joseph Getchell got himself into trouble again. He had some unorthodox views concerning the Christian religion, and he dared to utter them publicly. It was his opinion that "all men should be saved," not just a few. When it was pointed out to him that Christ had sent out his disciples to preach that "whoever *repents* and *believes* shall be saved," not everyone, Getchell answered, "If it be so, he was an imperfect savior and a fool." Getchell would go further: "There is no God, Devil, or Hell!"

For uttering such blasphemies, Getchell got off with a relatively mild sentence, considering that he had committed a capital offense. It was ordered that he be pilloried and "have his tongue drawn forth out of his mouth, and pierced through with a hot iron." Perhaps, for Getchell, it was an even milder sentence than the authorities realized, considering how he loathed Salem prison. But the town had replaced the old jail with a new one in 1684, and the accommodations, if still primitive, were at least relatively unused.

There were a good many Putnam family events during the fall of 1684. On October 4th Jonathan and Lydia Potter Putnam had their first child, Lydia, and later on Nathaniel's daughter Elizabeth married George Flint of Salem Village. Carolina John and his wife Hannah were blessed on November 5th with the birth of their first son, Samuel.

In England's occult world there were only two events of note during the year: The witch Alice Holland was hanged at Exeter, and Richard Bovet published his book *Pandaemonium* which espoused the dying trade of witchery in England and replied to Wagstaffe's book of 1669 and Webster's of 1677.

Among the scientists, Edmund Halley was introduced to Sir Isaac Newton, of whom he had heard much, and they struck up a friendship. Halley took it upon himself to encourage Newton to publish the findings he had made regarding the laws of motion and of gravity, for Newton was modest to a fault.

Judge Philip Smith of Hadley, Massachusetts, was something quite different — he was a hypochondriac. At the turn of the year he fell gravely ill, and he was convinced that the cause of his affliction was Mary Webster who had the previous year been acquitted of witchcraft by the General Court, despite the fact that it was largely Judge Smith whose testimony had sent her to Boston. He was convinced that Goody Webster was merely getting even with him for his action against her.

As Judge Smith got well into his illness George Corwin died in Salem on January 6th, 1685, but the weather was so cold, and the ground so frozen, that his coffin was put away temporarily until a grave could be dug in the spring. In Hadley Smith alternated between lamenting that Goody Webster had caused his sickness and crying out, "Lord, stay thine hand! It is enough…it is more than thy frail servant can bear!" Some thought he said this in agony, but others were sure it was joy they heard in his voice.

In a moment of lucidity Judge Smith told his brother, "Be sure to have a care of me, for you shall see strange things. There shall be a wonder in Hadley! I shall not be dead when 'tis thought I am!" Then he lapsed into delirium again, thrashing about, seeming to speak in tongues, calling out now and again that he was tormented in various parts of his body. He saw the apparition of Mary Webster in the room during his convulsions, and many people smelled the disagreeable odor of something like musk hanging about the house. They were horrified to see Judge Smith's body flush red, then cover itself with a rash, and the rash turn into blisters. They had heard of such a disease, but no one had ever seen smallpox in Hadley before. It was so strange that it was not hard to believe the judge was possessed by the Devil.

At the height of his suffering some young men of the village went out to procure relief for the sick man. They went to Mary Webster's house, dragged her out into the cold in nothing more than her houseclothes, beat her, hung her upside down, rolled her in the snow, and left her for dead in a drift. While this medical treatment was taking place a good many observers noted that Judge Smith, for once, "slept as a weary man" might.

Nor were the sick man's torments the only things that led the villagers to believe that there was a witch's hand in it: His medicine containers were emptied invisibly; there were scratching noises about the bed while his hands and feet were still. There was a flame seen in the bed, and it looked as though there were an animal beneath the covers with Mr. Smith, but no one could catch it. The bed shook while men tried to hold it down. Strong arms could not bend him to sit up.

The judge died on January 10th. The grand jury that inspected his corpse found one breast swelled, his genitals burned or wounded, his back bruised, and a number of holes in his skin that looked as though they had been made with awls — people remembered that at least one other corpse in the area had looked the same, and then, too, the case had been diagnosed as witchcraft.

But after Smith had been pronounced dead there seemed to be no change in the body from Saturday morning to Sunday sunrise. At that point the corpse was taken from its bed and found to be warm still. The following night his face continued to look fresh, but the night after, his face was tumefied and discolored black and blue — fresh blood ran down his cheek among the hairs of his beard, as though nails had scratched at the scabbing blisters on his face. There were more noises in the room where the corpse lay — noises no one made. Despite the winter weather, a grave was hacked out of the frozen ground and he was hurried to his final repose.

But there was after all a resurrection in Hadley. Somehow Mary Webster had managed to make it out of the drift where the village boys had left her and get back to her house. She survived, and as soon as ever she could, she moved out of town to Boston.

Charles II, King of England, died on February 6th. Ten days later the Catholic James II ascended the throne, but it was a while before the terrible news reached New England. Two days before the crowning there was an unusual double baptism in Salem: Carolina John's son, Samuel, and his wife, Hannah, were welcomed into the ranks of the presumed saved by the Rev. John Higginson.

In the spring Edward Bishop and his wife Bridget moved out of Salem into Salem Village, near the Beverly line, where they opened "a house of refreshment for travelers" and attended, for convenience's sake, the church of the Rev. John Hale in Beverly, but they kept their ties with their former community, and when the ground had thawed sufficiently to allow the easy interment of the corpse of George Corwin, the Bishops attended the burial service in Salem.

Afterward a number of Salem Villagers and others were riding back home, including Elizabeth Balch, wife of Benjamin Balch, Jr., and her sister Abigail Woodbury. The two women were mounted on a single horse. As they approached Crane River Commons, Edward Bishop, with Bridget riding pillion behind him, overtook the sisters. It was obvious the Bishops had been arguing, for Edward rode into the stream precipitately and Bridget cried, "You will throw me into the water!"

"No matter if I do," Edward replied. He urged his horse up to the riding women and the two parties rode along together, Bridget scolding, "You are riding too fast! You will do me a mischief!"

Again Edward said, "It is no matter what is done to you." Then, turning to Abigail and Goody Balch he said, "She has been a bad wife to me since we were married," and he listed a number of grievances against Bridget. When he said, "But now, of late, she is worse than ever she has been before. The Devil comes bodily to her, and she is familiar with him. She sits up all night with the Devil." He continued in this line — none of the women saying much of anything until they reached the Bishops' tavern.

At the point of parting, finally Elizabeth Balch gathered up her outrage and reproved Bishop for having spoken in such a manner about his wife. Edward reined in his horse, looked at her, and said, "It was nothing but the truth." He nudged his horse through the gate, and the women rode on, wondering among themselves.

Something that Roger Williams had said years earlier was coming back to haunt the people of Massachusetts now that the charter had fallen. Williams had said that the lands on which the white people lived was not theirs because it had not been paid for. Few people, in other words, had deeds in writing from the native owners, and it was therefore conceivable that the king could simply claim that all the land in the colonies belonged to him. It was a restive situation, and people were beginning to think of Indians as something more than simply savages roving the woods.

In May John Ho[d]gkins, Sagamore of the Penacook tribe, began to display his ability with the English language by addressing a series of letters to Gov. Simon Bradstreet and others. One, dated May 15th, read,

"Honour Mr. Governor,

"Now this day I com hour house, I want se you, and I bring my hand at before you I want shake hand to you if your woship when please then you receve my hand, then shake your hand and my hand. You my friend because I remember at old time, when live my grant father and grant mother then Englishmen come this country then my grant father and Englishmen they make a good govenant, they friend allwayes, my grant-father leving at place called Malameke rever, other name chef Nattukkog and Punukkog that one rever great many names, and I bring you this few skins at this first time I will give you my friend. This all Indian hand."

The Sagamore and fourteen others signed the letter. The government had been having trouble with drunken Indians, which was one of the reasons Salem had imposed its curfew. Sagamore Hogkins sent another letter to the Governor:

"Please your worship,

"I will intreat you matther you my friend, now this if my Indian he do you long pray you no put your law because some my Idins fooll some men much love drunk then he no know what he do, may be he do mischief when he drunk if so pray you must let me know what he done because I will ponis him what he have done you, you my friend if you desire my business then sent me I will help you if I can."

On March 17th Jonathan Putnam was chosen surveyor of highways of Salem Village, and a few weeks later he attended the strangest wedding ceremony Salem had ever seen. On April 23rd his cousin, Deliverance Putnam, Lt. Thomas' daughter, married Jonathan Walcott of Salem Village. He was a widower with six children by his first marriage, including two girls named Hannah, 18, and Mary, who had been born in 1675. But that was only the half of it, for, at the same time, Jonathan's cousin Benjamin, Nathaniel's son, made his vows before Rev. Mr. Higginson and to his adoptive cousin, Hannah Walcott.

It was the romantic talk of the village for many weeks, but Deliverance discovered shortly that it was anything but romantic to be, suddenly, the stepmother of six children ranging in ages from seven to nineteen. Even at that, though, she counted herself lucky, for she was twenty-nine years old. Not long after this spectacular connubial explosion, in May, Jonathan and his wife Lydia Putnam baptized their daughter, Lydia, in Salem First Church.

In June Harvard College graduated its class, and among the graduates was another Mather prodigy — Nathaniel, Cotton's brother — who took his baccalaureate at the age of sixteen.

John Rogers, forty-three years of age, lived near the Carrier farm in Billerica, not very peacefully. After a disagreement of some sort, Martha Carrier threatened him, as she was wont to do, but this time there seemed to be repercussions, for shortly afterward two of Rogers' sows disappeared. He searched for them and eventually found one over by the Carriers' place. Not long thereafter one of his best milking cows dried up, and he suspected someone was creeping into his barn to milk it on the sly. He sat up in the barn all one night to watch — no one came near the cow, yet in the morning it gave little milk still, nothing like the plenitude it used to give twice a day. Perhaps it wasn't someone physically tampering with his animals. Perhaps Goody Carrier had been consorting again with her sister Mary Toothaker, who was the practicing white witch in town and known to her clientele as Aunt Toothaker.

Samuel Webber was living in Casco, Maine, where George Burroughs was the minister. Webber had heard about the prodigious strength of the man of God, and during a visit Webber finally got to talk about it with him. Burroughs didn't offer to demonstrate, but he did tell Webber that he had put his fingers into the bung of a barrel of molasses, lifted it up, carried it around, and set it down again. Webber was impressed with the story, and a preacher wouldn't make up something like that, would he?

Twenty-one-year-old Francis Lane was hired by James Howe of Ipswich to cut posts and rails. Lane made a better bargain of it when he, in turn, hired John Pearly to help him. When they had finished, they delivered the products to the Howe homestead. At that point it became patent that Elizabeth Howe was unhappy about something — perhaps the fact that Lane had seemed to get the better of her husband through the sub-contracting arrangement: Lane had no doubt been overpaid in the first place. Goody Howe was going to get her money's worth in one way or another. She told Lane, "I do not believe these posts and rails will do, because John Pearly helped you get them. If you had got them alone, I believe they would have done."

Francis Lane took James Howe out to accept delivery, but Howe inspected the posts first, and several unaccountably broke and split. Howe made Lane get thirty or forty more, and while Lane was working Goodman Howe went back home to tell his wife what had happened. She said, "I told him before that they would not do because John Pearly helped about them."

During the summer John Bly, Sr., and his seven-year-old son were at the old Bishop place in Salem where Edward and Bridget had lived before they moved out to their tavern on the Beverly line. John was taking down the house, and while he was working on the foundation he discovered, secreted in some holes in the wall, several "poppits" or dolls made of rags and hog bristles. He pulled them out of the holes and peered at them — there were, he was astonished to see, headless pins stuck into the puppets, with the points outward. The dolls were dressed in red woolen clothes.

Ebenezer Putnam, fourth child and second son of Sgt. Thomas and Ann Carr Putnam, was born on July 25th, and on August 19th George and Elizabeth Putnam Flint had their first child, Elizabeth, On the 8th of September the Selectmen of Salem ordered that shipments of Barbados cotton that had arrived in the harbor were to be unloaded at Baker's Island and quarantined there, for another smallpox epidemic was loose in the Caribbean.

Neither Salem nor Boston, being port towns, were unused to Satan's scourge; therefore, they were constantly on the alert to take preventive measures whenever they could. Still, frequently smallpox would run its course through an entire family and neighborhood, and at those times no one except those who had already lived through the infection or the related disease, cowpox, or who had been exposed and proven immune, would go anywhere near the sufferers. For the sick people, it was like living in Hell without succor.

After the harvest had been gathered, Edward and Mary Hale Putnam welcomed their third child, a son named Elisha, into the world, and at about the same time one of the children of Samuel Shattuck, the Quaker dyer, came down with a virulent disease. The boy ran a high fever and went into convulsions. Dr. John Swinnerton, who was called in, was unable to diagnose the disease. He shrugged, said, "The boy is bewitched," and bled him. It was about all he felt he could do, and it was.

While Sonny Shattuck was suffering one Saturday his parents and some of their neighbors decided that, where medicine was useless, magic might prevail: They cut off a lock of his hair, and the child shrieked. They put the hair into a spider — a legged cast-iron skillet — of boiling water that stood on the hearth, but as soon as they left the room they heard the spider crash to the floor. Everyone rushed back, but saw nothing living in the room, so they put the spider back, refilled it, and sat watching to make sure nothing else untoward happened.

After the hair had been boiling a while, Mary Parker came to the house and asked Shattuck if he wanted to buy some chickens. Shattuck told her, "No," and she left. Shattuck went back to the hearth where Mrs. Henry Williams, wife of Shattuck's hired man, had been eavesdropping. She said, "It is a pity you did not ask to see her chickens, for I believe she has none to sell." Goody Williams suggested that Shattuck send to Mary's house to buy some. Shattuck thought that was a fine idea, so he did it.

Not long after he had been sent the messenger returned with the news that Mary Parker told him she had no chickens. Goody Williams said, "I thought not. Parker had none three weeks before." Everyone present agreed that the doctor had been right — witchcraft *had* been involved in this business, and they had uncovered the witch with their countercharm.

A few days later John and Mary Parker and another man brought as a witness came to the Shattuck home. Mary confronted Samuel: "Did you say I have bewitched your child?"

"I do believe you have," Shattuck replied.

"You are a wicked man!" Mary was red in the face. "The Lord avenge me of you! The Lord bring vengeance upon you for this wrong!" she cried.

But Goody Williams, unflurried, asked, "Why did you come to this house last Saturday?"

"To sell chicken," Mary said angrily.

"Why did you not let Shattuck have them when he sent for them?"

"Because I had sold them."

"To whom?"

Mary named a man, and a messenger was sent to ask him if it were true. Mary fidgeted while they waited for word, and when it came it was that the man said he had never bought chickens of John and Mary Parker.

"You have lied to us," Shattuck said.

For a moment Mary was baffled, but then she said, "My son carried them to sea with him."

It was John Parker's turn to be baffled. He was a mariner, often away from home, and he knew little of what his wife did while he was away. Perhaps she had sold some chickens to someone, but of one thing he was certain. He raised his eyebrows at his wife and said, "That is not true, for our son went to sea last Friday, and if he had carried them to sea you could not have brought them here the Saturday following."

Mary could think of nothing to say — she could not confess at so late an hour that she had merely been curious about Sonny's illness and had come a-prying. She whirled on her heel, stalked into the sickroom where Mrs. Shattuck sat at the bedside, and hissed at her, "You are a wicked woman for speaking ill of me. I hope I shall see the downfall of you." She turned and left in a great rage.

Eventually, Shattuck's son recovered from the disease, but it had left him ravaged, both physically and mentally, for the high fevers had caused permanent brain damage.

The seamen on the waterfront often brought news of far places, and Salem heard that there was witchcraft in Maryland as well that year — five had been tried for the crime, and one of them, Rebecca Fowler, had been executed.

In England James Scott, Duke of Monmouth and putative bastard son of Charles II by his mistress Lucy Walters, had landed from Holland at Taunton with eighty-two followers on May 23rd. He had raised his standard and claimed the crown. He had gathered a rag-tag "army" but, shortly, was arrested and on July 15th had been beheaded.

As 1686 began, Putnams continued to generate inhabitants of Salem Village. January 27th saw the birth of Ann Walcott, daughter of Jonathan and Deliverance Putnam Walcott. April Fool's Day brought forth George Flint, Jr., first son and second child of George and Elizabeth Putnam Flint. A month later, on May 5th, the head of the Putnam family, Landlord Thomas Putnam, Lieutenant of Salem, died at the age of seventy-one and passed the family title on to his brother Nathaniel. The church was filled to overlowing in Salem for the funeral service.

All in all, however, Thomas' passing caused but a pause in the rhythm of life in Salem and its environs. Capt. John Putnam, Jr. — who had been promoted to the rank of Captain — was again elected Deputy from Salem, though the election was of dubious legal validity, considering the state of the former Charter; still, someone had to govern, and the king had not yet sent the new Royal Government to the colony.

The town of Salem issued Capt. Putnam an order that he was not to resist if, in fact, the General Court received official word that the Charter had been lost. The order, dated May 18th, read in part, "That, in case Mr. Dudley &c., said to be nominated and authorized by his Majesty to erect another government here and do publish a legal nullification of our charter, and a commission from the King for their acceptance of the government here, then our instructions to you is: That you give no countenance to any resistance, but peaceably withdraw yourself as representing us no longer."

The will of Capt. John's eldest brother was proved on July 8th. He left several estates in Salem and Salem Village. The main Salem estate had a town residence and lands that extended from the north side of Essex Street to the North River. He left the eastern portion of this to his son Sgt. Thomas , and the western half to his only child by Mary Veren Putnam, Joseph. Another estate on the western side of St. Peter's Street went to Edward. Each of his children got land in Salem Village, including a piece of meadow. He left his faithful servant Joseph Stacey eleven acres of property.

A family fight set in, and a court battle ensued, for Thomas' children by his first wife, Ann Holyoke Putnam, felt that Mary Veren, his second wife, had induced the old man to give far too much to Joseph. The effort to break the will failed, and the other sons and daughters, all of them older, could do little thenceforth but resent their half-brother Joseph and his mother.

During the summer Elizabeth Howe of Ipswich went to Rev. William Hubbard and asked to be allowed to join the Ipswich church. The minister put her request to the church members who considered her case, each person of the congregation being asked to give witness for or against the applicant. Mary Cummings, who was a member, gave witness that Mrs. Howe had been spreading rumors about the way the

Cummingses had treated their mare for "the stomach ache" a couple of years earlier, and she informed the church that Mrs. Howe lied when she stated that the mare had received "brimstone and oil." Everyone knew that they had used a pipe and tobacco.

As a result Elizabeth Howe was blackballed and a short time afterward Isaac Cummings, Jr., missed his mare. He looked everywhere for her for three days; then, on the fourth day, the mare showed up near the house looking — so it seemed to the Cummingses and the neighbors who gathered to inspect it — the worse for wear: It appeared to have been ridden hard and ill-used by whoever had borrowed it. They began to spread their own rumors of what they thought had happened.

It was not long before Elizabeth Howe heard how her family was being calumniated, and she launched a counterattack in the rumor mills. She said that the Cummingses were keeping the mare out of the public view so that they would not have to prove their allegations. Mary Cummings escalated by telling her son to take the horse and show it about, which he did. The next round of escalation saw Elizabeth going gossiping that Isaac Cummings, Jr., and his girl friend had ridden the horse double since the spring. Mary Cummings hotly denied that any such thing had ever happened — her son was a nice young man who did not ill-use creatures.

Perhaps it gave the Salem Village parishioners some sort of relief to see neighboring parishes having troubles for a change, as in the Howe case, and in that of Bridget Bishop in Beverly. The Rev. John Hale received a visit from Christine, wife of John Trask of Salem, who lived near the Beverly line, like the Bishops, and so brought his family to Mr. Hale's meetinghouse. Mrs. Trask asked the minister that he refuse to allow Bridget to take communion until she had answered for offenses committed at her roadhouse: Keeping unreasonable hours, allowing too much drinking and carousing, playing at shovel board. The woman was corrupting the morals of minors and causing family discords. Goody Trask assured Mr. Hale she knew what she was talking about, for she had gone to the nearby Bishops' place, scolded the proprietors, and thrown the shovel board pucks into the fire. Mr. Hale told her he could not do as she requested, but he informed her of how to go about taking legal action.

The next night Christine Trask became "distracted," and continued so. Mr. Hale went to the Trask house to pray and fast with the family, and Goody Trask recovered for a while, then collapsed at Sabbath Day service.

She was an amazement to the congregation, writhing about on the Lord's floor that way. Nothing Mr. Hale could do after that was of avail. She continued in her distraction, threatening suicide, for a good while. Then, one day, Rev. Mr. Hale was present with her when she asked him to send for Edward Bishop so that she could make friends with him. The minister asked, "Have you wronged Edward Bishop?"

Christine answered, "Not that I know of, unless it were in taking his shovel board pieces when people were at play with them and throwing them into the fire. If I did evil in it," she said, "I am very sorry for it."

The next day — about a month after her request that Goody Bishop be excluded from the Lord's Supper — Christine Trask committed suicide by cutting her throat with a pair of scissors.

At the end of August Benjamin and Hannah Walcott Putnam had their first child, a boy who was named Nathaniel Putnam III after his grandfather, Landlord Nathaniel who was engaged, with the other men of the town, in a long overdue action. On the 11th of October it was brought to a successful end when Salem bought its lands from the Naumkeag Indians. Sagamore George accepted payment — twenty pounds — and made his mark on the document that at last gave the townsfolk title to the lands on which they had lived for over half a century.

Nine days later Joseph Knight, 38, and Nathaniel Clark, Jr., of Newbury went into the woods to fetch their horses back to their farms, and there, running through the trees with a little dog, they saw Susannah Martin. The woman bent to pick it up and tuck it under her arm. When the men drew close enough to see better, they discovered that the "dog" had turned itself into a keg. Approaching Susannah, Joseph said to her, "That keg was a little dog."

"So it was," Nathaniel agreed. They turned and left Susannah staring after them.

Knight and Clark rounded up their horses, but when they attempted to get them to pass over a causeway the animals shied and began running around a hillock. It was impossible. For the better part of the day they tried to get the herd across, but the horses kept shying and breaking loose until a young man with a yoke of oxen came along, made it across, and the horses followed.

Carolina John and Hannah had their second son and fifth child, Josiah, on October 29th. The next month Joseph Hutchinson had had enough of the wrangling of his fellow parishioners and their jabbering about who had title to the church lands. Since he had donated the site of the Salem Village meetinghouse, he felt a symbolic gesture was in order, so he erected a fence all around his property, and left the parishioners an opening on the road side.

Everyone was furious, and the parish went to court about it. When he was ordered by the court to explain his action he filed a deposition on November 27th which read,

"First, as to the covenant they spoke of, I conceive it is neither known of by me or them, as will appear by records from the Farmers' Book.

"Second, I conceive they have no cause to complain of me for fencing in my own land; for I am sure I fenced in none of theirs. I wish they would not pull down my fences. I am loath to complain, though I have just cause.

"Third, for blocking up the meetinghouse, it was they did it, and not I, in the time of the Indian wars, and they made Salem pay for it. I wish they would bring me my rocks they took to do it with; for I want them to make fence with.

"Thus, hoping this honored Court will see that there was no just cause to complain against me, and their cause will appear unjust in that they would in an unjust way take away my land, I trust I shall have relief; so I rest, your honor's servant,

"Joseph Hutchinson."

A meeting of the parish was called for December 10th at which it was proposed that the Rev. Mr. Deodat Lawson be ordained, but the church members were squabbling so much that nothing of substance occurred.

While the Salem Villagers were haggling among themselves, King James II had created a "Dominion of New England" of the northern American colonies, which included New York and New Jersey as well as Connecticut, Rhode Island, Plymouth Colony, Massachusetts Bay, and the northern territories of Maine and New Hampshire. The former alliance of the New England Confederation quietly fell.

Ten days after the Salem parish meeting the King's Governor, Sir Edmund Andros, arrived in Boston. He came ashore at Governor Leverett's Wharf where he was welcomed — not enthusiastically — by the interregnum government of Massachusetts, of which Joseph Dudley was President. The new Governor and the Council walked through the streets of Boston escorted by Colonial soldiers to the Town House. There, a portion of Andros' commission was read in public and he took the oath of office. Eight Council members were sworn in, and Massachusetts officially became a Royal Province. Samuel Sewall wrote in his diary that evening, "I heard a gun or two, as I supposed, which made me think Sir Edmund might be come."

On Christmas eve sixty redcoats landed at Pool's Wharf and marched through Boston to their station.

The first annual almanac published by John Tulley appeared for 1687, and it was the first also that included day-to-day astrological weather forecasts and such saws as, "When the small stars are obscured at night, beware of tempests in the offing." The Salem Villagers should have paid attention, but at last they did agree on something: At a meeting held on January 17, 1687, they chose "Capt. Putnam, Jr., Lt. Jonathan Walcott, Ensign Thomas Flint, and Cpl. Joseph Herrick" as a committee — perhaps they thought that the military could force harmony — "for to transact with Joseph Hutchinson, Job Swinnerton, Joseph Porter, and Daniel Andrews about their grievances relating to the public affairs of this place; and, if they cannot agree among themselves, that then they shall refer their differences to the honored Major Gedney and John Hathorne, Esqs., and to the Reverend Elders of the Salem Church, for a full determination of those differences."

The parish committee could accomplish nothing, and the committee of arbitration, with William Brown added, was called in from Salem. The arbitrators investigated, consulted, and drew up a report that read in part,

"*Loving Brethren, Friends, and Neighbors,* Upon serious consideration of, and mature deliberation upon, what hath been offered to us about your calling and transacting in order to the settling and ordaining the Rev. Mr. Deodat Lawson, and the grievances offered by some to obstruct and impede that proceeding, our sense of the matter is this, — first, that the affair of calling and transacting…hath not been so inoffensively managed as might have been, — at least, not in all the parts and passages of it; second, that the grievances…are not in themselves of sufficient weight to obstruct so great a work, and that they have not been improved so peaceably and orderly as Christian prudence and self-denial doth direct; third, to our grief, we observe such uncharitable expressions and uncomely reflections tossed to and fro as look like the effects of settled prejudice and resolved animosity, though we are much rather willing to account them the product of weakness than willfulness; however, we must needs say, that, come whence they will, they have a tendency to make such a gap as we fear, if not timely prevented, will let out peace and order, and let in confusion and every evil work." The report went on to offer some advice for the settling of grievances, and it suggested "that you desist, at present, from urging the ordination of the Rev. Mr. Lawson, till your spirits are better quieted and composed."

The referees and the elders of Salem Old Church — the Revs. John Higginson and Nicholas Noyes — signed the report and submitted it on February fourteenth. On the 18th the Salem Villagers accepted the report in general, but not in its particulars; however, they did take some advice of the report — they went through their record book and re-voted every entry in it that in any way had caused contention. They made a new record book, but decided that they would keep the old one handy as well. The new book was submitted to the major contenders of the parish for approval and eventual adoption. Somehow, the old record book was misplaced in the shuffle, but at first no one noticed that it was missing. There was, however, an immediate casualty: The Rev. Mr Deodat Lawson gave up and went back to Boston, a widower, for his wife and daughter had both died in Salem Village during his residence there.

While all this was going on, on February 2nd Jonathan and Lydia Potter Putnam had their second child, yet another member of the clan named Elizabeth, and Gov. Andros was beginning to prove that those people who had been denied the vote in the Puritan colony were going to gain nothing under the new government, for there was to be no vote for anyone, inasmuch as there was to be no assembly. Andros would govern like a petty king. He dismissed the General Court, wiped off the books the Colonial court system and set himself up as the supreme arbiter of justice, introduced the Anglican worship to Boston, and levied a unilateral set of taxes.

The levies Andros imposed were upon all estates in the Colonies, to the rate of a penny per pound of assessed valuation, plus a poll tax of twenty pence — although there were to be no polls; import duties of one cent per pound, and an excise tax on liquors. The estate tax was an outrage especially because Andros declared that the old Charter had been illegal; therefore, all grants of land made under it were without force. Owners of property had to reapply to own their own lands and obtain new patents by paying out large fees. He laughed to scorn such documents as those exhibited in evidence by Salem showing it had purchased its territory from the Indians. For one thing, the documents were brand new, drawn up during the tenure of the interregnum government, and not even signed by the original natives of the place. Salem had given away twenty pounds to the savages who had no doubt used the money to get drunk.

Ipswich was the first town to resist. The Selectmen voted "that inasmuch as it is against the privilege of English subjects to have money raised without their own consent in an Assembly or Parliament, therefore they will petition the King for liberty of an Assembly before they made any rates." Andros threw the Rev. Mr. John Wise and other "principal persons" of Ipswich into jail without the right of *habeas corpus*, tried them in Boston with a packed jury, and fined them ruinously. Rebellion began to spread, its watchwords, "No taxation without representation," or words to that effect.

Samuel Smith of Boxford, twenty years of age, was in Topsfield one evening visiting Isaac and Mary Easty. At one point in the conversation he said something that Mary took to be rude, and she said to him, "I would not have you be so rude in discourse, for you might rue it hereafter." When Smith left that evening, about a quarter of a mile from the Easty house, near a stone wall, he felt a blow on his shoulder — from what source he could not tell: The stone wall rattled, and his horse shied. He began to wonder what Mary had meant by her threat.

One evening in April — perhaps the same one — Increase Mather surreptitiously and in disguise left his house and went to the waterfront where he boarded a ship bound for England. His son, Cotton, at his home in the town sat and worried about his father's safety, for Increase meant to go to London to persuade the King to grant Massachusetts a new charter. If Andros had known, of course he would have stopped the proceeding and committed Increase to durance vile.

The Boston minister sailed without difficulty, however, and while he was en route Joseph Beacon of Boston had a strange experience. While he was lying in bed at about 5 a.m. on May 2nd, Beacon had a vision of his brother in England: He was wearing a Bengal gown and a kerchief about his head. He looked deathly pale, and there was a wound on the side of his forehead. Startled, Joseph said, "What's the matter, brother?"

The vision replied, "Brother, I have been most barbarously and injuriously butchered by a debauched, drunken fellow to whom I never did any wrong in my life." He described the murderer and added, "Brother, this fellow, changing his name, is attempting to come over to New England in the *Fox* or *Wild*. I would pray you on the first arrival of either of these to get an order from the Governor to seize the person whom I have now described, and then do you indict him for the murder of me, dear brother. I'll stand by you and prove the indictment." Waving farewell, the apparition vanished.

Four days later, on May 6th, Increase Mather arrived safely in England. There, he was dismayed to discover that the Catholic James II had issued a Declaration of Indulgence that authorized Protestant dissenters *and* Catholics to worship publicly. It soon became apparent, however, that the Puritans preferred an alliance with Anglicans to an alliance with James and Catholics, so few ministers and local authorities observed the Declaration, and it got very little publicity in the churches.

In midsummer Sir Isaac Newton's great work, *Philosophiae Naturalis Principia Mathematica* was published. It was the central document for which the New Philosophers had been waiting, for it put the hallmark of the new Age of Science on the dying Age of Magic.

In New England, late in May, a maypole had been raised in Charlestown, but the outraged elders had cut it down. It was not merely a pagan custom, it was a symbol that times had changed in New England. Those who had erected the first maypole simply went back out and put up a larger one, winding it about with a garland of flowers.

At the end of June Joseph Beacon of Boston received word from England that in April his brother had gone out one evening to call a coach for a lady who had been visiting him. On the street he had met a drunk with a doxy on his arm. Beacon had accidentally brushed against him in haste. The drunk had rushed into a nearby tavern, enraged, grabbed a firefork from the hearth, come back into the street and struck Beacon on the forehead. Beacon had not died until May 2nd at 5 a.m. in London. The drunk had tried to board a ship, but he was seized by Beacon's friends, taken before authority, and prosecuted. However, the man had somehow managed to get off, and he disappeared from view, much to the helpless frustration of Joseph and his brother's friends.

One summer Sunday in Salem Village John Cook, thirteen, was in bed at sunrise when Bridget Bishop appeared at the window, grinned at him, and swatted him in the side of the head. The boy could have sworn she left through a crevice the size of a rat hole. At noon the same Lord's Day, while Cook was holding an apple and standing in the room where his mother was sitting a few feet away, Bridget Bishop reappeared, though only John could see her. She walked across the floor, the apple flew out of John's hand and landed in his startled mother's lap. Again Bridget disappeared, her evil work done.

At the Samuel Shattuck home there was a conspiracy undertaken between the dyer and a stranger who stopped by. While Shattuck was conversing with the man the visitor cast a pitying glance at Shattuck's boy and said, "We are all born, some to one thing and some to another."

"And what," Shattuck asked him, "do you say this child is born to?"

"To be bewitched, and he is bewitched."

Shattuck replied, "You do not know."

"I do know," the stranger said. "You have a neighbor that is a witch, and she has had a falling-out with your wife. She has said in her heart your wife is a proud woman, and she will bring down her pride in this child."

What the stranger said rang a bell — Shattuck recalled that his wife had told him that once Bridget had come and told her to beat Henry Williams, the Shattucks' servant, for some blunder or incivility. When Mrs. Shattuck had refused, Bridget had left muttering...muttering curses, it seemed obvious through hindsight, for not long afterward Shattuck's son had been stricken. Perhaps, after all, it was Goody Bishop and not Mary Parker who had hexed his boy. Shattuck told the stranger, "There is such a woman as you speak of."

"Where does she live, for I would go and see her if I knew how." It didn't occur to Shattuck to question why, if the stranger knew everything else, he didn't know this bit of information.

Shattuck gave the stranger directions as to how he could find Goody Bishop's roadhouse and added, "Go ask her for a pot of cider."

The stranger nodded his head — he understood. Shattuck had given him an excuse for going to the Bishops' place, and at the same time the ruse would provide him with the means they needed to break her spell, for they had to obtain some article that she had touched. "And," the stranger told the dyer, "I will have the child scratch her face," for that, too, would break the spell — drawing the blood of the witch. Shattuck watched the stranger walk off with his boy.

He saw them come back not much later, empty-handed and his son's face bleeding. Astonished, he asked, "What has happened?"

The stranger told him that they had arrived at Goody Bishop's, knocked, and the witch had answered the door. The Shattuck boy had been coached, but he had been too eager. Bridget had asked, "What would you have?"

The stranger had replied, "A pot of cider," and at that point Sonny had tried to scratch her face. Bridget had avoided the attempt — it was not well coordinated — and had scratched his own face instead.

"You shall have none!" she cried, "Get out!" She had picked up a handy spade, backed them both out the door, and screamed at the Shattuck boy, "Thou rogue! Why do you bring this fellow to plague me?"

The Quaker dyer was disappointed, but the stranger reassured him. Before he left he said, "I will fetch blood of her." He went away and nothing was changed: Sonny Shattuck continued to have his falling-down fits.

John Atkinson, a middle-aged man, arranged to swap cows with one of Susannah Martin's sons. Atkinson had bought his cow from the Rev.

Mr. Wells of Amesbury. The Martin boy picked up Atkinson's cow at the minister's house, but when Atkinson went to get young Martin's animal it soon became apparent that his mother was unhappy about the trade. Nevertheless, Atkinson took the cow and tried to lead it to the river.

The cow was balky, so Atkinson hobbled and tethered it at last to a tree. The cow broke free, and when Atkinson and his helpers tried to catch her to lead her down to the ferry, she charged at them and drove them into the water up to their waists. Finally, after a great struggle, the cow was led onto the ferry, at which point she became as docile an animal as one could wish — water, in which people were baptized, was always effective in breaking the spell of a witch.

During the summer Nathaniel Putnam's daughter Mary was wed to John Tufts of Charlestown and moved to her bridegroom's village. Deliverance, third daughter and fifth child of Sgt. Thomas and Ann Carr Putnam, was born on the 11th of September, and on November 1st Edward and Mary Hale Putnam had their fourth child and fourth son, Joseph. On October 2nd Benjamin Putnam and Hannah Walcott Putnam baptized their first child, Josiah Putnam, at Salem First Church, and their second boy, one-year-old Nathaniel Putnam, was baptized by Mr. Higginson on November 6th. During the winter James and Sarah Putnam brought their baby Bartholomew Putnam into the world.

A girl named Martha Lawrence was living with Goodwife Wilmot Reed and her husband in Marblehead, and she was hired out as a servant to Goodwife Sarah Simms for her keep. Mrs. Simms one day noticed that some of her linen was missing, and she suspected she knew who had taken it. She asked Charity Pitman to accompany her to the Reeds' home, for she intended to demand the return of her property. Charity consented.

When they arrived an argument ensued, Mammy Reed denying that Martha had done any such thing as steal. Exasperated, Mrs. Simms told Wilmot, "If you will not deliver them, I will go to Salem to Mr. Hathorne's and get a special warrant for your servant girl."

Mammy Reed replied, "I wish you may never minger or cacare if you do."

Mrs. Simms and her friend Charity left. It was not long until Goody Simms was taken with "the distemper of the dry bellyache" — she found that she was plagued by an inability to urinate and with chronic constipation.

Jonathan and Deliverance Putnam Walcott had their second child, Thomas Putnam, on the 25th of March, 1688, and on April 12th Benjamin and Hannah Walcott Putnam were blessed with the arrival of Tarrant Putnam, their third child. In the spring a young man who owned a famous name died in Salem and was buried in the Charter Street Cemetery. He was Nathaniel Mather, and he had given promise of great things. Following in the footsteps of his brother Cotton, he had already published two almanacs; he had lived through the smallpox in 1678, but was brought low early in life by a cancer that had spread from his thigh.

Increase Mather could not attend his son's funeral, since he was still in England, but Cotton and many other relatives and notables from Boston came to see him put to rest. His gravestone read,

> "An aged person
> that had seen but
> Nineteen Winters
> in the World."

The news that spring was anything but good. The Indians were rising again in a war that was being called the French and Indian War. King James was still determined to see to it that Catholics as well as Protestants had the right of free worship, and Increase Mather was making little headway in London against the Lords of Trade and Plantations. All sorts of rumors were circulating, including one that came down from Casco with the fishers and coasters — that the Rev.

George Burroughs could read people's minds. But there were others closer to home:

John Wilds of Topsfield heard in the rumor mill that Mary Reddington, John Reddington's wife, had been whispering that Sarah, his own wife, had bewitched her. Wilds went to Reddington, confronted him, and said, "I will arrest you for your wife's defaming my wife."

Reddington asked him not to "For," he said, "it will but waste my estate. My wife will have done with it in time. I know nothing Mary has against your wife." It was left at that for the time being..

Later Wilds asked his brother Averill Wilds to approach Mrs. Reddington, who had persisted in her libels. Averill obliged. He told Mary Reddington, "If you have anything against my sister-in-law, I will be a means to help you bring them out."

Mary replied, "I know of no harm Sarah Wilds has done me." Averill went back and gave John a report of the conversation.

But there were further turns of the wheel. Ephraim Wilds, twenty-three, son of John and Sarah, had been courting a daughter of Goody Simons; however, then he heard that her mother had said his mother had done her a wrong. He, too, decided on a confrontation. As a witness he took Mark Howe along with him when he went to see Goody Simons and present her with what he had heard.

William Simons protested, "I have never had any grounds to think any harm of your mother, but only what Mary Reddington said about her." Angry, Ephraim spun on his heel and left, for good. He dropped his courtship of the Simons girl, and that, in its turn, infuriated Mrs. Simons. A great grudge sprang up among the three families and ripened toward a harvest of bitter fruit.

In April James II issued another Declaration of Indulgence, but this time he gave the bishops direct orders to read it in their churches. Seven of the bishops presented a petition to James that pointed out his suspension of the religious laws of England was illegal. They asked him to rescind his order and the Declaration. The king refused, and on the

Sunday he had prescribed for the reading, ministers throughout the country, including the bishops, failed to read his proclamation.

James charged the seven bishops with sedition and brought them to trial. The judges and jury found them not guilty. The country went wild. Increase Mather wrote letters back to New England to keep the clergy and other important colonists informed of the developing situation. It began to look as though another revolution might take place. The news, when it arrived in America, gave many folk great hope. Perhaps another Divine Providence was at hand.

On June 5th Jonathan and Deliverance Putnam Walcott's infant son, Thomas, died. On the first of July there was a double baptism: Deliverance, ten-month-old daughter of Sgt. Thomas Putnam, Jr. and Ann Carr Putnam, and Joseph, sixth child and fourth son of Carolina John and Hannah Cutler Putnam were initiated by Mr. Higginson at Salem First Church.

Seven leaders of Parliament on July 30th — both Tories and Whigs — quietly asked William of Orange, the Protestant husband of Mary Stuart, King James' daughter, if he wouldn't be so good as to come to England to lead an uprising and overthrow the Catholic despot. When William received the letter he was disposed kindly to the proposition.

Increase Mather could get nothing done while things were in such turmoil. Being himself the compiler of an anthology of spectral marvels, he was interested to buy and read a copy of Nathaniel Crouch's new book *The Kingdom of Darkness*. It was an illustrated collectaneia of the most grotesque and horrible stories imaginable.

In New England his son, Cotton, was involved in a real-life witchcraft story. In midsummer the four children of John Goodwin, a mason of Boston, began to have fits and convulsions immediately after one of them, Martha, fourteen, had a quarrel over a missing item of clothing with Carline Glover, an Irish washerwoman whose mother,

Mary Glover, had an evil reputation because her late husband had circulated about the neighborhood that Mary was "undoubtedly a witch."

Gammer Glover had intervened in the argument between her daughter and Martha Goodwin, and she had cursed the girl. Martha had almost immediately been taken with fits, and soon her sister Mercy, seven, and her brothers Nathaniel, sixteen, and John, fourteen, were in the Devil's toils as well.

At night the young people slept well enough, but as soon as ever it was cockcrow, they would commence to be tormented again. Their tongues would be stuck out to great lengths, then swallowed; their jaws thrown out of joint by monstrous yawns, then clapped back together again and locked; their necks would be as though boneless one moment, then too rigid to bend; they were tormented with all sorts of diabolical aches and pains. At devotions they would be struck deaf so that they could not hear the Scriptures. They would go limp, then stiff, and no one could straighten their bodies.

Neighbors at first suggested that the Goodwins try white magic, but Goodman Goodwin refused; instead, two doctors — one of them Dr. Thomas Oakes — were called in for consultation. When Oakes had taken stock of the situation he said, "This can be nothing but an hellish witchcraft."

Goodwin turned to the Boston clergy. Cotton Mather, with his local colleagues, came to hold a day of fasting and prayer at the Goodwin home. The treatment was effective in the case of the youngest child, Mercy, much to Rev. Mr. Mather's delight: He had at last proved himself in the field against the Adversary in a head-to-head confrontation. The other three children, however, continued to be possessed.

Mr. Goodwin had no other recourse except to turn to the courts. He filed a complaint with the magistrates against Gammer Glover. She was arrested, thrown into prison, searched, examined, and indicted.

At her trial, which was held in Salem, Mary Glover refused to answer the question "How do you plead?" She claimed to be able to speak nothing but Gaelic, though she had been known to speak English well enough before. Finally, after she had been asked the question many times, instead of pleading Gammer Glover confessed, and more than confessed — she bragged about her powers as a witch. She told the court through interpreters that the reason she had been unable to plead was that another witch had cast a spell that prevented her from speaking in any but a language that no one, it was to be hoped, could understand.

A search of the witch's house produced solid evidence that what she was saying before the bar was the truth, for the authorities found a number of poppits made of rags and stuffed with goat's hair. Gammer Glover said that she used these to torment people — she would wet her finger with spittle and stroke the dolls, and the people they represented would be tormented.

Cotton Mather wrote that as she stood in court "the woman kept still stooping and shrinking, as one that was almost pressed unto death with a mighty weight upon her" — a visual representation, perhaps, of the English law that required a person who refused to plead to be pressed with weights until a plea was entered. "But one of the images being brought unto her, she oddly and swiftly started up, and snatched it into her hand: But she had no sooner snatched it than one of the children," who were present in court, "fell into sad fits before the whole assembly." And present in that assembly were a number of young people of Salem and Salem Village who were mightily impressed with the performance.

The judges thought there might be some trickery involved in the exhibition, so they experimented by making Gammer Glover grasp the dolls out of the view of the Goodwin children — still they had fits, even though they didn't know, according to Mather, when the witch took the dolls.

William Stoughton, the chief judge, asked her if she had any character witness, "any to stand by you?"

Gammer Glover, looking up into the air, replied, "No, he is gone."

"Who is gone?" Judge William Stoughton asked.

"My Prince," she replied.

The witch was put back into prison. The next night she was heard whining and expostulating with her Prince who, she accused, had deserted her, and it was, she told the empty air, "because you have served me so basely and falsely that I have confessed all."

The court appointed five physicians to examine her and give in their opinion as to whether the woman was merely mad. While the doctors were with her, however, she seemed to be completely lucid and quite pleasant for several hours. One of them asked her, "What do you think will become of your soul?"

Gammer Glover replied, "You ask me a very solemn question, and I cannot well tell what to say to it."

"What is your religion?"

"I am a Catholic of Rome," she replied.

"Can you say your Pater Noster?"

"Yes," she said, and started off quite readily, but there were one or two parts of the prayer, the doctors noticed, that were difficult for her. She stumbled then admitted, "I cannot repeat it aright if I might have all the world." Proof positive of her guilt!

Others were testifying in the case meanwhile, and the fits were beginning to spread. The son of Arthur Hughes caught the affliction. Hughes told the court his boy would cry out in the night that "a black person with a blue cap" tortured him and tried to pull his bowels out while he was in bed. Goody Hughes had gone to the prison to see Gammer Glover and ask, "Why do you torture my poor lad at such a rate?"

Glover had replied, Hughes said, "Because of the wrong I have received of you. I came at him as a black person with a blue cap, and with my hand in the bed, would have pulled his bowels out, but could not." Mrs. Hughes denied that she had ever in the world given the witch cause for revenge, and Gammer Glover relented. She asked to see the

Hughes boy. When he was ushered into her cell she wished him well and he was no longer afflicted.

Mary Glover was convicted and sentenced to be hanged. After her condemnation Cotton Mather visited her several times to question her. She told him that she had gone to coven meetings with four other people, and her Prince had been present as well. Mather said, "Your Prince has cheated you."

"If it be so," Gammer Glover replied, "I am sorry for that!" Mather put several other questions to her that she would not answer. She said, "I would fain give you a full answer, but my spirits will not give me leave." When Mather asked her if he would pray with her the witch said, "I cannot consent without my spirits' leave."

The people of Salem attended the trial in crowds, and no one missed the Sunday when the Rev. Mr. Cotton Mather was invited to be guest preacher at Salem First Church. The meetinghouse was not large enough to hold everyone who wanted to see and hear the man with the famous name speak on such an important subject as witchcraft.

Mather did not disappoint them. In his best oratorical style, embellished with exempla out of the world of horrors and delivered filled to bursting with hellfire and brimstone, he gave them a sermon that raised the hackles for years afterward and filled the Salemites with an awe that encouraged them to see witches even in the sunlit fields and meadows of the New England countryside.

At 11 p.m. on August 16th the people of the colony thought that the Catholic King had been deposed or that they were being attacked when they heard bells ringing and cannon being fired. They rushed out of their houses to learn the news and were vastly disappointed or relieved, depending on which conclusion it was to which they had jumped: James II had been blessed with a son, a Catholic heir to the English throne. In August Tarrant Putnam, Benjamin's son, was baptized in Salem, and on the 29th of September Mary Putnam was born to Carolina John and Hannah.

William of Orange sailed for England from Holland with troops for the invasion of England to which he had been invited — the ships weighed anchor on November 5th. He landed in the west of England and issued a rallying call to which many men responded. James marched to meet him, but along the route his troops melted away into the landscape, and the king found it expedient to return to London before he arrived at the field of battle.

When the news reached New England's shores there was great rejoicing: An expectation began to grow that Massachusetts would receive a new charter as soon as ever the new Protestant king understood the calamities Sir Edmund Andros had wrought. Everyone expected to see Increase Mather step off the next ship, but a good many ships docked, and the only Mather anyone saw was Cotton who was growing to be as famous as his father. His involvement in the Glover case had helped to make his name a household word everywhere in New England.

Gammer Glover was brought to the gallows on Thursday, November 15th, but before she died she told the assembled multitude that at her death the Goodwin children could expect no relief, for there were other witches involved in their torment. The moment after she swung off the ladder her prophecy was shown to be true, for nothing happened to give the children respite from their torment. Indeed, they began to have fits worse than before: They barked at each other, then purred; they would roast and sweat, then complain of the cold and shiver with goose bumps. They would scream that their heads were nailed to the floor, and no one could raise them. One of them dreamt something was growing under his skin — an examination discovered a brass pin stuck there, near a rib. And they would fly across the floor, like geese, swiftly, only their toes touching the ground. Cotton Mather and the other ministers continued to try to help them; Cotton himself took under his wing particularly the oldest girl, Martha, who had begun the flap in the first place.

Mather wrote, "...I took her home to my own family, partly out of compassion to her parents, but" being a noted scientist as well, "chiefly that I might be a critical eye-witness of things that would enable me to confute the *sadducism* of this debauched age."

The Salem Village parishioners on November 15th appointed a committee whose members were Capt. John Putnam, Jr., Joshua Ray, Sr., and Francis Nurse. They were empowered to approach the Rev. Mr. Samuel Parris and ask him to become the fourth minister of Salem Village. Parris was, in the pecking order of the unofficial ecclesiastical hierarchy, the bottom of the barrel, lower even than George Burroughs who had at least graduated from Harvard, though he had afterwards become a backwoods preacher down East.

Parris had attended Harvard, but he had never graduated, and any community of New England — if it could not have an Englishman out of Oxford or Cambridge — at least expected to have a Harvardian. Worse still, Parris had not gone straight into the ministry; rather, he had become a businessman in Barbados. It was through this connection that the Putnams became acquainted with the man, for the late Thomass' second wife, Mary Veren Putnam, had property and other interests in Barbados. It was not until he had failed in business that Parris had returned to New England and taken up his cross.

Mather was continuing to help Martha Goodwin bear hers. At first, after he got her under his care, the girl "continued to do well for some days, applying herself to actions of industry and piety. But November 20, 1688, she cried out, 'Ah! They have found me out!' and immediately she fell into her fits; wherein we soon observed that she would cough up a ball as big as a small egg into the side of her windpipe, that would near choke her, till by stroking and by drinking it was carried down." Much more terrible effects were produced as time went by, and Mather's treatments of prayer and fasting proved ineffective.

The Salem Village church on November 25th was asked to stay after service, and the members voted to request "Mr. Parris to take office." But Parris was in no hurry to bring his period of probation to an end.

Being a former businessman, he wanted to strike the best bargain he could. He played the waiting game, and the parishioners began to fidget, then to become impatient, and some began to grow angry. On the 10th of December the people formed another committee made up of Lt. Nathaniel Putnam, Sgt. Thomas Fuller, Joshua Ray, Sr., and Sgt. Nathaniel Ingersoll. These men were to be "messengers to know whether Mr. Parris would accept of office."

In Boston Martha Goodwin and her sister celebrated Christmas in an unusual way for Puritan girls. Mather wrote, "When Christmas arrived, both she at my house and her sister at home were by the demons made very drunk, though we were fully satisfied they had no *strong drink* to make them so; nor would they willingly have been so to have gained the world. When she began to feel herself drunk, she complained, 'Oh! They say they will have me to keep Christmas with them. They will disgrace me when they can do nothing else.' And immediately the ridiculous behaviors of one drunk were, with a wondrous exactness, represented in her *speaking*, and *reeling*, and *spewing*, and anon *sleeping*, till she was well again."

In England William of Orange called for a constituent assembly to be convened. He had also captured James II, but — keeping in view what had happened when Charles I had been executed, he wisely allowed the deposed monarch to escape to France.

The constituent assembly of England met on the 22nd of January 1689, and after long debate about what to do — to ask Mary to be Queen and William I to be Consort, or offer him the Crown outright — the crown was given to them jointly. The Toleration Act was passed, which allowed all sects except Catholics and Unitarians to worship freely. The Puritans didn't like it, but it was better than having a Catholic state. The coronation took place on February seventeenth.

In unwitting New England life went on as usual with Andros still in command. Early in the year Dorcas Hoar was ill in bed at her home in Beverly. Several people had gathered to watch over her including her son-in-law Christopher Read and his wife Joan, Dorcas' daughter. At one point in the evening they went into Dorcas' room to check on her only to discover she was gone. Frightened, everyone rushed outdoors to look for her but Joan, who was the last person out, cried, "Someone is holding my foot on the stairs!" Christopher made a light, and they found that it was Dorcas, fully dressed and wearing a cloak, who had hold of Joan's ankle.

In Boston Martha Goodwin and the other children seemed at last to be responding to treatment. Cotton Mather wrote, "The ministers of Boston and Charlestown kept another day of prayer and fasting for Goodwin's afflicted family, after which the children had a sensible, but a gradual abatement of their sorrows, until perfect ease was at length restored unto them. The young woman dwelt at my house the rest of the winter, having by a virtuous conversation made her self enough welcome to the family. But ere long, I thought it convenient for me to entertain my congregation with a sermon on the 'memorable providences' wherein these children had been concerned.... When I had begun to study my sermon, her tormentors again seized upon her and managed her with a special design, as was plain, to disturb me in what I was then about.

"In the worst of her extravagances formerly, she was more dutiful to myself than I had reason to expect. But now her whole carriage to me was with a *sauciness* which I was not used anywhere to be treated withal. She would knock at my study door, affirming that 'some below would be glad to see you,' though there was none that asked for me" except, of course, Martha. "And when I chid her for telling what was false, her answer was, 'Mrs. Mather is always glad to see you!' She would call to me with numberless impertinences — and when I came down, she would *throw* things at me, though none of them could ever hurt me; and she would hector me at a strange rate for something I was doing above, and threaten me with *mischief* and *reproach*, that should revenge it. Few tortures now attended her, but such as were provoked. Her frolics were numberless, if we may call them hers." But finally, after help from others of the clergy, the Goodwin children settled down and became good little Christians.

In early April rumors began to arrive in New England about events in the old country, and things began to be stirred up. John Winslow arrived in Boston with a copy of King William's proclamation, and he was called before Sir Edmund Andros who requested to see the document. Winslow refused to show it to him; Andros threw him into jail.

On April 7th in Salem Village Jonathan and Lydia Potter Putnam had their third daughter, Ruth, but all was not delight in the settlement, for William Goode and his wife, Sarah, who were destitute lodgers in the home of Samuel and Mary Abbey, fell into contention with their landlords who gave them board and lodging in return for work — it was Sarah who caused the trouble to begin with — and they were evicted. The Goodes, having nowhere to go, became semi-vagabonds; their children ran wild.

On the 8th of April a mob gathered about the Governor's house in Boston, though the colony still had had no official word of anything from England. The crowd grew large and violent. Andros, being without a great number of English troops, saw nothing for it but to give himself up. He was thrown into prison by the "Council for the Safety and Conservation of the Peace," which was merely a euphemism for the old government, or what was left of it. The fourteen-man English garrison followed Andros' example; Castle Rock and the frigate *Rose*, both in Boston harbor, surrendered the next day, and a bloodless coup had been effected.

The old governor, Simon Bradstreet — who was eighty-nine years of age — was made President of the Council and former Gov. John Winthrop's son Waite Winthrop was made commander of the colonial militia. Then people began to be apprehensive about how the English government would view this mini-revolution.

The Devil manifested himself to William Barker of Salem Village. He was a Black Man with a cloven foot, and he put this proposition to Barker: He would pay Barker's debts and see to it that he lived comfortably; for his part, Barker was to cede his soul to the powers of darkness. It was the Devil's plan to begin his own coup by taking over Salem Village and then spreading out into the countryside. Barker made his pact and was taken to a Sabbat that had been called by Bridget Bishop and the former minister of Salem Village, Rev. George Burroughs. One hundred and five young blades, some of them armed with rapiers, gathered together at the assembly and, at the sound of a trumpet, fell to drinking wine and eating bread at the site of the Sabbat, which was a field nearby the meetinghouse.

The Rev. Samuel Parris had never answered the inquiry of Nathaniel Putnam's committee, put to him in December; the congregation waxed extremely irritable about the situation, especially some of the younger people, so on April 29th acting "Deacons Nathaniel Ingersoll and Edward Putnam, Daniel Ray, Thomas Fuller, Jr., and John Tarbell came to Mr. Parris from the meeting-house" where a conclave of the parish had been held. They told Parris, "Being the aged men had had the matter of Mr. Parris' settlement so long in hand, and effected nothing," it was thought to try and see what the younger men could manage to bring about. It was a perfect situation for a businessman. The new committee was eager to show how well it could succeed, and in its haste it agreed to several of Parris' demands, the fulfillment of which the committee had no right to guarantee.

Parris was to have sixty pounds per year, one-third of which was to be paid in currency and the rest in supplies at standard rates. But Parris wanted, also, an escalator clause in his contract: "When money shall be more plenteous, the money part to be paid me shall accordingly be increased" to a larger proportion than one-third of the total salary; he wanted an inflation clause — "though corn or like provisions should arise to a higher price than you have set, yet, for my own family use, I shall have what is needful at the price now stated, and so if it fall lower," which was unlikely; he wanted his rates to be paid by Salem Village alone, not by any other town or portion of towns, for he knew that Salem Village would never be able to coerce Topsfield to levy rates for him, for instance; no one was to pay his portion of the rate in provisions that were unacceptable to Parris; the minister, in addition to his annual salary, was to have free firewood supplied by the parish; two ratemakers were to be appointed annually to levy and collect Parris' salary.

So far it was only a tight bargain, but the next provision was unheard-of: Each Sunday people could pay a portion of their rate through sealed contributions, but only those contributions which were sealed "in papers" and made by those "dwelling within our bounds," were "to be accounted a part of the sixty pounds." In other words, if Topsfielders or others turned in contributions, they were to be perquisites, not part of Parris' salary; further, should anyone drop unsealed money into the collection box — a visitor or an anonymous donor — it, too, was to go to the minister and not be counted as part of his maintenance. Finally, if Salem Village should grow — and Parris knew it would — then he was to receive a proportionally larger salary. On the other hand, if it should shrink, then Parris would rebate part of his rate on petition of individuals, and he would be the final judge of what was reasonable. Of course, Parris would also have the use of the lands belonging to the parish.

This last provision, however, Parris somehow came to understand meant that he was to *own* the parish lands, including the parsonage, for good and all, even if he were to retire or be replaced by someone else in time, and the church lands were to be so much his that he could will them away to his heirs and assigns at his death. No one was fully aware that Parris thought any such thing at the time, unless some of the younger men, in their zeal to strike a bargain, said something at the meeting that planted the notion in Parris' mind.

On May 7th Capt. John Putnam, Jr. and his brother Nathaniel were chosen Selectmen of Salem, and Sgt. Thomas Putnam, Jr., became constable. Jonathan Putnam was promoted to the rank of Captain of the Salem Village militia. A parish meeting was held in Salem Village on May 17th to discuss the terms of agreement with Rev. Samuel Parris, and some objected to the fifth and seventh conditions. In the draft document these words had been added to the fifth clause: "And Mr. Parris to find himself firewood, and…to keep the ministry house in good repair"; but his salary had been raised from 60 to 66 pounds to cover the firewood. The draft added, "Mr. Parris shall also have the use of the ministry-pasture, and the inhabitants to keep the fence in repair." The seventh clause made no mention of perquisites derived from the contributions of outsiders. Thus, the person most agitated by the draft document was Mr. Parris himself, and some of his staunchest supporters joined him in his irritation. Mr. Parris was serving his probationary time; however, it had become clear that it was not he, but the Salem Village church, that had to come up to snuff. He continued to preach and minister while another meeting was called for June 18th.

During the late spring in Beverly John Neal, who was working for Thomas Whitridge, found a stray chicken that was damaging his master's cornfield. He killed it and afterward discovered that it belonged to Dorcas Hoar. Neal returned the dead bird to Dorcas who, in a passion, declared "That should be the worst week's work that you ever did!"

Deliverance Putnam Walcott, Jonathan Walcott's wife, gave birth to a son on the fifth of June, and the parents named him Thomas, after their baby who had died the previous year. At the Salem Village parish meeting held June 18th "it was agreed and voted by general concurrence that, for Mr. Parris' encouragement and settlement in the work of the ministry amongst us," the draft contract was to be in force. The document's provisions were entered in the record book.

During the summer Francis Nurse's wife Rebecca went to the home of Benjamin and Sarah Houlton to berate Goodman Houlton because his pigs had gotten into her field — despite the fact that the pigs were yoked — for Rebecca's fence was down in several places. Nothing Mr. Houlton could say would calm her down. Goody Nurse called to her son, Benjamin, to "go and get a gun and kill the pigs, and let none of them go out of the field!" Not long after this encounter Goodman Houlton suffered a stroke as he was coming into the house, and a series of strokes followed till, on a midnight, he died.

Mary Putnam was born, the fifth child and first daughter, to the family of Deacon Edward and Mary Hale Putnam on August 14th, and on the 30th of that month Sgt. Thomas and his wife Ann Putnam had another child for whom little hope was held out.

Simon Willard, thirty-nine, went to Falmouth, Maine, on Casco Bay, and he stayed in the home of Robert Lawrence. They got to speaking of various things, and Mr. Lawrence introduced the subject of the local parson, Rev. Mr. George Burroughs, who was also visiting and present in the room. He commended Mr. Burroughs' strength to Willard; he said, "We could none of us do what he could do, for Mr. Burroughs can hold out his gun with one hand." The company were astonished, but Burroughs affirmed that he could do it. He showed the folk present where he held the gun to perform the feat — behind the flintlock. It was a rifle with a seven-foot barrel. Burroughs, being a modest man, refused to perform, but Willard picked it up, held it where Burroughs had shown him, and couldn't lift it with both hands. Later Willard, still skeptical, mentioned it to Capt. Wormall, but the Captain assured him that Burroughs could do what he said.

At another gathering Burroughs was present when some members of Capt. Edward Sergeant's garrison were talking about the minister's ability to lift a barrel of molasses out of a canoe by himself and carry it to shore. The short, stocky preacher told the men, and Simon Willard who was there as well, that he had carried one barrel that was like to have hurt him, but Willard took this to mean that the ground was rough and he might have strained a leg, not that the effort was too much for him. He shook his head in wonder.

Meanwhile in Salem Village Burroughs' successor, the Rev. Mr. Samuel Parris, continued in his delusion that he owned the parish property of Salem Village outright, though it had been pointed out to him that an entry in the record book for the year 1681 forbade the property, through an entailment, from ever being sold to anyone else. Parris told his friends that, if such were the case, he would never be ordained. He was passionate about it. His backers were so anxious to have him ordained that they conceived a plot. They called a rump parish meeting for October 10th, and there "it was agreed and voted that the vote in our record book of 1681 that lays, as some say, an entailment upon our ministry house and land, is hereby made void and of no effect; one man only dissenting" — somehow, a maverick had gotten into the meeting.

Then "It was voted and agreed by a general concurrence, that we will give to Mr. Parris our ministry house and barn, and two acres adjoining to the house; and that Mr. Parris take office amongst us, and live and die in the work of the ministry among us; and, if Mr. Parris or his heirs do sell the house and land, that the people may have the first refusal of it, by giving as much as other men will. A committee was chosen to lay out the land, and make a conveyance of the house and land, and to make the conveyance in the name and in the behalf of the inhabitants unto Mr. Parris and his heirs." The entry was made in the record book, but no one signed it.

On August 30th Deacon Edward Putnam and his wife baptized their daughter Mary at Salem First Church. The French and Indian War struck Salem when a raiding party of braves killed Nicholas Reed, a servant of Deacon Putnam and John Bishop. In Boston Cotton Mather had gotten Gammer Mary Glover's case whipped into shape for publication, and he brought it out in his *Memorable Providences Relating to Witchcrafts and Possessions.*

If any outsider were to wonder who constituted the rump meeting that gave away the Salem Village church property to Rev. Samuel Parris, its outlines became clear when, on the 10th of November, twenty-four members of the settlement were officially set off from Salem Parish and allowed to form their own church and parish. Of the two dozen, fourteen were Putnams or their spouses, including Deliverance Putnam Walcott. Conspicuously absent from the roster was Joseph Putnam. On November 19th the Rev. Nicholas Noyes ordained Mr. Parris as minister; Rev. Samuel Phillips and Rev. John Hale of Beverly joined in the laying-on-of-hands.

During the fall Margaret Reddington, a sixty-seven-year-old woman, visited Isaac and Mary Easty in Topsfield. The two women talked of deaths and illnesses — in particular of an infirmity that plagued Margaret. Not long after Goody Reddington went home she fell into a state of depression that — as Robert Burton in his *The Anatomy of Melancholy* had pointed out, was likely to occur. She soon got worse rather than better. On the Thursday before Thanksgiving a specter of Mary Easty visited Goody Reddington and offered her a piece of meat. Margaret became ill that afternoon, but she gathered her strength and told the ghost, "'Tis not fit for the dogs, and I will have none of it," whereupon Mary vanished.

On Sunday, November 24th, Nathaniel Ingersoll was voted Deacon of Salem Village church, but only on probation. Though he had been associated with the church of Salem for twenty years, was a founder of Parris' own church, and had already filled the post of Deacon for some time, Parris felt he ought to serve a further term of trial.

During the winter James and Sarah Putnam became the parents of James, Jr., as did George and Elizabeth Putnam Flint of Thomas — named after his dead brother — on December 16th. The day after, the infant of Sgt. Thomas and Ann Carr Putnam that had been born at the end of August died: Ann was not the sort of woman who bore such afflictions with patience, resignation, and a trust in the will of the Lord. She grieved mightily, and her dark moods increased as each new burden was placed on her shoulders.

It had been several months since William and Sarah Goode had been evicted by Samuel and Mary Abbey, but at last the worst began to happen: The Abbeys' cattle started to sicken and die.

Priscilla Stacey, William Stacey's daughter, fell victim to illness as well — she "suddenly screeched out, and so continued in an unusual manner for about a fortnight, and so died in a lamentable manner," according to her father. Until her sudden illness, he said, she had been "a likely, thriving child." Stacey suspected that Bridget Bishop had a hand in the curious death, but others suspected that it was Satan's scourge and refused to come near.

At about the same time Sarah Goode went to the home of Thomas and Sarah Gadge and asked to come in. Mrs. Gadge, however, refused to let her enter because, she said, "I am afraid you have been with them that have smallpox."

Sarah fell to mumbling and then said aloud, "If you won't give me leave to come in, then let me borrow what I came for."

Goody Gadge shook her head, said, "I wish not to have traffic with you," and slammed the door. The next morning one of the Gadge's cows died in a remarkable way, perhaps of cow pox, smallpox's cousin.

In England John Partridge, who was busy preparing the new edition of his astrological almanac, enjoyed a wealthy Christmas, for he was not only doing well in a business way, he had followed William Lilly's example in every way possible, even unto marrying a rich widow during the year.

Robert Boyle, who was living in London, had done some backsliding from his scientific days. He was in ill health and living with his sister in Pall Mall. For some time he had been easing out of his public engagements, and at last he requested that visitors not come to see him except on extraordinary business, for he wished to devote his remaining days to the study of alchemy and the attempt to transmute base metals into gold by means of the Philosopher's Stone. He had resolutely sworn not to study atomic theory in order to keep his mind uncluttered until his own experiments showed him what was what, and what was not — but he was not ignorant of the works of the alchemists. During 1689 he had helped in the successful attempt to repeal the English law against multiplying silver and gold. Boyle — a tall, slender, pale man — worked among his retorts and furnaces painstakingly, and despite himself, came slowly closer to a scientific understanding of the building blocks of matter.

Chapter Nine

Benjamin and Hannah Walcott Putnam welcomed the new year of 1690 by becoming the parents of their first daughter and fourth child, Sarah, on the 8th of January. They would of course baptize their little girl, as was the normal rule in Salem Village — no one thought twice about it except, of course, during the time of the Anabaptist heresy. But Samuel Parris, anxious to bring intellectual discourse to the town, brought up the subject at a church meeting held at the home of Capt. John on February 20th.

Parris asked, "Who are the proper subjects of baptism?" The Villagers wondered how he would answer it, but Parris did not keep them waiting long: "Covenant-professing believers and their infant seed." It was not the way the farmers would have phrased it, but they saw nothing wrong with the answer once they thought about it. Parris asked them to vote on whether they agreed, and the affirmative won unanimously. But the evening wasn't over.

"How far," Parris continued, "may we account such infant seed, and so to be baptized?" The Putnams and their neighbors frowned and looked at each other uneasily. When Parris proposed an answer and put it to the vote, only a majority said "Aye," and two or three said "Nay." No one counted the abstentions. Nevertheless, it was a successful evening for Mr. Parris. The parishioners went home impressed with the depth of erudition shown by this Harvard dropout. Two days later Mr.

Parris in Salem Village baptized James Putnam, Jr., son of James, Sr. and Sarah, and he duplicated the ritual that same day for Elizabeth Putnam, daughter of Benjamin and Hannah Walcott Putnam.

In March Sarah Goode went to the home of Zachariah Herrick to ask if she could stay there overnight, for since her eviction she and her family had been wandering the countryside, staying now in one barn, now in another, getting work here and there, as they could. Herrick refused the old woman, and she left grumbling. When the door was closed Herrick turned to Henry his son and Jonathan Batchelor and said, "Follow her and see that she goes away clear, lest she should lie in the barn and set it afire by smoking of her pipe."

The young men went out. They stood watching the witch as she went through the dooryard, and when they saw her pause near the barn they called, "Begone!"

Goody Goodee turned to them. "Then it shall cost your father one or two of his cows," she said. Two weeks later Goodman Herrick's cows began to get loose, unaccountably.

The French and Indian War continued. In outlying settlements throughout New England, but particularly to the northeast, the Indians were depredating, killing, and taking many prisoners into Canada. One of these was a girl named Mercy Short whose mother, father, brother, and sister had been murdered in a raid on Salmon Falls, New Hampshire.

In April Sir William Phips — a native of Maine who had been knighted — was appointed by the General Court to lead the colonial forces in an attack on Port Royal. Phips had served the government before, the Province government, as sheriff under Andros. Though he was a bluff, not very well-educated man, a sea captain who had made his fortune by discovering a sunken ship full of treasure (which had been the cause of his knighthood), he was trusted and deemed a good soldier by President Bradstreet and his Council. His attack on Port Royal was completely successful — an easy victory. He was given a hero's welcome on his return.

In Salem Village among the Putnams there was a good deal of activity in the spring. A fifth daughter and eighth child, Susannah, was born to Carolina John and Hannah Cutler Putnam on April eleventh. Ten days later Joseph Putnam married Elizabeth Porter of Salem Village, the niece of Judge John Hathorne. Edward Putnam was made a freeman of Salem, as was his cousin Jonathan whose one-year-old daughter Ruth was baptized by Mr. Parris on April 27th.

On that same day Martha Corey was admitted as a member of the Salem Village church; her husband, Giles, was getting to be an elderly man. Capt. John Putnam, Jr. ., deeded a hundred acres of land to his sons Jonathan and James, and in May his brother, Landlord Nathaniel, was chosen both a Selectman of Salem and Salem's Deputy to the General Court.

In Maine, Casco was again under attack by the Indians. A relief party was being assembled under Capt. Cedrick Walt at Great Island in Piscataway. Two of the assembling soldiers were Thomas Hardy and Joseph Ring who was from Salisbury. Before they sailed Hardy invited Ring to join a game of shovel board that some of the men were playing, but they were betting and Ring said, "I have no money to wager." Hardy told Ring that was no problem, and he lent him two shillings. They played, and Hardy won back the lent money. Ring could not repay what he owed.

In Casco itself Lt. Richard Honeywell, Thomas and John Greenslit, and the Rev. George Burroughs were at the home of Capt. Joshua Scott of Blackpoint. The Indian raid was underway, but the people had been told help was in the offing, and no one was inclined, yet, to take to the woods. At the Scott home the people gathered there witnessed at last some of the proverbial strength of the minister. When the demonstration was over Thomas Greenslit told people that he had seen Burroughs insert his forefinger into a rifle with a six-foot barrel and lift it, holding it out at arm's length; further, he had seen Burroughs lift a barrel with only his two fingers stuck into the bung; he had carried it that way from the stage depot to the stage door without setting it down along the way. Those to whom he told the story were amazed beyond measure — or skeptical.

When the Indians had finally finished with Casco it was a ruin, but once again George Burroughs managed to be one of the survivors. He took his family and migrated down the coast a way to Wells where he was granted 150 acres of land.

Indians hit Salem itself and Godfrey Sheldon was killed, but for the most part life held to its routine. Samuel Preston had an argument with Martha Carrier who had moved into Andover with her parents' family, the Allens — she had had to fight her way in, for the townspeople considered her to be a sloven, the next thing to a vagabond. She let her children run wild and fought with her neighbors, as she had done in Billerica with John Rogers who had subsequently had so much trouble with his sows and cow, and with Preston who subsequently lost the prerequisite cow.

Martha Carrier's sister in Billerica was Aunt Mary Toothaker — wife of Dr. Roger Toothaker and a white witch — who had in that town the same sort of reputation that Mother Goose had in Salem, that Mammy Reed bore in Marblehead, and that Mary Webster wore in Hadley and Boston. Martha Carrier was *persona non grata* to the selectmen of Andover, but she managed to stick.

In June Joseph Ring, back from Casco, was on his way to Hampton when he met Thomas Hardy on the way. Hardy asked him for the two shillings he had lent him, but Ring said he didn't have it. Two weeks later Ring again ran into Hardy on the road from Boston. Hardy, in a company of people on horseback, passed Ring, then turned back and invited him to go to Mrs. Whit's for a drink. Ring refused. Hardy returned to his companions and, in a group, they turned about and galloped down on Ring, frightening him — but they passed on by and Joseph was left alone.

Martha Dutch, thirty-four, and Alice Parker of Salem were standing in the street near the wharves one day when they saw John Jarman coming ashore, safely returned from a voyage. Martha said to her companion, "What a great mercy it is for to see them come home well. Through mercy, my husband has gone and come home well many times. I do hope he will come home this voyage well also."

"No, never more in this world," Alice replied. A chill ran down Martha's spine.

In July Samuel Preston again had words with Martha Carrier, but she had the last word. "You lost a cow lately," she told him, "and it should not be long before you lose another." Martha was as good as her word.

Sir William Phips attacked Quebec in July, and Eleazer Putnam, Capt. John's son, went with him as a member of William Raymond's company. This time Phips had no luck.

David Balch of Beverly became ill, and in his delirium witches tormented him. His father, Benjamin, was distraught, but when the boy was relatively lucid a visitor, Marie Gadge — the former Widow Wood — asked David if he could identify his tormentors. David replied, "Goody Wilds and her daughter and Goody Hoar, and another woman of Marblehead that I know not." Goody Gadge could only assume he meant Mammy Wilmot Reed.

Benjamin asked, "Are they with you in the room?"

"They are whispering together at my bed foot," David told him. "Oh! Strike at them!" he cried, and Gabriel Hood, who was also present, took his sword and sliced at the place where the witches stood. "You have hit Goody Wilds!" David shouted. "She is going out at the door! But Goody Hoar is here still, and she torments me!" He asked the Lord to help him and the crowd in the room said, "Amen."

The first newspaper ever published in America, sponsored by Benjamin Harris and titled *Publick Occurrences Both Foreign and Domestic*, appeared in Boston on September 25th, but it was unlicensed by the government that suppressed it the same day.

In October, on the road from Hampton, New Hampshire, a group of men and women on horseback overtook Joseph Ring; sure enough, Thomas Hardy was once more of the party, and Ring thought he recognized Susannah Martin as well. Hardy rode up to Ring and demanded his two shillings. Ring had no intention of paying him back and Hardy threatened to tear him apart, but nothing happened, and again Ring found himself alone on the road.

Ring began to tell people he was being haunted by spectral shapes, one of which was a Black Man who offered him a book to sign; another was Thomas Hardy, and still a third was Susannah Martin. He saw many strange sights, for he was transported to Sabbats where the group of men and women assembled to conduct their occult business, tempting him in many ways — but always Joseph remained virtuous and rejected their blandishments.

George and Elizabeth Putnam Flint became the parents of their fifth child, Nathaniel, on October 21st, and in November Martha Carrier lived up to her name:

Boston and Salem, being port towns, were rather well used to the ravages of Satan's scourge. Every year for as long as people could remember, at least one or two cases showed up in the settlements, but it did not run through whole populations the way it did in European cities, for during the winter especially many of the farms were almost completely isolated from one-another and from the center of town. Salem Village had far fewer cases than Salem did. Here and there, scattered about New England, there were settlements that knew almost nothing of the disease. Andover had been particularly blessed, for the smallpox had never struck the village at all — not until Martha Carrier brought it to town in November 1690, perhaps after a visit to her sister in Billerica. It ran like searing flame through her family and spread through the village, for by the time the Allens and the Carriers were quarantined, it was too late. Martha herself survived, and others did as well, but during the month of November several people succumbed to Satan's scourge.

Edward Putnam was proposed, on Sunday, November 30th, as Deacon of Salem Village church — a position that he, like Nathaniel Ingersoll, had more or less formally been filling for a time. It was a cold day and the parishioners didn't wish to discuss the matter then, so a meeting was set for Thursday, December third.

At that meeting Edward was again put forward by Mr. Samuel Parris who made the suggestion that perhaps another name ought to be advanced as well, but the room — three-fifths full of Putnams — did not respond to the idea, and Edward was affirmed unanimously. Parris made it clear that Edward, too, would have to undergo a probationary period — such honors were not to be handed out lightly, for the Lord's work was of too great moment for hasty decisions. Edward accepted the position under the conditions Parris enunciated.

On Sunday, December 7th, Parris made a great point after evening services of informing his congregation — at least "those of the church that were ignorant of it" — that Edward had been chosen deacon pro-tem. From this he dovetailed into a lecture against absences and followed up by questioning his people about whether they were ready to propose that Nathaniel Ingersoll be permanently vested with the Deaconship — he was confirmed, but no date of ordination was set. Parris concluded by asking that "there be a more open and liberal contribution by the communicants, that so the deacons may have wherewith[al] to furnish" the communion table with something a bit better than merely the "two pewter tankards" that were currently available.

Abigail Hobbs, a young woman of Topsfield, noted for her saucy tongue, had what seemed to some of her neighbors to be peculiar — not to say astonishing — habits. One day fifteen-year-old Lydia Nichols asked Abigail, "How do you durst lie out overnights in the woods alone?"

Abigail tossed her head and replied, "I am not afraid of anything, for I have sold myself body and soul to the Old Boy."

Another girl who had lain out in the woods, but against her will — Mercy Short, taken by Indians to Canada in March — was rescued in December. She was brought to Boston where a position was found for her as a domestic servant, for she had to earn her keep, being the orphan that she was. The failed invader of Canada, Sir William Phips, made another trip to England during the winter, and the smallpox epidemic continued to ravage Andover. By the end of the year nine victims were dead.

A New Year's baby appeared in Salem Village in 1691. William was born to Jonathan and Deliverance Putnam Walcott. The couple had four children, of whom three lived, their first, Thomas, having died within three months of his birth in 1688. Some of the children of Jonathan's first marriage still were living at home, and one of these was the younger girl, Mary. She had been ten years old when her father remarried, and she had never been able to accept with a good grace the half-siblings produced by her stepmother. In 1691 she would be sixteen years old and, being an adolescent, was not always able to control her resentments and willfulness.

Martha Carrier's brother, John Allen, died in Andover of the smallpox during the first month of the year, but the epidemic began to wane leaving in its wake a village tormented with grief and fear. Irrationally, a good many of the town's inhabitants blamed Martha for having introduced Satan's scourge to the village — worse, she had lived while so many others had died. She was treated as though she still carried the seeds of the disease.

Elsewhere in Andover social visits were resuming, and on one occasion John Farnham and Samuel Wardwell had occasion to drop in at the Martin home. While the folks were conversing, Farnham brought up the topic of prognostication; he asked Wardwell to tell his fortune. Wardwell agreed, studied his subject, and told him, "You are in love with a girl, but you shall be crossed and will go to the southward."

Farnham was surprised; he admitted that such a thought had been on his mind. Wardwell continued, "You had like to be shot with a gun, and shall have a fall off your horse."

On another occasion during the winter Wardwell told James Bridges he was in love with a girl of fourteen — Bridges owned it to be the truth, and he marveled to his neighbors how Wardwell could have known.

Smallpox was a factor in the life of Salem Village early in the year, and the Rev. Mr. Samuel Parris' "Negro lad," a member of a family of slaves he had brought with him from Barbados, died of what some thought was the pox. Perhaps it was not, however, because the young man's parents — a couple named John Indian, a Carib, and Tituba, an African — did not catch it, nor did members of the Parris household. The child must have had a first name, but no one ever called him anything but "Boy." Nor did anyone use the slave family's last name, if they had one other than "Indian." The bereaved parents grieved mightily at the young man's death, particularly the father, John Indian, whom Parris began to think might have been mentally unhinged by the experience.

Joseph Putnam, the outcaste, and his wife Elizabeth Porter Putnam, were blessed with their first baby, Mary, on the second of February. Not only were the parents delighted, so were the babe's paternal grandmother, twice-widowed Mary Veren Putnam, and the Porter family. Little Mary's maternal uncle, Judge John Hathorne, visited the Joseph Putnam home and brought with him small gifts for mother and child.

Giles Corey in his old age got religion and followed the example of his third wife, Martha, by becoming a member of Salem First Church a year after she had been admitted to the Village congregation. The fact astonished many of the inhabitants who could not imagine how one of Corey's repute could be counted as one of the Saved. His application to join the Village church had been rejected, for the stories that had circulated about his life were almost as much a part of lore as those of Mammy Wilmot Reed, the witch of Marblehead. The Salem Villagers could not imagine what Rev. Mr. Higginson and the mother church were thinking when they agreed to take in the old reprobate.

As for Mammy Reed — parents used her name to coerce children to behave. They told their youngsters that if Mammy Reed wished it, a bloody cleaver would be found in a bad child's bed, and after that the girl or boy would sicken and die. Mammy could cause milk to curdle as it left the cow, and butter new-churned would turn to wool if she touched it.

In March Benjamin Abbott, thirty, was granted some land by the town of Andover, near the farm of the Allens. When Abbott's land was laid out by the selectmen Martha Carrier — completely recovered from her illness — became angry, for she felt her family's land had been impinged upon. She told anyone who mentioned the topic, as her nephew Alan Toothaker and Ralph Farnham did, "I will stick as close to Benjamin Abbott as the bark sticks to the tree." She went on to predict that Abbott "should repent of it before seven years come to an end."

Abbott, who had been under treatment by a local physician, was in for a long bout of illness, according to Goody Carrier, for she continued to rail at a great rate. "Dr. Prescott shall never cure him!" she told Toothaker and Farnham. "I shall hold his nose so close to the grindstone as ever it was held since his name was Benjamin Abbott!" Soon afterward, Abbott's foot began to swell, and then he developed an infection in his side which festered so badly that Dr. Prescott lanced it — a great deal of corruption ran out of the sore.

Joseph Benham was the son of John Benham who had migrated from England to Dorchester, Massachusetts, in 1630. In 1657 Joseph had married Winifred King of Boston, and in 1670 he had taken his family into Connecticut to settle in the Meriden-Wallingford area located between Hartford and New Haven not far from the Hanging Hills of Meriden. The Benhams' farm was on the main street of Wallingford, on the east side of the road. On the last Tuesday in April 1691, Joseph Benham had had enough of his neighbors and their insinuations. They had been talking about his wife behind her back, calling her a witch and other evil names, and some of them had evidently dared to go so far as to make a public complaint about her to the authorities. The Selectmen of town came to the Benham farm to investigate the allegations for themselves.

Joseph blew up at them. He told them to their faces, "You are no more fit for townsmen than dogs!" The men faced each other, but Joseph was outnumbered. He was told that the constable would come calling shortly. The town council left, and Mr. Benham sat down before the fire trembling. His wife came to comfort him and to thank him for standing up for her.

On April 26th Rev. Samuel Parris baptized Timothy, son of Sgt. Thomas and Ann Carr Putnam, and on May the 8th Capt. Jonathan and Lydia Potter Putnam became the parents of their fifth child, but first son, Jonathan, Jr. He was baptized two days later in the Village.

During the late spring saucy Abigail Hobbs and her mother, Deliverance, visited the family of young Margaret Knight. While the older people were conversing Abigail asked, "Margaret, have you been baptized?"

"Yes," Margaret answered.

"My mother has not baptized," Abigail said, "but I will baptize her." She got up, went to a bucket standing nearby, took some water in her hand. While Margaret looked on in bewilderment Abigail went to Deliverance, sprinkled the water in Goody Hobbs' face and said, "I do baptize you in the name of the Father, Son, and Holy Ghost." Everyone sat staring at the girl in shocked dismay.

On Election Day Nathaniel Putnam once more became Salem's Deputy to the General Court, and so did his brother, Capt. John. On the 31st of May, at a church meeting, Samuel Parris said to his congregation, "The ordination of Brother Ingersoll has already been voted a good while since, and I thought to have consummated the affair a good time since, but have been put by, by the diversity of occurrents; and, seeing it is so long since, I think it needless to make two works of one, and therefore intend the ordination of Brother Putnam together with Brother Ingersoll in the deaconship, if you continue in the same mind as when you elected him; therefore, if you are so, let a vote manifest it." The vote was overwhelmingly in favor, if not actually unanimous — Parris had some small doubt which.

The same day William Goode spoke with his wife, Sarah, and mentioned a "sad incident" had occurred to two of Samuel Abbey's cows, both of them having died within a half hour of each other. Sarah was cold. She replied, "I care not if Abbey lost all the cattle he had."

Ever since Alice Parker had told Martha Dutch, nearly a year earlier, that she would never see her mariner husband in this world again, Martha had been worrying about his safety. Her worst fears were realized and confirmed when she received word that her man had died while he was overseas. The Widow Dutch knew whom to blame for her loss.

On the 15th of June in New Haven a County Court was held at which "Joseph Benham of Wallingford" was "presented for speaking words in reproach against the Townsmen," i. e., Selectmen "of Wallingford...." Three witnesses appeared against him and he confessed to the charge; "he was fined to pay 5 shillings into the County Treasury before the 1st of November next for his so traducing and vilifying said Townsmen." The trial did nothing to keep his neighbors from muttering against his wife, nor did the fine completely satisfy the Selectmen.

At about the same time in Andover another sore developed in Benjamin Abbott's groin. Dr. Prescott had to lance that boil as well. Strange things were happening in Andover and elsewhere. Some of Abbott's cattle sickened, and one died after it had given birth; others came out of the woods with their tongues hanging out and otherwise acting strangely.

Demons were sighted in Gloucester on Cape Ann, by many of the inhabitants. The creatures wore white waistcoats, blue shirts with white breeches. Their hair was full, bushy, and black. Some dared to suggest it was French and Indians people saw, but others asked how it was possible for mere men to float above the houses and glide through the air over the fields; how they could appear and vanish, then reappear at great distances? The town was baffled and amazed. For three weeks the phenomena continued, and the villagers barricaded themselves in the town garrison. Whenever someone saw, or thought he saw something, the militia would fire its guns into the woods, but no one was ever hurt. News of the horrible events spread swiftly throughout the countryside, and sixty militiamen from Ipswich were sent out to relieve the beleaguered folk at Gloucester, for even the prayers and fasting of the town's minister, Rev. John Emerson, had been of no avail against the Devil's uniformed legions.

On Sunday, June 28th, Deacon Ingersoll was ordained in Salem Village, but with regard to Edward Putnam's vestiture — it was Rev. Samuel Parris' turn to wait. Edward wanted more time to think things over — such matters were weighty. Meanwhile, he continued to serve in the office of Deacon without ordination.

In next-door Andover John Farnham had a series of accidents — he was nearly shot with a gun he was carrying when his horse stumbled and threw him. The gun flew out of his hand as he was falling, turned in the air, and hit the ground at about the same time Farnham did. The blast missed him but tore the foliage alongside the path, which was a good thing because he was hopelessly in love with a girl who did not requite his devotion. Remembering what Wardwell had told him, he decided to go to Salem and ship aboard a coaster to southward.

Rev. Mr. Samuel Parris, ever a lover of complication where simplicity might have served, and of pomp rather than Puritan plainness, kept his congregation after services on Sunday, August 9th, and "proposed to the church whether they were free to admit to baptism, upon occasion, such as were not at present free to come up to full communion." It was a confusing proposition: To baptize someone and not allow that person full communion in the church. He told them, "There is a young woman, by name Hannah Wilkins, the daughter of our Brother Thomas Wilkins, who much desired to be baptized, but yet did not dare to come to the Lord's Supper. If you have nothing against it, I shall take your silence for consent, and in due time acquaint you with what she has offered me to my satisfaction, and proceed accordingly." The church members had no idea whether they were pro or con such a procedure. Parris accordingly took their silence for assent…to whatever it was he had said.

Carolina John and Hannah Putnam became the parents on August 16th of a mixed pair of twins, Rebecca and Carolina John, Jr. The house was filled to overflowing afterward with family members who came to see and admire the unique babies. No time at all was lost in baptizing them in the Salem Village Church where Mr. Parris officiated a week later, Sunday, August twenty-third. The minister made a public ceremony of the baptism after services, and he blew things up even larger by reintroducing the case of Hannah Wilkins. Parris wrote an account of the event in his journal that evening:

"Hannah Wilkins, aged about twenty-one years, was called forth, and her relation" — her justification for baptism and church membership — "read in the full assembly" by Mr. Parris from the pulpit as Hannah stood in the congregation, "and then it was propounded to the church, that, if they had just exceptions, or, on the other hand, had any thing farther to encourage, they had opportunity and liberty to speak. None said any thing but Brother Bray Wilkins (Hannah's grandfather) who said that, for all he knew, such a relation as had been given and a conversation suitable (as he judged hers to be) was enough to enjoy full communion. None else saying any thing, it was put to vote whether they were so well satisfied as to receive this young woman into membership, and therefore initiate her therein by baptism. It was voted full."

Parris proceeded, then, to make the day a truly gala affair with a third baptism, though Hannah Wilkins would not be a full communicant, according to her own wishes. But the middle of the following week she changed her mind and wished to take communion. Since she was already legally a full member, entitled to take communion at the Lord's Supper, Parris really had to do nothing, but on Sunday,

August 30th, he put the question once more to a vote of the church. Of course, Hannah was given permission, needlessly, to take communion with the other members, which accordingly was done, it being Communion Sunday.

Capt. Jonathan Putnam on the same day was chosen "commissioner to join with the Selectmen in taking a list of the male persons and estate of the town" of Salem Village. It was becoming a very settled place, for the commission's report showed 402 heads of families residing in town.

At the end of September Joseph Ring and his brother Jarvis were in the woods outside Salisbury, hewing wood. Jarvis drove the team home with a load, leaving Joseph to finish up. As soon as Jarvis was out of sight, Thomas Hardy of Piscataway appeared to Joseph who was, "by some impulse," forced to follow Hardy to a deserted house "half a mile away." There, before the roaring fire, Joseph found two women — Susannah Martin and a stranger — drinking (no doubt hard) cider at the hearth. Much against his will, Joseph was forced to spend the night with his two-shilling nemesis and the bibbing witches.

Warfare resumed among the Salem Village parishioners on the 8th of October. As in previous years, with the former ministers, a sizeable minority of opponents to Parris and his ways had formed; their antagonism was brought into the open when Parris, after Lecture Day services, kept the congregation while he complained that he had received no firewood for the winter. He told the farmers, "I am so bare of firewood that I am forced publicly to desire the inhabitants to take care that I may be provided for. Had it not been for Mr. Corwin, who brought me some wood, being then at my house, I should hardly have any to burn." A church meeting was called for October 16th where the situation was to be confronted.

On the appointed day the meeting was held, and Parris' enemies made sure that they were present — they constituted a majority. Nathaniel Putnam was chosen moderator, and the church records were searched for the agreement that had been made with the minister on June 18th, 1689. The entry was read, and the pertinent portion pointed out: Because his salary had been increased to 66 pounds from the 60 originally agreed upon, "Mr. Parris to find himself firewood."

Someone at the meeting said that he thought Mr. Parris "would not comply with that entry." An argument ensued until someone else suggested "it were best to send for Mr. Parris to resolve the question." A messenger was sent out, and Parris came in to the meeting. The entry in the records was read to him — he turned apoplectic.

"I never heard or knew any thing of it," he told his parishioners angrily, "neither can or will I take up with it, or any part of it! They were knaves and cheaters that entered it!"

It was obvious to those gathered that Parris was talking about more than just firewood, for the entry implied that he had no right to the church properties either — the firewood issue was a dodge Parris was using in order to clear his title to the parsonage and its lands according to the terms of the unsigned entry that had been made, just prior to his ordination, by his friends at their rump meeting. Or so it appeared to those who had set their faces against their pastor. They questioned who it was that were "knaves and cheaters."

Nathaniel Putnam replied to Mr. Parris' outburst, "Sir, then there is only proposals on both sides, and no agreement between you and the people?"

"No more, there is not!" Parris answered hotly, "for I am free from the people, and the people free from me!" He stalked out.

When he was gone the church members present elected a committee of Parris' enemies. A motion was made to instruct the committee to raise a rate for the provision of firewood to the minister, and it was defeated. Then a warrant was written calling for a special meeting of the Villagers at which an investigation was to be conducted into the circumstances of, and agreements made prior to, Mr. Parris' ordination; in particular, the committee wanted to know whether all the meetings that were held during that time had been legally called, and whether the actions taken during those meetings had brought into question the right and title of the Church to its ministry and properties.

Parris, when he heard of the meeting's actions — and he heard of them that day — calmed down sufficiently to attempt to head off his opponents at the pass. On the first of November he called for a meeting of the "brethren" at the parsonage — which he termed "my house" in his journal — the next day at an hour and a half past sundown.

Seventeen people came to the meeting — it was far from being a full complement of members. Parris said to those who had bothered to show up, "Brethren, I have not much to trouble you with now, but you know what committee, the last town-meeting here, were chosen — and what they have done, or intend to do — better than I. But, you see, I have hardly any wood to burn. I need say no more, but I leave the matter to your serious and godly consideration."

After Parris sat down the meeting decided that Capt. John Putnam, Jr, and the deacons, Nathaniel Ingersoll and Edward Putnam, were to go to the committee and ask them to set a rate for the minister's supplies. The trio of go-betweens was to report back on November 10th, when another church meeting had been called.

In Wallingford, Connecticut, Goodman Joseph Benham on the same day had begrudgingly gone to pay his five shillings in fine to the county. He had obtained no relief from his neighbors who continued to accuse his wife of the most atrocious and diabolical behavior.

In the hiatus between meetings in Salem Village, too, preternatural occurrences continued, and in Chelmsford, Massachusetts, Martha Sparks was arrested by Deputy Governor Thomas Danforth and committed to Boston Prison on a charge of practicing witchcraft.

On the appointed day the deacons and the captain arrived to make their report, but there were few to listen, for besides Parris and his emissaries the only people who bothered to attend were Sgt. Thomas Putnam, Jr., Thomas Wilkins, and Peter Prescott. Parris was considerably put out by the lack of response to his summons, and no less so with the report of his messengers: "The Committee did not see good to take notice of our message, without they had some letter to show under the church's and pastor's hand." Of course, it was impossible, under the circumstances, to get a majority of the church to sign such a letter, or approve of one.

Mr. Parris was so busy rushing from meeting to meeting, from church member to member shoring up his defenses and attempting to mount an offensive of his own — not to mention writing his sermons and attending to his ordinary duties (no doubt despite the chill in the parsonage) — that he took no notice whatsoever of the activities of his daughter, Elizabeth, her cousin, Abigail Williams, and some of the other girls of the parish, including Annie Putnam, Sgt. Thomas' daughter, and Mary Walcott, Annie Putnam's step-cousin, who were gathering in the house from time to time, as their parents came to consult with their pastor.

When Parris poked his nose out of the study he would see a group of them — sometimes a pair, sometimes more — gathered about his slave Tituba who seemed to be telling them stories. As often as not, John Indian would be hovering at the fringes of the circle of young people, busying himself about some small task, but listening intently nonetheless.

Parris was much too preoccupied to notice the girls' wide eyes, or to diagnose their silences as the effect of fascinated fright at what they were hearing. As for Mrs. Parris — she was only too glad to have the girls taken care of while she chatted with the wives of her husband's supporters. Sometimes the girls took care of themselves, talking quietly, if Tituba were busy elsewhere. Mrs. Samuel Parris had no way of knowing that they were talking of the Gloucester apparitions, of Mammy Reed of Marblehead, of Martha Sparks' arrest in Chelmsford, even of the locally legendary late Mother Goose about whom their mothers had often spoken in sober tones.

To accompany these stories of evil omen, some of the girls, in particular Annie Putnam and Mercy Lewis who lived with Annie's family, there were the bleak history lessons of Salem Village delivered in lectures at home by Goody Ann Putnam who recounted grievances she and hers had sustained in the town since she was a little girl living with her sister and brother-in-law, the Rev. and Mrs. James Bailey. Mrs. Putnam seemed to have the memory of an elephant when it came to such anecdotes, and the two girls were steeped in the lore of neighborhood misdemeanors and vendettas going back to times before they were born.

At services on Sunday, November 15th, Parris called for yet another meeting, to be held at Nathaniel Putnam's home at noon three days later, "to spend some time in prayer, and seeking God's presence with us, the next Lord's Day, at his table, as has been usual with us, some time before the Sacrament." The prayer meeting was held, and transformed into another political session when Parris addressed them on a topic close to his heart:

"Brethren," he said, "several church meetings have been occasionally warned, and sometimes the appearance of the brethren is but small to what it might be expected, and particularly was it so at the meeting that was called to be held on the tenth instant last. I do not desire to warn meetings unnecessarily, and, therefore, when I do, I pray you will regularly attend them.

"Furthermore," he continued, "I have scarce wood enough to burn till the morrow — Nathaniel Putnam rolled his eyes — and I pray that some care may be taken about it."

Those people who had attended, Parris himself had taken care, were his supporters. After his exhortation he proposed several points, all of which were unanimously voted:

"1. That it was needful that complaint should be made to the next honored County Court, to sit at Salem, the next third day of the week, against the neglects of the present committee.

"2. That the said complaint should be drawn up, which was immediately done by one of the brethren, and consented to.

"3. That our brethren, Nathaniel Putnam, Thomas Putnam, and Thomas Wilkins, should sign said complaint in behalf of the church.

"4. Last, that our brethren Captain John Putnam. and the two deacons, should be improved to present the said complaint to the court.

"In the mean time, I desire the brethren that care might be taken that I might not be destitute of wood."

It was winter. All Hallows Eve had come and gone, and Thanksgiving. Cotton Mather's *Memorable Providences* had become so popular that an edition had been published in London where Increase Mather continued to dicker with the King over a charter — it was Increase who had arranged to have the English edition of his son's book printed.

Priscilla Chub, thirty, had a thing or two on her mind to say to that young rakehell Abigail Hobbs, and at the first opportunity she chastised Abigail for her wicked carryings-on and disobedience to her parents. Abigail was derisive. "I care nothing what anybody says to me," she told Priscilla, "for I have seen the Devil and sealed a bargain with him."

Dread illness struck again, this time in Beverly, where it took the life of William Hoar and left Dorcas a widow. A grand jury was impaneled to investigate the strange death, and the men gathered at the Hoar home to view the corpse. Goodman Hoar's body was lying, garbed, on the bed when they were led into the room. One of the jurors, John Richards, turned to Goody Hoar and said, "It is necessary that the naked body of the deceased should be viewed."

Dorcas reacted passionately — she wrung her hands, stamped her feet on the floor, and cried, "You wicked wretches! What do you think — I have murdered my husband?"

As a matter of fact, some of the jurors recalled that, in 1668, Dorcas had prophesied that she would be better off after her husband had died. The jury chastised her for becoming so overwrought. They assured her that this was the normal proceeding. Finally, she was calmed down, and they got on with their business.

In England Richard Baxter published an important witchcraft book, *Certainty of the World of Spirits*. It supported all of the folklore, myths, superstitions and religious grounds traditional to the subject. It and Mather's book were anachronisms, for Baxter's contemporaries had been turning away from the issue of witchcraft in England, and no witches had been tried in a considerable length of time.

While the Rev. Mr. Samuel Parris was engaged with his lawsuit against the Salem Village Church and with his political intrigues during the winter, the number of girls who orbited Tituba grew and fluctuated. Besides the minister's daughter Elizabeth Parris, nine, there were her cousin Abigail Williams, eleven; Mary Walcott, sixteen, a near neighbor; Annie Putnam, twelve, Mary's step-cousin, and Mercy Lewis who often came with Annie Putnam inasmuch as she was a servant of Sgt. Thomas and Ann Carr Putnam. On occasion she also worked for Carolina John, and when Rev. George Burroughs had been the Salem Village minister, Mercy had lived in his family for a while, having no family of her own. Other neighbors of the Parrises were Susannah Sheldon, eighteen, and Elizabeth Booth, sixteen, both of whom had taken to dropping in and listening to Tituba's stories of phantasms and witchery. They were joined frequently by Elizabeth Hubbard, seventeen, the niece of Mrs. William Griggs, who lived with Dr. William Griggs' family as a servant; by another servant, Sarah Churchill, twenty, maid of George Jacobs, and Mary Warren, also twenty, maidservant of John and Elizabeth Proctor.

Tituba's influence, by January of 1692, had gone beyond mere storytelling. She had introduced the girls to some of the divinatory arts and to sympathetic magic. Tituba was a good teacher, for she gave her girls a thorough education in folklore. This, added to the fire and brimstone theology to which they all had been born, and that Mr. Parris reinforced twice each week from the pulpit, together with all the rumors and news of occult manifestations that were currently taking place in New England — such as those that had been laid out on the printed page by Cotton and Increase Mather of recent years in books that were easily available — wrought heavily on the girls' minds. When they secretly got together in twos and threes to experiment with scrying and fortunetelling, they had the exquisite knowledge that if their parents and employers knew what they were up to they would be horrified. On the other hand, the young people knew for a fact that there were many witches, both white and black, who had been practicing more or less openly in the community and the area for years without having incurred any real reprobation. The Gammer Glover case had been an exception, and anyway, she had been a Catholic.

Moreover, the girls knew that nearly everyone from time to time applied some sort of magic to situations where nothing else seemed to be of avail. Even the doctors used remedies that seemed not to be entirely medical when they came to treat a particularly difficult case, and when they were baffled they would as often as not shake their heads and excuse their lack of skill by saying, "There is an evil hand in it," or something suchlike. There was not one of the girls who had not been indoctrinated at an early age into the mysteries of the birth process, an event ringed around with superstition and presided over by the midwife, who was held in no little awe by the girls and the men of the villages particularly. The midwife was, to all intents and purposes, half priestess when she was practicing her calling, and she herself knew it. There was not one midwife anywhere who was not to some degree an herb-doctor, and an herb-doctor was one remove from the witch, if that much.

But what the girls did not foresee in their experiments was that some of the younger members of the juvenile coven might take things too seriously. These were delicious games they were playing when, though they didn't know the technical terms, they practiced onychomancy — scrying into their waxed or oiled fingernails; Bibliomancy, as Increase Mather himself, and even some of their parents did when they allowed the Bible to fall open of itself to prophetic passages; chiromancy — palmistry; or cosquinomancy, divining by means of a sieve balanced on a rod or pincers. Had they known these names, the sounds would only have added occult glamour to their practices.

The trouble was that Elizabeth Parris particularly was too impressionable. She was the minister's daughter, and she was much more aware than the others that what they were doing was truly sinful. She was filled with feelings of guilt and impending damnation, but she — like Rev. Hale's daughter Rebecca in 1678 when she feared the power of Goody Hoar — could say nothing to her father, for she would be ostracized by her friends. They would all get into terrible trouble, and Tituba the witch would take revenge upon her.

As the year got under weigh Edward Bishop, Bridget's husband, was required to answer a complaint before Judge John Hathorne. Bishop did not see fit to respond, and the constable was dispatched to the Bishop tavern to arrest him and bring him forcibly, if necessary, before the magistrate. Bishop was fined for his failure to answer a summons.

One day in January a neighbor burst into the home of John Bullock, thirty-six, and cried, "Mary Parker is lying outdoors upon the dirt and snow! If you do not take her in she will perish!"

As it happened, some of his Andover neighbors were visiting at the time, and he asked them to come out and help him get her, but when they reached the scene it seemed to them the woman was already dead. A crowd of people had gathered around, and one of them — another neighbor, Martha Dutch — told Bullock, "I have sometimes seen Goody Parker taken with this kind of fit before," so one of the men bent, lifted Mary Parker, and slung her over his shoulder. He turned to carry her inside, but he slipped on the ice and Mary fell off onto some stones — she did not react.

Everyone was sure that if she hadn't been dead before, she was now. The men picked her up, carried her corpse to her own house, and laid it on the bed. They began to remove her clothes to put her under the covers, but suddenly the dead woman sat up, opened her eyes, and laughed into their faces.

In Salem Village on January 25th, Deacon Edward and Mary Hale Putnam welcomed into the world their sixth child and second daughter, Prudence. Her name ought to have been a byword with the Villagers, but it was not, for one day early in February Betty Parris and her cousin Abigail Williams, who lived with the Parrises, decided to practice what was called — had they known it — oomancy.

This method of scrying was reputed to be one of the most effective possible ways of looking into the future. The girls took an egg and a pot of water; then, bending their heads over the lip, they cracked the egg and let its contents slowly ooze into the water. As the white and yolk slid into the pot the girls gazed at it to see what shapes and forms the egg would take, for these were the shapes of the future. What the girls saw set Betty Parris to screaming: In the water there was the silhouette of a coffin.

When Elizabeth's parents rushed into the room asking what had happened, they got no answer that made any sense. All they saw was a pot of water with an egg floating in it. Mrs. Parris took her daughter and tried to calm her down, but the little girl could not stop trembling and crying. Abigail was frightened speechless. Nothing the Parrises could do would calm Elizabeth, so Dr. Griggs was called in.

The good doctor was perplexed by the case. There was nothing physically wrong with either girl. Though he tried as best he could to tonic Betty into a calmer state over the next few days, his treatments were ineffective. At last he gave up and fell back on the old excuse for his ignorance: He diagnosed her ailment as caused by witchcraft, which indeed, for a change, it was.

Abigail was in little better shape. Though she did not tremble constantly like Betty, whenever she was asked what had happened to set her cousin off, Abigail began to kick and scream, partly to avoid having to answer and thereby getting into trouble, partly because the question reminded her of what she had seen in the pot.

The fantasmal infection began to spread. Other members of Tituba's club started to exhibit signs of "suffocation of the mother," and one of these was Mary Walcott whose aunt Mary, Samuel Sibley's wife, was a neighbor of the Parrises. Goody Sibley decided to take matters into her own hands, inasmuch as the doctors were doing no good. She approached John Indian and asked him to make a witch cake.

The method was simple: Take corn meal, mix it with the urine of the bewitched person, bake the cake before the fire and, when it was done, feed it to a dog which would take the spell into itself, thereby hurting the witch who cast the enchantment and freeing the afflicted person. Unfortunately for everyone concerned, by the time Mary Sibley attempted her white magic countercharm, Mr. Parris' antennae were deployed and vibrating sensitively. Mrs. Sibley and John Indian were caught. Under interrogation they broke down and told what they knew of what had been going on under Parris' very nose all winter. Pandora's box was opened.

An astonished and horrified Samuel Parris railed at a great rate in admonition of Mary, John and Tituba, but now he knew what his next step had to be. The ministers of the area — Higginson, Noyes, Hale, and others — assembled to witness the contortions of the girls. There was no doubt that Dr. Griggs had been correct. The clergymen prayed and fasted with Betty and her family, and Mr. Parris called for public and private fasting and prayers in his congregation. He began to do some research into the subject of diabolical possession, too, and the first book at which he looked was William Perkins' 1608 *Damnable Art of Witchcraft,* for he had a copy in his library. Mr. Hale and the other ministers had books as well — Cotton Mather's *Memorable Providences* was one, everyone had a copy of that; Mr. Hale owned Joseph Glanvill's *Saducismus Triumphatus,* and Increase Mather's *Illustrious Providences* was also on peoples' shelves, not to mention the witchcraft pamphlets of England, especially those of trials in which Sir Matthew Hale had been involved, including *A Trial of Witches.* Soon there was a considerable reference library on the subject passing from hand to hand in Salem Village, Salem, Beverly, Andover, and the other towns of the area.

On February 12th in Boston Cotton Mather celebrated his thirtieth birthday. He had begun to hear rumors of unusual occurrences taking place in Salem Village, and he took care to keep himself informed of the developments there. It sounded like the beginnings of another Goodwin Children case.

Mr. Parris and the other ministers began to preach admonitory and oracular sermons in the pulpits of their meetinghouses, and soon everyone in the entire area knew what was going on. The tormented girls suddenly found themselves to be celebrities: People crowded into their homes to witness for themselves the hand of the Devil at work.

No one knew who the witches were who were tormenting the girls, for no names had yet been mentioned by any of the young ladies, though Tituba had confessed to Parris that in Barbados her former mistress had taught her how to find a witch. She was, however, the prime suspect because of her original complicity in the situation, and on Thursday, February 25th, there was proof positive: Annie Putnam Putnam, Sgt. Thomas's daughter, cried out that she was being tortured by Tituba, Sarah Osburn, and another person whom she did not know. Elizabeth Hubbard screamed that her tormenter was the specter of Tituba.

Sarah Osburn's name surprised many people. She had been the wife of Robert Prince, a well-to-do man of a socially respectable family who, when he died young, left his widow with two children. Rebecca Prince Putnam, Capt. John's wife, had been sister-in-law to Sarah Osburn when she had been married to Sarah's brother. It had been expected that Sarah would remarry when Robert died, but when she did it scandalized the community.

The young Widow Prince had needed male help around her farm; for fifteen pounds she had bought from one of her neighbors the contract of an indentured servant, an Irishman named Alexander Osburn. When he had lived with and worked for the widow a while, she married him. She had been ostracized socially, and in retaliation she had taken to staying away from church-meeting. Though she was thus a reprobate, no one had ever accused her of practicing witchcraft before.

So there were three witches in town, two of them identified. Everyone wondered which of the multitude of likely suspects was the third, and on Saturday, February 27th, their curiosity was gratified, for Annie Putnam Putnam had another visit from the specter of the anonymous witch: She obligingly told the child her name was Sarah Goode, and she accompanied her self-incrimination with some pinches for good measure. That same day Betty Hubbard was visited by the phantom of Sarah Osburn who pinched the teenager most dreadfully.

If there were people in the community of Salem Village who had their doubts about the validity of these spectral sightings, they kept their own counsel — all but one. No sooner had he been apprised of the situation and seen the convulsive behavior of the girls than Joseph Putnam derided the whole business. He refused to have anything whatever to do with the mania into which his relatives and the rest of the town were falling, and at every opportunity he spoke his mind.

However, Joseph was no fool and when, to his incredulous amazement, he saw that things were getting serious, he withdrew himself completely from intercourse with his relatives and neighbors. Though Joseph had property in Salem itself, it soon became clear that even there people were becoming entrapped in the Devil's snare and he would do well to take his immediate family to live with his mother, Mary Veren Putnam, in the old family home east of Hathorne's Hill.

When the girls began to cry out on people, Joseph also realized he was to a degree vulnerable, though he had his defenses, for he was a Putnam, though outcaste, and his wife was the niece of Judge Hathorne of the Village. Nevertheless, he cut himself off completely from the outside world, not even visiting his Salem holdings. He and his family carried guns at all times, and he kept horses constantly saddled in the barn in case he should need them at a moment's notice. Everyone knew the situation and avoided mentioning his name as the specters multiplied in the New England countryside.

On Sunday, February 28th, before they went to meeting to be edified by the doom and damnation sermon of Mr. Parris, Joseph Hutchinson,

Sgt. Thomas Putnam, Jr., Deacon Edward Putnam, and Thomas Preston filed complaints of witchcraft against Sarah Goode, Sarah Osburn, and Tituba Indian. Elizabeth Hubbard was again tormented, this time by Sarah Goode.

The next day — February 29th, as 1692 was a leap year — warrants were issued for the arrest of the three women for their tormenting of Betty Parris, Abby Williams, Annie Putnam, and Betty Hubbard. The witches were arrested and given a body search for witch teats. After the search committee, composed of women, made its report, William Goode saw something — a wart or a teat — a little below the right shoulder of his wife. He had never noticed it before, so he asked Goody Ingersoll whether she hadn't seen it when Sarah was inspected by the women. The witches were booked for a preliminary examination before Magistrates John Hathorne and Jonathan Corwin on the morrow. Meanwhile, the apparition of Sarah Osburn visited Mercy Lewis; the witch wanted the nineteen-year-old to sign the Devil's Black Book.

On the morning of March 1st Giles Corey rose from his bed, had his breakfast, and prepared to go into town to see the examination. Martha Corey had more sense. She told her husband to stay as far away as ever he could from that business, but Corey simply snorted and saddled his horse. Martha, her voice rising higher and higher, expostulated with him and then, when he had gone back into the house after something, she undid the cinch and slid the saddle off Giles' mount. When he saw what his wife had done the old man was greatly irritated. He swore at her, put the saddle back on, and rode off down the path.

Corey thought he was going to be late, but when he arrived at Ingersoll's tavern, where the inquisition was scheduled to be held, he found that the magistrates were moving the proceedings to the meetinghouse to accommodate more people. At last things were arranged; Corey found a spot from which he could see what was going on — there were folks hanging in at the windows, crushed together inside, mobbing the stairs. Corey mused that it had taken the Devil to fill up the meetinghouse so.

Rev. Mr. Samuel Parris began with public prayer, then Constable George Locker brought Sarah Goode forward, and Marshal George Herrick brought in the other two women, elbowing his way to the front of the room. The judges were seated on a platform behind a table, and Locker helped Goody Goode up onto another table so that she would be visible to everyone in the room. The tormented girls were placed between the judges' bench and the witness stand. As soon as the witches appeared, the afflicted persons went into tremendous public agonies. Eventually things quieted down enough so that the constables could report that searches had been made of the homes of the accused, but that no poppits or other occult paraphernalia had been uncovered.

Judge John Hathorne read the charges accusing Sarah Goode of having afflicted the children and — a surprise — Goody Sarah Bibber, wife of John Bibber of Wenham. People murmured among themselves about it and craned their necks to see who this outsider was. No one knew how she had gotten involved. As the questioning got underway it became apparent that Magistrate Jonathan Corwin was going to be nothing more than Hathorne's silent partner. He took notes while Hathorne put the questions.

"Sarah Goode," Hathorne asked, "What evil spirit have you familiarity with?" From the very first it was apparent to everyone in the room that the judge was going to act as devil's advocate and not as an impartial observer.

Sarah Goode faced the judge and replied, "None."

"Have you made no contract with the Devil?"

"No."

"Why do you hurt these children?"

The girls were the main spectacle at the examination. They writhed about on the floor kicking and screaming that the witch was pinching and tormenting them. The greatest spectacle among them, though, was Goody Bibber, a grown woman, who was thrashing about with the best of them. No one present could imagine a person acting so unless they were terribly ill or afflicted by the Devil. It just wasn't otherwise conceivable — an amazing experience for everyone. No wonder Hathorne had no doubt of the women's guilt.

"I do not hurt them," Goody Goode replied. "I scorn it." The audience looked at one another in wonder. She must be guilty — how could she remain unaffected by the obvious tortures of the afflicted persons? Just look at how they tumbled!

"Who do you employ, then, to do it?"

Sarah Goode snorted. "I employ no body."

Hathrone was growing impatient. "What *creature* do you employ, then?"

"No creature, but I am falsely accused."

"Look upon the children," Hathorne told her. She did so and they went into convulsions screaming, "It is Goody Goode! Oh! Oh! She pinches! She hurts!"

"How came they to be thus tormented?" Hathorne asked the witch.

"What do I know? You bring others here, and now you charge me with it."

"Why, who was it?"

"I do not know but that it was some you brought into the meeting house with you."

"We brought you into the meeting house."

"But you brought in two more." Evidently Goody Goode had not been unaffected after all. She was merely certain that *she* hadn't hurt the children — she scorned to do it. If it were not she, then it may have been the others who had been named.

"Who was it then that tormented the children?"

She hesitated, and then committed a fatal mistake. She tacitly admitted she knew who was doing it, and that made her complicity in the witchcraft plain — "It was Osburn," she said. There was no turning back now that she was committed to something other than simple denial. Her manner to this point had been hostile, but now a note of whining began to enter her voice, and she was on the defensive.

"What is it you say when you go muttering away from peoples' houses?" Hathorne asked her.

Now the pipe-smoking old vagrant added perjury to her testimony, but she had some idea of the possible consequences, for she put it off a moment. She said, "If I must tell, I will tell."

"Do tell us then," Hathorne urged impatiently.

"If I must tell, I will tell — it is the Commandments. I may say my Commandment, I hope?"

"What Commandment is it?"

Now, truly, she was on the hook and she knew it. Hathorne's technique of "quick and cross questions," which was right out of Michael Dalton's *Country Justice*, Richard Bernard's *Guide to Grandjurymen*, and Sir Matthew Hale's Bury St. Edmunds trials of 1662, as set forth in the pamphlet published in 1682.

"If I must tell, I will tell," Sarah Goode repeated, "It is a psalm."

Hathorne was inexorable. "What Psalm?"

Goody Goode's mind raced as she tried to think of something, then finally she mumbled something that sounded like part of a psalm and Hathorne turned to her husband in the audience. "Why did you say of your wife that you were afraid that she either was a witch or would be one quickly?"

William Goode was startled. Evidently one could say nothing whatever any more without its being poured into the wrong ears. "Have you ever seen anything by her?" John Hathorne continued.

"No," Goodman Goode answered, "not in this nature, but it was her bad carriage to me, and indeed, I may say with tears that she is an enemy to all good." And with that Sarah Goode's doom was sealed, for not even her husband would stand by her.

Sarah Osburn was the next to be examined. She was led forward and a repetition of Sarah Goode's examination took place. The bewitched persons fell to fits after accusing her of hurting them, but she denied she had any hand in it. Then she introduced a major issue into the proceedings. "Perhaps the Devil goes about in my likeness," she said.

The ministers present — and there were several of them — understood that this was a crucial statement. The question, much debated, was, "Can the Devil appear in the likeness of a person without that person's specific agreement?" If the answer to that were *no*, then spectral evidence, such as that which the girls were giving, was admissible as proof of guilt; if the answer were *yes*, then spectral evidence was useless. The Devil could appear in the shape of King William if he wished, or Cotton Mather, for that matter, though there must be *some* limit to his power.

Sarah Osburn continued to maintain her innocence, but she, too, made a fatal mistake, out of fear.

"What familiarity have you with Sarah Goode?" Hathorne asked. Knowing Sarah Goode's reputation, and suspecting where Hathorne might go, "None," Goody Osburn lied, but noticing Hathorne's sharpened glance, added, "I have not seen her these two years."

"Where did you see her then?"

"One day a-going to town."

"What communications had you with her?"

"I had none, only, 'How do you do?' or so. I did not know her by name."

Hathorne saw his opening. "What did you call her, then?"

She hesitated, saw her mistake too late, could think of no way out of her own trap, and gave up. "I called her Sarah," she said limply.

Hathorne pounced. "Sarah Goode saith that it was you that hurt the children." Goody Goode was a convicted witch already, to his mind, though no trial had yet been held, and her accusation was thus that of a conspirator.

Goody Osburn fell back on the defense that had already, so quickly, been eroded. "I do not know but that the Devil goes about in my likeness to do hurt."

Hathorne would test that. He asked the children to stand up and face the witch. Could they identify this specific woman as the one whose specter afflicted them? "Yes," they said unanimously, this was one of the women, down to every item in her dress. The children in the morning, before the examination, had been taken to see Mrs. Osburn in her cell, and when they had fallen into their contortions she had told them, "I am more like to *be* bewitched, than that I *am* a witch."

Hathorne asked her why she had said that.

"I was frighted one time in my sleep," she said, "and either saw, or dreamed that I saw, a thing like an Indian, all black, which did prick me in my neck and pull me by the back part of my head to the door of the house."

"Did you ever see anything else?"

"No," she said, but she was contradicted by voices out of the audience. One spectator called, "She said once that she 'would never be tied to that lying spirit any more.'"

Hathorne turned again to Goody Osburn. "What lying spirit is this?" he asked. "Hath the Devil ever deceived you and been false to you?"

"I do not know the Devil. I never did see him."

"What lying spirit was it, then?"

"It was a voice that I thought I heard." A murmur swept the crowd.

"What did it propound to you?"

"That I should go no more to meeting, but I said I would, and did go the next Sabbath Day."

"Were you ever tempted further?"

"No," she said, but again she was contradicted out of the audience: It was her husband's voice that called, "She has not been to meeting for a year and two months."

Goody Osburn's head snapped around angrily in Alexander Osburn's direction, and then her eyes began to fill with despair. The audience was full of prosecutors who were allowed to speak, and she had not even one defender, nor could count on the man who shared her life and estate.

"Why," John Hathorne asked, "did you yield thus far to the Devil as never to go to meeting since?"

"Alas!" she cried, "I have been sick and not able to go." Would that she had it to do over again.

Before Tituba ever came to her examination there was abundant evidence against her, and she knew it — for one thing, witch teats had been found during her body search; for another, she had told Samuel Parris, "My mistress in my own country was a witch, and she taught me how to find a witch — but *I* am not a witch." Her master had without doubt told the magistrates everything she had said, and they would be prepared for her. Tituba's only hope was to turn prosecution's witness, which is what she did.

Judge John Hathorne's preliminary questions had turned into a ritual litany already. When he asked her if she hurt the children or had familiar spirits she replied in the negative. "Who was it, then, that hurt them?" Hathorne asked Tituba.

"The Devil, for aught I know," she replied.

"Did you ever see the Devil?"

"The Devil came to me," Tituba said — a gasp went through the meetinghouse — "and bade me serve him."

"Who have you seen?"

"Four women sometimes hurt the children."

"Who were they?"

"Goody Osburn and Sarah Goode, and I do not know who the others were. Sarah Goode and Osburn would have me hurt the children, but I would not, and there was a tall man of Boston that I did see."

"When did you see them?"

"Last night at Boston."

Although Hathorne knew that Tituba could not have been in Boston the night before, he asked her nevertheless, "What did they say to you?"

"They said, 'Hurt the children.'"

"And did you hurt them?"

"No!" Tituba was emphatic. "There is four women and one man — *they* hurt the children, and they lay all upon me, and they tell me if I will not hurt the children, they will hurt me."

"But did you not hurt them?" They writhed on the floor.

Hathorne won at last — "Yes," Tituba replied, "But I will hurt them no more."

"Are not you sorry you did hurt them?"

"Yes," she said contritely.

"And why, then, do you hurt them?"

"They say, 'Hurt the children or we will do worse to you.'"

"Who have you seen?"

"A man come to me and say, 'Serve me.'"

"What service?"

"Hurt the children! And last night there was an appearance that said, 'Kill the children,' and if I would not go on hurting the children they would do worse to me."

"What is this appearance you see?"

"Sometimes it is like a hog, and sometimes like a great dog — I did see it four times."

"What did it say to you?"

"It...the black dog said, 'Serve me,' but I said, 'I am afraid.' He said if I did not, he would do worse to me."

"What did you say to it?" Hathorne was not used to confessions yet, and he was being redundant. Tituba answered at length, however, amplifying her earlier remarks:

"'I will serve you no longer.' Then he said he would hurt me, and then he looked like a man and threatens to hurt me. He had a yellow bird that kept with him, and he told me he had more pretty things that he would give me if I would serve him."

"What were these pretty things?"

"He did not show me them."

"What also have you seen?"

"Two rats — a red rat and a black rat."

"What did they say to you?"

"They said, 'Serve me.'"

"When did you see them?"

"Last night, and they said, 'Serve me,' but I said I would not."

"What service?"

"Hurt the children."

"Did not you pinch Elizabeth Hubbard this morning?"

"The man brought her to me and made me pinch her."

"Why did you go to Thomas Putnam's last night and hurt his child?"

"They pull me and haul me and make me go."

"And what would they have you do?"

"Kill her with a knife." The audience drew in its breath.

Rebecca Putnam Fuller's father-in-law, Lt. Thomas Fuller, said from the spectators, "When the child saw these persons and was tormented by them, she did complain of a knife — that they would have her cut off her head with a knife."

Others who had been at the Putnam home the evening before and seen Annie Putnam in one of her fits affirmed that what Fuller said was true. Hathorne nodded — it was just as he had suspected, but here was confirming testimony that spectral evidence was valid, for Tituba had been in jail at the time, and there had been no chance for collusion. He forgot that, before the examination that very morning, the children had been with the prisoners.

"How did you go?" Hathorne asked the woman.

"We ride upon sticks and are there presently."

Hathorne clarified his question: "*How* did you go — what did you ride upon?"

"I ride upon a stick or pole, and Goode and Osburn behind me; we ride taking hold of one another. Don't know how we go, for I saw no trees nor path, but was presently there when we were up."

"Why did you not tell your master?"

"I was afraid. They said they would cut off my head if I told."

"Would not you have hurt others if you could?"

"They said they would hurt others, but they could not." And with that sentence Tituba nailed down the defense against another argument, for if one were to ask, "Why should a witch be able to hurt one person but not another?" the answer would be, "A witch may only hurt by God's permission, and then hurt only those people whom God has allowed the witch to harm."

"What attendants hath Sarah Goode?"

"A yellow bird — and she would have given me one."

From the gallery another voice interrupted. Little Dorcas Goode called, "My mother has three birds, one black, one yellow, and the birds hurt the children!"

Judge Jonathan Corwin and Ezekiel Cheever, who was acting as court recorder, took a note, and Hathorne went on. "What meat did she give it?" he asked.

"It did suck between her fingers."

"Did not you hurt Mr. Corwin's child?" Judge Jonathan Corwin glanced sharply at Tituba as she gave her answer. It was satisfactory:

"Goody Goode and Goody Osburn told that they did hurt Mr. Corwin's child, and would have had me hurt him, too, but I did not."

"What hath Sarah Osburn?"

"Yellow dog, and she had a thing with a head like a woman with two legs and wings, and it turns into a woman. Abigail Williams, that lives with her Uncle Parris, said that she did see the same creature, and it turned into the shape of Goody Osburn."

"What else have you seen with Osburn?"

"A thing all over hairy — all the face hairy — and a long nose, and I don't know how to tell how the face looks; is about two or three foot high, and goeth upright like a man — it hath only two legs — and last night it stood before the fire in Mr. Parris' hall." A babble went up from the spectators at the gruesome description. Hathorne rapped his hand on the bable for silence.

"Did not you see Sarah Goode upon Elizabeth Hubbard last Saturday?" It was a leading question; it was clear that, like a prosecuting attorney, he had most of the facts before ever he got into court. And, of course, since lawyers were not allowed to practice in Massachusetts Bay, he *was* prosecuting attorney *and* judge, and each defendant had to be his or her own defense, so they were at a huge disadvantage.

Tituba replied, "I did see her set a wolf upon her to afflict her." There was a spate of confirmations from the courtroom. She continued, "I saw a cat with Goode another time."

"What clothes doth the man go in?"

"In black clothes sometimes, sometimes serge coat of another color. A tall man with white hair, I think." Tituba was beginning to tire.

"How doth the woman go?"

"One had a black silk hood, with a white silk hood under, with a topknot, and another wore a serge coat with a white cap."

"Do you see who it is that torments these children now?" For the girls had commenced falling to fits once more.

"Yes, it is Goody Goode — she hurts them in her own shape."

"And who is it that hurts them now?" for the fits had changed their character even as she spoke.

Tituba replied, "I am blind now. I cannot see."

The court gave Marshal George Herrick custody of Sarah Goode and ordered him to deliver her to Ipswich jail. Other arrangements had been made for Tituba and Sarah Osburn. Herrick took Goody Goode home to his house and set a guard over her for the night.

Later in the evening, when William Allen and John Hughes were on their way home from Ingersoll's Ordinary — where all the men had gathered after the trial to drink beer and talk about what had happened — they saw a strange beast that vanished into the shadows beside the path. When the men screwed up their courage to approach the spot, three women rose up out of the brush and ran away. Though it was pitch dark, Allen and Hughes had no doubt who they were and, like their neighbors far and wide, they resolved to make a deposition in the case that told the story of this staggering experience.

In the morning, when George Herrick got up and went to check on his prisoner, the men who had been guarding Sarah Goode reported that she had been gone — barefoot and barelegged — for some time during the night. Herrick was quite angry, but at last his prisoner was intact and recaptured. She was ordered to get ready to go to Ipswich, for she was not to be examined again that day, though Tituba and Goody Osburn were.

Samuel Braybrook had been assigned the job of delivering Sarah to Ipswich jail; he found the task almost more than he could handle. She swore and railed at him constantly. Thrice she jumped off her horse and tried to run away or refused to remount. She said to Braybrook, "I would not own myself to be a witch unless it were a proud one. There is but one evidence of it, and that an Indian; therefore, I fear not." Fortunately for Braybrook her actions had made him as wary as a cat, and he was able to foil the witch when she attempted to commit suicide en route.

Meanwhile, Tituba and Sarah Osburn were being examined again in Salem Village. Their testimony added nothing substantially new to the case: Tituba reaffirmed her confession and her accusation of the other two women; Sarah Osburn simply fell back on denials. The court tried the test of the witch's touch on the afflicted girls and Sarah Bibber — it was effective.

At eight that evening, as he was coming from Samuel Sibley's house — Sibley was husband of Mary Sibley who had requested the witch cake, and the uncle of Mary Walcott — John Hughes saw a great white dog following him. Frightened, he got to his home without incident, but when he was in bed, in a locked room, a great light appeared, and he saw a large gray cat at the foot of the bed. William Allen, at his place, had a more direct experience: He saw Sarah Goode in his bedroom.

By the time George Herrick got to bed he had been admonished by the court for his lapse of vigilance and informed that, during the days of her examination, Sarah Goode was to be brought back and forth the ten miles each way from and to Ipswich jail, and never allowed to remain in town overnight. He was told also that during Tuesday night Elizabeth Hubbard had been hurt by Sarah Goode who appeared to her barefoot and barelegged. Fortunately, Samuel Sibley had been watching Elizabeth that night, and he had struck out at Goody Goode's specter — Herrick's wife told him that, indeed, she had noticed that Sarah Goode had a wound on her arm before she left for Ipswich. It had been a bad day for the marshal. He resolved to do better.

On Wednesday Tituba and Sarah Osburn were once more examined. The next day, Thursday Lecture Day, Annie Putnam was tormented in the meetinghouse, at services, by two people, one of whom was a woman she didn't know, but she could identify the other person: It was Sarah Goode's five-year-old daughter, Dorcas.

On Saturday, March 5th, Tituba and Sarah Goode underwent examination once more, and there was a birth in the Putnam family: Carolina John Putnam and Hannah Putnam welcomed a daughter, Sarah, to the fold — their thirteenth child, born prematurely, only seven months after the twins. On Sunday her cousin Annie Putnam was again pinched most mortally by the woman who had afflicted her at meeting on the third, only this time she was able to identify her tormenter: It was Elizabeth Proctor.

The three original witches on Monday the 7th were sent to Boston Jail to wait for trial. There was a lapse of four days while the Salem Villagers took a spell to absorb what had happened and to make trips to the homes of the afflicted girls to witness for themselves the trials the creatures were put to.

Friday the 11th of March was to be a solemn day of prayer and fasting in the community, and Mr. Samuel Parris invited the ministers of Essex County to meet in his home that day to observe the ritual and the girls, who were also to be present. The clergymen duly assembled and there, between and during prayers, they observed the girls' fits. Annie Putnam added a highlight to the affair by accusing Martha Corey of torturing her most grievously. When they heard of it, some of the town wits wondered aloud how it came about that it was Martha, and not her husband Giles, who had been accused.

On the morning of Saturday, March 12, Sarah Putnam, the newly born daughter of Carolina John and Hannah Cutler Putnam was baptized at the Salem Village meetinghouse. Deacon Edward Putnam and Ezekiel Cheever attended the ritual; afterward, at 10:00 a.m., they fell to talking at Ingersoll's Ordinary about Annie Putnam's accusation of Martha Corey. They knew that Joseph Putnam derided the whole thing, and they thought it were best to attempt a test to see whether Annie's visions were credible. Edward and Ezekiel agreed to meet in the afternoon at Sgt. Thomas Putnam's house, there to request Annie Putnam, while she was being tormented, to take good notice of what Martha Corey was wearing so that they could compare the specter's dress with the living person's actual apparel, "so we might see whether she was not mistaken." This was important, for Annie Putnam had cried out on a member of the church; further, it was a test of spectral evidence *per se*.

At the appointed time Edward and Ezekiel met at Sgt. Thomas' house. When they had made known to Annie Putnam what they intended, the girl told them that Goody Corey had come and blinded her and said, "My name is Goody Corey. You shall see no more before it is night, because you should not tell what clothes I have on. Then I will come and pay you off."

To an objective observer it would have been clear that Annie Putnam had been tipped-off about the impending test. Although the men's plans had been torpedoed, they went to the Corey farm anyway, to salvage what they could of the experiment and to find what the accused witch had to say about the blinding. The speed of communication in the Village was also blinding, for when they arrived in the late afternoon Goody Corey said, "I know what you are come for — you are come to talk with me about being a witch, but I am none. I cannot help peoples' talking of me." She knew that her husband had been telling the story of how she had tried to stop him from going to the first day's examination, and that her taking the saddle off his horse had rendered her vulnerable to suspicion.

Edward Putnam replied, "It is the afflicted person that did complain of you that was the occasion of our coming here."

Then Goody Corey astonished the men. "But does she tell you what clothes I have on?" They should not, under ordinary circumstances, have been surprised, for that morning after the baptism others had heard Edward and Ezekiel laying out their plan over beer at Ingersoll's, and there had been ample time for word to get back to the Coreys. Goody Corey had taken good care to change her clothes to something unusual before the experimenters arrived.

The men did not reply; Martha asked again, eagerly, "But does she tell you what clothes I have on?" Ezekiel and Edward were thinking about what Annie Putnam had told them just before they went to Martha.

"No, she did not," they replied at last, "for she told us that you came and blinded her and told her that she should see you no more before it was night, that so she might not tell us what clothes you had on."

Martha found this to be ironic, and she murmured something with a smile on her lips. But the men misread her response. Perhaps Martha herself did not realize at that moment what her eager question might mean under the circumstances.

Edward and Ezekiel began to discuss the witchcraft phenomena of the Village, but Martha was interested only, it seemed, in stopping the gossip about her. She made another blunder. "I do not think," she said, "that there are any witches." Her remark was equivalent to a confession of atheism, in itself a capital offense, and it had been a member of the church who said such a thing!

The two men immediately contradicted her — they told her they were satisfied that the first three who had been accused were indeed witches.

"If they are," Martha said, showing her own brand of the Christian charity that was sweeping the town, "we cannot blame the Devil for making witches of them, for they are idle, slothful persons and mind nothing that is good. But you have no reason to think so of me, for I have made a profession of Christ and rejoice to go and hear the word of God."

Deacon Putnam had his answer ready to demolish that defense. He replied, "It is not your making an outward profession that will clear you from being a witch, for it has often been so in the world that witches have crept into the churches."

Martha was shattered by the evaporation of all her arguments and ploys, and she began to understand what all of this that had taken place during the interrogation might mean. She fell into despair — and sealed her doom. "The Devil is come down amongst us in a great rage!" she cried. "God has forsaken the world!"

Ezekiel Cheever and Deacon Edward returned to Sgt. Thomas' house to find that, true to her word, the shape of Goody Corey had not bothered Annie Putnam all afternoon. It was enough. They prepared to write their deposition to the court. That night Martha Corey's specter greatly afflicted Annie Putnam, and the next day she was tortured by a woman she knew only by sight — it was discovered to be Rebecca Nurse, whom she had seen in church meeting that very day.

When word got out into the community about this new revelation, the entire village was horrified. Mrs. Nurse was highly regarded as a good and compassionate woman. The loyalty of her family was absolute, and they were outraged, for they had known her only as the best wife, mother, aunt and grandmother that anyone had ever had.

By the middle of March one of the possessed girls had been removed from the field of action by her father. Rev. Samuel Parris had sent his daughter Betty to live in Salem with the family of Stephen Sewall. She continued to be "distracted" and to act like the other possessed girls, but the Sewalls kept her well under cover while the Devil stalked rampant through Salem Village. There were plenty of replacements; people hardly thought about or missed her.

The new witch Elizabeth Proctor tormented Abigail Williams on March 14th. Deacon Edward Putnam and Ezekiel Cheever that same day planned an extension of their experiment when they arranged to have Mrs. Corey come to the Sgt. Thomas Putnam, Jr. home for a further test — no sooner had she walked into the room where Annie Putnam was than the girl had a convulsion and accused the old woman. She was cured by the witch's touch.

It was time for concerted effort. After the experiment Sgt. Thomas, Deacon Edward, Carolina John — who had been appointed a deputy constable of Salem Village —, Ezekiel Cheever, and others organized the Committee of Vigilance, the purpose of which was to seek out the witches in town methodically, for by this time it was obvious that there were many. The vigilantes, using the bewitched girls, would operate in much the same way that Matthew Hopkins, the Witch-Finder General of England, had worked.

The next day Abigail Williams saw the shape of Rebecca Nurse, which tormented her. Encounters were breaking out all over town, and irreparable divisions were occurring among the people. One day a family would be saying that it was high time these witches were found out, and the next, to their astonishment and horror, one of their own members would stand accused. It was difficult to make about-faces under the circumstances; all people could do was to admit there were witches, indeed, but one's own mother or aunt could not be one of them. However, it was the possessed girls who had the final say, and the infection was spreading to other communities.

Alan Toothaker found himself confronted by Richard Carrier in Andover on March 15th. Carrier stuck out his chin and asked him if it were true what he had heard — that Toothaker was going about saying that his mother was a witch. Toothaker didn't deny it, and the young men fought. Carrier pulled Toothaker to the ground by his hair and pinned him there.

Allen cried, "Let me rise!" Richard let him up so that the action could continue. Toothaker stumbled to his feet, took a great swing, missed, and fell flat on his back. Carrier pounced on him and held him down. Toothaker rasped, "I yield. You are best man." At that moment, he told folks afterward, he saw the specter of Martha Carrier, not Richard, sitting on his chest, but when he got up the witch had disappeared. It had not been a fair fight.

On Wednesday, March 16th, Rebecca Nurse again tormented Abigail Williams. The good old witch tempted the innocent girl to jump into the fire in the hearth and to sign the Devil's Book. Having heard all over town that Rebecca was about to be accused of witchcraft formally, Israel Porter and Elizabeth Hathorne Porter, who was Judge John Hathorne's sister and the mother-in-law of the arch-rebel Joseph Putnam, went with Daniel Andrews and Peter Cloyse to see the old woman and warn her. When they arrived at the Nurses' homestead they found Rebecca ill in bed. They told her how sorry they were to see her so and asked her how long she had been ailing.

"About a week now," she replied.

"How is it otherwise with you?"

"I bless God for it," Rebecca said. "I have more of His presence in this sickness than sometimes I have had, but not so much as I desire. But I will, with the Apostle, press forward to the mark." She began to speak of the current afflictions of the Village, and particularly of those of the Parris household. "How I grieve for them," she told her visitors, "though I have not been to see them for that I had formerly some fits, which folk said were terrible to behold. But I pity them with all my heart, and go to God for them."

Rebecca did not remember her fits, for she, unlike the girls — except for Elizabeth Parris — had been truly delirious. She had run a high temperature, had had convulsions, had seen visions of God and his angels; but now, "after about a week," or a little more — perhaps a day or two since the first symptoms of the disease — she had passed the crisis and was beginning to recover. "But I hear," the sick woman went on, "that there are persons spoke of that are as innocent as I."

Her visitors told her, "It is a heavy thing to say, but you are one of those," for news of Rebecca Nurse's convulsions and visions had reached the ears of the girls. Since she was not one of them, because she had had Satan's scourge, Rebecca Nurse must perforce be a member of the Salem Village coven.

"I?" Rebecca asked, astonished. "Well, if it be so, the will of the Lord be done." She lay still, stunned, for a while. Then, "Well, as to this thing, I am as innocent as the child unborn. But surely, what sin hath God found out in me, unrepented of, that He should lay such an affliction upon me in my old age?"

Giles Corey fetched one of his oxen out of the woods on Thursday "about noon," as he told his neighbors, all of whom were swapping portentous stories but not necessarily, like Giles, about their own wives and relatives. The ox, "lying down in the yard," Giles said, "I went to raise him to yoke him, but he could not rise but dragged his hinder parts as if he had been hipshot, but after did rise." This was the second strange occurrence concerning animals to take place that week on the Corey farm, for, Giles said, "I had a cat strangely taken on the sudden, and did make me think she would have died. Presently my wife bade me knock her in the head, but I did not, and since, the cat is well!"

The next day there was a new possessed person in Salem Village. Goodwife Ann Carr Putnam lay down in midafternoon to take a nap, exhausted by the fits of her daughter Annie and Mercy Lewis. Immediately she was "almost pressed and choked to death" — it was the specter of Martha Corey who wanted her to sign a red book with a black pen.

Mrs. Putnam was again visited by the specter of Martha Corey on Saturday, but the witch had a companion in this visit — Rebecca Nurse. Ann was fearfully tormented, greatly to the dismay of the Sergeant, his family and friends. Henry Kenny and Sgt. Thomas swore out a warrant for the arrest of Goody Corey for her phantom's abuse of Mrs. Putnam,

Annie Putnam, and Mercy Lewis — all members of Thomas' household — and for afflicting as well Abby Williams — Parris' niece — and Betty Hubbard, Dr. William Griggs' maidservant. Even at the moment they were making their complaint before the magistrates Abigail was crying out on Rebecca Nurse again.

The Rev. Mr. Deodat Lawson arrived back in Salem Village that afternoon and lodged at Ingersoll's inn. He had been invited back to town by Mr. Parris to preach a guest sermon to his old parishioners, but when he had settled into his room he discovered that there were perhaps ulterior motives for folks' calling him back to the scene of his former religious afflictions: He was told that the bewitched girls had been saying in some of their fits that a witch or witches unknown had murdered his wife and daughter, both of whom were buried in a local cemetery. He went immediately to visit the home of Samuel Parris.

There, he found Abby Williams in the midst of a fit: She ran into the fireplace — as though to fly up the chimney — scattering firebrands about the house; the assembly quickly stamped out the sparks. It was an extraordinary sight. At Ingersoll's that evening Lawson saw another demonstration of the power of Satan, for Mary Walcott was present. She was bitten on the wrist by invisible teeth, but the toothmarks were not invisible: Lawson saw them with his own eyes.

Though a warrant had been sworn out for her arrest that day, in the evening Martha Corey was still free and at home with her husband. They were sitting by the fire when Matha said, "Let us go to bed."

Giles replied, "I would go to prayer first." He did so, but his mind was so befuddled that, as he phrased it, "I could not utter my desires with any sense, nor open my mouth to speak."

Martha noticed Giles' condition and said, "I am coming to you," which she did. Oddly, after she had laid hands upon him, Giles found that he could pray again. It was a suspicious circumstance, particularly in view of the fact that, as he told people next day, "Another time, going to duties, I was linterrupted for a space, but afterward I was helped according to my poor measure. My wife hath been wont to set up after

I went to bed, and I have perceived her to kneel down on the hearth as if she were at prayer, but heard nothing."

Rev. Lawson went next door to the meetinghouse the following morning to conduct the service, but he had never stepped into a church scene like this one. Several of the bewitched girls were present, and they were being tormented in the very House of the Lord, as were two matrons — Sarah Bibber and Gertrude Pope. Martha Corey was present in the assembly. It was an appalling and an humbling experience. Things calmed down, however, when the congregation rose to sing the psalm, but as soon as they were done, and before Mr. Lawson could step forward to the pulpit, Abby Williams cried out, "Now read your text!" Lawson kept his public composure and read. When he was finished Abigail called once more, "It's a long text!"

Mrs. Pope interrupted Lawson's sermon early to call out at him, "Now, there is enough of that!" But he managed to go on at length.

At the afternoon service Mr. Lawson had reference to his morning text, and again Abby broke in. "I know of no doctrine you had! If you did name one, I have forgotten it." Everyone present was made uncomfortable by the outbursts, but Lawson put the best face on it that he could, and people said he had done himself credit. Later on Mary Walcott saw the shape of Rebecca Nurse, and so did Elizabeth Hubbard, but the specter hurt neither of them. Abigail Williams was, however, tormented by Goody Nurse for the fourth time.

Samuel Barton, twenty-eight, and John Houghton, twenty-three, went to Sgt. Thomas' house to attend upon the afflicted there — such visits were now no longer made merely out of curiosity; they were a form of insurance. While they were there the men were witnesses to a curious argument that took place between Mrs. Putnam and Mercy Lewis. Ann said, "Mercy, you cried out on Goody Proctor in your fit."

"I did not cry out of Goody Proctor," the girl replied warmly, "Nor nobody. I did say, 'There she is!' but did not tell you who."

Thomas broke in to correct her. "You cried out of Goody Proctor," he said.

"Yes, you did," Goody Putnam confirmed.

"Well, if I did, it was when I was out of my head," Mercy told them, "for I saw nobody."

Mrs. Putnam had very few fits that day, for her time had been too broken up with services, with arguments with Mercy, and so forth and so on. In many ways it was truly a day of rest. The morrow would be a busy day, though, for Martha Corey was to be examined.

On Monday morning at the meetinghouse the Rev. Mr. Nicholas Noyes began with prayer. Deodat Lawson was present as well, in a good seat to the fore of the room with other preachers. George Herrick brought in Goody Corey, and the girls fell to fits, accusing her of afflicting them.

Mr. Hathorne looked at Goody Corey. "You are now in the hands of authority. Tell me, now, why do you hurt these persons?"

"I do not," Martha said.

"Who doth?"

"Pray, give me leave to go to prayer."

"We do not send for you to go to prayer; but tell me why you hurt these?"

"I am an innocent person. I never had to do with witchcraft since I was born. I am a gospel woman."

"Do not you see these complain of you?" The children continued to have fits. Martha was nibbling at her nails and fidgeting, and whatever movement she made had its effect on the bewitched persons. It began to appear that, unwittingly, Martha Corey was introducing something new into witchcraft — or the girls were introducing it: So far no witch dolls or "poppits" had been discovered in the house searches of the accused witches. Now, at Martha Corey's examinations, it began to be seen that this particular coven had no need of such contrivances, for they were using their own bodies as "images" of the girls. If Martha bit her lip, Annie Putnam was bitten; if she pinched her hands, Mercy Lewis was pinched until Herrick held Martha's hands still; if the witch stamped her foot, Goody Gertrude Pope — now a full-fledged Afflicted Person — gasped as though she were being trodden upon.

Goody Corey replied to Hathorne's question, "The Lord open the eyes of the magistrates and ministers! The Lord show His power to discover the guilty! I desire to go to prayer."

Hathorne ignored her request. "Tell us then who hurts these children?"

"I do not know."

"If you be guilty of this fact, do you think you can hide it?"

"The Lord knows."

"Well, tell us what *you* know of this matter."

"Why, I am a gospel woman, and do you think I can have to do with witchcraft too?"

John Hathorne got at last to the most damaging evidence against Goody Corey — the Edward Putnam-Ezekiel Cheever experiment. "How could you tell, then," he asked, "that the child was bid to observe what clothes you wore, when some came to speak with you?"

Before she could reply Cheever warned from the spectators, "Do not begin with a lie!"

Hathorne asked Deacon Edward to rise and read his deposition, which he bagain to do. He got as far as, "…she replied, 'But does she tell you that clothes I have on?'" when Hathorne broke in to ask Martha, "Who told you that?"

Goody Corey answered, "He said that the child said," and Cheever called, "You speak falsely!"

Hathorne persisted. "Why did you ask if the child told what clothes you wore?"

"Because I heard the children told what clothes the others wore." She knew that the bewitched girls were passing information and details back and forth among each other at every opportunity, but that to outsiders their knowledge would appear to be preternatural. Edward Putnam did not wait for her to amplify, but recommenced reading his and Cheever's deposition:

"We made her no answer to this at her first asking, whereupon she asked us again, with very great eagerness, 'But does she tell you what clothes I have on?'"

Once again Hathorne interrupted the testimony to ask, "Why did you ask if the child told what clothes you wore?"

Martha realized that no one was going to believe her information had simply come through the rumor mill; therefore, like others before her, she lied, expecting to be backed up by someone loyal to her. She said, "My husband told me the others told."

"Who told you about the clothes? Why did you ask that question?" Hathorne pounded at the point. He saw that the old witch had been flustered and that she had begun to crack.

"Because I heard the children told what clothes the others wore," she repeated.

"Goodman Corey," Judge Hathorne called to Giles, "did you tell her?"

"Nay," Corey said.

The magistrate snapped his head back to Martha. "Did not you say your husband told you so?"

Martha did not reply, but fidgeted worse than ever and bit her lip. The children screamed.

"Who hurts these children?" Hathorne asked again. "Now look upon them!" She did so and they were vigorously tormented.

"I cannot help it," Martha said in a small voice. "I wish to go to prayer."

"Did not you say you would tell the truth why you asked that question? How came you to the knowledge?"

Martha's answer was so simple and quiet that not everyone heard it: "I did but ask," she said. That knowledge had been the easiest thing in the world to come by. Everyone knew of the plan that had been hatched by the Deacon and Ezekiel Cheever after Sarah Putnam's baptism the morning of the day they visited Martha, but no one in the courtroom raised his voice to confirm the fact.

"You dare thus to lie in all this assembly!" Hathorne roared indignantly. "You are now before authority," he reminded her; "I expect the truth — you promised it! Speak, now, and tell who told you what clothes?"

But Martha had been speaking the truth, except for the lie about her having gotten the information from Giles. If she remembered who, specifically, had told her about the Putnam plot, and she mentioned that person's name, there would, she knew, be another witch in town before the night was out. She kept her counsel and said firmly, but in despair, "Nobody."

"How came you to know that the children would be examined what clothes you wore?"

"Because I thought the child was wiser than anybody if she knew." Martha's words confused Hathorne, for it was not a reply unless one accepted Martha's previous statement that she had gotten her information through rumor and, further, unless people knew — as some of those in court did — that Martha had deliberately changed her clothes with no witnesses present after she heard that Edward Putnam and Ezekiel Cheever were on their way.

John Hathorne was not privy to this information, so he said, "Give an answer!" You said your husband told you."

"He told me the children said I afflicted him," and this was the truth.

"How did you know what they came for?" Hathorne asked, waving in the direction of Cheever and the Deacon. "Answer me this truly — will you say how you came to know what they came for?"

"I had heard speech that the children said I troubled them, and I thought that they might come to examine."

In the audience there was someone who knew that Martha Corey was shielding him or her. When Hathorne asked, "But how did you *know* it?" Martha replied, "I *thought* they did."

Hathorne could hear the lie. Exasperated, he said, "Did not you say you would tell the truth?" *Who* told you what they came for?"

"Nobody."

"*How did you know?*"

"I did *think* so."

"But you said you *knew* so!"

The tormented children had an explanation. Mary Walcott and Abigail Williams cried, "There is a Black Man whispering in her ear!"

A murmur swept the room — so Martha did have legal counsel after all! Her invisible attorney stood beside her and told her what to reply to Hathorne's interrogation. The Black Man was an inept barrister. Hathorne accepted what the children said as gospel, and he asked, "What did he say to you?"

"We must not believe," Martha told him as pointedly and calmly as she could, "all that these distracted children say."

But of course, John Hathorne could, and did. "Cannot you tell what that Man whispered?"

"I saw nobody," Martha answered; nor had anyone else present except the tortured girls.

"But did not you hear?"

"No."

The girls experienced at that moment the most excruciating tortures, and there was bedlam in the court for a while. Finally the officers, ministers, parents, and others got things under better control and Hathorne could go on. He had been mightily impressed with the display. He told Martha solemnly, "If you expect mercy of God, you must look for it in God's way, by confession. Do you think to find mercy by aggravating your sins?"

"A true thing."

"Look for it, then, In God's way."

"So I do."

"Give glory to God and confess, then!" Judge Hathorne intoned, taken by the spirit of the moment.

"But I cannot confess," Martha replied simply. She meant one thing — that it would be the greatest sin to do so, but Hathorne thought she meant that the Devil was preventing her. He was incredulous that she could have been unmoved by the tremendous agonies of the girls.

"Do not you see how these afflicted do charge you?" he asked, exasperation in his voice.

"We must not believe distracted persons," Martha said firmly.

From the gallery the Rev. Nicholas Noyes rose to say indignantly, "It is the judgment of all that are here present that they are bewitched, and only you say they are distracted."

"Who do you employ to hurt them?" Hathorne went on.

"I employed none."

"Did not you say our eyes were blinded and you would open them?"

"Yes, to accuse the innocent."

John Hathorne picked up a deposition submitted by Henry Crosby and read a portion of it. Crosby had sworn that Martha Corey had said in his presence, "Annie Putnam will not be able to stand before me, for not even the Devil can stand before me." But Martha had been proved wrong to the whole town that day, as she was well aware. Again, Hathorne chose to interpret her remark as meaning something other than what Martha had intended.

"Why cannot the girl stand before you?"

"I do not know." It was useless to argue.

"What did you mean by that?"

Martha sighed. "I saw them fall down."

"It seems to be an insulting speech, as if they could not stand before you. Tell me," Hathorne asked, referring to something one of the girls had just shouted from the crowd, "what was that turning upon the spit by you?"

"You believe the children that are distracted. I saw no spit."

"Here are more than two that accuse you for witchcraft. What do you say?"

"I am innocent."

Hathorne took Crosby's deposition and read some more of it aloud. Then he turned once more to the accused witch. "What did you mean by that — the Devil cannot stand before you?"

"I never said so," Martha replied, but voices in the room rose to refute her lie. "What can I do?" she asked after the outburst, "Many rise up against me."

"Why, confess," Hathorne told her.

"So I would, if I were guilty."

"Here are sober persons," Hathorne said, indicating the poeople who had just called Martha a liar. "What do you say to them? You are a 'gospel woman'; will you lie?"

Abigail Williams cried out, "Next Sabbath is a sacrament day, but she shall not come there."

"I do not care," Martha said. She was weary and beginning to slump noticeably.

"You charge these children with distraction. It is a note of distraction when persons vary in a minute, but these fix upon you. This is not the manner of distraction."

"When you are all against me, what can I help it?"

"Now tell me the truth, will you? Why did you say that the magistrates' and ministers' eyes were blinded, you would open them."

Martha straightened and laughed. "I deny it," she said.

"Now tell us how we shall know who doth hurt these if you do not?"

"Can an innocent person be guilty?"

Do you deny these words?"

"Yes."

"Tell us who hurts these. We came to be a terror to evildoers. You say you would open our eyes — we are 'blind'"

"If you say I am a witch."

"You said you would show us."

"I deny it."

"Why do not you now show us?"

"I cannot tell; I do not know."

"What did you strike the maid at Mr. Thomas Putnam's with?"

"I never struck her in my life," Martha replied indignantly.

Some of the girls railed from the floor that they had seen the old witch do it.

"There are two that saw you strike her with an iron rod," Hathorne admonished her.

"I had no hand in it."

"Who had? Do you believe these children are bewitched?"

"They may, for aught I know. I have had no hand in it."

"You say you are no witch. Maybe you mean you never covenanted with the Devil. Did you ever deal with any familiar?"

"No, never."

"What bird was that the children spoke of?" From the accusers several voices cried, "She had a bird that sucked her," and suchlike words. "What bird was it?" Hathorne repeated.

"I know no bird."

"It may be you have engaged you will not confess, but *God* knows," Hathorne told her angrily.

"So he doth," Martha replied calmly.

"Do you believe you shall go unpunished?"

"I have nothing to do with witchcraft."

"Why was you not willing your husband should come to the former session here?"

"But he came, for all." She raised her eyes and stared into the audience. The girls shrieked.

"Did not you take the saddle off?"

"I did not know what it was for."

John Hathorne raised his brows. "Did not you know what it was for?"

"I did not know that it would be to any benefit," she amended.

Someone from the audience, perhaps a member of the Committee of Vigilance, called, "She would not have us help to find out witches."

Hathorne continued, "Did not you say you would open our eyes? Why do you not?"

"I never thought of a witch." She snorted.

"Is it a laughing matter to see these afflicted persons?"

"I did not laugh at them," Martha said, but voices from the audience contradicted her. "Ye are all against me," Martha said bitterly, "and I cannot help it."

"Do not you believe there are witches in the country?" Hathorne pressed forward, for he had information regarding her apostasy.

"I do not know that there is any."

"Do not you know that Tituba confessed it?"

"I did not hear her speak."

"I find you will own nothing without several witnesses, and yet you will deny for all."

Martha bit her lip and the children were nipped. Ezekiel Cheever pointed out the fact from his point of vantage. "You bit your lip," Hathorne said to her.

"What harm is there in it?" Martha asked.

The Rev. Mr. Noyes rose. "I believe it is apparent," he said, "she practiceth witchcraft in the congregation: There is no need of images."

"What do you say," Hathorne queried her, "to all these things that are apparent?"

"If you will all go hang me, how can I help it?"

"Were you to serve the Devil ten years? Tell how many."

Martha Corey laughed at the absurdity. The children flew into paroxysms. One of them called, "She has a yellow bird that did use to suck between her fingers."

"What bird is it?" Hathorne asked her, and she laughed again. George Herrick was told to look between Martha's fingers for a mark. No sooner had he let go her hands than the tortures of the children were redoubled. They cried, "Oh! She pinches! Oh!" and the girl who had just spoken called, "It is too late now, for she has removed a pin and put it on her head." Herrick searched Martha's hair, found a pin, and handed it to Hathorne who was grim. "Why do not you tell," the judge said over the bedlam, "how the Devil comes in your shape and hurts these? You said you would."

"How *can* I know how?" Martha asked him in exasperation.

"Why did you say you would show us?"

Martha had already answered that question any number of times, and there was no getting through, so she merely laughed bitterly once more.

"What book is that you would have these children write in?"

This was something new. "What book?" Martha was hardly a literary person. "Where should I have a book?" she asked. "I showed them none, nor have none, nor brought none." She was emphatic, but the afflicted girls cried out again that there was a man whispering in her ears.

"What book did you carry to Mary Walcott?" Hathorne insisted.

"I carried none. If the Devil appears in my shape…."

Anthony Needham called from the audience, "John Parker some time ago thought this woman was a witch."

Hathorne ignore him. "Who is your god?" he asked her.

"The God that made me."

"What is His name?"

"Jehovah."

John Hathorne saw that this line of questioning was going poorly, for she was saying the sacred names clearly. She was supposed to stumble.

"Do you know any other name?" he asked Martha.

"God Almighty," she said loudly and firmly.

"Doth *he* tell you, that you pray to, that *he* is God Almighty?" Hathorne thought this might prove a fruitful avenue for exploration. If Martha thought she talked with a spirit that called himself God…but she avoided the trap by asking Hathorne her own question:

"Who do I worship but the God that made me?"

Hathorne tried next to catch her in a false catechism. "How many gods are there?" he asked.

"One," she said.

"How many persons?"

"Three."

"Cannot you say, 'So there is one God in three blessed persons?'" Hathorne asked testily. He was nitpicking.

Martha replied, "'So there is one God in three blessed persons.'"

Hathorne gave up that line of questioning as unprofitable and, indeed, damaging to the case he thought he had been building so cleverly. He needed some spectacular material. "Do not you see these children and women are rational and sober as their neighbors when your hands are fastened?" for George Herrick had secured Martha's arms again after the last outburst. The possessed people picked up their cue and all were seized with fits. Herrick still had hold of her arms. but bystanders said, "She is squeezing her fingers." Herrick said, "She hath bit her lip," and immediately the afflicted were in an uproar.

"Tell why you hurt these," Hathorne said, back at last on firm ground, "or who doth."

Again Martha denied having had any part in the performance. Gertrude Pope was so irritated by her denial that she threw her muff at the witch. It missed, and while the crowd was murmuring she bent down, took off a shoe, hurled it, and this time struck Martha Corey in the head. Martha cried out, "Oh!" and tried to get her hands loose, but Herrick had them securely and all she could do was shake her head, at which the girls all shook theirs and screamed. Hathorne banged his hand for silence but did not admonish Mrs. Pope. When things quieted down somewhat he asked, "Why did you say, if you were a witch you should have no pardon?"

"Because I am a gospel woman," Martha gasped. But there was still so much agitation in the audience that Hathorne abruptly broke things off and ordered that Martha be remanded to Salem Jail to await trial.

Later that day Mary Walcott was tormented by Dorcas Goode; Abigail was visited with affliction at the spectral hands of Rebecca Nurse for the fifth time, and by Elizabeth Proctor for the second. Goodwife Annie's mother, Ann Carr Putnam, had few fits herself, but she was weak from her ordeals...and pregnancy.

The next day, Tuesday the 22nd, Rebecca Nurse's shade renewed its attack upon Mrs. Ann Putnam just after dawn. Goody Nurse was dressed only in a shift, and she carried a little red book that she wished Ann to sign. The witch threatened, Goody Putnam said, "to tear the soul out of my body, blasphemously denying the blessed God and the power of the Lord Jesus Christ to save my soul; and denying several places of scripture which I told her of to repel her hellish temptations."

For two solid hours Mrs. Putnam was grievously tormented, and then intermittently the rest of the day. While she was undergoing her hellish temptations, some of the Villagers were collecting a petition in behalf of the Proctor family; it said, in part, "they lived Christian life in their family, and were ever ready to help such as stood in need...." Among those who signed the document was Constable George Locker.

Deacon Edward and Jonathan Putnam swore out warrants against little Dorcas Goode and Rebecca Nurse on Wednesday. Goody Nurse tormented Abigail Williams a sixth time, and Goody Ann Putnam was visited by Rebecca's spirit also. Deodat Lawson went to pray with the afflicted family of Sgt. Thomas Putnam, Jr., but when he and the family had finished their orisons, they discovered that Mrs. Putnam had fallen into another of her trances.

Sgt. Thomas, took his wife off the bed where she lay, her face contorted, her mouth drawn to one side, and tried to settle her on his lap. At first she was so stiff they couldn't bend her body, but finally she loosened up and sat on her husband's knees, only to launch into a St. Vitus-like lap dance of arms and legs and to have a conversation with Rebecca Nurse.

"Begone! Begone! Begone!" she cried, "Are you not ashamed, a woman of your profession, to afflict a poor creature so? What hurt did

I ever do you in my life? You have but two years to live" — Lawson noted the prophesy — "and then the Devil will torment your soul; for this your name is blotted out of God's Book, and it shall never be put in God's Book again; be gone, for shame! Are you not afraid of that which is coming upon you? I know, I know what will make you afraid — the wrath of an Angry God! I am sure that will make you afraid! Begone! Do not torment me — I know what you would have!" Lawson was sure she meant her soul "— but it is out of your reach; it is clothed with the white robes of Christ's righteousness."

Then she seemed to argue with Rebecca about a scripture text. She was completely hysterical and seemed to be trying to speak: "I will tell, I will tell; it is, it is, it is…," but she couldn't get it out. Then at last the dam broke; she said, "It is the third chapter of the Revelations!"

Lawson wrote in his journal later that evening, "I did something scruple the reading it, and did let my scruple appear, lest Satan should make any superstitiously to improve the word of the Eternal God. However, though not versed in these things, I judged I might do it this once for an experiment. I began to read, and before I had near read through the first verse, she opened her eyes and was well." Mrs. Putnam had been tormented for about half an hour. Thomas and the others present in the room told Lawson that Goody Putnam had often been relieved by someone's reading texts that she named in her traumas.

Thursday was Lecture Day. At 8:00 a.m. five-year-old Dorcas Goode was arrested and sent in custody to Ingersoll's tavern. Lawson saw her there and he thought she looked "hale and well as other children."

Lawson attended the examination, and Rev. John Hale of Beverly opened with a prayer. Hathorne asked the afflicted girls, who were having fits — as was Mrs. Ann Putnam — whether Rebecca Nurse were the one who was hurting them. They answered affirmatively, and the magistrate, who was evidently unsure of himself in his dealing with this woman who had been, to the best of his knowledge, a model member of the community for as long as he could recall, said to her, "Goody

Nurse, here are two — Ann Putnam the child and Abigail Williams — complains of your hurting them. What do you say to it?"

"I can say," she responded, "before my Eternal Father I am innocent, and God will clear my innocency."

John Hathorne replied, "Here is never a one in the assembly but desires it. But if you be guilty, pray God discover you!"

Henry Kenny in the throng, however, disagreed with what Hathorne had said about everyone wishing her innocent. He rose. Hathorne asked, "Goodman Kenny, what do you say?"

"I do believe she is guilty," Kenny said. "Since this Nurse came into the house, I have been seized with an amassed condition." He sat down.

Mrs. Ann Putnam also disagreed. She was writhing and screaming out upon Rebecca. Hathorne turned to his defendant and said, "Here are not only these" — he swept an arm toward the children — "but here is the wife of Mr. Thomas Putnam who accuseth you by creditable information…both of tempting her to iniquity and of greatly hurting her."

"I am innocent and clear," Rebecca told him, "and have not been able to get out of doors these eight or ten days." She had been ill, as everyone knew.

The judge turned to Edward Putnam. "Give in what you have to say," he requested.

Deacon Putnam rose and told the court he had seen the children afflicted by Mrs. Nurse. Hathorne asked, "Is this true, Goody Nurse?"

"I never afflicted no child — no, never in my life."

"You see these accuse you. Is it true?"

"No."

"Are you an innocent person relating to this witchcraft?"

Before she could answer, Mrs. Ann Putnam cried out, "Did you not bring the Black Man with you? Did you not bid me tempt God and die? How oft have you eat and drunk your own damnation?"

Rebecca spread out her arms and cried, "Oh, Lord, help me!" The afflicted went into tremendous convulsions. Mr. Lawson felt suffocated.

He needed air. He got up and went outdoors and listened to the screeching as he walked back and forth between the meetinghouse and Ingersoll's tavern.

Inside the court Hathorne faced Goody Nurse. "Do you not see," he asked, "What a solemn condition these are in? When your hands are loose, the persons are afflicted."

Mary Walcott and Betty Hubbard cried, "She is hurting me! She bites! She pinches!" This was an about-face for both girls who had been maintaining all morning that Goody Nurse had never hurt them. Now, she was tormenting them grievously. Mrs. Ann Putnam was beside herself with the outrage of hearing Rebecca Nurse repeat over and over again that she was innocent, innocent, innocent. Mrs. Putnam went into prodigious paroxysms.

Outdoors Deodat Lawson heard her give "such a hideous screech…as did amaze me." The assembly "was struck with consternation, and they were afraid that those that sat next to them were under the influence of witchcraft."

Mrs. Putnam was at last subdued by her husband and others and carried screaming from the courthouse. As soon as she hit fresh air she calmed down to a degree.

Judge John Hathorne, when things got quieter, said to Rebecca, "It is very awful for all to see these agonies, and you an old Professor" — professor of the faith — "thus charged with contracting with the Devil, by the effects of it, and yet to see you stand with dry eyes when there are so many wet."

"You do not know my heart," Rebecca told him.

"You would do well, if you are guilty, to confess and give glory to God."

"I am as clear as the child unborn."

Hathorne's faith in spectral evidence faltered for a moment, seeing this good old woman standing calmly amid the havoc, maintaining her innocence. "What uncertainty there may be in apparitions, I know not." Never before had he said such a thing. "Yet this with me strikes hard upon you," he continued amid the bedlam of screaming girls, shouting men, weeping women, "that you are, at this very present moment, charged with familiar spirits," for the girls were screeching and pointing in various directions at Mrs. Nurse's apparently multiple apparitions, imps and so forth, that were scattered through the courtroom, even up into the spring air above the seething people, and at Rebecca Nurse herself, where the afflicted saw her invisible parasites suckling at her body.

"This is your bodily person they speak to," Hathorne said to her. "They say now they see these familiar spirits come to your bodily person. Now, what do you say to that?"

"I have none, sir."

"If you have, confess and give glory to God! I pray God clear you if you be innocent; and if you be guilty, discover you. Therefore give me an upright answer: Have you any familiarity with these spirits?"

"No," she responded, "I have none but with God alone."

"How came you sick? — for there is an odd discourse of that in the mouths of many."

Goody Nurse misunderstood him, for Hathorne was speaking of her recent illness. "I am sick at my stomach," she replied.

"Have you no wounds?" Hathorne meant pock-marks, but somehow Mrs. Nurse's case of Satan's scourge had left her with no overt scars.

"I have but old age."

"You do know whether you are guilty and have familiarity with the Devil, and now, when you are here present, to see such a thing as these testify there is a Black Man whispering in your ear, and birds flying about you — what do you say to it?"

"It is all false," she said. "I am clear."

"Possibly you may apprehend you are no witch, but have you not been led aside by temptations in that way?"

"I have not."

"What a sad thing it is that a church member here," Martha Corey, "and now another of Salem, should be thus accused and charged."

Things had calmed down considerably until Hathorne said that; then, Gertrude Pope fell into a massive convulsion and all the others followed suit.

Tell us," Hathorne said amid the hubbub, "have you not had visible appearances more than what is common in nature?" He was talking about the hallucinations Rebecca had seen in her illness.

"I have none, nor never had in my life," Rebecca said, and it was literally the truth, for she remembered nothing of what she had shouted under the influence of delirium while she had been ill. All she knew was what people had told her. The only thing of which she was certain was that she had been terribly sick.

"Do you think these" — Hathorne pointed to the writhing females before him — "suffer voluntarily or involuntarily?"

"I cannot tell."

"That is strange! Everyone can judge."

"I must be silent."

"They accuse you of hurting them, and if you think it is not unwillingly, but by design, you must look upon them as murderers."

No truer words could have been spoken under the circumstances, but Rebecca shook her head. "I cannot tell what to think of it."

However, Hathorne insisted that he receive a definite answer. Finally Rebecca said, "I do not think so. I did not understand aright what you said."

"Well, then, give an answer now — to you think these suffer against their wills or not?"

"I do not think these suffer against their wills." There was bedlam in the court again.

"Why did you never visit these afflicted persons?"

"Because I was afraid I should have fits too." In whatever way Rebecca moved her body the girls and afflicted women went into violent fits. John Hathorne pursued Rebecca.

"Is it not an unaccountable case," he asked her, "that when you are examined these persons are afflicted?"

"I have got nobody to look to but God," Rebecca said. She stirred her hands and the accusers were violently afflicted.

"Do you believe these afflicted persons are bewitched?"

"I do believe they are," she replied. It was an interesting proposition — that the girls were bewitched, but not against their wills — but Hathorne did not pick up on it, assuming perhaps that he had at last gotten the correct answer, or that Rebecca had continued to misunderstand his question, which she had not.

"When this witchcraft came upon the stage," Hathorne lectured, using probably the appropriate metaphor, "there was no suspicion of Tituba — she professed much love to that child, Betty Parris, but it was her apparition did the mischief. And why should not you also be guilty — for your apparition doth hurt also?" He had at last come down again on the right interpretation of spectral evidence.

Rebecca cast a sharp look at the judge. "Would you have me belie myself?" Elizabeth Hubbard twisted her head in imitation of the old woman; Abby Williams cried, "Set up Goody Nurse's head! Elizabeth's neck will be broke!" Herrick and others reached and forced Goody Nurse's head back aright.

After the interruption, Rev. Samuel Parris was asked by the judges to read the deposition of Mrs. Ann Putnam, which he did. When he had finished Hathorne asked, "What do you think of this?"

"I cannot help it. The Devil mayhap appears in my shape." It was a blind alley. The court no longer entertained any doubt about the Devil's ability to appear in anyone's likeness without that person's consent. Rebecca Nurse was sent to Salem Prison.

Little Dorcas Goode's examination was an anticlimax. Annie Putnam, Mary Walcott, and Mercy Lewis went into fits and said that the child was biting, pinching, and choking them. They showed the court sets of teeth marks on their arms. Pins were found on the bodies of the afflicted. Dorcas had no idea at all of what was going on, but she was wide-eyed and frightened at the strange proceedings. The evidence against her was overwhelming, however, so she was sent to join her mother in prison, which in some ways was a blessing.

Deodat Lawson delivered the afternoon lecture. His text was Zachariah iii:2, "And the Lord said unto Satan, 'The Lord rebuke thee, O Satan! Even the Lord that hath chosen Jerusalem rebuke thee: Is not this a brand plucked out of the fire?'" In his sermon he warned, "Give no place to the Devil by rash censuring of others, without sufficient grounds, or false-accusing any willingly. — It is a time of temptation among you, such as never was before: Let me entreat you not to be lavish or severe in reflecting on the malice or envy of your neighbors, by whom any of you have been accused lest, whilst you falsely charge one another…the grand Accuser (who loves to fish in troubled waters) should take advantage upon you. — And, if innocent persons be suspected, it is to be ascribed to God's pleasure…by representing of such" by specters "to the affliction of others…. This giving place to the Devil, avoid! — for it will have uncomfortable and pernicious influence upon the affairs of this place, by letting out peace, and bringing in confusion and every evil work, which we heartily pray God, in mercy to prevent."

But Giles Corey was persuaded to give in a deposition in evidence against his wife; in it he told of the trouble he had had in praying, and of the strange behavior of his ox and cat. He voiced his suspicions about his seemingly praying wife, and the lack of sound as she moved her lips.

As soon as Rebecca Nurse was in chains in Salem Prison Mrs. Ann Carr Putnam had much ease and was not given to fits for a while.

On the morning of Friday, March 25th, Martha Corey, Rebecca Nurse, and Dorcas Goode were transferred from Salem Prison to Boston. That same morning Joseph Putnam got his first public convert to lonely rebellion. Samuel Sibley met John Proctor near Mr. Phillips' house; others were present as well. The men asked Phillips, "How do the folks do in the Village?"

Phillips replied, "I heard they were very bad last night, but I have heard nothing this morning."

John Proctor said, "I am going to fetch home my jade" — he was referring to his maidservant, Mary Warren, one of the possessed girls…in fact, one of the two oldest of them, at twenty, with Sarah Churchill. "I left her there last night and had rather given forty cents than let her come up."

Sibley asked, "Why do you talk so?"

"If they were let alone, sir," Proctor told him, "we should all be witches and devils quickly. They should rather be had to the whipping post. But I will fetch my jade home and thrust the Devil out of her."

He had worked himself up to wrath, and he said more to the same purpose while the men stood around uncomfortably and cast furtive glances at each other. Suddenly Proctor burst out with, "Hang them! Hang them!" Then he added, "When she" — Mary Warren — "was first taken with fits I kept her close to the wheel and threatened to thrash her, and then she had no more fits till the next day I was gone forth, and then she must have her fits again, forsooth!" John Proctor was in trouble as soon as the group broke up.

The same day Rev. Samuel Parris called in Mary Sibley and told her he was going to ask her on Sunday to make a public confession and apology for her part in the making of the witch cake last February 25th. She broke into tears and agreed.

Elizabeth Parris, one of the other originators of the trouble, had a fit that day at the home of Capt. Stephen Sewall, where she was in sequestration in Salem. During her fit she said that the Black Man had come to her and offered her a golden city. Mrs. Sewall told her, "It is the Devil, and he was a liar from the beginning. You must tell him so when next he comes to you." Betty obeyed her instructions.

On Saturday John Proctor's specter tortured Mary Warren, and the apparition of his wife, Elizabeth, appeared to Mercy Lewis and grievously hurt her.

The next day was Communion Sunday. The entire parish — no one dared be absent from church meeting except those who had been arrested, or were about to be — crowded into the meetinghouse to see Samuel Parris rise to deliver his sermon. It was, he announced, "Christ Knows How Many Devils There Are in His Church," on the text John vi:70-71, "Jesus answered them, 'Have not I chosen you twelve, and one of you is a devil?'"

No sooner had Mr. Parris finished his preliminaries than Sarah Cloyse, sister of Rebecca Nurse, rose from her pew, stalked out, and slammed the door behind her. Her action startled everyone, and there was a murmur of disapprobation and shock among the congregation, but Mr. Parris continued in a moment.

After the sermon, but before communion, Parris gave the congregation a synopsis of the beginning of the witchhunt. He pointed out that it was Mary Sibley's dabbling in the occult, through unwitting ignorance, by making the witch cake that began it all. He asked the church members to vote on whether to allow her to remain a member of the church if she made a public confession of her errors. All voted "Aye" by raising their hands.

Then the minister said, "Sister Sibley, if you are convinced that you herein did sinfully, and are sorry for it, let us hear it from your own mouth." Mary rose, confessed her transgression and expressed her remorse. When she was finished Parris said, "Brethren, if herein you have received satisfaction, testify it by lifting up your hands." It was another unanimous affirmative vote.

At two p.m. Mrs. Ann Putnam was bitten by Rebecca Nurse again, and the specter beat her with a ghostly chain six times in half an hour, leaving link marks on her, including "one remarkable one, with six streaks across her arm," according to Edward Putnam's verification of the fact, which he witnessed.

By Monday the 28th suspicion was beginning to grow among a number of people that there was more to these possessions than met the eyes of the afflicted, but there was little visible opposition yet. John

Tarbell, son-in-law of Rebecca Nurse, proved to be a brave man, however, when he went to the home of Sgt. Thomas Putnam, Jr., with Samuel Nurse and asked some hard questions. He inquired of the Sergeant, "Did young Ann that was afflicted first speak of Goody Nurse, before others mentioned her to her?" No one but Annie Putnam had been afflicted in the household up to that point.

Putnam replied, "She told us that she saw the apparition of a palefaced woman that sat in her grandmother's seat, but did not know her name."

Tarbell pressed on. "But who was it that told her it was Goody Nurse?"

Mercy Lewis said, "It was Goody Putnam that said it was Goody Nurse."

"No," Mrs. Putnam broke in, "it was you who told her."

"It was you!" Mercy cried.

"No, Mercy, you told her," Mrs. Putnam said, and they broke into an argument about it.

During the day some of the afflicted girls were at Deacon Ingersoll's inn. Among the others present were William Raymond, twenty-six, and Daniel Elliot; the conversation going about concerned the examinations of several accused witches. Raymond said, "I heard that Goody Proctor is to be examined tomorrow."

Goody Ingersoll replied, "I do not believe so, for I have heard nothing of it."

Suddenly the girls cried out, "There, Goody Proctor!" "Old witch! I'll have her hang."

Mrs. Ingersoll swiveled irritably upon them and said, "Here now, we shall have no more of that!"

The girls stopped, then began to giggle among themselves.

William Raymond said to one of them, "I believe you lied, for I saw nothing." He might have been in trouble if Goody Ingersoll, who was immune, had not said to the child, "You did tell a lie. There was nothing."

The girl replied, "I did it for sport." Pouting, "For we must have some sport."

On Tuesday Abigail Williams was tormented by Elizabeth Proctor for the third time, and on Thursday, the last of the month, by Rebecca Nurse a seventh time. A public fast was held for the afflicted persons. Abigail Williams said that the witches held Sacrament that day in a house at Salem Village where they ate red bread and drank something red: Evidently the witches took the miracle of transub-stantiation quite literally.

Mercy Lewis had a fit on April Fool's Day, and in it she saw the specters eating red bread "like man's flesh," and they wanted her to share it, but she refused. She spat and said, "I will not eat; I will not drink — it is blood and flesh. That is not the Bread of Life; that is not the Water of Life! Christ gives the Bread of Life. I will have none of it."

But she also saw a glorious Man in White in a grand place that had neither candle nor sun but was full of radiance and light. There was a great multitude present, and they sang hymns and psalms. She asked the angel, "How long shall I stay here? Let me be along with you."

That night Stephen Bickford was in bed at the house of James Darling, sober and fully awake in his opinion. Rebecca Nurse and Elizabeth Proctor appeared to him and gave him a "great pain" in the neck.

On Saturday the second the shape of Elizabeth Proctor visited Abigail Williams for the fourth time; the next day, Sunday, the girls accused Sarah Cloyse of taking communion with the Devil. They saw her at a witch's sacrament and Mary Walcott cried out in her fits, "O Goodwife Cloyse! I did not think to see you here! Is this a time to receive the sacrament? You ran away on the Lord's Day and scorned to receive it in the meetinghouse, and is this a time to receive it? I wonder at you!"

Deliverance Putnam Walcott's husband Jonathan, Mary's father, and Nathaniel Ingersoll filed complaints on Monday against Elizabeth

Proctor and Sarah Cloyse. Abigail Williams had a fit and cried out, "What, Goodman Proctor, are you come too? Are you come to show you can pinch as well as your wife?" Mrs. Ann Putnam, whose fits had considerably diminished for several days, recommenced to be tormented on April 5th. The night of Wednesday, April 6th, Abigail Williams beat her breast and cried out that John Proctor was pinching her.

Joseph Putnam made one of his rare public appearances Thursday. He was more than ever vehemently opposed to the witchhunt, but there was little he could do except protect himself against the hysteria that had swept the Village. He made a symbolic gesture, however, when, on the 7th, he rode his horse, his one-year-old daughter Mary cradled in his arms, all the way to Salem to be baptized, bypassing the Salem Village meetinghouse and the parsonage of Samuel Parris. Afterward, he returned the same way. The Villagers who saw him ride by thought that they, too, were seeing a ghost.

Although Joseph Putnam was outspoken in his condemnation of his neighbors' demonic possessions, he was not the only Putnam who either disapproved of or, for other reasons, wanted to have as little to do with the whole affair as possible. Benjamin Putnam, his cousin Nathaniel's son, stayed clear of things and quietly supported the Goodes, of all people, who were attached to his farm. Two other cousins — James Putnam and John Putnam III, Capt. John's boys — kept themselves uninvolved as well. It was hard enough, what with the rest of the family so deeply embedded in the Devil's moil. But John Proctor was not circumspect at all. He said at Ingersoll's tavern that day, having heard that John Indian was to testify against his wife on Monday, "If I had John Indian in my custody, I would soon beat the Devil out of him!"

The next day, Friday, warrants were issued against Elizabeth Proctor and Sarah Cloyse. Carolina John Putnam, in a conversation that day, said of Rebecca Nurse and her sister Sarah Cloyse, "It is no wonder they are witches, for their mother was so before them." He soon came to regret this outburst, for on Saturday, April 9th, he was taken violently ill with convulsions and a high fever. His example, however, did nothing to dampen the aggressions of the people, for at a gathering at the home of Philip Knight, which included Thomas Nichols and John Willard, in speaking about everyone involved in any way with the witchhunt Willard said, "Hang them! They are all witches!" He had good cause to be disgusted, for as a deputy constable he had his share of dirty work to do, and he hated what he was seeing.

His colleague, deputy constable Carolina John Putnam, grew worse on Sunday, but on Monday he began to be better. His high fever and convulsions stopped, much to the relief of his family. It had been a spectacular demonic possession and, except for John Indian, who was also one of the afflicted persons, Carolina John had been the only adult male in the Village to be so visited by the fiends of Hell.

Chapter Ten

The scene of the witchcraft cases was transferred from Salem Village to the mother town, Salem, on Monday, April 11, and several judges were sent down from Boston to join John Hathorne and Jonathan Corwin on the bench. Thomas Danforth, the Deputy Governor, was to preside, and sitting as well were Samuel Sewall, James Russell, Isaac Addington, and Samuel Appleton.

The Rev. Nicholas Noyes began the hearing with prayer. There was a huge crowd present in the Salem meetinghouse — people from everywhere in the area were present, for this was to be an extraordinary examination, the proceedings having been given the stamp of approval of the Government by the presence on the bench of some of the Council who comprised the interim government of Massachusetts. Simon Bradstreet, the ancient Governor, was not present because of his age and the fact that he was largely a figurehead of the revolutionary government, but Danforth, who was really the acting governor, was there on the bench and he, unlike Bradstreet, who had squelched so many witchcraft cases, had actually arrested Martha Sparks for witchcraft in 1691; in fact, she was at that moment still in prison.

The first witness to be called was not one of the accused witches but John Indian who had helped to begin the hunt and since had been converted to one of the possessed people, despite the fact that he had actually practiced white magic when he baked his witch cake. Danforth asked him, "John, who hurt you?"

"Goody Proctor first," the West Indian replied, "and then Goody Cloyse."

"What did she do to you?"

"She brought the book to me."

"John, tell the truth — who hurts you? Have you been hurt?"

"The first was a gentlewoman I saw."

"Who next?"

"Goody Cloyse."

"But who hurt you next?"

"Goody Proctor."

"What did she do to you?"

"She choked me and brought the book."

"How oft did she come to torment you?"

"A good many times, she and Goody Cloyse."

"Do they come to you in the night as well as the day?"

"They come most in the day."

"Who?" Danforth wanted to see if he could catch John Indian in a mix-up, but he got the same answer.

"Goody Cloyse and Goody Proctor."

"Where did she take hold of you?"

"Upon my throat, to stop my breath."

"Do you know Goody Cloyse and Goody Proctor?"

"Yes," John Indian said, pointing, "here is Goody Cloyse."

Mrs. Cloyse broke in to ask, "When did I hurt thee?"

"A great many times," John answered with equanimity.

"Oh, you are a grievous liar!" she said, outraged.

Danforth continued, "What did this Goody Cloyse do to you?"

"She pinched and bit me till the blood came."

"How long since this woman came and hurt you?"

"Yesterday, at meeting."

"At any time before?"

"Yes, a great many times."

John Indian was dismissed and Mary Walcott brought to the stand. She was asked, "Mary Walcott, who hurts you?"

"Goody Cloyse," the young woman said.

"Did she bring you the book?"

"Yes."

"What was you to do with it?"

"To touch it and be well." But she was not well yet, for at that moment she fell to a fit that put a crimp in the questioning for awhile, until Goody Cloyse's witch's touch was put to use and she recovered.

"Doth she come alone?" Danforth asked her, resuming.

"Sometimes alone, and sometimes in company with Goody Nurse and Goody Corey, and a great many I do not know." She went into convulsions again, and the court called Abby Williams.

"Abigail Williams, did you see a company at Mr. Parris' house eat and drink?"

"Yes, sir — that was in the Sacrament."

"How many were there?"

"About forty, and Goody Cloyse and Goody Goode were their deacons."

"What was it they drank?"

"They said it was our blood, and they had it twice that day."

Mary Walcott had again recovered, so she was asked again, "Have you seen a White Man?" The judge referred to her glorious vision of the man in shining raiment.

"Yes, sir, a great many times," she replied.

"What sort of a man was he?"

"A fine, grave man, and, when he came, he made all the witches to tremble."

Abigail Williams confirmed it. "We had such a sight at Deacon Ingersoll's," she told the court.

"Who was at Deacon Ingersoll's then?" Danforth queried.

"Goody Cloyse," Mary replied, "Goody Nurse, Goody Corey, and Goody Goode."

Sarah Cloyse, fainting, called for water and sat down heavily. At that, a number of the afflicted people went to fits and called, "Oh! Her spirit has gone to prison to her sister Nurse!" John Indian did tumbles, the girls screamed and raved and, one by one, they were gathered up, brought to Goody Cloyse; the witch was made to touch them, and one by one they came to their senses, such as they were. At last the chaos was returned to a semblance of order, and Elizabeth Proctor was called to testify.

The Court addressed her: "Elizabeth Proctor, you understand whereof you are charged; viz., to be guilty of sundry acts of witchcraft. What say you to it? Speak the truth." Turning to the possessed people, Danforth admonished them, "And, so, you that are afflicted, you must speak the truth, as you will answer it before God another day. Mary Walcott, doth this woman hurt you?"

Danforth's warning evidently got the girls to thinking of Future Punishment if they lied, for Mary said, "I never saw her so as to be hurt by her."

"Mercy Lewis, does she hurt you?" But Mercy was struck dumb and couldn't answer. "Ann Putnam, does she hurt you?" Annie Putnam, too, was stricken mute. "Abigail Williams, does she hurt you?" Abby's hand was involuntarily stuffed into her mouth. Turning to the Indian at last, the judge asked, "John, does she hurt you?"

John Indian evidently didn't worry so much about the Throne of Judgment. He replied, "This is the woman that came in her shift and choked me."

"Did she ever bring the book?"

"Yes, sir."

"Are you sure of it?"

"Yes, sir."

Danforth asked Annie Putnam and Abby Williams once more to reply, but still they were dumb and having fits. At last the judge turned to Mrs. Proctor, "What do you say, Goody Proctor, to these things?"

"I take God in Heaven to be my witness," she said, "that I know nothing of it, no more than the child unborn."

By this time Annie Putnam Putnam had recovered herself, so Danforth queried her a third time, "Ann Putnam, does this woman hurt you?"

Annie Putnam had her courage back. "Yes, sir," she said, "a great many times."

Mrs. Proctor shot the girl a piercing glance and she, with her fellow accusers, was thrown into the most violent agonies, which subsided at length and the questioning resumed. "She does not bring the book to you, does she?"

"Yes, sir, often, and she hath made her maid set her hand to it."

"Abigail Williams, does this woman hurt you?"

"Yes, sir," Abigail finally was able to say, "often."

"What would she have you do with it?"

"To write in it, and I shall be well." Then Abigail addressed a startled Goody Proctor and asked directly, "Did not you tell me that your maid had written?" This was a revelation — that the witches had converted Mary Warren, one of the possessed girls, to the Devil's cause. It was a revelation, but it did not surprise the quiet cynics of Salem Village, for Mary Warren had been stricken with conscience and, perhaps, John Proctor's switch, when her mistress had been cried out upon; she seemed no longer to be possessed but rather to deny the validity of her former fits.

Goody Proctor composed herself and replied, "Dear child, it is not so. There is another judgment, dear child." The kindness of her reply threw Abigail and Annie into contortions again. When they were able to speak they cried, "Look you! There is Goody Proctor upon the beam!" and they pointed toward the rafters. Everyone craned but saw nothing more than dust in the beams of the sunlight that came through the windows.

John Proctor looked with the rest, and then he called out, "It is a lie. There is nothing to be seen." No sooner had he made his accusation than he himself was accused. The girls and John Indian cried out hysterically, "John Proctor is on the beam with his wife! He is a wizard!"

Danforth asked, "Ann Putnam, who hurt you?"

"Goodman Proctor, and his wife, too." One of her cohorts in possession cried, "There is Proctor going to take up Mrs. Pope's feet!" No sooner said than done: Gertrude's legs were knocked out from under her and she fell to the floor.

"What do you say," Danforth called, "Goodman Proctor, to these things?"

"I know not," he said. "I am innocent."

Abigail screamed, "There is Goodman Proctor going to Mrs. Pope!" The woman was taken by the Devil. She screeched, "There is Sarah and Goode hurting Mercy Lewis and John Indian!" Both were remorselessly tortured instantly. "Goodman Proctor is going to Mary Walcott!" Mary was tortured.

Hathorne, who had been holding his tongue impatiently, at last burst forth. "You see," he said vehemently, "the Devil will deceive you — the children could see what you was going to do before the woman was hurt. I would advise you to repentance, for the Devil is bringing you out!"

Abigail gasped out of her convulsions, "There is Goodman Proctor going to hurt Goody Bibber!" On cue, Sarah Bibber was drawn into the melee.

Benjamin Gould was called to give his evidence in the case, and he said, "I saw Goodman Proctor and his wife, and Goodman Corey and his wife, and Goody Cloyse, Goody Nurse, and Goody Griggs in my chamber on Thursday night last." Now there was truly havoc, for no one had ever said anything about Dr. William Griggs' wife, Betty Hubbard's aunt, and Giles Corey had not yet been accused; in fact, he had been a witness for the prosecution against his own wife. Elizabeth Hubbard was in a dead trance, and had been so since the beginning of the examination — she did not react when Gould accused her aunt.

Goody Proctor was still on the stand; Abigail Williams and Annie Putnam tried to strike at her, but there was a spell on the witch — as Abby's hand descended to meet the witch's head, her fist was forced open, the force of her blow was diminished, and all she could do at last was touch lightly the woman's hood. Immediately she cried, "My fingers burn!" Annie Putnam clutched her head and sank to her knees, moaning, as though she had taken the full force of the blow instead.

Friends of the Proctors had given in to the court a petition on their behalf. It said in part, "We never had the least knowledge of such a nefarious wickedness in our...neighbors" the Proctors "since they have been within our acquaintance. Neither do we remember any such thoughts in us concerning them, or any action by them...no more than might be in the lives of any other persons of the clearest reputation as to any such evils. What God may have left them to, we cannot go into God's pavilion clothed with clouds of darkness round about. But as to what we have ever seen or heard of them, upon our consciences, we judge them innocent of the crime objected."

However, mere testimonials of character could not stand beside such Pandemonium as reigned in the meetinghouse at that moment. The examination clearly could not continue, and Danforth called on the Rev. John Higginson to close with prayer amid the screeching and cavorting of the allegedly bewitched people. The hearings were adjourned until the next day.

That night Samuel Sewall wrote in his diary that he had gone to Salem "where, in the meeting-house, the persons accused of witchcraft were examined; was a very great assembly; 'twas awful to see how the afflicted persons were agitated. Mr. Noyes prayed at the beginning, and Mr. Higginson concluded. Vae, Vae, Vae, witchcraft!"

The next day was a repeat performance of the first day. John Indian and Abigail Williams cried out upon John Proctor in their fits, but there was one island of calm in the center of the screaming bewitched: Mary Walcott sat knitting. While Abigail was seized with a torment Mary was asked if she saw Goodman Proctor hurting her, but Mary was struck dumb and went on knitting. At last she was able to articulate words, and she said, yes, Proctor had hurt Abigail.

Annie Putnam was asked to sign the Devil's Book; Betty Hubbard was struck dumb; so was Mercy Lewis. John Indian cried out to the dog under the table to "come away, for Goodman Proctor is sitting on your back." Then he said to Goody Cloyse, "Oh, you old witch!" and fell to a fit: Marshal George Herrick and three men could hardly hold him. Mary went on knitting quietly, from time to time breaking her silence to confirm all the things that were happening to the others. Suddenly, she was stirred to action. "There," she said, "Goody Cloyse has pinched me now." Shortly afterwards she added, ""Oh! Yonder is Goodman Proctor and his wife, and Goody Nurse and Goody Corey and Goody Cloyse and Goode's child. Oh! Goodman Proctor is going to choke me!" She was choked.

Rev. Samuel Parris was called upon to give evidence against John Proctor — an imposing moment, to see the Village minister on the stand rather than taking notes, for he was one of the clerks of the inquisition. The Proctors and Sarah Cloyse were transferred from Salem Prison to Boston at the end of the day's examinations.

In Salem Village at midnight there was more trouble at the home of Carolina John and Hannah Putnam: Their infant daughter, Sarah, grew violently ill with high fever and convulsions. The family sent immediately for a doctor and Mother Elizabeth Hutchinson Putnam. Both arrived immediately. Despite the fact that the child had obviously contracted a contagious disease, inasmuch as her father was still suffering from the same illness, Mother Putnam, no sooner than she had seen Sarah, said, "I fear there is an evil hand upon her." When Dr. William

Griggs' medicaments had no effect, the diagnosis of witchcraft was confirmed.

During the day Abigail Williams was tormented by the specters of Elizabeth Proctor a fifth time, and by Rebecca Nurse an eighth.

Sarah Putnam continued very ill on Thursday, April 14th, and her sickness was added to the thousand rumors that were circulating through the towns of Salem Village, Salem, Andover, and the others in the area. People marveled most, however, at the news that Mary Warren, Proctor's maid, had told the authorities that the bewitched people "do but dissemble." The relatives of the accused — many of them at least — were inclined to agree. Even Dr. Griggs, now that his own wife had been cried out upon, was beginning to wonder whether his quick diagnoses of witchcraft had been judiciously arrived at. Joseph Putnam, for his part, had no doubts at all in his seclusion.

Sarah, the three-month-old daughter of deputy constable Carolina John Putnam and his wife Hannah, died on Friday, April 15. Her father, recuperating at last from the pox that had killed her, told people that the baby's demise "was enough to pierce a stony heart, for she was near five hours a-dying."

Mercy Lewis cried out upon Abigail Hobbs for the first time on Sunday the 17th, as did Mary Walcott. The next day warrants were issued for the arrest of Giles Corey, Abigail Hobbs of Topsfield, and Bridget Bishop, on complaint of Constable Carolina John Putnam and Ezekiel Cheever, members of the Committee of Vigilance. The afflicted people had confirmed Benjamin Gould's identification of Corey but not that of Goody Griggs, and she escaped. Marshal George Herrick took the others into custody and brought them to Nathaniel Ingersoll's inn. Mercy Lewis and Mary Walcott were both tormented again by Abigail Hobbs.

The examinations of April 19th were held in Salem Village again, the Council having returned to Boston, and the proceedings were once more in the hands of John Hathorne and Jonathan Corwin. The first to be questioned before the bar was Abigail Hobbs — she was easy to crack. She had been boasting of having made a pact with the Devil, and of being on familiar terms with "The Old Boy" for some time. Everyone knew it; she knew it. There was little for her to do, under the circumstances, than to stand where her rebellious heart, and her clever little head, told her to stand. It was a satisfactory beginning. No sooner had she begun to confess than the bewitched girls stopped having fits.

Abigail told the court that "Judith White, a Jersey maid that lived with Joseph Ingersoll at Casco, but now lives at Boston, with whom I was very well formerly acquainted, came to me yesterday in apparition, together with Sarah Goode, as I was going to examination and advised me to fly and not to go to be examined. I told them that I would go and that I would confess all that I knew. They told me also that Goody Osburn was a witch. Judith White came to me in fine clothes, in a sad-colored silk mantle with a topknot and hood.

"The Devil in the shape of a man came to me and would have me to afflict Ann Putnam, Mercy Lewis, and Abigail Williams and brought their images with him in wood, like them, and gave me thorns and bade me prick them into these images, which I did accordingly, into each of them one, and then the Devil told me they were afflicted, which they were and cried out they were hurt by me. I was at the great meeting in Mr. Parris' pasture when they administered the Sacrament and did eat of the red bread and drink of the red wine at the same time."

When her examination was finished, rather than being taken out of the court, she was allowed to stand near the bewitched girls, her new allies.

The recidivist Mary Warren was next, and no sooner had she appeared than the girls fell to fits. John Hathorne said to her, "Mary Warren, you stand here charged with sundry acts of witchcraft. What do you say for yourself — are you guilty or not?"

"I am innocent," the young woman replied.

"Hathorne turned to the afflicted. "Hath she hurt you?"

Some of the girls were struck dumb. Elizabeth Hubbard cried, "She is tormenting me!" and went into convulsions. Hathorne turned back to Mary. "You were a little while ago an afflicted person; now you are an afflicter. How comes this to pass?"

"I look up to God and take it to be a great mercy of God."

"What! Do you take it a great mercy to afflict others?" Hathorne had a marvelous ear for double entendre where none was intended.

Betty Hubbard, who had come out of her fit, said from the floor where she lay prostrate, "After she was well Mary said we did but dissemble!" The devils took her and the other girls again, and Goody Gertrude Pope joined them. For a few moments John Indian seemed unaffected, then he, too, went into his tumbling act. Abigail Hobbs, the new recruit, flailed about with the best — she screamed that Mary Warren's specter was coming to hurt her.

Hathorne said, pointing at Abigail Hobbs, "Well, here was one just now that was a tormenter in her apparition, and she owns that she had made a league with the Devil." Mary sat still, staring at Abigail, as though she were thinking things over, then she, too, had a fit: Double backslide. It was an immobile, blind, deaf and dumb trance she went into. One of the other girls cried, "She was going to confess, but Goody Corey and Proctor and his wife came in, and their apparitions struck her down and said she would tell nothing." Annie Putnam and the other girls confirmed.

Mary stayed rigid and mute for a while, then suddenly she started up, saying, "I will speak! Oh! I am sorry for it, I am sorry for it!" She wrung her hands, then fell back into her trance; came to and tried to speak, but her jaws locked and between her clenched teeth she cried, "Oh, Lord, help me! Oh, good Lord, save me!" She began to writhe, then again cried, "I will tell, I will tell!" and fell back over into a dead swoon.

After a bit she cried again, "I will tell — they did! they did! they did!" only to fall back over once more. She recovered to a degree yet again, cried, "I will tell! They brought me to it!" and back into her coma. Her seizures continued until the judges ordered her taken out and Bridget Bishop brought in; instead, George Herrick brought Mary in once more when the fresh air outdoors had seemed to revive her. She had a few more fits, then the examination continued. John Hathorne asked her, "Have you signed the Devil's Book?"

"No."

"Have not you touched it?"

"No. She said I shall not speak a word, but I will! I will speak, Satan! — she says she will kill me. Oh! She says she owes me a spite and will claw me off! Avoid, Satan! For the name of God, avoid!" She raised her arms as though to ward off an attack by someone, then fell into a fit out of which she cried, "Will ye? I will prevent ye in the name of God...."

Hathorne tried to ask, "Tell us, how far have you yielded?" when Mary came around, but she merely went into another fit.

"What did they say you should do, and you should be well?" Hathorne asked, but Mary bit her lips so that she could not speak. The afflicted people had become quiet when she began to confess, and they remained that way until she was once more sent out.

Bridget Bishop came forward. The girls were stricken, as usual, but Hathorne asked the first question eventually. "Bridget Bishop," he said, "you are now brought before authority to give account of what witchcrafts you are conversant in."

"I take all these people," the innkeeper said, surveying the room, "to witness that I am clear."

Hathorne addressed the accusers. "Hath this woman hurt you?"

"Yes, oh, yes, she is the one," Betty Hubbard, Annie Putnam, Abby Williams and Mercy Lewis cried.

Hathorne addressed Bridget again: "You are here accused by four for hurting them. What do you say to it?"

"I never saw these persons before, nor I never was in this place before." It seemed a peculiar thing to say, inasmuch as she had lived in Salem most of her life.

Mary Walcott cried out, "My brother Jonathan struck her shape, and I saw that he tore her coat in striking — I heard it tear."

Hathorne said to Marshal Herrick, "Search her." Several people did — at last they found what seemed to be a tear in her clothing. Judge Corwin made a note.

"Goody Bishop, what contract have you made with the Devil?"

"I have made no contract with the Devil. I never saw him in my life."

Annie Putnam called out, "She calls the Devil her God!"

"What say you," Hathorne asked, "to all this that you are charged with? Can not you find in your heart to tell the truth?"

"I do tell the truth. I never hurt these persons in my life. I never saw them before."

Mercy Lewis said, "Oh, Goody Bishop, did you not come to our house the last night, and did you not tell me that your master made you tell more than you were willing to tell?"

"Tell us the truth in this matter," Hathorne admonished her. "How came these persons to be thus tormented and to charge you with the doing of it?"

"I am not come here to say I am a witch," Bridget told him squarely, "to take my life."

"Who is it that doth it if you do not? They say it is your likeness that comes and torments them and tempts them to write in the book. What book is it that you tempted them with?"

"I know nothing of it. I am innocent."

Samuel Braybrook rose and said, "She told me today that she had been accounted a witch these ten years, but she said she was no witch, so the Devil cannot hurt her."

Bridget nodded her head. "I am not a witch," she agreed. All the girls were agreeing as well, heads nodding.

Hathorne looked at them, then at Bridget. "Have not you given consent that some evil spirit should do this in your likeness?"

"No! I am innocent of being a witch. I know no man, woman, or child here."

Another voice was raised at that point: Marshal Herrick asked her, "How came you into my bedchamber one morning, then, and asked me whether I had any curtains to sell?" He turned to the bench. "She is by some of the afflicted persons charged with murder."

Hathorne asked, "What do you say to these murders you are charged with?"

"I hope I am not guilty of murder." She rolled her eyes toward the rafters, and the girls mimicked her.

"They say," Hathorne continued, "you bewitched your first husband, Goodman Wasselby, to death." He fixed her with a stare.

"If it please your Worship," Bridget replied, "I know nothing of it." She shook her head; the girls' heads shook, and they fell to fits.

"What do you say to these things here, these horrible acts of witchcraft?"

"I know nothing of it. I do not know whether there be witches or no."

"Why," Hathorne said, "if you have not wrote in the book, yet tell me how far you have gone?"

"I have no familiarity with the Devil."

"How is it, then, that your appearance doth hurt these?"

"I know nothing of it. I am innocent to a witch."

"Why, you seem to act witchcraft before us by the motion of your body, which seems to have influence upon the afflicted." The girls were miming Bridget's every move.

"I know not what a witch is," Bridget told him.

"How do you know, then, that you are *not* a witch?" Hathorne smiled at his own cleverness.

Bridget was merely puzzled. "I do not know what you say," she told him.

The judge frowned. He rephrased his question so her simple mind could fathom it: "How can you know that you are no witch, and yet not know what a witch is?"

"I am clear. If I were any such person, *you* should know it."

Hathorne blanched, then recovered himself. He leaned forward, louring. "You may threaten," he told Bridget, "but you can do no more than you are permitted. It may be you do not know that any have confessed today, who have been examined before you, that they are witches?"

"No. I know nothing of it."

John Hutchinson and John Lewis rose in the audience. "That is a lie." "We told her," they said.

"Why, look you," Hathorne said, "you are taken now in a flat lie."

"I did not hear them."

Disgusted, Hathorne dismissed her. When she was again outdoors in the custody of Samuel Gould he asked her, "Were you not troubled to see the afflicted persons so tormented?"

"No," the old witch told him, "I was not troubled for them."

"Do you think they were bewitched?"

Bridget shrugged and said, "I cannot tell what to think about them."

Giles Corey was examined next, but the proceedings could not get under weigh until his hands were bound so that his specter would stop hurting the afflicted people. At last things got quiet enough so that Hathorne could say to him, "You see these accuse you. What do you say to it?"

"I know nothing of it." He shook his head: All the girls' heads, and the afflicted women's, and John Indian's began to shake. "I am innocent," Corey said stonily. Although he wasn't sure about his wife, at least he knew for sure that *he* was no witch.

"What! Is it not enough to act witchcrafts at other times, but must you do it now, in the face of authority?"

"I am a poor creature," Giles replied, "and cannot help it."

"Do not you see you hurt them?"

"I do not hurt them. I am innocent."

"Why do you tell such wicked lies against witnesses?" Hathorne turned to George Herrick and said, "Loosen one of his hands." Herrick complied, and the girls went into fits again. Corey cocked his head to look at them — several other heads were cocked. He drew in his cheeks in wonderment — other cheeks were sucked in.

Goody Bibber cried, "Oh! He is the one! He hath tormented me and is a murderer! He called my husband a 'damned devilish rogue!'"

The old man raised his brows. "I know nothing of it. I am innocent."

But Hathorne had a pertinent question to ask: "Did not you say that your wife is a witch?"

"No," Corey had the brass to reply, though to speak truly, he had not said so in so many words, but he had intimated it strongly; he *had* called her a liar in court. "We did but disagree," he finished lamely.

"Did not you often argue?"

"I did but say, 'Living to God and dying to sin,' and she found fault with me for it. I did believe it was all right to say it."

Sarah Bibber cut in once more — "He told me he saw the Devil in his cow house in the shape of a dog and was much frighted."

"It is not so," Corey said.

"But Hathorne was interested. "What did you see in the cow house? Why do you deny it?" Several people in the gallery rose to affirm that he had told them he was frightened in his barn. Hathorne asked again, "Well, what do you say to these witnesses? What was it frighted you?"

"I do not know that ever I spoke the word in my life."

"Is it not true that you have thought to make away with yourself and charge it upon your son?" Shocked murmurs rippled through the audience. "It is a very great sin."

But Giles Corey fell silent and refused to say anything more. At last, furious, Hathorne dismissed him and committed all those that had been examined that day to prison.

Most of the men who had been present at the hearing retreated to Ingersoll's Ordinary, but the judges followed their prisoners to Salem prison in order to try to conclude, in camera, their examination of Mary Warren. In her cell Mary admitted to having signed the Devil's Book.

"Did not you know it was the Devil's book when you signed?" she was asked.

"No. But I thought it was no good book."

"After you had made your mark in the book, what did you think then?"

"Then I thought it was the Devil's Book."

"How did you come to know your master and mistress, Goodman Proctor and his wife, were witches?"

"The Sabbath eve after I had put up my note for thanks in public my mistress," Elizabeth Proctor, "appeared to me and pulled me out of the bed and told me that she was a witch and had put her hand to the Book. She told me this in her bodily person. And she said that I might have known she was a witch if I had but minded what books she read in."

"What did she say to you before you tormented the children?"

"The night after she told me she was a witch she in her person told me that I and her son John, would quickly be brought out for witches.

"Giles Corey's shape," she continued, "told me the night before that the magistrates were going up to the Farms to bring down more witches to torment me."

Giles Corey was in another cell of the prison being examined at the same time, and Mary was sent for to come to his cell. When she heard the message she fell into a fit; when at last she came to she said that Corey's specter had appeared and told her not to go into the room where he was. Her examiners thought this would be a fine opportunity, once again, to try Edward Putnam's spectral evidence test, so Mary was asked what Corey's specter had been wearing in her vision. She replied that he had on a coat of a certain color, a cord about his waist, and a white cap. There were chains on his legs.

Mary was forced then to go to Corey's cell — and he was wearing what she said he wore. Corey was told to look at her; he did so, and she was tormented. When she came around again she charged him to his face with having caused her torment. She told the authorities present that Corey, while they were both in prison, had threatened her that he would "fix her for it" because she had caused her master to ask more for a piece of meadow than Corey was willing to give.

Meanwhile at Ingersoll's tavern Edward Bishop, Bridget's husband, was drinking beer and watching John Indian kicking up a ruckus. Finally he had had enough. He got up, said, "Here, now, we shall have no more of *that*!" and gave him a lash or two with a stick. John Indian immediately quieted down and the men went on drinking and conversing.

Afterwards Bishop and others were riding home. John Indian, mounted pillion behind a man, had another fit: He sank his teeth into the man's shoulder. The man yelled loudly at which Edward Bishop rode up alongside and lashed John Indian a few times until he came to himself and let go.

"John not do that any more," the Indian said.

"I doubt not," Bishop said to the company in general. "I could cure them all with the same medicine."

Not long after he left the company of riders Edward Bishop was cried out upon.

The possessed girls were busy. Abigail Hobbs had implicated a number of people in Topsfield, Ipswich, Salem Village, and Salem; Mercy Lewis cried out upon George Jacobs, and in the evening Annie Putnam saw the shape of the Rev. Mr. George Burroughs of Casco. She exclaimed, "Oh! Dreadful! Dreadful! What? Are ministers witches too? What is your name, for I will complain of you, though you be a minister, if you be a wizard."

Burroughs' specter tortured her — she was racked and choked. He tempted her to write in his book, but she refused with loud cries: "I will not write in your book though you tear me to pieces! It is a dreadful thing that you who are a minister that should teach children to fear

God, should come to persuade poor creatures to give their souls to the Devil. Oh! Dreadful! Tell me your name that I may know who you are!"

Instead of doing so, however, Burroughs tortured her again, once more requested that she put pen to book. When Annie refused, Burroughs' apparition told her, obligingly, "My name is George Burroughs. I have had three wives. I bewitched the first two of them to death, and I killed Mrs. Lawson" — Rev. Deodat Lawson's wife — "because I was so unwilling to leave Salem Village, and I killed Mr. Lawson's child because he went to the Eastward with Sir Edmund, and I preached so to the soldiers, and I bewitched a great many soldiers to death at the Eastward when Sir Edmund was there, and I made Abigail Hobbs a witch and several witches more, and above a witch, I am a conjuror as well."

Warrants were issued on Thursday, April 21st, against William and Deliverance Hobbs, Abigail's parents; Nehemiah Abbott; Mary Easty, and Sarah Wilds — all of Topsfield or Ipswich; Edward Bishop and Sarah Bishop, and Mary Black, Negro servant of Nathaniel Putnam — of Salem Village; and Mary English of Salem, wife of the wealthy merchant Philip English who had heard he was to be cried out upon and had fled. The warrants were issued on the complaint of Sgt. Thomas Putnam, Jr. and John Buxton.

Mary Warren was again examined in prison by the Rev. Mr. Nicholas Noyes who showed her a Bible and asked her if this was not the book she had been asked to sign — they showed her her mark in it and asked her to touch it. She did so and said, "No, I see I was deceived."

"Did you not tell Mercy Lewis that you had signed a book?"
"No."
"Did not your mistress bring you a book to sign?"
"No, but my master brought one."
"Did you sign it?"
"No, unless putting my finger to it was signing."

"Did you not see a spot where you had put your finger?"

"There was a spot."

"What color was the spot?"

"It was black." This is the first recorded instance of a fingerprint being used as evidence in a criminal trial.

"Did not your master John Proctor threaten to run hot tongs down your throat if you did not sign?"

"No. He threatened to burn me out of my fit."

"Did you make a mark in the book?

"I made no mark but with the tip of my finger."

"What did you dip your finger in when you made the mark?"

"Nothing but my mouth." In order to make a black mark, then, her fingers must have been exceedingly dirty.

"Was your finger wet when you touched the book with it?"

"I know not that it was wet, or whether it was wet with sweat or with cider I had been drinking of" — hard cider, no doubt — "I know not. But my finger did make a mark, and the mark was black."

"Were there any there but your master and mistress when you were threatened with the tongs?"

"None but them. My master put my hand to the book, and my finger made a black spot, which made me tremble. Then I was undone body and soul and cried out grievously. They told me it was my own voluntary act. I would have denied it, but they told me the Devil could have done nothing if I had not yielded, and that I, for ease to my body — not for any good to my soul — had done it. With this I much grieved and cried out. My master and mistress threatened to drown me and to make me run through the hedges," a much worse threat than drowning, evidently, especially after having already been drowned.

"Have you not seen your master and mistress since you came to prison?"

"I thought I saw my master, and I daresay it was he."

"What did he say to you?"

"Nothing." She fell into a fit, recovered herself and cried, "I will tell! I will tell! I will tell! Thou wicked creature, it is you stopped my mouth, but I will confess the little that I have to confess."

"Who would you tell of?" Mary was asked. "Is it Goody Proctor or no?" Leading questions were good questions.

"O! Betty Proctor — it is she," Mary cried, "it is she I lived with last! It shall be known, thou wretch! Hast thou undone me body and soul?" Turning away from the apparition to Noyes, Mary said, "She said also she wishes she had made me make a thorough league."

"What was your finger blackened with when you touched the book?"

"I knew not that my finger was black till I see it blacken the book, and after I put my finger to the book I eat bread and butter, and my finger blacked the bread and butter also."

"What does your mistress now say to you?"

"My mistress bids me not tell your Honors that she is a witch." Mary went into convulsions again, came out of them and cried, "My master now bids me not to tell that he had sometimes gone to make away with himself, for he told me that he had been about sometimes to make away with himself because of his wife's quarreling with him." Another fit.

When she was again herself Noyes asked, "How do you know Goodwife Proctor was a witch?"

"I will tell! I will tell!" Mary shrieked. "My mistress told me I might know she was a witch if I hearkened to what she used to read. My mistress had many books, and she carried one book with her to Reading" — an appropriately named town not far away — "when she went to see her sister."

"Did you know your mistress was a witch before you touched the book?"

"My mistress told me she had set her hand to the Devil's book that same night that I was thrown out of bed, which was the same night after she had a note of thanksgiving put up at the meetinghouse. My mistress came to me in her body, not her shape as far as I know, and she said she was a witch."

"Have you seen any of the witches since you came to prison?"

"I have seen Goodman Corey and Sarah Goode — they brought the book to me to sign."

The inquisitors pressed her further, but she would not say that she knew John Proctor was a witch or wizard. She was asked whether she didn't know her finger would make a mark if she touched the book with it.

"No," she replied, "but my master and mistress asked me to read, and the first word I read was 'Moses.' The next word I could not tell what it was, but my master and mistress bade me if I could not pronounce the word I should touch the book."

"Why will you not tell the whole truth?"

"I had formerly not told all the truth because I was threatened to be torn in pieces if I did, but now I will, and have told the truth."

"Did you not suspect it was the Devil's Book that you touched?"

"I did not suspect it before I see my finger blacked it."

"Why did you yield to do as you did?"

"My master said if I would not, when I was in my fit I should run into the fire or water, if I would, and destroy myself, and he would not lift a finger to save me."

"Have you not been instrumental in afflicting the children?"

"No, but when I heard they were afflicted in my shape I began to fear it was the Devil."

"Do you have images to stick pins or thorns into to hurt people?"

"No."

"Did the Devil never ask your consent to hurt in your shape?"

"No. I heard my master and mistress tell of images and of sticking of thorns in them to hurt people."

"Do you know of any images in the house?"

"No."

"Do you know of any ointment they had in the house?" For the tradition was that witches used salves made of the grease of dead babies to smear themselves so that they could fly through the air.

"My mistress ointed me once for some ail I had, but it was with ointment that came from Mrs. Bassett of Lynn. The color of it was greenish." Noyes made a note, and Mrs. Bassett was a marked woman.

"How did it smell?"

"Very ugly to me."

Noyes asked her, "How many times did you touch the book?"

"When I touched the book I went to put my finger to another line, but still my finger went to the same place where my finger had blacked it."

The minister said, "Then you touched the book twice. Did you not suspect it to be the Devil's book before you touched it the second time?"

"I feared it was no good book."

"What do you mean by 'no good book'?"

"A book to deceive."

At eleven o'clock Benjamin Hutchinson was with Abigail Williams. The girl said, "There stands a little black minister that lived at Casco Bay — he says so. He says that he has killed three wives, two for himself and one for Mr. Lawson, and that he had made nine witches in Salem Village. He says he can hold out the heaviest gun that is in Casco Bay with one hand."

Hutchinson asked, "Where about does this little man stand?"

Abigail pointed — "Just where the cart wheel went along."

Hutchinson, who was holding a three-tined pitchfork, threw it to the spot. Abigail fell to the ground in a short fit. When it was over she said, "You have torn his coat, for I heard it tear."

"Whereabouts?" Hutchinson asked.

"To one side," she replied.

The pair of them walked along to Ingersoll's together, entered the main room, and Abigail, cried, "There he stands!"

"Where? Where?" Hutchinson asked, drawing his rapier, but Abigail said, "He is gone." Then, a moment later, "There is a gray cat!"

"Where?" Hutchinson asked again, "Whereabouts doth she stand?"

"There!" Abigail cried, pointing. Hutchinson struck at the spot; Abigail fell into a fit. When it was over she told him, "You killed her, and immediately Sarah Goode came and carried her away." It was noon.

Lecture was held in the tavern that day because of the examinations that were taking place, and afterward Abigail Williams and Mary Walcott had several fits and said, "William Hobbs and his wife go, both of them, along the table!" Hutchinson hauled out his trusty blade again, whiffled it through the air. "You have stabbed Goody Hobbs in her side!" they screeched, "and scratched her eye, but now the room is full of shapes!"

Hutchinson and Edward Putnam flailed about, parrying and thrusting at shadows. At last, having seen enough of invisible gore, the girls said, "You have killed a great black woman of Stonington, and an Indian that came with her, for the floor is all covered with blood." Hutchinson and Putnam stood panting, having fought well and hard for the Lord, but they were startled to defensive postures once more when the girls looked out the window and called, "There is a great company of them on a hill, and there are three of them as lies dead — the black woman, the Indian, and one other that we know not." It was four in the afternoon.

Thomas Putnam heard the news of Abigail Williams' crying out upon George Burroughs by evening, but it was no news to him, for his own daughter Annie, had done so as well. He had written a letter to Judges John Hathorne and Jonathan Corwin that read in part, hinting darkly, "We thought it our duty to inform your Honors of what we conceive you have not heard, which are high and dreadful — of a wheel within a wheel, at which our ears do tingle." Thomas hoped God would prepare them that they "may be a terror to evil-doers and a praise to them that do well...."

In the evening the constable went to the great English mansion in Salem to arrest Mary English. She had already retired, but the servants let him in and escorted him to the lady's bedchamber where he read her the warrant for her arrest. She thanked him; he placed guards about the house for the night.

In the morning Mary English came downstairs, prayed with her family, kissed her children, and told the constable, "Let us go, then. I am ready to die."

Ephraim Wilds was constable of Topsfield. When Marshal George Herrick of Salem came with a warrant for the arrest of William and Deliverance Hobbs, Wilds did his duty. No sooner had Goody Hobbs been taken into custody than she accused Sarah Wilds, Ephraim's mother, of being a witch. The constable said that, when he had arrested her, Deliverance "did show a very bad spirit when I seized her — one might almost see revenge in her face, she looked so maliciously on me. As for my mother — I never saw any harm by her upon any such account, neither in word nor action, as she is now accused of."

The examinations of April 22nd were held in Salem Village. John Hathorne and Jonathan Corwin were on the bench when Sarah Wilds was led in and the girls fell to their preliminary fits. Hathorne asked the girls, "Hath this woman hurt you?"

One replied, "Oh! She is upon the beam!"

Goody Bibber, who had never seen Sarah Wilds before, cried, "I see her now upon the beam!" and fell into contortions.

Hathorne turned to Sarah: "What say you to this? Are you guilty or not?"

"I am not guilty, sir," she answered.

The girls cried out, "She is guilty! She hurts us now!" and gyrated some more.

"What do you say," Hathorne asked again, "are you guilty?"

"I thank God, I am free."

One of the girls shrieked, "She made me sign the Book!"

"Here," Hathorne told Goody Wilds, "is a clear evidence that you have been not only a tormenter, but that you have caused one to sign the book the night before last. What do you say to this?"

"I never saw the book in my life, and I never saw these persons before."

The girls stepped up their contortions.

"Did you never consent that these children should be hurt?"

"Never in my life."

The girls screamed, "She hurt John Hemmings' mother?"

"I deny it," Sarah Wilds said.

Captain James Howe, Jr., rose to tell the story of how the witch had killed John Hemmings' mother. The girls cried, "She is upon the beam!" and had more fits. Sarah Wilds was taken away and Deliverance Hobbs brought in.

Jidge John Hathorne began by asking the bewitched folks, "Mercy Lewis, do you know her that stands at the bar?" Mercy was struck dumb. Hathorne asked another, "Do you know her?" Another dumbshow. But Annie Putnam piped up, "It was Goody Hobbs, and she hath hurt Mercy very much." John Indian said, "I saw her," and he was choked for having volunteered the information. Mary Walcott said that yesterday had been the first time she had seen Goody Hobbs as a tormenter.

Hathorne turned to Goody Deliverance Hobbs to ask, "Why do you hurt these persons?"

"It is unknown to me," she replied.

"How come you to commit acts of witchcraft?"

"I know nothing of it."

"It is you or your appearance. How comes this about? Tell us the truth."

"I cannot tell."

"Tell us what you know in this case," Hathorne cajoled. "Who hurts them if you do not?"

"There are a great many persons hurts us all."

"But it is *your* appearance."

"I do not know it."

"Have you not consented to it, that they should be hurt?"

"No, in the sight of God and man, as I shall answer another day."

"It is said you were afflicted. How came that about?"

"I have seen sundry sights."

"What sights?"

"Last Lord's Day, in this meeting house and out of the door, I saw a great many birds, cats and dogs, and heard a voice say, 'Come away!'"

"What have you seen since?"

"The shapes of several persons."

"What did they say?"

"Nothing."

"What! Neither the birds nor persons?"

"No."

"What persons did you see?"

"Goody Wilds and the shape of Mercy Lewis."

Hathorne was stunned, as was the rest of the court. "WHAT is that!" he exclaimed, "Did neither of them hurt you."

"None but Goody Wilds, who tore me almost to pieces."

"Where was you then?"

"In bed."

"Was not the book brought to you to sign?"

"No."

"Were not you threatened by anybody if you did not sign the book?"

"No, by nobody."

"What were you tempted to, under your affliction?"

"I was not tempted at all."

"Is it not a solemn thing, that last Lord's Day you were tormented, and now you are become a tormenter, so that you have changed sides! How comes this to pass?"

Abigail Williams and Annie Putnam cried, "There is Goody Hobbs upon the beam." "She is not at the bar — we cannot see her there!"

"What do you say to this?" Hathorne asked, "that though you are at the bar in person, yet they see your appearance upon the beam, and whereas a few days past you were tormented, now you are become a tormenter? Tell us how this change comes — tell true."

"I have done nothing."

"What! Have you resolved you will not confess? You can tell how this change comes."

Deliverance Hobbs looked at John Indian and the others — they fell to fits at her evil eye. Hathorne said, "Tell us the reason of this change — tell us the truth. What have you done?"

"I cannot tell."

"Have you signed to any book?"

"It is very lately, then."

"When was it?" Hathorne queried, looking quite satisfied.

"The night before the last."

"Will the Lord upen your heart to confess the truth? Who brought the book to you?"

"It was Goody Wilds."

"What did you make your mark with in the Book?"

"Pen and ink."

"Who brought you the pen and ink?"

"They that brought the book — Goody Wilds."

"Did they threaten you if you did not sign?"

"Yes — to tear me in pieces."

"Was there any else in the company?"

"No, sir."

"What did you afflict others by? Did they bring you images?"

"Yes."

"Who brought the images?"

"Goody Wilds and Goody Osburn."

"What did you put into those images?"

"Pin, sir."

"Well, tell us, who have you seen of this company>"

"None but those two."

"Have not you seen many?"

"No, I heard last night a kind of thundering."

"How many images did you use?"

"But two."

"Nay, there is more afflicted by you; you said more — well, tell us the truth. Recollect yourself."

"I am amazed," Goody Hobbs said, meaning she was confused.

"Can you remember how many were brought?"

"Not well, but several were brought."

"Did they not bring the image of John Nichols' child?"

"Yes."

"Did not you hurt that child?"

"Yes."

"Where be those images, at your house?"

"No, they carried them away again." By now, none of the afflicted were having fits; they merely sat and listened with great interest.

"When?" Hathorne asked.

"They carried some then, and some since."

"Was it Goody Wilds in body, or appearance?"

"In appearance."

"Was there any man with them?"

"Yes, a tall Black Man with a high-crowned hat."

"Do you know no more of them?"

"No, sir."

After her public examination Deliverance Hobbs was asked in private, "Did you receive any hurt yesterday?"

She answered, "Yes, in my right side, like a prick, and it was very sore."

"When was it done?"

"When I was in a trance."

The magistrates ordered a committee of women to conduct a body search of Mrs. Hobbs to verify the fact, and it was verified: they found a sore spot on her side. The confessed witch also complained that she had something in her left eye as a result of her torture, like dust. Marshal Herrick looked and said, "Why, so there is!"

Goody Hobbs' husband William was brought in next. Hathorne asked the girls, "Hath this man hurt you?"

"No," answered Goody Bibber; all the rest said, "Yes."

"What say you, are you guilty or not?" Hathorne asked.

"I can speak in the presence of God safely, as I must look to give account another day, that I am as clear as a new-born babe," Goodman Hobbs told the judge.

"Clear of what?" Hathorne urged him.

"Of witchcraft."

"Have you never hurt these?"

"No."

"Have not you consented that they should be hurt?"

Abigail Williams cried, "He is going to Mercy Lewis to hurt her!" Mercy had a fit, then passed Hobbs' specter on: "He is coming to Mary Walcott!" she cried, and Mary fell to horrible tortures.

John Hathorne was visibly affected, poor man. "How can you be clear," he asked Hobbs, "when the children saw something come from you and afflict these persons?" All the children, according to Samuel Parris, the court clerk, "fell to fits and hallooed and suffered greatly." Hathorne asked Hobbs, "When were you at any public religious meeting?"

"Not in a pretty while," Hobbs told him.

"Why so?"

"Because I was not well. I had a distemper."

"Can you act witchcraft here, and by casting your eyes, turn folks into fits?"

"You may judge at your pleasure," Hobbs replied coolly, "my soul is clear."

"Do not you see you hurt them by your look?"

"No. I do not know it."

"You did not answer to that question. Don't you overlook them?"

"No, I don't overlook them."

"What do you call that way of looking upon persons and striking them down?"

"You may judge at your pleasure."

"Well, but what do you call it?"

"It was none of I."

"Who was it, then?"

"I cannot tell who they are."

Abigail Williams cried, "He is going to hurt Mercy Lewis!" who fell into a fit, as did the others.

"Why, they say they see you going to hurt persons, and immediately there are hurt persons. Can you now deny it?"

"I can deny it to my dying day," Hobbs answered firmly.

"What is the reason that you go away when there is any reading of the scripture in your family?"

"I deny it."

Nathaniel Ingersoll and Thomas Haynes rose to testify that Goodman Hobbs' daughter, Abigail, had told them he did so.

"As soon as your daughter — and after her today your wife — confessed, they left off torturing others, and so would you if you would confess. Can you still deny that you are guilty?"

"I am not guilty."

"If you put away God's ordinances, no wonder that the Devil prevails with you to keep his counsel. Have you never had any apparition?"

"No, sir."

"Did you never pray to the Devil that your daughter might confess no more?"

"No, sir."

"Who do you worship?"

"I hope I worship God only."

"Where?"

"In my heart."

"But God requires outward worship too, yet you do not worship Him in public, nor in your family."

"I worship Him in my heart."

"Yet you do not worship Him in your family, if your family speak the truth. Have not you given the Devil advantage over you thereby?"

Hobbs was silent awhile, thinking. Then he said, "Yes."

"Have not you known a good while how that your daughter was a witch?"

"No, sir."

"Do you think she is a witch now?"

"I do not know."

"Well, if you desire mercy from God, own the truth."

"I do not know anything of that nature."

"What do you think ails these people?" Hobbs was silent. "Why do not you answer what it is that ails them?"

"I do not know what ails them. I am sorry, but it is none of I."

"Do you think they are bewitched?"

"I cannot tell." He continued to deny any knowledge of what ailed the afflicted people, his wife and daughter, and at length he was dismissed.

Mary Easty, sister of Rebecca Nurse and Sarah Cloyse, was brought in for examination. She was fifty-eight years old, the mother of seven. After the ordinary preliminaries Judge John Hathorne asked, "Do not you see you are guilty? It would be well to confess."

"Would you have me accuse myself?" Mary asked incredulously.

"How far have you complied with Satan?"

"Sir," the woman answered with great dignity. "I never complied, but prayed against him all my days."

"Confess, if you be guilty."

"I will say it, if it was my last time — I am clear of this sin."

Hathorne asked the girls, "Are you certain this is the woman?" They all affirmed it with wild torments. Annie Putnam came to and said, "That is the woman! It was like her, and she told me her name." The girls mimicked Mary Easty's every gesture: When the witch bowed her head the girls cried, "Put up her head, for while her head is bowed, the necks of these are broken!" Once more Hathorne put the question to the girls. "*Is* this the woman?" — but the afflicted people gestured that they had been struck dumb, until Annie Putnam bellowed, "Oh! Goody Easty, Goody Easty, you are the woman! You are the woman!"

"What do you say to this?" Hathorne asked Mrs. Easty.

"Why, God will know."

"Nay," Hathorne contradicted her, having caught her on a fine point of doctrine, "God knows now."

"I know He does," she replied.

"What did you think of the actions of others before your sisters came out? Did you think it was witchcraft?"

"I cannot tell."

"Why, do not you think it is witchcraft?"

"It is an evil spirit, but whether it be witchcraft, I do not know."

Hathorne sent her away, having received no satisfaction at all.

Nehemiah Abbott's examination was unusual. At first there was the regular scene with Abbott protesting his innocence and Mary Walcott saying, "I have seen his shape," Annie Putnam crying, "I see him upon the beam!"

Hathorne told Abbott, "Your guilt is certainly proved," which probably ought to have meant that the hearing was superfluous. "If you would find mercy in God, you must confess."

"I speak before God," Abbott replied, "that I am clear from this accusation."

"What! In all respects?"

"Yes — in *all* respects." The girls went dumb at Abbott's words. Annie Putnam said, "He is surely the man who hurts me!" and fell into a seizure — but Mary Walcott said, "I am not sure it is he." It was a clear cue for Annie Putnam who screamed out of her trance, "Did you put a mist before my eyes?"

Mercy Lewis confirmed the incredible fact: "It is not the man," and the court examination came to a halt. Abbott was sent out while others were examined.

Later, he was brought back in, but there were so many people crowding about him and hanging in at the windows that Hathorne said, "Take him abroad into the daylight so that the afflicted may see him." Abbott went outside with the girls and magistrates. Several of these spoke quietly with him, and each of the afflicted girls cleared him. Mary Walcott said, "He is very like unto the one I saw, but he has not the wen." Abbott, to the utter amazement of the onlookers, was set free.

Nathaniel Putnam's slave Mary Black was examined. The girls maintained that she hurt them, and when Hathorne said, "These persons say you hurt them. What do you say to it?" Mary replied, "I do not hurt them."

"Who hurts them, then?"

"I do not know."

"Is it your shape hurts them?"

"I cannot tell."

Annie Putnam said, "Her master saith a man sat down upon the form with her about a twelvemonth ago." A murmur ran through the crowd — if that man had been white, Mary had at the very least breached a social taboo.

"What did the man say to you?" Hathorne asked.

"He said nothing."

Hathorne asked the girls, "Doth this Negro hurt you?"

"Yes! Yes!" they cried.

Back to Mary: "Why do you hurt them?"

"I did not hurt them."

"Do you prick witch sticks?"

"No. I pin my neck-cloth."

"Will you take out the pin and pin it again?"

Mary Black complied, and the girls were tormented. Mary Walcott showed that she had been pricked in the arm and blood was running from the wound; likewise, Abigail Williams was pricked in the stomach, Mercy Lewis in the foot. It was quite clear the black woman was guilty and she was sent to prison with the others.

In jail Mary Warren said to Edward Bishop and some of the others that evening, in a rational moment away from the eyes of the authorities, "The magistrates might as well examine Eleazer Keysar's daughter that has been distracted many years, and take notice of what she said as well as any of the afflicted girls, for when I was afflicted I thought I saw the apparitions of a hundred persons, for my head was so distempered that I could not tell what I said. When I was well again I could not say that I saw any of the apparitions at the time foretold."

On Sunday Susannah Sheldon was at meeting when the shape of Philip English stepped over a pew and pinched her. He and the phantom of Sarah Goode accosted her later and asked her to sign the Devil's Book. On Monday the 25th English again pinched Susannah; on Tuesday she was accosted by two women and a man who brought books for her to touch. She refused. She didn't know where they lived, but one of them told her they lived in the Village.

He offered her the book again, but she told them she didn't know their names. One of the women told her she was "Old Goodman Buckley's wife" Goody Buckley and that the other woman was her daughter, Mary Buckley. Now would Susannah touch the book?

"No," Susannah said, for the woman hadn't told her how long she had been a witch. "Ten years," the harridan said obligingly as she opened her dress, took "two little things like young cats," put them to her breast and suckled them. The things had no hair on them, and ears like a man's jutted out of their heads. Still Susannah wouldn't sign the book; therefore, the witch pinched her in lieu of anything worse that she might have been able to do, like the man, who knocked her on the head, and then they went away.

The next day, Wednesday, a woman appeared to Susannah — the witch sat on the doorstep and laughed at the girl, came into the house, hopped up and down, and offered her the book to touch, promising she wouldn't pinch her if she did it. There was a scene like that of the preceding day, and the witch said her name was Goodwife White. Later on in the day Goody Buckley and Mary Buckley came back with books, but this time they carried Susannah away to a wood near which William Shaw was plowing. The farmer heard a noise in the woods, went to investigate, and found Susannah Sheldon lying there in a swoon.

Saturday was a day of warrants. They were issued for the arrest of Philip English, merchant of Salem; Sarah Merrill and Dorcas Hoar of Beverly, and Susannah Martin of Amesbury. The complainants were Sgt. Thomas Putnam, Jr. and Capt. Jonathan Walcott. In Boston Elisha Hutchinson, a magistrate, issued a surreptitious warrant for the arrest of Rev. George Burroughs of Wells, Maine.

When George Herrick, Marshal of Essex County on Monday, May 2nd, went to arrest Philip English, he was still missing, but the Marshal did take into custody Sarah Merrill and Dorcas Hoar. Orlando Begley, constable of Amesbury, apprehended the "short old woman" and quite neat witch Susannah Martin who scorned to get her clothing wet in foul weather.

When Dorcas Hoar was examined, after the diabolical preliminaries in the courtroom Betty Hubbard said, "This woman has afflicted me ever since last Sabbath was seven nights, and hurt me ever since, and she choked her own husband." Mary Walcott affirmed that the witch's specter had told her the same thing.

Abigail Williams testified, "This is the woman that I saw first, before Tituba Indian or any else." Ann Putnam was equally positive: "This is the woman that hurts me; the first time I was hurt by her was the Sabbath was seven nights." Susannah Sheldon informed John Hathorne and Corwin that "She hurt me last Monday night," and Abigail Williams said, "She told me and Annie Putnam that she choked a woman lately at Boston." Annie Putnam nodded — "That is what she said."

"Why do you pinch me?" Abigail cried.

Marshal George Herrick had the answer: "She pinched her fingers together, and the girl was hurt." Everyone crowded around to see the ghastly red mark.

"Dorcas Hoar," John Hathorne intoned, "Why do you hurt these?"

"I never hurt any child in my life," The palmist replied.

"It is you or your appearance."

"How can I help it?"

"What is it from you that hurts these?"

"I never saw worse than myself."

"You need not see worse," Hathorne quipped. "They charge you with killing your husband."

"I never did," she said to the judge, then, to the children, "nor never saw you before."

One of the girls said, "You sent for Goody Gale to cut your head off."

"What do you say to that?" Hathorne asked, leaning forward and fixing her with a baleful stare.

"I never sent for her on *that* account!"

"What do you say about killing your husband?"

Before Goody Hoar could answer Susannah Sheldon broke in: "She came in with two cats and brought me the book!" Susie fell into a fit and screamed, "You told me your name was Goody Buckley!"

"No, I never did. I never saw thee before," Dorcas replied formally.

Someone called, "What black cats were those you had?" Mary Walcott, Sue Sheldon, and Betty Hubbard cried, "Look! See! He is there!" "A Black Man is whispering in her ear!"

Dorcas' composure broke. "Oh! You are liars!" she fumed. "God will stop the mouth of liars!" Just then Hathorne noticed that Goody Bibber was staring into space toward the roof. He asked, "What did you see, Goody Bibber?" But the woman was struck dumb. Hathorne turned again to the accused. "What! Can you have no heart to confess?"

Mrs. Hoar had gathered herself once more. She replied calmly, "I have nothing to do with witchcraft."

"They say the Devil is whispering in your ear."

"I cannot help it if they do say it."

"Cannot you confess what you think of these things?"

"Why should I confess what I do not know?"

"Oh, Goody Hoar!" Susie howled, "Do not kill me!" and fell to the floor. When she came round again she said, "I saw a Black Man whispering in her ear, and she brought me the Book!"

"I have no book but the Lord's Book." This was dangerous ground, for evidence had been given in that she had told fortunes out of a book for years, but Hathorne unaccountably let his opportunity pass. He asked, "What Lord's Book?" Perhaps it was merely what he considered to be a subtle question, but if so its subtlety was lost upon his witch, or she was cleverer than he gave her credit for. "*The* Lord's Book," she replied.

"Oh!" the afflicted people cried, "There is one whispering in her ears!"

Dorcas leaned forward toward them, squinted and hissed, "There is somebody will rub your ears shortly." Everyone fell into convulsions, including Mercy Lewis.

"Why do you threaten they should be rubbed?" Hathorne queried, the Book forgotten.

"I did not speak a word of rubbing," Dorcas had the effrontery to tell the court, but the spectators all began chiming in to affirm that she had, indeed, done so. "My meaning was," Goody Hoar told Hathorne, "God would bring things to light."

"Your meaning for God to bring the thing to light," the judge informed her, "would be to deliver these poor afflicted ones, not that He would rub them. This is unusual impudence, to threaten before authority," Hathorne bridled. "Who hurts them now?"

"I know not." The girls were flailing about, trying to keep unseen hands from rubbing them.

"They were rubbed after you threatened them," Hathorne said, signaling the Marshal and other officers who bent and tried to bring the girls to the witch for her touch, but they fought away. "What is the reason these cannot come near you?"

"I cannot help it," Dorcas groaned, "I do them no wrong. They may come, if they will."

"Why, you see they cannot come near you," the judge told her.

"I do them no wrong," the accused witch said, all her confidence evaporated, knowing she had condemned herself.

"Do you know this woman?" John Hathorne asked the accusers when the spic-and-span old woman Susannah Martin was arraigned before the bench.

Abigail Williams affirmed their acquaintance: "It is Goody Martin. She hath hurt me often." But Elizabeth Hubbard shook her head — "I have not been hurt by her." John Indian agreed: " Have not seen her," he said. Mercy Lewis recognized her, though — she pointed at the witch and dived into a small fit. Annie Putnam took a good look and threw her glove at Mrs. Martin.

Mrs. Martin laughed.

"What! Do you laugh at it?" Hathorne asked, enraged by her behavior. People were beginning to treat his court with contempt.

"Well may I laugh at such folly," Susannah said to him.

"Is this folly? The hurt of these persons?" Hathorne was trembling with anger.

"I never hurt man, woman or child." Mrs. Martin was quite calm, though chaos was beginning to brew in the meetinghouse.

Mercy cried, "She hath hurt me a great many times — and pulls me down!" She fell down. Mrs. Martin laughed again at the ridiculous display. Mary Walcott said, "This woman hath hurt me a great many times as well." She screamed, "She afflicts me!" and was afflicted.

"What do you say to this?" asked the judge.

"I have no hand in witchcraft."

"What did you do? Did not you give your consent?"

"No, never in my life."

"What ails these people?" Hathorne pointed.

"I do not know."

"But what do you think?"

Goody Martin sniffed. "I do not desire to spend my judgment upon it."

"Do not you think they are bewitched?"

"No, I do not think they are."

"Tell me your thoughts about them."

"Why, my thoughts are my own, when they are in, but when they are out, they are another's and I am no longer their master."

Hathorne's cat-quick mind saw his opportunity, and he pounced upon it: "You said, 'their master' — who do you think is their Master?" he asked, indicating the bewitched folk.

"If they be dealing in the black art, you may know as well as I."

"Well, what have you done towards this?"

"Nothing."

"Why, it is you or your appearance."

"I cannot help it."

"That may be your Master," Hathorne said, playing upon his conceit.

"I desire to lead myself according to the Word of God."

"Is this" — he aimed at the sprawling figures on the floor — "according to God's word?"

"If I were such a person, I would tell you so."

The girls redoubled their bouts of wild hysteria. Obviously, their efforts to this point had had little effect upon the heinous neat witch.

"How comes your appearance just now to hurt these?"

"How do *I* know?" Susannah answered curtly.

"Are not you willing to tell the truth?"

"I cannot tell. He that appeared in Samuel's shape — a glorified saint — can appear in anyone's shape."

"Do you believe these children do not say true?"

"They may lie, for aught I know."

"May not you lie?"

"I dare not tell a lie if it would save my life." In fact, the safest way to stay off the gallows ladder was, indeed, to confess, even if the confession were a lie.

"Then you will speak the truth?"

"I have spoke nothing else. I would do them any good I may."

"I do not think you have such affections for them whom, just now, you insinuated had the Devil for their master."

Betty Hubbard was gyrating at a great rate. Herrick said, "I saw her pinch her hand." Bedlam once more. All the afflicted cried, "There! She is sitting on the beam," and so forth. Hathorne told her soulfully, "Pray God discover you if you be guilty!"

"Amen, Amen," Susannah replied. "A false tongue will never make a guilty person."

Hathorne had never seen such insolence. Mercy screamed, "You have been a long time coming to the court today! You can come fast enough in the night!"

"No, sweetheart," Mrs. Martin said to her unctuously, and Mercy fell to a wild, rolling fit — so did everyone else. John Indian howled, "She bites! She Bites!"

"Have you no compassion for these afflicted!" Hathorne shouted, rising out of his seat and leaning toward Susannah.

"No, I have none," she said, fixing him with her clear eye.

"There is a Black Man with her! He is telling her what to say!" The questioning had gone very badly. "He is whispering into her ear!" Goody Bibber, who had been mute this long time, was at last moved to articulation. "Yes! Yes!" she wailed, "Yes, it is so! There is a Black Man beside her!" Everyone strained to get a look at the witch's Advocate; unfortunately, normal eyes could see not even a shadow.

"Approach her!" Hathorne ordered the girls, but they couldn't get near her without hysteria; neither could Goody Bibber. John Indian bawled, "I will kill her if I come near her!" He scratched and clawed to draw nigh, but failed and went into tumbles. It was a good thing he did, because if he had harmed, or even touched a white woman, he could have been hanged himself.

"What is the reason," Hathorne asked, "these cannot come near you?"

"I cannot tell. It may be the Devil bears me more malice than another."

"Do not you see how God evidently discovers you?"

"No, not a bit for that." But now the crowd had become a mob and voices everywhere called out, "Yes, yes, God discovers her!" and more to the same effect. Hathorne told the witch smugly, "All the congregation think so."

Susannah shrugged. "Let them think what they will."

"What is the reason these cannot come nigh?"

"I do not know; but they *can* if they *will*. Or else, if you please, I will come to them."

"What is the Black Man whispering to you?" Hathorne asked, confounded by his inability even to crack this aged female.

"There was none whispered to me," she said.

Susannah Martin, Lydia Dustin of Reading, Dorcas Hoar, and Sarah Merrill of Beverly were sent to Boston jail.

Later in the day Sarah Bibber was tortured by the specter of Sarah Goode who pressed the breath out of her thirty-six year old body and also pinched her child, whom the matron was holding, so that John Bibber had to take it — but it continued to be tortured till it writhed out of his arms and hurt itself.

That evening in Wells, Maine, the Rev. George Burroughs was sitting in the hall eating his supper when Field Marshal John Partridge rode up, burst into the house, arrested him, and without an explanation bundled the minister off on the familiar road to Salem.

Tuesday, May 3rd, was Election Eve. John Willard, who had acted as deputy constable during the early part of the proceedings, had helped in making arrests, and had come to view the entire witchhunt — everything about it and everything in it — as sheer madness. He had dropped out of the limelight subsequently, and the rumor mill had begun grinding out stories about him after he had shouted that they ought to hang everyone, not just the accused witches. Willard was a latecomer to Salem Village, having formerly lived in Groton. He was related to the large clan of Bray Wilkins by marriage to Margaret Knight, and on the third he went to his kinsman Henry Wilkins to ask him to go to Boston with him to vote in the election. He agreed. Not long afterward Daniel Wilkins approached his father and asked, "Are you going to Boston with John Willard?"

"That I am," Henry replied.

Daniel flushed. "It were well if Willard were hanged!"

Wilkins was startled, for he had never heard his son say anything like that before.

Old Bray Wilkins decided he, too, would vote in Boston, and he told his wife to make ready.

Deliverance Hobbs was examined again on the third. Hathorne asked her, "What have you done since, whereby there is further trouble in your appearance?"

Deliverance was amazed to hear of it, for she thought that her confession would have taken care of further manifestations of her spirit. "Why, nothing at all," she replied.

"But have not you since been tempted?"

"Yes, sir, but I have not done it, nor will not do it."

"Here is a great change since we last spake to you, for now you afflict and torment again. Now tell us the truth," he told her as the girls flopped about. "Who tempted you to sign again?"

Evidently double jeopardy, a new wrinkle, was to apply in this court, so it was of no use to lie to such a clever barrister. "It was Goody Bishop," Deliverance answered. "She would have me to set my hand to the Book, but I would not, neither have I. Neither did I consent to hurt them again."

"Was it true that Goody Wilds appeared to you and tempted you?"

"Yes, that was true."

"Have you been tempted since?"

"Yes, about Friday or Saturday night last."

"Did they bid you that you should not tell?"

"Yes, they told me so."

"But how far did they draw you or tempt you, and how far did you yield to temptation?"

"I did not yield."

"But do not you acknowledge that what you formerly told us was true?"

"Yes."

"And you did sign then at the first, did you not?"

"Yes, I did, it is true."

Then Hathorne put on the record the reason for this new accusation, for Deliverance had evidently told someone she was going to recant. "Did you promise them to deny at last what you said before?"

"Yes, I did, and it was Goody Bishop that tempted me to deny all that I had confessed before."

"Do not you know the man with the wen?" Hathorne was trying to discover who the specter was that had been confused with Nehemiah Abbott.

"No, I do not know who it is. All that I confessed before is true."

Hathorne decided to check her memory. "Who were these you named formerly?"

"Osburn, Goode, Burroughs, Bishop, Wilds, Corey and his wife, Nurse, Proctor and his wife."

"Who were with you in the chamber when you were tempted to sign the second time, on Friday or Saturday night last?" Hathorne was checking the notes he had on the table before him.

"Wilds and Bishop, Goode, and Osburn, and they had a feast both of roast and boiled meat, and did eat and drink and would have had me to eat and drink with them, but I would not, and they would have had me sign, but I would not then, nor when Goody Bishop came to me."

"Nor did not you consent to hurt these children in your likeness?"

"I do not know that I did," she replied dubiously, eyeing the girls.

"What is it you have to tell which you cannot tell yet?"

"I have nothing more to tell."

The specter of Rebecca Nurse told Mary Walcott that she had had a hand in the deaths of Benjamin Houlton, John Harrod, Rebecca Shepard and others, and in the evening the Rev. Mr. George Burroughs appeared to Annie Putnam again, asked her to sign his book; when she refused he said, "My two first wives will appear to you presently and tell you a great many lies, but you should not believe them." Immediately, two phantoms put in an appearance: They were women in winding sheets with kerchiefs about their heads. They turned to Burroughs looking "very red and angry" and said, "You have been a cruel man to us. Our blood does cry for vengeance against you. We shall be clothed with white robes in Heaven when you are cast into Hell." Apparently Hell was not a place that intimidated Annie Putnam herself.

Burroughs vanished. The women turned to Annie Putnam: Their color had changed — now they "looked as pale as a white wall." They told the tirl, "We were Mr. Burroughs' two first wives. He hath murdered us."

One said, "I was his first wife. He stabbed me under the left arm and put a piece of sealing wax on the wound." She pulled aside her winding sheet and showed Annie Putnam. The phantom continued, "I was in the house where Mr. Parris now lives when it was done."

The other moaned, "Mr. Burroughs and his present wife did kill me in the vessel as I was coming to see my friends, for he and that woman" — she meant Burroughs' third wife — "would have one another."

Both the ghosts charged Annie Putnam to tell the magistrates these things "before Mr. Burroughs' face, and if he does not own to them, we do not know but we shall appear there in the court." It was a hair-raising prospect to the Salem Villagers until they thought about it — and then they realized they would probably be able to see no more of these shades than they had of all the others.

As May 4th dawned John Willard and Henry Wilkins were on their way to Boston, as were Mr. and Mrs. Bray Wilkins, but in a separate party. Mrs. Wilkins was not particularly happy about it, for her husband was eighty-one and not in the most rugged physical condition, but he would have it no other way. The two parties did not sight each other on the road, but when Bray reached Lt. Richard Way's house at noon they found many people dining there, including Rev. Mr. and Mrs. Deodat Lawson. Way was Mrs. Wilkins' brother, and they chatted together about the occurrences in Salem Village until John Willard and Bray's brother Henry came in, walked over to Bray's table, and sat down. Bray thought that Willard gave him a strange look, but they spoke a few minutes; then Bray and his wife stepped into the next room to eat. Suddenly he felt ill; he went to the outhouse to relieve himself, but found his urine stopped up. As he described it, "I had no benefit of nature, but was like a man in a rock." He told his wife, "I believe

Willard has done me wrong," though it was more likely his prostate gland or a kidney stone.

The herb doctor and white witch Mary Webster, formerly of Hadley and now of Boston, was summoned to Bray's aid. She gave him a large mug of bearberry tea, but when nothing happened immediately she asked him, "Have none of those evil persons in Salem Village done you damage?"

"I cannot say they have, but I am sore afraid they have," Bray replied.

Mary the practicing witch shook her head. "I do fear so too."

Warrants were issued in Salem Village against George Jacobs and his granddaughter Margaret Jacobs, and the specter of George Burroughs came a-visiting Annie Putnam again. Burroughs in person appeared in Salem under arrest in custody of Field Marshal John Partridge who turned him over to the local authorities. The minister was not put in prison but given lodging at Thomas Beadle's Inn. Abigail Williams was haunted by Rebecca Nurse for the ninth time.

That night Samuel Sewall in Boston wrote in his diary, "Election-Day, Major Hutchinson and Capt. Greenough's company attend, Mr. Moody preaches. Dine at Wing's. The election Capt. Johnson of Woburn is left out, and Maj. Richards chosen again. Sir William Phips had the most votes, viz. 969. No treat at the Governor's but beer, cider, wine." In Salem Capt. John Putnam, Jr. was elected Deputy for the fifth time.

The next day, Thursday, May 5th, Eleazer Keysar, forty, was at Beadle's in Salem socializing with Capt. Daniel King and others, and the inevitable topic of conversation was the upstairs guest. King said to Keysar, "Will you not go up and see Mr. Burroughs and discourse with him?"

"It does not belong to me," Keysar replied, "and I am unwilling to make or meddle with it."

King said, huffily, "Are you not a Christian? If you are a Christian, go and see him, and discourse with him."

Keysar set his glass on the table and told King measuredly, "I do believe it does not belong to such as I am to discourse with him, he being a learned man."

King began to grow angry. "I believe he is a child of God," he said, "a choice child of God, and God will clear his innocency."

But Keysar's back was up too. He cleared his throat and looked at the Captain. "My opinion or fear is that he is the chief of all the persons accused for witchcraft, or the ringleader of them all," Keysar said. "If he is such a one, his Master has told him by now what I have said of him."

Captain King flew into a rage and began to rail at Keysar. A wary hush settled over the room, and Keysar forebore to speak further until the situation had been glossed over by the others present.

Nevertheless, that afternoon Keysar did in fact have occasion to be in Mr. Burroughs' chamber, and it seemed to him that Burroughs "did steadfastly fix his eyes" upon him.

After his day at the tavern Keysar went home and, he wrote in a deposition given in later, "The same evening, being in my own house, in a room without any light, I did see very strange things appear in the chimney, I suppose a dozen of them, which seemed to me to be something like jelly that used to be in the water, and quivered with a strange motion, and then quickly disappeared. Soon after which, I did see a light up in the chimney, about the bigness of my hand, something above the bar, which quivered and shaked, and seemed to have a motion upward, upon which I called the maid, and she, looking up the chimney, saw the same; and my wife looking up could not see any thing. So I did and do conclude it was some diabolical operation!"

On Friday, May 6th, Daniel Wilkins — while his father and uncle were still away at Boston — grew ill up on Will's Hill in Salem Village. In the evening George Burroughs' specter appeared to Mercy Lewis, tortured her, and tried to get her to sign his book, which she refused to do. Then he brought her "a new-fashion book which he did not use to bring." He told her, "You might write in this book, for it is a book that was in my study when you lived with my family."

Mercy replied, "I do not believe you, for I was often in your study, but I never saw that book there."

Burroughs replied, "I had several books in my study which you never saw, and with them I could raise the Devil. I bewitched Mr. Shepard's daughter." Burroughs was referring to Rebecca Shepard, daughter of the late Rebecca Putnam Shepard — Mrs. John Shepard, alias Widow John Fuller.

"How can you go," Mercy asked, "to bewitch her now you are kept at Salem?"

"The Devil is my servant," Burroughs informed her. "I sent him in my shape to do it." He tortured her again, threatened to kill her "For," he said, "you shall not witness against me."

Lydia Wilkins, who had been attending her brother Daniel in his illness, came down with the contagion on May 8th. Her father and uncle yet were away in Boston where Bray Wilkins was still feeling ill himself. And the young Wilkins people were not the only ones who were down with the spread of Satan's scourge. Cases were being reported all over Salem Village. Carolina John Putnam — now Constable John — was recovered from his own affliction; he and his family had buried Sarah, who had succumbed to the pox, and none of that family doubted that the witches were responsible. The Constable threw himself into his work with a will and a vengeance.

The next day, Monday, William Stoughton and Samuel Sewall came down from Boston to join John Hathorne and Jonathan Corwin on the bench, but the first examination of the day was held in private, only the magistrates and ministers present.

Burroughs was asked when he had last partaken of the Lord's Supper, for he maintained that he was a full communicant of the congregation at Roxbury. "It has been so long since, I cannot tell," Burroughs told the interrogators.

"Have you not been to church when the Lord's Supper was served?"

"I was at meeting at Boston part of one day when it was served, and again at Charlestown part of a Sabbath, but I did not partake at either time."

"Why did you not?"

"I do not recall."

"Is it not true that your house at Casco is haunted?" Burroughs was a bit confused — he no longer lived at Casco, but at Wells. Nevertheless he answered, "It is not true."

"Is it not? Doth it not have toads in it?"

"It hath toads, but it is not haunted." It seemed a fine distinction to the judges.

"We have it by report that you made your wife to swear," — swear, that is, not to tell his secrets to the Putnams when they lived together. "What do you say to it?"

"I deny it."

"When she wished to write to her father, did you not forbid it without your consent?" This was all material that had been provided by Mrs. Ann Carr Putnam who had been Mrs. Burroughs' gossip.

"I deny it."

"Is it not true that, of your children, none but the eldest is baptized?"

"It is true."

"How comes this to pass?"

Burroughs did not answer, and the judges decided that it might be better to adjourn to the public gallery. No sooner had they all walked in than the afflicted people went into paroxysms of agony — screams, thrashings-about, wails, ululations: virtual Pandemonium. It lasted a long time, but eventually William Stoughton and the others managed to get things a bit settled and to take testimony from the accusers. Susannah Sheldon said, "This is the man who murdered his two wives. They came to me in their winding sheets and told me so."

Burroughs was asked to turn about to face Susie — he looked back over his shoulder and almost all the afflicted were knocked down; Susie and Annie Putnam gasped that he brought the Book for them to sign. Finally, the judges asked, "What do you think of these things?"

"It is an amazing and humbling Providence," Burroughs admitted, "but I understand nothing of it." He mused for a moment, then said, "Some of you may observe that, when they begin to name my name, they cannot name it."

Annie Putnam and Susannah testified that he murdered his two wives and two of his children. Some of the bewitched had such terrible fits that they were ordered to be carried out of the courtroom. Sarah Bibber managed to rasp out, "This is the man that has hurt me in his shape, but I have not seen him in his presence" — that is, in the flesh — "before this." Assumedly Burroughs had never seen her either, so why would he have tormented her? However, logic was lacking at that time, and Burroughs was too confused to think of it.

Mary Warren told the court that Burroughs, when he wished to call a Sabbat in Rev. Mr. Parris' field, blew a trumpet "to summon the witches to their feasts" — it could be heard rolling against the hills of Lynn and Gallows Hill in Salem, its spectral notes echoing down the Merrimac to Cape Ann and west to Andover, but its blast was audible only to the members of the coven.

The depositions of Abigail and Deliverance Hobbs and Eleazer Keysar were read; Capt. Simon Willard, John Brown, and John Weldon testified to the reality of the myths regarding his strength: He held up a great gun with one hand, even with but one finger stuck in the barrel; Capt. John Putnam, Jr. affirmed the truth of the stories. Capt. William Wormall testified about the barrel of molasses, but he said that Burroughs held the gun in front of the lock and rested its butt on his chest. John Brown told a story about a barrel of cider, but denied that his family was frightened by a white calf in his house. Capt. Putnam deposed that Burroughs forced his wife to enter into a covenant with him, and Abigail Hobbs submitted evidence from prison that Burroughs made her sign the Devil's Book.

A body search of the minister had revealed nothing. At great length, Burroughs was quizzed and finally sent back to confinement. The evidence was overwhelming — at least to Stoughton and Hathorne, if not to Sewall and Corwin; but Sewall, at least, was enormously impressed.

Sarah Churchill, George Jacobs' maidservant, was examined as well, and afterward Mercy Lewis was tormented by George Proctor for the second time. At Ingersoll's Inn the ghosts of William Shaw's first wife, Widow Cook, Goodman Johns and his child, appeared to Susannah Sheldon and accused the specter of John Willard, which was also present, of having killed them; then they turned red as blood, faced eighteen-year-old Susannah, and told her to inform Hathorne. Willard's phantom pulled out an insubstantial knife and told her that if she dared to do so, he would cut her throat.

As soon as Willard heard that he had been cried-out upon he went to Bray Wilkins — who had recuperated sufficiently to have come back from Boston — and asked him and some neighbors to pray with him. Bray told Willard, "I was going out and cannot stay, but if I should come home before night, I should not be unwilling." Bray left the house and Willard, too, departed in anger.

Susannah Sheldon was visited by the specter of Elizabeth Colson and asked to sign the Devil's Book — the witch offered the young woman "a black piece of money" and said that if she "might touch that" she "shall be well." Sarah Bibber and Elizabeth Hubbard both were terrorized by the apparition of George Burroughs for the first time officially.

On Tuesday, May 10th, Sarah Osburn died in prison, the first casualty among the current crop of accused local witches. Warrant was issued for the arrest of John Willard, and George Jacobs was arrested and examined; his granddaughter, Margaret, was arrested as well by Constable Joseph Neal of Salem.

Jacobs was quite a tall old man with white hair who walked with the aid of two canes. He was informed by the court, "Here are them that accuse you of acts of witchcraft."

"Well," he replied, "let us hear who are they and what are they."

Abigail cried out, "He is the one who hurts me!" and fell to a fit to be tied. Jacobs laughed.

"Do you laugh at these?"

"Because I am falsely accused. Your worships — all of you! Do you think this is *true*?" Jacobs was incredulous.

"Nay, what do you think?"

"*I* never did it."

"Who did it?"

"Don't ask me."

"Why should we not ask you?" Sarah Churchill was gagging and pointing at the defendant. "Sarah Churchill accuseth you — there she is."

Jacobs looked with a wide eye at the woman. "I am as innocent as the child born tonight. I have lived thirty-three years here in Salem."

"What then?"

"If you can prove that I am guilty, I will lie under it."

Sarah Churchill said, "Last night I was afflicted at Deacon Ingersoll's...." Mary Walcott broke in, "It was a man with two staves!" "...it was my master," Sarah finished.

Jacobs reproachfully looked at his maid and said, "Pray do not accuse me." Then he turned to the bench: "I am as clear as your worships. You must do right judgments."

"What book did he bring you, Sarah?" the judge asked, ignoring the old man.

"The same that the other woman brought," Sarah replied.

"The Devil can go in any shape," Jacobs told the court.

"Sarah," Stoughton asked, "Did he not appear on the other side of the river and hurt you? Did you not see him?"

"Yes, he did," she replied.

"Look here," Stoughton said, turning to Jacobs, "she accuses you to your face. She charged that you hurt her twice. Is it not true?"

"What would you have me say?" the old man asked, leaning on his canes. "I never wronged no man in word nor deed."

"Here are three evidences," Stoughton told him, fanning out three depositions."

"You tax me for a wizard. You may as well tax me for a buzzard. I have done no harm."

"Is it no harm to afflict these people?"

"I never did it."

"But how comes it to be in your appearance?"

"The Devil can take any likeness."

"Not without their consent."

"Please, your worship," Jacobs begged, "It is untrue. I never showed the book. I am silly about these things as the child born last night."

"That is your saying. You argue you have lived so long, but what then? Cain might have lived long before he killed Abel, and you might live long before the Devil had so prevailed on you."

"Christ hath suffered three times for me."

"What three times?"

"He suffered the cross and the gale — "

Sarah Churchill interrupted and said, smugly, "You had as good confess if you are guilty."

Jacobs faced her and asked, "Have you heard that I have any witchcraft?"

"I know you live a wicked life," she replied.

To the judge Jacobs said, "Let her make it out."

"Doth he ever pray in his family?" the judge asked her.

"Not unless by himself," she answered.

"Why," the judge asked Jacobs, "do you not pray in your family?"

"I cannot read."

"Well, but you may pray for all that. Can you say the Lord's Prayer? Let us hear you."

Jacobs gave it a try and failed — the courtroom murmured disapprovingly; there were exclamations of "He is guilty!" "He may not say the prayer!"

"Sarah Churchill," the judge said, "when you wrote in the Book, you was showed your master's name, you said."

"Yes, sir."

"If she say so," Jacobs said, "if you do not know it, what will you say?"

"But," the judge replied, "she saw you or your likeness tempt her to write."

"One in my *likeness*," the old man corrected him. "The Devil may represent any likeness."

Again the bench ignored Jacobs. "Were you not frighted, Sarah Churchill, when the representation of your master came to you?"

"Yes."

"Well!" Jacobs exclaimed, exasperated, "Burn me or hang me! I will stand in the truth of Christ. I know nothing of it."

"Do you know nothing of getting your son George and his daughter Margaret Jacobs to sign the Devil's Book?"

"No, nothing at all," Jacobs said, coldly. The hearing was adjourned.

The same apparitions that had appeared to her the day previous appeared again to Susannah Sheldon, and there was a similar scene, but the shining White Man appeared with the phantoms who told her to go to Judge John Hathorne despite Willard's threats. The shining man said to her that if she went to tell Mr. Hathorne she would be all right going and coming, but she would be afflicted before the judge.

Susannah replied, "Hunt Willard away and I will believe what you say."

The shining man held up his hand and Willard's specter vanished.

Two hours later the ghosts reappeared, including Willard. Susannah asked them where their wounds were; they replied, "There will come an angel from heaven and will show them," and forthwith the angel came.

As she described the vision, Susannah "asked what the man's name was that appeared to me last, and the angel told me his name was Southereh, and the angel lifted up his winding sheet and out of his left side he pulled a pitchfork tongue and put it in again, and likewise he opened all the winding sheets and showed all their wounds, and the White Man told me to tell Mr. Hathorne," etcetera.

In the evening the apparitions of John Willard, Elizabeth Colson, and an old man Susannah didn't know, tempted her with books and money. Willard suckled two black pigs at his breasts, Elizabeth Colson suckled a yellow bird, and the old man suckled a snake. A Black Man put in an appearance, and the three witches prayed to him.

The next day, Monday the 11th of May, Susannah as she came to the town bridge saw Willard and the old man of her vision the previous night — they were riding on the water in a dish, as in one of Mother Goose's old rhymes. The witches landed by George Hacker's house, and the three of them, including Hacker, offered her the Devil's Book to sign.

George Jacobs was indicted the day after he was first examined, and examined once more at Thomas Beadle's Inn. Each of the afflicted identified him individually; Jacobs continued to maintain his innocence; testimony against him was read, and Jacobs denied it. Hathorne asked, "Are not you the man that made disturbance at a lecture in Salem?"

"No great disturbance," Jacobs replied. "Do you think I use witchcrafts?"

"Yes, indeed," Hathorne replied.

"No, I use none of them," the old man said, bridling, insulted.

The magistrates also examined Margaret Jacobs at Beadle's. She confessed, and Joseph Flint went into the other room where George was sitting to tell him, "Your granddaughter has confessed."

"What did she confess?" Jacobs asked.

"She confessed she was a witch, or that she had set her hand to the Devil's Book."

"Jacobs exclaimed, "She was charged not to confess!"

"Who charged her not to confess?" Flint inquired suspiciously.

Jacobs paused before he answered; then, "If she were innocent and yet confessed, she would be accessory to her own death," he said. It didn't answer Flint's query, but it was an important point, or might be if it proved not to be true what people were saying: That it was safer to confess than to maintain one's innocence. Nevertheless, it would be an important consideration before the ultimate Throne of Judgment if Puritan theology were up to the mark.

Elizabeth Hubbard and Mercy Lewis were both afflicted by John Willard that day, but Sarah Churchill experienced a visitation of another sort. She went to Sarah Ingersoll, thirty, the mate of Samuel Ingersoll. The young matron was amazed to see the twenty-year-old young woman weeping and wringing her hands. Goody Ingersoll asked, "What do you ail?"

"I have undone myself," Miss Churchill cried.

"In what?"

"In belying myself and others in saying I set my hand to the Devil's Book, but I never did."

"I believe," Goody Ingersoll told her, "that you set your hand to the book."

"No, no, no! I never, *never* did," Sarah wailed.

"Then what made you say you had??"

"Because they threatened me and told me they would put me into the dungeon, and put me along with Mr. Burroughs." The maid paced up and down after Mrs. Ingersoll, complaining.

Finally, exasperated, the woman asked, "Then why do not you deny you wrote in it?"

"Because," Sarah said with great frustration evident in her voice, "I have stood out so long in it that now I durst not. If I told Mr. Noyes but once I set my hand to the book, he would believe me, but if I told him a hundred times I had not, he would not believe me."

On the 12th of May Constable Carolina John Putnam of Salem Village reported to the court that John Willard had fled. Putnam was directed to raise a hue and cry after the fugitive.

Mary Warren was examined in prison again. She was asked, "Did you not know that it was the Devil's Book when you signed it?"

"I did not know it then," she replied, "But I know it now. To be sure, it was the Devil's Book. In the first place, to be sure, I did set my hand to the Devil's Book. I have considered of it since you were here last, and it was the Devil's Book my master Proctor brought to me, and he told me if I would set my hand to that book I should believe, and I did set my hand to it, but that with which I did it was done with my finger. He brought the book and told me if I would take the book and touch it, I should be well, and I thought then that it was the Devil's Book."

"Was there not your consent to hurt the children when you were hurt?"

"No, sir. But when I was afflicted my master Proctor was in the room and said, 'If you are afflicted I wish ye were more afflicted — you and all of them!' I said, 'Master, what makes you say so?' He answered, 'Because you go to bring out innocent persons.' I told him that that could not be, and whether the Devil took advantage at that to afflict them, I know not. And one night talking about them I said I did not care though they were tormented if they charged me."

"Did you ever see any poppits?"

"Yes. Once I saw one made of cloth in Mistress Proctor's hand."

"Who was it like, or which of the children was it for?"

"I cannot tell whether for Annie Putnam or Abigail Williams — for one of them it was, I am sure. It was in my mistress' hand."

"What did you stick into the poppit?"

"I did stick in a pin about the neck of it as it was in Proctor's hand."

"How many more did you see afterwards?"

"I do not remember that ever I saw any more…yes! I remember one, and that Goody Proctor brought a poppit unto me of Mercy Lewis, and she gave me another, and I stuck it somewhere about the waists, and she appeared once more to me in the prison, and she said to me, 'What are you got there?' And she told me that she was coming here herself, in person. I had another person that appeared to me — it was like to Mary Walcott — and it was a piece of stick that she brought me to stick into it. And somewhere about her arms I stuck it in."

"Where did she bring it to you?"

"Up at Proctor's. Goody Proctor told me she had been a witch these twelve years and more; Ann Pudeator told me that she had done damage and told me that she had hurt James Coy's child, taking it out of the mother's hand."

"Who brought the last to you?"

"My mistress. And when she brought it, she brought it in her own person. And her husband with his own hands brought me the Book to sign, and he brought me an image which looked yellow, and I believe it was for Abigail Williams — it being like her — and I put a thing like a thorn into it. This was done by his bodily person after I had signed. The night after I had signed the book, while she was thus confessing, Parker appeared and bit me extremely on my arms." This was a lot of poppits to conjure up after she could at first remember only one.

"Who have you seen more?"

"Nurse and Cloyse, and Goode's child, after I had signed."

"What said they to you?"

"They said that I should never tell of them nor anything about them, and I have seen Goody Goode herself."

"Was that true of Giles Corey — that you saw him? That he afflicted you the other day?"

"Yes. I have seen him often, and he hurts me very much. And Goody Bishop hath appeared to me and afflicted me and brought the Book to tempt me. And I have seen Goody Corey: The first night I was taken I saw, as I thought, the apparition of Goody Corey and catched at it, as I thought, and caught my master in my lap, though I did not see my master in the place at the time; upon which my master said, 'It is nobody but I — it is my shadow, as you see.'

"But my master was not before me that I could discern. But catching at the apparition that looked like Goody Corey I caught hold of my master and pulled him down in my lap. Upon which he said, 'I see there is no heed to any of your talkings, for you are all possessed by the Devil — for it is nothing but my shape.'

"I have seen Goody Corey at my master's house in person, and she told me that I should be condemned for a witch as well as she, and would cry out and bring out all."

"Was this before you had signed?"

"Yes, before I had my fits."

"Now tell the truth about the mountebank. What writing was that?"

"I do not know. I asked her what it was about, but she would not tell me, saying she had promised not to let anybody see it."

"Well, but who did you see more?"

"I don't know any more."

"How long hath your master and mistress been witches?"

"I don't know, they never told me."

"What likeness or appearance have you had to bewitch you?"

"They never gave me anything."

It was a grueling task to interview Mary Warren, for her testimony was often interrupted by fits. She reimplicated a number of people between times: Mrs. Parker was said to have hurt Mary Warren's sister and was the cause of her becoming dumb; the woman was also supposed to have killed Michael Chappleman aboard a ship in Salem Harbor — he had died of a pain in his side.

Goody Ann Pudeator's specter had told Mary she had thrown John Turner off a cherry tree and nearly killed him, and Goody Parker said she had cast away Capt. Price's ketch, of which Thomas Westgate had been master — Venus Colefax had been aboard as well, and John

Lapshorne — they had foundered at sea. There were evidently few things that happened in Nature that were natural.

Rev. Mr. George Burroughs, too, with the women, Mary implicated in maleficia perpetrated against cattle and horses. Goody Pudeator — or Poindexter — had killed her husband "about seven or ten years since"; further, she had been instrumental in drowning Goodman Orn's son in the harbor and had bewitched John Scarlet's boy as he was going to sea, and the master of the vessel had had to turn about to bring him home. Finally, Burroughs told Mary that he had killed his wife off Cape Ann.

Abigail Hobbs was examined in Salem Prison the same day. She was asked, "Did Mr. Burroughs bring you any of the poppits of his wives to stick pins into?"

"I do not remember that he did," she replied.

"Did he bring any of his children, or of the Eastward soldiers?"

"No."

"Have you known of any that have been killed by witchcraft?"

"No. Nobody."

"How came you to speak of Mr. Burroughs's wives yesterday?"

"I don't know." For a confessed witch, Abigail was being singularly uncooperative.

"Is that true about Davis' son of Casco, and of those of the Village?"

"Yes, it is true."

"What service did he put you upon? And who are they you afflicted?"

"I cannot tell who, neither do I know whether they died."

"Were they strangers to you that Burroughs would have you afflict?"

"Yes."

"And were they afflicted accordingly?"

"Yes."

"Can't you name some of them?"

"No. I cannot remember them."

"Where did they live?"

"At the Eastward."

"Have any vessels been cast away by you?"

"I do not know."

"Have you consented to the afflicting of any others besides those at the Village?"

"Yes."

"Who were they?"

"I cannot tell, but it was of such who lived at the fort side of the river about half a mile from the fort toward Capt. Brackett's."

"What was the hurt you gave to them by consent?"

"I don't know."

"Was there anything brought to you like them?"

"Yes."

"What did you stick into them?"

"Thorns."

"Did some of them die?"

"Yes. One of them was Mary Lawrence that died."

"Where did you stick the thorns?"

"I do not know."

"Was it about the middle of her body?"

"Yes, and I stuck it right in."

"What provoked you? Had she displeased you?"

"Yes, by some words she spoke of me."

"Who brought the image to you?"

"It was Mr. Burroughs."

"How did he bring it to you?"

"In his own person, bodily."

"Where did he bring it to you?"

"Abroad a little way off from our house."

"And what did he say to you then?"

"He told me he was angry with that family."

"How many years since was it?"

"Before this Indian war."

"How did you know Mr. Burroughs was a witch?"

"I don't know."

"How long have you been a witch?"

"I made two covenants with the Devil, first for two years, and after that for four years. I have been a witch these six years."

"Did the maid complain of pain about the place you stuck the thorn in?"

"Yes, but how long she lived, I don't know."

"How do you know Burroughs was angry with Lawrence's family."

"Because he told me so."

"Where did any other live that you afflicted?"

"Just by the other toward James Andrews', and they died also."

"How many were they — more than one?"

"Yes."

"And who brought those poppits to you?"

"Mr. Burroughs."

"What did you stick into them?"

"Pins. And he gave them to me."

"Did you keep those poppits?"

"No, he carried them away with him."

"Was he there himself with you in bodily person?"

"Yes, and so he was when he appeared to tempt me to set my hand to the Book. He then appeared in person, and I felt his hand at the same time."

"Were they men, women, or children you killed?"

They were both boys and girls."

"Was you angry with them yourself?"

"Yes, though I don't know why now."

"Did you know Mr. Burroughs' wife?"

"Yes."

"Did you know of any poppits pricked to kill her?"

"No, I didn't."

"Have you seen several witches at the Eastward?"
"Yes, but I don't know who they were."

Between examinations warrants were issued against Ann Pudeator of Salem, widow, and Alice Parker, wife of John Parker of Salem. They were arrested the same day and sent to Boston jail to join George Jacobs, Giles Corey, William Hobbs, Edward Bishop, Sarah Bishop, Bridget Bishop, Sarah Wilds, Mary Black, and Mary English. In Salem Prison there were Mary Easty, Deliverance Hobbs, Abigail Hobbs, Margaret Jacobs, Abigail Soames, Mary Warren, Sarah Proctor, and Sarah Churchill, for word of her confession to Goody Ingersoll had been reported immediately, and she had been cried out upon. Sarah Proctor, too, was in Salem jail; others were in Ipswich and Cambridge jails.

On Friday the 13th, day of ill omen, Annie Putnam cried out upon Elizabeth Hart of Lynn, and on Saturday a warrant was issued for her arrest along with those of Thomas Farrar of Lynn, Daniel Andrews, George Jacobs, Jr., and his wife Rebecca, Goody Sarah Buckley and her daughter Mary Whitridge — all of Salem Village; Elizabeth Colson of Reading, and Bethia Carter of Woburn. Constable Carolina John and the other officers searched for Daniel Andrews and George Jacobs, Jr., but they were not to be found.

When Rebecca Jacobs was to be arrested she resisted the constable at first — she was a partially "distracted" woman, and not much inclined to reason, but Carolina John Putnam persuaded her that she would be allowed to return presently. Her four children were left behind, including a baby — some of them followed after their mother, crying, until neighbors came and took them in. Since her husband George had fled, there was no one else to keep the family. The madwoman was put into a cell, the squalor of which amazed her. She screamed that she was to be allowed to go home to her children, but no one listened.

Bray Wilkins was still having difficulty urinating, and he felt quite ill, but well enough to visit with his grandson Daniel Wilkins, who was sick unto death, like his sister Lydia, who had likewise been infected. Mercy Lewis and some of the other accusers came to Will's Hill on Saturday, as did Constable Carolina John who had himself only recently recovered from contagion, and seen his child Sarah die of it. They all recognized Satan's scourge for what it was, and Mercy articulated its cause for them when she said she saw John Willard tormenting Daniel and — a spectral double feat — sitting on Bray's stomach, hurting him.

The constable, ever alert, struck at Willard's phantom — immediately Bray was eased of his pain and Mercy threw a fit, but Daniel continued to suffer.

In Boston that evening there was another event of great importance: Governor Sir William Phips arrived aboard the frigate *Nonesuch*, and with him the man who had been most instrumental in securing Phips the post, Increase Mather. They carried with them the new Charter for Massachusetts. Eight companies of soldiers escorted the party to Increase's home, but there were no volleys, as it was Sabbath Eve. Cotton Mather made a short note of his father's arrival in his diary, and that evening William Stoughton replaced Thomas Danforth as Deputy Governor.

At meeting in Andover on Sunday twelve-year-old Phoebe Chandler was approached by Martha Carrier while the psalm was being sung. She shook the child by the shoulder and asked her where she lived. Phoebe didn't answer, for she knew that Goody Carrier knew her, since they were near neighbors. Martha greatly frightened the impressionable child.

In Lynn Elizabeth Hart was arrested, and a new warrant issued for the arrest of the fugitive John Willard, on complaint of Thomas Fuller, Jr., and Benjamin Wilkins, Sr., for acts of injury inflicted upon Bray Wilkins and Samuel Wilkins — still another member of the Wilkins family had come down with smallpox; there was no mention of Daniel or Lydia.

On Monday the 16th Sir William Phips took his oath of office at Boston Townhouse. Simon Bradstreet delivered up the reins of government to him under the new charter granted the province by

William III. Bradstreet had already made his plans to retire to Salem, which numbered 1700 inhabitants when he left office. Before he slipped into quiet obscurity he denounced the witchhunt, but he was far too old and decrepit to be able to take a hand in quelling this latest and greatest mass mania, manifestations of which he had competently fought for decades.

In the evening in Salem Village Mercy Lewis saw John Willard choking Daniel Wilkins, who died black in the face, gasping for breath: He could not breathe because of Willard's attack…or the swelling of pustules in his windpipe.

John Parker, constable of Reading, had to turn in a report that Elizabeth Colson had fled, evidently to Boston to take ship for another country. The authorities had better success on Tuesday the 17th when John Willard was caught in Lancaster, arrested, and turned over to Constable Carolina John Putnam of Salem Village. Susannah Sheldon was attacked by Willard's specter, and Bray Wilkins' condition was eased; but, then, in place of the urinary blockage, he found that he, as he put it, "was vexed with a flowing of water so that it was hard to keep myself dry." His granddaughter found herself in even worse condition: She died of the pox and followed her brother to the place of Salvation.

On Wednesday, May 18th, Rebecca Jacobs was examined, but it was a useless exercise. The woman was almost as distracted as the accusers, and made as little sense.

John Willard was brought before the court by Constable Putnam, indicted, and examined. A body search revealed no witch teats. Evidence was given in against him by various people including Lydia Nichols and Margaret Knight who deposed that Mrs. Willard had been at her father's house in Groton when she "made a lamentable complaint how cruelly her husband had beaten her; she thought herself that she should never recover of the blows he had given her.

"The next morning he was got into a little hole under the stairs, and then she thought something extraordinary had befallen him. Then he ran out at the door and up a steep hill almost impossible for any man to run up, as she said; then she took her mare and rode away, fearing some evil had been intended against her. And when she came to the house of Henry or Benjamin Willard, or both, went to look after him, and met him running in a strange, distracted manner."

Thomas Bailey continued the story. He said that "I being at Groton some short time after Willard, as the report went, had beaten his wife, I went to call him home and, coming home with him in the night, I heard such a hideous noise of strange creatures that I was much affrighted, for I never heard the like noise.

"I fearing they might be some evil spirits, I enquired of Willard what it be that made such a hideous noise. He said they were locusts. The next day…Willard's wife with a young child, and her mother, were riding upon my mare between Groton and Chelmsford, and I was leading. Being willing to go on foot a little, they desired me to ride. I took my mare to let her feed a little there, and I heard the same noise again, whereat my mare shied and got away from me."

The only witnesses against Sarah Buckley were the girls. Her examination was a standard operation, and she was sent to prison to await trial with the others, despite several character references by Rev. William Hubbard of Ipswich, Rev. John Higginson of Salem First Church, and Rev. Samuel Cheever.

An anomaly occurred when the child accusers changed their minds about Mary Easty and she was released. Except for Nehemiah Abbott, no one else had ever been turned loose after being accused. The gossip of the town could not account for it. Elizabeth Booth accused Mary Warren of trying to get her to sign the Devil's Book, and she was joined by Betty Hubbard.

A warrant was issued against Dr. Roger Toothaker of Billerica; Constable Joseph Neal arrested him, and he was sent to Boston Jail along with John Willard, Thomas Farrar, and Elizabeth Hart.

In England that day Elias Ashmole died and bequeathed the remainder of his antiquities to the Ashmolean Museum at Oxford.

Two days later — Friday, May 20th — Samuel Abbey went to the home of Carolina John Putnam at 9 a.m. There, he found Mercy Lewis in the midst of dreadful anguish. Carolina John asked Abbey to fetch Annie Putnam from Sgt. Putnam's, which he set off to do immediately. When he got to the Sergeant's he found Abigail Williams there as well and fetched them both. On their way the girls saw the specters of Mary Easty, Mary Whitridge, and John Willard afflicting Mercy — and it was true, as they confirmed when they arrived at Carolina John's. They sent for Mary Walcott — she, too, as she came in, said, "There is the apparition of Goody Easty choking Mercy, pressing her breasts with both hands and putting a chain about her neck."

Next, Betty Hubbard was sent for, and she, too, saw Goody Easty: The girls had recanted their recantation completely. By that time a great crowd had gathered to watch Mercy who was undergoing a marathon torment, but eventually she began to take turns on and off with Betty Hubbard.

Marshal Herrick was sent for. When he arrived he looked in at the spectacle, turned, and left at a gallop. Not long after, Mary Easty was rearrested and brought to Thomas Beadle's in Salem to await examination.

Dr. Roger Toothaker was examined as well. Thomas Gadge testified that Dr. Toothaker of Billerica, whose family had long been associated in one way or another with the Carriers of Andover and who was, in fact, the husband of Mary Allen, Martha Carrier's sister, had come to Gadge's house in Beverly in the spring, "and we discoursed about John Marston's child of Salem, that was then sick and having unwonted fits, and likewise another child of Philip White's of Beverly, who was then strangely sick.

"I persuaded Toothaker to go and see these children, but Toothaker answered he had seen them both already, and that his opinion was they were under an evil hand. Further, he said that his daughter had killed a witch. I asked him how she did it. He answered readily that his daughter "had learned something from him," for Toothaker, like the late Dr. Zerubabel Endicott, was a practicing sympathetic magician.

"I asked, 'By what means did she?'" Gadge continued, "and he said that there was a certain person bewitched, and that person complained of being afflicted by another person that was suspected by the afflicted person. Further, Toothaker said that his daughter got some of the afflicted person's urine, and put it into an earthen pot and stopped the pot very close, and put it into a hot oven, and stopped up the oven, and the next morning the suspected person was dead."

There was little doubt that Roger Toothaker, like Bridget Bishop and several others under indictment, was in fact a practicing warlock, but he was the first of the Massachusetts Bay witch doctors to be arrested, though Dr. Griggs had come close when his wife was cried out upon but not indicted. There were many other non-medical witches, however, such as Toothaker's wife Mary, who was known in Billerica as Aunt Toothaker, and Toothaker's daughter. Like the doctors, they also practiced sympathetic magic, and they were as likely to be accusers as accused, or witnesses against their innocent fellows, or simply lying low. It should have been patently obvious, especially to the judges, that all sorts of people were technically witches who were not among the accused, but stood to witness against solid church members who would have thought it anathema to use charms or curses. Had the authorities thought about it in these terms, they might well have come to the conclusion that the Devil had plotted to bring the Bay and God's people to their knees, and that they were deluded, but not in the way they had originally supposed. A few people were, in fact, beginning to ponder along these lines, but as yet they were very few.

While the examinations were going on at Beadle's inn and elsewhere, Mercy Lewis' anguish continued under the gaze of many eyes including those of Capt. Jonathan Putnam, James Darling, Benjamin

Hutchinson, and Samuel Braybrook. At midnight Marshal Herrick returned, and the torment went on.

Toward dawn Mercy's fits grew weaker. Herrick was still watching, but he had been busy that day, and he finally fell asleep. However, first thing in the morning Mary Easty was examined, he heard by report, and he left to go home for a nap. Later in the day Sgt. Thomas Putnam, Jr., and Carolina John complained against Goodwife Sarah Basset of Lynn, Widow Susannah Root of Beverly, and Sarah Proctor of Salem Village.

In Boston Cotton Mather wrote in his diary, "For my own part, I was always afraid of proceeding to convict and condemn any person as a confederate with afflicting demons upon so feeble an evidence as a 'spectral representation'. Accordingly, I ever testified against it, both publicly and privately; and in my letters to the judges I particularly besought them that they would by no means admit it; and when a considerable assembly of ministers gave in their advice about the matter, I not only concurred with their advice, but it was *I* who drew it up."

He continued his entry: "In this evil time, I offered at the beginning, that if the 'possessed' people might be scattered far asunder, I would singly provide for six of them, and we would see whether, without more bitter methods, prayer with fasting would not put an end unto these heavy trials."

Mather's offer had been ignored by the judges and other officials, yet again he attempted to resolve a paradox by defending the judges in his journal for their actions, despite the fact that, in his opinion, they were wrong in their procedures and were likely to convict innocent people of crimes they had not committed.

Nathaniel Ingersoll and Thomas Raymond complained against Benjamin Proctor, Mary Derish of Lynn, Mrs. Sarah Pease of Salem, and procured warrants for their arrest on Monday, May 23rd. Marshal Herrick appointed Carolina John his deputy to serve the warrant on Benjamin Proctor. Putnam did his duty and took Proctor into custody: He was sent to Boston Jail along with rearrested Mary Easty, Susannah Root, Mary Bassett, Abigail Soames, Sarah Pease, and Sarah Proctor.

Elizabeth Carey was the wife of Captain Nathaniel Carey of Charlestown, and the Captain wrote an account of his spouse's ordeal: "I having heard some days that my wife was accused of witchcraft," he said, "being much disturbed at it, by advice we went to Salem Village, to see if the afflicted did know her. We arrived there 24 May; it happened to be a day appointed for examination. Accordingly, soon after our arrival Mr. Hathorne and Mr. Corwin, etc., went to the meetinghouse which was the place appointed for that work.

"The minister began with prayer. And having taken care to get a convenient place, I observed that the afflicted were two girls of about ten years old, and about two or three others of about eighteen. One of the girls talked most, and could discern more than the rest.

"The prisoners were called in one by one, and as they came in were cried out of, etc. The prisoner was placed about seven or eight foot from the justices, and the accusers between the justices and them. The prisoner was ordered to stand right before the justices, with an officer appointed to hold each hand lest they should therewith afflict them. And the prisoner's eyes must be constantly on the justices, for if they looked on the afflicted they would either fall into their fits or cry out of being hurt by them.

"After examination of the prisoners — who it was afflicted these girls, etc. — they were put upon saying the Lord's Prayer as a trial of their guilt. After the afflicted seemed to be out of their fits they would look steadfastly on some one person, and frequently not speak (and then the justices said they were struck dumb), and after a little time would speak again.

"Then the justices said to the accusers, 'Which of you will go and touch the prisoner at the bar?' Then the most courageous would adventure, but before they had made three steps would ordinarily fall down, as in a fit. The justices ordered that they should be taken up and carried to the prisoner, that she might touch them. And as soon as they were touched by the accused the justices would say, 'They are well,' before I could discern any alteration, by which I observed that the justices understood the manner of it. Thus far I was only as a spectator. My wife also was there part of the time, but no notice taken of her by the afflicted except once or twice they came to her and asked her name.

"But I having an opportunity to discourse with Mr. Hale (with whom I had formerly acquaintance), I took his advice what I had best do, and desired of him that I might have an opportunity to speak with her that accused my wife, which he promised should be, I acquainting him that I reposed my trust in him.

"Accordingly he came to me after the examination was over and told me I had now an opportunity to speak with the said accuser, viz., Abigail Williams, a girl of eleven or twelve years old, but that we could not be in private at Mr. Parris' house as he had promised me. We went therefore into the alehouse" — Ingersoll's Ordinary — "where an Indian man attended us who it seems was one of the afflicted. To him we gave some cider. He showed several scars that seemed as if they had long been there, and showed them as done by witchcraft, and acquainted us that his wife, who also was a slave, was imprisoned for witchcraft.

"And now instead of one accuser, they all came in, who began to tumble down like swine, and then three women were called in to attend them. We in the room were all at a stand to see who they would cry of, but in a short time they cried out, 'Carey!' And immediately after, a warrant was sent from the justices to bring my wife before them, who were sitting in a chamber nearby waiting for this.

"Being brought before the justices, her chief accusers were two girls. My wife declared to the justices that she never had any knowledge of them before that day. She was forced to stand with her arms stretched out. I did request that I might hold one of her hands, but it was denied me; then she desired me to wipe the tears from her eyes and the sweat from her face, which I did; then she desired she should lean herself on me, saying she should faint.

"Justice Hathorne replied, she had strength enough to torment those persons and she should have strength enough to stand. I speaking something against their cruel proceedings, they commanded me to be silent or else I should be turned out of the room.

"The Indian before mentioned was also brought in to be one of her accusers. Being come in, he now (when before the justices) fell down and tumbled about like a hog, but said nothing. The justices asked the girls, 'Who afflicts the Indian' They answered, 'She' (meaning my wife), 'and now she lies upon him.' The justices ordered her to touch him, in order to his cure, but her head must be turned another way lest, instead of curing, she should make him worse by her looking on him, her hand being guided to take hold of his. But the Indian took hold on her hand and pulled her down on the floor in a barbarous manner. Then his hand was taken off and her hand put on his, and the cure was quickly wrought.

"I, being extremely troubled at their inhumane dealings, uttered a hasty speech (that God would take vengeance on them, and desired that God would deliver us out of the hands of unmerciful men). Then her *Mittimus* was writ. I did with difficulty and charge obtain the liberty of a room, but no beds in it. If there had, could have taken but little rest that night.

"She was committed to Boston Prison, but I obtained a *Habeas Corpus* to remove her to Cambridge Prison, which is in our County of Middlesex. Having been there one night, next morning the jailer put irons on her legs (having received such a command). The weight of them was about eight pounds. These irons and her other afflictions soon brought her into convulsion fits, so that I thought she would have died that night. I sent to entreat that the irons might be taken off, but all entreaties were in vain, if it would have saved her life, so that in this condition she must continue."

Judges John Hathorne and Jonathan Corwin transferred Sarah Goode and Tituba to Boston Jail on May 25th; on the same day Mr. and Mrs. Joseph Bailey were also on their way to Boston, but not under arrest, merely on business. When they came within sight of John

Proctor's house Joseph felt a hard blow on his breast "which caused great pain in my stomach," he said, "and amazement in my head," but he saw no one but his wife mounted pillion behind him. When they drew opposite the house he saw Proctor at a window and Goody Proctor just outside the door.

Joseph told his wife to look, but she saw no one except a little girl at the door. Half a mile beyond, Joseph was struck speechless. "If you cannot speak, hold up your hand," his wife said; he did so. No sooner had he moved than he could speak once again.

When they reached the Ipswich road, he received another blow that caused him so much pain he could not sit his horse.

Joseph dismounted and saw a woman coming toward them in the near distance, though his wife saw nothing where he pointed. When finally he remounted, he noticed that the woman had transformed herself into a cow grazing in the field.

The Baileys got to Boston without further trouble, but on their return when they reached Newbury Joseph was pinched and nipped "by something invisible," yet that passed as well, and he returned to normal.

On May 26th, Thursday, Rebecka, wife of John Ballard of Andover was ill. Goodman Ballard, certain that it was another manifestation of evil, sent to Salem Village for Annie Putnam to attend his wife and discover whether or not his theory that witchcraft was involved was correct.

Annie Putnam, despite the fact that such a trip could only mean more tortured agony for her if the theory proved out, was pleased to oblige. She and Mary Walcott traveled up together, and the whole town appeared to greet them and accompany them to the meetinghouse where the Rev. Mr. Thomas Barnard offered prayer. Then everyone went with the girls to the Ballard home. There, Annie Putnam and Mary saw Martha Carrier tormenting Goody Rebecka Ballard. Immediately, all sorts of Andover names began to be mentioned and arrangements were made to have the girls continue their scrying at the meetinghouse where they were joined in their fits by some local young people including Phoebe Chandler and Timothy Swan.

In England, Elias Ashmole was buried at the Church of the Great Lambeth in Surrey.

Chapter Eleven

On Friday, May 27th, Governor William Phips' Council established a special court to take up the cases of the imprisoned witches, none of whom, including Martha Sparks who had been arrested in 1691, had yet been tried: "Ordered, that a Special Commission of Oyer and Terminer be made out to William Stoughton, John Richards, Nathaniel Saltonstall, Waite Winthrop, Bartholomew Gedney, Samuel Sewall, John Hathorne, Jonathan Corwin, and Peter Sergeant, Esquires, assigning them to be justices, or any five of them (whereof Stoughton, Richards, and Gedney to be one)," to hear crimes in Suffolk, Essex, and Middlesex Counties. Stoughton was to be Chief Justice.

Thomas Newton was appointed King's Attorney, Capt. Stephen Sewall — Samuel's brother and the keeper of Elizabeth Parris — was assigned to be Clerk of the Court. The post of Marshal was abolished, and that of Sheriff substituted. George Corwin the Younger, twenty-six — grandson of the late Salem merchant of the same name — was given that post and, under him as Deputy Sheriff, the former Marshal George Herrick was appointed.

Governor Phips was preparing to leave Boston to go to Maine and "the Eastward" on frontier business. The new justices set about collecting a legal library, and soon they had Joseph Keeble's *Common Law*, a chapter of which, on "Conjuration," was of particular relevance; the pamphlet on Sir Matthew Hale's trial of the Bury St. Edmunds witches, *A Trial of Witches*; Joseph Glanvill's *Saducismus Triumphatus*; Richard Bernard's *Guide to Grandjurymen*; Richard Baxter's *Certainty of the World of Spirits*; Richard Bovet's *Pandaemonium*, and Cotton Mather's *Memorable Providences Relating to Witchcraft*.

The next day, Saturday, Thomas Putnam and Benjamin Hutchinson entered a formal complaint against Elizabeth Carey of Charlestown, after her examination, and Joseph Houlton and Jonathan Walcott complained against Martha Carrier of Andover, Goodwife Elizabeth Fosdick of Malden, Mammy Wilmot Reed of Marblehead, Sarah Rice of Reading, Elizabeth Howe of Topsfield, Capt. John Alden of Boston, William Proctor of Salem Village, Capt. John Flood of Rumney Marsh, Aunt Mary Toothaker and her daughter of Billerica, Nehemiah Abbott of the Topsfield-Wenham line — he had been allowed to go free and was rearrested. Warrants for the apprehension of Martha Carrier and Mammy Reed were also issued.

That same day Phoebe Chandler was sent by her mother to carry beer to the men working in the woodlot in Andover. When she got within the fence she heard Martha Carrier's voice in the bushes saying, "What do you do here, and whither are you going?" Phoebe saw no one, was frightened, and ran to the men. She told them what she had heard, but they paid little attention and Phoebe went home. About two hours later her mother sent her back with more beer. On her way home again, near the place she had heard the voice, Phoebe heard it again — this time over her head. It said, "You shall be poisoned within a few days." Later in the day Phoebe's parents thought it would be as well if she went to her sister Allen's farm to stay for a while.

Activity did not diminish much on the Lord's Day, May 29th. After meeting, Clement Codum, sixty, was carrying Betty Hubbard back home on horseback, the girl riding pillion. She told Codum, "Ride faster."

"Why?" he asked.

"Because the woods are full of devils. There!" she pointed, and "There they be!"

Codum spurred his horse, though he saw nothing. After they had gone on a while at a canter Elizabeth said, "You may ride softer now, for we have outridden them."

"Are you not afraid of the Devil?" the old man asked the child.

"No, I can speak with the Devil as well as with you," she informed him.

James Houlton, too, was becoming familiar with the Old Boy. He had a fit in which he was tormented by John and Elizabeth Proctor and their son William and daughter Sarah Proctor: They pressed the breath out of him with their hands. Abigail Williams was similarly afflicted by the specter of Rebecca Nurse.

Constable Ephraim Wilds of Topsfield arrested Elizabeth Howe, and when Martha Carrier was taken into custody in Andover, four of her children were apprehended as well, including eight-year-old Sarah Carrier.

Philip English, the fugitive merchant of Salem, was found and arrested on Monday the 30th by Deputy Marshal Jacob Manning. Nathaniel Putnam III and Joseph Whipple swore out a complaint against Elizabeth Fosdick of Malden and Elizabeth Paine of Charlestown; Peter Tufts of Charlestown joined them in the complaint "for acts of witchcraft by them committed on his Negro woman."

In Topsfield the newly arrested Elizabeth Howe asked her brother-in-law John Howe to accompany her to Salem Village for her examination upon the morrow. He replied, "If you had been sent for upon almost any account but witchcraft, I would go with you, but on that account I would not for ten pounds. But if you are a witch, tell me how long you have been one and what mischief you have done, and then I will go with you, for you have been accused by Samuel Perley's child and suspected by DeaconCummings for witchcraft."

Elizabeth's reaction was anger, but she continued to importune him until finally he replied, "I do not know but that I might come tomorrow."

Cotton Mather's sentiments were before the court in the form of a letter on the last day of May. His observations were the same as those he had expressed in his diary: He was sure God approved of the work of the Court, though he warned them against putting too much weight on spectral evidence. In the case of the Salem Village witchcrafts, though it was possible for specters to be sent to torment people without the intermediation of witches, "there is cause enough to think that it is a horrible witchcraft which hath given rise to the troubles wherewith Salem Village is at this day harassed, and the indefatigable pains that are used for the tracing this witchcraft are to be thankfully accepted and applauded among all this people of God."

He also made the point that, although witchcrafts proceeded on an ethereal plane, their effects were nevertheless real; therefore, crimes committed through witchcraft were equally real, and their perpetrators punishable by law. The best evidence on which to convict was "a credible confession," for there were those that were not credible, but he felt the Court would be able to differentiate between the two sorts. He opposed torture to extract confessions, but espoused, rather, "cross and swift questions" in a "cross-examination". Other solid evidence was the paraphernalia of sympathetic magic, such as poppits and witch teats: Surgeons were competent to judge whether a body mark were natural or preternatural, and so, probably, were midwives. Last, he recommended leniency in lesser cases, as in those involving people who had been duped into making a demonic pact through ignorance or innocence.

At least a hundred accused witches were in the Massachusetts Bay jails awaiting examination and trial on the last day of May, and other warrants and arrests were being issued and made all the time: On the 31st a warrant was issued for the arrest of Capt. John Alden; he was arrested and examined, all at once — on the bench were John Hathorne, Jonathan Corwin and Bartholomew Gedney. Many others were also examined that day.

When Mammy Wilmot Reed was questioned, to nearly every query she replied either, "I cannot tell," or "I know nothing about it." The girls had their fits cured by her touch, and when she was asked insistently for her opinion regarding what ailed the accusers, including John Indian, all she would say was, "My opinion is that they are in a sad condition." She was sent back to jail wearing the invisible crown of the Queen of Understatement.

Deputy Marshal Jacob Manning delivered Philip English to the Court, but in Topsfield when the time came for Elizabeth Howe to be taken for her examination, her brother-in-law found an excuse to go to Ipswich instead of accompanying her.

At Goody Elizabeth Howe's examination Mercy Lewis and Mary Walcott "fell into a fit quickly" after the witch came in. Mary Walcott cried, "This is the woman pinched me and choked me this month." Annie Putnam said she had been hurt three times by the witch. "What say you to this charge?" Hathorne asked. "Here are them that charge you with witchcraft."

"If it was the last moment I was to live," Betty Howe replied, "God knows I am innocent of anything in this nature."

"Did not you take notice that now when you looked upon Mercy Lewis she was struck down?"

"I cannot help it."

"You are charged here, what do you say?" Hathorne asked crossly.

"I am innocent," she repeated, "of anything of this nature."

"Is this the first time that ever you were accused?"

"Yes, sir."

"Do not you know that one at Ipswich hath accused you?"

"This is the first time that ever I heard of it."

"You say that you never heard of these folks before."

Mercy Lewis and Abby Williams cried out that she was tormenting them, and Annie Putnam had a pin stuck into her hand by Mrs. Howe's phantom.

"What do you say to this?" Hathorne asked again.

"I cannot help it."

"What consent have you given?"

Mary Warren "cried out she was pricked," and Abby Williams that she was pinched: The prints on her arm were exhibited.

"Have not you seen some apparition?"

"No, never in all my life."

"Those that have confessed — they tell us they used images and pins; now, tell us what *you* have used."

"You would not have me confess that which I know not?" It was more question than statement. Her evil eye cut down Marry Warren; she and Annie Putnam cried that Goody Howe's specter was torturing Mary Walcott; Susie Sheldon said, "This is the woman that carried me yesterday to the pond" — she fell into a fit, was carried to the witch, and was cured by taking hold of Goody Howe's arm.

"You said," Hathorne told her, "you never heard before of these people."

"Not before the warrant was served upon me last Sabbath Day."

John Indian yelled, "O! She bites!" and fell to a grievous fit. He, too, was cured by the touch, but only after being forced, for he clawed away from the evil woman.

"What do you say to these things? — they cannot come to you."

"Sir, I am not able to give account of it."

"Cannot you tell what keeps them off from your body?"

"I cannot tell, I know not what it is."

"That is strange, that you should do these things and not be able to tell how." The examination was concluded; Rev. Samuel Parris signed his notes and handed them over to the Court.

William Proctor was indicted and examined, as was Martha Carrier's daughter Sarah. Hathorne asked her, "How long have you been a witch?"

"Ever since I was six years old," Sarah told him.

"How old are you now?"

"Near eight years old in November next."

"Who made you a witch?"

"My mother — she made me set my hand to a book."

"How did you set your hand to it?"

"I touched it with my fingers, and the book was red. The paper of it was white."

"Where was the place you did it?"

"It was in Andrew Foster's pasture."

"Did you see the Black Man there?"

"I never have seen the Black Man, but Elizabeth Johnson was there."

"Who also was there?"

"My aunt Toothaker and my cousin."

"When was it they were there?"

"When I was baptized."

"What did they promise to give you?"

"A black dog."

"Did the dog ever come to you?"

"No."

"But you said you saw a cat once — what did it say to you?"

"It said it would tear me in pieces if I would not set my hand to the Book."

"Who was it baptized you?"

"It was my mother, and the Devil was not there, and my mother said when she baptized me, 'Thou are mine for ever and ever. Amen.'"

"How did you afflict folks?"

"I pinched them."

"Did you have poppits?"

"No, I had none, but I went to them and afflicted them."

"How did you go, in your body or your spirit?"

"In my spirit, and my mother carried me."

"How did your mother carry you, when she was in prison?"

"She came like a black cat."

"How did you know it was your mother?"

"The cat told me so — that she was my mother."

"Whom did you afflict?"

"I hurt John Phelps' child last Saturday."

"Did anyone help you do it?"

"Elizabeth Johnson joined with me."

"How did you do it?"

"I had a wooden spear as long as my finger — Elizabeth Johnson give it me, and she had it of the Devil."

"Did you see the Devil?"

"No, I never did."

"Were you ever at the witch meeting at the Village?"

"No, I never did go."

When Sarah's mother Martha Carrier was examined Abigail Williams, Elizabeth Hubbard, Susannah Sheldon, Mary Walcott, and Annie Putnam identified her; Susie said she saw a Black Man talking with her before the bench. Hathorne asked, "What Black Man did you see?"

Martha replied, saucily, "I saw no Black Man but your own presence."

"Can you look upon these and not knock them down?"

"They will dissemble if I look upon them."

"You see you look upon them, and they fall down!"

"It is false. The Devil is a liar. I looked upon none but you since I came into the room."

The girls went into more fits and made accusations. Martha said to the judge, "It is a shameful thing that you should mind these folks that are out of their wits."

Hathorne asked her if she didn't see the ghosts of thirteen people whom Martha had murdered in Andover, most of them dead of smallpox since she had introduced the disease to town: They were lying all over the court, according to the girls.

"If I do speak, you will not believe me," Martha said.

The girls cried, "You do see them!"

The witch turned upon them and cried, "You lie!" Then, to the judges, "I am wronged!"

The girls were afflicted with so many horrible convulsions, contortions, hallucinations and turbulences that the magistrates saw no use in going on with the examination, so Goody Carrier was carried away and ordered to be closely bound. As soon as she was gone, the girls "all had strange and sudden ease. Mary Walcott told the magistrates that this woman told her she had been a witch these forty years." Martha Carrier was indicted.

William Proctor was examined and indicted, as was John Alden, the most famous man accused of witchcraft in America.

Alden was standing in the courtroom, having heard that he had been cried out upon, but none of the girls had ever seen him in the flesh. When someone informed them that Alden was present, they went into wild fits and cried, "Alden! Alden!" The judges attempted an unfortunate experiment — they asked, "Who is it in the room that hurts you?"

The girls were too tormented to say anything, but finally Annie Putnam, gagging, speechless, pointed at another military man, one Captain Hill. It was terribly obvious that a mistake had been made. Annie Putnam sensed the shock through the arms of her father, Sgt. Thomas, who was supporting her with his hands under her shoulders. Quickly, he bent and whispered in her ear, and Annie Putnam found her voice. "Alden! Alden afflicts me!"

The magistrate asked, "Have you ever seen Capt. Alden?"

"No."

"How do you know it is Alden?"

"The man told me so." Indeed he had, but "the man" was her father.

The court was adjourned into the street where a ring of people was set out with Annie Putnam in the center. She finally had the right man now, in the broad daylight; she pointed at him and cried, "There stands

Alden! A Bold fellow, with his hat on before the judges. He sells powder and shot to the Indians and French, and lies with Indian squaws and has papooses!"

Deputy Sheriff George Herrick took Alden into custody, confiscated his sword, and several hours later John Alden was brought to the meetinghouse where he was required to stand on a chair where everyone might see him. The girls had further fits: Alden's phantom pinched them. Hathorne told Herrick to hold Alden's hands open so he could no longer hurt the children.

Alden asked the magistrates, "Why should you think I should come to this Village to afflict these persons that I never knew or saw before?"

Justice Barholomew Gedney told him, "Confess, and give glory to God."

"I hope to give glory to God, and that I never satisfy the Devil. I appeal to all you who ever knew me, did you ever suspect me to be such a person? I challenge anyone to bring in anything, on their own knowledge, that might give suspicion of my being such a one."

Justice Gedney replied, "I have known you many years, and have been at sea with you, and I always looked upon you to be an honest man. But now I see cause to alter my judgment."

"I am sorry for that," Alden told him, "but I hope God will clear up my innocency so that you will recall your former judgment again. I hope I shall, with Job, maintain my integrity till I die."

Gedney ordered him, "Look upon your accusers." Alden did so — they were knocked down like so many bowling pins. Gedney said to the Captain, "You see that your look strikes them down."

"What reason can be given," Alden asked Gedney, "why my looking upon you does not strike you down as well?"

But that question had been answered long since: The Devil could do only what he was permitted by God to do, and God certainly would not give him permission to knock down judges of a Puritan court. Gedney ignored the question and ordered the girls to be brought forward so that the test of the witch touch could be administered; it worked, miraculously. Affronted, Alden declared, "It is a Providence of God that He suffers these creatures to accuse innocent persons."

The Rev. Nicholas Noyes rose to ask Alden, "Why should you offer to speak of the Providence of God? God, by His Providence, governs the world and keeps it in peace." He went on to preach a short sermon on the subject.

When Noyes had finished Alden turned to Bartholomew Gedney again and assured him, "There is a lying spirit in them. I can assure you, there is not a *word* of truth in all that they say of me."

But Gedney told Herrick, "Take him away. The examination is ended," and Alden was remanded to Boston Jail.

John Howe got back to Topsfield from Ipswich about sunset, and not long afterward he was standing in his dooryard talking with his neighbor about his sister-in-law's examination that day when suddenly his sow, that had six piglets, squealed, jumped into the air, and fell down. Startled, Howe exclaimed, "I think my sow is bewitched.! I think she is dead!"

The neighbor laughed — but it turned out to be true. The neighbor, sober now that they had confirmed the sow's demise, suggested, "Cut off her ear." He did so, and that night John's hand — the one that had held the knife — was full of paralysis and pain.

On the first of June Sarah Rist of Reading was arrested and sent to Boston Jail, but Rebecca Nurse and other prisoners in Boston were transferred to Salem Prison. When she arrived Rebecca was indicted by the grand jury and evidence was given in against her. At the same time that Mrs. Ann Carr Putnam's deposition was being read in court, she suddenly had a recurrence of her worst fits: Rebecca Nurse attacked her in all her elderly fury. Her specter told Mrs. Putnam, "Now I am come out of prison I have power to afflict you, and now I will afflict you all day long and will kill you if I can, for I have killed Benjamin Houlton and John Fuller and Rebecca Shepard."

This was going back some distance in time, for John Fuller had been the first husband of Rebecca Putnam, Capt. John's daughter. Fuller had died in 1675, three years after their marriage. Rebecca Putnam Fuller had been remarried to John Shepard and subsequently had died herself. Mercy Lewis on May 6th had accused George Burroughs of having bewitched Rebecca Shepard the younger, and Mary Walcott had earlier accused Rebecca Nurse of having helped in the girl's witch-murder.

Goody Nurse's phantom went on to inform Goody Ann Putnam that she and her sister Goody Cloyse, together with Goody Bishop, had killed Carolina John's infant daughter Sarah on the 15th of April because the Constable had said of the sisters, "It is no wonder they are witches, for their mother was so before them." The trio of witches had tried to kill John himself but, unfortunately, he had recovered from his own attack of Satan's scourge, so they had to settle for the murder of his child.

No sooner had Goody Putnam been told these things than the ghosts of six children in winding sheets appeared, called her Aunt — which terrified Ann — and told her they were the murdered children of her sister Goody Carr Baker of Boston. Their murderers, they informed Mrs. Putnam, were Goody Rebecca Nurse and Elizabeth Carey of Charlestown and an old deaf woman of Boston. The murdered babies charged Ann to go and tell these things to the magistrates, or else they would tear her to pieces, for their blood cried out for vengeance.

Following this onslaught of ectoplasm, Goody Putnam had to withstand yet another sordid visit, this time by the three stillborn or early dead infants of her sister Mrs. Mary Carr Bailey, wife of Salem's first minister; they told her that Rebecca had also murdered them.

In court Mrs. Mary English corroborated the fact that Mary Warren had told Edward and Sarah Bishop and Mary Easty that the magistrates might just as well examine Eleazer Keysar's mad daughter as the "afflicted persons."

Prison proved too much for Sarah Churchill, and she re-entered the ranks of the haunted by confessing that Widow Ann Pudeator had brought her the Book to sign, which she had done. She had seen Bridget Bishop who told her she had killed John Trask's child recently. Her master George Jacobs also had afflicted her and called her a "bitch witch" and assorted other ill names. It was, indeed, true that Goody Pudeator had brought her three poppits in the likenesses of Mercy Lewis, Annie Putnam, and Betty Hubbard, which she stuck with thorns.

Timothy and Deborah Perley deposed that after an argument over boards with Elizabeth Howe the Perley cows refused to give much more than a spoonful of milk, and they used to be good cows fed on good English pasture, but within four days they had gotten back to normal.

Deborah Perley swore further that her daughter Hannah had fits when she saw Elizabeth Howe's apparition going in and out of the oven. When Deborah asked why her daughter spoke so badly of Mrs. Howe, who had always been so loving toward her, the girl said, "If you were afflicted, as I am, you would talk as bad of her."

Later, when she saw Mrs. Howe and the girl again being friendly and loving, Deborah asked Hannah, "Why are you so loving to Goody Howe when you are together?" Hannah replied, "I am afraid to do otherwise, for then Goody Howe would kill me."

The Rev. Mr. Samuel Phillips, minister of Rowley, refuted the testimony of the Perleys. He had gone, with another minister of Rowley, Rev. Edward Payson, to visit Hannah Perley in one of her fits, and she had not mentioned Mrs. Howe. After the fit was over Mrs. Howe had asked the girl whether she had ever hurt her. Hannah had answered, "No, never, and if I did complain of you in my fits, I know not that I did so."

Mr. Phillips also swore that the girl's brother Samuel had looked out a window when the minister was outdoors with the girl and called to Hannah, "Goodwife Howe is a witch! Say she is a witch!" but Hannah said nothing of the kind, and the minister rebuked the boy. Phillips added in his deposition, "No wonder that the child in her fits did mention Goodwife Howe, when her nearest relations were so frequent in expressing their suspicions in the child's hearing when she was out of her fits."

Rev. Mr. Payson supported Phillips' testimony that Hannah, who went into a fit after her mother spoke tartly to her, did not mention Mrs. Howe, and that when Mrs. Howe came in later, took the child by the hand, and asked whether she had ever done her any hurt, Hannah answered, "No, never." Many of her neighbors submitted depositions supporting Goodwife Howe — they carried no weight whatsoever with the Court.

The magistrates continued to refer to the bewitched girls as "afflicted persons," as did all circumspect people in public places. But when George Jacobs' felicitous expression "bitch witches" became known through Sarah Churchill's testimony, in private some few individuals when they knew they were speaking with friends, picked up the phrase and applied it as they thought it ought to be applied.

Joseph Putnam was picking up converts to his point of view fairly rapidly by the beginning of June, but very few were willing to stand in the open and declare their feelings except, now and then, the relative of an accused witch, or one of the witches in person. But Joseph Fowler submitted a deposition that read, "Goodman Bibber and his wife lived at my house, and I did observe and take notice that Goodwife Bibber was a woman who was very idle in her calling, and very much given to tattling and tale-bearing, making mischief among her neighbors and very much given to speak bad words, and would call her husband bad names, and was a woman of a very turbulent and unruly spirit."

The new Court of Oyer and Terminer met for the first time in Salem Court House on June 2, 1692. At 10:00 a.m. Dr. J. Barton and a committee of women conducted body searches of Bridget Bishop, Rebecca Nurse, Elizabeth Proctor, Alice Parker, Susannah Martin, and Sarah Goode. The searchers found in the first three women "a preternatural excrescence of flesh between the pudendum and anus, much like to teats and not usual in women, and much unlike to the other three...." A committee of eight men inspected the body of John Proctor, but found nothing unusual.

John Hathorne and Jonathan Corwin issued a warrant for the arrest of Elizabeth Paine and Elizabeth Fosdick, and the same day the former was arrested. During the day Susannah Sheldon saw the apparitions of Rebecca Nurse and the deceased Goodman John Harwood who accused the witch of having murdered him by pushing him off his cart and striking the breath out of his body.

A new afflicted person arrived on the scene when Hannah Cutler Putnam, wife of Constable Carolina John, saw the specters of Samuel Fuller and Lydia Wilkins in winding sheets in her own home. The phantoms told her to inform Judge John Hathorne that John Willard had murdered them; if she did not, they would tear her into pieces. John Willard's very own specter, also present, with little sense of self-preservation confirmed the ghosts' statements and added he had further murdered an entire mass of men, women, and children of both sexes, including Samuel Fuller, Lydia Wilkins, Mrs. William Shaw, Rebecca Putnam Fuller, "Aaron Way's child and Benjamin Fuller's child," Philip Knight's child "with the help of William Hobbs, and Jonathan Knight's child, Ezekiel Cheever's children," also with Hobbs' help, and, to boot, Carolina John and Hannah Cutler Putnam's own daughter "Sarah, six weeks old." The invisible corpses were piling up, sometimes murdered more than once by more than one person, an anomaly that seems to have gone unnoticed by the Court. Later in the day Joseph Fuller's ghost arrived to tell Hannah he had been killed by Goody Corey.

Rev. Francis Dane of Andover submitted a testimonial in behalf of Martha Carrier to the Court; in it he swore that the reports against the woman "have been scandalous and unjust," and they would not bear the light. "As for such things as charms," he said, "and ways to find their cattle — I never heard, nor do I know any neighbor that ever did so; neither have I any grounds to believe it," having lived forty years in Andover. He admitted there "was a suspicion of Goodwife Carrier" among some of the townsfolk, but he put no credence in it.

With regard to the other accused people, "had charity been put on, the Devil would not have had such an advantage against us, and I believe many innocent persons have been accused and imprisoned: The conceit of specter evidence as an infallible mark did too far prevail with us; hence, we so easily parted with our neighbors of honest and good report, and members in full communion; hence, we so easily parted with our children, when we knew nothing in their lives — nor any of our neighbors' — to suspect them. And thus things were hurried on; hence, such strange breaches in families." Rev. Mr. Dane believed that many people had lied and confessed to being witches merely to save themselves, while those who did not confess were condemned.

Concerning his daughter, Elizabeth Johnson, he said, "I never had ground to suspect her; neither have I heard any other to accuse her till, for specter evidence "— given in by Annie Putnam and Mary Walcott — "she was brought forth. But this I must say — she was weak, and incapacious fearful, and in that respect I fear she hath falsely accused herself and others." She was one of many Andover people who had confessed and become themselves accusers.

Dane continued, "Not long before she was sent for she spoke as to her own particular that she was sure she was no witch." As for her daughter Elizabeth Dane the younger, Dane's granddaughter, "she is simplish at best, and I fear the common speech that was frequently spread among us — of their liberty if they would but confess, and the like expressions used by some — have brought many into a snare."

At four in the afternoon the search committee that had examined Bridget Bishop's body in the morning, reexamined it and found it to be "in a clear and free state from any preternatural excrescence as formerly seen by us, as also Rebecca Nurse. Instead of that excrescence" they had formerly seen, now there was only an insensitive area of dry skin. Nor was there anything to be found on Elizabeth Proctor's body. "And as for Susannah Martin, whose breast in the morning search appeared to us very full, the nibs fresh and starting, now at this searching" they were "all lank and pendant...."

When Bridget Bishop was being brought up the streets of Salem to the Court House for her trial, as she was passing the meetinghouse she glanced at it, and there was a loud noise inside. People ran in to see what was wrong: To their amazement — and to that of Cotton Mather when he heard the report — they found a board torn out of the wall and lying on the other side of the chamber.

Bridget Bishop was tried and condemned to death.

The next day, Friday, John Proctor's shape hurt Sarah Bibber — it wanted her to swallow "drink as red as blood," but she refused. Phoebe Chandler, still visiting at her sister Allen's farm in Andover, was stricken — just as Martha Carrier's voice had predicted: Half her right hand was swollen and painful, and part of her face as well.

Abigail Williams deposed to the Court that she had seen the apparition of Rebecca Nurse "at a sacrament, sitting next to the man with a high-crowned hat at the upper end of the table, and that she had had a hand, with her sister Goody Cloyse, in the murders of Goodman Harwood, Benjamin Porter, and Rebecca Shepard, among others.

Deputy Marshal Samuel Gookin arrested Elizabeth Foster and delivered her to the court. Sheriff George Corwin went to the Proctors' house to seize John Proctor's goods and provisions for the crown, as was done in all cases. He sold some of the cattle at half-price, butchered some and put the rest up for the West Indies; he threw the beer out of its barrel and confiscated the barrel; emptied out a pot of broth and took the pot — he left nothing in the home for the support of the Proctor children.

On June 4th Edward Putnam and Thomas Raymond complained against Mary Ireson of Lynn; Hathorne, Gedney, and Corwin issued a warrant for her arrest. John Proctor asked Rev. Nicholas Noyes to pray with him, but Noyes refused because the old man would not confess he was a witch. James Howe, a blind man, came to visit his wife in jail, as he did regularly, riding pillion behind one of his daughters, Mary or Abigail, commuting from their distant farm located off the beaten track. And Sgt. Thomas and Ann Carr Putnam had a new daughter that day whom they named Abigail. Jonathan Putnam thought that, now she had been relieved of her pregnancy and safely delivered of her child, Ann would perhaps have fewer fits.

By Sunday, June 5th, Phoebe Chandler had recovered pretty well from an attack of poison ivy, so she went to meeting in Andover. She sat in her accustomed place, and noticed that Richard Carrier was looking at her — her hand began to pain her as it had done while she was ill. This symptom was followed by a strange burning in her stomach, and finally she was struck deaf so that she could not hear the prayer nor the singing until the last few words of the hymn.

The same day Joseph Hutchinson, Sr., had a discussion with Abby Williams. He said, "Abigail, I have heard you speak often of a book that has been offered you."

"There are two books," she replied. "One is a short, thick book, and the other is a long book."

"What color is the book of?"

"They are as red as blood."

"Have you seen the books opened?"

"I have seen it many times."

"Did you see any writing in the book?"

"There are many lines written, and at the end of every line there is a seal."

"Who brought the book to you?"

"It was the Black Man."

"Who is the Black Man?"

"The Devil."

"Are you not afraid to see the Devil?"

"At the first I was," she replied, "and I did go from him, but now I am not afraid. I can talk with him as well as I can with you."

On Monday the 6th a warrant was issued against Ann Doliver of Gloucester. She was the daughter of the Rev. John Higginson of Salem who had, on May 18th, submitted a written testimonial in behalf of the accused witch Sarah Buckley.

Mary Tyler of Andover, when she was first arrested, said, "I have no fears upon me, and do think that nothing can make me confess against myself," but when she was taken to Salem her brother John Bridges rode along with her and kept saying, "You must needs be a witch, since the afflicted persons accuse you and at your touch were raised out of their fits. You must confess to it."

But Mary continually replied, "I am no witch; I know nothing of witchcraft. I beg you not to urge me to confess." But she was lying to her brother, as he well knew, for she it was who, together with her husband Job and the rest of her family, had accused John Godfrey in 1659 and 1665 of being a witch. The shoe was merely now on the other foot. The difference between the two situations was that, in the earlier cases Simon Bradstreet had been in charge, and he had quashed them; in 1692 Bradstreet sat doting and feeble in his chair in his retirement home in Salem while the witches flew over his head and Goody Tyler rode to her rendezvous with the Court of Oyer and Terminer.

When she got to Salem she was taken to a room and placed in it with her brother John on one side and Rev. John Emerson on the other. Both told her, "You are certainly a witch. You see the Devil before your eyes at this very moment." Mr. Emerson tried to beat the phantom away from her eyes with his hand. "You must confess."

But Mary replied, "I am innocent. I wish myself in a dungeon than that you should treat me so."

"Well, I see you will not confess," Emerson told her over and over; "Well, I will now leave you, and then you are undone, body and soul, forever!"

Her brother John, too, importuned her to confess, for in doing so she surely would not lie.

"Good brother, do not say so," Mary wept, "for I shall lie if I confess, and then who shall answer unto God for my lie?"

"You are a witch," Bridges insisted, "for God would not suffer so many good men to be in such an error about it, and you will be hanged if you do not confess," which was the important point.

The two men kept at her for so long that Mary thought she was going to lose her wits and her life until, finally, she broke down and agreed to everything that Emerson and Bridges put into her mouth, but the pangs of conscience she experienced were worse than anything else she had felt since she was cried out upon — and certainly greater than she had experienced in the Godrey affair.

Mary Osgood found herself in a similar situation, but she was left to invent times and names as her examiners asked their questions. When they asked, "How long have you been a witch?" She had replied, "I do not know."

"You do know the time," she was told.

She thought back and recollected that about twelve years before, after she had had her last child, she had undergone a spell of sickness and become melancholy: Mary had been a victim of what would much later be termed post-partum depression. She thought that time might be "as proper a time to mention as any," and so she replied, "I have been a witch twelve years."

"How did the Devil appear to you?" she was asked.

"I did not see the Devil," she replied.

"You did see the Devil," she was told, "for you were a witch and he must needs appear unto you."

"Yes," Mary agreed, "the Devil did appear to me."

"In what creature's shape did he appear?"

Mary hadn't thought of these things before, but her inquisitors were insistent — she had put the first foot upon the ladder, and she had to go on. She said the first thing that came to mind: "He came in the shape of a cat," for some time before her arrest she remembered that as she went out her front door she had seen a cat. And so, step by step, she was led to confess more and more specific disinformation. The same thing happened to others, including Eunice, the wife of Deacon John Fry.

On June 8th the newly elected General Court of Massachusetts met in Boston and resolved that all the old laws of the Colony that were not repugnant to English law would remain in force for the time being, while new laws were being written.

In Salem Village the ghost of Lawrence Shafling appeared to Elizabeth Booth and told her, "Elizabeth Proctor killed me because your mother would not send for Dr. Griggs to give me physic, and also because Goody Proctor was not sent for when first I was taken sick."

The uneasy spirit of Robert Stone, Sr., also appeared and told Betty that John Proctor and his wife killed him over a quarrel; his son, Robert Stone, Jr., told her the Proctors had killed him, too, because he had taken his father's part. One after the other, ghost after ghost paraded through Betty's field of vision that Wednesday: Hugh Jones told her they had killed him because he had not paid for a pot of cider; Elizabeth Shaw had been dispatched by Mrs. Proctor and John Willard because she had not used the services of those doctors Mrs. Proctor had recommended; Mrs. John Fulton died because she would not sell her apples. But the most impressive of the phantasms was that famous local sorcerer-physician, Dr. Zerubabel Endicott.

It seemed that Goody Proctor was a medical competitor of the good Doctor, and he had been killed because he and she "differed in their judgments about Thomas Very's wife." Further, the old witch had tried to kill Goody Endicott as well, and though she couldn't do it, she had nevertheless lamed the doctor's wife a good while.

The specter of Giles Corey appeared to Elizabeth Wardwell on Lecture Day, Thursday, June 8th; she saw it enter the Andover meetinghouse and take his wonted place among the men "in the middlemost seat by the post." He left with the congregation after the service, as Mary Walcott was pleased to corroborate.

June 10th was the day that had been set by the Court of Oyer and Terminer for the execution of Bridget Bishop. The site of the hanging was to be at the top of the nearly inaccessible hill that dominated Salem, and the gallows tree was to be an oak on the peak of the hill at the head of the winding path that was the only passable rout up the promontory.

At the bottom of the hill lived the coffin maker, Caleb Buffham. He knew that the corpses would be buried without coffins; but he knew, too, that the relatives of the executed people would wish to disinter the corpses from their shallow graves, put them in coffins, and carry them away for decent burial elsewhere. He stood ready to offer his services, and a helping hand in the arrangements as well as the labor.

The gallows oak was visible from most points in Salem, though everyone who could climb the hill would surely be on hand to witness this ultimate punishment — early in the morning people on foot struggled along the narrow, stony trail to the top so that they could arrange to have good spots for viewing. But Elizabeth Parris, in her place of detention in Stephen Sewall's home, was not allowed even to look out a window toward what would thenceforth be known as Gallows Hill for fear that the sight of the fruit of the Hanging Oak would cause her to be reminded of her original scrying and cause a recurrence of the hysteria that had begun the Salem Village witchhunt.

Before Bridget Bishop was turned off the ladder, Thomas Maule, the Salem Quaker who had fought poltergeists with urine in New Hampshire during 1682, gossiped within the hearing of the Rev. John Hale. Maule's wife had testified against Bridget at her trial, and Maule himself said, "If I were asked to pray with Goody Bishop today, I would not, for I believe she is guilty of that sin the Scripture saith we must not pray for it, For I believe she is a witch and covenanted with the Devil and hath forsaken God — and that is the sin we ought not to pray for. I could have come in a witness against her, if I would. I believe she bewitched to death a child of mine, and I believe most of those in prison are witches." But even Maule did not believe they were *all* witches.

Sarah Bibber saw the specter of George Jacobs at the gallows when Bridget was hanged — a Black Man was helping him to stand, thus freeing one of his hands so that he could beat Mary Walcott with one of his two canes.

Two days later, on Sunday, there was an eclipse of the sun which terrified the people of Massachusetts, and particularly those of Salem Village — so much so, indeed, that no fits or visions were reported. But in Boston the amateur astronomer Thomas Brattle, who had expected the phenomenon, observed the darkening of the sun through his telescope and made notes about it.

On Wednesday, June 15th, after several days of quiet occasioned by the execution of Goody Bishop and the solar eclipse, the clergy of Massachusetts gave in its opinion to the Court of Oyer and Terminer officially. In the final draft, which had been penned by Increase Mather, though the original had been written by his son, the ministers said, "We judge that, in the prosecution of these and all such witchcrafts, there is need of a very critical and exquisite caution, lest by too much credulity received only upon the Devil's authority, there be a door opened for a long train of miserable consequences, and Satan get an advantage over us; for we should not be ignorant of his devices."

The document recommended, also, great care "toward those that may be complained of, especially if they have been persons formerly of an unblemished reputation." Further, at preliminary examinations, the ministers recommended "that there be admitted as little as possible of such noise, company, and openness as may too hastily expose them that are examined," and that no questionable tests of witchcraft be used. They averred that "a demon may by God's permission appear, even to ill purposes, in the shape of an innocent, yea, and a virtuous man." The clergymen recommended that evidence of the "evil eye" and the "witch's touch" be disallowed. But the memo concluded with a recommendation that the government proceed with "the speedy and vigorous prosecutions of such as have rendered themselves obnoxious" as witches.

On Saturday, June 18th, Rev. Samuel Parris and Capt. John Putnam, Jr. were at the home of Jonathan Putnam who had been taken seriously ill. They sent for Mercy Lewis. When she arrived she was asked whether any witches tormented Jonathan, but she was immediately struck dumb. Mercy was told to lift her hand if the answer were yes —

she lifted the hand and went into a trance. When she awakened she said that she saw Rebecca Nurse and Goody Carrier holding Jonathan's head.

In Boston on Monday, June 20th, the servant maid Mercy Short, who had been rescued from the Indians after the massacre of her family, was asked by her mistress to go on an errand to Boston Prison. While she was there, Sarah Goode from her cell, her pipe clamped unfilled between her teeth, asked the young woman for "a little tobacco."

Mercy stooped to the floor, picked up a handful of wood shavings, threw them in the witch's face, and said, "That's tobacco good enough for you!"

Sarah started back rubbing her eyes; when she had cleared them she fixed the girl with her gimlet gaze and uttered a curse against her.

Mercy Short was immediately catapulted into paroxysms of agony in a fit of epic proportions. The Rev. Mr. Cotton Mather, who often haunted the corridors of the prison to question the witches, was called into the case immediately, and he prescribed fasting and prayer. He personally directed the exorcism, and determined to stick it through to the end.

Susannah Sheldon was at the home of William Shaw on Tuesday, June 21st; present, besides Deborah and William Shaw, was William Batter. The adults were witnessing a fit the eighteen-year-old was undergoing: Somehow a rope had been tied around her hands so tightly that it had to be cut to be removed. While she was in her fit Susannah named Sarah Goode as her tormenter. The bitch witch had had three similar, earlier fits in which her hands had been tied — the first time she had said it was Widow Lydia Dustin who hurt her, but the third and fourth times it had been Goody Goode. Whenever Susannah touched the rope — and she touched it often — something invisible bit her. It was a new twist, a fact that awed the onlookers.

Four days later, on Saturday, Nathaniel Saltonstall, one of the justices of the Court of Oyer and Terminer, resigned his post, being "very much dissatisfied with the proceedings of it."

The next day Sarah Goode's apparition pulled Susannah Sheldon's head down behind a chest and tied her hands together with a wheel band. To add insult to rope tricks, the tobacco-craving witch choked her as well. On Monday the 27th Sarah Bibber was attacked by the shape of Rebecca Nurse, and Elizabeth Booth by Elizabeth Proctor's shade. The old woman told Betty, "Neither you nor your mother would believe I am a witch, but I will make you know it before I have done with you!" Evidently there was an iota of doubt about it somewhere, so self-incrimination was required to remove all doubt.

Rebecca Nurse petitioned the Court on June 28th "That, whereas some women did search your petitioner at Salem, as I did then conceive for some supernatural mark, and then one of the said women which is known to be the most ancient, skillful, prudent person of them all as to any such concern did express her self to be of a contrary opinion from the rest, did then declare that she saw nothing in or about your Honor's poor petitioner but what might arise from a natural cause. And I then rendered the said persons a sufficient known reason as to myself of the moving cause thereof, which was by exceeding weaknesses descending partly from an overture of nature and exigencies that have befallen me in the times of my travails.

"Therefore, your petitioner humbly prays that your Honors would be pleased to admit of some other women to enquire into the great concern — those that are most grand, wise, and skillful; namely, Mrs. Higginson, Sr.; Mrs. Durkstone; Mrs. Woodbury (two of these being midwives); Mrs. Porter, together with such others as may be chosen on that account, before I am brought to my trial.

"All which I hope your Honors will take into your prudent consideration, and find it requisite so to do, for my life lies now in your hands, under God. And being conscious of my own innocence, I humbly beg that I may have liberty to manifest it to the world, partly by the means above-said."

Two other petitions were presented to the court in her behalf as well, and it was evident from them that some minds were beginning to change — some minds that one might have thought would be the last to reverse themselves:

Nathaniel Putnam submitted a paper to the Court that said of Goody Nurse, "I have known her differ with her neighbors, but I never knew or heard of any that did accuse her of what she is now charged with."

A petition saying much the same thing was submitted by thirty-nine of her neighbors. Among the signers were several Putnams, including Capt. John and his wife Rebecca Prince Putnam; Benjamin; Spinster Sarah, Old John's daughter; Sarah, James Putnam's wife; Lydia, and Joseph — who might have been expected to come to Goody Nurse's defense. But the most surprising signer of all was Jonathan Putnam who had been one of the two people to swear out the original complaint. Two other signers were Israel Porter and Elizabeth Hathorne Porter, brother-in-law and sister of Judge John Hathorne.

The Court of Oyer and Terminer met for the second time in Salem the next day, June 29th, and tried several people. At Sarah Goode's trial one of the bitch witches went into a fit, came to, and accused the witch of having stabbed her spectrally with a knife that broke. She exhibited a piece of the blade of the knife, which had somehow transformed itself from ectoplasm into metal — it was an impressive stroke. But at the climactic moment a young man came forward out of the spectators, showed the court the broken haft of a knife, claimed that he had broken it yesterday and thrown away the piece of blade. An examination showed that the blade did, indeed, fit the haft. The court reproved the young man for lying before authority, and he was summarily dismissed. Sarah Goode was convicted and sentenced to death.

Rebecca Nurse, too, was tried. Her daughter, Sarah, testified that "being in the Court, this 29th of June, 1692, I saw GoodwifeBibber pull pins out of her clothes, and she held them between her fingers and clasped her hands around her knees. Then she cried out and said, 'Goody Nurse pinched me!'"

Capt. John. and Rebecca Putnam deposed with regard to Goody Nurse that "our son-in-law John Fuller, and our daughter Rebecca Shepard did both of them die a most violent death (and died acting very strangely at the time of their death); we did judge then that they both died of a malignant fever, and had no suspicion of witchcraft of any; neither can we accuse the prisoner at the bar of any such thing."

The evidence in defense of Rebecca Nurse was great: Accusers retracting their complaints, character references, the powerful Putnams rallying behind the woman — the jury felt compelled to bring in a verdict of "Not Guilty." But no sooner had they done so than the bitch witches were thrown into ghastly convulsions. One of the judges said, "I am not satisfied." Another, as he was leaving the bench, said, "We shall have her indicted anew." Judge William Stoughton intoned, "I would not impose upon the jury, but would you not care to reconsider your verdict because of what Goody Nurse said when Goody Hobbs was brought in?"

What had happened at the point to which Stoughton had reference was that Rebecca had exclaimed, "What! Do you bring her? She is one of us." Stoughton thought she had meant "one of us *witches*," and that she had thus inadvertently confessed.

The jury did reconsider, but it was hung, part believing Stoughton was right, the other part believing Goody Nurse had merely meant "one of us *prisoners*." They returned to court to ask Rebecca what she had meant, — the question was put by Thomas Fisk, the jury foreman. Goody Nurse, partially deaf, did not hear him and did not reply. The jury retired once more and, taking her silence to confirm Stoughton's view, brought in a final verdict of "Guilty."

The trials continued on Thursday, June 30th, and Friday, July 1st. At one of them a bitch witch, in the midst of a tremendous fit, shocked the crowd and dismayed the bench by crying out on the Rev. Mr. Samuel Willard of the Old South Church in Boston. There was a solemn silence in the Salem Court House for a moment, and then Chief Justice

Stoughton leaned forward, pierced the girl with a look as baleful as any evil eye, and informed her, "You are surely mistaken in the person you identify. Sheriff, remove this witness until she may come to her wits." Deputy Sheriff George Herrick removed the object of infamy forthwith.

The authorities also removed, at the end of the trials, the condemned persons including, besides Goody Goode and Goody Nurse, Susannah Martin, Elizabeth Howe, and Sarah Wilds.

Examinations recommenced immediately after the trials, on July 2nd, Saturday. Ann Pudeator was interrogated at Thomas Beadle's Inn. Hathorne said to Sarah Churchill, "You have charged her with bringing the Book to you."

"Yes," Sarah answered.

"Have you seen her since?"

"No."

"Goodwife Pudeator," Hathorne said, "You have formerly been complained of. We now inquire further — here is one person saith you brought her the Book, which is Sarah Churchill. Look on the person."

"I brought no book," Mrs. Pudeator replied.

Sarah contradicted her. "You did bring me the Book. It was at Goodman Jacobs'."

But Widow Pudeator, still looking at the judge, insisted, "I never saw the woman before now."

"This maid," Hathorne told her, "charged you with bringing her the Book at the last examination."

"I never saw the Devil's Book, nor knew that he had one."

Hathorne turned to the spectators. "Lt. Jeremiah Neal, what can you say of this woman?"

Neal stood forward. He said, "She has been an ill-carriaged woman, and since my wife has been sick of smallpox this woman has come to my house pretending kindness, and I was glad to see it. She asked whether she might use our mortar, which was used for my wife. I consented to it, but I afterward repented of it, for the nurse told me my wife was the worse since she was very ill of a flux which she had not seen before.

"When the officer came for Pudeator," he continued, "the nurse said, 'You are come too late,' for my wife grew worse till she died. Goody Pudeator had often threatened my wife."

When they were queried some of the bitch witches, including Betty Hubbard, testified that Goody Pudeator had tormented them. Mary Walcott swore that, though the witch hadn't hurt her, she had seen Widow Pudeator's specter in company with Rebecca Nurse.

Hathorne asked, "Goody Pudeator, what did you do with the ointments that you had so many of in hour house?"

"I never had ointment or oil," she answered, "but meat tried out in my house, since my husband died."

Constable Neal contradicted her: She had near twenty that had ointment or grease in them, a little in each container."

"I never had any ointment but neatsfoot oil in the house."

"But what was in these things the constable speaks of?" Hathorne insisted.

"It was grease to make soap of."

"But why did you put them in so many things, when one would have held all?"

Mrs. Pudeator mumbled something unintelligible, and Neal said, "The ointments were of several sorts."

John Hathorne turned to a trusted witness. "Sarah Bibber," he asked, "did you ever see this woman before now?"

"No," Mrs. Bibber replied, but Annie Putnam chimed in, "I never have seen her until she came to Salem Town last," and fell to a fit.

"Take the girl by the wrist, widow," Hathorne ordered. She did so, Annie Putnam recovered, Mary Warren fell to fits, and she, too, was cured by the witch's touch.

After morning service and Sacrament on Sunday in Salem Church, the Rev. Nicholas Noyes spoke to the congregation. "It is propounded to the church by the Elders," he said, "that our sister Rebecca Nurse, being convicted a witch by the Court and condemned to die, should be excommunicated. All those who concur in this judgment will please to signify by the raising of hands." The vote was unanimous.

At the afternoon service Goody Nurse was brought before the congregation in chains, placed conspicuously in the center aisle, and Mr. Noyes read the excommunication. It was a solemn moment.

The next day Candy, the black Barbados slave of Margaret Hawkes, was examined. Hathorne asked, "Candy, are you a witch?"

The woman answered, "Candy no witch in her country. Candy's mother no witch," she went on gratuitously, but none of the judges did more than raise an eyebrow. "Candy no witch, Barbados. *This* country, mistress give Candy witch." And Sarah Hawkes stood accused.

The judge wanted to be clear on this point — "Did your mistress make you a witch in this country?"

"Yes, in this country mistress give Candy witch."

"What did your mistress do to make you a witch?"

"Mistress bring Book and pen and ink; make Candy write."

"Show us what you wrote." Hathorne pushed his inkwell, pen and paper across the bench, and the Deputy Sheriff brought them to the slave. She made her mark.

"How did you afflict or hurt these?" He indicated the girls.

"You let me go, I show you," she said. "Candy come back."

The judges let her go outdoors with the deputy sheriff for a few minutes, and when she came back she had with her a handkerchief with two knots in it, a rag with one knot, a piece of cheese, and some grass. At the sight of all this paraphernalia the bitch witches went into spasms, and when they at last came to normalcy Annie Putnam cried, "The Black Man and Goody Hawkes and Candy are by the poppits! They pinch them!" and there were more fits.

When order was once again restored, the examination room, against all the advice of the clergy, was turned into an occult laboratory. When a piece of the rag was burned, one of the afflicted girls was burned on the hand. No one bothered to point out that it was the judge who was at that moment practicing witchcraft. When another scrap was put into a tankard of water, two were choked as though drowning, and a third ran out of the building toward the river as though to jump in, but was stopped before anything could happen. Candy was forced to eat the cheese, and that night her belly burned. Margaret Hawkes, when she heard what Candy had done, chose to confess.

Thomas Fisk, foreman of the jury that had first acquitted and then condemned Rebecca Nurse, wrote an explanation of the jury's action for her relatives. Mrs. Nurse herself wrote an explanation of what had happened: "I being informed that the jury brought me in guilty upon my saying that Goodwife Hobbs and her daughter were of our company — but I intended no otherways than as they were prisoners with us, therefore did then, and yet do, judge them not legal evidence against their fellow prisoners. And I being somewhat hard of hearing, and full of grief, none informing me how the court took up my words, and therefore had not opportunity to declare what I intended when I said they were of our company." But her plea fell upon ears deafer than her own.

Bray Wilkins on Tuesday, July 5th, had a bloody urination while he was arguing with neighbors about his grandson John Willard — some of them maintained that he was innocent, but Bray said, "It was not I nor my son Benjamin, but the testimony of the afflicted persons, and the jury's verdict concerning the murder of my grandson, Daniel Wilkins, that would take away his life if anything does." After the disagreement he went home to change his pants and write another deposition. Shortly, his copious waters became a blockage once again, and he had a recurrence of his pains.

Rebecca Nurse's case had been appealed upward to the government, and somehow it had reached the ears of Governor William Phips away to Eastward. On July 6th he granted her a reprieve. Immediately the Committee of Vigilance raised an outcry against the Governor's decision, and it became evident that a widening split had developed among the Putnams. The members of the vigilantes, including Sgt. Thomas Putnam, Jr., Deacon Edward Putnam, Carolina John Putnam, Deacon Nathaniel Ingersoll, and Ezekiel Cheever — none of whom had signed the petition on behalf of Mrs. Nurse — sent riders to Boston to protest the governor's action.

During the next few days the lobbyists for the Committee of Vigilance were entirely successful, and the reprieve was waived. Once more Goody Nurse faced the gallows. Rev. Samuel Parris' staunchest supporters, who comprised most of the Committee, had won their greatest victory.

Ann Foster of Andover was examined on July 15th, and after some initial grilling she broke down and confessed that "The Devil appeared to me in the shape of a bird at several times, such a bird as I never saw the like before."

"How do you hurt these?" she was asked.

"The Devil gave me the gift of the evil eye."

"Why do you think that the bird was the Devil?"

"Because he came white and vanished away black, and the Devil told me that I should have this gift and I must believe him, and he told me I should have prosperity."

"How many times did he appear to you?"

"Three times, and was always as a bird, and the last time was about half a year since and sat upon a table."

"What did he look like?"

"He had two legs and great eyes."

"When did he promise that you should have prosperity?"

"It was the second time of his appearance that he promised me prosperity."

"Who told you to hurt these people?"

"It was Carrier's wife about three weeks ago that came and persuaded me to hurt them."

Ann Foster's interrogation continued the next day. "Who made you a witch?" she was asked.

"It was Goody Carrier."

"How did she come to you, in her shape or her body?"

"She came to me in person."

"When was it she came?"

"It was about six years ago and told me if I would not be a witch the Devil would tear me in pieces and carry me away, and then I promised to serve the Devil."

"What did you do?"

"I bewitched a hog of John Lovejoy's to death, and I hurt some persons in Salem Village."

"Did you hurt any others?"

"Goody Carrier came to me and would have me bewitch two children of Andrew Allen's."

"How did you do it?"

"I had two poppits made and stuck pins in them to bewitch Allen's children, by which one of them died, the other very sick."

"Did you go to the meeting at Salem Village?"

"Yes, Goody Carrier came and told me of the meeting and would have me go, so we got upon sticks and went on the journey."

"Who did you see there?"

"Mr. Burroughs the minister was there, and he spake to us all — there was then twenty-five persons met together."

"Did you hurt Timothy Swan?"

"Yes, I tied a knot in a rag and threw it into the fire to hurt him."

"Did you hurt any others?"

"Yes, I did hurt the rest that complained of me by squeezing the poppits like them and so almost choked them."

Two days later, on the 18th, Ann Foster was questioned again in her room at the prison — she was a goldmine of occult information, but this time she began to repeat herself, though some details were new: She had agreed to serve the Devil two years, "upon which he promised me prosperity but never performed it." Indeed, it was remarkable how little prosperity there was among most of the accused witches. As she and Martha Carrier were going to the Sabbat in Salem Village "the stick broke as we were carried in the air above the tops of the trees, and we fell, but I did hang fast about the neck of Goody Carrier, and we were presently at the Village, but I was then much hurt of my leg." Though there were only twenty-five present at the meeting she "heard some of the witches say that there was three hundred and five in the whole country, and that they would ruin that place, the Village."

Besides Burroughs there were at the meeting two men, "and one of them had gray hair." Ann, contrite, told the judges that she "formerly frequented the public meeting to Worship God, but the Devil had such power over me that I could not profit there, and that was my undoing." She recalled another act of murder that had been committed: "About three or four years ago Martha Carrier told me she would bewitch James Hobbs' child to death, and the child died in twenty-four hours."

After the judges left, the Rev. John Hale asked Ann further questions. "Did you ride to the witches' meetings on a stick?"

"Yes."

"What did you do for victuals?"

"I carried bread and cheese in my pocket. I came before the meeting with the Andover folk to Salem Village, and we sat down together under a tree and eat our food, and I drank water out of a brook to quench my thirst."

"Where was the meeting?"

"Upon a grassy place by a cart path, and there was sandy ground in the path with the marks of horses' feet." She said further, "I am in fear that Mr. Burroughs and Martha Carrier will kill me, for they appeared to me and brought a sharp-pointed iron like a spindle, but four-square, and threatened to stab me to death with it because I had confessed my witchcraft and told of them that they were with me at meeting. It was Martha Carrier that made me a witch."

Tuesday, July 19th, was the day of execution that had been set by the Court of Oyer and Terminer for those who had been convicted earlier in the month. As Rebecca Nurse mounted the ladder to the oak on Gallows Hill in Salem, there was a hush that settled over the crowd except for a few angry murmurs here and there. When she was turned off, there was a communal gasp and loud sobbing from some of the people. Susannah Martin, Elizabeth Howe, and Sarah Wilds took their turns.

When Goody Sarah Goode turned to face the crowd she did not, like her sister witches, pray before the hangman's push, but glared fiercely out at the spectators. The Rev. Nicholas Noyes stood before the tree and called on her, as she would save her soul, to confess at the eleventh hour. He said, "You are a witch, and you know that you are."

Sarah fixed him with her evil eye and replied clearly, "You are a liar. I am no more a witch than you are a wizard, and if you take away my life, God will give you blood to drink."

The tree was festooned that day with five corpses of women. They were taken down and shallow graves scratched out among the stones. Caleb Buffham the coffin-maker was in touch with the families of the women, and he had been busy making arrangements for the dark hours to follow.

Mary Lacey, Ann Foster's daughter, was examined on Thursday, July 21st. She said that her mother, Martha Carrier, and she all rode on the same pole to the Salem Village Sabbat, and that the pole broke not far from the Village. She said also that three or four years earlier she had seen Mary Bradbury, Elizabeth Howe, and Rebecca Nurse baptized by "the Old Serpent" at Newbury Falls: The Devil carried her in his arms to the baptism and showed her how to use nearly any sort of rag or cloth — "Imagine it to represent such and such a person," he had told her, "then whatsoever she doth to that rag or cloth so rolled up, the person represented thereby will be in like manner afflicted." She admitted to having hurt Timothy Swan and others in such a manner. She was taken out of the examination room and her mother brought in.

She stood before Justices Bartholomew Gedney, John Hathorne, Jonathan Corwin, and Capt. John Higginson. Gedney said to her, "Goody Foster! You remember we have three times spoken with you, and do you now remember what you then confessed to us? You have been engaged in very great wickedness, and some have been left to hardness of heart to deny; but it seems that God will give you more favor than others, inasmuch as you relent. But your daughter here hath confessed some things that you did not tell us of. Your daughter was with you and Goody Carrier when you did ride upon the stick."

"I did not know it," Goody Foster said.

"How long have you known your daughter to be engaged?"

"I cannot tell, nor have I any knowledge of it at all."

"Did you see your daughter at the meeting?"

"No."

"Your daughter said she was at the witches' meeting, and that you yourself stood at a distance off and did not partake at that meeting, and you said so also; give us a relation from the beginning until now."

"I know none of their names that were there, but only Goody Carrier."

"Would you know their faces if you saw them?"

"I cannot tell."

"Were there not two companies in the field at the same time?"

"I remember no more."

Mary Warren broke in to say, "Goody Carrier's shape told me that Goody Foster had made her daughter a witch."

Hathorne addressed Mrs. Foster, "Do not you acknowledge that you did so about thirteen years ago?"

"No," Ann replied, "and I know no more of my daughter's being a witch than what day I shall die upon."

"Are you willing your daughter should make a full and free confession?"

"Yes."

"Are you willing to do so too?"

"Yes."

"You cannot expect peace of conscience without a free confession," Gedney said.

"If I knew any thing more, I would speak it to the utmost." Ann set her lips in a firm line. The justices conferred among themselves — obviously, when it came to her daughter, Mrs. Foster was less than totally cooperative. They decided to bring the two together. Mary Lacey was sent for.

When she came into the room the first thing she did when she saw her mother was to say, "Oh! Mother! How do you do? We have left Christ, and the Devil hath got hold of us. How shall I get rid of this evil one? I desire God to break my rocky heart that I may get the victory this time."

Gedney leaned forward ferociously and said, "Goody Foster! You cannot get rid of this snare, your heart and mouth is not open!"

Nor were her eyes, for she seemed to be praying. "Who is it? The Devil?" Hathorne asked.

"I did not see the Devil," Ann replied, "I was praying to the Lord."

"What Lord?"

"To God."

"What God do witches pray to?" Hathorne asked.

"I cannot tell. The Lord help me!"

The magistrate turned to the daughter. "Goody Lacey! Had you no discourse with your mother when riding?"

"No, I think I had not one word," she answered.

"Who rid foremost on that stick to the Village?"

"I suppose my mother."

Mrs. Foster contradicted her — "Goody Carrier was foremost!"

"Goody Lacey! How many years ago since they were baptized?"

"Three or four years ago, I suppose."
"Who baptized them?"
"The Old Serpent."
"How did he do it?"
"He dipped their heads in the water, saying they were his and that he had power over them."
"Where was this?"
"At Fall's River."
"How many were baptized that day?"
"Some of the chief; I think they were six baptized."
"Name them."
"I think they were of the Higher Powers," she replied. The examination was terminated, the women taken out, and Goody Foster's granddaughter, Mary Lacey the younger, was led in. Mary Warren fell into a violent fit.

Hathorne bellowed at the girl, "How dare you come in here and bring the Devil with you to afflict these poor creatures?" Mary Lacey was made to touch Mary Warren, who immediately recovered. Gedney said to the child, "You are here accused of practicing witchcraft upon Goody Ballard; which way do you do it?"

"I cannot tell. Where," she asked, looking around the room wonderingly, "is my mother that made me a witch, and and I knew it not?"

"Can you look upon that maid Mary Warren and not hurt her?" The girl tried to do it, but Mistress Warren toppled over. "Do you acknowledge now that you are a witch?"

Wide-eyed, greatly impressed with her manifest power to do damage, Mary said, "Yes."

"How long have you been a witch?"
"Not above a week."
"Did the Devil appear to you?"
"Yes."

"In what shape?"

"In the shape of a horse."

"What did he say to you?"

"He bade me not to be afraid of anything, and he would not bring me out, but he has proved a liar from the beginning."

"When was this?"

"I know not; above a week."

"Did you set your hand to the Book?"

"Nay."

"Did he bid you worship him?"

"Yes, he bade me also afflict persons."

"You are now in the way to obtain mercy if you will confess and repent."

"The Lord help me!"

"Do not you desire to be saved by Christ?" Hathorne asked ponderously.

"Yes."

"Then you must confess freely what you know in this matter."

At last Mary understood what was expected of her. She said, "I was in bed and the Devil came to me and bade me obey him, and I should want for nothing, and he would not bring me out."

"But how long ago?"

"A little more than a year."

"Was that the first time?"

"Yes."

"How long was you gone from your father, when you ran away?"

"Two days."

"Where had you your food?"

"At John Stone's."

"Did the Devil appear to you then, when you was abroad?"

"No, but he put such thoughts in my mind as not to obey my parents."

"Who did the Devil bid you afflict?"

"Timothy Swan. Richard Carrier comes often o'nights and has me to afflict persons."

"How many of you were there at a time?"

"Richard Carrier and his mother, and my mother and grandmother."

"How many more witches are there in Andover?"

"I know no more but Richard Carrier."

On Friday, July 22nd, a large group of her neighbors submitted a petition in behalf of Mary Bradbury. They deposed that "she had always been a religious and good woman, nor ever heard anything evil of her; moreover, she was always willing to help her fellows."

Richard Carrier, when he was interrogated, was asked by the judges, "Have you been in the Devil's snare?"

"Yes," he replied.

"Is your brother Andrew ensnared by the Devil's snare?"

"Yes."

"How long has your brother been a witch?"

"Near a month."

"How long have you been a witch?"

"Not long."

"Have you joined in afflicting the afflicted persons?"

"Yes."

"You helped to hurt Timothy Swan, did you?"

"Yes."

"How long have you been a witch?" he was asked again. This time he was more specific.

"About five weeks."

"Who was in company with you when you covenanted with the Devil?"

"Mrs. Bradbury."

"Did she help you afflict?"

"Yes."

"Who was at the Village meeting when you were there?"

"Goody Howe, Goody Nurse, Goody Wilds, Proctor and his wife, Mrs. Bradbury, and Corey's wife."

"What did they do there?"

"Eat, and drink wine."

"Was there a minister there?"

"No, not that I know of."

"From whence had you your wine?"

"From Salem, I think it was."

"Goodwife Bishop there?"

"Yes, I knew her," Richard said.

John Proctor wrote a letter to the Boston clergy on Saturday, July 23rd; in it he maintained that he and his fellow prison inmates were innocent and that he and the others had been accused by five confessed witches: Two of the five were Martha Carrier's sons. These young men refused to confess anything until the prison keeper and others had tied them "neck and heels till the blood was ready to come out of their noses; and it is credibly believed and reported this was the occasion of making them confess what they never did, by reason they said one had been a witch a month, and another five weeks, and that their mother made them so, who has been confined here this *nine* weeks. My son, William Proctor, when he was examined, because he would not confess that he was guilty when he was innocent, they tied him neck and heels till the blood gushed out at his nose, and would have kept him so 24 hours if one more merciful than the rest had not taken pity on him and caused him to be unbound.

"These actions are very like the Popish cruelties. They have already undone us in our estates, and that will not serve their turns without our innocent blood. If it cannot be granted that we can have our trials at Boston, we humbly beg that you would endeavor to have these magistrates changed, and others in their room [stead]; begging also and beseeching you, that you would be pleased to be here — if not all, some of you — at our trials, hoping thereby you may be the means of saving the shedding of our innocent blood."

The Salem Village witchhunt had spread as far south as the Meriden-Wallingford section of Connecticut and involved again the family of Joseph Benham who, in 1691, had threatened the Selectmen of Wallingford for encouraging people to say vile things of his wife, Winifred. But the gossip and rumors had failed to die down, and with the Salem Village firestorm they were intensified.

"At a meeting of the authority of New Haven, 25th of July, 1692, Joseph Benham of Wallingford appeared according to summons before the authority this day," the Connecticut clerk of the court recorded. "And being examined upon complaint, and evidence being brought against him that he had lately threatened to charge his gun with two bullets and shoot Goody Parker if she came into his house about such matters or things, upon which examination he, the said Benham, confessed he said threatening words in part being, as he said, provoked by the said Parker's casting some reflections (in her speech) about witchcraft upon his wife, yet not intending mischief to said Parker, and blaming himself for his passion and such threatening expressions.

"The Authority having considered the case and finding (besides his past confession) the said threatening words clearly proved by two witnesses, viz., Sarah Howe, Sr. , and Abigail Atwater, did order the said Joseph Benham to acknowledge himself and his estate bound in a recognizance of fifty shillings to the county treasury that he shall keep the King's peace towards all Their Majesties' subjects, especially the said Joseph Parker and Hannah Parker his wife and their family.

"And his said recognizance to stand good against him until November County Court next, and then he to appear for his release as the Court shall see cause, and in the meantime to pay just fees for the prosecution."

But the neighbors of the Benham family had no intention of allowing the November trial to be merely a suit for assault. They set about immediately to collect evidence and depositions that Goody Winifred Benham was a witch.

In the evening of July 26th the family of Rebecca Nurse went to Gallows Hill with Caleb Buffham, exhumed her body, and removed it to the family plot.

The next day Anthony Checkley replaced Thomas Newton as King's Attorney to the Court of Oyer and Terminer. In prison Mary Lacey the younger said to her mother and grandmother before witnesses, "Oh, mother, why did you give me to the Devil?"

"I am very sorry at the heart for it," the matron replied, "it was through that Wicked One."

"Repent, mother, and call upon God!" the girl cried. "Oh, mother, your wishes are now come to pass, for how often have you wished that the Devil would fetch me away alive?" The disobedient little runaway wept. "Oh! Lord!" she prayed, "Comfort me and bring out all the witches!"

Then, turning to Goody Foster, "Oh, grandmother, why did you give me to the Devil? Why did you persuade me?" the old woman was shaking her head bemusedly. "Oh! Grandmother," the girl cried, "do not deny it!"

The next day Mary Bradbury wrote out an answer to the charges that had been placed against her. She claimed to be totally innocent. "I am the servant of Jesus Christ," she said, "and have given myself up to him in all his holy ordinances, in utter contempt and defiance of the Devil and all his works as horrid and detestable...." Mary referred the magistrates to her brethren and neighbors who knew her — indeed, many had testified in her favor — "and unto the searcher of all hearts for the truth and uprightness of my heart therein (human frailties, and unavoidable infirmities excepted, of which I bitterly complain every day)."

Goodwife Bradbury's husband Thomas also submitted a petition that read, "We have been married fifty-five years, and she hath been a loving and faithful wife to me. Unto this day she hath been wonderfully laborious, diligent, and industrious in her place of employment, about the bringing up of our family (which have been eleven children of our own, and four grandchildren). She was both prudent and provident; of a cheerful spirit; liberal and charitable. She being now very aged and weak and grieved under her affliction, may not be able to speak much for herself, not being so free of speech as some others may be.

"I hope her life and conversation hath been such amongst her neighbors as gives a better and more real testimony of her than can be expressed by words."

A new witch bitch appeared on the scene when Rebecca Wilkins on July 29th accused her kinsman John Willard of tormenting her. The next day, a Saturday, Willard again afflicted her.

Capt. Nathaniel Carey had been active in Charlestown while his wife languished in prison. He wrote, "The trials at Salem coming on, I went thither to see how things were there managed, and finding that the specter-evidence was there received, together with idle, if not malicious stories against people's lives, I did easily perceive which way the rest would go, for the same evidence that served for one would serve for all the rest." He returned to Cambridge to his wife and, he wrote, "I acquainted her with her danger; and that if she were carried to Salem to be tried, I feared she would never return. I did my utmost that she might have her trial in our own county, I, with several others, petitioning the judge for it, and were put in hopes of it; but I soon saw so much, that I understood thereby it was not intended, which put me upon consulting the means of her escape, which through the goodness of God was effected, and she got to Rhode Island, but soon found herself not safe when there, by reason of the pursuit after her. From thence she went to New York, along with some others that had escaped their cruel bonds, where we found his Excellency Benjamin Fletcher, Esq., Governor, who was very courteous to us.

"After this, some of my goods were seized in a friend's hands, with whom I had left them, and myself imprisoned by the sheriff, and kept in custody half a day and then dismissed. But to speak of their usage of the prisoners, and their inhumanity shown to them, at the time of their execution, no sober Christian could bear; they had also trials of cruel mockings, which is the more, considering what a People for Religion — I mean the profession of it — we have been, those that suffered being many of them church members, and most of them unspotted in their conversation, till their Adversary, the Devil, took up this method for accusing them"

On the way to meeting on Sunday, the last of July, Rebecca Wilkins was again waylaid by the specter of John Willard.

August first saw Increase Mather and seven other ministers meet at Cambridge to discuss John Proctor's petition. At that meeting, according to Increase, "The question then discoursed on was whether the Devil may not sometimes have a permission to represent an innocent person as tormenting such as are under diabolical molestations." The ministers, their advice having been ignored by the Court of Oyer and Terminer with regard to spectral evidence, had only a clear choice: Either they could maintain their former position, which would be an attack on the Court's proceedings, or they could modify their opinion, in order to justify what the court had done.

They chose to do the latter. They agreed "That the Devil may sometimes have a permission to represent an innocent person as tormenting such as are under diabolical molestations, but that such things are rare and extraordinary, especially when such matters come before civil judicature." In other words, God would surely not be so disrespectful of the Court as to *allow* the Devil to torture the afflicted persons; *ergo*, it was the witches' own shapes, with their personal permissions, that pinched the girls, and not Satan in disguise. And for sure, it wasn't a bunch of vicious young witch bitches being malignant all on their own who were lying about the things they were seeing but that no one else could see. And no one seemed to ask the question why it was that the accused witches would, in *court,* and before the public, choose to send their self-accusatory ethereal phantoms to torment the "afflicted persons."

A great cover-up had begun at the hands of the clergy of the Puritan Bay. The ministers chose to condemn a woman or man to death rather than to let the suspicion develop that the authorities had made immense mistakes and had killed innocent people for nonexistent crimes. But it was too late. A great many people, now, were beginning to see things all too clearly, yet those who had been at the center of the witchhunt, rather than admitting they had themselves been deluded, hardened in their positions, a knot of fear and bitterness at their hearts. And they had for backers the great mass of the uninvolved population, who knew for a fact that there were many evil people in the colony, most of them very likely, and some of them certainly, witches.

The Age of Witchcraft, and with it the system of sympathetic magic, was nevertheless rapidly coming to an end in August of 1692. Logic and rationalism were beginning to creep strongly into the witchhunt. The eighteenth century, the Age of Reason, lurked over the horizon; science was growing rapidly as a system, and the Salem Village explosion was the last gasp of the old system before it lapsed into desuetude in the western, European world. The Boston ministers, by their action, had patently succeeded, not in defending authority, but in undermining its credibility and the credibility of the Puritan religion itself. This, added to the political realities of the period and the growth of the doctrine of tolerance, not to mention the successful founding of colonies of diverse religious backgrounds in America, sounded the knell of intolerance and dogma as viable policies of the Massachusetts government. But the last gasp of the oldest system in the world — that of magic — had not, on August fifth, yet fallen to a dying sigh.

The third session of the Special Court of Oyer and Terminer was convened in Salem the same day that the ministers met, its purpose to try John and Elizabeth Proctor, Rev. George Burroughs, John Willard, George Jacobs, Sr., and Martha Carrier.

Elizabeth Proctor pleaded pregnancy, and she was returned to jail until after the birth of her child.

At George Jacobs' trial there was a parade of witnesses, including sixteen-year-old John Derish, who became a new name among the accusers. He testified that the late John Small and his dead wife, Anne, appeared to him and told him to go to John Hathorne and inform him that Jacobs had killed them — if he did not, the specters would tear him to bits. Some people wondered why, with all the threats to do so, no one yet had been dismembered in Massachusetts Bay.

Also, according to Derish, Mary Warren's mother's ghost turned up with a "White Man" to say that Mary Parker and Bridget Bishop had killed her. The boy was afflicted likewise by Giles Corey, John and Sarah Wilds, Elizabeth and Joseph Proctor, Philip and Mary English — they all threatened to rip him to shreds if he didn't sign the Devil's Book. Nor were these all: Goodies Sarah Pease and Deliverance Hobbs and the latter's daughter Abigail Hobbs also descended upon him like the Mongol hordes, not to mention a woman named Mary who lived at the upper end of Boston and went about "in black clothes, hath but one eye with a crooked neck," but who would not — an unusual circumstance, and a wise move for a witch — tell him her last name. But it was not necessary: Everyone knew he was talking about Mary Webster.

Deputy Sheriff George Herrick testified that he had searched the body of the old man — in the presence of the jailer William Dunton and Constable Joseph Neal — and found a witch teat. It was under his right shoulder and was one-quarter-inch long "or better, with a sharp point drooping downwards so that I took a pin...and ran it through the said teat, but there was neither water, blood, nor corruption, or any other matter" in it, which might have indicated that it wasn't a teat at all. Dunton testified that Jacobs never felt a thing.

The opinion of the Rev. John Wise of Ipswich and a number of the inhabitants of that town was in direct contravention to that of the Boston ministers. Mr. Wise submitted a petition containing a number of signatures in behalf of John Proctor that stated God "sometimes may permit Satan to personate, dissemble, and thereby abuse innocents and such as do, in the fear of God, defy the Devil and all his works." Nor had Mr. or Mrs. Proctor, to the knowledge of their neighbors, ever done anything like what they were charged with. A number of Salem Village people presented a similar petition.

Both George Jacobs and John Proctor were convicted.

The trial of George Burroughs was held on both August 2nd and 3rd, there were so many witnesses against him. At first the bitch witches had such a great number of fits and were struck so dumb at Burroughs' entry into the courtroom in Salem that no one could accuse him. But after a great while Justice Gedney asked the minister, "Who do you think hinders these witnesses from giving their testimonies?"

"The Devil, I suppose," Burroughs answered.

"How comes the Devil so loath to have any testimony borne against you?"

Burroughs didn't know how to answer. The girls complained, "He bites!" and they showed the tooth marks. The court ordered Burroughs to bite a stick; the judges compared the stick with the bite marks on the children's arms, and sure enough — !

Mercy Lewis in her fit said, "George Burroughs carried me away to a very high mountain where all the kingdoms of the world lay below and said, 'I will give all these to you if you will but write in my Book, and if you do not I will throw you down and break your neck,' but I told him, 'They are none of yours to give, and I will not write if you throwed me down on a hundred pitchforks.'"

True to their word, Burroughs' two murdered wives appeared to Annie Putnam right there in court. She told the judges, "They cry, 'Vengeance! Vengeance!'" The other girls were asked if they saw the specters there, and of course they did.

Hathorne asked Burroughs, "Do not you see the apparitions of your dead wives?"

"I know nothing of it," he replied, baffled.

"You are not a large man," Hathorne noted, "yet it is said you have performed feats beyond the strength of a giant. What do you say to it?"

"It is not true."

"Did not you hold out a gun seven foot in the barrel with one hand?"

"An Indian was there, and held it out at the same time."

Annie Putnam broke in, "It was the Black Man, or the Devil, who looks like an Indian. It was Hobbamock," she told the Court, "who was with him in the appearance of a man."

"Did you not carry a barrel full of molasses or cider from a canoe to the shore without help?" a judge queried.

"It is no great thing," he replied. "It was a cask, not a barrel."

"Here is testimony that you caught up with your wife and her brother Richard preternaturally quick when you had been left far behind" — the judge waved a deposition at him — "and you chided her for speaking of you and told her you knew their thoughts" (a new charge: Burroughs was a telepath); "that Rucke was startled and said that the Devil himself did not know so far, and that you replied, 'My God makes known your thought to me.'"

"Rucke and my wife left a man with me when they left me," Burroughs said, implying that he had a witness. But Thomas Rucke, who was present in Court, stood forth and called, "That is false!"

Gedney asked Burroughs, "What was the man's name?"

Burroughs did not answer.

"Why do you not reply? Is it because you only stepped aside to put on your invisibility so that you might listen to them in a fascinating mist?" It was a fascinating question.

Rather than answer, Burroughs submitted a paper to the Court that read, in part, "There neither are, nor ever were, witches that, having made a compact with the Devil, can send a Devil to torment other people at a distance." The magistrates read it; then Gedney asked, "Did you write this?"

"Yes," Burroughs replied. It was a stupid lie because the one thing no one should have doubted was that this court was widely and deeply read in the literature of witchcraft.

"You are a liar!" he was told. "This paper is transcribed from the book of Thomas Ady." The eyes of judge and accused locked: They both knew they were talking about the 1655 skeptical treatise titled *A Candle in the Dark*. Now Burroughs was accused of *two* new charges — telepathy and plagiarism!

Caught in an untenable position, Burroughs, like his colleagues in Boston, chose to bluster it out. "I took none of it out of any book," he maintained.

"How does it happen, then, that this sounds so much like the other?"

"A gentleman gave me the discourse in a manuscript," Burroughs said, "from whence I transcribed it." It was a mealy-mouthed reply that nevertheless meant he himself had not written the paper. The Court was disgusted, and the parade of witnesses and storm of depositions continued unabated, but they were no longer needed — they were but window dressing to justify the condemnation of an ordained minister.

The affidavit of Samuel Sheldon was read. He said that the day before the trial Burroughs appeared to him and asked if Sheldon "would go to the village tomorrow to witness against him." When Sheldon answered he would, Burroughs' specter told him that before that happened he would be killed. That hadn't happened, obviously.

Later, at Ingersoll's, the shade reappeared and told Sheldon, in direct contradiction of the details as they had been revealed to Annie Putnam, that he had smothered his first wife and choked the second, together with his two children. He had also killed three other children in Maine.

After his condemnation Burroughs said to the magistrates, "I am innocent, yet I justify you in your verdict, for there are many positive witnesses against me, but I die by false witnesses." His justification of the Court gave some faint satisfaction to the ministers of Boston.

In addition to George Jacobs, John Proctor and Burroughs, John Willard and Martha Carrier were convicted by Friday, August fifth.

On Tuesday the 9th, Robert Pike, magistrate of Salisbury, wrote a letter to Judge Jonathan Corwin in which he attacked the methods of the Court. It was his opinion that the specters seen by the afflicted people "are more commonly false and delusive than real, and cannot be known when they are real and when feigned, but by the Devil's report, and then not be believed, because he is the Father of Lies.

"1. Either the organ of the eye is abused and the senses deluded, so as to think they do see or hear some thing or person, when indeed they do not, and this is frequent with common jugglers.

"2. The Devil himself appears in the shape and likeness of a person or thing, when it is not the person or thing itself; so he did in the shape of Samuel.

"3. And sometimes persons or things themselves do really appear, but how it is possible for any one to give a true testimony, which possibly did see neither shape nor person, but were deluded; and if they did see anything, they know not whether it was the person or but his shape. All that can be rationally" — the word appeared in the records for the first time — "or truly said in such a case is this — that I did see the shape or likeness of such a person, if my senses or eyesight were not deluded: And they can honestly say no more, because they know no more, except the Devil tells them more, and if he do, they can but say he told them so. But the matter is still incredible: First, because it is but their saying the Devil told them so, if he did so tell them, yet the verity of the thing remains unproved, because the Devil was a liar and a murderer (John viii:44), and may tell these lies to murder an innocent person."

Pike's letter went on at great, and closely reasoned length, but it was addressed to a man who was in too deeply to back out.

Margaret Jacobs, too, wrote a letter to the Court; however, hers was not an exercise of rationality, but of conscience: She recanted her confession. She said that whereas she was "closely confined here in

Salem jail for the crime of witchcraft — which crime, thanks be to the lord! I am altogether ignorant of... — ...I was cried out upon by some of the possessed persons of afflicting them, whereupon I was brought to my examination; which persons at the sight of me fell down, which did very much startle and affright me.

"The Lord above knows I knew nothing in the least measure how or who afflicted them. They told me without doubt I did, or they would not fall down at me. They told me if I did not confess I should be put down in the dungeon and...hanged; but if I should confess, I should have my life — the which did so affright me...my own vile, wicked heart, to save my life, made me make the...confession I did — which confession...is altogether false and untrue.

"The very first night after I had made confession I was in such horror of conscience that I could not sleep, for fear the Devil should carry me away for telling such horrid lies. I was...sworn to my confession, as I understand since, but...at that time was ignorant of it, not knowing what an *oath* did mean. —

"What I said was altogether false against my grandfather and Mr. Burroughs, which I did to save my life and to have my liberty. But the Lord, charging it to my conscience, made me in so much horror that I could not contain myself before I had denied my confession, which I did, though I saw nothing but death before me — choosing rather death with a quiet conscience than to live in such horror, which I could not suffer. — Upon my denying my confession I was committed to close prison where I have enjoyed more felicity in spirit, a thousand times, than I did before in my enlargement." —

On August 11 Faulkner was examined. Hathorne. Corwin, and Capt. Higginson presided. The preliminaries out of the way, Hathorne said to her, "You are here apprehended for witchcraft."

"I know nothing of it," returned.

"Look upon the afflicted!"

The bitch witches fell down.

"Do not you see?"

"Yes, but it is the Devil does it in my shape."

Mary Warren testified, "I saw her shape two months ago, but she did not hurt me till last night."

"Annie Putnam agreed, adding, "And last night she pulled me off my horse."

Mary said, "I have seen her in company with other witches, but was not hurt by her till lately." Faulkner had a handkerchief in her hand that she was nervously wringing. When the girls noticed it they cried, "She hurts us with the handkerchief!"

Abigail threw the offending object onto the table, and the girls cried, "There are the shapes of Daniel Eames and Capt. Flood sitting on the handkerchief!" Both these men were in jail under arrest. The fits went on, and the court watched in amazement as Mary Warren was dragged under a table by invisible hands. The test of the witch's touch was administered, and the girls were cured.

Hathorne asked, "Will not you confess for the credit of your town?" Evidently it would be an act of civic-mindedness. From the audience her cousin Elizabeth Johnson called, "Oh, confess, Abigail! Confess!"

But the accused witch said, "I refuse to do it. God does not require me to confess to that which I am not guilty of."

In prison on August 12th George Jacobs wrote a new will, and on Wednesday the 17th Cotton Mather wrote John Foster of the Governor's Council and Samuel Sewall of the Court of Oyer and Terminer, "I do still think that when there is no further evidence against a person but only this: That a specter in their shape does afflict a neighbor, that evidence is not enough to convict...." His treatment of Mercy Short had been entirely successful; the girl was acting normally once more.

After church service on Sunday, August 14th, Rev. Samuel Parris said to his members, "Brethren, you may all have taken notice that, several Sacrament Days past, our brother Peter Cloyse, and Samuel Nurse and his wife, and John Tarbell and his wife have absented themselves from communion with us at the Lord's Table — yea, have very rarely, except our Samuel Nurse, been with us in common public worship. Now, it is needful that the church send some persons to them to know the reason of their absence. Therefore, if you be so minded, express yourselves."

No one objected — though everyone knew why the absent members had not been coming to church — or even said anything, so Nathaniel Putnam and the two deacons were appointed as emissaries.

The following Thursday Margaret Jacobs visited Rev. George Burroughs in his cell and asked his forgiveness for her false testimony. He gave it and prayed with her, as she had done with her grandfather, who had written into his will subsequently that she was to receive ten pounds in silver.

Friday, August 19th, was a day of execution. As the cart bearing the condemned couple — George Jacobs, Sr., John Proctor, John Willard, Martha Carrier, and the Rev. Mr. George Burroughs — proceeded slowly up Gallows Hill, at one point it got stuck. The bitch witches, who walked alongside, informed the crowd, as people put their shoulders to the wheels, "The Devil hinders it."

At the gallows oak the crowd was ominously quiet; when George Proctor and John Willard died bravely and well, the silence began to grow into an angry murmur. Cotton Mather had come up from Boston to be present at this execution of a colleague; he sat upon a horse while the hangings took place. Samuel Sewall was in the crowd, as were several ministers — Rev. Messrs. Simms, John Hale, Nicholas Noyes, and Samuel Cheever among others.

Martha Carrier, like the others before her, died protesting her innocence. And when George Burroughs mounted the ladder he spoke to the gathering of Puritans, said he was innocent, delivered a short oration, and ended with a flawlessly executed recitation of the Lord's Prayer.

The display, as it was meant to do, amazed the crowd, for no witch was supposed to be able to manage such a feat, and he was quickly turned off the ladder before the assembly could assimilate his achievement. While the little dark minister was swinging and dying Cotton Mather on his horse shouted, "They all died by righteous sentence! Mr. Burroughs was not an ordained minister." That was an incomprehensible remark. "That he could recite the Lord's Prayer is no proof of his innocence, for the Devil often has been transformed into an angel of light" — another remarkable statement.

The corpses were cut down and hastily buried among the rocks in shallow graves. Burroughs was tumbled into a gash in the ground along with John Willard and Martha Carrier. When the soil was shoveled in, the gravediggers were in too great a hurry to get away, for they left the preacher's hand and chin uncovered, as well as a foot of one of the others. There were many people who left Gallows Hill weeping that day.

The Court the same day postponed the trial of Margaret Jacobs owing to her illness, but John Hathorne and his inquisition team were undeterred by anything, for a panel examined Rebecca Eames of Boxford. She was quick to confess. The authorities asked her, "Who came with the Devil when he made you a witch?"

"A ragged girl," she answered. "They came together, and they persuaded me to afflict, and I afflicted Mary Warren and another fair face — it was about a quarter year ago — I did it by sticking of pins."

"But did you afflict Swan?"

"Yes, but I am sorry for it."

"Where had you your spear?"

"I had nothing but an awl."

"Was it with your body or your spirit that you came to hurt these maids?"

"With my spirit."

"Can you ask them forgiveness?"

"I will fall down on my knees to ask it of them."

As the examination proceeded Rebecca was asked who went with her on her journeys of affliction. She would not admit that anyone went with her, but some of the bitch witches told the court her son Daniel

Eames had gone along. The examiner asked her, "Did you not say the Devil baptized your son Daniel?"

"He told me so."

"But did you not touch the Book nor lay your hand on book nor paper?"

"I laid my hand no nothing without it was a piece of board."

"Did you lay your hand on the board when he bade you?"

"Yes." She told the panel that she gave her son Daniel to the Devil when he was two years old. She was asked to beg forgiveness of Mary Warren; Rebecca did so, and the bitch witches forgave her. She said, "If I did give my son Daniel to the Devil it was in an angry fit. I do not know but I might have done it, nor I do not know he is a witch, but I am afraid he is."

Daniel rose from the spectators and said, "Mother, do not confess I am a witch!" But Rebecca went on to say that the reason she was afraid he might be one was that he "used dreadful bad words when he was angry, and bad wishes." Asked how old he was, Mrs. Eames replied, "Twenty-eight."

"You have been long a witch, then, if you gave your son to the Devil at two years old. Have you been a witch twenty-six years?"

"No, I cannot remember but seven years, and have afflicted about a quarter of a year."

"But if you have been a witch so long, why did you not afflict before, seeing you promised it to the Devil?"

There was no way out of her web of contradictions, and Rebecca floundered. Finally she was asked in what shape the Devil appeared to her.

"I cannot tell," she said, "except it was a mouse."

Margaret Jacobs wrote her father on August 20th, Saturday, to explain her accusation of her grandfather. The letter was similar to her petition to the court, but briefer. She closed by writing, "My mother, poor woman, is very crazy, and remembers her kind love to you...."

The specter of Giles Corey went to the home of John Derish that day and said, "I want some platters, for I am going to have a feast. I've a good mind to ask your dame, but she would not let me have them." Corey took the dishes and, half an hour later, returned them without saying a thing.

During the night one of George Jacobs' grandsons, without the aid of Caleb Buffham, went to Gallows Hill, exhumed the body of his grandfather and took it, strapped to a shying horse, home to the farm for interment.

On Sunday Mrs. Benjamin Hutchinson could hardly bear the splitting headache that had begun soon after the executions and had grown since.

William Barker was arrested on Monday, and he quickly confessed. Capt. Bradstreet examined Elizabeth Johnson on August 30th, Tuesday, and afterward she was examined again in court. At first she denied her culpability, but later she told the Court, "I own I am angry at what the possessed folk say of me and that they bring my kindred out, and I do wish them ill, and my spirit being raised, I know not but that the Devil might take advantage. But it is the Devil, and not I, that afflicts them."

The justices were not sure whether or not this was a confession, but it was as far as Elizabeth was willing to go. They decided that it was not a confession. Her cousin Johnson, also named Elizabeth, was taken with a fit. The gallery laughed and people said, "Her sister Johnson will come out against her next!"

On the last day of the month Nathaniel Putnam and the two deacons, Edward Putnam and Nathaniel Ingersoll, reported back to Rev. Samuel Parris regarding the church's absentees: John Tarbell was ill with the disease that was still going around, and Peter Cloyse could not be found at home, since he was often visiting his wife in Ipswich prison. So much for the Nurse relatives; with reference to Goodman Francis Nurse himself — the delegation chose not to ask him why he had been so often absent from God's house.

The arrested witches of Andover were confessing as fast as they could, but there would be few others to join them. Dudley Bradstreet, magistrate of Andover, having issued about fifty warrants of arrest, at last refused to issue any more — and he was cried out upon himself. His brother, John Bradstreet, was accused as well, but not of afflicting the bitch witches or his neighbors; rather, he was cried out upon for having bewitched a dog. Both the Bradstreets fled before the hounds of Hell, John making for Piscataqua in Maine. Unable to find him, the Andover citizens executed the dog instead: It was the only bitch witch to suffer such a fate.

The frustrated Andover people accused an anonymous Gentleman of Boston (Perhaps Robert Calef, a cloth merchant) of afflicting them, but the gentleman acted in an extraordinary manner: He sent a writ of arrest for slander to the town, and all new accusations ceased generally against those not already cried out upon. William Barker admitted in writing while he was in prison that he had attended the Sabbat in Salem Village, having been summoned to it by the Devil's trumpet. His vehicle had been a stick that he rode to the Village where he witnessed, but did not partake of, a Black Communion. The Devil had taken him by the hand and flown his spirit to Salem where he had afflicted Martha Sprague, Rose Foster, and Abigail Martin — this last was peculiar, because his "enticers" had been Abigail Martin, Elizabeth Johnson, and Ann Foster. It was the Devil's plan to destroy Salem Village through his witches, and to begin at the parsonage, undermine the church of God, and set up Satan's kingdom, when all would be well. The plan appeared to be working.

Samuel Wardwell, the Wizard of Andover, was examined on Thursday, September 1st, and he was quick to admit to being "sensible I was in the snare of the Devil. I used to be much discontented, so that I could get no more work done, and I was foolishly led along with telling of fortunes, which sometimes came to pass. I used also, when any creature came into my field, bid 'the Devil take it!' and it may be the Devil took advantage of me by that."

Constable Foster testified that "Wardwell told me once in the woods that when he was a young man he could make all his cattle come round about him when he pleased."

Asked to tell the truth, Wardwell said, "Once in a discontented frame, I saw some cats, together with the appearance of a man who called himself a Prince of the Air and promised me I should live comfortably and be a captain if I would honor him, which I promised to do, and this was twenty years ago.

"The reason of my discontent was because I was in love with a maid named Barker who slighted my love. But the Black Man never performed anything of his promise, and the Devil would be angry when I would go to prayer in my family. At this time I signed the Devil's Black Book with a mark like a square, with a black pen, and the Devil brought me the pen and ink. I covenanted with the Devil until I should arrive to the age of sixty years, and I am now about the age of forty-six years." Wardwell admitted to having afflicted several persons, to having been baptized by total immersion at Shawshin River, and it was his belief that he had renounced his former Christian baptism.

On September 2nd Bartholomew Gedney, John Hathorne, Johnathan Corwin, and John Higginson examined Mary Parker. The gang of bitch witches had grown considerably, and it now numbered among its members Hannah Post, Sarah Bridges, and Sarah Phelps. They went into wild displays of hysteria, working themselves up to great pitches of perverse excitation when the judges asked, "How long have you been in the snare of the Devil?" and Mary replied, "I know nothing of it. There is another woman of the same name in Andover."

But Martha Sprague cried, "She is the right one!" and was struck down by the witch's evil eye. Mary Lacey cried out upon her and was cured by the witch's touch. William Barker maintained that she had been seen in the company of witches, and Mary Wardwell agreed. Mary Warren achieved a spectacular mania when it was found she had a pin stuck into her hand and blood running out of her mouth: She had bitten her tongue.

Mrs. Jane Hutchinson had another of her terrible headaches on Sunday, the fourth. She groaned to her husband Benjamin, "I believe I have an evil hand upon me."

Goodman Hutchinson left immediately and went to find Mary Walcott to whom he said, "My wife is very ill. Will you come and look to see if you can see anybody upon her?" Mary was glad to oblige.

No sooner had the bitch witch arrived in the Hutchinson home than she exclaimed, "Oh, yes, your two next neighbors, Sarah Buckley and Mary Whitridge, are upon her."

Hutchinson thanked her and rode for the sheriff to ask him if he couldn't do something to keep the two witches, who were in his jail, from tormenting Jane Hutchinson. Sheriff George Corwin, too, was pleased to help — he put fetters on the women, for iron circlets were known to be an effective antidote to witch spells, the powers of witches theoretically having something to do with magnetism, though the scientific details of the phenomenon had not been thoroughly investigated. By the time Hutchinson returned to his home Mrs. Hutchinson was already feeling better.

On Wednesday the seventh of September depositions were taken in evidence against Ann Pudeator, primarily sworn by the bitch witches who said the woman had tormented them at her examination on July 2nd at Thomas Beadle's tavern.

Mary Towne of Topsfield, who had been summoned to Salem to testify against Mary Easty excused herself, for she and her daughters, who also had been summoned, "are in a strange condition, and most of us can scarce get off our beds, we are so weak, and not able to ride at all. As for my daughter Rebecca — she hath strange fits: Sometimes she is knocked down of a sudden." The next day Mary and Rebecca Towne were again commanded to come to Salem to testify — and Lady Mary

Phips, in the absence of her husband the Governor, granted Abigail Faulkner a reprieve!

Mary Osgood, wife of Capt. John Osgood of Andover, was examined that day, the 8th, before Hathorne and the others, including John Higginson, who took the notes. She told the magistrates, "About eleven years ago, when I was in a melancholy state and condition, I used to walk abroad in my orchard; and upon a certain time I saw the appearance of a cat at the end of the house, which yet I thought was a real cat.

"However, at that time it diverted me from praying to God, and instead I prayed to the Devil. About that time I made a covenant with the Devil who, as a Black Man, came to me and presented me a book, upon which I laid my finger, and that left a red spot. Upon my signing the Devil told me he was my God, and that I should serve and worship him, and I believe I consented to it.

"About two years ago I was carried through the air, in company with Eunice Fry, the Deacon's wife; Ebenezer Baker's wife, and Goody Tyler, to Five Mile Pond, where I was baptized by the Devil, who dipped my face in the water and made me renounce my former baptism and told me I must be his, soul and body, forever, and that I must serve him, which I promised to do. The renouncing my first baptism was after my dipping, and then I was transported back again through the air, in the same company, in the same manner as I came, and I believe we were carried upon a pole."

Judge John Hathorne asked, "How many persons were upon the pole?"

"As I said before, four persons, and no more but those I named before."

"Who was it you afflicted?"

"John Sawdy, Martha Sprague, and Rose Foster, and I did it by pinching my bedclothes and giving consent the Devil should do it in my shape."

"Was the Devil able to afflict in your shape without your consent?"

"No."

"Who is it hurts these?" Hathorne asked, pointing to the writhing girls.

"I do it with the glance of my eye. As I was coming down to Salem to be examined, I and the rest of the company with me stopped at Mr. Phillips' to refresh ourselves, and the afflicted persons, being behind us upon the road, came up just as I was remounting again and were then afflicted, and cried out upon me, so that I was forced to stay until they were all past, and I only looked that way towards them."

"Do you know the Devil can take the shape of an innocent person and afflict?" one of the judges asked again.

"I believe he cannot."

"Who taught you this way of witchcraft?"

"Satan, and he promised me abundance of satisfaction and quietness in my future state, but never performed anything, and I have lived more miserably and more discontented since, than ever before.

"I, in company with Goody Parker, Goody Tyler, and Goody Dane, had a meeting at Moses Tyler's house last Monday night to afflict, and I and Goody Dane carried the shape of Mr. Dane, the minister, between us to make persons believe that Mr. Dane afflicted."

"What hindered you from accomplishing what you intended?"

"The Lord would not suffer it so to be, that the Devil should afflict in an innocent person's shape."

"Have you been at any other witch meetings?"

"I know nothing thereof, as I shall answer in the presence of God and His people."

The afflicted girls fell to fits and cried, "There is a Black Man whispering in her ear!"

Hathorne asked, "What does he say to you?"

"He stands before me," Goody Osgood answered, "and tells me that what I have confessed is a lie, but what I have confessed is true, and I put my hand to it."

Hathorne turned to the gallery and called, "Captain Osgood, do you judge your wife to be any way discomposed?"

Osgood stood forward. "Having lived with her so long," he told Hathorne, "I do not judge her to be any ways discomposed, but I have cause to believe what she has said is true."

The bitch witches nodded their heads, and among them now stood little Mary Lacey, Elizabeth Johnson, Jr., Hannah Post, Rose Foster and Mary Richardson. They had all been cured by the witch's touch, and the witch's words.

On Friday, September 9th, Rev. Deodat Lawson's sermon of March 24th was published under the title, "Christ's Fidelity, the Only Shield against Satan's Malignity", and the Court of Oyer and Terminer sat for its fourth session. Alice Parker, Dorcas Hoar, and Mary Bradbury were convicted.

Giles Corey, when he was brought before the court for trial and asked how he pled, replied "Not guilty" to the charge, but when he was asked by the magistrates, "How will you be tried?" Corey refused to repeat the formal answer, "By God and this Court," for he realized that there was no hope for mercy in Salem, no more than he himself had had for his wife. He stood mute.

Stoughton said to the old man, "If you do stand mute before the Court you must, under the laws of England, be stood to *peine fort et dure*. You shall be pressed with weights until you plead, or until you are dead." Corey did not respond. After a consultation with the other magistrates Stoughton said, "You must be asked the question thrice, according to law. Take him away," he said to George Herrick, "but bring him before the Court on the morrow."

Corey had made out a deed in jail — duly executed and witnessed — making over his property to his two sons-in-law William Cleves of Beverly and John Moulton of Salem and cutting out his two other sons-in-law who, as he himself had done, had given evidence against Martha Corey. The deed was legal, unlike a will such as John Proctor's, for a will made by someone who was under indictment and subsequently convicted could not stand. If Corey were not convicted of any crime, his property was his own to dispose of, not the Crown's.

On Saturday Martha Corey was convicted. Samuel Wardwell repudiated his confession and was scheduled for trial. Giles Corey was again brought forward and asked how he would be tried — again he stood mute. The magistrates decided to give him a week before they asked him the third and final time, so that he could think things over.

At Sunday services on September 11th Rev. Samuel Parris preached two sermons in Salem Village from Revelations xvii:14 on the subject, "These shall make war with the Lamb, and the Lamb shall overcome them: For He is Lord of lords and King of kings; and they that are with Him are called and chosen and faithful." The two sermons, taken together, were given the overall title, "The Devil and His Instruments Will Be Warring Against Christ and His Followers". After meeting, Parris excommunicated Martha Corey *in absentia*.

The Court convicted Mary Easty on Monday the 12th, and the next day it also tried and condemned Ann Pudeator.

Mary Easty petitioned Governor Phips, the Court of Oyer and Terminer, and the ministers. She maintained her innocence, of course, but the main point of her letter was this:

"I petition to your Honors, not for my own life — for I know I must die, and my appointed time is set — but the Lord, He knows it is that, if it be possible, no more innocent blood may be shed, which undoubtedly cannot be avoided in the way and course you go in. I question not but that your Honors do, to the utmost of your power, in the discovery and selection of witchcraft and witches, but by my innocence I know you are in the wrong way. The Lord in His infinite mercy direct you in this great work, if it be His blessed will that no more innocent blood be shed. I would humbly beg of you that your Honors would be pleased to examine these afflicted persons strictly, and keep them apart some time, and likewise to try some of these confessing witches — I being confident there is several of them has belied themselves and others, as will appear — if not in this world, then in the world to come, whither I am now going."

Nathaniel and Deacon Edward Putnam, together with Deacon Nathaniel Ingersoll, went to Salem prison to inform Martha Corey of her excommunication. According to their report the witch was "very obdurate, justifying herself, and condemning all that had done anything to her first discovery or condemnation." She refused to pray with her visitors and would barely speak to them. They read the sentence of excommunication to her, but she merely glared, though no one was struck down by her evil eye.

On Thursday, September 15th, Ann Pudeator petitioned the Court "That the evidence of John Best, Sr., John Best, Jr., and Samuel Pickworth which was given in against me in court were all of them altogether false and untrue. Besides, John Best hath been formerly whipped, and likewise is recorded for a liar." She repudiated as well the testimony of Sarah Churchill and Mary Warren. Goody Pudeator maintained her innocence and ignorance of "the crime of witchcraft, for which I am condemned to die, as will be known to men and angels at the great Day of Judgment, begging and imploring your prayers of grace in my behalf, and your poor and humble petitioner shall forever pray, as she is bound in duty, for your Honors' health and happiness in this life, and eternal felicity in the world to come."

Nearly a month after George Burroughs was hanged, new affidavits giving evidence against him were procured from Thomas Greenslit and others by the Committee of Vigilance and inserted into the trial records. There was more to Greenslit's testimony than met the eye, for he was the son, by a former marriage, of Ann Pudeator, who was fighting for her life in every way she knew how. Greenslit's effort to save his mother, and her petition, were futile.

The witchhunt in Connecticut had spread from Wallingford to Fairfield, where a number of people were accused. A Court of Assistants was called to deal with the situation, and it was able to dispose of most of the cases by proclamation of dismissal. However, two women — Mercy, wife of Thomas Disbrow, and Elizabeth Clawson — had been swum and, according to witnesses, both "swam like cork" with their hands and feet bound together. The two were indicted and tried, but the result was a hung jury: All members except one thought both women were guilty. The court adjourned to ask the advice of the Connecticut General Court, which was to sit in October. In Wallingford the people were in full cry at the heels of Winifred Benham.

The Court of Oyer and Terminer in Salem on Saturday, September 17th, tried and convicted Margaret Scott, Mammy Wilmot Reed, Samuel Wardwell, Mary Parker, Abigail Faulkner, Rebecca Eames, Mary Lacey and her mother Ann Foster, and, astonishingly, Abigail Hobbs.

A great many people testified against Abigail Faulkner. Mary Easty and her sister Sarah Cloyse petitioned the court to allow them defense counsel and supportive evidence in the way of character testimonials entered in their behalf by Rev. Mr. Joseph Capen, their pastor in Topsfield, and others including their children and relatives; and to require corroborative evidence to support the allegations of the bitch witches and other spectral evidence accusers. All was in vain.

Giles Corey was once more asked to plead, also in vain. It was his last chance. At noon he was sentenced to *peine forte et dure*, led to an open field near the jail, laid on his back, and stones placed on top of him. Periodically he was asked whether he had changed his mind, but he replied nothing each time, and each time another stone was added to the pile. On the first day of his torture he was allowed only "three morsels of the worst bread," as per the law, and no water.

At noon on Sunday Giles Corey completed his first twenty-four hours of pressing. On the second day of his ordeal he was allowed only "three draughts of standing water," by law. During his ordeal his friend, Capt. Richard Gardner, importuned and tried to reason with him, but all Corey would say, once, was "More weight!" As the pressure increased, Giles' tongue began to protrude from his mouth.

After services that day Rev. Nicholas Noyes again officiated at the rite of excommunication, this time for Giles Corey who, unlike his wife, was a member of the Salem church, not that of Salem Village. Noyes had decided not to wait for Corey's conviction, for he was likely to die without being damned first by the church. Noyes entered in his records that Corey was "either guilty of the sin of witchcraft, or of throwing himself upon sudden and certain death, if he were otherwise innocent." Suicide was a mortal sin. Noyes' superior, Higginson, refused to take part.

But Corey's death was anything but "sudden." On the morning of September 19th Giles was offered the first of three morsels of the worst bread, without water, that he was allowed on his alternate-day diet, but he refused, or was unable, to eat it. At noon, after forty-eight hours of pressing, the old yeoman died — he was 81 years of age.

Caleb Buffham was called in by Corey's sons-in-law. As the old man's body, still with its tongue protruding, was carted through the streets of Salem, a bystander with a cane reached out with his stick and, with its tip, attempted to poke the tongue of the corpse back into its mouth. Almost immediately this incident was picked up by the growing anti-witchcraft underground and distorted for propaganda purposes: It was rumored that Corey's tongue had been poked back into his mouth by someone while he was still dying. Buffham and the Corey kin gave the old man a secret burial.

That night Annie Putnam was haunted by Jacob Goodell's ghost who appeared in winding sheets to tell her that, long before she had been born, "Giles Corey murdered me by pressing me to death with his feet, but the Devil there appeared to him and covenanted with him, and promised him that he should not be hanged." It seemed to the Committee of Vigilance and to Sgt. Thomas Putnam, Jr., the head vigilante and Annie Putnam's father, a wonderful justification for Corey's strange death, and justification was needed, for the pressing had turned many people's stomachs, and the tide was now turning strongly against the witchhunt in Salem Village and Essex County, though it was popular elsewhere.

Captain John Alden, like many others, had decided that it were best to eschew a visit to Salem during the current session of the Court of Oyer and Terminer, so, with help, he engineered an escape from Boston Prison and departed for a milder climate.

On September 20th Sgt. Thomas Putnam, Jr., wrote Judge Samuel Sewall in Salem to tell him of his daughter's vision of the evening previous. Putnam said that Annie Putnam told him the ghost of Joseph Goodell "also said that Giles Corey was carried to the court" for the murder, and that his father, Thomas Putnam, Sr., "knew the man and the thing was done before she was born." The good Sergeant did not mention the date, 1676, nor the fact that the case had been dismissed for lack of evidence.

Cotton Mather was still following the Salem Village Witchhunt with great interest, and he had decided to write a book about it — he sent to the Clerk of the Court, Stephen Sewall, to ask for some trial transcripts for his researches.

Something unusual happened on Wednesday, Sept. 21st, the day before the date set for the next executions: For the first time a number of convicted witches confessed. It was the last hope, for no confessed witch had ever been hanged by the Court of Oyer and Terminer — only those who refused to confess went to the gallows. Abigail Hobbs had originally confessed in April, and she had entered the ranks of the accusing girls, but she had recanted, and now she re-recanted. Mary Lacey and her mother Ann Foster also re-confessed; the others who confessed were Dorcas Hoar and Rebecca Eames, The rest stood fast, preferring to lose their lives rather than their souls.

Just before her execution the specter of Mary Easty appeared to seventeen-year-old Mary Herrick, one of the later of the afflicted people, and said to her, "I am going upon the ladder to be hanged for a witch, but I am innocent, and before a twelvemonth be past, you shall believe it." Mary Herrick said nothing about her vision, for she was certain at the time that Goody Easty was guilty.

Those who would not confess to their alleged crimes were carted up to Gallows Hill on Thursday, September 22nd. Cotton Mather did not attend this hanging, but the justices of the Court of Oyer and Terminer were present.

Widow Ann Pudeator, Alice Parker, Margaret Scott, and Mammy Wilmot Reed each mounted the ladder, said her piece and prayer, and was turned off. The Wizard of Andover, Samuel Wardwell, addressed the crowd out of the grim weather as he stood upon the last rung. The executioner was smoking a pipe beside him, adding smoke to the gray clouds overhead, and a stray current of air wafted a puff into the Wizard's face which made him choke as he spoke. The bitch witches cried, "The Devil does hinder him with smoke!"

Widow Martha Corey protested her innocence, looked at Samuel Parris and said, "I yet am a Gospel woman," prayed, and was turned off. Rev. Nicholas Noyes observed, "What a sad thing it is to see eight firebrands of Hell hanging there!"

It had been a dry fall, which had stunted the few crops available for harvest in the area, but on this day a drizzling rain fell upon Gallows Hill, soaking through everyone's clothing, dripping from hat brims, and through the branches of the oak, quenching the firebrands of Hell. Famine threatened to follow the harvest, for so many people had been involved in the witchhunt — busy sitting on juries, having visions, giving witness, writing depositions, serving warrants and so forth — that many of the yeomen had been unable to plant properly or tend adequately their normal crops. Many who were present at the executions that day felt something final and foreboding about these hangings.

The same feeling haunted the magistrates of the Court of Oyer and Terminer. After the executions Chief Justice Stoughton, Justices John Hathorne and Samuel Sewall, and Clerk of the Court Stephen Sewall rode to Boston through the rain to see Rev. Cotton Mather and discuss his proposed book, *Wonders of the Invisible World*.

It was the intention of the magistrates to persuade Mr. Mather to slant his book in such a way as to defend the Court against the rising tide of disapprobation that threatened to engulf the witchhunt. The discussion with Mather was successful in persuading him to the view of Authority. Stoughton and Sewall took an oath to stand behind him in his literary endeavor, and Stephen Sewall volunteered to ride post-haste back to Salem in order to gather and send Mather the court records he needed. The great Salem Village Whitewash was under weigh.

When the meeting was over the Rev. Mr. Cotton Mather saw his visitors to the door, then went directly to his study, sat down, took pen, ink, and a clean journal. He opened it, left the first page blank for Stoughton's promised endorsement and, on the second page, wrote, "I live by neighbors that force me to produce these undeserved lines."

The next day the Court of Oyer and Terminer adjourned because the General Court of Massachusetts was to meet for its fall term. Stoughton set the first Tuesday in November as the date for the next session for the purpose of resuming the witchcraft trials. Meanwhile, the examinations went on, but in a rather desultory fashion: The steam had gone out of the proceedings, and remorse was setting in among the citizenry.

Job Tookey of Beverly had been cried out upon when he said, "I am not the Devil's servant, but the Devil is mine!" It was typical of the same sort of arrogance that had gotten him into trouble with his master Dr. Richard Knott in 1682. At that time he had spent three months in jail, mocked and teased by the man who owned his indenture.

The bitch witches cried out that Tookey's specter was going from one to the other of them, knocking them about. Hathorne said, "These accuse you of hurting them. What do you say to it?"

Tookey gazed at the pile of twisting bodies and replied, "If they really see any such thing, it is not I, but the Devil in my shape, that hurts the people." But that question had long since been settled.

Susie Sheldon, Mary Warren and Annie Putnam said and corroborated that, "two women and two men and a child are here, and they rose from the dead." "They cry, 'Vengeance! Vengeance!'" Tookey nor anyone else besides the girls could see a thing and no one could hear anything over the noise. Suddenly, however, there was silence as the girls were stricken dumb, their eyes popping and staring, every gaze fixed on the same place. The Court could do nothing but believe the truth of this horrible manifestation of the undead.

At last Mary Warren regained the use of her voice and screeched, "There are three men, and three women, and two children! They are all in their winding-sheets: They look pale upon us, but red upon Tookey — red as blood!" She gasped a bit, then continued, frightened beyond measure, "There is a young child under the table, crying out for vengeance!"

Elizabeth Booth looked under the table and was struck speechless at what she saw. Before the examination was over everyone who had died at Royal Side within living memory had come forward to say that the trial of Job must take place forthwith, for he had murdered them all. Gedney, Corwin and Hathorne shipped him off to durance vile.

While the hunt had been going on a local figure of great eminence had passed from the scene. Richard Moore, one of the original colonists of the Plymouth Plantation, died in Salem, an octogenarian. His tombstone was erected in the Charter Street Cemetery; it read,

> Here
> Lyeth buried
> Ye body of Capt.
> Richard Moore
> Aged 84 years
> Died 1692

One of the last of the Pilgrims had lived to witness what his faith had wrought in New England.

Several incidents put the quietus at last to the witchhunt. Lady Mary Phips, in the absence of her husband the Governor, had granted a reprieve to Abigail Faulkner, and the witch bitches had subsequently cried out upon her. It was a scandal, but then the girls dared to accuse Mrs. John Hale, wife of the minister of Beverly, and public opinion rose to crescendo in the belief that the afflicted persons had overreached, and obviously perjured themselves.

Then, too, stories of heroism were circulating widely, such as that of the son who, when she had been cried out upon, hid his mother in the woods in a wigwam. During the woman's escape it was said that she had broken her leg; the son had set it and kept her supplied and hidden until the witchcraft delusion should be over.

Finally, there was a procedural situation that had developed. The composition of the juries at the trials was changing. Formerly, juries had been composed only of Freemen, who were church members; now, under the new Charter, juries were to be composed of all those men who were landholders. Consequently, the Salem Village and Salem minister, including two of the most rabid witch hunters in the colony — Rev. Nicholas Noyes and Samuel Parris — would no longer have the power they had formerly wielded to influence the Salem juries. Samuel Parris had acted as court recorder for many of the inquisitions and trials, and both ministers had participated as inquisitors themselves, witnesses against the accused witches, and orators fanning the flames of the delusion from the pulpit. Not to mention that the whole outrage had begun in the home and household of Samuel Parris.

The General Court of Connecticut, too, met in October to consider, among other things, the cases of Mercy Disbrow and Elizabeth Clawson of Fairfield who had been the objects of a hung jury. Before the magistrates acted, however, they solicited the opinion of the Connecticut clergy in regard to the case, for the Salem backlash was beginning to swell to the south as well.

In Manchester, New Hampshire, the daughter of Goodman Pitman was haunted by a specter in a sheet. She snatched at the invisible being, tore off a corner of the sheet — and it became visible, like the broken knife of Salem. Goodman Pitman took the torn piece of cloth from his daughter; the specter tried to wrest it away from him, but he held on to it.

On October 3rd Increase Mather, at a gathering of Boston area clergymen, read the manuscript of a short treatise he had written entitled *Cases of Conscience*. It unequivocally attacked the validity of spectral evidence; however, the elder Mather undercut his position by adding a postscript that maintained the judges of the Court of Oyer and Terminer were "wise and good men" who "have acted with all fidelity according to their light...." He insisted that none of the witches had been condemned merely on the basis of spectral evidence. He himself had been present at Burroughs' trial and judged it to be a fair one.

So, with his treatise, Increase Mather joined with his son in a cover-up of the culpability of the Court for having proceeded on erroneous principles. Then fourteen of the members of the Massachusetts clergy entered into the conspiracy by approving of, and signing, the preface to the book.

Nor was the Committee of Vigilance yet done. Having invaded Andover with such success, the afflicted girls were taken on the road to Gloucester, which somehow — unaccountably, considering the specters that had hovered about the town the previous year — had remained relatively isolated from the trials.

But opposition to the Massachusetts proceedings was spread by this time far and wide, even to New York, where Joseph Dudley, formerly of Massachusetts and at that time an official of New York, wrote out a set of questions regarding witchcraft and addressed them to the Dutch and French Calvinist ministers of his province, and to the Rev. John Miller, Anglican chaplain to the King's forces in New York.

Mr. and Mrs. Edward Bishop III had been two of those who had escaped from prison. Sheriff George Corwin sent to seize Bishop's goods, but one of Bishop's sons borrowed ten pounds to pay Corwin for the materials to be seized. The Sheriff was amenable and gave young Bishop a receipt for the sum. Another mundane event occurred on October 7th: George and Elizabeth Putnam Flint had their seventh child, Mercy — their family, like Joseph Putnam's, had stayed clear of the hunt from the beginning, and their infant daughter was well named.

On October 8th Thomas Brattle of Boston, a mathematician and astronomer in touch with the leading scientists of England, circulated in samisdat, like Increase Mather, the manuscript of a treatise titled *A Full and Candid Account of the Delusion Called Witchcraft Which Prevailed in New England*. The manuscript was unlike any other 17th century American document in that it was highly literary and satirical in tone — like some of the satires that were beginning to appear in England. Brattle directly attacked the witchcraft court, pointed out that the occurrences at Salem Village were no part of the New Philosophy, but mere "Salem superstition and sorcery." It was Brattle's opinion that what was taking place in Salem Village was "not fit to be named in a land of such light as New England is." He closed by writing, "I am afraid that ages will not wear off that reproach and these stains which these things will leave behind them upon our land."

By Tuesday, October 11th, the library of samisdat manuscripts circulating in Boston and its environs had increased. Cotton Mather's written-to-order *Wonders of the Invisible World* was completed, though with great difficulty, for Stephen Sewall had not kept his promise to send Cotton the court records pell-mell. He had procrastinated a long while, perhaps in order to augment the records with post-execution testimony. When finally he honored his commitment, Mather rushed to finish. Chief Justice Stoughton and Justice Sewall read the completed final draft, found it accurate, and endorsed it. A copy was hurried to the printer who feverishly began to set it in type while other handwritten copies were being passed about.

Sewall also read Rev. Samuel Willard's letter, "Epistle to Mr. Increase Mather's *Cases of Conscience*" in manuscript. The purported author of this treatise was, peculiarly, one of those fourteen ministers who had endorsed Mather's book. It was Willard's opinion that there was a schism between the ministers, who opposed spectral evidence, and the popular belief that the witchcraft trials had been fair. Willard felt there could not be a "procedure in court," according to Sewall, "except there be some better consent of ministers and people."

There was no doubt in Sewall's mind as to the author of the manuscript, but when it shortly began to circulate as a printed pamphlet titled *Some Miscellany Observations on Our Present Debates Respecting Witchcrafts, in A Dialogue between S. & B.*, by P. E. & J. A., Philadelphia, Printed by William Bradford, for Hezekiah Usher," many people were confused. The putative authors were Philip English of Salem, and John Alden of Boston, both fugitives from the trials. Usher, the supposed publisher, had also fled the colony; the "Dialogue between S. & B." meant "Salem and Boston."

But the pamphlet was not published in Philadelphia — it came from a Boston press. The reason for Willard's subterfuge was that Governor Phips had forbade any publishing in Massachusetts on the subject of witchcraft — except for Cotton Mather's official apologia — which was the reason, likewise, why Brattle's letter and some of the others were circulated only in samisdat.

By October 11th Governor Phips had returned from the Eastward to discover that his wife had been accused as a witch while he was away. The list of questions posed by New York's Joseph Dudley to the various New York Clergymen, together with the answers to those questions, was forwarded to Phips: The ministers unanimously agreed that spectral evidence was inadmissible in a court of law.

On the twelfth Phips wrote William Brathwayt, Clerk of England's Privy Council, a letter saying he had "forbidden the committing of any more that shall be accused without unavoidable necessity," and that he would protect "Those that have been committed...from any suspicion of any wrong done to the innocent." Sir William asked the King's advice. On the same day in Salem Village James and Sarah Putnam welcomed their fourth child, Nathan, into the visible world.

Samuel Sewall talked with one of his fellow judges, Thomas Danforth, on Saturday, October 15th. It was Danforth's opinion that the Court could not proceed unless the people, many of whom were still in favor of the witchhunt, and the ministers, who opposed spectral evidence, were reconciled. Cotton Mather's *Wonders of the Invisible World* appeared in its first American edition at about the same time. Published in Boston, copies of the book soon were circulating throughout the colonies.

In Salem Arthur Abbott on Saturday was ill. He sent for Daniel Epps and Capt. Thomas Wade of Ipswich to be witnesses of his will. When they arrived he informed them that he wished to make certain amends for testimony he gave in against Goody Proctor in court — testimony that had been questioned by Samuel Appleton. It seemed that in court Abbott had insisted upon certain specific dates, but he should not have done so, for he was uncertain of the times. However, as to what had happened in the Proctor home — that which he swore to had been the truth.

The General Court of Connecticut on October 17th received from the Connecticut ministers the opinion the Court had solicited. Some of the ministers believed that the child accuser who had cried out upon Goodies Elizabeth Clawson and Mercy Disbrow (or Desborough) might have been counterfeiting her fits of possession; others, that she suffered from suffocation of the mother — hysteria — "improved by craft." It was the ministers' opinion that the evidence regarding bewitchment of cattle was slender testament against the women.

In Massachusetts the next day the Revs. Francis Dane and Thomas Barnard of Andover, together with twenty-eight others, petitioned the government on behalf of the confessed Andover witches and criticized the Court's practices. Increase Mather traveled to Salem on the 19th to interview the Andover witches in prison — he found that they were recanting their confessions. Six women wrote out a complete retraction:

"We whose names are underwritten, inhabitants of Andover, when that horrible and tremendous judgment, beginning at Salem Village, in the year 1692, by some called witchcraft, first breaking forth at Mr. Samuel Parris's house, several young persons, being seemingly afflicted, did accuse several persons for afflicting them; and many there believing it so to be, we being informed that, if a person was sick the afflicted person could tell what or who was the cause of that sickness: John Ballard of Andover, his wife being sick at the time, he, either from himself, or by the advice of others, fetched two of the persons called the afflicted persons from Salem Village to Andover, which was the beginning of that dreadful calamity that befell us in Andover, believing the said accusations to be true, sent for the said persons to come together to the meeting-house in Andover, the afflicted persons being there.

"After Mr. Barnard had been at prayer, we were blindfolded, and our hands were laid upon the afflicted persons, they being in their fits, and falling into their fits at our coming into their presence, as they said: And some led us, and laid our hands upon them; and then they said they were well, and that we were guilty of afflicting them. Whereupon we were all seized as prisoners, by a warrant from the justice of the peace, and forthwith carried to Salem; and by reason of that sudden surprisal, we knowing ourselves altogether innocent of that crime, we were all exceedingly astonished and amazed, and consternated and affrighted, even out of our reason; and our nearest and dearest relations, seeing us in that dreadful condition, and knowing our great danger, apprehended there was no other way to save our lives, as the case was then circumstanced, but by our confessing ourselves to be such and such persons as the afflicted represented us to be, they, out of tenderness and pity, persuaded us to confess what we did confess. And, indeed, that confession that it is said we made was no other than what was suggested to us by some gentlemen [i. e., the magistrates], they telling us that we were witches, and they knew it, and we knew it, which made us think that it was so; and, our understandings, our reason, our faculties almost gone, we were not capable of judging of our condition; as also the hard measures they used with us rendered us incapable of making our defence, but said anything, and everything which they desired, and most of us what we said was but in effect a consenting to what they said.

"Some time after, when we were better composed, they [the authorities] telling us what we had confessed, we did profess that we were innocent and ignorant of such things; and we hearing that Samuel Wardwell had renounced his confession, and was quickly after condemned and executed, some of us were told we were going after Wardwell."

Mary Osgood, Mary Tyler, Deliverance Dane, Abigail Barker, Sarah Wilson, and Hannah Tyler signed the document.

Judge Samuel Sewall wrote in his diary for October 26th that a bill had been sent in to the General Court "about calling a fast, and convocation of ministers, that [we] may be led in the right way as to the witchcrafts. The reason and manner of doing it is such that the Court of Oyer and Terminer count themselves thereby dismissed: 29 nos and 33 yeas to the bill. William Hutchins and several other interested persons there, in the affirmative." Hidden between the lines was a measure of bitterness, for by "interested persons" Sewall meant neighbors, relatives or friends of people who had been cried out upon, such as Captain Dudley Bradstreet and Lt. Henry True.

The Connecticut Court reassembled on October 28th, and the jury rendered a verdict of "Guilty" in the case of Mercy Disbrow, "Not guilty" as to Elizabeth Clawson. The magistrates requested the jury to reconsider its verdict. The judges — Samuel Willis, William Pitkin, and Nathaniel Stanley — cited as authority William Perkins' *Discourse of the Damned Art of Witchcraft,* Richard Bernard's *Guide to Grandjurymen,* and Increase Mather's samisdat *Cases of Conscience*, but the jury reaffirmed its verdict, the Court accepted it, and the governor signed a death warrant against Mercy Disbrow.

In Massachusetts Samuel Sewall asked Governor Phips and his Council if the Court of Oyer and Terminer should sit the following week as scheduled. He received only a "great silence." Justice James Russell put Sewall's question again to Gov. Phips on October 29th, expressing "some fear of inconvenience" if the Court should fail to meet. This time Phips gave a firm reply: "It must fall." The witchhunt was officially over.

The next day in Salem Village there took place an event of great irony: Chief Vigilante Sgt. Thomas Putnam, Jr. and his afflicted wife Ann Carr Putnam brought the newest sibling of bitch witch Annie Putnam to the meetinghouse of the Rev. Samuel Parris to be baptized.

Chapter Twelve

The Committee of Vigilance died hard. In November the bitch witches journeyed again to Gloucester to look for witches, but Sgt. Thomas Putnam, Jr., and his fellow vigilantes were no longer given any credence whatsoever by the authorities, much to the bilious anger of the former Court of Oyer and Terminer. Furthermore, cracks began to appear in the façade of the Committee itself, and soon Sgt. Thomas and Carolina John Putnam found themselves standing alone behind the crumbling structure of spectral evidence.

Rebecca Fox wrote a petition to Gov. Phips requesting the release of her daughter, Rebecca Jacobs, who was "well known to be a person crazed, distracted, and broken in mind…these twelve years and upwards.

"However, for (I think) above this half-year" she "has lain in prison, and yet remains there, attended with many sore difficulties. —

"Some have died already in prison, and others have been dangerously sick; and how soon others, and, among them, my poor child, by the difficulties of this confinement may be sick and die, God only knows."

Thomas Barrett of Chelmsford sent another petition to the Governor on behalf of his daughter, Martha Sparks, who had been incarcerated since 1691, before the Salem Witchhunt had even begun. Goodman Barrett wrote, "She hath lain in Boston prison for the space of twelve months and five days, being committed by Thomas Danforth, Esq., the late Deputy Governor, upon suspicion of witchcraft, since which no evidence hath appeared against her in any such matter; neither hath any given bond to prosecute her, nor doth anyone at this day accuse her of any such thing...."

The Benhams of Wallingford, Connecticut, benefited from the reversal of affairs in Boston and Salem when, the second Wednesday in November, the County Court met in New Haven before Robert Treat, Gov. William Jones, Deputy Gov. Andrew Leet, Capt. Moses Mansfield, and Thomas Trowbridge.

"Winifred Benham of Wallingford," the clerk wrote, "being summoned to appear at this Court for examination upon suspicion of witchcraft, was now present. And the witnesses were called to testify what they had to say in the case, and accordingly gave in their testimonies in writing, which were read in the hearing of the said Winifred. And she being called to say what she had to say for herself, her general answer was that she knew nothing of the matters testified, and was not concerned therein. She also gave in some testimonies for herself which were read.

"The Court having heard and considered all the evidences against the said Winifred Benham and not finding sufficient grounds of conviction for further prosecution (at present) of the said Winifred, do therefore at this time dismiss the business, yet advising the said Winifred Benham solemnly to reflect upon the case and grounds of suspicion given in and alleged against her. And told her if further grounds of mischief done to the bodies or estate or any preternatural acts proved against her, she might justly fear and expect to be brought to trial for it."

The problems of the Benhams were far from over, for their neighbors truly hated them, and the action of the Court did nothing to soothe the folk of Wallingford, who were sure the Court had committed an injustice. But Mrs. Benham went home, equally determined to stick it out.

Mary Herrick went to see the Rev. John Hale of Beverly on November 14th to tell him that she had been haunted for two months by Mary Easty, who had declared to the maid that she was innocent. She told Hale that she would not have spoken if she had not also lately seen Mrs. Hale in her visions, but the appearance of the minister's wife had convinced Mary that her astral sightings must be the delusion of the Devil.

Governor Phips dismissed charges against Abigail Faulkner of Andover for lack of evidence, thus putting his imprimature on the action of Lady Mary Phips while Sir William had been away from Boston, and the General Court on November 22nd called special sessions of the Superior Court of Judicature in order to bring to trial those still under indictment for witchcraft. Several members of the Witch Court were appointed to the new Superior Court: Stoughton was once more Chief Justice; Sewall, John Richards, and Waite Winthrop were Justices, and Thomas Danforth was the fourth. It looked as though it were merely another hanging tribunal, but Phips, in reconstituting it, made sure that the judges had changed their procedures, and that spectral evidence would no longer be allowed.

Samuel Sewall wrote in his diary for that day, "I prayed that God would pardon all my sinful wanderings, and direct me for the future. That God would bless the Assembly in their debates, and that would choose and assist our judges &c., and save New England as to enemies and witchcrafts, and vindicate the late judges, consisting with His Justice and holiness, &c., with fasting."

The same day Mercy Short, Cotton Mather's patient, began having fits again, so violent that "many strong men with an united force," according to Mather, "could not well carry her." She shrieked, she chattered gaily, she was impudent, and alternately melancholy — she "imagined herself in a desolate cellar, where day or night could not be distinguished."

She was smitten with anorexia and ate nothing for days on end, once going without food for fifteen days, and the Devil appeared to her as a

Black Man with cloven feet. Mather attended her religiously with prayer and fasting.

William Hobbs was released from prison on 200 pounds bond raised by his neighbors John Nichols and Joseph Towne on the understanding that he would appear at the January session of the Superior Court, and that same day, December 14th, Eleazer Putnam, Capt. John's son, married Hannah Boardman of Ipswich and moved with her to Topsfield.

Mercy Short spent Christmas Day by hallucinating a dancing party. She said, according to Mather, that the specters "were going to have a dance, and immediately those that were attending her most plainly heard and felt a dance, as of barefooted people upon the floor, whereof they are ready to make an oath before any lawful authority." No one who had lived through the Salem Village Witchhunt would have doubted there would be plenty of witnesses willing to do just that, but Cotton Mather's contradictory early stance against just such sorts of spectral evidence was official policy at last, and the authorities ignored his hints.

Mather was in a remarkable and ambiguous position: He had been transformed from an early critic of the methods of the trials into a defender of the Witch Court. He had been minimally involved in the main cases, had attended few of the proceedings, but he had always been a propagandist for witchcrafts, despite his interest in science — had Dorcas Hoar or one of the other confirmed seers of Massachusetts Bay been able to look into the future through Dr. John Dee's crystal egg, they would have seen both Cotton and his father fighting vehemently against public opinion in a few years in favor of inoculation for smallpox.

It was the position he now took that identified him as the major figure among the proponents of witchcrafts and started him and his religion on the swift slide downward. As he had early helped to begin the mania, now he was attempting to prolong it. However, the remorse that was beginning to set in was much too strong to yield once again to the Devil's delusions. There was another "great silence" settling over Massachusetts as many people stopped talking about witchcraft at all, avoiding the painful subject in everyday discourse. Cotton and his father Increase were practically alone in their harping upon the matter. Cotton began to notice that people avoided his presence when they could, and he lamented bitterly in his journals that his motives were being misunderstood.

On the third of January, 1693, the new-old Superior Court of Judicature met in sessions with the mandate to settle the cases of all accused witches remaining in the prisons, though mere acquittal was no guarantee of release, since the indicted people would first have to settle such matters as court costs, board, and other expenses incurred in their arrest, transportation, and trial. Fifty-two people were indicted by the grand jury.

Trials began for the madwoman Rebecca Jacobs, Margaret Jacobs, Sarah Buckley, Job Tookey, Hannah Tyler, Candy, Mary Marston, Elizabeth Johnson, Abigail Barker, Mary Tyler, Sarah Hawkes, Mary Wardwell, Mary Bridges, Hannah Post, Sarah Bridges, Mary Osgood, Mary Lacey the younger, Sarah Wardwell, Elizabeth Johnson the younger, and Margaret Post. William Hobbs, who had been released on 200 pounds bond — on the advice of the friends who had raised the bond — failed to appear for trial, and his bond was forfeit.

In the trials, which were held in Salem, spectral evidence was given no weight. Of all those tried in January only three were convicted on their own confessions. Two of these, Elizabeth Johnson the younger and Mary Post, were retarded people; the third was Sarah Wardwell, wife of the executed Samuel Wardwell, Wizard of Andover. The baby of Elizabeth Proctor having been born while the convicted witch was in prison, she, together with four other previously convicted witches and the three new convicts, were sentenced to death, and Chief Justice Stoughton signed their death warrants.

However, on the advice of the King's Attorney General, Governor Phips issued a reprieve for all eight until such time as His Majesty's will in the matter should be known. Stoughton, when he heard the news, was furious. He said, disgustedly, "We were in a way to have cleared the land of these witches! Who it is that obstructs the course of justice I know not. The Lord be merciful to the country!" He resigned his position; the resignation not being accepted, he refused to sit for the remainder of the sessions.

In England on the 26th of January the Privy Council discussed Phips' letter, and the Duke of Nottingham was ordered to draft a reply for the Queen's signature.

Mercy Short was still having her fits during the winter and early spring in Boston, and on March 9th Cotton Mather overheard her spelling out a word the devils were showing her in one of their three books. Shortly afterwards, though, Mather's efforts began to be rewarded by a distinct improvement in the girl's condition. On the 15th of the month the witch metaphysician cured Mercy — again.

Queen Mary Stuart approved Nottingham's letter to Phips on April 15th, signed it, and commanded that it be sent to New England. It said essentially nothing, but its equivocations were suffused with urgings to moderation and circumspection in the matter.

While the letter was on the way the April sessions of the Court were being held, and Phips found himself on his own. A good many people weren't waiting for the Queen — they were breaking jail in clusters, and no one was sent after them very swiftly or ordered to search very hard for the fugitives. Many others, accused, with warrants issued for their arrest, simply were not taken into custody. William Hobbs surrendered himself to the court, as did John Alden. Stoughton resumed his seat on the bench with the others when the Court was moved from Salem to

Boston, and the justices did their best to browbeat the remaining accused witches into confession, which was about the only way left that would convince a jury to convict.

Justice Thomas Danforth roared at eighty-year-old Sarah Daston, whom everyone believed to be notoriously a witch, and against whom there was more than spectral evidence, "Woman, woman, repent! There are shrewd things come against thee!" However, Goody Daston was having none of that. Though she could not be convicted, neither could the Court allow her to wander the streets bewitching innocent citizens, so it kept her in prison until she died.

The Court was more successful with half-crazed Mary Watkins who, when she was caught attempting to strangle herself, confessed voluntarily. The jury returned a verdict of *ignoramus* in her case, was asked to reconsider, and came back again with the same verdict. Like Sarah Daston, she was sent back to jail, for, as an impoverished indentured servant, she had no way of paying the fees that were requisite in order to set her free.

Eight members of Salem Village Church, on April 21st, withdrew from communion with their brethren. They were Nathaniel Ingersoll, Edward Putnam — the two deacons, Aaron and William Way, Peter Cloyse, Samuel Nurse, John Tarbell, and Thomas Wilkins. They wrote an explanation to Rev. Samuel Parris: The afflicted girls made so much noise in their possessions and delusions in church that people could not hear the service. Furthermore, they were afraid they would be cried out upon — an astonishing remark to come from former members of the Committee of Vigilance such as Ingersoll and Putnam. They were offended by Parris' harping on the "dark and dismal mystery of iniquity" working among the people of the Village; they could not, in good conscience, join in the requests Parris made in his prayers regarding the late witchcrafts.

So much for public worship. As for communion, they were offended with the minister because his opinions regarding witchcraft were unorthodox, "differing from the opinion of the generality of orthodox ministers of the country," who had repudiated spectral evidence; because he continued to believe in the accusations of the afflicted — as Rev. George Moxon had done in Springfield forty years earlier, for to do otherwise would be to admit that one had been deceived by one's own daughter's hysteria; because he had laid aside "charity towards his neighbors, and especially those of his church, when there is no apparent reason, but for the contrary." Also, because Parris encouraged the girls to accuse witches; because he gave his oath to what they believed to be perjured testimony in some of the trials; because he wrote prejudiced accounts of the statements of the afflicted persons; because several points of his doctrine — if Christian, were "unsafe," and because the minister persisted in those unsafe principles and justified his practice, giving the signers no satisfaction, "but rather offending and dissatisfying" them.

Since no one at all appeared to charge John Alden before the Court in Boston, he was discharged by proclamation, as was William Hobbs, whose bond was also remitted. In May, Phips discharged Mary Black by proclamation, and about one-hundred-fifty other people as well, for he had finally received Queen Mary's letter.

Margaret Jacobs, however, like many another, remained in prison after the general pardon because she could not pay the requisite fees. Her executed grandfather's property had been confiscated by the sheriff; her father had fled overseas; her mother had been arrested when she had been, was at best mad at any rate, and there was no one to whom she could look for help. But compassion reared its head in the form of a stranger named Goodman Gammon who, having heard of her case, took it upon himself to pay what was due, and she was released.

In Connecticut, too, Mercy Disbrow was reprieved, but on a technicality, until the next General Court. The magistrates found that, illegally, one of the jurors who sat in her case had left for New York in mid-trial and been replaced by another man. But it was the feeling of the judges, also, that she had been convicted on insufficient evidence.

At the May elections in Boston every judge of the late court of Oyer and Terminer was elected to the Governor's Council, including Nathaniel Saltonstall, who had resigned. However, the other judges took some satisfaction in the knowledge that Samuel Sewall, who had not resigned, got more votes.

Cotton Mather wrote, "'Twas upon the Lord's day, the 10th of September, 1693, that Margaret Rule, after some hours of previous disturbance in the public assembly, fell into odd fits, which caused her friends to carry her home, where her fits in a few hours grew into a figure that satisfied the spectators," in particular the Rev. Cotton Mather himself, "of their being preternatural. Some of the neighbors were forward enough to suspect the rise of this mischief in an house hard by, where lived a miserable woman who had been formerly imprisoned on the suspicion of witchcraft, and who had frequently cured very painful hurts by muttering over them certain charms, which I shall not endanger the poisoning of my reader by repeating."

The woman in question was a white witch of long-standing, Mary Webster, who had several times previously been in trouble, especially in Hadley, but who somehow had managed to avoid being arrested during the Witchhunt despite the fact that she had been cried out upon. She it was who had treated Bray Wilkins when, on Election Day the previous year, he had been stricken at the sight of John Willard.

"This woman had," Mather wrote on, "the evening before Margaret fell into her calamities, very bitterly treated her and threatened her. But the hazard of hurting a poor woman that might be innocent, notwithstanding surmises that might have been more strongly grounded than those, caused the pious people in the vicinity," i.e., Cotton Mather, "to try rather whether incessant supplication to God alone might not procure a quicker and safer ease to the afflicted than hasty prosecution of any supposed criminal. And accordingly, that unexceptionable course was all that was ever followed. Yea (which I looked on as a token for good), the afflicted family was as averse as any of us all to entertain thoughts of any other course."

On September 13th a Boston merchant named Robert Calef, who had become the most outspokenly bitter and pertinacious critic of the Salem Village Witchhunt, and particularly of Cotton Mather, upon whom he fastened like a bulldog, went to see Margaret Rule, having heard that both Cotton and Increase Mather would be present. Between thirty and forty people were gathered in the room with her. Increase sat on a stool, and Cotton on the bed.

Cotton spoke to the young woman: "How do you do?" Margaret did not answer, so Cotton continued, "What? Do these a great many witches sit upon you?"

"Yes."

"Do you not know there is a hard Master?"

Margaret threw a fit, then lay stark still. Cotton put his hand to her nose and mouth to feel for breath, brushed her face with his glove, then rubbed her stomach and asked others to do the same, saying, "It eases her." Margaret at length revived, and Cotton repeated his question.

Finally she answered, "Yes." Cotton resumed his rubbing and Margaret Perd, an attendant upon the girl, began to assist him, at which Margaret Rule said to her angrily, "Don't you meddle with me!" and pushed the woman's hand away.

Mather waved his hand before the maiden's eyes and asked, "Do you see the witches still?"

"No," she replied.

"Do you believe?"

"Yes."

"Do you believe in" — Cotton dared not say the word "God," for fear the Devil would give her another fit — "in you know Who?"

"Yes."

"Would you have other people do so too — to believe in you know Who?" — evidently the Devil didn't know Whom Cotton had in mind.

"Who is it that afflicts you?"

"I know not — there is a great many of them."

Increase Mather asked, "Do you know the specters?" someone present said, "If she does, she will not tell."

Cotton threw out another leading question: "You have seen the Black Man, haven't you?"

"No."

Disappointed, Cotton said, "I hope you never shall. You have had a Book offered you, haven't you?"

"No." Another disappointment.

Crestfallen, Cotton changed the subject — "The brushing of you gives you ease, does it not?" He knew that it did, so he was sure to get a yes this time.

"Yes," Margaret said; she turned a bit and groaned.

"Now the witches scratch you and pinch you and bite you, don't they?"

"Yes."

Cotton put his hand on her stomach — and felt something alive! "Father," he said, "touch here!" Increase's hand joined that of his son on the young woman's abdomen. "Do you feel a live thing in the bed?"

"No," Increase answered, feeling about, "that is only fancy."

Cotton turned again to Margaret: "The great company of people increase your torment, don't they?"

"Yes," she told him obligingly.

Cotton asked the crowd to withdraw. One woman said, "I am sure I am no witch. I will not go." Several others muttered the same and stayed; others left.

Cotton asked Margaret, "Shall we go to pray?" Margaret went into another trance, but this time the attendants waved a hat and brushed her head with it. When she came to, Cotton asked again, but spelled the word "P-R-A-Y." Obviously, he felt the Devil did not know how to spell.

Margaret answered, "Yes"; Increase and Cotton prayed over her for half an hour. During prayer, when the ministers thought the maid had gone into another trance they beckoned people to use the hat on her, and when they had finished Cotton asked, "You did not hear when we were praying, did you?"

"Yes," Margaret answered, which reply set Cotton aback.

He tried yet another leading question: "You don't hear always? You don't hear sometimes past a word or two, do you?"

"No."

Cotton turned to the assembly and remarked, "This is just another Mercy Short."

Margaret Perd contradicted him — "She is not like her in her fits."

"What does she eat or drink?" Cotton asked.

"Not eat at all, but drinks rum," he was told.

"Take heed," Cotton said, "you young people, by this example. It is a sad thing to be so tormented by the Devil and his instruments." Especially by Demon Rum.

A seaman, who was sure to know, remarked, "This is the Devil all over!"

The ministers got up and withdrew. After they had left Margaret Rule said to the women attendants present, "Begone!" But when the remaining people began to leave Margaret took the seaman's hand and said, "The company of the man is not offensive to me."

Margaret Perd whispered to Robert Calef, "He was once her sweetheart." As he was leaving the room Calef heard Margaret Rule say, pulling the seaman into his seat again, "You shall not go tonight."

By September 18th Margaret Rule had fasted for eight days, subsisting entirely on a liquid diet. Though she had been hungry occasionally, if anyone brought her food, her teeth would set, and she would have convulsions. Now and then, though, she could get a spoonful of rum through her lips and past her teeth.

The next day Calef went to see the girl again and found her looking fresher. She was having a screaming fit, and several people were rubbing her in various places. One said to Calef, "The brushing does put the devils away, if we brush or rub in the right place; therefore, we brush and rub in several places, and when we do it in the right place she can fetch her breath." Soon Margaret Rule came out of her fit and went into a merry talking jag.

A young man entered the room and said to her, "How do you do?"

"Very bad, but at present a little better," she replied.

He stayed awhile, talking, then said, "I must be gone. Good night."

Margaret seemed troubled. "I like your company," she told him, "and I would not have you go till I am well, for I shall die when you are gone." Then she muttered, "They did not put a clean cap on me, but let me lie so, like a beast. I shall lose my fellow!" She fidgeted. "I wonder," she mused, "that any people should be so wicked as to think I am not afflicted, but that I dissemble."

A young woman present said, "If they were to see you in this merry fit they would say you dissembled indeed."

Margaret replied, "Mr. Mather says this is my laughing time now; I must laugh now. Mr. Mather was here this evening."

"How long," the young woman asked, "has he been gone?"

"He stayed alone with me in the room a half hour and told me there were some that came for spies to report about town that I am not afflicted. I had no fits while he was here, and he asked me if I knew how many times he had prayed for me today. I said I could not tell, and he replied he had prayed for me nine times today."

Margaret Rule's attendants told Calef, "Sometimes she is in a fit such that none can open her joints. There came an old iron-jawed man and tried, but could not do it. Her head cannot be moved from the pillow."

Calef — the spy — and others tried it and had no difficulty, but he was afraid of offending the attendants who cried, "You will break her neck!" so he didn't lift her head very far off the pillow.

The attendants told Calef, "Mr. Mather will not go to prayer with her any more when people are in the room."

Margaret Perd exclaimed, "I smell brimstone!" and one other person agreed with her. No one else smelled anything, or suggested that perhaps someone had broken wind. Perd and the other person backed down: "I cannot tell what it is I smell," and Goody Perd continued, "I wish I had been here when Mr. Mather was here."

Another attendant replied, "If you had been here, you might not have been permitted in, for her own mother was not suffered to be present."

Calef later wrote up his account of his visits to Margaret Rule, circulated it in samisdat, and it was not long before the Mathers heard of it — they complained of slander. Calef was brought before the court and bound over to sessions to answer the charge. Mather's complaint was that Calef's account erred by omission. Calef contended that he had written out everything that he knew of the situation and could not be responsible for what he did not know. He had offered, he said, to meet Mather to show him what he had written, but his arrest had intervened. Mather never appeared in court to press charges against Calef.

On the 24th of November Calef renewed his offer to meet with Cotton, but the minister did not pick up the gauntlet. An English edition of the *Wonders of the Invisible World* h ad been published in London, as was an editon of Lawson's *A Further Account of the Trials of the New England Witches* which included Increase Mather's *Cases of Conscience Concerning Withccrafts*. All of these treatises dealt with the Salem trials.

While the Calef-Mather battle of words was going on, Ipswich sessions of the county court, in an aftermath trial, found Sarah Post of Andover "Not guilty" of witchcraft, and the fits of Margaret Rule diminished, eventually petering out. Tituba Indian was sold back into slavery to pay for her fees, and Mary Watkins asked for a new master: She was released once more to indentured servitude.

On the 15th of January 1694 Cotton Mather answered Robert Calef's charges in a letter, and three days later Calef rebutted. Samuel Sewall, in his diary for January 19th wrote, "This day Mrs. Prout dies after sore conflicts of mind, not without suspicion of witchcraft." In February Calef wrote Mather again to complain that the minister hadn't yet come to grips with any of his offers and charges. While Calef was waiting for a reply from Mather, he decided to take on the entire clergy of Boston on March 18th in still another letter; then, on April 16th, he resumed his one-sided dialogue with Cotton.

Philip English, who had been Salem's wealthiest merchant before he was cried out upon and had his goods and chattels seized by the grandson of his old mercantile rival, Sheriff George Corwin, sued to recover before Superior Court. The seizure, however, was held to be legal, and fifteen hundred pounds in property was forfeit to the Crown.

The Rev. Samuel Parris presided over a completely splintered congregation, and he was forced to reassess his conduct and actions. Finally, he read from the pulpit his "Meditations for Peace", which to a degree retreated from his former positions — but it was not to a sufficient degree for some of his dissident parishioners who refused to attend services or pay rates. His "confession" of November 26th, which admitted that God had laid a heavy Providence upon him and his family, said only, at last, "were the same troubles [to occur] again…I should not agree with my former apprehensions in all parts."

The parish war continued into 1695 when Parris' enemies asked for a council of mediation to be formed to hear their complaints. Sixteen were appointed, including the ministers Increase Mather as moderator, Cotton Mather, Samuel Willard, and James Allen. On April 3rd the council recommended reconciliation, but reckoning that might not occur, it suggested that Parris ought to leave without any character damage, so far as the council members were concerned. The report did nothing to quench the smoldering flame of Salem Village. On the 3rd of May the dissenters wrote the Boston churches for permission to get rid of Parris. The signers of the petition numbered well over sixty people, including sixteen church members.

In 1695, too, Thomas Maule, the Quaker of Salem, published *The Truth Held Forth and Maintained*, in which he affirmed his belief in witchcraft and the punishment of death for anyone who murdered by witchcraft. But he had a rather unlimited definition of the word "witch": Anyone who was not a Quaker.

In 1696 Thomas Maule was haled into Salem Court accused of having written a book filled with unsound doctrine. His defense was that the only proof the court had that he was its author was his name on the title page, and that name was nothing but his specter and thus was spectral evidence.

The jury brought in a verdict of "Not guilty," which left the judge, Thomas Danforth, "much dissatisfied." When he asked the jury to explain its thinking the foreman replied that "the book was not sufficient evidence, for that Thomas Maule's name was thereunto set by the printer." Furthermore, the jury felt itself incompetent to judge of unsound doctrines, "they not being a jury of divines."

Danforth accepted the verdict, but admonished the jury "that though Thomas Maule had escaped the hands of men, yet he had not escaped the hand of God."

Maule protested that the Puritan court was persecuting yet another Quaker "as their fathers before had done."

Danforth cried, "Take him away! Take him away! Take him away!"

On Christmas Eve Samuel Sewall's son Samuel Sewall, Jr., read to him in Latin from Matthew xii:7: "If ye had known what this meaneth, 'I will have mercy and not sacrifice,' ye would not have condemned the guiltless." Sewall, not thinking of divination by Bibliomancy, took it instead as a Providence of God that this passage should have been read under the circumstances in which he found himself, for the Lord had seen fit to lay the heavy hand of tribulation upon his family.

On the 14th of January 1697 Massachusetts held a day of penance for Salem Village's catastrophe. Samuel Sewall wrote the draft of the proclamation calling for the day, the Governor's Council having rejected Cotton Mather's version because it said, "Wicked sorceries have been practiced in this land, and, in the late inexplicable storms from the Invisible World" mistakes had been made.

At church meeting on the 15th Sewall handed in to Rev. Mr. Samuel Willard a confession of his errors. Willard read the document from the pulpit while Sewall stood up in the congregation:

"Samuel Sewall, sensible of the reiterated strokes of God upon himself and family; and being sensible, that as to the guilt contracted upon the opening of the late Commission of Oyer and Terminer at Salem (to which the order for this day relates) he is, upon many accounts, more concerned than any that he knows of, desires to take the blame and shame of it, asking pardon of men, and especially desiring prayers that God, who has an unlimited Authority, would pardon that sin and all other his sins; personal and relative: and according to His infinite Benignity and Sovereignty, not visiting the sin of him, or of any other, upon himself or any of his, nor upon the land: But that He would powerfully defend him against all temptations to sin, for the future; and vouchsafe him the efficacious, saving conduct of His Word and Spirit."

Sewall's fellow judge William Stoughton, on the other hand, maintained, "I feel no personal remorse. I acted out of conscience, and my silence at the public Fast Day is sufficient."

That night Cotton Mather lamented into his diary that he was "afflicted last night with discouraging thoughts, as if unavoidable marks of the Divine Displeasure must overtake my family for my not appearing with vigor enough to stop the proceedings of the judges when the inextricable storm from the Invisible World assaulted the country...."

On the 24th of May Sgt. Thomas Putnam, Jr., died of a contagious disease involving high fever, convulsions, hallucinations, and great agony. His wife, Ann Carr Putnam, became infected as well, and on the 8th of June Satan's scourge claimed her for a victim as well. Little Annie Putnam— no longer so little — was an orphan, a frightened and chastened one at this further Providence of God. She and Mercy Lewis, who also had somehow survived the family's disease, were taken into the homes of relatives in Salem Village.

Samuel Parris took his case to the Inferior Court of Common Pleas on July 21st. The Court app[ointed three arbitrators — Waite Winthrop, Elisha Cook, and Samuel Sewall — to recommend a solution. The Village appointed as its attorneys four people, including two relatives of Rebecca Nurse — John Tarbell and Samuel Nurse; Daniel Andrews, and the Village hero, Joseph Putnam. They argued that Parris had been in error in 1692, and the law required the town to maintain only an "orthodox and blameless" rector. The arbitrators recommended that Parris be severed from his connection with the Village with back salary and a cash payment for the disputed church property.

With great alacrity the Villagers raised the requisite cash, paid off Parris, sent him packing, and settled, at long last, on a good and mild man for their next preacher, the Rev. Joseph Green who set about circumspectly and gently healing the gaping wound that had festered for so long in the community.

In Connecticut Mercy Disbrow had long since ceased to be an issue; but in Wallingford during the late summer of 1697 Mrs. Winifred Benham and her daughter, Winifred the younger, were cried out upon by some children who claimed the Benham females' specters were tormenting them. Involved in the case was Satan's scourge.

Evidently Joseph Benham had caught one of the milder forms of smallpox — perhaps cowpox — for the spots he developed on his body disappeared after the illness had run its course, and left no scars. But the Benhams' baby had not been so lucky — the disease had been enough to kill it, and to send the pack of child accusers — nurtured by years of rumor and malicious gossip on the part of their parents — howling off in full cry after Mrs. Benham. Mother and Daughter Benham were seized, searched several times for witch teats (none were found), and swum. They were rescued before they drowned, but the fact that they floated was enough for the Rev. Mr. Samuel Street, the local pastor, who excommunicated them before their trial.

Mrs. Samuel Street and Deacon Hall had appeared at Mrs. Benham's hearing in July of 1692 and, with Goody Parker, "mentioned many peculiar things as grounds for suspicion of witchcraft reflecting upon Goody Winifred Benham, then also present, whereupon the Authority desired and advised Mr. Street and others of Wallingford concerned, to consider of the matter being weighty, and to prepare such evidences as could be come at for the further discovery and conviction of the party suspected if guilty, or clearing if innocent, and the said suspected person being a member of their church, 'twas left with Mr. Street that he and the church should consider what did nor might belong to them, hoping God would direct them on their seeking counsel from Him," etcetera. On that occasion the minister had forborne, but no longer. Yet he had been wary, and for five years he had been collecting evidence against one of the lambs of his flock. This time he would have his pound of flesh, and her life as well.

The Benhams were examined August 31st at "a special County Court by order of the Governor held at New Haven" before the Governor himself, William Jones; the Deputy Governor, Major Moses Mansfield; and Robert Treat, but between the hearing — which bound the Benham women over for trial — and the October trial itself, cooler heads prevailed than those of the ravening Wallingford citizens, and on October 7th in Hartford the jury "Returned upon the bill 'Ignoramus.' That is, 'not proven.'" The Benhams returned to their community, but the possessed children continued to cry out upon them, and in the fall the family packed up and fled into New York jurisdiction.

On November 19th the Salem jurors signed a joint confession of their errors, though they continued to believe that the Devil had been the cause of everything: He had deluded the people, though the delusion was not of the sort that at first they had thought.

On the same day Samuel Sewall spoke with the Rev. John Hale of Beverly about a book that Hale proposed to write about the witchcrafts of 1692. Sewall wrote in his diary, "I fear lest he go to the other extreme." But Hale had no intention of doing that.

Epilogue

As Connecticut had begun the New England witchcrafts, so it ended them with the Benhams' exile, and the Wallingford case was the last ever to be prosecuted in America. There would be only one other in the Western World — an anachronism in 18th century England.

When Philip English's archenemy, the former Sheriff George Corwin, died, English sued for recovery of a debt Corwin owed him, a debt unrelated to Corwin's seizure of English's estate. He warned the Corwin family that he would seize the corpse of the Sheriff until the debt was paid if the family tried to bury him in any cemetery located off their own property. The family was forced to inter Corwin temporarily on the home farm property.

The Nurse family returned to the flock of Rev. Joseph Green in Salem Village during 1699, and the following year Robert Calef published in England his attack on the Mathers and on the witchcraft mania of 1692, *More Wonders of the Invisible World*. In it he included all his letters to Cotton Mather and others, together with very biased accounts of events that had taken place, including Margaret Rule's possession. Many copies of the book were brought into the country. One of these was the center of a final Matherian ritual of exorcism conducted by Increase in Harvard Yard and designed to indicate that there was no Matherly love lost between the ministers and the merchant: Increase Mather burned it.

In the following year, 1701, some of the Mathers' parishioners banded together to publish a rebuttal to Calef's volume, *Some Few Remarks upon a Scandalous Book,* but few paid any attention, preferring the Calef work over yet another painful apologia.

John Hale's book, *A Modest Inquiry into the Nature of Witchcraft,* appeared in 1702. Though it affirmed a belief in witchcraft, it rejected all the traditional proofs of Satanism. Recalling Candy's dolls and the way the judges had manipulated the poppits to hurt the bitch witches, just as though the Court itself were witches, Hale reached the conclusion that it was a person's own belief in witchcraft that hurt him. No one had ever before come closer to the truth.

Though others had hinted at this very thing quite often throughout the history of witchcraft, Hale put it in such plain and clear terms that intelligent people were forced to agree that the system of sympathetic magic operated largely on the psychological level, rather than on the physical or spiritual levels, but that there was such a close tie between the mind and the body that the mind could, indeed, influence the body to a degree, and cause it to manifest physical symptoms that were, in every way, "real," for as long as those who witnessed the symptoms believed in their reality as well. If it was "man's faith about it" that made maleficia possible, Hale reasoned, then "the reason why any suspected person is...concerned is not because they are guilty, but because they are suspected." Hale never said it, and perhaps he never thought it, but exactly the same arguments could have been made against religion in general.

In 1703 Martha Corey's excommunication was revoked, but "six or seven" of the congregation dissented. Attainders of those who had sued — Abigail Faulkner, Sarah Wardwell, and Elizabeth Proctor — were reversed, but not those of people who had not sued that their bills of attainder be reversed.

In 1706 Annie Putnam stood in the Salem Village Church while the Rev. Joseph Green read her confession from the pulpit — but nowhere did she truly confess, for again, what had happened was a delusion of the Devil:

"I desire to be humbled before God for that sad and humbling Providence that befell my father's family in the year about" — she was uncertain of the date — "1692; that I, then being in my childhood, should by such a Providence of God be made an instrument for the accusing of several persons of a grievous crime, whereby their lives were taken away from them, whom now I have just grounds and good reason to believe they were innocent persons. And that it was a great delusion of Satan that deceived me in that sad time, whereby I justly fear I have been instrumental, with others, though ignorantly and unwittingly, to bring upon myself and this land the guilt of innocent blood; though what was said or done by me against any person I can truly and uprightly say before God and man, I did it not out of any anger, malice, or ill-will to any person, for I had no such thing against one of them, but what I did was ignorantly, being deluded of Satan."

On the 25th of May 1709 Philip English and twenty-one others who had been, or whose relatives had been accused, indicted, arrested, or executed, petitioned the General Court to restore their honor and estates. Cotton Mather, in a sermon delivered on November 2nd, supported them.

In May, 1710, the General Court appointed a commission to collect information and evidence in the Philip English petition. One of the documents the commission collected was a deposition submitted by William Goode on September 13th:

"1. My wife, Sarah Goode, was in prison about four months and then executed.

"2. A sucking child died in prison before the mother's execution.

"3. A child," Dorcas Goode, "of four or five years old was in prison seven or eight months, and being chained in the dungeon was so hardly used and terrified that she hath ever since been very chargeable, having little or no reason to govern herself. And I

leave it unto the honorable Court to judge what damage I have sustained by such a destruction of my poor family, and so rest
"Your Honors' humble servant,
William Goode."

In October of 1711 the Commission submitted its report to the General Court, which began to settle with those people whose names were listed. Some of the cases dragged on at great length, and the Burroughs family —engaged in intra-family strife of extreme nature, sued in 1750.

Despite its attempt to be thorough, the Commission missed some names, and at the time of the writing of this book, 1974, attainders still had not been reversed in the cases of Bridget Bishop, Elizabeth Johnson, Susannah Martin, Alice Parker, Ann Pudeator, Wilmot Reed, and Margaret Scott.

As for the bitch witches of Salem Village: Some were married and became respectable matrons; others, according to common report, became women of less than savory repute. As for Annie Putnam: She died young and unmarried in 1716, aged thirty-seven.

In 1719 Thomas Fleet, the son-in-law of Elizabeth Vergoose of Salem Village, published in Boston the book titled *Mother Goose*.

During the smallpox epidemic of 1721 Cotton Mather inoculated his family with cowpox serum and saved his son by doing so. But fate spurned him, and the public rejected him likewise. The citizens of Massachusetts Bay watched his fall through a series of bitter calamities, and it would be a long while before the world of medicine realized how prescient he had been in the matter of inoculation against Satan's scourge and other diseases.

APPENDIX A
THE LINEAGE OF
MAY LAURA PUTNAM TURCO

I.   ? Roger de Puteham, Hertfordshire, c. 1086.
II.

    II. ? Simon de Puteham, Herts, c. 1199.

III. ? Ralph de Pudeham, Stivecle, Buckinghamshire, c. 1200-1249.

    IV. ? William de Puttenham, Bucks, c. 1250.

    V. ? John de Puttenham, Bucks, c. 1279-1294.

    VI. John de Puttenham m. Agnes; Puttenham; Bucks, c. 1306.

VII. Thomas Puttenham m. Helen Spigornell; Bucks, c. 1272-1307;
    *Roger
    James.

    VIII. Roger Puttenham m. Aline, Herts, c. 1322;
    *Roger

    IX. Sir Roger Puttenham m. Margery; Tring, Bucks, c. 1310-79;
    *Henry
    Roger
    Robert.

    X. Henry de Puttenham; Bucks, c. 1380;
    ? William

XI. William Puttenham m. Margaret de Warbleton; Puttenham & Penne;
    b. c. 1380;
    *Henry, b. c. 1402
    ? Robert, living 1406-28

? John, rector of Tewin, Herts (resigned 21 June 1453
? Thomas, vicar of Ambrosden, County Oxford, 1458.

XII. Henry Puttenham m. Elizabeth, widow Goodluck; Puttenham & Penne, b. c. 1402
*William, b. c. 1430.

XIII. William Puttenham m. Anne Hampden; Puttenham, Penne, Sherfield, Warbleton &c., c. 1430-92.
Sir George
Edmund, of Puttenham
*Nicholas, of Penn, b. c. 1460
Frideswide
Elizabeth
Alionore
Brigide
Agnes

XIV. Nicholas Puttenham, Putnam Place, Penn, b. c. 1460
John of Penn
*Henry, b. c. 1480.

XV. Henry Putnam, Penn, b. c. 1480
*Richard, of Eddlesborough & Woughton, b. c. 1500
John, of Slapton & Howbridge
Thomas, of Eddlesborough.

XVI. Richard Putnam m. Joan (2nd wife?), Edlesborough & Woughton, b. c. 1500
*John, of Wingrave
Harry, of Woughton
Joan

XVII. John Putnam m. Margaret, Rowsham, Wingrave, b. c. 1520
*Nicholas, b. c. 1540
Richard, of Wingrave

Thomas, of Towsham
Margaret, of Wingrave.

XVIII. Nicholas Putnam m. Margaret Goodspeed, Wingrave, b. c. 1540
Anne, bapt. 12 Oct. 1578
*John, bapt. 17 Jan. 1579
Elizabeth, bapt. 11 Feb. 1581
Thomas, bapt. 20 Sep. 1584.

XIX. John Putnam m. Priscilla Deacon, Hemel Hempstead, Herts; Aston Abbotts, Bucks, & Salem, Mass., b. c. 1579; d. Salem Village (Danvers), 30 Dec. 1662
Elizabeth, bapt. 20 Dec. 1612
Thomas, bapt. 7 Mar. 1615; d. Salem Village, 5 May 1686
*Nathaniel, bapt. 11 Oct. 1619; d. Salem Village, 23 Jul. 1700.
Sara, bapt. 28 Jul. 1624
John, bapt. 27 May 1627; d. Salem Village, 7 Apr. 1710.

XX. Nathaniel Putnam m. Eliz. Hutchinson, b. Aston Abbots, Bucks, c 1619; d. Salem Village, 23 Jul. 1700
Samuel, 1652
Nathaniel, 1655
*John, b. Salem Village, 26 Mar. 1657
Joseph, b. 1659
Elizabeth, b. 1662
Benjamin, b. 1664
Mary, b. 1668

XXI. Constable "Carolina John" Putnam m. Hannah Cutler, b. Salem Village, 26 Mar. 1657; d. Sep. 1722
Carolina John was Constable of Salem Village at the time of the Witchhunt of 1692. During the hunt he was stricken by smallpox, as was his daughter, Sarah, born on 5 March 1692, who died of the disease six weeks later. Sarah Putnam's birthdate in the Parish records is apparently given as 1695, but this is impossible:

According to Hannah Putnam's testimony in the trial of John Willard (see Woodward in the bibliography below, p. 275), "…this deponent's child Sarah 6 weeks old" died of Willard's curse. This entry seems to have escaped the notice of Eben Putnam in his genealogy (see bibliography below, p. 56), which repeats the error and is otherwise confusing on this issue.

Hannah, 1679
Elizabeth, 1680
Abigail, 1682
Samuel, 1684
*Josiah, 29 Oct. 1680
Joseph, 1687
Mary, 1688
Susanna, 1690
Joshua,
David (or Daniel?)
Rebecca, 1691
John, 1691
Sarah, b. Salem Village, 5 Mar. 1692; d. six weeks later
Amos, 1697 (ancestor of the Putnams of Houlton, Maine, including Thomas Putnam Packard, first cousin of Jean Cate Houdlette Turco, wife of Lewis Putnam Turco, son of Luigi Turco and May Laura Putnam Turco)
Priscilla 1699.

XXII. Josiah Putnam m. Ruth Hutchinson, b. Salem Village, 29 Oct. 1686; d. Danvers, 5 Jul. 1766

Asa, 1714
Enos, 1716-1780
*Josiah, b. 3 Mar. 1719
Peter, 1724
Elizabeth, 1725
Elisha, 1728
Ruth, 1732.

XXIII. Josiah Putnam, Jr., m. Lydia Wheeler, b. Brookfield, 14 Aug. 1721, d. 17--; b. Salem Village, 3 Mar. 1719, d. Warren, MA, 4 Feb. 1795

*Asa, b. 10 Aug.. 1743; d. 7 Sep. 1795

Lydia
Thankful, 1747
Josiah III, 1750
Ruth, 1752
Mary, 1759.

XXIV. Asa Putnam m. Anna Collins, b. Danvers, Aug. 1743, d. 7 Sep. 1795
Perley, 1767
Lewis, b. 22 Aug 1769 (namesake of the Author)
Serephina, 1722
Ebenezer, 1729
Josiah, 1781
Alfred, 1784
*Sewall, b. 23 Sep. 1786
Sylvia, 1789.

XXV. Sewall Putnam m. Rebecca Shepard, b. 4 Nov. 1791, d. 25 Feb. 1838; b. Brattleboro, VT, 23 Sep. 1786, d. So. Trenton NY, 2 Mar (?)
Albert, 1809
Sarah Louisa, 1811
*Harvey, b. 25 Nov. 1812; d. 1863
Amanda, 1814
Savina, 1816
Anna, 1820
Mary Elizabeth, 1822
Charles Sewall, 1824
Hester, 1827
George Washington, 1831
Alfred, 1833.

XXVI. Harvey Putnam M. Surinda Dewey, b. Deerfield MA, 24 Mar. 1833; d. Eureka KS, 20 Nov 1899; b. 25 Nov. 1812; d. Princeton IL, 14 Jan. 1863
Lillian, 1855
*William Herbert, b. 18 Sep. 1857; d. Superior WI 22 Oct. 1949

Savina, 1863.

XXVII. William Herbert Putnam m. Laura Christina Larsen (second wife), b. Manistee MI, 5 Dec. 1874; d. Superior WI, 13 Jan. 1952; b. Princeton IL, 18 Sep 1857; d. Superior WI 22 Oct. 1949
Myrtle Cara, 1896
Harvey Herbert, 1897
*May Laura, b. Wayne NB, 1 May 1899; d. Bristol CT 25 Nov. 1985
Arnold Louis, 1900
Floyd Arthur, 1902
Lillian Mabel, 1905
Edwin Irving, 1906
Russell Sewall, 1908
Elmer Theodore, 1910.

\XXVIII. May Laura Putnam m. Luigi (n) Turco, b. Riesi, Sicily, 28 May 1890; d. Meriden CT, 18 Sep. 1968; b. Wayne NB, 1 May 1899; d. Bristol CT 25 Nov. 1985
*Lewis Putnam, b. 2 May 1934
Gene Laurent, b. 25 Feb. 1939.

XXIX. Lewis Putnam Turco m. Jean Cate Houdlette, b. Meriden CT 29 May 1934; b. Buffalo NY 2 May 1934
Melora Ann, b. Meriden CT 21 Jul. 1960
Christopher Cameron, b. Oswego NY 23 Jan. 1973.

BIBLIOGRAPHY

Adams, Charles Francis, *Three Episodes of Massachusetts History,* in two volumes, Boston: Houghton, Mifflin, 1892.

Allen, Rowland H., *The New England Tragedies in Prose*, Boston: Nichols & Noyes, 1869.

Anonymous, *A Universal Biographical Dictionary*, Hartford: Silas Andrus, 1833.

Baring-Gould, William S. & Ceil, *The Annotated Mother Goose*, New York: Clarkson N. Potter, 1962.

Besse, Joseph, *A Collection of the Sufferings of the People Called Quakers*, in two volumes, London: Luke Hinde, 1753.

Bois, John, *Translating for King James*, ed. Ward Allen, Nashville: Vanderbilt University Press, 1969.

Bolté, Mary, and Eastman, Mary, *Haunted New England*, New York: Weathervane, 1972.

Bovet, Richard, *Pandaemonium*, East Ardsley: E. P. Publishing, 1975.

Boyer, Paul, and Nissenbaum, Stephen, *Salem Possessed*, Cambridge: Harvard University Press, 1974.

———, *Salem-Village Witchcraft,* Boston: Northeastern University Press, 1972.

Bradford, William, *Bradford's History "Of Plymouth Plantation," from the Original Manuscript,* etc., Boston: Wright & Potter, 1898.

Bridenbaugh, Carl, *Vexed and Troubled Englishmen, 1590-1642*, New York: Oxford University Press, 1968.

Brooks, C. Harry, *The Practice of Autosuggestion*, New York: Dodd, Mead, 1922.

Burr, George Lincoln, *Narratives of the Witchcraft Cases*, New York: Barnes & Noble, 1975.

Burt, Henry M., *The First Century of the History of Springfield: The Official Records from 1636 to 1736*, in two volumes, Springfield, 1898.

Burton, Robert, *The Anatomy of Melancholy*, ed. Floyd Dell and Paul Jordan-Smith, New York: Tudor, 1927.

Calef, Robert, *More Wonders of the Invisible World*, Bainbridge: York Mailprint, 1972.

Carlson, Laurie Winn, *A Fever in Salem*, Chicago: Ivan R. Dee, 1999.

Carrell, Jennifer Lee, *The Speckled Monster, A Historical Tale of Battling Smallpox*, New York: Dutton, 2003.

Christian, Paul, *The History and Practice of Magic*, tr. James Kirkup & Julian Shaw, in two volumes, New York: Citadel, 1963.

Crowley, Aleister, *Magick in Theory and Practice*, Secaucus: Castle, 1991.

Culpepper, Nicholas, *The English Physician Enlarged...English Herbs*, London: Thomas Kelly, 1850.

Dee, John, *A True and Faithful Relation of What Passed for Many Years Between Dr. John Dee and Some Spirits*, etc., edited, with a Preface, by Meric. Casaubon, London: D. Maxwell for T. Garthwait, 1659.

Demos, John Putnam, *Entertaining Satan: Witchcraft and the Culture of Early New England*, New York: Oxford University Press, 1982.

De Lys, Claudia, *A Treasury of American Superstitions*, New York: Philosophical Library, 1948.

Devore, Nicholas, *Encyclopedia of Astrology*, New York: Philosophical Library, 1947.

Dow, George Francis, *Every Day Life in the Massachusetts Bay Colony*, Boston: Society for the Preservation of New England Antiquities, 1935.

Drake, Samuel G., *Annals of Witchcraft in New England*, etc., New York: Burt Franklin, 1977.

———, *The Witchcraft Delusion in New England*, in three volumes, New York: Burt Franklin, 1970.

Duffy, John, *Epidemics in Colonial America*, Baton Rouge: Louisiana State University Press, 1979.

Erikson, Kai T., *Wayward Puritans*, New York: John Wiley, 1966.

Essex Institute Historical Collections, Vol. IX: *Salem Town Records, 1630-1690*, Salem: Essex Institute, 1869.

Evans-Wentz, W. Y., *The Fairy-Faith in Celtic Countries*, New York: University Books, 1966.

Federal Writers' Project, *Massachusetts*, Boston: Houghton, Mifflin, 1937.

Federmann, Richard, *The Royal Art of Alchemy*, tr. Richard H. Weber, Philadelphia: Chilton, 1969.

Felt, Joseph B., *The Annals of Salem from Its First Settlement*, Salem: Ives, 1827.

Fiery, Ann, *The Book of Divination*, San Francisco: Chronicle Books, 1999.

Frazer, James George, *Folk-Lore in the Old Testament: Studies in Comparative Religion, Legend and Law*, Abridged Edition, New York: Tudor, 1923.

———, *The Golden Bough: A Study in Magic and Religion*, Abridged Edition, New York: Macmillan, 1940.

Geneva Bible, The, A Facsimile of the 1560 Edition, Madison: University of Wisconsin Press, 1969.

Gillespie, C. Bancroft, & Curtis, George Munson, *A Century of Meriden, Connecticut*, Meriden: City of Meriden, 1906.

Gilpin, Richard, *Daemonologia Sacra*, Edinburgh: Thomas & John Turnbull, 1800.

Givry, Grillot de, *Witchcraft, Magic, and Alchemy*, tr. J. Courtenay Locke, New York: Bonanza, n.d.

Goodspeed, Edgar J., tr., *The Apocrypha*, New York: Random House, 1959.

Greven, Philip J., Jr., *Four Generations: Population, Land, and Family in Colonial Andover, Massachusetts*, Ithaca: Cornell University Press, 1970.

Guazzo, Francesco Maria, *Compendium Maleficarum*, Facsimile reprint of the 1929 edition tr. E. A. Ashwin, edited with notes by Montague Summers. New York: Barnes & Noble, 1970.

Hale, John, *A Modest Inquiry into the Nature of Witchcraft,* Bainbridge: York Mail-Print, 1973.

Hansen, Chadwick, *Witchcraft at Salem*, New York: Mentor, 1969.

Harrison, G. B., ed., *The Trial of the Lancaster Witches A. D. MDCXII*, London: Peter Davies, 1929.

Hayward, John, *The New England Gazetteer,* Concord: Israel Boyd & William White, 1839.

Hoffer, Peter C. & Hull, N. E. H., *Murdering Mothers: Infanticide in England and New England 1558-1803*, New York: New York University Press, 1984.

Hutchinson, Thomas, *The History of Massachusetts*, etc., Vol. I, Salem: Thomas C. Cushing, 1795.

———, *the History of the Colony and Province of Massachusetts Bay*, ed. Lawrence Shaw Mayo, in three volumes, Cambridge: Harvard University Press, 1936.

Johnson, Edward, *Wonder-Working Providence*, ed. J. Franklin Jameson, New York: 1910.

Kimball, Henrietta D., *Witchcraft Illustrated*, etc., Boston: George A. Kimball, 1892.

Kittredge, George Lyman, *Witchcraft in Old and New England*, Cambridge: Harvard University Press, 1929.

Kors, Alan C. and Peters, Edward, eds., *Witchcraft in Europe 1100-1700*, Philadelphia: University of Pennsylvania Press, 1984.

Kunze, Michael, *Highroad to the Stake, A Tale of Witchcraft*, Chicago: University of Chicago, 1987

Lawson, Deodat, *A Further Account of the Trials of the New England Witches, with the Observations of a Person Who Was upon the Place Several Days When the Suspected Witches Were First Taken into Examination*: See Mather, Cotton, *Wonders*, below.

Leighton, Martha E., *The Lineage of Reuben Leighton*, Ithaca: n. p., c. 1950.

Levin, David, *Cotton Mather, The Young Life of the Lord's Remembrancer, 1663-1703*, Cambridge: Harvard University Press, 1978.

Lieber, Francis, ed., *Encyclopedia Americana*, second edition, in fourteen volumes, Philadelphia: Sears, Roebuck, 1836.

Lilly, William, *An Introduction to Astrology*, London: Bell & Daldy, 1870.

Marks, Joseph E. III, ed., *The Mathers on Dancing*, Brooklyn: Dance Horizons, 1975.

Mather, Cotton, *The Diary*, ed. Worthington Chauncey Ford, in two volumes, New York: Frederick Ungar, 1957.

——, *Magnalia Christi Americana*, ed. Thomas Robbins, in two volumes, Hartford: Silas Andrus, 1852.

——, *On Witchcraft*, New York: Bell, 1974.

——, *Selected Letters*, ed. Kenneth Silverman, Baton Rouge: Louisiana State University Press, 1971.

——, *The Wonders of the Invisible World*, etc., *To Which Is Added, A Further Account of the Tryals of the New England Witches* by Deodat Lawson [see Lawson, above], and

Mather, Increase, *Cases of Conscience Concerning Witchcrafts and Evil Spirits Personating Men*, London: John Russell Smith, 1862.

——, *Remarkable Providences Illustrative of the Earlier Days of American Colonisation*, London: Reeves and Turner, 1890.

McIntyre, Ruth A., *William Pynchon: Merchant and Colonizer 1590-1662*, Springfield: Connecicut Valley Historical Museum, 1961.

Melton, J. Gordon, *Encyclopedia of Occultism & Parapsychology*, Detroit: Gale, 1996.

Messadie, Gerald, *A History of the Devil*, New York: Kodansha International, 1996.

Michelet, Jules, *Satanism and Witchcraft: A Study in Medieval Superstition,* tr. A. R. Allinson, New York: Citadel, 1939.

Miller, Perry, *The New England Mind from Colony to Province,* Boston: Beacon, 1961.

———, *The New England Mind: The Seventeenth Century*, Boston: Beacon, 1961.

Monter, E. W., *Witchcraft in France and Switzerland*, Ithaca: Cornell University Press, 1976.

Mudge, Z. A., *Witch Hill: A History of Salem Witchcraft*, New York: Carlton & Langham, 1870.

Nevins, Winfield S., *Witchcraft in Salem Village*, New York: Burt Franklin, 1971.

Oesterreich, Traugott K., *Possession and Exorcism,* New York: Causeway, 1974.

[Perley, M. V. B.], *A Short History of the Salem Village Witchcraft Trials*, Salem: The Author, 1911.

Perley, Sidney, *The History of Salem, Massachusetts*, in three volumes, Salem: The Author, 1924.

Peters, Edward, *The Magician, the Witch, and the Law*, Philadelphia: University of Pennsylvania Press, 1978.

Peters, Samuel, *General History of Connecticut From Its First Settlement Under George Fenwick, Esq. To Its Latest Period of Amity with Great Britain; Including A Description of the Country, and Many Curious and Interesting Anecdotes* in *Papers and Proceedings of the Connecticut Valley Historical Society, 1876-1881,* Vol. I, Springfield: Connecticut Valley Historical Society, 1881.

Powers, Edwin, *Crime and Punishment in Early Massachusetts, 1620-1692*, Boston: Beacon, 1966.

Priest, Josiah, *The Anti-Universalist, or, History of the Fallen Angels of the Scriptures*, Albany: J. Munsell, 1839.

Proctor, John W., *Centennial Celebration, At Danvers, Massachusetts, June 16, 1852*, Boston: Dutton & Wentworth, 1852.

Puttenham, George, *The Arte of English Poesie*, ed. Hilton Landry, Kent: Kent State University Press, 1970.

Putnam, Eben, *A History of the Putnam Family in England and America,* Salem: Salem Press, 1891.

———, *The Putnam Lineage,* Salem: Salem Press, 1907.

Putnam, Harold, *The Putnams of Salem Village,* Vero Beach: Penobscot Press, 2001.

Quincy, John, *Pharmacopoeia Officinalis Extemporanea. Or, A Complete English Dispensatory, in Four Parts,* "Twelfth edition, enlarged and corrected," London: Thomas Longman, 1742.

Robbins, Rossell Hope, *Encyclopedia of Witchcraft and Demonology,* New York: Crown, 1959.

Robertson, William, *The History of the Discovery and Settlement of America,* New York: Harper & Bros., 1839.

Robotti, Frances Diane, *Chronicles of Old Salem,* New York: Bonanza, 1948.

Rohmer, Sax, *The Romance of Sorcery,* New York: Causeway, 1973.

Rollins, Hyder Edward, *The Pack of Autolycus, or Strange and Terrible News of Ghosts, Apparitions...as told in Broadside Ballads of the Years 1624-1693,* Port Washington: Kennikat, 1969.

Russell, Jeffrey B., *A History of Witchcraft,* New York: Thames & Hudson, 1983.

Savage, James, *A Genealogical Dictionary of the First Settlers of New England,* reprint edition in four volumes, Baltimore: Genealogical Publishing, 1972.

Schmidt, Philip, *Superstition and Magic,* Westminster: Newman, 1963.

Scot, Reginald, *The Discoverie of Witchcraft,* Carbondale: Southern Illinois University Press, 1964.

Scott, Sir Walter, *Letters on Demonology and Witchcraft,* Ware: Wordsworth Editions, 2001.

Sebald, Hans, *Witch-Children from Salem Witch-Hunts to Modern Courtrooms,* Amherst: Prometheus Books, 1995.

Sewall, Samuel, *The Diary,* ed. M. Halsey Thomas, in two volumes, New York: Farrar, Straus & Giroux, 1973.

Sibly, Ebenezer, *A New and Complete Illustration of the Occult Sciences,* etc. (commonly known as *Sibly's Astrology*), in two volumes, London: C. Stalker, 1790.

Smith, Joseph H., ed., *Colonial Justice in Western Massachusetts (1639-1792): The Pynchon Court Record,* Cambridge: Harvard University Press, 1961.

Starkey, Marion L. *The Devil in Massachusetts: A Modern Inquiry into the Salem Witch Trials*, New York: Knopf, 1950.

——, *The Tall Man from Boston*, New York: Crown, 1975.

Summers, Montague, *The Geography of Witchcraft* ; New York: University Books, 1965.

——, *The History of Witchcraft and Demonology*, New York: University Books, 1956.

Taylor, John M., *The Witchcraft Delusion*, New York: Gramercy, 1995.

Thomas, Keith, *Religion and the Decline of Magic*, New York: Scribner, 1971.

Thompson, C. J. S., *The Mystery and Romance of Astrology*, New York: Causeway, 1975.

Turco, Lewis, compiler, *Sources of Witchcraft Used in Research for The Devil's Disease [Satan's Scourge]*, Oswego: n. p., 1976, a bound volume of various items including 1) Anonymous author, *Relation of a Memorable Piece of Witchcraft, at Welton, Near Daventry*, etc., Northampton: Taylor and Son, 1867; 2) "Witchcraft in Springfield: Hugh and Mary Parsons," from Burt (see above), *The First Century of Springfield*; 3) "William Pynchon" from McIntyre (see above), *William Pynchon: Merchant and Colonizer*; 4) "Martha and Rebeccah Moxon," from *Peters's History of Connecticut* (see above); 5) "William Pynchon" from Smith (see above), *Colonial Justice*, etc.; 6) The Springfield Witchcrafts," a manuscript article by Lewis Putnam Turco; 7) "Vergoose, Isaac," from Savage (see above), *Genealogical Dictionary*; 8) "Mary Oliver," and "Dorothy Talby," from Winthrop (see below), *Journal*; 9) "The Metamorphosis of Tituba, or Why American Intellectuals Can't Tell an Indian Witch from a Negro" by Chadwick Hansen, annotated in ink by Turco, from *The New England Quarterly* for March, 1974; "Susannah Martin," from Leighton (see above), *The Lineage of Reuben Leighton*; 10) "The Salem Witchcraft" from Hutchinson (see above), *History of the Colony and Province...*; 11) "The Wallingford Witchcraft" from Gillespie and Curtis (see above), *A Century of Meriden*; 12) "The Lineage of May Laura Putnam" derived from Putnam, Eben (see above), *The Putnam Lineage*; 13) autograph letter signed by John Greenleaf Whittier datelined "Oak Knoll [the Salem Village Putnam homestead], 11th Mo 22 1879"; 14) "May Laura Putnam's Maternal Grandparents," an official transcript; 15) "Essex Institute Itinerary Points of Historical Interest in Salem," from Nov. 26, 1913; 16) Publishing prospectuses for Sidney Perley (see above), *History of Salem*, Vol I, for Vol. II, and for the set; 17) "Voluntary Commendations" for the Perley *History*, and 18) "The Ancient Ways," an old map of Salem and environs.

Upham, Caroline E., *Salem Witchcraft in Outline*, Salem: Salem Press, 1891.

Upham, Charles W., *Lectures on Witchcraft*, Boston: Carter, Hendee, & Babcock, 1831.

——, *Salem Witchcraft*, in two volumes, New York: Frederick Ungar, 1969.

Waite, Arthur Edward, *The Book of Ceremonial Magic*, New York: Bell, 1969.

——, *Complete Manual of Occult Divination*, in two volumes, New Hyde Park: University Books, 1972.

Walker, D. P. *Unclean Spirits*, Philadelphia: University of Pennsylvania Press, 1981.

Wallis, Charles L., *Stories on Stone: A Book of American Epitaphs*, New York: Oxford, 1954.

Webber. C. H., and Nevins, W. S., *Old Naumkeag: An Historical Sketch of the City of Salem and the Towns of Marblehead, Peabody, Beverly, Danvers, Wenham, Manchester, Topsfield, and Middleton*, Salem: A. A. Smith, 1879.

Wedeck, Harry E., *Dictionary of the Occult*, New York: Philosophical Library, 1956.

——, *A Treasury of Witchcraft*, New York: Philosophical Library, 1961.

Weisman, Richard, *Witchcraft, Magic, and Religion in 17th-Century Massachusetts*, Amherst: University of Massachusetts Press, 1984.

Wendover, Sanford H. et al., *150 Years of Meriden [CT]*, Meriden: City of Meriden, 1956.

White, Beatrice, *Cast of Ravens, the Strange Case of Sir Thomas Overbury*, London: John Murray, 1965.

White, Henry, *The Early History of New England*, Concord: I. S. Boyd, 1842.

Williams, Charles, *Witchcraft*, New York: New American Library, 1959.

Willis, Charles Murray, *Shakespeare and George Puttenham's The Arte of English Poesy*, St. Leonards-on-Sea: Upso, Ltd., 2003

Wilson, Colin, *The Occult*, New York: Random House, 1971.

Winthrop, John, *Original Narratives of Early American History, 1630-49*, ed. J. Franklin Jameson: New York, 1908.

Winwar, Frances, *Puritan City*, New York: National Travel Club, 1938.

Woods, William, ed. *A Casebook of Witchcraft*, New York: G. P. Putnam's Sons, 1974.

[Woodward, W. Elliot, ed.], *Records of the Salem Witchcraft*, two volumes in one, New York: Lennox Hill, 1972.

Woolley, Benjamin, *The Queen's Conjuror, The Science and Magic of Dr. John Dee, Adviser to Queen Elizabeth I*, New York: Henry Holt, 2001.

Worsencroft, Mona Esty, *An Echo from Salem*, Stafford: American History Press, 1981.

Yates, Frances A., *The Occult Philosophy in the Elizabethan Age*, London: Routledge and Keegan Paul, 1979.

Zolar, *The History of Astrology, The Complete Illustrated Story of Man's First Science*, etc., New York: Arco, 1972.

INDEX

-A-

Mary Abbey, 449, 456
Thomas Abbey, 358
George Abbot, Archbishop of Canterbury, 103
Arthur Abbott, 681
Benjamin Abbott, 467, 469
Nehemiah Abbott, 549, 563, 575, 597, 607
Abigail, 132, 159
Abigail Atwater, 647
Abingdon, 78
Samuel Abbey, 449, 456, 469, 598
Samuel Aborne, Sr., 319
Absolute Predestination, 5, 19, 85
Academy of the Lincei, 122
Acadia, 139, 315. *See* Nova Scotia
Achurch-cum-Thorpe Waterfield, 40, 151
Adam's decline from Grace, 5
Isaac Addington, 531
Addled Parliament, 100
Adept, 11, 67, 82
Adjutant von Buchheim, 60
The Advancement of Learning, 79
Advertisement to the Jurymen of England, 265
Thomas Ady, 273, 655
afflicted person, 507
Agamenticus, 209, 214
Agawam River, 165
Age of Magic, 434
Age of Reason, 651
Age of Science, 434
Age of Witchcraft, 651
Agnes Browne, 97
Agrippa, 21
air pump, 282, 287
Albany, 123
alchemist, 3, 75, 201
alchemy, 12, 26, 29, 67, 68, 72, 89, 227, 456

Aldeburgh, Kent, 216
Aldeburgh, Suffolk, 213
John Alden, 607, 609, 614, 615, 673, 680, 690, 692
alembic, 6
Alexander, 23
William Alford, 165
Algonquin Grammar, The, 220
Algonquin Indians, 305
Elizabeth Allen, 345; *see* Elizabeth Allen Endicott
Hannah Dummer Allen, 323
James Allen, 321, 323, 345, 347, 366, 699
John Allen, 232, 341, 465
Mary Allen, 598
Rachel Chandler Allen, 607
Andrew Allen, 638
William Allen, 192, 495, 496
Isaac Allerton, 138
All Hallows Eve, 44
almanac, 50, 177, 206, ,207, 236, 291, 316, 318, 340, 389, 391, 400, 430, 456
Alschain, 3
Altair, 3
Ambrose, 139
America, 7, 31
American Pilgrims, *See* Pilgrims
Amesbury, 323-326, 330, 331, 333, 341, 348, 437, 566
Amsterdam, 83, 87
amulet, 260
Anabaptist heresy, 203, 219, 320, 458
The Anatomy of Melancholy, 118, 258, 455
Andover, 186, 284, 285, 301, 314, 318-320, 626, 357, 398, 461, 463, 465, 467, 469, 470, 480, 482, 501, 539, 581, 595, 598, 604, 607, 608, 613, 620-624, 639, 645, 663, 664, 666, 674, 678, 681, 682, 687, 698
Launcelot Andrewes, 78
Daniel Andrews, 375, 376, 431, 502, 594, 702
James Andrews, 593
John Andrews, 275
Thomas Andrews, 275, 413
Sir Edmund Andros, 430, 445, 449, 549
angel, iv, 54, 84

Anglican Church. *See* Church of England
Princess Anne of Denmark, 42
anorexia, 687
anti-Catholic regulations, 227
anti-Darrellites, 64
Antidote against Atheism, 265, 310
Antigua, 185
Antinomianism, 165, 167, 202
Samuel Appleton, 356, 531, 681
Apocalypse of John, 84
Apocrypha, 91, 134
apocryphal, 84
Apostles, v
The Apprehension and Confession of Three Notorious Witches, 39
April Fool's Day, 425, 528
Aquarian, 302
Aquiday, 188
Aquilla, 3
Arbella, 139
Lady Arbella, 154
Arcetri, 176
Archbishopric of Canterbury, 18
archeology, 242, 263
Samuel Archer, 359
Arctic, 31
Dr. Arder, 257
Anne Putnam Argett, 1, 28, 59, 65, 75, 93,
William Argett, 75, 93
Joan Argoll, 214
Aries, 278, 285
Aristotelianism, 4, 39
The Arte of English Poesy, 40
Articles of Confederation, 202
Elias Ashmole, 206, 221, 242, 245, 263, 310, 320, 340, 365, 391, 408, 598,
Assistants, 138, 140, 207, 220, 261, 272, 274, 283, 383, 391
Jacob Astley, 210
Aston Abbotts, 2, 31, 59, 65, 74, 75, 91, 93, 97, 101, 103, 104, 107, 108, 111, 121, 124, 129, 135, 146, 147, 151, 160, 166, 176, 178, 191
astrology, i, ii, 3, 38, 50, 69, 74, 82, 107, 118, 126, 130, 148, 150, 177, 194, 200, 245, 257, 260, 291, 305, 317, 320, 329, 358, 365, 380, 381,

390, 391
astronomer, 38, 50, 61, 64, 74, 107, 110, 122, 148, 176, 628, 679
Astronomia Nova, 89
Astronomiae Instaurate Progymnosmata, 68
Astronomiae Pars Optica, 77
astronomy, 3, 5, 77, 82, 102, 177, 380
Mother Atkins of Pinner, 48
John Atkinson, 436
Sarah Atkinson, 347
Atlantic Ocean, 7, 109, 111
Attorney General, 366, 370, 690
Mrs. Atwater, 267
John Aubrey, 236
Augsberg, 94, 107
Ann Austin, 277
Avebury, 236, 242
Aylesbury, 1, 2

-B-

Anthony Babington, 32
Sir Edmund Bacon, 298
Sir Francis Bacon, 79, 101, 110, 127
Mary Baguley, 358
Rev. James Bailey, 326, 343, 372, 374, 375, 377, 378, 388, 409, 476
Joseph Bailey, 603
Mary Carr Bailey, 344, 367, 617
Nicholas Bailey, 273
Thomas Bailey, 597
Ebenezer Baker, 666
Mary Osgood Baker, 617, 625, 666, 683, 689
Benjamin Balch, Jr., 418
Benjamin Balch, Sr., 418, 462
Elizabeth Balch, 418, 419
John Balch, 130, 157, 187
John Ballard, 604, 682
Rebecka Ballard, 604, 643
Richard Bancroft, 63, 77
Banqueting House, 237
Baptist. *See* Anabaptist heresy

Barbados, 307, 315, 382, 391, 392, 422, 446, 466, 483, 635
Mary Barber, 97
William Barber, 220
Bard, 102
Barebone Parliament, 263
Abigail Barker, 664, 683, 689
William Barker, 450, 662-664
Thomas Barnard, 604, 681, 682
Jacob Barney, 243, 273, 280, 282
Barnstable, 100
Thomas Barrett, 685
Dr. Philip Barrow, 41
Henry Barrowe, 49
Henry Bartholomew, 257, 304, 338
barter system, 186
Samuel Bartlett, 350, 374
Harry Bartholomew, 318
Mary Bartlett, 350
John Bartoll, 220
J. Barton, 619
Samuel Barton, 505
Basel, 68
Mary Bassett, 256, 553, 600
Stephen Batchellor, 162
Goodwife Batchelor, 273
Jonathan Batchelor, 459
Bath, England, 389
King Stephen Bathory, 29, 31
Edmund Batter, 243, 320, 338, 378
William Batter, 629
Richard Baxter, 477, 607
The Bay Psalm Book, 185
Joseph Beacon, 433, 434
beadle, 141, 175
Samuel Beadle, 406, 414
Thomas Beadle, 577, 665
Beadle's Inn, 586, 598, 599, 633
Simon Beaumont, 248
Bedford, 217
Bedfordshire, 1

Beelzebub, 54
Richard Beers, 354
Orlando Begley, 566
Richard Bellingham, 136, 152, 184, 191, 271, 274, 277, 290, 293, 360
bell-ringer, 141
Belvoir Castle, 106
John Benham, 467
Joseph Benham, 467, 469, 474, 647, 702
Winifred Benham, Sr., 467, 647, 648, 671, 686, 702, 703
Winifred Benham, Jr., 702
Mr. Bent of Abbey, 326
Berkshire, 77
Bermudas, 91, 100, 104, 185
Richard Bernard, 130, 488, 607, 683
John Best, Jr., 670
John Best, Sr., 670
Bethlem, 22
Beverly, 277, 309, 312, 319, 322, 340, 348, 352, 354, 357, 366, 370, 372, 375, 394, 395, 405, 406, 418, 422, 427, 448, 452, 455, 462, 477, 482, 518, 566, 572, 598, 600, 668, 675, 677, 687, 704
John Bibber, 486, 573
Sarah Bibber, 486, 496, 505, 536, 546, 555, 572, 573, 581, 582, 619, 622, 627, 630, 631, 634
Bible, 4, 75, 78, 79, 82-84, 86, 89, 91, 92, 99, 162, 185, 297, 302, 305, 323, 400, 410, 479, 549
bibliomancy, 479, 700
bicameral legislature, 207
Stephen Bickford, 528
Arthur Bill, 97
Billerica, 421, 461, 463, 597-599, 607
Bilson Boy, 109, 117; *see* William Perry
Bishop of Lichfield, 103
Bishop of London, 27, 60
Bishop of Norwich, 8
Bishop of Salisbury, 78
Bishop of Winchester, 16
Bridget Bishop, 384, 390, 411, 412, 427, 435, 450, 456, 539, 541, 542, 594, 599, 618, 619, 621, 622, 626, 627,646 ,652 ,708. *See* Bridget Oliver, 334, 365, 367, 371, 372, 379 *and* Bridget Wasselby, 278, 302, 303, 315, 316

George Bishop, 294
Hannah Bishop, 266
John Bishop, 454
Sarah Bishop, 549, 594, 617
Edward Bishop, Jr., 266, 290, 319, 345, 379, 411, 418, 428, 379, 480, 548, 549, 565, 594, 617
Edward Bishop, Sr., 183, 211
Edward Bishop III, 678
Thomas Bishop, 249
bitch witch, 618, 629, 632, 663, 665, 684
Mary Black, 549, 564, 565, 594, 692
Black Book, 485, 664
Black Communion, 663
black magic, iv
Black Man, 45, 265, 450, 463, 510, 519, 521, 525, 559, 568, 572, 586, 612, 613, 623, 627, 635, 654, 664, 666, 667, 688, 695
Black Paternoster, 44
Black Tom Tyrant, 184. *See* Thomas Wentworth
black witch, iv
black woman, 554
Blackfriars, 312
Blackpoint, 460
Henry Blaisdell, 284, 330, 331
blasphemy, iv, 256
Blessing of the Bay, 145
Block Island, 163
Blocula, 329
John Bly, Sr., 422
John Bois, 78, 83, 84 91
Joseph Bois, 186
John Booker, 305, 320, 365
Bloody Brook, 355
Board of Selectmen, 141
Jane Bocking, 297
Anne Bodenham, 123, 133, 260, 264
Jean Bodin, 8
Bodleian Tower, 390
Blanche Bodortha, 230, 244
Rice Bodortha, 230, 244
Body of Liberties of Massachusetts Bay, 188-189, 195

Bohemia, 51, 230, 244, 305
Book of Canons, 167, 169
Book of Common Prayer, 3, 73, 143, 151
Book of Discipline, 256
The Book of St. Dunstan, 30
A Book of the Witches Lately Condemned and Executed at Bedford, 98
Elizabeth Booth, 478, 597, 526, 630, 676
James Booth, 355
Boston, 120, 126, 143, 146, 152, 153, 156, 162, 165-168, 170, 172, 183, 192, 193, 195, 199, 201, 206, 208, 211, 217, 221, 223, 226, 229, 231, 232, 234, 242, 255-257, 261, 262, 266, 272, 274, 275, 277, 281, 283, 286, 291, 292, 294, 301, 306-308, 312-314, 321, 339, 345-347, 350-352, 355, 359, 361, 362, 366, 371, 373, 376, 388, 391-393, 401-403, 405, 409, 410, 414, 416, 418, 423, 430, 432-434, 438, 440, 441, 447-449, 454, 461-464, 467, 474, 482, 491, 524, 531, 538-540, 506, 567, 573, 576-580, 582, 594-596, 600, 604, 606, 607, 617, 626, 628, 629, 632, 637, 646, 651, 652, 655, 659, 674, 678-681, 686, 687, 690-694, 699
Boston Bay, 120, 126
Boston Church, 162, 191
Boston churches, 699
Boston Ephemeris, 400
Boston Harbor, 152, 208, 232, 313
Boston North Church, 302
Boston prison, 229, 306, 497, 572, 597, 600, 603, 616, 629, 673, 685
Boston Townhouse, 595
Earl of Bothwell, 46
Edward Bottome, 97
Elizabeth Bottome, 93, 97, 100
George Bottome, 93
Richard Bottome, 100
Margaret Bourdon, 333
Mrs. Nehemiah Bourne, 217, 223
Richard Bovet, 416, 607
Edmund Bowen, 265
Mary Bowen, 220
Thomas Bowen, 220
William Bowen, 273
Boxford, 413, 433, 660
Boxworth, 78

Boy. *See* Boy Indian.
The Boy of Bilson, or A True Discovery of the Late Notorious Impostures of Certain Romish Priests in Their Pretended Exorcism or Expulsion of the Devil Out of a Young Boy, Named William Perry, 109, 121
boy of Burton, 74
Richard Boyle, Earl of Cork, 194
Robert Boyle, 194, 207, 268, 282, 287, 291, 294, 305, 310, 373, 456
Boyle's Law, 291
Capt. Brackett, 592
Mary Bradbury, 342, 376, 377, 391, 640, 645, 646, 648, 668
Thomas Bradbury, 377, 648
William Bradbury, 342
Dorothy Bradford, 114
William Bradford, 114, 115, 145, 153, 155, 680
Anne Bradstreet, 376
Dudley Bradstreet, 663, 683
John Bradstreet, 238, 262, 662, 663
Capt. Simon Bradstreet, 142, 287, 301, 314, 349, 376, 383, 406, 419, 449, 459, 531, 595. 624
Tycho Brahe, 38, 42, 55, 61, 64, 74
Braintree, 224, 232
William Branch, 242, 246
William Brathwayt, 680
Thomas Brattle, 628, 679
Samuel Braybrook, 496, 543, 600
Capt. Breedon, 291
William Brend, 286
John Bridgeman, Bishop of Chester, 150
Sarah Bridgeman, 276
Edmund Bridges, 368, 369
James Bridges, 465
John Bridges, 624
Sarah Bridges, 664, 689
Mary Bridges, 689
Brielhaven, 20
John Brinley, 389
Britain's Royal Star, or An Astrological Demonstration of England's Future Felicity, 293
British Museum, 12
Edward Bromley, 106

Sir Robert Brooke, 317
Brookline, 177
Brother Glassap, 54
Brother Radulphus, 54
Brotherhood / Sisterhood of the Initiate / Adepts, 88
Capt. Christopher Brown, 348 , 351
Elizabeth Brown, 323, 325
Henry Brown, 396
James Brown, 314
John Brown, 581
Richard Brown, 259
William Brown, 275, 323, 326, 371, 431
Agnes Browne, 97
Charles Browne, 267, 276, 287
John Browne, 143
Robert Browne, 2, 8, 10, 18, 28, 32, 33, 40, 151
Samuel Browne, 143
Thomas Browne, 200
Capt. Bubb, 329
John Bucke, 270
Buckingham, 123
Buckinghamshire, 1, 66,128, 260
Mary Buckley, 565-567
Sarah Buckley, 565, 594, 597, 623, 665, 689
Caleb Buffham, 627, 640, 648, 662, 672
Peter Bulkel[e]y, 364, 373
John Bullock, 480
Edward Burcham, 211, 231
Rev. George Burroughs, 334, 352, 388-391, 393, 402-406, 408, 409, 410, 421, 439, 446, 450, 453, 454, 460, 461, 478, 548, 549, 554, 566, 573, 575-582, 587, 591-593, 617, 638, 639, 651, 653-660, 670, 678, 708
Mrs. George Burroughs, 393
Goodwife Burt, 328, 388, 240
Jonathan Burt, 240
Isaac Burton, 292
John Burton, 283
Robert Burton, 118, 258, 455
The Burton Boy, 55
Bury St. Edmunds, Suffolk, 2, 19, 212, 220, 296, 298, 303, 488, 606
The Bury St. Edmunds Witches, 400

Burying Point, 296
Peter Busgutt, 176
Isaac Buswell, 363
Susannah Buswell, 363
William Butler, 41
John Buttolph, 296
John Buxton, 405, 549
Buzzard's Bay, 70

-C-

Robert Calef, 663, 694, 696, 698-699, 705-706
California, 7
John Calvin, 4
Calvinism, 2, 10, 13, 19, 125, 219, 249, 678
Cambridge, Massachusetts, 41, 74,78 ,82, 83, 86, 89, 91, 138, 172, 173, 177, 185, 187, 205, 211, 217, 232, 258, 288, 305, 322, 446, 594, 649, 650
Cambridge Platform, 232
Cambridge Prison, 603
Cambridge University, 74, 79, 187
Canada, 459, 464
A Candle in the Dark, 273, 655
Candy, 635, 636, 689, 706
Archbishop of Canterbury, 18, 60, 77
Canterbury, 18, 125
Cape Ann, 100, 104, 122, 126-128, 130, 144, 157, 186, 357, 469, 581, 591
Cape Cod, 70, 100, 112
Cape Sable, 315
Joseph Capen, 671
Capricorn, i, 311
Elizabeth Carey, 601, 607, 617
Nathaniel Carey, 601, 649
Caribbean, 422
Carmelite, 102
George Carr, 341, 376
James Carr, 342
Robert Carr, Viscount Rochester, 89, 90, 93, 98-101, 122, 306
Andrew Carrier, 645
Martha Carrier, 421, 461-463, 465, 467, 502, 595, 598, 604, 607, 608,

611, 613, 614, 620, 622, 629, 638, 639, 640, 641, 642, 646, 651, 656, 659, 660
Richard Carrier, 501, 623, 645
Sarah Carrier, 608, 611
carrier pigeons, 234
Joan Carrington, 234
John Carrington, 234
Laird of Carschogill, 43
Bethia Carter, 594
George Cartwright, 306
Gov. John Carver, 115
Meric. Casaubon, 287, 322, 343, 364
Casco, Maine, 214, 217, 352, 359, 387, 388, 402, 407, 409, 410, 421, 438, 453, 460, 461, 540, 548, 552, 580, 591
John Case, 358
Thomas Case, 392
Case's Crew, 392
Cases of Conscience Concerning Withccrafts, 678, 683, 698
Giovanni Domenico Cassini, 389
Castle Island, 152, 208, 313, 449
Castle of Benatky, 61
Castle of Zerner, 51
Castle of Zobeslau, 51
caterpillar scourge, 221
Catholicism, 4, 5, 8, 10, 13, 18, 32, 34, 42, 46, 64, 67, 76, 79, 96, 115, 122, 123, 125, 147, 169, 227, 237, 257, 261, 343, 381, 418, 434, 438, 440, 443, 444, 447, 479
Catholic plot, 384
catted chimney, 178, 211
Cavalier Parliament, 293, 301
William Cecil, Lord Treasurer Burghley, 8, 17
census, 323
center of gravity, 38
Certainty of the World of Spirits, 477, 607
John Chaddock, 206
Richard Chamberlain, 397
Samuel de Champlain, 83
Mary Chandler, 297
Phoebe Chandler, 595, 605, 607, 622, 623
Susan Chandler, 297,

Mrs. William Chandler, 318
Michael Chappleman, 590
Charity, 119
Charles I of England, 122, 124-126, 130, 132, 152, 155, 170, 184, 185, 187, 195, 198, 207, 225, 228, 233, 235-237, 447
Charles II of England, 237, 244, 291, 294, 306, 316, 340, 343, 349, 373, 390, 394, 418, 425
Charles River, 100, 101
Charlestown, 140, 142, 143, 178, 208, 229, 231, 232, 280, 434, 437, 448, 580, 601, 607, 608, 617, 649
Charon, 85
Charter, 677
Charter for Massachusetts, 595
Charter of Massachusetts Bay, 373
Charter Street Cemetery, 438, 676
John Chase, 383
Geoffrey Chaucer, 16
Anthony Checkley, 648
Ezekiel Cheever, 263, 494, 498, 500, 501, 507, 509, 514, 539, 620, 637
Samuel Cheever, 597, 659
Chelmsford, Essex, 14, 39, 209-213, 216, 228
Chelmsford, Massachusetts, 474, 475, 597, 685
Chelmsford Sessions, 209, 216, 228
Chesapeake Bay, 80
Cheshire, 63
Chester, 64
Chichester, 89
Chickatabot, Sagamore of Naponsett, 153
Henry Chickering, 234
Chickering-Townsend Bishop farm, 266
Chief Justice of Common Pleas, 79, 98
Chief Justiceship of the King's Bench, 98
Robert Child, 220
Child petition, 307
Chiltern Hills, 1
China, 88
chirurgery, 315. *See* surgery
Christ, v
Christ Church, Oxford, 105, 118
Christ's College, Cambridge, 86

"Christ's Fidelity, the Only Shield against Satan's Malignity," 668
Christian II of Saxony, 72
Christian IV of Denmark, 38, 61
Christianity, i-iii
Christmas, 7, 48, 97, 114, 228, 235, 300, 306, 310, 318, 362, 430, 447, 456, 688, 700
Priscilla Chub, 477
Benjamin Church, 361
Sarah Churchill, 478, 525, 582-585, 587, 594, 618, 619, 633, 670
church member, 141
Church of England, 2, 3, 8, 18, 32, 33, 38, 40, 61, 64, 71, 73, 74, 76, 86, 125, 136, 143, 151, 167, 219, 293, 301, 312, 347, 432, 434
Church of Rome, iv, 4, 7
Church of the Great Lambeth, 605
Jane Clark, 109, 117
Mary Clark, 280
Nathaniel Clark, Jr., 428
Walter Clark, 397
William Clark, 224
Elizabeth Clarke, 209
Clavis Astrologiae Elimata or, A Key to the Whole Art of Astrology, 329
Elizabeth Clawson, 671, 677, 681, 683
Clayworth Hall, 56-57
Clerk of the Court, 606, 673, 674
Clerk of the Market, 306
William Cleves, 668
Clevethon, 80
Constable Clifford, 355
Lord Cliftonhall, 43
Peter Cloyse, 502, 658, 662, 691
Sarah Cloyse, 526, 528, 529, 534, 538, 562, 671
Constable Clifford, 355
Thomas Cobbett, 205, 266, 269, 393
Robert Cocker, 199
Robert Codman, 227
Clement Codum, 607
Sir Edward Coke, Chief Justice of Common Pleas, 117, 130, 132, 156
Thomas Colby, 17
Ann Cole, 300, 305
Eunice Cole, 270, 271, 277, 302, 313, 346, 383, 385

John Cole, 300
Robert Cole, 159
William Cole, 270, 302
Anne Coleman, 280
Thomas Coleman, 277
Henry Coley, 329, 340, 390, 391
Christopher Collins, 188, 266
Mrs. Christopher Collins, 266
Cologne, 13, 70
Elizabeth Colson, 582, 586, 594, 596
Anthony Colve, 346
Richard Coman, 412
William Coman, 412
Commentary on Alchabitius, 200
Commission, 179
Commission of Oyer and Terminer at Salem, 701
Commission of the Peace, 66
commissioners, 141
Committee of Review at Cambridge, 91
Committee of Vigilance, 501, 513, 539, 636, 637, 670, 672, 678, 685, 691
Common Law, 606
Commons, 76, 125, 185, 194, 390
communion, 1, 427, 464, 470, 471, 526, 528, 621, 659, 691
Communion Sunday, 472, 526
compulsory distraint of knighthood, 135
compulsory education, 228
Roger Conant, 126, 127, 130, 133, 144, 157, 163, 178, 377
Concord, 70
Congregation of the Index, 102
Congregationalism, 28, 205, 219, 232
conjuration, 606
conjuror, iv, 26, 27, 56, 76, 549
Bennet Conley, 59
Connecticut, 155, 165, 193, 222, 226, 232, 267, 281, 283, 292, 305, 311, 327, 334, 335, 338, 355, 356, 362, 430, 467, 474, 647, 670, 677, 681, 683, 686, 692, 702, 705
Connecticut River, 165, 222, 226, 354
Considerations for the Better Settling of Church Government, 132
constable, 141, 176
Constitution, 313

consumption. *see* tuberculosis
contagious magic, iii
conventicle, 2
Conventicle Act, 312
Lady Ann Conway, 310
Elisha Cook, 702
John Cook, 435
Widow Cook, 582
Anthony Ashley Cooper, Earl of Shaftesbury, 394
Thomas Cooper, 105, 248, 252
John Copeland, 280, 282
Copernican theory, 58, 99, 102, 105, 122
Copernicus, 4, 102, 147
copper lode, 234
Giles Corey, 241, 249, 275, 288, 295, 358-360, 368, 369, 460, 466, 485, 498, 503, 524, 536, 539, 545-547, 552, 589, 594, 626, 652, 662, 668, 671-673
Martha Corey, 358, 360, 460, 466, 485, 497, 498, 500, 503-506, 509, 511, 514, 516, 521, 524, 646, 668-670, 674, 706
Joan Coriden, 214, 216
Earl of Cork, 207
Cornet, 301
Ensign Corning, 322
Goodman Cornish, 209
George Corwin, Jr., 606, 622, 665, 678, 699, 705
Capt. George Corwin, Sr., 173, 257, 280, 288, 290, 301, 349, 368, 416, 418
John Corwin, 338
Judge Jonathan Corwin, 224, 348, 378, 472, 485, 486, 494, 531, 539, 554, 555, 579, 603, 606, 609, 620, 641, 656
Cosimo II, Grand Duke of Tuscany, 90
cosquinomancy, 479
John Cotta, 124
Henry Cotton, 78
John Cotton, 143, 170, 195, 221, 302
Robert Couch, 326
Goodwife Coulter, 385
George Coulton, 249
Council for the Affairs of New England, 111, 119, 153
Council for the Safety and Conservation of the Peace, 449

Council of Assistants, 154
Council of Plantations, 349
Council of State, 234
Council of the North, 184
countercharm, 424, 484
Country Justice, 107, 273, 488
county court of Boston, 232
County of Middlesex, 603
Court of Assistants of the Massachusetts Bay Company, 140-142, 152, 157, 158, 161, 261, 272, 283, 308, 346, 350, 352, 371, 383, 402, 405, 670
Court of Massachusetts, 184
Court of Oyer and Terminer, 619, 624, 626, 628, 629, 631, 640, 648, 650, 651, 658, 668, 669, 671, 673-675, 678, 683-685
Covenant with God, 204
covenant with the Devil, 76
Covent Garden, 291
cover-up, 651, 678
Cowes, 139
Mary Cowper, 58
Robert Cowper, 61
cowpox, 423, 702, 708
James Coy, 589
Cracow, Poland, 21, 30, 73, 75
Matthew Cradock, 136, 138, 153, 154, 180
Crane River, 243, 394
Crane River Commons, 418
Credulity and Incredulity, 323
Randolph Crew, 103
Croatoan, 47
Sir John Croke, 70
Francis Cromwell, 48
Sir Henry Cromwell, 42, 49
John Cromwell, 359
Lady Cromwell, 42, 48, 130
Oliver Cromwell, 130, 196, 199, 204, 207, 210, 233, 237, 244, 257, 260, 261, 264, 268, 275, 284
Philip Cromwell, 377
Richard Cromwell, 284, 291
Thomas Cromwell, 360

Dr. Crosby, 326, 342
Henry Crosby, 511
Crossen, 72
cross-examination, 609
Nathaniel Crouch, 440
Nicholas Culpepper, 260
Mary Cummings, 426, 427
Crown of Thorns, 328
Crown officers, 200
crucible, 6
Cublington, 2
Rose Cullender, 296-298, 400
Isaac Cummings, Jr., 427, 608
Deacon Isaac Cummings, Sr., 412, 427
Alice Cunny, 39
Joan Cunny, 39, 40
Dr. Curtz, *See* Dr. Jacob Kurtius
Eliza Cutler, 373
Samuel Cutler, 287, 373

-D-

Daemonologia Sacra, 282
Michael Dalton, 107, 273, 488
Damnable Art of Witchcraft, 482
Lord De la Warre. *See* Thomas West, Lord De la Warre
Deliverance Dane, 683
Elizabeth Dane, 621
Francis Dane, 620, 681
Samuel Danforth, 311
Thomas Danforth, 474, 531, ,595, 681, 686, 687, 691, 700
Richard Danton, 334, 335
John Danvers, 260
Danvers, Massachusetts, 260. *See* Salem Village,
Brian Darcy, 14
Virginia Dare, 38, 47
James Darling, 528, 599
Thomas Darling, 53, 55, 57, 74
John Darrell, 33, 54, 57, 60, 63
Nathaniel Davenport, 357

Richard Davenport, 154, 157, 162, 173, 183, 184, 199, 203, 208, 313, 348
Sarah Daston, 691
Davenport Hill, 189
Andrew Davis, 349
Capt. John Davis, 31
Stephen Day, 173, 177, 185
The Day of Doom, 300
day of humiliation, 137, 261, 275, 325, 372
De Cometis, 107
De Fundamentis Astrologiae, 69
De Harmonica Mundi, 107
De Mundi Aethereii, 74
De Praestigiis Daemonum, 52, 55
De Revolutionibus Orbium Coelestium, 102
deacon, 141
John Deacon, 63
Priscilla Deacon, 91
Deacons of Hemel Hempstead, 93
Death, 85
Declaration of Indulgence, 434, 439
Dedham, 232, 281
Arthur Dee, 37, 87, 146, 221, 245
Jane Dee, 11, 36
Dr. John Dee, 3, 6, 8, 10, 19, 20, 26, 39, 45, 46, 49-51, 58, 60, 62, 70, 71, 74, 76, 80, 84, 87, 206, 221, 242, 258, 287, 322, 688
Deer Island, 355
Deerfield, 354
democracy, 227
demon, iii
demonology, 52, 55, 73, 82, 105, 209, 245, 273, 323. *See* witchcraft
Demonology and Theology, 245
Demonomania of Witches, 8
demons, iii
Elizabeth Denham, 385
Daniel Dennison, 349, 371
depression, 118. *See* melancholy
Deputies, 140, 207
Derbyshire, 32, 53
John Derish, 652, 662
Mary Derish, 600

Desborough, 681. *See* Disbrow
A Description of New England, 103
Robert Devereux, Earl of Essex, 204
Alison Device, 95
Elizabeth Device, 95
James Device, 95
Janet Device, 96, 149
Devil, iii, 4, 25, 32, 33, 35, 43-45, 48-50, 54, 55, 57, 57, 70, 88, 92, 95, 103, 121-123, 133, 150, 166, 187, 204, 209, 210, 212, 213, 223, 232, 233, 235, 238, 242, 250, 253, 255, 256, 258, 262, 265, 267, 270, 271, 276, 279, 281, 292, 297, 300, 310, 320, 322, 329, 333, 338, 339, 346, 350, 352, 364, 370, 380, 411, 415, 417, 419, 441, 450, 470, 477, 483-486, 488-491, 500, 511-515, 518, 520, 521, 523-525, 528, 536, 540, 541, 543, 544, 546, 549, 550, 552, 561, 562, 568, 571, 572, 579, 583-585, 588, 590, 593, 599, 608, 612, 613, 615, 621, 523-625, 627, 628, 637-640, 642-645, 648, 650, 653, 654, 656-664, 666, 667, 672, 674, 675, 687, 689, 694-696, 703, 707
Devil's Book, 502, 538, 542, 547, 551-553, 555, 565, 581, 585-588, 597, 633, 652
"The Devil and His Instruments Will Be Warring Against Christ and His Followers," 669
The Devil's Delusions, 242
Devil's mark, 39, 43, 150, 209, 229, 265, 267, 277, 297, 300, 402, 485, 491, 596, 609, 702. *See* witch teat
diabolical possession, 109, 212
Dialoghi delle Nuove Science, 176
Dialogical Discourse, 64
Dialogo dei Due Massini Sistemi del Mondo, 147
Dialogue, 105
Dialogue Concerning Witches and Witchcrafts, 50, 71
Johann Wolfgang Dienheim, 67
George Dill, 183
Dioptrice, 94
Mercy Disbrow, 671, 677, 681, 683, 692, 701
Nicholas Disbrow, 406
Thomas Disbrow, 406
Discourse of the Damned Art of Witchcraft, 86, 105, 683
Discovery of the Fraudulent Practices of John Darrell, 61
Discovery of the Imposture of Witches, 389
The Discovery of Witchcraft, 73, 105, 273

The Discovery of Witches, 228
Diseworth, 110
Displaying of Supposed Witchcraft, 364
Diverse Voyages Touching the Discovery of America, 15
divination, 1, 8, 200
Divine Displeasure, 701
Divine Providence, 91, 232, 440
Divine Right of Kings, 73, 76, 125
divining, 400, 479
Doctor Lamb's Darling, *See* Anne Bodenham
doctrine of absolute predestination, 61
John Dodge, 358
William Dodge, Jr., 358
William Dodge, Sr., 243
Ann Doliver, 623
Dominion of New England, 430
Dorchester, 122, 126-128, 130, 144, 191, 239, 240, 258, 467,
Anthony Dorchester, 239
Sarah Dorchester, 239
Dr. Dorrington, rector of Warboys, 48
Dorset, 269
Dorsetshire, 208
Dover, 273, 277, 291, 326
Robert Downer, 326
Emanuel Downing, 173, 174, 199, 208, 211, 241, 263
George Downing, 199, 211, 243
Lucy Downing, 173, 174
Sir Francis Drake, 7, 32
Robert Drake, 271
Drayton Beauchamp, 2
drought, 268, 361
Drummer of Tedworth, 305
William Drury, 299, 304
Joseph Dudley, 394, 430, 678, 680
Robert Dudley, Earl of Leicester, 19
Thomas Dudley, 142, 146, 152, 154, 163, 185
Elizabeth Due, 268-270, 315
The Duke's Devil. See Dr. John Lamb
Dunbar, 244
Gillis Duncan, 42, 43, 44

Dundee, 28
Jonathan Dunen, 392
Henry Dunster, 187
William Dunton, 652
Amy Duny, 296-298, 400
Ann Durent, 297
Dorothy Durent, 296
Mrs. Durkstone, 630
Lydia Dustin, 572, 629
Dutch, 32, 39, 47, 64, 83, 86, 98, 101, 104, 123, 192, 202, 300, 306, 309, 320, 346, 351, 353, 361, 363, 678
Goodman Dutch, 228
Grace Dutch, 267
Martha Dutch, 461, 469, 480
Mary Dyer, 170
dynamics, 39

-E-

Eagle, 139. See Arbella
Daniel Eames, 658, 661
Dorothy Eames, 398
Rebecca Eames, 660, 671, 673
Earth, 4
Earth Sign, i
earthquake, 172
East India Company, 63
Eastern Army, 207
Easthampton, Long Island, 281, 294
Eastward. *See* Maine
Isaac Easty, 293, 433, 455
John Easty, 293
Mary Easty, 433, 455, 549, 562, 563, 594, 597, 598, 600, 617, 665, 669, 671, 673, 687
Nathaniel Eaton, 173
Theophilus Eaton, 136
eclipse of the sun, 628
Edinburgh, 28, 43, 55, 245
Anna Edmunds, 346
Alexander Edwards, 238

Sarah Edwards, 238
Susanna Edwards, 400
Thomas Edwards, 201
Elders, 162
The Elect, i, 5, 303
Election, 573
Electors of Saxony, 72
Elementary education, 228
John Eliot, 220, 305, 347, 355
Sir John Eliot, 135, 147
Elizabeth I of England, 3, 7, 19, 20, 26, 30, 32, 37, 63, 71
Daniel Elliot, 527
Edmund Elliot, 330, 331
Sir George Ellis, 120
John Elston, 145
Gervaise Elvis, 99
John Emerson, 470, 624
George Emery, 164, 322
Emmanuel College, Cambridge, 167
Elizabeth Allen Endicott, 266, 315, 316, 321, 323, 323, 626
John Endicott, Jr., 266, 315, 316, 321, 376
Governor John Endicott, Sr., 132-134, 136, 138-140, 142, 144, 146, 153, 157, 158, 163, 165, 167, 168, 176, 178, 189, 196, 207, 208, 231, 234, 262, 266, 273, 274, 282, 287, 291, 294, 299, 312, 313, 345, 366, 376, 396
Samuel John Endicott, 392
Zerubabel Endicott, Jr., 377
Dr. Zerubabel Endicott, Sr., 270, 315, 316, 337, 366, 376, 407, 408, 410, 599, 626
England, 83, 109, 115, 125, 126, 132, 168, 189, 240, 242, 244, 257, 262, 358, 438
Mary English, 549, 555, 594, 617, 652
Philip English, 349, 549, 565, 566, 608, 610, 652, 680, 699, 705, 707
English Catholics, 3
English Commonwealth, 264
The English Physician, 260, 265
English Revolution, 200
Enkhuyssen, Holland, 64, 67
epilepsy, 40, 77
Episcopacy, 194, 219

Episcopal Church of England. See Church of England
"Epistle to Mr. Increase Mather's Cases of Conscience," 679,
Epitome Astronomiae Copernicanae, 105
Daniel Epps, 334, 353, 390, 681
Essay for the Recording of Illustrious Providences: Wherein an Account Is Given of Many Remarkable and Very Memorable Events Which Have Happened in This Last Age, Especially in New England, 414. See *Illustrious Providences*, 414
Essex, England, 14, 15, 50, 209, 213
Countess of Essex. See Frances Howard
Essex County, 164, 287, 304, 351, 354, 497, 566, 606, 673
Essex County Court, 304, 351, 399, 402, 406
Essex Street, 180, 249, 286, 290, 415, 426. See
estate tax, 432
Agnes Evans,
Mrs. Benjamin Evans,
Master Evans,
James Everell,
evil, iv, 5
evil eye, 558, 611, 628, 633, 637, 640, 664, 670
The Examination, Confession, Trial, and Execution of Joan Williford, Joan Coriden, and Jane Holt, 216
excise tax, 432
excommunication, 175, 203
Exeter, 416

-F-

Edward Fairfax, 120
Daniel Fairfield, 192, 193, 262, 267, 275, 338, 670, 677
Thomas Fairfax, 210
falconry, 139
falling sickness. *See* epilepsy
Fall's River, 643
familiars, 39, 43, 210, 212, 214
Farms. *See* Salem Village
John Farnham, 465, 470
Ralph Farnham, 467
Thomas Farrar, 594, 597
Edmond Farrington, 159

Fasciculus Chemicus, 146
Fatemon, 80
Abigail Faulkner, 657, 658, 666, 671, 677, 687, 706
Guy Fawkes, 79
Faversham, Kent, 214, 216
Fellow of the Royal Society, 305
Benjamin Felton, 325, 342, 361, 377
John Felton, 133
Edward Fenner, 49
Goodman Fern, 20
ferry, 173
Dr. John Fian, 43, 46
Robert Filmer, 265
Goodwife Finch, 291
Andreas Firmorshem, 23
Fish Street, 163
Mary Fisher, 277
Fisherton Anger, Wiltshire, 260, 264
fishing, 119, 127, 154, 159, 163, 183, 262, 315
Thomas Fisk, 632, 636
William Fisk, 345
John Fiske, 168
Nicholas Fiske, 148, 194, 245
James Fitzmaurice, 18
Five Mile Pond, 666
Flagellum Daemonum: Exorcismos, 52
Thomas Fleet, 708
Benjamin Fletcher, 649
Elizabeth Putnam Flint, 406, 416, 422, 425, 432, 455, 459, 463, 679
George Flint, Jr., 425
George Flint, Sr., 416, 422, 425, 455, 463, 679
Joseph Flint, 586
Mercy Flint, 679
Nathaniel Flint, 463
Thomas Flint, 357, 369, 430, 455
William Flint, 281, 287
Capt. John Flood, 607, 658
Florence, 47, 102, 148, 194
Joan Flower, 106
Margaret Flower, 106

Philippa Flower, 106
Ralph Fogg, 187
folk medicine, 229
Goodman Footman, 209
Simon Forman, 74, 87, 89, 90, 93, 94, 110, 124
Fort Nassau, 101
Fortune Theatre, 133
fortune-telling, 322, 400, 407, 479
Fra Foscarini, 102
Elizabeth Fosdick, 607, 608, 620
Andrew Foster, 612
Ann Foster, 349, 350, 637, 638, 640, 641-643, 648, 663, 671, 673
Elizabeth Foster, 622
Ephraim Foster, 399
Constable John Foster, 664, 658
Rose Foster, 663, 666, 668
Fourth of July, 164
Thomas Fowle, 221
Joseph Fowler, 619
Rebecca Fowler, 425
Rebecca Fox, 685
France, 135
Frankfurt, 70
J. G. Frazer, ii
Frederick II of Denmark, 42, 61
Duke Frederick of Würtemburg, 72
freemen, 141, 314, 677
Alice Freeman, 58
The Freeman's Oath, 173
free will, 401
Freiburg, Breisgau, 67
French, 8, 18, 39, 67, 104, 361, 469, 615, 678
French and Indian War, 438, 454, 459
James Friend, 345
Friends. *See* Quakers
Nicholas Fromonds, 23
Frost Fish Brook, 189
Fruit of Knowledge, 5
Eunice Fry, 625, 666
John Fry, 625

A Full and Candid Account of the Delusion Called Witchcraft Which Prevailed in New England, 679
A Full and Plain Evidence Concerning Witches, 394
A Full and True Relation, 350
Dr. Fuller, 326
Benjamin Fuller, 620
John Fuller, 342, 385, 387, 579, 616, 617, 632
Joseph Fuller, 620
Rachel Fuller, 395-387
Rebecca Putnam Fuller, 493, 617, 620. *See* Rebecca Putnam, Rebecca Putnam Shepard
Samuel Fuller, 138, 620
Thomas Fuller, Jr., 450, 595
Thomas Fuller, Sr., 369, 383, 395, 447, 493
John Fulton, 626
John Furbush, 320
fustian spinsters, 187
Fustis Daemonum, 52

-G-

E. G., Gent., 263
John Gadbury, 245, 261, 269, 287, 293, 381, 389
Marie Gadge, 462
Sarah Gadge, 456
Thomas Gadge, 456, 598
Gaelic, 442
Gainesborough, 71, 80
Goodwife Gale, 567
Galileo Galilei, 13, 38, 47, 55, 58, 88, 90, 94, 98, 101, 102, 122, 147, 153, 176, 194, 200
Gallows Hill, 180, 193, 581, 627, 640, 648, 659, 666, 662, 674
Goodman Gammon, 692, 693
Lyon Gardiner, 283
George Gardner, 306
Joseph Gardner, 265
Capt. Richard Gardner, 671
Samuel Gardner, Jr., 366, 394
Samuel Gardner, Sr., 366
Thomas Gardner, 126, 162, 168, 273

Elizabeth Garlick, 281, 283
John Gaule, 219, 227, 228
Judge Bartholomew Gedney, 376, 388, 606, 609, 615, 616, 641, 664,
John Gedney, 187, 262, 271, 352, 410, 431
Susannah Gedney, 411
Gemini, 129, 344
General Court, 138, 141, 145, 152-154, 157, 158, 162, 165, 184, 186, 194, 203, 205, 211, 215, 220, 221, 224, 227, 239, 244, 255, 256, 261, 272, 274, 275, 277, 281-283, 286, 293-294, 299, 301, 305, 207, 309, 311-313, 315, 316, 321, 334, 335, 340, 343, 346, 352, 361, 365, 371, 376, 377, 383, 340, 343, 346352, 361, 365, 371, 376, 377, 383, 387, 407, 408, 410, 416, 426, 452, 459, 460, 468, 626, 671, 675, 677, 681, 683, 687, 692, 707, 708
Geneva Bible, 92
Gentleman of Boston, 663
Joseph George, 545
Mary Godfry, 385, 386
Mehitabel Godfry, 386
Sarah Godfry, 386
Goodwife Gent, 192
John Getchell, 169, 257
Joseph Getchell, 352, 377, 384, 399, 415
Samuel Getchell, 346
Gibson family, 288-289
George Gifford, 50, 71, 105
Margaret Gifford, 388
Sir Humphrey Gilbert, 20
John Giles, 405
Goodman Gillow, 173
Richard Gilpin, 282
John Gingle, 290, 293, 360
Joseph Glanvill, 310, 373, 389, 394, 482, 607
Glastonbury, 10
Glastonbury Plain, 3, 242
Johann Rudolph Glauber, 332
Gloucester. England, 304
Gloucester, Massachusetts, 207, 267, 469, 475, 623, 678, 685
Carline Glover, 440
Gammer Mary Glover, 70, 71, 441, 442, 444, 454, 479
John Gloyd, 368, 370

God, iv, 6
Mr. Goddard, 264
Mrs. Goddard, 260
John Godfrey, 186, 267, 275, 276, 284, 285, 287, 301, 314, 624
John Godfry, 385, 386
Gammer Elizabeth Godman, 267, 272
William Goffe, 291
Lydia Golbert, 267
Enoch Golden, 266
The Golden Bough, ii
Goodall's Hill, 324
Dorcas Goode, 494, 497, 517, 518, 523, 524, 707
Sarah Goode, 449, 456, 459, 469, 484-489, 491, 494-497, 540, 552, 554, 565, 573, 603, 619, 629-631, 640, 707
William Goode, 449, 456, 469, 485, 488, 707, 708
Jacob Goodell, 358, 360, 372
Joseph Goodell, 673
Robert Goodell, 358
Robin Goodfellow, 406
Alice Goodrich, 53-55
Goodspeed family, 106
John Goodwin, 440, 441
Martha Goodwin, 440, 441, 445-448
Mercy Goodwin, 441
Nathaniel Goodwin, 441
Samuel Gookin, 622
Sir Ferdinando Gorges, 70, 79, 81, 100, 104, 111, 119, 130, 294, 340, 364, 387
Bartholomew Gosnold, 70, 80
Charles Gott, 137
Benjamin Gould, 536, 539
Jeremy Gould, 128, 146, 160, 166
Nathan Gould, 285
Phoebe Gould, 91, 93, 147, 180
Samuel Gould, 545
Thomas Gould, 369
Zaccheus Gould, 88, 91, 93, 108, 121, 128, 135, 146, 147, 180, 202
Governor Leverett's Wharf, 430
Governor's Council, 658, 693, 700
Grace, iv

Joseph Grafton, 185
Richard Graham, 47
grand and petit jurors, 141
Grand Island, 397
Grand Jury, 305
Grand Remonstrance, 195
Gratz, Germany, 50, 55, 62
Richard Graves, 159, 168, 176, 192, 201, 211, 227, 271
Gravesend, 20
Samuel Gray, 368, 372
Great Bay, 398
Great Fire of London, 316
Great God Pan, 92.
Great Island, 460
Great Plague, 316
The Great Protestation, 117
Great Swamp, 345, 367
Great Turk, 25
Greek, 84
Greek gods of nature, 92
Joseph Green, 702, 705, 706
Greenhead, 95
Daniel Greenleaf, 351
John Greenslit, 460
Thomas Greenslit, 460, 670
Nathaniel Greensmith, 300, 305
Rebecca Greensmith, 300, 305
Greenwich, 20
John Greenwood, 49
Elizabeth Gregory, 77
Richard Grenville, 32
Gresham College, 269
Hannah Grey, 348
William Griggs, 478, 481, 504, 536, 539, 626
Mrs. William Griggs, 478
Sir Harbottle Grimston, 213
Groton, 338, 339, 573, 596, 597
Guardian angels, 200
Philipp Jakob Guestenhoever, 49
Guiana, 104

Guide to Grandjurymen, 130, 209, 235, 488, 607, 683
Gunpowder Plot, 79
Ann Gunter, 77
Reuben Guppy, 359
Goodman Gutch, 228
Peter Gwinne, 51
Gyor, 60

-H-

habeas corpus, 433, 603
George Hacker, 586
Hades, 84
Hadley, 354, 402, 405, 406, 416-418, 461, 577, 693
D. Hageck, 22
Henry Haggett, 279
Richard Hakluyt, 15
John Hale, 231, 280, 309, 312, 335, 370, 394, 418, 427, 455, 518, 627, 639, 659, 677, 687, 704, 706
Mary Hale, 391. *See* Mary Hale Putnam
Sir Matthew Hale, 212, 216, 268, 296, 298, 303, 340, 482, 488, 606
Rebecca Hale, 370, 480
Hales, 188
Deacon Hall, 703
Mary Hall, 309, 314
Ralph Hall, 306, 309, 314
Edmund Halley, 362, 389, 408, 416
Henry Hallywell, 394
Halfway Covenant, 281
Hamburg, 70
William Hamilton, 67, 73, 87
Hammer of Witches, . See Malleus Maleficarum
John Hampden, ,
Hampton Court, 75, 226
Hampton, New Hampshire, 75, 226, 270, 271, 277, 302, 313, 326, 346, 349, 383, 385, 387, 388, 361, 462
Hand of God, 84
Hanging Hills, 467
Hanging Oak, 627
Jacob Hanssen, 64, 67

Capt. Joseph Hardy, 243
Thomas Hardy, 460-463, 472
Benjamin Harris, 462
Elizabeth Harris, 214
Katherine Harrison, 327, 334, 335, 344, 346
Thomas Harrison, 63, 64
John Harrod, 575
Samuel Harsnett, Bishop of York, 19, 55, 60, 63, 77-79, 89, 91, 132, ,
Elizabeth Hart, 594, 595, 597
Hartford, 202, 222, 226, 235, 300, 311, 406, 467, 703
Edmund Hartlay, 56
John Harvard, 167, 173, 187
Harvard College, 165, 183, 187, 199, 275, 280, 291, 326, 334, 354, 368, 421, 446, 458
Dr. Harvey, 150
Harwich, 213
John Harwood, 620
Thomas Hastings, 374
Hatfield, 354, 374
Judge John Hathorne, 377, 431, 460, 466, 480, 485, 486, 488, 490, 502, 507-511, 513, 515, 519, 520, 522, 531, 549, 540, 542, 554-556, 560, 562, 567, 569, 579, 585, 603, 606, 609, 620, 631, 641, 652, 660, 664, 666, 674
Justice William Hathorne, 162, 178, 184, 195, 207, 211, 220, 224, 228, 241, 243, 244, 270, 278, 280, 290, 304, 318, 362, 371, 391
Hathorne's Hill, 484
Hatorask, 47
Haverhill, 301
Margaret Hawkes, 635. 636
Jane Hawkins, 170
John Hawkins, 414
Sarah Hawlins, 347
John Haynes, 152, 161
Sarah Ingersoll Haynes, 262
Thomas Haynes, 285, 405, 561
William Haynes, 262
Richard Head, 320
Heaven, 5
Heawelon, 80
Hebrew, 84

Hebrew texts for the Apocrypha, 92
Helen Jenkinson, 97
Hell, 84
Hemel Hempstead, 91
John Hemmings, 556
Ruth Hemingway, 348
Henrietta Maria of France, 125, 152
Henry III of France, 19
herb lore, i, 133, 260, 364, 382
Hercules, 3
heresy, 4, 256
Hermes Trismegistus, 82
Hermetic Brotherhood, 98
Hermetic dragon, 6
Hermeticism, 82
Herriard, 18
Deputy Sheriff George Herrick, 486, 495, 496, 506, 514, 516, 538-539, 541, 543, 545, 555, 560, 566, 567, 598, 600, 606, 615, 633, 652, 668;
Marshal George Herrick. *See* Deputy George Herrick
Henry Herrick, 459
Joseph Herrick, 345, 358, 430
Mary Herrick, 673, 687
Zachariah Herrick, 459
Hersham, 245, 332, 390, 391
Hertfordshire, 1, 15, 91
Johann Hevelius, 332
Ann Hibbins, 272, 274, 275
William Hibbins, 192, 272
Francis Higginson, 137, 139, 142, 288
John Higginson, 288, 290, 305, 309, 318, 320, 340, 343, 359, 372, 418, 432, 537, 597, 623, 641, 664, 666
Mrs. Higginson, 630
Capt. Hill, 614
Hingam, 222
His Majesty's Commissioners, 308
The Historic Report of a Break-Down of Gold by Means of an Anti-Elixir, 373
history, 118
Histrio-Mastix, 151
Dorcas Hoar, 322, 335, 352, 370, 395, 405-407, 448, 452, 462, 477, 566, 567, 572, 668, 673, 688

William Hoar, 322, 371, 477
Hoarstones, 149
Henry Hobart, 106
Hobbamock, 166, 267, 328, 355, 406, 654
Abigail Hobbs, 464, 468, 477, 539, 541, 548, 549, 561, 581, 591, 594, 652, 671, 673
Deliverance Hobbs, 468, 549, 554, 555, 556, 558-560, 573, 581, 594, 632, 652
James Hobbs, 639
William Hobbs, 549, 554, 555, 560, 594, 620, 688-690, 692
Carl Hodges, 17
John Ho[d]gkins, 419
Christopher Holder, 280, 282
Isabel Holdred, 284
John Holgrave, 157
Holland, 15, 18, 19, 64, 74, 63, 86, 88, 104, 111, 123, 124, 340, 425, 445
Alice Holland, 416. See Ann Holyoke Putnam
Henry Holland, 46
Richard Hollingsworth, 168, 192, 239
William Hollingsworth, 348
Mary Holman, 288, 289
Winifred Holman, 288
Deborah Holmes, 166
Mrs. William Holmes, 292
Jane Holt, 214, 216
Holy Office, 102
Ann Holyoke,
Edward Holyoke, 201
Prudence Holyoke, 201
Holyrood Castle, 43
Homeopathic Magic, iii. *See* Sympathetic magic
Nathaniel Homes, 245
Richard Honeywell, 460
Gabriel Hood, 462
Mr. Hooke, 272
Thomas Hooker, 152, 158
Matthew Hopkins, 209, 214, 216, 219, 224, 228, 230, 501
Edmund Hopwood, 52
horoscope, i, 90, 287
Millicent Horsley, 61

Antonio Hortado, 396, 405
Mary Hortado, 396, 405
John Houghton, 505
Benjamin Houlton, 452, 575, 616
James Houlton, 608
Joseph Houlton, Jr., 357
Joseph Houlton, Sr., 192, 262, 409, 607
Sarah Houlton, 452
House of Burgesses of Virginia, 107, 123
House of Commons, 76, 117, 125, 134, 317, 390
House of Correction, 302, 306, 308
House of Deputies, 207, 383, 391
House of Lords, 127, 390
Frances Howard, Countess of Essex, 89, 93, 98, 99
Thomas Howard, Earl of Arundel, 127
Abigail Howe, 622
Elizabeth Howe, 422, 426, 427, 607, 608, 610, 611, 618, 633, 640, 646
James Howe, Jr., 412, 556
James Howe, Sr., 422, 622
John Howe, 292, 608, 616
Mary Howe, 622
Sarah Howe, 647
Elizabeth Hubbard, 478, 483-485, 493, 495, 497, 504, 505, 520, 523, 536, 537, 538, 540, 541, 542, 566, 568, 569, 571, 582, 587, 597-598, 607, 613, 618, 634
William Hubbard, 426, 597
Henry Hudson, 88, 98
Hudson River, 104
Arthur Hughes, 362, 443
Goodwife (Mrs. Arthur) Hughes, 443
John Hughes, 495, 496
Lewis Hughes, 71
Huguenots, 135
Cornelius Hulett, 268
John Humphrey, 130, 154, 169, 192, 262
Susan Humphrey, 154
Huntingdon, 217
Huntingdonshire, 48, 219
William Hutchins, 683
Alice Hutchinson, 231

Anne Hutchinson, 156, 162, 165, 167, 170, 173, 188, 204;
Benjamin Hutchinson, 553, 600, 607, 662, 665
Elisha Hutchinson, 566
Francis Hutchinson, 213
Jane Hutchinson, 665
John Hutchinson, 342, 545
Joseph Hutchinson, 285, 383, 429-431, 484, 623
Richard Hutchinson, 231, 301
William Huxley, 99, 100, 111
Hveen, 38
hydrostatic balance, 38
Elizabeth Hynes, 263
hysteria, 40, 121, 529, 571, 572, 627, 664, 681, 692

-I-

idolatry, 256
idols of the cave, 110
idols of the market place, 110
idols of the theatre, 110
idols of the tribe, 110
ignoramus, 691, 703
Illustrious Providences, 414, 482
imp, 39, 43
import duties, 432
incorruptibility of the heavens, 77
incubi, 210. 212
Independents, 234
Boy Indian, 466
John Indian, 466, 482, 529-534, 536, 538, 541, 545, 548, 556, 558, 569, 571, 572, 610, 611
Tituba Indian, 466, 475, 478, 480-483, 485, 491-497, 503, 514, 523, 567, 603, 698
Indian Agricultural School, 238
Indian corn. *See* maize
Indians, 47, 70, 116, 118-120, 126, 128, 129, 131, 133, 145, 146, 148, 153, 156, 159, 163, 165, 166, 182, 202, 204, 220, 238, 245, 279, 347, 352, 354-356, 359, 363, 377, 419, 420, 433, 438, 459-461, 464, 469, 615, 629
indigo, 182

Infanta, 122
Inferior Court of Common Pleas, 702
Hannah Ingersoll, 403
John Ingersoll, 359
Joseph Ingersoll, 440
Nathaniel Ingersoll, 345, 375, 403, 447, 450, 455, 463, 464, 474, 528, 561, 600, 637, 662, 670, 691
Richard Ingersoll, 192, 194, 208, 262
Samuel Ingersoll, 587
Sarah Ingersoll, 587
Ingersoll's Inn, 404, 504, 527, 539, 582, 655
Mary Ingham, 363
inoculation, 688, 708
Inquisition, 101, 102, 147, 148
Instrument of Government, 264
Invisible College, 82, 110, 122, 200, 261, 268, 305, 310. *See also* Hermetic Brotherhood
Ipswich, 152, 162, 168, 173, 182, 188, 191, 202, 215, 217, 227, 238, 254, 273, 275, 280, 282, 302, 306, 316, 323, 356, 254, 273, 275, 280, 282, 302, 306, 316, 323, 356, 369, 376, 382, 388, 393, 406, 412, 422, 426, 433, 470, 496, 548, 549, 594, 597, 610, 616, 652, 662, 681, 688, 698
Ipswich Court, 348
Ipswich House of Correction, 304, 495-497
Ipswich River, 254
Ipswich road, 604
Ipswich Sessions, 324, 448, 402
Ireland, 18, 60, 73, 194, 244, 261
William Ireland, Jr., 405
Mary Ireson, 622
Irish, 237
Ironsides, 196, 200, 207
isochronism of the pendulum, 13
Israel, 631

-J-

Elizabeth Jackson, 70, 71
"Dr." Jacob, 296
George Jacobs, Jr., 350, 594

George Jacobs, Sr., 350, 363, 478, 548, 577, 582, 585, 586, 594, 618, 619, 627, 651-653, 656, 658, 659, 662
Margaret Jacobs, 577, 582, 585, 586, 594, 656, 659-661, 689, 692
Rebecca Jacobs, 594, 596, 685, 689
Jamaica, 318
James I of England, 76, 98, 103, 107, 111, 117, 119, 122, 123, 124
James II of England, 418, 430, 434, 438, 439, 444, 447
James VI of Scotland, 42, 43, 55, 71
James River, 81
James, Sagamore of Saugus, 153
Erasmus James, 183, 247, 257
Jane James, 183, 220, 247, 257, 319
Jamestown, 81, 88, 91, 100, 111
John Jarman, 461
John Jeffray, 120
Maud Jeffray, 120
Goodman Jennings, 259
Goodwife Jennings, 259
Samuel Jennings, 397
Jesuit, 4
Jewel, 139
Jewish, i
Goodman Johns, 582
Lady Arbella Johnson, 139, 140, 154
Elizabeth Johnson, 612, 613, 621, 658, 662, 663, 689, 708
Elizabeth Johnson, Jr., 668, 689
Isaac Johnson, 136, 139, 142, 357
Mary Johnson, 234, 235
Capt. Christopher Jones, 112
Griffin Jones, 241
Hugh Jones, 626
Margaret Jones, 229, 231, 232
Thomas Jones, 230, 232
William Jones, 199, 686, 703
Judaism, iii
judges, 200
Jupiter, i
Justice of Common Pleas, 268

-K-

Joseph Keeble, 606
Sergeant Keeling, 298
Keeper of the Rolls, 66
Arthur Kelley, 34
Edward Kelley, 9, 10, 13, 19, 21-23, 25-27, 33-35, 40, 51, 62, 69, 287, 323, 373
Joan Kelley, 13, 20
Ursula Kempe, 14, 15
Simon Kempthorne, 277
Elizabeth Kendal, 258
Kennebec River, 81, 83
Henry Kenney, 304, 375, 503, 519
Kent, 15, 263
Johannes Kepler, Jr., 332
Johannes Kepler, Sr., 50, 55, 58, 62, 65, 69, 74, 77, 89, 94, 101, 105, 107, 110, 119, 130 ,142
Katherine Kepler, 110
Francis Kerry, 304
Kesmark, 21
Kettle Island, 156
Key into the Language of America, 146
Eleazer Keysar, 565, 577, 581, 617
Kildwick, 149
John Kimball, 325, 330, 331
Daniel King, 577
Thomas King, 200
William King, 319
King James Bible, 78, 85, 86, 91, 92, 134
King Philip, 37, 335, 353, 355, 356, 358. 361
King Philip's War, 355
The Kingdom of Darkness, 440
King's Attorney, 606, 648
King's Bench, 17, 89
King's Commissioners, 309, 311, 312, 315, 346
King's Council, 150
Kingston, 332, 358
John Kitchen, 249
Elizabeth Knapp, 267, 338, 339.

Charles Knight, 357
Jonathan Knight, 620
Joseph Knight, 428
Margaret Knight, 468, 573, 596
Philip Knight, 530, 620
Elizabeth Knot, 242
Richard Knott, 675
Heinrich Kramer, 52
Dr. Jacob, 296
Dr. Jacob Kurtius, 25, 27, 29

-L-

Mary Lacey, Jr., 643, 689
Mary Lacey, Sr., 640, 642, 648, 664, 668, 671, 673
ladder, 175. *See* scaffold
Alice Lake, 258
Dr. John Lamb, 81, 82, 87, 89, 122, 123, 133
Dr. Lamb's Darling. *See* Anne Bodenham
Lamb of God, iv, v
Lambeth, 60, 74, 89, 94, 103, 329, 358
Lambeth Marsh, 329
Lambeth Palace, 60
Lanark, Scotland, 258
Lancashire, 56, 95, 97, 149
Lancashire witches, 209
Lancaster, 9, 10, 52, 596
Lancaster Castle, 95
landholder, 141
landlord, 302
Francis Lane, 422
Philpot Lane, 74
George Langdon, 247
Hannah Langdon, 247
John Lapshorne, 591
Count Adalbert Lasky, 19, 20, 21, 23, 30
Last Supper, v
Latin, 84
William Laud, Archbishop of London, 132, 151, 153
Law of Contact, ii, iii

law of elliptical orbits, 89
law of equal areas, 89
law of refraction of light, 77
Law of Similarity, ii
laws of motion and of gravity, 416
Martha Lawrence, 437
Mary Lawrence, 592
Robert Lawrence, 453
Rev. Deodat Lawson, 339, 388, 409, 410, 430-432, 504-506, 517, 520, 524, 549, 553, 576, 668
Lawrence Leach, 178
Robert Leach, 358
Lecture Day, 137, 172, 191, 202, 472, 497, 518, 626
Andrew Leet, 686
Leicester, 103, 109, 110, 115
Leicestershire, 81
Leigh, 56
Thomas Leighton, 211, 231
Leighton Buzzard, 2
Leonburg, Germany, 110, 119
Lethe, 85
Letters on the Solar Spots, 98
Hazen Levitt, 387
John Lewis, 545
Mercy Lewis, 475, 478, 485, 503-506, 523, 525, 527, 528, 534, 536, 538-540, 542, 543, 548, 549, 556, 557, 560, 561, 564, 565, 568, 569, 578, 582, 587, 589, 595, 596, 598, 599, 610, 617, 618, 628, 653, 701
Leyden, 87, 108, 124, 176
Leyden Pilgrims, 104, 105
Libra, 107, 378
licensing, 299
The Life and Death of Mother Shipton, 320
William Lilly, 110, 124, 125, 128, 129, 146, 148, 150, 194, 200, 206, 207, 211, 221, 234, 245, 258, 261, 291, 305, 310, 312, 316, 329, 332, 389-391, 456
Lincoln, 106
Earl of Lincoln, 130
Lincoln's Inn Fields, 126, 154
Lincolnshire, 71, 128
Linz, 101

Johannes Lippershey, 86
Liskeard, 108
literature, 118, 299, 379, 655
Little Castleton, 40
Little John. *See* "Carolina" John Putnam
Mary Lloyd, 400
George Locker, 486, 517
John Lombard, 245
John Londer, 410
London, 1, 3, 7, 8, 10, 12, 15, 18, 20, 63, 66, 70, 74, 79-83, 87-90, 94, 98, 99, 101, 103, 104, 110, 111, 119, 123, 125, 128, 129, 133, 136, 138, 145, 148, 150, 155, 184, 187, 194, 196, 200, 207, 208, 211, 226, 245, 260, 261, 269, 282, 287, 305, 310, 312, 317, 320, 332, 358, 373, 394, 400, 401, 410, 433, 435, 438, 445, 546, 477, 698
London Company, 79, 80, 87, 88, 104, 111, 119, 123
Long Island, 203, 283, 292, 294, 309, 314, 392
Long Marston, 2
Long Meadow, 238, 240
Long Parliament, 204, 205
Constable Lord, 284
Lord Chamberlain of England, 100
Lord Cornwallis, 298
Lord Deputy of Ireland, 184
Lord Protector, 264
Lords, 237
Lords Commissioners for Plantations in General, 153
Lords of Trade and Plantations, 361, 366, 370, 373, 410 438
Ellen Lothrop, 245, 263
Thomas Lothrop, 245, 263, 354
John Lovejoy, 638
John Lowes, 213
Lowestoft, Suffolk, 296, 298
Lubeck, 20
Roger Ludlow, 256, 267, 268
John Lyford, 126
Lyme Regis, 358
Lynn, 146, 148, 152, 159, 162, 165, 168, 173, 181, 182, 185, 188, 190, 193, 199, 201, 203, 205, 211, 231, 234, 259, 266, 269, 290, 301, 328, 335, 352, 357, 553, 581, 594, 595, 600, 622.
Lynn Bay, 181

Lyon, 142

-M-

Dame Euphane Macalzean, 43, 46
Madeira, 315
Madimi, 35, 287,
Magi, 6, 82, 86
magic, ii, iii, 8, 9, 13, 33, 45, 56, 60, 262, 333, 349, 364, 386, 406, 408, 414, 423, 479, 651
magician, ii
magistrate-for-life law, 184
Maidstone, 263
Maine, 81, 101, 185, 207, 214, 340, 352, 359, 388, 393, 421, 430, 453, 459, 460, 606, 655, 663
maize, 112, 157, 162, 225, 239, 365. *See* Indian corn
Malden, 355, 607, 608
Maldon, 50
Maleficia (*plural*; maleficium, *singular*), 50, 212, 214, 305, 344, 591, 706
malignant fever, 217
Malleus Maleficarum, 52
Man in White, 528
Man of the Signs, 177
Manchester, 51, 678
Manchester College, 52, 71
mandrake, 172
Manhattan Island, 98, 101, 104, 123, 127, 309
mania, 118.
Manichaeism, iii
Jacob Manning, 608, 610
Nicholas Manning, 362
Manningtree, 209, 220, 228
Moses Mansfield, 686, 703
Canoness Agnes von Mansfield, 13
Mansfield, Nottinghamshire, 33
Manton's Neck, 161
Marblehead, 159, 183, 220, 239, 247, 257, 319, 328, 357, 399, 437, 461, 462, 466, 475, 607
Marblehead Neck, 158
John March, 351

Ma-Re Mount. *See* Merry Mount
Marmaduke Perry, 183, 184
Mars, i
Marshal General, 275
Marshal of Salem, 405
Sara Marshfield, 231, 392
Widow Thomas Marshfield, 231, 238, 241, 243, 256
John Marston, 361, 598
Marston Moor, 207,
Mary Marston, 689
George Martin, 324, 325, 330, 331, 395
Mary Queen of Scots, 18, 32, 34, 42
Martha's Vineyard, 339
Abigail Martin, 663
Mary Martin, 217, 223
Susannah Martin, 323-326, 330, 333, 341, 347, 428, 436, 463, 472, 566, 569, 572, 619, 621, 633, 640, 708
Martin Marprelate, 38
Maryland, 425
John Mason, 111, 163
Mr. Mason, 264
Massachusetts Bay, 126-128, 130, 136, 140, 142-144, 146, 153, 154, 160, 166, 173, 176, 179, 194, 201, 203, 216, 228, 238, 277, 281, 284, 290, 301, 305, 307, 316, 340, 349, 364, 366, 370, 376, 430, 495, 599, 609, 652, 688, 708
Massachusetts Bay Company, 132, 140
Massachusetts Charter, 401, 410
Massachusetts General Court, 207
Massasoit, 116, 119, 122, 335
Jeffrey Massey, 285
mathematician, 3, 25, 118, 329, 679
Rev. Cotton Mather, 302, 355, 368, 400, 401, 421, 433, 438, 440-442, 444, 445, 448, 454, 477, 478, 482, 489, 595, 600, 607, 609, 622, 629, 658-660, 673-675, 679-681, 687, 688, 690, 693, 694, 697-701, 705, 707, 708
Rev. Increase Mather, 275, 302, 303, 339, 355, 393, 401, 414, 433, 434, 438, 440, 445, 447-479, 482, 595, 628, 650, 678, 679, 681, 683, 694, 695, 698, 699, 705
Nathaniel Mather, 421, 438
Toby Matthew,

John Matthews, 238, 246
Thomas Maule, 397, 627, 699, 700
Samuel Maverick, 224, 306
Widow Maverick, 342
Maximilian, 24
Mayflower, 109, 111, 112, 115, 117
Maypole of Merry Mount, 128, 129, 139
John Meade, 59
William Meade, 59
medicine, 118
medicine men, 166
meetinghouse, 141
"Meditations for Peace," 699,
Melampronoeia, 394
melancholia, melancholy, 118, 169
Memorable Providences Relating to Witchcrafts and Possessions, 454, 477, 482, 607
Girolamo Menghi, 52
Gerardus Mercator, 31
Ernest Merchant, 90, 110, 124
merchantman, 208
Meriden, 467, 647
Merlin, 3
Merlinus Anglicus Junior, 206, 236, 389, 391
Merlinus Liberatus, 389
Goodwife Merrick, 256
Thomas Merrick, 240, 250, 252
Sarah Merrill, 566, 572
Merrimac River, 341, 581
Merry Mount, 130, 138, 202
Messiah, 327
Metacom, 335, 353, 358
meteorology,
Middleburg, 365
Middleburgh in Zealand, Holland, 10
Middlecub, 33
Middle Temple, 340
Middlesex County, 48, 606
midwifery, i, 360, 382
Mile Brook, 189, 336,

Military Commission, 158
militia, 66, 132, 145, 164, 301, 321, 371, 450, 452, 470
Militia Bill, 198
John Milk, 299, 303
Millenary Petition, 73-75,
John Miller, 678
Joseph Miller, 290
Sarah Miller, 253, 254
Thomas Miller, 248, 254
John Milton, 176, 204
Pieter Minuit, 127
John Mitchell, 327
Mr. Mitton, 217, 223
mittimus, 603
Moderate Intelligencer, 213
A Modest Inquiry into the Nature of Witchcraft, 706
Justice John Momperson, 299, 304
Monarchy or No Monarchy, 258
Monas Hieroglyphica, 24
Monatiquot River, 120
monster, 170, 173
Richard Montague, 125
Caleb Moody, 306, 353, 354
Deborah Moody, 180, 165, 192, 203, 222
moon, i
moons of Jupiter, 90
Capt. Caleb Moore, 347, 369,
Jane Moore, 369
Richard Moore, 676
Mora, 329
George More, 61, 63
Henry More, 265, 310, 394
Prudence Morgan, 254
More Wonders of the Invisible World, 705
Francis Morris, 16, 17
Elizabeth Morse, 306, 314, 318, 327, 344, 349, 351, 353, 354, 379, 382, 383, 391
William Morse, 306, 327, 344, 349, 351, 353, 360, 379, 391
Mortlake, 3, 6, 20, 22, 45, 71, 87

Thomas Morton, Bishop of Lichfield, 115, 120, 121, 126, 128, 131, 132, 138, 142, 202, 207, 208, 214
Patrick Moscrop, 43
Samuel Mosely, 357
Henry Moses, 362
A Most Certain, Strange, and True Discovery of a Witch, Being Overtaken by Some of the Parliamentary Forces, 204
The Most Strange and Admirable Discovery of the Three Witches of Warboys, 49, 204
Mother Goose. *See* Elizabeth Vergoose
"Mother Shipton, Her Life," 211, 320
John Moulton, 668
Mount Agamenticus, 214
Mount Hope, 361
Mount Wollaston, 126
Rev. George Moxon, 165, 215, 222, 225, 226, 228, 239, 245, 252, 256, 262, 692
Martha Moxon, 223, 225, 226, 246, 250, 257
Rebecca Moxon, 226, 246, 250, 257
Munich, 70
murder, 39, 46, 49, 51, 56, 95, 96, 101, 169, 183, 184, 212, 223, 224, 255, 258, 263, 291, 314, 359, 385, 434, 544, 617, 636, 639, 656, 673
mute, 174, 293, 534, 541, 572, 668, 669
Mysteria Stephanica, 29
Mystery of Witchcraft, 105
Mystic River, 140, 145
mysticism, 6

-N-

Valentine Nabod, 200
Nahant, 181
Nantasket, 126, 142
Barbara Napier, 43, 46
Narragansett Bay, 118, 161, 355, 356, 406
Naseby, 210
Natick Indians, 361
National Covenant, 169
native Americans, 127

The Nativity of the Late King Charles Astrologically and Faithfully Performed, 287
Naumkeag, 120, 126-128, 130, 132, 133, 136. *See* Salem
Naumkeag Indians, 428
Navigation Act, 257
Navy, 200
Constable Jeremiah Neal, 452, 633, 634
John Neal, 452
Joseph Neal, 582, 597, 652
The Neck, 180
Neckar Valley, 72
necromancer, 206
necromancy, 33
necrophiliac charms, 45
Anthony Needham, 515
Negroes, 170
William Nelson, 385
Neponset River, 173
Netherlands West India Company, 104
Joan Neville, 291
New Amsterdam, 346
New England, 101, 104, 105, 111, 120, 121, 124, 126, 128, 130, 138, 139, 142, 143, 145, 146, 148, 152-155, 160, 161, 166-168, 170, 172, 173, 178, 183, 185, 188, 196-198, 202, 204, 205, 208, 216, 217, 220, 221, 225, 229, 235, 236, 242, 288, 294, 398, 301, 302, 306, 309, 312, 313, 315, 318, 321, 328, 340, 345, 347, 352, 355, 361, 363, 366, 393, 401, 410, 414, 418, 430, 434, 440, 444-446, 448, 449, 459, 463, 478, 484, 676, 687, 690, 705
New England Almanac, 311
New England Confederation, 202, 355, 356, 430
New England Council, 130
New England Judged, 294
New Experiments Phsyico-Mechanical Touching the Spring of Air and Its Effect, 291
New Hampshire, 273, 326, 346, 396, 430, 459, 627, 678
New Haven, 193, 202, 204, 233, 266, 272, 273, 467, 469, 647, 686, 703
New Jerusalem, 204
New Model, 207, 210, 225, 264
New Netherland, 123
New Netherlands, 305, 309

New Order, 110
The New Philosophy, ii, 4, 39, 200, 400, 679
New Planters, 134
New School, 132, 151, 194
New Testament, 84
New World, 31, 74, 89, 103, 104, 107, 137, 140, 145, 177, 319, 310
New York, 300, 309, 311, 314, 327, 334, 335, 344, 346, 351, 430, 649, 678, 703
The New Philosophy, ii, 208
The New School, 125
The New World, 40, 70
Newbury, Massachusetts, 162, 204, 205, 306, 314, 318, 325-327, 330, 342-344, 347, 349, 351, 353, 360, 379, 380, 391, 428, 604
Newbury Falls, 640
Newcastle, New Hampshire, 397
Newfoundland, 20
Christopher Newport, 80
News from Scotland, 46
Newton, 146, 165, 172. *See* Cambridge, Massachusetts
Isaac Newton, 416, 434
Thomas Newton, 606, 648
Niantic Indians, 361
John Nichols, 292, 559, 688
Lydia Nichols, 464, 596
Col, Richard Nichols, 306
Thomas Nichols, 530
William Nichols, 257, 270
Joseph Nicholson, 290
Charles Nicolet, 301
night watch, 141
Nonesuch, 595
Norfolk, 2, 15, 213
Norman Street, 290
Edward Norris, Jr., 268
Edward Norris, 168, 192, 203, 205, 249, 268, 283, 288
Sir Francis North, 399
North America, 83, 88, 127
North Berwick, 44, 46
North Kingston, 356
North Moreton, 77

North River, 180, 426
Northampton, Massachusetts, 276, 349, 350, 352, 373, 376
Northamptonshire, 40, 97, 151, 217
Northern Virginia, 109, 111,
Northwest Passage, 31, 88, 98
John Norton, 275, 301
"Norumbega et Virginia," 147,
Norwich, 2, 63, 64
Nottingham, 57, 200
Duke of Nottingham, 690
George Nowell, 136
nova, 76
Nova Scotia, 100, 139
Nova Steriometria Doliorum, 101
Novum Lumen Chymicum, 75
Novum Organum, 110
Roger Nowell, 95
Rev. Nicholas Noyes, 432, 455, 506, 511, 531, 549, 616, 622, 634, 640, 659, 672, 674, 677
Benjamin Nurse, 453
Francis Nurse, 283, 284, 304, 366, 376, 407, 446, 451, 662
Rebecca Nurse, 366, 452, 453, 500-503, 505, 517, 518, 521, 523, 524, 526-529, 533-539, 562, 575, 577, 608, 616, 617, 619-622, 629-636, 640, 646, 648, 702
Samuel Nurse, 527, 658, 691, 702
Sarah Nurse, 631
Alice Nutter, 96
Christopher Nutter, 96
Robert Nutter, 95

-O-

Oak Knoll, 294, 320, 336
occult, 4-6, 10, 37, 77, 105, 124, 215, 221, 263, 265, 281, 310, 315, 364, 373, 376, 380, 386, 388, 402, 414, 416, 463, 478, 479, 486, 526, 635, 638
Goodwife Odell, 268
Colonel Okye, 211
Old Chattox, 95, 98. *See* Anne Whittle
Old Demdike, 95, 98. *See* Elizabeth Southern

Old Planters, 134, 144, 157
Old Testament, 84
John Oldham, 132, 163
Bridget Oliver. *See* Bridget Bishop, Bridget Wasselby
Mary Oliver, 175, 176, 183, 202, 220, 224, 228, 235, 239, 240, 243, 244, 254, 278
Thomas Oliver, 176, 235, 244, 278, 293, 296, 316, 334, 335, 367, 377
One God, iii
onychomancy, 479. *See* scrying
oomancy, 481
Orchard Farm, 147
Original Sin, 1
Orion, 3
Goodman Orn, 591
Alexander Osburn, 483, 490
Sarah Osburn, 483-485, 488, 489, 494-497, 558, 582
Capt. John Osgood, 666
Mary Osgood. *See* Mary Osgood Baker
Capt. William Osgood, 186, 287, 395, 668
Ouroboros, 6
Thomas Overbury, 93, 98, 99, 101
Oxford, 9, 15, 74, 82, 132, 154, 261, 269, 282, 291, 390, 408, 446, 598
Oyster Bay, 292

-P-

Pacific Ocean, 7
pact with the Devil, iv
Deborah Pacy, 296, 297
Elizabeth Pacy, 297
Padua, 47, 90
Margaret Page, 201, 216, 224, 227
Elizabeth Paine, 608, 620
Palace of the Inquisition, 148
Peter Palfrey, 130, 157
Pall Mall, 456
John Palmer, 242
palmistry, 322, 335, 352, 370, 399, 479, 567
Pandaemonium, 416, 607
Paqutwock, 47

Paracelsus, 294, 365
Paradise, 5
parish clerk, 141
Parish Committee, 343, 374, 388
parish meeting, 141
Alice Parker, 461, 469, 590, 594, 619, 667, 668, 674, 708
Hannah Parker, 647, 703
John Parker, 280, 370, 414, 424, 515, 594, 596
Joseph Parker, 647
Mary Parker, 414, 415, 423, 424, 436, 480, 590, 652, 664, 671
Parliament, 3, 8, 32, 73, 76, 79, 92, 100, 108, 117, 123, 125-127, 130, 132-135, 155, 184, 185, 187-189, 194-196, 198, 200, 204, 206, 208, 211, 213, 219, 221, 222, 225, 234-237, 257, 263, 312, 317, 347, 390, 433, 440
Parliament House, 123
Parliamentary Commission of Oyer and Terminer, 212
Parliamentary Commissioners, 225
Parliamentary Committee, 211
Elizabeth Parris, 475, 478, 480, 481, 485, 500, 502, 523, 525, 606, 627
Rev. Samuel Parris, 446, 450, 452, 454, 455, 458, 464, 466, 468, 470, 478, 482, 486, 491, 497, 500, 504, 523, 525, 526, 529, 538, 560, 611, 628, 637, 658, 662, 669, 674, 677, 682, 684, 691, 699, 702
Mrs. Samuel Parris, 475, 481
Hugh Parsons, 165, 215, 226, 230, 231, 233, 235, 238-243, 245, 247, 248, 250, 252-254, 256, 261, 276
John Parsons, 352
Joseph Parsons, 253, 276, 340
Joshua Parsons, 246, 255
Mary Bliss Parsons, 253, 256, 276, 350, 352, 374
Mary Lewis Parsons, 215, 231, 233, 235, 238, 239, 246, 249, 352-356, 258, 276
Samuel Parsons, 231, 239, 240
John Partridge, 291, 389, 456, 573, 577. *See* Field Marshal Partridge
Pater Noster, 443
Pawtucket Indians, 104
Edward Payson, 618
John Pearly, 422
Madeline Pearson, 328
Sarah Townsend Pearson, 328
Henry Pease, 247

Sarah Pease, 600, 652,
peers, 200
Edward Peggy, 348
peine forte et dure, 668, 671
Joseph Peirce, 357
William Peirce,
Pemaquid, 185
Pembroke Hall, Cambridge, 78
Penacook Indians, 419
Pendle, 95, 149
William Penn, 408
Penobscot River, 101
Agnes Pepwell, 77
Mary Pepwell, 77
Pequot Indians, 163, 183
Margaret Perd, 694, 696, 697
perjured testimony, 692
Elizabeth Perkins, 267
Luke Perkins, 393
William Perkins, 86, 105, 265, 449, 482, 489, 683
Deborah Perley, 618
Hannah Perley, 618
Samuel Perley, 608, 618
Timothy Perley, 618
William Perry, 109, 115, 117
Rev. Hugh Peter, 158, 159, 163, 175, 189, 191, 199, 227, 291
Joan Peterson, 260, 263
Petition of Right, 132, 134, 155, 160, 184
John Phelps, 369, 613
Sarah Phelps, 664
Philip of Spain, 32, 37
Sir Edward Philips, 118
Charles Phillips, 667
Mary Phillips, 210, 213, 216, 217
Samuel Phillips, 455, 618
Sarah Phillips, 412
Philomaths, 310, 312, 329
Philosopher's Stone, 11, 20, 51, 67, 69, 72, 73, 75, 456
Philosophiae Naturalis Principia Mathematica, 434
Philosophical Transactions, 332, 362

philosophy, 118
Lady Mary Phips, 666, 677, 687
Governor William Phips, 459, 462, 465, 577, 595, 606, 669, 680, 684, 687, 690
physic, 122. *See* medicine
Henry Pickering of Christ's College, 41
John Pickering, 178
Samuel Pickworth, 670
Capt. William Pierce, 142, 173
Robert Pike, 656
Samuel Pikeworth, 357
Pilgrims, 109
Pilniewinks, 43, 45
pine tree money, 262
Pisa, 38
Piscataqua, 663
Piscataway, 460, 472
Pisces, 101, 259, 285
Peter Pitford, 247
William Pitkin, 683
Charity Pitman, 437
Goodman Pitman, 678
plagiarism, 655
plague, 104, 125, 128, 153, 155, 234, 310, 315-317
plague of locusts, 234. *See* cicada
planetarium, 242
planetary influences, 260
Platform of Church Government, 256
Plum Island, 341
Plymouth Colony, 79, 81, 100, 114-116, 118-122, 126, 127, 131, 132, 136, 138, 142, 144-146, 153, 155, 161, 163, 202, 207, 217, 222, 292, 355, 356, 361, 363, 392, 430, 676
Plymouth Company, 79, 81, 100
Plymouth, England, 217
A Poem of Chemistry, 51
A Poem of the Philosopher's Stone, 51
Poindexter – see Pudeator
James Poland, 369
poll tax, 432
poltergeist, 304, 379, 380

Pontifical Court, 94
Pool's Wharf, 430
Widow Poole, 258
William Poole, 257
Gertrude Pope, 505, 507, 516, 522, 536, 541
Pope Paul V, 102
Pope Sixtus V, 33
George Popham, 81
poppit, ii, 422, 442, 486, 506, 588, 589, 591, 593, 609, 612, 618, 635, 638, 706
Port House, 168
Port Royal, 459
Port Seton, 64
Benjamin Porter, 622
Elizabeth Hathorne Porter, 502, 630, 631
George Porter, 282
Israel Porter, 391, 502
John Porter, Jr., 304, 306, 308, 309, 312, 313
John Porter, Sr., 273, 281, 290, 306, 307
Joseph Porter, 391, 431
Portsmouth, 274, 275, 277, 299, 326
possession. *See* demonic possession
Hannah Post, 664, 668, 689
Margaret Post, 689
Mary Post, 689
Sarah Post, 698
John Potts, 98
Caleb Powell, 379, 380, 382
Powers of Darkness, iv
Practical Magic, iii
Prague, 22, 29, 33, 37, 61, 64, 74, 75, 77, 89, 97
Prebend of Canterbury, 323
prehistoric temple, 236
Joan Prentice, 40
Presbyterianism, 28, 76, 152, 167, 205, 219, 226, 228, 232
Dr. Prescott, 467, 469
Mrs. Prescott, 385
Peter Prescott, 358, 474
John Pressey, 324, 333
Thomas Preston, 407, 485

Samuel Preston, 461, 462
Capt. Price, 590
Walter Price, 301, 378
John Pride, 192
Robert Prince, 282, 483
Sarah Prince, 483
Martin Pring, 75
Privy Council, 17, 18, 32, 66, 98, 200, 680, 690
Benjamin Proctor, 600
Elizabeth Proctor, 478, 497, 501, 505, 517, 525, 528, 529, 534, 539, 547, 608, 619, 621, 626, 630, 651, 652, 689, 706
George Proctor, 582, 659
John Proctor, Jr., 547
John Proctor, Sr., 316, 358, 368, 369, 478, 524, 525, 529, 535, 536, 538, 550, 552, 604, 608, 620, 622, 626, 646, 650, 651, 653, 656, 659, 668
Joseph Proctor, 652
Sarah Proctor, 594, 600, 608
William Proctor, 607, 608, 611, 614, 646
A Prodigious and Tragical History, 263
Katherine Prout, 698
Marah Pressey, 333
profanation of the Lord's Day, 256
Promised Land, 124
prophecy, 8, 211
The Prophecy of Mother Shipton in the Reign of Henry VIII, 194
proportional compass, 58
Protectorate, 264, 275, 284, 291
Protestantism, v, 3, 11, 28, 34, 39, 42, 44, 84, 122, 123, 135, 205, 219, 237, 257, 293, 434, 438, 440, 445
Providence, 163
Providence of God, 146, 170, 171, 204, 313, 347, 401, 616, 700, 701, 707
William Prynne, 151, 154, 168, 187
psychology, 118
Ptolemaic theory, 77, 99
Publick Occurrences Both Foreign and Domestic, 462
Pullen Point, 209
Puritan army, 196, 207
Ann Pudeator, 589, 590, 594, 618, 633, 665, 669, 670, 674, 708
Puritanism, i, 4, 28, 38, 76, 86, 132, 154, 163, 196
Putnam family, 111, 176, 178

Abigail Putnam, 395, 411, 623

Ann Carr Putnam, 344, 367, 372, 376, 378, 389, 406, 422, 437, 440, 455, 468, 478, 503, 505, 517-520, 524, 526, 529, 580, 616, 617, 622, 684, 701

Ann Holyoke Putnam, 201, 205, 214, 234, 244, 259, 269, 277, 288, 296, 314, 426

Ann Putnam, 214, 296, 453, 476, 517, 523, 567

Ann Putnam, Jr. *See* Annie Putnam

Annie Putnam, 296, 378, 379, 475, 478, 483-485, 493, 497-501, 503, 504, 506, 511, 519, 523, 527, 534-538, 540-543, 548, 549, 554, 556, 558, 563, 564, 567, 569, 575-577, 581, 588, 594, 598, 604, 510, 611, 613, 614, 618, 621, 634, 635, 653-655, 658, 672, 673, 676, 684, 701, 706, 708

Bartholomew Putnam, 437

Benjamin Putnam, 310, 420, 428, 437, 438, 458, 459, 529, 631

Deliverance Putnam Walcott, 277, 280, 420, 425, 437, 438, 440, 452, 455, 465, 528

Eben Putnam, 712

Ebenezer Putnam, 322

Edward Putnam, Jr., 395

Edward Putnam, Sr., 269, 335, 395, 406, 423, 450, 453, 454, 460, 463, 470, 474, 480, 485, 498, 499, 501, 507, 509, 517, 519, 526, 547, 554, 622, 637, 662, 670, 691s

Eleazer Putnam, 314, 462, 688

Elisha Putnam, 423

Elizabeth Hutchinson Putnam, 266, 271, 278, 288, 301, 323, 538

Elizabeth Porter Putnam, 460, 466

Elizabeth Putnam, 7, 28, 59, 65, 97, 121, 146, 288, 301

Elizabeth Whipple Putnam, 398

Hannah Boardman Putnam, 688

Hannah Cutler Putnam, 373, 377, 440, 460, 498, 620

Hannah Putnam, 302, 320, 377, 388, 395, 396, 416, 429, 444, 471, 497, 538, 539, 712

Hannah Walcott Putnam, 421, 428, 437, 438, 458, 459

Holyoke Putnam, 406

James Putnam, Jr., 455, 459

James Putnam, Sr., 294, 321, 437, 455, 459, 460, 529, 631, 681

Capt. John Putnam, Jr., 104, 111, 129, 146, 160, 180, 196, 205, 231, 234, 262, 266, 267, 270, 272, 278, 282, 285, 292-294, 299, 302, 304, 305, 313, 314, 316, 320, 323, 326, 330, 338, 340, 342, 345, 346, 348, 349,

359, 360, 362, 363, 265-367371, 374-376, 383, 388-391, 393-395, 403, 404, 406, 409, 410, 425, 446, 452, 460, 468, 474, 477, 529, 577, 581, 628, 631, 632

Carolina John Putnam, 278, 285, 336, 337, 353, 358, 373, 377, 388, 395, 411, 416, 429, 429, 440, 444, 460, 471, 478, 497, 498, 529, 530, 538, 539, 579, 5878, 594, 596, 598, 620, 637, 685

John Putnam, Sr., 9, 28, 32, 34, 40, 47, 59, 60, 65, 66, 70, 74, 75, 79-81, 83, 87, 88, 91, 93, 94, 98, 100, 103, 104, 106, 107, 121, 128, 135, 146, 147, 151, 160, 166, 178, 180, 181, 182, 188, 189, 193, 196, 199, 208, 225, 257, 261, 266, 271, 278, 281, 301, 302, 353, 357, 393, 717

John Putnam III, 321, 529

Jonathan Putnam, 285, 321, 387, 388, 393, 398, 406, 416, 420, 421, 432, 440, 449, 452, 460, 465, 468, 472, 517, 599, 623, 628, 631

Joseph Putnam, 327, 328, 335, 426, 437, 440, 455, 460, 466, 484, 498, 502, 524, 529, 539, 619, 631, 679, 702

Josiah Putnam, 429, 437

Lydia Potter Putnam, 406, 416, 421, 432, 449, 468, 631

Lydia Putnam, Jr., 421

Margaret Goodspeed Putnam,

Margaret Putnam, i, 7, 28, 31, 58, 97, 99, 106

Mary Hale Putnam, 395, 406, 423, 347, 453, 480

Mary Putnam, 244. *See* Mary Putnam Tufts

Mary Veren Putnam, 316, 318, 327, 426, 446, 466, 484

Nathan Putnam, 681

Nathaniel Putnam, Jr., 271

Nathaniel Putnam, Sr. 107, 121, 129, 160, 178, 180, 182, 184, 185, 196, 231, 241, 243, 254, 265, 266, 271, 275, 278, 281, 282, 284, 285, 287, 288, 294, 301, 304, 306, 310, 314, 315, 318, 320, 323, 326, 335, 338, 339, 341, 343, 344, 346-348, 350, 363, 364, 366-369, 372, 374, 378, 383, 389, 394, 395, 407, 416, 425, 428, 437, 447, 450, 452, 468, 472, 473, 476, 549, 564, 631, 659, 662, 670

Nathaniel Putnam III, 428, 608,

Nicholas Putnam, i, 6, 27, 31, 58, 59, 106

Phoebe Putnam, 124, 160

Priscilla Gould Putnam, 93, 97, 99, 101, 103, 107, 121, 129, 151, 93, 107, 121, 129, 151, 160, 179, 199, 234, 257, 278, 309, 320,

Prudence Putnam, 296, 299, 395, 480

Rebecca Prince Putnam, 262, 266, 278, 285, 294, 302, 314, 335, 342, 346, 483, 631

Rebecca Putnam, 320, 337, 342, 471, 493, 579, 632

Ruth Putnam, 346, 460
Samuel Putnam, 266, 416
Sarah Putnam, 121, 160, 234, 320, 342, 437, 455, 458, 497, 498, 508, 538, 539, 579, 595, 617, 620, 631, 681, 712
baby Sarah Putnam, 269
Susannah Putnam, 335, 460
Tarrant Putnam, ,
Thomas Putnam, Jr., 318, 319, 322, 327, 372, 376, 378, 379, 389, 394, 395, 420, 440, 468, 474, 485, 501, 517, 527, 549, 554, 566, 600, 614, 637, 672, 673, 684, 685, 701
Thomas Putnam, Sr., 28, 59, 65, 101, 121, 129, 160, 178, 180, 185, 188, 199, 201, 202, 205, 211, 214, 231, 234, 235, 244, 259, 266, 269, 272, 273, 277, 280, 282, 283, 285, 286, 288, 290, 296, 301, 302, 311, 314-316, 318, 322, 327, 341, 343, 350, 352, 362, 364, 366, 374, 375, 388, 389, 391, 395, 410, 425, 438, 446, 673
Thomas Putnam III, 389
Timothy Putnam, 468
William Putnam, 465
Puttenham. 1, 2. *See also* Putnam
George Puttenham, 15, 17, 40, 51, 58
Mary Puttenham, 16, 17
Richard Puttenham, 15, 32, 33, 58, 59, 65, 135
Puttenhams of Sherfield, Southampton, 15, 58
John Pym, 118, 195
John Pynchon, 262
William Pynchon, 136, 142, 165, 222, 226, 239, 245, 250, 255, 256, 262

-Q-

Quakerism, 277-278, 281-282, 305
Quakers, 275, 280, 281, 283, 286, 287, 290, 294, 299, 305, 309, 384, 392, 397, 408, 423, 436, 627, 699, 408, 700
quarantine, 422
Quebec, 83, 104, 462
The Question of Witchcraft Debated, 329
Quinborough, 20
Quirinal Palace, 94

-R-

Thomas Rabbet, 14
Ragley Castle, 310
Sir Walter Raleigh, 20, 31, 34, 37, 70, 89, 99
Edward Randolph, 361, 364, 373, 401
Ranters, 275
James Ratcliffe, 80
rationalism, 393, 651
Ratisbon, Germany, 142
Daniel Ray, 146, 450
Joshua Ray, 446, 447
John Raymond, 357, 358
Thomas Raymond, 358, 600, 622
William Raymond, 358, 462, 527
Christopher Read, 448
Joan Hoar Read, 448
Simon Reade, 80, 87, 89
Reading, 281, 551, 572, 594, 596, 616
John Reddington, 439
Margaret Reddington, 455
Mary Reddington, 439
Anne Redfearn, 95
Dr. Reed, 328, 329, 388
Nicholas Reed, 454
Philip Reed, 328, 386, 388
Mammy Wilmot Reed, 437, 438, 461, 462, 466, 475, 607, 609, 671, 674, 708
Refrigeration, 127
Religio Medici, 200
religion, ii
Religious Freedom, 203
resident Governor of the colony of Massachusetts Bay, 138
Restoration, 343
John Reynolds, 75
Rhode Island, 163, 166, 171, 188, 204, 283, 308, 309, 355, 356, 361, 397, 430, 649
Robert Rich, Earl of Warwick, 213
John Richards, 394, 477, 606, 687
Joshua Richardson, 349

Mary Richardson, 668
Jarvis Ring, 472
Joseph Ring, 460-462, 472
Sarah Rist, 616
ritual, v
Roanoke Island, 32, 38, 47,
Alexander Roberts, 104
Edmund Robinson, 149, 150, 364
Isaac Robinson, 169
John Robinson, 71, 74, 80, 83, 87, 104, 109, 124, 127, 235, 415
Robinson Pilgrims, 108
Henry Roby, 271, 386
Viscount Rochester. *See* Robert Carr
Ann Rogers, 314
Goodman Rogers, 309
John Rogers, 421, 461
Rogheda, 237
Roman Catholic Church, v, 125
Rome, 98, 122
Susannah Root, 600
Margaret Roper, 33, 54
George Ropes, 241
Count Wilhelm von Rosenberg, Viceroy of Bohemia, 37
Lord Henry Ross, 106
Mary Ross, 392
Francis Ross, Earl of Rutland, 106
Roundheads. *See* Puritan army
John Rouse, 283
Richard Rowland, 319,
Rowley, 262, 267, 275, 349, 376, 618
Roxbury, 262, 275, 348, 357, 383, 388, 579
Royal Charter, 313
Royal Collector of Customs for New England, 373
Royal Colony, 417
Royal Prerogative, 93. *See* Royal rule of England
Royal Province, 430
Royal rule of England, 92
Royal Side, 391, 676
Royal Society of London, 305, 310, 332, 362, 400. *See* Invisible College
Royalists, 196, 207, 210, 219, 233

Richard Rucke, 654
Thomas Rucke, 288, 393, 654
Emperor Rudolph II of Germany, 13, 19, 24, 33, 51, 60, 61, 64, 59, 75, 89, 97
Rudolphine Tables, 130
Margaret Rule, 693-698, 705
Rumney Marsh, 607
Rump Parliament, 263
Rush-Bearing ceremony, 27
James Russell, 531, 684
Countess of Rutland, 106
Rutterkin, 106

-S-

Sabbat, 95, 96, 149, 150, 450, 581, 639, 640, 663
Sacred Animal, iv
Sacred Books, 82
sacrifice, iv
sadducism, 446
Saducismus Triumphatus, 394, 482, 607
William Saffold, 312
Sagamore, 153, 419, 420
Sagamore George, 428
Saggiatore, 122
Sagittarius, 3
St. Albans, 242
St. Andrews, 28
St. Barholomew's Day, 301
St. Cecilia's Day, 195
St. Giles, 151, 169
St. James, 237
St. John's College, Cambridge, 78, 86,
St. Mary's Church, 57
St. Olave's, 33, 40
St. Osyth, 14
St. Paul's Cross, 133
St. Peter, 16
St. Peter's Street, 426
Sainthood, 6

Salem, 120, 137-140, 142-146 ,152-154, 156-166, 168-170, 172-176, 178-189, 191-196, 198, 199, 201-204, 207-209, 211, 215, 220-335, 227, 229, 231, 234, 235, 239, 240, 243-245, 249, 254, 257, 260-263, 265-269, 271, 273, 275, 277-280, 282-288, 290-294, 296, 299, 301, 303-307, 309-311, 313-316, 318, 320-323, 325-328, 330, 334, 335, 338, 340-342, 344-351, 353, 357, 359, 361-363, 365-369, 371, 372, 374-379, 382-384, 387, 388, 390, 391, 394, 397, 405, 411, 414, 416, 418, 420, 422, 423, 425, 426, 428, 430-432, 437, 438, 442, 444, 452, 461, 463, 468, 470, 476, 482, 484, 500, 521, 525, 529, 531, 537, 539, 547-549, 555, 566, , , , , , , , 573, 577, 579, 581-583, 586, 590, 594, 596, 598, 600, 608, 622-624, 625, 627, 630-632, 640, 646, 649, 651, 653, 665, 667, 668, 670-673, 675-678, 680-682, 686, 689, 690, 698-700, 703

Salem Board of Selectmen, 243

Salem Church, , 137, 142, 144, 158, 159, 162, 174, 176, 192, 201, 203, 211, 225, 231, 244, 266, 277, 280, 282, 283, 290, 309, 319, 335, 340, 372, 374, 375, 409, 431, 634, 672

Salem Common, 415

Salem Court, 368

Salem Court House, 619

Salem Farms, 168, 182, 184, 186, 188, 410. *See* Salem Village, Danvers.

Salem First Church, 421, 432, 437, 440, 444, 454, 466, 597. *See* Salem Church.

Salem Harbor, 154, 170

Salem Head, 184

Salem Latin Grammar School, 168, 268

Salem meetinghouse, 183, 272, 275, 321, 348, 363, 531

Salem Militia, 352, 371

Salem Neck, 168

Salem Parish, 455

Salem Prison, 355, 377, 399, 415, 516, 523, 524, 538, 547, 591, 594, 616, 657

Salem school public education, 209

Salem Selectmen, 261

Salem sessions, 229, 279

Salem Village, 188, 189, 191, 203, 231, 254, 257, 259-261, 265, 266, 271, 277, 278, 282, 284, 288, 289, 295, 301, 302, 304, 319, 321, 322, 325, 330, 340-343, 345, 348-350, 352, 354, 357, 358, 360, 364-367, 371, 373, 374, 378, 379, 383, 387-389, 391, 393-395, 398, 405, 406, 409, 410, 416, 418, 420, 425-427, 429, 432, 435, 442, 446, 449-452, 454,

458-460, 463, 465, 466, 470, 472, 474, 475, 480, 482-484, 496-498, 501, 503, 504, 528, 529, 531, 535, 538, 539, 548, 549, 553, 555, 565, 573, 576-579, 588, 594, 596, 600, 601, 604, 607-609, 626-628, 638-640, 647, 651, 653, 663, 669, 672, 673, 677, 679, 681, 682, 684, 688, 699, 700, 702, 705, 708

Salem Village Church, 389, 452, 455, 463, 471, 478, 691, 706

Salem Village Whitewash, 675

Salem Village Witchhunt, 673, 685, 694

Salisbury, 265, 304, 314, 323, 325, 326, 341, 342, 344, 346, 376, 391, 395, 396, 460, 472, 656

Salmesbury witches, 96

Salmon Falls, New Hampshire, 396, 405, 459

William Salter, 313

Nathaniel Saltonstall, 606, 629

Richard Saltonstall, 136, 152

Saltpans, 43, 45

Salvation by the Grace of God, 63, 67

Salvation by Works, 86, 163

Salvation of the Elect, 5, 109

Samoset, 116

Agnes Sampson, 43, 46

Agnes Samuel, 48

John Samson, 322, 352, 371, 407

Alice Samuel, 41, 46, 48

John Samuel, 48

Don Guglielmo de San Clemente, 22

Santa Maria sopra Minerva, 148

Satan, iv, 47, 81, 84, 88, 92, 104, 105, 139, 153, 174, 210, 212, 217, 225, 228, 242, 255, 261, 264, 265, 282, 289, 300, 339, 364, 456, 504, 518, 524, 542, 562, 628, 650, 653, 663, 667, 707, 708. *See* Devil

Satan's scourge. *See* smallpox.

Barnabas Saul, 10

Satanism, 706

Saturn, i

Saugus. *See* Lynn

Saugus River, 181

John Sawdy, 666

scaffold, 174

Scandinavia, 329

John Scarlet, 591

schism, 256
Scholasticism, 4, 39
School House Lane, 168
Count Adolph von Schwarzenburg, 60
Science, ii, 4, 5, 39, 69, 79, 94, 110, 118, 242, 401, 651, 688
scire facias, 410
Scituate, 292, 363
Reginald Scot, 55, 73, 105, 273
Scotland, 28, 64, 169, 244
Scots, 257
James Scott, Duke of Monmouth, 425
Joshua Scott, 460
Margaret Scott, 671, 674, 708
Scottish army, 194, 207
Scottish Commissioners, 228
Scottish Presbyterian Calvinism, 18
Joshua Scottow, 272
Hieronymous Scotus, 13
Scribe of the Gods. *See* Hermes Trismegistus
Scrooby, 80, 83
Thomas Scruggs, 165
scrying, 10, 12, 26, 31, 36, 478, 479, 481, 604, 627
Peter Sergeant, 606
Goodman Sears, 223
David Seaton, 42
Alexander Seton, 64, ,67 ,68 ,70-72, 75, 221, 373
second death, 85. *See* Death
secondary schools, 228
secret ballot, 137
Secret Name, iii, 6
Secretary of State, 349
sector. *See* proportional compass
sedition, 168, 440
Elizabeth Seger, 311
Select Cases of Conscience, 219
Selectmen, 141, 164, 166, 201, 216, 222, 224, 271, 272, 275, 278, 280-282, 287, 293, 295, 303, 304, 311, 315, 316, 318, 319, 322, 325, 330, 334, 335, 340, 345, 347, 348, 350, 359-361, 362, 367, 371, 377, 382, 385, 422, 433, 452. 460, 468, 469, 472, 647. *See* Board of Selectmen
Selectmen of Salem, 164, 166

Michael Sendigovius, 72, 75, 221
separation of powers between Church and State, 204
Separatism, 8, 83, 88, 104, 142
Capt. Edward Sergeant, 453
Setauket, Long Island, 306, 314
Bessy Sewall, 247, 253, 255, 256
Jane Sewall, 360
Samuel Sewall, Jr., 700
Justice Samuel Sewall, Sr., 430, 531, 537, 577, 579, 606, 658, 659, 673, 674, 681, 683, 684, 687, 693, 698, 700-702, 704
Stephen Sewall, 500, 525, 606, 627, 673-675, 679
sexton, 141
Lawrence Shafling, 626
William Shakespeare, 102
Samuel Shattuck, 286, 294, 384. 423, 435
Deborah Shaw, 629
Elizabeth Shaw, 626
William Shaw, 566, 582, 620, 629
Shawshin River, 664
Gilbert Sheldon, Archbishop of Canterbury, 332
Godfrey Sheldon, 461
Samuel Sheldon, 655
Susan Sheldon, 568, 676,
Susannah Sheldon, 478, 565-567, 580, 582, 585, 596, 613, 620, 629, 630
John Shepard, 579, 617
Rebecca Putnam Shepard, 575, 579, 616, 617, 622, 632
Sherborne, 89
Sherfield, 16, 17
Goodwife Sherman, 207
Robert Sherringham, 298
ship money, 155, 160, 166, 167
Shippen's, 404
Mercy Short, 459, 464, 629, 658, 687, 688, 690, 696
Short Parliament, 185
Mary Sibley, 481, 482, 496, 525, 526
Richard Sibley, 283
Samuel Sibley, 405, 481, 496, 497, 524
William Sibley, 405
Siderius Nuncius, 90
Sienna, 148

Sarah Simms, 437, 438
Simon, Baccalaureate of Prague, 22
James Simons, 293
Samuel Simons, 301
William Simons, 301, 439
Jonathan Singletary, 285, 301
six-mile extent boundary order, 184
Rev. Samuel Skelton, 137, 144, 147, 148, 152, 156, 165
Mrs. Samuel Skelton, 144
The Skeptical Chemist, 294
Francis Skerry, 335
Henry Skerry, 359, 403, 405
slavery, 170, 177, 362, 698
Charles Sledd, 258
Anne Small, 652
John Small, 652
smallpox, 81, 88, 91, 111, 139, 155, 156, 242, 365, 371, 374, 417, 422, 423, 438, 456, 463, 465, 595, 613, 633, 688, 702, 708, 712
Henry Smith, 232, 246
James Smith, 319
Capt. John Smith, 88. 100, 103, 111, 145, 290
John Smith of Husbands Bosworth, 81, 102
Margaret Smith, 232
Nathaniel Smith, 386
Philip Smith, 416
Roger Smith, 81
Samuel Smith, 391, 433
Sarah Smith, 233
John Soam, 298
Abigail Soames, 594, 600
solar eclipse, 305, 628
solemn day of prayer and fasting, 497
Solemn League and Covenant, 205, 207
Solicitor General, 366, 370
Some Few Remarks upon a Scandalous Book, 706
Some Miscellany Observations on Our Present Debates Respecting Witchcrafts, in A Dialogue between S. & B., by P. E. & J. A., 680
William Somers, 57, 60, 63
Earl of Somerset, Treasurer of Scotland, 102
Americus Sontag, 24

sorcery, ii, iv, 3, 6, 10, 39, 41, 50, 80, 89, 122, 263, 298, 309, 679
soul, iv
South Kingston, 356
South Lambeth, 340, 365
South River, 168, 180, 288, 306
Southampton, 100, 109, 110
Southereh, 586
Elizabeth Southern, 95
Southold, 392
Southwark, 33
Cassandra Southwick, 280
John Southwick, 290
Josiah Southwick, 283
Lawrence Southwick, 278, 280
Spain, 76, 122, 123, 264
Spanish Armada, 37
Spanish boots, 45
Spanish Main, 264
Martha Sparks, 474, 475, 531, 606, 685
Speaker of the House of Deputies, 134, 211, 220, 228, 244, 278, 290,
Special Commission, 376, 606
specie, 186
spectral evidence, 50, 121, 212, 216, 226, 297, 319, 489, 493, 498, 520, 523, 547, 609, 650, 671, 678, 680, 681, 685, 687-689, 691, 692, 700
Speedwell, 109, 110, 118
John Spencer, 186
Mary Spencer, 149, 150
Octavious Spinola, 24
Thomas Spooner, 291
Martha Sprague, 663, 664, 666
Jacob Springer, 52
Springfield, 166, 215, 222, 225-228, 230-233, 235, 238, 239, 241, 243, 245, 247, 250, 254, 256, 262, 268, 276, 350, 376, 692
Squanto, 116
Joseph Stacey, 426
Priscilla Stacey, 456
William Stacey, 365, 371, 372, 456
Stafford, 109, 117
Capt. Stagg, 208
Stalbridge, 208, 269

Stamford, 29
standing mute, 174
Miles Standish, 112, 116, 126, 131
Nathaniel Stanley, 683
Mary Staples, 268
Thomas Staples, 268
Star Chamber, 136, 154
Nicholas Starkey, 56
Starry Messenger, 211
State Puritanism, 205
John Stearne, 209, 220
Rebecca Stearns, 289
John Stebbins, 253, 373, 376
Mrs. John Stebbins, 254
Stephanus of Alexandria, 29
Goodman Stephens, 168
Stetin, Pomerania, 20
Elias Stileman, 167, 241, 366
John Stone, 644
Stewkeley, 2, 31, 40, 59, 65, 97
Stoke Poges, 132, 156
Robert Stone, Jr., 626
Robert Stone, Sr., 626
Stonington, 554
Israel Stoughton, 191
Justice William Stoughton, 364, 373, 394, 442, 443, 579, 580, 582-584, 595, 606, 632, 633, 668, 674, 675, 679, 687, 689, 690, 701
Stow-on-the-Wold, 210
Straits of Magellan, 7
Strasbourg, 69
Stratford, Connecticut, 256
Stratford-upon-Avon, 102
Alice Stratton, 232
Samuel Street, 703
Mrs. Samuel Street, 703
Mary Stuart, Queen of Scots, 440, 447, 690, 692
study atomic, 456
Governor Pieter Stuyvesant, 305
Elizabeth Style, 310
Ann Styles, 264

John Styles, 379, 380, 382
Styx, 85
succubus, 210, 300
suffocation of the mother, 40, 64, 77, 481, 681. *See* hysteria
Suffolk, 19, 213, 217
Suffolk County, 306, 348, 606
Suffolk Sessions in Bury St. Edmunds, 213
sugar, 182
Sugar Loaf Hill, 354
suicide, 90, 124, 428, 496, 672, 691
A Summary Answer, 64
Sun, 4
Superior Court of Judicature, 687, 689
Supernatural Sight, 207
Surrey, 245, 605
Swagustago River, 387
Swallow, 277
Swan, 119, 120
Timothy Swan, 605, 638, 641, 645
Sweden, 305, 329
swimming, 210, 212, 300
Job Swinnerton, 431
John Swinnerton, 423
Dinah Sylvester,
symbolism, v
Samuel Symonds, 152
sympathetic magic, ii-iv, 8, 44, 96, 118, 212, 270, 315, 348, 364, 386, 398, 413, 478, 599, 609, 651, 706
synod of the churches, 152, **204**, 221, 232, 281

-T-

Talbot, 139
Difficulty Talby, 174
Dorothy Talby, 169, 174
John Talby, 278, 280
tall man of Boston, 491
Jonathan Taylor, 250, 252, 254
Tarazed, 3
John Tarbell, 407, 450, 527, 658, 662, 691, 702

Tarrantine Indian War, 104
Tarrantine Indians, 101
Taunton, 335, 353, 425
taxation without reprsentation, 132, 160, 433
teacher, 141
Tedworth, Wiltshire, 299, 304
telepathy, 655
telescope, 88, 305
Temperance Lloyd, 400
Test Act, 347
testing, 210, 212, 216, 300
Thames, 94, 320
Thanksgiving, 194, 455, 477
Anthony Thatcher, 183, 220
Theatrum Chemicum Britannicum, 263
Theoretical Magic, iii
theory of the variation of the magnet, 408
theory of vision, 77
Thirty Years War, 105
Sir Amyas Paulet, 34
Thomas, Lord Paulet, 17
Thomas, Lord Windsor, 81, 89
Thomas Thompson, 320
Edward Thomson, 113
Goodman Thomson, 232
William Thomson, 224
David Thorlowe, 14
Grace Thorlowe, 14
Mr. Thorndyke, 241
Thorpe, 263
Thoth, 82
Thou shalt not suffer a witch to live, 86
thrawing, 43, 44, 45
Jane Throckmorton, 40, 41
Sir John Throckmorton, 17
Robert Throckmorton, 47
Throckmorton family, 48
John Tilly, 163
tithing, 368, 374, 409
Tituba. *See* Tituba Indian.

tobacco, 310
Toleration Act, 447
"tonnage and poundage" taxes, 134
Job Tookey, 399, 675, 689
Alan Toothaker, 467, 501
Aunt Mary Toothaker, 421. 461, 599, 607
Roger Toothaker, 461, 597-599,
Topsfield, 202, 216, 257, 282, 285, 286, 292, 295, 302, 311, 315, 345, 357, 366, 374, 433, 439, 451, 455, 464, 539, 548, 549, 555, 607, 608, 610, 616, 665, 671, 688
Tories, 390, 440
torture, 45, 53, 148, 212, 443, 560, 609, 650, 671. *See* testing
Tower of London, 89, 99
Isabella Towle, 385, 387
town herdsman, 141
Town House, 430
town meeting, 141
Jacob Towne, 292
John Towne, 293
Joseph Towne, 293, 688
Mary Towne, 665
Rebecca Towne, 665
Township Privileges, 367
Tranent, 42
transmutation, 11
Transubstantiation, v
Ann Putnam Trask, 318, 362
Christine Trask, 427, 428
John Trask, 427, 618
Sarah Trask, 318
William Trask, 157, 163, 281, 316, 318, 362
treasure, 459
Treasurer of Scotland, 99
Robert Treat, 686, 703
Treatise Against Witchcraft, 46
Treatise of Witchcraft, 104
A Treatise Proving Spirits, Witches, and Supernatural Operations by Pregnant Instances and Evidences, 343
Treaty of Westminster, 351
Trebona, Bohemia, 34, 37

The Trial, Condemnation, and Execution of Three Witches; viz., Temperance Lloyd, Mary Lloyd, and Susanna Edwards, 400
A Trial of Witchcraft, 124
A Trial of Witches, 303, 482, 607
A Trial of Witches at the Assizes Held at Bury St. Edmunds, 298
Susannah Trimmings, 273
Tring, 1, 2
Trinidad, 206
Thomas Trowbridge, 686
Gebhard Truchsess von Waldburg, Archbishop of Cologne, 13
Henry True, 683
A True and Exact Relation, 216
A True and Faithful Relation, 287. 323
A True and Just Record, 14
A True Relation of the Arraignment of Eighteen Witches at St. Edmundsbury, 216
The Truth Held Forth and Maintained, 699
tuberculosis, 239. *See* consumption
Thomas Tuck, 395
John Tufts, 437
Mary Putnam Tufts, 323, 444, 453, 454, 465, 466, 529
Peter Tufts, 608
John Tulley, 430
Turkey Company, 8
turned off, 175, 225, 232, 627, 640, 659, 674
John Turner, 590
Tyborn, 260
Hannah Tyler, 624, 666, 667, 683, 689
Job Tyler, 287, 314, 624
Mary Tyler, 287, 624, 683, 689
Moses Tyler, 287, 667
typographical error, 84

-U-

Uffcot, 304
Ulm, 130
Capt. John Underhill, 161, 163
James Underwood, 272
Union Jack, 157

Unitarians, 447
universal franchise, 227
universal panacea, 98
University at Cologne, 52
University of Pisa, 13
Phineas Upham, 355, 357
Joan Upney, 40
Uraniborg, 38, 42, 61, 74
Pope Urban VIII, 122
Uriel, 12, 29, 35, 287
Hezekiah Usher, 680
Francis Usselton, 279

-V-

Vagabond Act, 294
Vale of Aylesbury, 1, 31
Dr. Van der Linden, 67
Henry Vane, 159, 163, 167
Judith Varlet, 305
Samuel Vassall, 136
Richard Vaughan, Bishop of Chester, 64
Bernard Veach, 395
Venice, 88
venting of corrupt and pernicious opinions, 256
Venus Colefax, 590
Mary Veren. *See* Mary Veren Putnam
Nathaniel Veren, 316
Philip Veren, Jr., 305
Philip Veren, Sr., 167
Elizabeth Vergoose, 279, 303, 315, 335, 337, 708
Elizabeth Proctor Very, 478, 497, 501, 505, 517, 525, 528, 529, 534, 539, 547, 608, 619, 621, 626, 630, 651, 652, 689, 706
Thomas Very, 626
George Villiers, Duke of Buckingham, 122, 127, 133
Sarah Vinson, 267
Virginia, 37, 47, 80, 81, 100, 104, 107, 123, 145, 185, 268, 305, 315, 363
Virgo, 288, 327
voters, 141

-W-

Thomas Wade, 681
William Wade, 99
John Wagstaffe, 329
Abraham Walcott, 369
Ann Walcott, 425
Jonathan Walcott, 388, 394, 420, 425, 430, 438, 452, 518, 566, 607
Mary Walcott, 475, 478, 481, 496, 504, 505, 510, 515, 517, 520, 523, 528, 533, 534, 536, 538, 539, 542, 554, 556 ,560 ,563-565 ,567 ,568 ,570 ,575 ,583 ,589 ,598 ,604 ,610 ,611 ,613 ,614 ,617 ,621 ,626 ,627 ,634, 665
Thomas Walcott, 452
Wales, 10, 30
Joan Walford, 273, 274, 277, 326
Thomas Walford, 273
Goodwife Walford, 274, 277, 326
John Walker, 63
Wallingford, Connecticut, 467, 469, 474, 647, 670, 686, 702, 703, 705
Sir Francis Walsingham, 33
Cedrick Walt, 460
Lucy Walters, 425
Henry Walton, 205
Walton Church, 391
Walton-in-the-Dale, Lancaster, 9
Wampanoag Indians, 361
wampum, 186, 199
Warboys, Essex, 46, 48
Warboys, Huntingdonshire, 40
Hester Ward, 268
Nathaniel Ward, 173, 188
Elizabeth Wardwell, 626
Samuel Wardwell, 398, 465, 663, 669, 671, 674, 683, 689
Mary Wardwell, 664, 689
Sarah Wardwell, 689, 706
Mary Warham, 15
William Warham, Archbishop of Canterbury, 15
Sir William Warham of Malsanger, 15
Paul Waring, 9
warlock, iv, 20, 133, 599

Mary Warren, 478, 525, 535, 539-541, 547, 549, 565, 581, 588, 590, 594, 597, 611, 617, 634, 641, 643, 652, 658, 660, 661, 664, 670, 676
Warwick, 308
Bridget Wasselby. *See* Bridget Bishop, Bridget Oliver.
Wat the cobbler, 126
water pollution, 140
Richard Waterman, 309
Watertown, 259, 262, 354
Mary Watkins, 691, 698
Aaron Way, 620, 691
Henry Way, 145
Richard Way, 576
William Way, 691
Samuel Webber, 421
Rev. John Webster, 149, 364
Mary Webster, 402, 405, 406, 416-418, 461, 577, 652, 693
William Webster, 402
Bessie Weems, 333
Jane Weir, 333
John Weir, 194, 245
Margaret Weir, 333
Thomas Weir, 237, 258, 332
Welcome, 232
Daniel Weld, 357
John Weldon, 581
John Wells, 351
Mrs. John Wells, 351
Mrs. Thomas Wells, 360
Rev. Mr. Wells, 437
Wells, Maine, 461, 566, 573, 580
Welsh, 11, 30
Wenham, 201, 227, 345, 357, 372, 376, 383, 389, 391, 486, 607
Thomas Wentworth, Lord Strafford, 184
Wessagusset, 120, 122, 126, 131
Thomas West, 91, 278
Thomas West, Lord De la Warre, 91
West Indies, 170, 185, 234, 622
West Jersey, 379
Westchester, 327, 334, 335, 344
John Westgate, 414

Thomas Westgate, 590
Westminster, 16, 78
Westminster Confession, 232
Francis Weston, 157, 172, 202
Thomas Weston, 119
Wethersfield, Connecticut, 234, 235, 327, 334
Johann Weyer, 52, 55
Weymouth, 119, 120
Edward Whalley, 291
Wheatley, 261
Thomas Wheeler, 266, 269
John Wheelwright, 342
Whig, 390, 440
Joseph Whipple, 608
Matthew Whipple, 227
Mrs. Whit, 461
Edward White, 117
John White, 38, 47,
Judith White, 540, 566
Philip White, 598
The White King's Prophecy, 207
White Magic, iv, 14, 441, 482, 532
White Man, 533, 585, 586, 652
white witch, i, iv, 14, 260, 296, 328, 360, 382, 421, 461, 577, 693
Whitehall, 196, 237
John Whitgift, Archbishop of Canterbury, 18, 49
Thomas Whiting, 165
Mary Whitridge, 594, 598, 665
Thomas Whitridge, 452
Anne Whittle, 95
Wicket-Shaw, 333
Wickford Hill, 356
William Wickham, Bishop of Lincoln, 48
Michael Wigglesworth, 300
Averill Wilds, 439
Ephraim Wilds, 439, 555, 608
Goodwife Wilds, 462, 556-559, 574, 646
John Wilds, 439, 652
Sarah Wilds, 439, 459, 555, 556, 594, 633, 640, 652
Benjamin Wilkins, Jr. 636

Benjamin Wilkins, Sr., 595
Bray Wilkins, 173, 290, 293, 343, 360, 375, 378, 471, 573, 576, 579, 582, 594-596, 636, 693
Daniel Wilkins, 573, 578, 579, 594, 596. 636
Hannah Wilkins, 470, 471
Henry Wilkins, 573, 576
Lydia Wilkins, 579, 595, 620
Rebecca Wilkins, 649, 650
Samuel Wilkins, 595
Thomas Wilkins, 470, 474, 476, 691
Benjamin Willard, 597
Henry Willard, 597
John Willard, 530, 573, 576, 582, 586-588, 595-598, 620, 626, 636, 649-651, 656, 659, 660, 693, 712
Samuel Willard, 338, 339, 632, 679, 699, 701
Simon Willard, 453, 581,
Willard's curse, 712
William I. *See* William of Orange
William III, 596
Abigail Williams, 475, 478, 481, 485, 494, 501, 502, 504, 505, 510, 512, 517, 519, 528, 529, 533, 535, 537, 540, 553, 554, 558, 560, 561, 565, 567, 569, 577, 588, 589, 598, 602, 608, 610, 613, 622
Henry Williams, 384, 423, 435
Mary Williams, 142
Roger Williams, 142-146, 152, 153, 156-159, 161, 163, 173, 177, 203, 419
Sir Joseph Williamson, 349
Joan Williford, 214, 216
Samuel Willis, 683
Will's Hill, 293, 578, 595
Deborah Wilson, 299
John Wilson, 286
Sarah Wilson, 683
Wiltshire, 236
Humphrey Winch, 103
Windmill Hill, 208
Lady Windsor, 18
Windsor, Connecticut, 155, 222, 225, 226, 267
Wingrave, Buckinghamshire, i, 1, 2, 7, 10, 15, 27, 31, 106
Edward Winslow, 119
John Winslow, 449

Josiah Winslow, 356
William Winter, 205
Winter Island, 163, 272, 346, 363
Henry Winthrop, 140
John Winthrop, Jr., 152, 305, 332, 362
John Winthrop, Sr., 138, 140, 167, 170, 172, 200, 206, 208, 216, 229, 232, 449
Waite Winthrop, 449, 606, 687, 702
John Wise, 433, 652
witch, ii, 133, 149
The Witch of Wapping, 263
The Witches of Huntingdon, 224
witch cake, 482, 496, 525, 526, 532
Witch Court, 687, 688
witch teats, 150, 209, 229, 265, 267, 277, 297, 300, 402, 485, 491, 596, 609, 702
witchcraft, iv, 8, 14, 40, 41, 43, 45, 47-49, 51-53, 55, 56, 64, 71, 78, 79, 81, 84, 86, 92, 95, 98, 105, 106, 110, 117-119, 130, 149, 142, 209, 211-213, 217, 222-224, 227, 229, 234, 235, 238, 244, 245, 252, 255, 256, 258, 260, 261, 263-265, 267, 272, 273, 276, 277, 281, 281, 288, 291, 292, 294, 298, 300, 304, 310, 311, 314, 323, 327-329, 338, 343, 344, 346, 350, 352, 354, 358, 363, 364, 374, 380, 384-386, 388, 394, 405, 406, 408, 416, 417, 424, 425, 440, 441, 444, 474, 477, 481-483, 485, 487, 499, 502, 506, 507, 511, 513, 514, 419, 520, 523, 231, 534, 537, 539, 540, 544, 556, 560, 563, 568, 570, 578, 583, 584, 591, 601, 602, 604, 608-610, 614, 624, 628, 632, 636, 639, 643, 647, 655, 657, 667, 669, 670, 672, 675, 677-680, 682, 686, 687, 689, 691, 693, 698, 700, 703, 705, 706
witchcraft persecution, 92
The Witches of Northamptonshsire: Agnes Browne, Joan Vaughan, Arthur Bill, Helen Jenkinson, Mary Barber, Witches, Who Were All Executed at Northampton the nd of July Last, 97
The Witches of Warboys, 57
witches' Sabbath, 200
Witchfinder General of Connecticut, 267. *See* Roger Ludlow
Witch-Finder General of England, 209 213, 219, 501. *See* Matthew Hopkins
witchhunt, 43, 226, 526, 529, 530, 573, 596, 627, 647, 651, 570, 673-675, 677, 681, 684, 688, 693
witch-pricker, 213

witch's bridle, 43
witch's touch, 230, 338, 496, 501, 533, 628, 634, 658, 664, 668
wizard, 25, 242, 536, 548, 552, 584, 640
Wizard of Andover, 689
Woburn, 395, 577, 594
Wokakon, 47
The Wonderful Discovery of the Witchcrafts of Margaret and Philip Flower, 106
The Wonderful Discovery of Witches in the County of Lancashire, 98
Wonders of the Invisible World, 674, 679, 681, 698
Ann Wood, 309
George Wood, 306, 309, 314
Joshua Wood, 405, 406
Marie Gadge Wood, 405, 406, 462
John Woodbridge, 380, 382
Abigail Woodbury, 418
Mrs. Woodbury, 630
Ann Woodbury, 290
John Woodbury, 128, 157, 167, 178
William Woodcock, 299
Jonathan Woodman, 344
Goodman Woods, 169
John Woods, 331
Mehitabel Woodworth,
Worcester, 89, 257
Worcester Castle, 89
Word of God, 85
Words of Power, 6
Capt. Wormall, 453
William Wormall, 581
Catherine Wright, 33
Elizabeth Wright, 54
Hannah Wright, 292
Gilbert Wright, 110, 124, 125, 128, 129
Mary Wright, 292, 294
William Wyman, 395
Cornelius Wytfliet, 47

-X-

-Y-

York, 120
Bishop of York. *See* Samuel Harsnett
Alice Young, 222, 226
Christopher Young, 201, 227

-Z-

Zion, 124
Zodiac, i, 3, 6, 177
Jacob Zwinger, 68

LEWIS TURCO began teaching in 1960 at what is now Cleveland State University, where he founded the Cleveland Poetry Center in 1962. In 1965 he began teaching at the State University of New York College at Oswego where he founded the Program in Writing Arts in 1968 and from which he retired in 1996. His *First Poems* appeared in 1960 as a selection of the Book Club for Poetry, and in 1968 he published *The Book of Forms: A Handbook of Poetics*, which has since become known in the field as The Poet's Bible. His book of literary criticism, *Visions and Revisions of American Poetry*, won the Poetry Society of America's Melville Cane Award in 1986, and his *A Book of Fears, Poems, with Italian Translations* by Joseph Alessia, won the Bordighera Bi-Lingual Poetry Prize in 1998. Two selections of poems from his 2002 collection of poems titled *The Green Maces of Autumn, Voices in an Old Maine House*, won the earlier Silverfish Review Chapbook Competition in 1989 and the Cooper House Chapbook Competition in 1990. A compendium of his rhymed and metered poems, *The Collected Lyrics of Lewis Turco / Wesli Court 1953-2004* appeared in 2004 and should be considered the companion volume to his collection of his non-traditional poetry, entitled *Fearful Pleasures: The Complete Poems, 1959-2007*. He lives in Dresden, Maine — with his wife, Jean, and cat, Sweetie-Pie — where he is currently working on a series of poems provisionally titled *Attic, Shed and Barn*.

www.ingramcontent.com/pod-product-compliance
Lightning Source LLC
Chambersburg PA
CBHW061946300426
44117CB00010B/1242